D0508143

Dictionary of
Accounting

Fourth edition

S.M.H. Collin

A & C Black • London

www.acblack.com

First published in Great Britain in 1992
by *Peter Collin Publishing*
Second edition published 2001
Third edition published 2004
This fourth edition published 2007
Reprinted 2009

A & C Black Publishers Ltd
36 Soho Square, London W1D 3QY

ISBN: 978 0 7136 8286 1

Text Production and Proofreading
Heather Bateman, Stephen Curtis, Katy McAdam, Howard Sargeant

This book is produced using paper that is made from wood grown in managed,
sustainable forests. It is natural, renewable and recyclable. The logging and
manufacturing processes conform to the environmental regulations of the
country of origin.

Text typeset by A & C Black
Printed in Spain by GraphyCems

Preface

This dictionary provides a basic vocabulary of terms used in accounting, from personal finance and investments to company accounts, balance sheets and stock valuations. It is ideal for students of accounting and for anyone who needs to check the meaning of an accountancy term, from people working in businesses who may not be professional accountants to translators or those for whom English is an additional language.

Each headword is explained in clear, straightforward English and examples are given to show how the word may be used in context. There are also quotations from newspapers and specialist magazines. Sample documents and financial statements are also provided.

Thanks are due to Hannah Gray and Sarah Williams for their invaluable help and advice during the production of this new edition.

Pronunciation

The following symbols have been used to show the pronunciation of the main words in the dictionary.

Stress has been indicated by a main stress mark (') and a secondary stress mark (ˌ). Note that these are only guides, as the stress of the word changes according to its position in the sentence.

Vowels		*Consonants*	
æ	back	b	buck
ɑː	harm	d	dead
ɒ	stop	ð	other
aɪ	type	dʒ	jump
aʊ	how	f	fare
aɪə	hire	g	gold
aʊə	hour	h	head
ɔː	course	j	yellow
ɔɪ	annoy	k	cab
e	head	l	leave
eə	fair	m	mix
eɪ	make	n	nil
eʊ	go	ŋ	sing
ɜː	word	p	print
iː	keep	r	rest
i	happy	s	save
ə	about	ʃ	shop
ɪ	fit	t	take
ɪə	near	tʃ	change
u	annual	θ	theft
uː	pool	v	value
ʊ	book	w	work
ʊə	tour	x	loch
ʌ	shut	ʒ	measure
		z	zone

A

AAA *abbreviation* American Accounting Association

AAPA *abbreviation* Association of Authorised Public Accountants

AARF *abbreviation* Australian Accounting Research Foundation

AAT *abbreviation* Association of Accounting Technicians

abacus /'æbəkəs/ *noun* a counting device consisting of parallel rods strung with beads, still widely used for business and accounting in China and Japan

abandonment /ə'bændənmənt/ *noun* an act of giving up voluntarily something that you own, such as an option or the right to a property □ **abandonment of a claim** giving up a claim in a civil action

abatement /ə'beɪtmənt/ *noun* a reduction in a payment, e.g., if a company's or individual's total assets are insufficient to cover their debts or legacies

ABB *abbreviation* activity-based budgeting

abbreviated accounts /ə,briːviːeɪtɪd ə 'kaʊnts/ *plural noun* a shortened version of a company's annual accounts that a small or medium sized company can file with the Registrar of Companies, instead of a full version

ABC *abbreviation* activity-based costing

ab initio /,æb ɪ'nɪʃiəʊ/ *phrase* a Latin phrase meaning 'from the beginning'

ABM *abbreviation* activity-based management

abnormal gain /æb,nɔːm(ə)l 'geɪn/ *noun* any reduction in the volume of process loss below that set by the normal loss allowance. Abnormal gains are generally costed as though they were completed products.

abnormal loss /æb,nɔːm(ə)l 'lɒs/ *noun* any losses which exceed the normal loss allowance. Abnormal losses are generally costed as though they were completed products.

abnormal spoilage /æb,nɔːm(ə)l 'spɔɪlɪdʒ/ *noun* spoilage that contributes to an **abnormal loss**

above par /ə,bʌv 'pɑː/ *adjective* referring to a share with a market price higher than its face value

above-the-line /ə,bʌv ðə 'laɪn/ *adjective* **1.** used to describe entries in a company's profit and loss accounts that appear above the line which separates entries showing the origin of the funds that have contributed to the profit or loss from those that relate to its distribution. Exceptional and extraordinary items appear above the line. ○ *Exceptional items are noted above the line in company accounts.* ◊ **below-the-line 2.** relating to revenue items in a government budget

abridged accounts /ə,brɪdʒd ə'kaʊnts/ *plural noun* financial statements produced by a company that fall outside the requirements stipulated in the Companies Act

absorb /əb'zɔːb/ *verb* **1.** to take in a small item so that it forms part of a larger one □ **a business which has been absorbed by a competitor** a small business which has been made part of a larger one **2.** to assign an overhead to a particular cost centre in a company's production accounts so that its identity becomes lost. ◊ **absorption costing**

absorbed overhead /əb,zɔːbd 'əʊvəhed/ *noun* an overhead attached to products or services by means of **overhead absorption rates**

absorption /əb'zɔːpʃən/ *noun* the process of making a smaller business part of a larger one, so that the smaller company in effect no longer exists

absorption costing /əb'zɔːpʃən ,kɒstɪŋ/ *noun* **1.** a form of costing for a product that includes both the direct costs of production and the indirect overhead costs as well **2.** an accounting practice in which fixed and variable costs of production are absorbed by different cost centres. Providing all the products or services can be sold at a price that covers the allocated costs, this method ensures that both fixed and variable costs are recovered in full. ◊ **marginal costing**

absorption rate /əb'zɔːpʃən ˌreɪt/ noun a rate at which overhead costs are absorbed into each unit of production

abstract /'æbstrækt/ noun a short form of a report or document ○ to make an abstract of the company accounts

abusive tax shelter /əˌbjuːsɪv 'tæks ˌʃeltə/ noun a tax shelter used illegally in order to avoid or reduce tax payments

Academy of Accounting Historians /əˌkædəmi əv ə'kaʊntɪŋ hɪˌstɔːriənz/ noun a US organisation, founded in 1973, that promotes the study of the history of accounting

ACAUS abbreviation Association of Chartered Accountants in the United States

ACCA abbreviation Association of Chartered Certified Accountants

accelerate /ək'seləreɪt/ verb to reduce the amount of time before a maturity date

accelerated cost recovery system /ækˌseləreɪtɪd 'kɒst rɪˌkʌvəri ˌsɪstəm/ noun a system used in the United States for calculating depreciation in a way that reduces tax liability

accelerated depreciation /ək ˌseləreɪtɪd dɪpriːʃɪ'eɪʃ(ə)n/ noun a system of depreciation which reduces the value of assets at a high rate in the early years to encourage companies, as a result of tax advantages, to invest in new equipment

acceleration /əkˌselə'reɪʃ(ə)n/ noun the speeding up of debt repayment

acceleration clause /əkˌselə'reɪʃ(ə)n ˌklɔːz/ noun US a clause in a contract that provides for immediate payment of the total balance if there is a breach of contract

acceptance /ək'septəns/ noun **1.** the act of signing a bill of exchange to show that you agree to pay it □ **to present a bill for acceptance** to present a bill for payment by the person who has accepted it **2.** a bill which has been accepted **3.** the act of accepting an offer of new shares for which you have applied

acceptance credit /ək'septəns ˌkredɪt/ noun an arrangement of credit from a bank, where the bank accepts bills of exchange drawn on the bank by the debtor: the bank then discounts the bills and is responsible for paying them when they mature. The debtor owes the bank for the bills but these are covered by letters of credit.

acceptance sampling /ək'septəns ˌsɑːmplɪŋ/ noun the process of testing a small sample of a batch to see if the whole batch is good enough to be accepted

accepting house /ək'septɪŋ 'haʊs/, **acceptance house** /ək'septəns haʊs/ noun a firm, usually a merchant bank, which accepts bills of exchange at a discount, in return for immediate payment to the issuer, in this case the Bank of England

Accepting Houses Committee /ək ˌseptɪŋ ˌhaʊzɪz kə'mɪti/ noun the main London merchant banks, which organise the lending of money with the Bank of England. They receive slightly better discount rates from the Bank.

acceptor /ək'septə/ noun a person who accepts a bill of exchange by signing it, thus making a commitment to pay it by a specified date

accident insurance /ˌæksɪd(ə)nt ɪn 'ʃʊərəns/ noun insurance which will pay the insured person when an accident takes place

accommodation /əˌkɒmə'deɪʃ(ə)n/ noun money lent for a short time

accommodation bill /əˌkɒmə'deɪʃ(ə)n ˌbɪl/ noun a bill of exchange where the person signing (the 'drawee') is helping another company (the 'drawer') to raise a loan

account /ə'kaʊnt/ noun **1.** a record of financial transactions over a period of time, such as money paid, received, borrowed or owed ○ Please send me your account or a detailed or an itemised account. **2.** a structured record of financial transactions that may be maintained as a list or in a more formal structured credit and debit basis **3.** (in a shop) an arrangement in which a customer acquires goods and pays for them at a later date, usually the end of the month ○ to have an account or a credit account with Harrods ○ Put it on my account or charge it to my account. ○ They are one of our largest accounts. **4.** a period during which shares are traded for credit, and at the end of which the shares bought must be paid for (NOTE: On the London Stock Exchange, there are twenty-four accounts during the year, each running usually for ten working days.) **5.** a customer who does a large amount of business with a firm and has an account with it ○ Smith Brothers is one of our largest accounts. ○ Our sales people call on their best accounts twice a month.

accountability /əˌkaʊntə'bɪlɪti/ noun the fact of being responsible to someone for something, e.g. the accountability of directors to the shareholders

accountable /əˈkaʊntəb(ə)l/ *adjective* referring to a person who has to explain what has taken place or who is responsible for something (NOTE: You are accountable **to** someone **for** something.)

account analysis /əˈkaʊnt əˌnæləsɪs/ *noun* analysis of a company's accounts with the aim of discerning how its activities affect its costs

accountancy /əˈkaʊntənsi/ *noun* the work of an accountant ○ *They are studying accountancy* or *They are accountancy students.*

accountancy bodies /əˈkaʊntənsi ˌbɒdiːz/ *plural noun* professional institutions and associations for accountants

accountancy profession /əˌkaʊntənsi prəˈfeʃ(ə)n/ *noun* the professional bodies that establish entry standards, organise professional examinations, and draw up ethical and technical guidelines for accountants

accountant /əˈkaʊntənt/ *noun* **1.** a person who keeps a company's accounts or deals with an individual person's tax affairs ○ *The chief accountant of a manufacturing group.* ○ *The accountant has shown that there is a sharp variance in our labour costs.* **2.** a person who advises a company on its finances ○ *I send all my income tax queries to my accountant.* **3.** a person who examines accounts

Accountants' International Study Group /əˌkaʊntənts ˌɪntənæʃ(ə)nəl ˈstʌdi ˌgruːp/ *noun* a body of professional accounting bodies from the United States, Canada, and the United Kingdom that was established in 1966 to research accounting practices in the three member countries. After publishing 20 reports, it was disbanded in 1977 with the foundation of the International Federation of Accountants.

accountant's liability /əˌkaʊntənts ˌlaɪəˈbɪlɪti/ *noun* the legal liability of an accountant who commits fraud or is held to be negligent

accountants' opinion /əˌkaʊntənts əˈpɪnjən/ *noun* a report of the audit of a company's books, carried out by a certified public accountant (NOTE: The US term is **audit opinion**.)

accountants' report /əˌkaʊntənts rɪˈpɔːt/ *noun* in the United Kingdom, a report written by accountants that is required by the London Stock Exchange to be included in the prospectus of a company seeking a listing on the Exchange

account code /əˈkaʊnt kəʊd/ *noun* a number assigned to a particular account in a numerical accounting system, e.g., a chart of accounts

account end /əˌkaʊnt ˈend/ *noun* the end of an accounting period

account executive /əˈkaʊnt ɪgˌzekjʊtɪv/ *noun* **1.** an employee who looks after customers or who is the link between customers and the company **2.** an employee of an organisation such as a bank, public relations firm or advertising agency who is responsible for looking after particular clients and handling their business with the organisation

account form /əˈkaʊnt fɔːm/ *noun* a balance sheet laid out in horizontal form. It is the opposite of 'report' or 'vertical' form.

accounting /əˈkaʊntɪŋ/ *noun* **1.** the work of recording money paid, received, borrowed, or owed ○ *accounting methods* ○ *accounting procedures* ○ *an accounting machine* **2.** accountancy, the work of an accountant as a course of study

'…applicants will be professionally qualified and have a degree in Commerce or Accounting' [*Australian Financial Review*]

Accounting and Finance Association of Australia and New Zealand /əˌkaʊntɪŋ ən ˌfaɪnæns əˌsəʊsieɪʃ(ə)n əv ɒs ˌtreɪliə ən njuː ˈziːlənd/ *noun* an organisation for accounting and finance academics, researchers and professionals working in Australia and New Zealand. Abbreviation **AFAANZ**

accounting bases /əˌkaʊntɪŋ ˈbeɪsiːz/ *plural noun* the possible ways in which accounting concepts may be applied to financial transactions, e.g. the methods used to depreciate assets, how intangible assets or work in progress are dealt with

accounting change /əˈkaʊntɪŋ tʃeɪndʒ/ *noun* any of various changes that affect a set of accounts, e.g. a change in the method of calculating the depreciation of assets or a change in the size, structure or nature of the company

accounting concept /əˈkaʊntɪŋ ˌkɒnsept/ *noun* a general assumption on which accounts are prepared. The main concepts are: that the business is a going concern, that revenue and costs are noted when they are incurred and not when cash is received or paid, that the present accounts are drawn up following the same principles as the previous accounts, that the revenue or costs are only recorded if it is certain that they will be incurred.

accounting control /əˈkaʊntɪŋ kənˌtrəʊl/ *noun* procedures designed to ensure that source data for accounts are accurate and proper, in order to prevent fraud

accounting conventions /əˈkaʊntɪŋ kənˌvenʃ(ə)nz/ *plural noun* the fundamental assumptions that govern the practice of accounting, e.g., consistency and prudence. ◊ **conceptual framework**

accounting cycle /əˈkaʊntɪŋ ˌsaɪk(ə)l/ *noun* the regular process of recording, analysing and reporting a company's transactions for a given period

accounting date /əˈkaʊntɪŋ ˌdeɪt/ *noun* the date on which an accounting period ends, usually 31st December for annual accounts but it can in fact be any date

Accounting Directives /əˈkaʊntɪŋ daɪˌrektɪvz/ *plural noun* a set of EU directives issued with the aim of regulating accounting procedures in member states

accounting entity /əˈkaʊntɪŋ ˌentəti/ *noun* the unit for which financial statements and accounting records are prepared, e.g., a limited company or a partnership. ◊ **reporting entity**

accounting equation /əˌkaʊntɪŋ ɪˈkweɪʒ(ə)n/ *noun* the basic formula that underpins double-entry bookkeeping. It can be expressed most simply as 'assets + expenses = liabilities + capital + revenue' where the debit amounts to the left of the equals sign must be equivalent to the credit amounts to the right. Also called **balance sheet equation**

accounting error /əˈkaʊntɪŋ ˌerə/ *noun* any accounting inaccuracy or misrepresentation that is the result of error, not intentional fraud

accounting event /əˌkaʊntɪŋ ɪˈvent/ *noun* a transaction recorded in a business's books of account

accounting fees /əˈkaʊntɪŋ ˌfiːz/ *plural noun* fees paid to an accountant for preparing accounts, which are deductible against tax

accounting information system /əˌkaʊntɪŋ ˌɪnfəˈmeɪʃ(ə)n ˌsɪstəm/ *noun* a system, usually computer-based, that processes information on a company's transactions for accounting purposes

accounting manual /əˈkaʊntɪŋ ˌmænjuəl/ *noun* a handbook or set of instructions that set out all procedures and responsibilities of those engaged in an entity's accounting systems

accounting period /əˈkaʊntɪŋ ˌpɪəriəd/ *noun* a period of time at the end of which the firm's accounts are made up

accounting policies /əˈkaʊntɪŋ ˌpɒlɪsiz/ *plural noun* the accounting bases used by a company when preparing its financial statements

accounting practice /əˈkaʊntɪŋ ˌpræktɪs/ *noun* the way in which accountants and auditors implement accounting policies

accounting principles /əˈkaʊntɪŋ ˌprɪnsɪp(ə)lz/ *plural noun* standards of accuracy and probity that apply to those carrying out accounting procedures

Accounting Principles Board /əˌkaʊntɪŋ ˈprɪnsɪp(ə)lz ˌbɔːd/ *noun* the US body which issued Opinions that formed much of US Generally Accepted Accounting Principles up to 1973 when the Financial Accounting Standards Board (FASB) took over that role. Abbreviation **APB**

accounting procedure /əˈkaʊntɪŋ prəˌsiːdʒə/ *noun* an accounting method developed by an individual or organisation to deal with routine accounting tasks

accounting profits /əˈkaʊntɪŋ ˌprɒfɪts/ *plural noun* the difference between revenue and the costs of production

accounting rate of return /əˌkaʊntɪŋ reɪt əv rɪˈtɜːn/ *noun* a method of valuing shares in a company where the company's estimated future profits are divided by the rate of return required by investors. Abbreviation **ARR**

accounting records /əˈkaʊntɪŋ ˌrekɔːdz/ *plural noun* all documents in which accounting information is recorded, used during the preparation of financial statements

accounting reference date /əˌkaʊntɪŋ ˈref(ə)rəns ˌdeɪt/ *noun* the last day of a company's accounting reference period. Abbreviation **ARD**

accounting reference period /əˌkaʊntɪŋ ˈref(ə)rəns ˌpɪəriəd/ *noun* **1.** the period for which a company makes up its accounts. In most, but not all, cases, the period is 12 months. **2.** the period for which corporation tax is calculated

accounting software /əˈkaʊntɪŋ ˌsɒftweə/ *noun* computer programs used to enter and process accounts information

accounting standard /əˌkaʊntɪŋ ˈstændəd/ *noun* an authoritative statement of how particular types of transaction and other events should be reflected in financial statements. Compliance with accounting standards will normally be necessary for financial statements to give a true and fair view. (NOTE: These principles are recommended by the Accounting Standards Board in the United Kingdom or by the FASB in the United States.)

Accounting Standards Board /ə ˌkaʊntɪŋ 'stændədz bɔːd/ *noun* a committee set up by British accounting institutions to monitor methods used in accounting. Abbreviation **ASB**

Accounting Standards Committee /əˌkaʊntɪŋ 'stændədz kəˌmɪti/ *noun* a UK accounting standards issuing body whose functions were taken over by the ASB in 1990. Abbreviation **ASC**

accounting system /ə'kaʊntɪŋ ˌsɪstəm/ *noun* the means used by an organisation to produce its accounting information

accounting technician /əˌkaʊntɪŋ tek 'nɪʃ(ə)n/ *noun* a person who assists in the preparation of accounts but who is not a fully qualified accountant

accounting unit /ə'kaʊntɪŋ ˌjuːnɪt/ *noun* any unit which takes part in financial transactions which are recorded in a set of accounts. It can be a department, a sole trader, a Plc or some other unit.

account payee /əˌkaʊnt peɪ'iː/ *noun* the words printed on most UK cheques indicating that the cheque can only be paid into the account of the person or business to whom the cheque is written, or be cashed for a fee at an agency offering a cheque cashing service

accounts /ə'kaʊnts/ *plural noun* detailed records of a company's financial affairs

accounts department /ə'kaʊnts dɪ ˌpɑːtmənt/ *noun* a department in a company which deals with money paid, received, borrowed, or owed

accounts manager /ə'kaʊnts ˌmænɪdʒə/ *noun* the manager of an accounts department

accounts payable /əˌkaʊnts 'peɪəb(ə)l/ *plural noun* money owed by a company

accounts receivable /əˌkaʊnts rɪ 'siːvəb(ə)l/ *plural noun* money owed to a company. Abbreviation **AR**

accounts receivable turnover /ə ˌkaʊnts rɪ'siːvəb(ə)l ˌtɜːnəʊvə/ *noun* a statistic showing on average how long customers take to pay money they owe for goods or services received

accrete /ə'kriːt/ *verb* **1.** (*of a fund*) to have interest added to it **2.** (*of assets*) to grow as a result of mergers, expansion or the acquisition of other interests

accretion /ə'kriːʃ(ə)n/ *noun* the process of adding interest to a fund over a period of time

accrual /ə'kruːəl/ *noun* a gradual increase by addition

accruals /ə'kruːəlz/ *plural noun* same as **accrued liabilities**

accruals basis /ə'kruːəl ˌbeɪsɪs/, **accruals concept** /ə'kruːəlz ˌkɒnsept/ *noun* a method of preparing accounts in which revenues and costs are both reported during the period to which they refer and not during the period when payments are received or made

accrue /ə'kruː/ *verb* **1.** to record a financial transaction in accounts when it takes place, and not when payment is made or received **2.** to increase and be due for payment at a later date ○ *Interest accrues from the beginning of the month.*

accrued dividend /əˌkruːd 'dɪvɪdend/ *noun* a dividend earned since the last dividend was paid

accrued expense /əˌkruːd ɪk'spens/ *noun* an expense that has been incurred within a given accounting period but not yet paid

accrued income /əˌkruːd 'ɪnkʌm/ *noun* revenue entered in accounts, although payment has not yet been received

accrued interest /əˌkruːd 'ɪntrəst/ *noun* interest which has been earned by an interest-bearing investment ○ *Accrued interest is added quarterly.*

accrued liabilities /əˌkruːd ˌlaɪə 'bɪlɪtiz/ *plural noun* liabilities which are recorded in an accounting period, although payment has not yet been made. This refers to liabilities such as rent, electricity, etc. Also called **accruals**

accrued revenue /əˌkruːd 'revənjuː/ *noun* same as **accrued income**

accumulate /ə'kjuːmjʊleɪt/ *verb* to grow in quantity by being added to, or to get more of something over a period of time ○ *We allow dividends to accumulate in the fund.*

accumulated depreciation /ə ˌkjuːmjʊleɪtɪd dɪˌpriːʃi'eɪʃ(ə)n/ *noun* the total amount by which an asset has been depreciated since it was purchased

accumulated earnings tax /ə ˌkjuːmjʊleɪtɪd 'ɜːnɪŋz ˌtæks/, **accumulated profits tax** /əˌkjuːmjʊleɪtɪd 'prɒfɪts ˌtæks/ *noun US* a tax on earnings above a specified limit which are unjustifiably retained in a business to avoid paying higher personal income tax

accumulated profit /əˌkjuːmjʊleɪtɪd 'prɒfɪt/ *noun* a profit which is not paid as dividend but is taken over into the accounts of the following year

accumulated reserves /ə,kjuːmjʊleɪtɪd rɪˈzɜːvz/ *plural noun* reserves which a company has put aside over a period of years

accumulation /ə,kjuːmjʊˈleɪʃ(ə)n/ *noun* the process of growing larger by being added to, or of getting more and more of something

ACH *abbreviation US* Automated Clearing House

acid test /,æsɪd ˈtest/, **acid test ratio** *noun* same as **liquidity ratio**

acquisition /,ækwɪˈzɪʃ(ə)n/ *noun* the takeover of a company. The results and cash flows of the acquired company are brought into the group accounts only from the date of acquisition: the figures for the previous period for the reporting entity should not be adjusted. The difference between the fair value of the net identifiable assets acquired and the fair value of the purchase consideration is goodwill.

acquisition accounting /,ækwɪ ˈzɪʃ(ə)n ə,kaʊntɪŋ/ *noun* a full consolidation, where the assets of a subsidiary company which has been purchased are included in the parent company's balance sheet, and the premium paid for the goodwill is written off against the year's earnings

across-the-board /ə,krɒs ðə ˈbɔːd/ *adjective* applying to everything or everyone ○ *an across-the-board price increase* or *wage increase*

act /ækt/ *noun* a law passed by parliament which must be obeyed by the people

active /ˈæktɪv/ *adjective* involving many transactions or activities ○ *an active demand for oil shares* ○ *an active day on the Stock Exchange* ○ *Computer shares are very active.*

active account /,æktɪv əˈkaʊnt/ *noun* an account, such as a bank account or investment account, which is used to deposit and withdraw money frequently

active partner /,æktɪv ˈpɑːtnə/ *noun* a partner who works in a company that is a partnership

activity /ækˈtɪvɪti/ *noun* something which is done, especially something which is involved in creating a product or a service

'...preliminary indications of the level of business investment and activity during the March quarter will provide a good picture of economic activity in the year' [*Australian Financial Review*]

activity-based budgeting /æk,tɪvɪti ,beɪst ˈbʌdʒɪtɪŋ/ *noun* the allocation of resources to individual activities. Activity-based budgeting involves determining which activities incur costs within an organisation, establishing the relationships between them, and then deciding how much of the total budget should be allocated to each activity. Abbreviation **ABB**

activity-based costing /ækˈtɪvɪti beɪst ,kɒstɪŋ/ *noun* a costing system used to assign overhead costs to specific items produced, by looking at specific cost drivers. Abbreviation **ABC**. ◊ **cost driver**, **activity driver**, **resource driver**

activity-based management /æk ,tɪvɪti ,beɪst ˈmænɪdʒmənt/ *noun* a system of management that uses activity-based cost information for a variety of purposes including cost reduction, cost modelling and customer profitability analysis. Abbreviation **ABM**

activity chart /ækˈtɪvɪti tʃɑːt/ *noun* a plan showing work which has been done, made so that it can be compared to a previous plan showing how much work should be done

activity cost pool /æk,tɪvɪti ˈkɒst ,puːl/ *noun* a grouping of all cost elements associated with an activity

activity driver /ækˈtɪvɪti ,draɪvə/ a type of cost driver which is used to quantify the activities involved in creating a product or service

activity driver analysis /æk,tɪvɪti ,draɪvər əˈnæləsɪs/ *noun* the identification and evaluation of the activity drivers used to trace the cost of activities to cost objects. It may also involve selecting activity drivers with potential to contribute to the cost management function with particular reference to cost reduction.

act of God /,ækt əv ˈgɒd/ *noun* something you do not expect to happen and which cannot be avoided, e.g. a storm or a flood (NOTE: Acts of God are not usually covered by insurance policies.)

actual /ˈæktʃuəl/ *adjective* real or correct ○ *What is the actual cost of one unit?* ○ *The actual figures for directors' expenses are not shown to the shareholders.*

actual cash value /,æktʃuəl kæʃ ˈvæljuː/ *noun* the amount of money, less depreciation, that it would cost to replace something damaged beyond repair with a comparable item

actual cost /ˈæktʃuəl kɒst/ *noun* the total cost of producing or buying an item, which may include, e.g., its price plus the cost of delivery or storage

actual price /ˌæktʃuəl 'praɪs/ *noun* a price for a commodity which is for immediate delivery

actuals /'æktʃuəlz/ *plural noun* real figures ○ *These figures are the actuals for last year.*

actuarial /ˌæktʃu'eəriəl/ *adjective* calculated by an actuary ○ *The premiums are worked out according to actuarial calculations.*

actuarial tables /ˌæktʃueəriəl 'teɪb(ə)lz/ *plural noun* lists showing how long people are likely to live, used to calculate life assurance premiums and annuities

actuary /'æktʃuəri/ *noun* a person employed by an insurance company or other organisation to calculate the risk involved in an insurance, and therefore the premiums payable by people taking out insurance

add /æd/ *verb* to put figures together to make a total ○ *If you add the interest to the capital you will get quite a large sum.* ○ *Interest is added monthly.*

add up /ˌæd 'ʌp/ *phrasal verb* to put several figures together to make a total ○ *He made a mistake in adding up the column of figures.*

add up to /ˌæd 'ʌp tʊ/ *phrasal verb* to make a total of ○ *The total expenditure adds up to more than £1,000.*

added value /ˌædɪd 'vælju:/ *noun* an amount added to the value of a product or service, equal to the difference between its cost and the amount received when it is sold. Wages, taxes, etc. are deducted from the added value to give the profit. ◊ **VAT**

addend /'ædend/ *noun* a number added to the augend in an addition

addition /ə'dɪʃ(ə)n/ *noun* **1.** a thing or person added ○ *The management has stopped all additions to the staff.* ○ *We are exhibiting several additions to our product line.* ○ *The marketing director is the latest addition to the board.* **2.** an arithmetical operation consisting of adding together two or more numbers to make a sum ○ *You don't need a calculator to do simple addition.*

additional /ə'dɪʃ(ə)nəl/ *adjective* extra which is added ○ *additional costs* ○ *They sent us a list of additional charges.* ○ *Some additional clauses were added to the contract.* ○ *Additional duty will have to be paid.*

additional personal allowance /ə ˌdɪʃ(ə)nəl ˌpɜːs(ə)n(ə)l ə'laʊəns/ *noun* a tax allowance which can be claimed by a single person who has a child of school age

living with them, formerly called the 'single-parent allowance'

additional premium /əˌdɪʃ(ə)nəl 'priːmiəm/ *noun* a payment made to cover extra items in an existing insurance

additional voluntary contributions /əˌdɪʃ(ə)nəl ˌvɒlənt(ə)ri ˌkɒntrɪ 'bjuːʃ(ə)nz/ *plural noun* extra payments made voluntarily by an employee to a pension scheme on top of the normal contributions, up to a maximum of 15% of gross earnings. Abbreviation **AVCs**

adequate disclosure /ˌædɪkwət dɪs 'kləʊʒə/ *noun* a comprehensive presentation of statistics in financial statements, such that they can be used to inform investment decisions

adjudicate /ə'dʒuːdɪkeɪt/ *verb* to give a judgment between two parties in law or to decide a legal problem ○ *to adjudicate a claim* ○ *to adjudicate in a dispute* □ **he was adjudicated bankrupt** he was declared legally bankrupt

adjudication /əˌdʒuːdɪ'keɪʃ(ə)n/ *noun* the act of giving a judgment or of deciding a legal problem

adjudication of bankruptcy /ə ˌdʒuːdɪkeɪʃ(ə)n əv 'bæŋkrʌptsi/ *noun* a legal order making someone bankrupt

adjudication tribunal /əˌdʒuːdɪ 'keɪʃ(ə)n traɪˌbjuːn(ə)l/ *noun* a group which adjudicates in industrial disputes

adjudicator /ə'dʒuːdɪkeɪtə/ *noun* **1.** a person who gives a decision on a problem ○ *an adjudicator in an industrial dispute* **2.** □ **the Adjudicator** official who examines complaints from individuals and businesses about how the Inland Revenue handles their affairs, but does not deal with questions of tax liability

adjust /ə'dʒʌst/ *verb* to change something to fit new conditions ○ *Prices are adjusted for inflation.*

'…inflation-adjusted GNP moved up at a 1.3% annual rate' [*Fortune*]

'Saudi Arabia will no longer adjust its production to match short-term supply with demand' [*Economist*]

'…on a seasonally-adjusted basis, output of trucks, electric power, steel and paper decreased' [*Business Week*]

adjustable rate mortgage /ə ˌdʒʌstəb(ə)l reɪt 'mɔːgɪdʒ/ *noun* a mortgage where the interest rate changes according to the current market rates. Abbreviation **ARM**

adjustable rate preferred stock /ə ˌdʒʌstəb(ə)l reɪt prɪˌfɜːd 'stɒk/ *noun* preference shares on which dividends are paid in line with the interest rate on Treasury bills. Abbreviation **ARPS**

adjusted gross income /ə,dʒʌstɪd grəʊs 'ɪnkʌm/ *noun US* a person's total annual income less expenses, pension contributions, capital losses, etc., used as a basis to calculate federal income tax. Abbreviation **AGI**

adjuster /ə'dʒʌstə/ *noun* a person who calculates losses for an insurance company

adjusting entry /ə,dʒʌstɪŋ 'entri/ *noun* an entry in accounts which is made to correct a mistake in the accounts

adjustment /ə'dʒʌstmənt/ *noun* **1.** an entry in accounts which does not represent a receipt or payment, but which is made to make the accounts correct **2.** a change in the exchange rates, made to correct a balance of payment deficit

administer /əd'mɪnɪstə/ *verb* to organise, manage or direct the whole of an organisation or part of one ○ *She administers a large pension fund.*

administered price /əd'mɪnɪstəd praɪs/ *noun US* a price fixed by a manufacturer which cannot be varied by a retailer (NOTE: The UK term is **resale price maintenance**.)

administration /əd,mɪnɪ'streɪʃ(ə)n/ *noun* **1.** the action of organising, controlling or managing a company **2.** an appointment by a court of a person to manage the affairs of a company

administration costs /əd,mɪnɪ 'streɪʃ(ə)n ,kɒsts/, **administration expenses** /əd,mɪnɪ'streɪʃ(ə)n ɪk,spensɪz/ *plural noun* the costs of management, not including production, marketing, or distribution costs

administrative expenses /əd ,mɪnɪstrətɪv ɪk'spensɪz/ *plural noun* same as **administration costs**

administrative receiver /əd ,mɪnɪstrətɪv rɪ'siːvə/ *noun* a person appointed by a court to administer the affairs of a company

administrative receivership /əd ,mɪnɪstrətɪv rɪ'siːvəʃɪp/ *noun* the appointment of an administrative receiver by a debenture holder

administrator /əd'mɪnɪstreɪtə/ *noun* **1.** a person who directs the work of other employees in a business ○ *After several years as a college teacher, she hopes to become an administrator.* **2.** a person appointed by a court to manage the affairs of someone who dies without leaving a will

ADR *abbreviation* American Depositary Receipt

ad valorem /,æd və'lɔːrəm/ *adjective* used to describe a tax or commission, e.g., Value Added Tax, that is calculated on the value of the goods or services provided, rather than on their number or size ○ *ad valorem duty* ○ *ad valorem tax*

ad valorem duty /,æd və'lɔːrəm ,djuːti/ *noun* the duty calculated on the sales value of the goods

ad valorem tax /,æd və'lɔːrem tæks/ *noun* a tax calculated according to the value of the goods taxed

advance /əd'vɑːns/ *noun* money paid as a loan or as a part of a payment to be made later ○ *She asked if she could have a cash advance.* ○ *We paid her an advance on account.* ○ *Can I have an advance of $100 against next month's salary?* ■ *adjective* early, or taking place before something else happens ○ *advance payment* ○ *Advance holiday bookings are up on last year.* ○ *You must give seven days' advance notice of withdrawals from the account.* ■ *verb* **1.** to pay an amount of money to someone as a loan or as a part of a payment to be made later ○ *The bank advanced him $100,000 against the security of his house.* **2.** to make something happen earlier ○ *The date of the shipping has been advanced to May 10th.* ○ *The meeting with the German distributors has been advanced from 11.00 to 9.30.*

advance payment guarantee /əd ,vɑːns 'peɪmənt gærən,tiː/, **advance payment bond** /əd,vɑːns 'peɪmənt ,bɒnd/ *noun* a guarantee that enables a buyer to recover an advance payment made under a contract or order if the supplier fails to fulfil its contractual obligations

adverse balance /,ædvɜːs 'bæləns/ *noun* the deficit on an account, especially a nation's balance of payments account

adverse opinion /,ædvɜːs ə'pɪnjən/ *noun US* an auditor's report that a company's financial statement is not a fair representation of the company's actual financial position

adverse variance /,ædvɜːs 'veəriəns/ *noun* variance which shows that the actual result is worse than expected. Also called **unfavourable variance**

advice /əd'vaɪs/ *noun* a notification telling someone what has happened

adviser /əd'vaɪzə/, **advisor** *noun* a person who suggests what should be done ○ *He is consulting the company's legal adviser.*

advisory /əd'vaɪz(ə)ri/ *adjective* as an adviser ○ *She is acting in an advisory capacity.*

advisory funds /əd'vaɪz(ə)ri ˌfʌndz/ *plural noun* funds placed with a financial institution to invest on behalf of a client, the institution investing them at its own discretion

AFAANZ *abbreviation* Accounting and Finance Association of Australia and New Zealand

AFBD *abbreviation* Association of Futures Brokers and Dealers

affiliated /ə'fɪlieɪtɪd/ *adjective* connected with or owned by another company ○ *Smiths Ltd is one of our affiliated companies.*

affiliated enterprise /əˌfɪlieɪtɪd 'entəpraɪz/, **affiliated company** /ə ˌfɪlieɪtɪd 'kʌmp(ə)ni/ *noun* company which is partly owned by another (though less than 50%), and where the share-owning company exerts some management control or has a close trading relationship with the associate ○ *one of our affiliated companies*

aftermarket /'ɑːftəˌmɑːkɪt/ *noun* a market in new shares, which starts immediately after trading in the shares begins

after tax /ˌɑːftər 'tæks/ *adverb* after tax has been paid

after-tax profit /ˌɑːftə 'tæks ˌprɒfɪt/ *noun* a profit after tax has been deducted

age analysis of debtors /ˌeɪdʒ ə ˌnæləsɪs əv 'detəz/ *noun* the amount owed by debtors, classified by age of debt

aged debtors analysis /ˌeɪdʒd 'detəz ə ˌnæləsɪs/, **ageing schedule** /'eɪdʒɪŋ ˌʃedjuːl/ *noun* a list which analyses a company's debtors, showing the number of days their payments are outstanding

agency /'eɪdʒənsi/ *noun* **1.** an office or job of representing another company in an area ○ *They signed an agency agreement* or *an agency contract.* **2.** an office or business which arranges things for other companies

agency bank /'eɪdʒənsi bæŋk/ *noun* a bank which does not accept deposits, but acts as an agent for another, usually foreign, bank

agency bill /'eɪdʒənsi bɪl/ *noun* a bill of exchange drawn on the local branch of a foreign bank

agency broker /'eɪdʒənsi ˌbrəʊkə/ *noun* a dealer who acts as the agent for an investor, buying and selling for a commission

agency worker /'eɪdʒənsi ˌwɜːkə/ *noun* a person who is employed by an agency to work for another company. He or she is

taxed as an employee of the agency, not of the company where he or she actually works.

agenda /ə'dʒendə/ *noun* a list of things to be discussed at a meeting ○ *The conference agenda* or *the agenda of* ○ *After two hours we were still discussing the first item on the agenda.* ○ *We usually put finance at the top of the agenda.* ○ *The chair wants two items removed from* or *taken off the agenda.*

agent /'eɪdʒənt/ *noun* **1.** a person who represents a company or another person in an area ○ *to be the agent for BMW cars* ○ *to be the agent for IBM* **2.** a person in charge of an agency ○ *The estate agent sent me a list of properties for sale.*

agent bank /'eɪdʒənt bæŋk/ *noun* a bank which uses the credit card system set up by another bank

agent's commission /ˌeɪdʒənts kə 'mɪʃ(ə)n/ *noun* money, often a percentage of sales, paid to an agent

age-related /'eɪdʒ rɪˌleɪtɪd/ *adjective* connected with a person's age

age-related allowance /ˌeɪdʒ rɪˌleɪtɪd ə'laʊəns/ *noun* an extra tax allowance which a person over 65 may be entitled to

aggregate /'æɡrɪɡət/ *adjective* total, with everything added together ○ *aggregate output*

aggregate demand /ˌæɡrɪɡət dɪ 'mɑːnd/ *noun* the total demand for goods and services from all sectors of the economy including individuals, companies and the government ○ *Economists are studying the recent fall in aggregate demand.* ○ *As incomes have risen, so has aggregate demand.*

aggregate risk /ˌæɡrɪɡət 'rɪsk/ *noun* the risk which a bank runs in lending to a customer

aggregate supply /ˌæɡrɪɡət sə'plaɪ/ *noun* all goods and services on the market ○ *Is aggregate supply meeting aggregate demand?*

AGI *abbreviation US* adjusted gross income

agio /'ædʒɪəʊ/ *noun* **1.** a charge made for changing money of one currency into another, or for changing banknotes into cash **2.** the difference between two values, such as between the interest charged on loans made by a bank and the interest paid by the bank on deposits, or the difference between the values of two currencies

AGM *abbreviation* Annual General Meeting

agreed /ə'griːd/ *adjective* having been accepted by everyone ○ *We pay an agreed* *amount each month.* ○ *The agreed terms of employment are laid down in the contract.*

agreed price /ə,griːd ˈpraɪs/ *noun* a price which has been accepted by both the buyer and seller

AICPA *abbreviation* American Institute of Certified Public Accountants

AIM *abbreviation* Alternative Investment Market

airmail transfer /ˈeəmeɪl ˌtrænsfɜː/ *noun* an act of sending money from one bank to another by airmail

alien corporation /ˌeɪliən ˌkɔːpə ˈreɪʃ(ə)n/ *noun US* a company which is incorporated in a foreign country

A list /ˈeɪ lɪst/ *noun* a list of members of a company at the time it is wound up who may be liable for the company's unpaid debts

all-in price /ˌɔːl ɪn ˈpraɪs/ *noun* a price which covers all items in a purchase such as goods, delivery, tax or insurance

all-in rate /ˌɔːl ɪn ˈreɪt/ *noun* **1.** a price which covers all the costs connected with a purchase, such as delivery, tax and insurance, as well as the cost of the goods themselves **2.** a wage which includes all extra payments such as bonuses and merit pay

allocate /ˈæləkeɪt/ *verb* **1.** to divide something in various ways and share it out ○ *How are we going to allocate the available office space?* **2.** to assign a whole item of cost, or of revenue, to a single cost unit, centre, account or time period

allocated costs /ˈæləˌkeɪtd kɒsts/ *plural noun* overhead costs which have been allocated to a specific cost centre

allocation /ˌæləˈkeɪʃ(ə)n/ *noun* the process of providing sums of money for particular purposes, or a sum provided for a purpose ○ *the allocation of funds to a project*

allot /əˈlɒt/ *verb* to share out

allotment /əˈlɒtmənt/ *noun* **1.** the process of sharing out something, especially money between various departments, projects or people ○ *The allotment of funds to each project is the responsibility of the finance director.* **2.** the act of giving shares in a new company to people who have applied for them ○ *share allotment* ○ *payment in full on allotment*

allow /əˈlaʊ/ *verb* **1.** to say that someone can do something ○ *Junior members of staff are not allowed to use the chairman's lift.* ○ *The company allows all members of staff to take six days' holiday at Christmas.* **2.** to give ○ *to allow 5% discount to members of staff* **3.** to agree to or accept legally ○ *to allow a claim* or *an appeal*

allow for /əˈlaʊ fɔː/ *phrasal verb* to give a discount for something, or to add an extra sum to cover something ○ *to allow for money paid in advance* ○ *Add on an extra 10% to allow for postage and packing.*

allowable /əˈlaʊəb(ə)l/ *adjective* legally accepted. Opposite **disallowable**

allowable deductions /əˌlaʊəb(ə)l dɪ ˈdʌkʃ(ə)ns/ *plural noun* deductions from income which are allowed by the Inland Revenue, and which reduce the tax payable

allowable expenses /əˌlaʊəb(ə)l ɪk ˈspensɪz/ *plural noun* business expenses which can be claimed against tax

allowable losses /əˌlaʊəb(ə)l ˈlɒsɪz/ *plural noun* losses, e.g. on the sale of assets, which are allowed to be set off against gains

allowance /əˈlaʊəns/ *noun* **1.** money which is given for a special reason ○ *a travel allowance* or *a travelling allowance* **2.** a part of an income which is not taxed ○ *allowances against tax* or *tax allowances* ○ *personal allowances* (NOTE: The US term is **exemption**) **3.** money removed in the form of a discount ○ *an allowance for depreciation* ○ *an allowance for exchange loss*

'…the compensation plan includes base, incentive and car allowance totalling $50,000+' [*Globe and Mail (Toronto)*]

allowance for bad debt /əˌlaʊəns fə bæd ˈdet/ *noun* a provision made in a company's accounts for debts which may never be paid

allowances against tax /əˌlaʊənsɪz ə ˌgenst ˈtæks/ *plural noun* part of someone's income which is not taxed

all-risks policy /ˌɔːl ˈrɪsks ˌpɒlɪsi/ *noun* an insurance policy which covers risks of any kind, with no exclusions

alternative cost /ɔːlˈtɜːnətɪv kɒst/ *noun* same as **opportunity cost**

Alternative Investment Market /ɔːl ˌtɜːnətɪv ɪnˈvestmənt ˌmɑːkɪt/ *noun* a London stock market, regulated by the London Stock Exchange, dealing in shares in smaller companies which are not listed on the main London Stock Exchange. Abbreviation **AIM** (NOTE: The **AIM** is a way in which smaller companies can sell shares to the investing public without going to the expense of obtaining a full share listing.)

alternative minimum tax /ɔːlˌtɜːnətɪv ˌmɪnɪməm ˈtæks/ *noun US* a way of calculating US income tax that is intended to ensure that wealthy individuals, corporations, trusts, and estates pay at least some tax regardless of deductions, but that is increasingly targeting the middle class. Abbreviation **AMT**

amalgamate /ə'mælgəmeɪt/ *verb* to join together with another group ○ *The amalgamated group includes six companies.*

American Accounting Association /ə,merɪkən ə'kaʊntɪŋ ə,səʊsieɪʃ(ə)n/ *noun* a US voluntary organisation for those with an interest in accounting research and best practice, which aims to promote excellence in the creation, dissemination and application of accounting knowledge and skills. Abbreviation **AAA**

American Depository Receipt /ə ,merɪkən dɪ'pɒzɪtri rɪ,siːt/ *noun* a document issued by an American bank to US citizens, making them unregistered shareholders of companies in foreign countries. The document allows them to receive dividends from their investments, and ADRs can themselves be bought or sold. Abbreviation **ADR**

American Institute of Certified Public Accountants /ə,merɪkən ,ɪnstɪtjuːt əv ,sɜːtɪfaɪd ,pʌblɪk ə'kaʊntənts/ *noun* the national association for certified public accountants in the United States. Abbreviation **AICPA**

amortisable /,æmɔː'taɪzəb(ə)l/ *adjective* being possible to amortise ○ *The capital cost is amortisable over a period of ten years.*

amortisation /ə,mɔːtaɪ'zeɪʃ(ə)n/ *noun* an act of amortising ○ *amortisation of a debt*

amortisation period /ə,mɔːtaɪ 'zeɪʃ(ə)n ,pɪəriəd/ *noun* the length of a lease, used when depreciating the value of the asset leased

amortise /ə'mɔːtaɪz/, **amortize** *verb* **1.** to repay a loan by regular payments, most of which pay off the interest on the loan at first, and then reduce the principal as the repayment period progresses ○ *The capital cost is amortised over five years.* **2.** to depreciate or to write down the capital value of an asset over a period of time in a company's accounts

amount paid up /ə,maʊnt peɪd 'ʌp/ *noun* an amount paid for a new issue of shares, either the total payment or the first instalment, if the shares are offered with instalment payments

amount realised /ə,maʊnt 'rɪːəlaɪzd/ *noun* money received from the sale or exchange of property

AMT *abbreviation* alternative minimum tax

analyse /'ænəlaɪz/, **analyze** *verb* to examine someone or something in detail ○ *to analyse a statement of account* ○ *to analyse the market potential*

analysis /ə'næləsɪs/ *noun* a detailed examination and report ○ *a job analysis* ○ *market analysis* ○ *Her job is to produce a regular sales analysis.* (NOTE: The plural is **analyses**.)

analyst /'ænəlɪst/ *noun* a person who analyses ○ *a market analyst* ○ *a systems analyst*

analytical review /,ænəlɪtɪk(ə)l rɪ'vjuː/ *noun* an examination of accounts from different periods for the purpose of identifying ratios, trends and changes in balances

angel /'eɪndʒəl/ *noun* an investor in a company in its early stages, often looking for returns over a longer period of time than a venture capitalist

annual /'ænjuəl/ *adjective* for one year ○ *an annual statement of income* ○ *They have six weeks' annual leave.* ○ *The company has an annual growth of 5%.* ○ *We get an annual bonus.*

'...real wages have risen at an annual rate of only 1% in the last two years' [*Sunday Times*]

'...the remuneration package will include an attractive salary, profit sharing and a company car together with four weeks' annual holiday' [*Times*]

annual accounts /,ænjuəl ə'kaʊnts/ *plural noun* the accounts prepared at the end of a financial year ○ *The annual accounts have been sent to the shareholders.*

annual depreciation /,ænjuəl dɪ,priːʃi 'eɪʃ(ə)n/ *noun* a reduction in the book value of an asset at a particular rate per year. ♢ **straight line depreciation**

annual depreciation provision /,ænjuəl dɪ,priːʃi'eɪʃ(ə)n prə,vɪʒ(ə)n/ *noun* an assessment of the cost of an asset's depreciation in a given accounting period

annual exemptions /,ænjuəl ɪg 'zempʃ(ə)nz/ *plural noun* the amount of income which is exempt from tax. For example, the first £8,500 in capital gains in any one year is exempt from tax.

Annual General Meeting /,ænjuəl ,dʒen(ə)rəl 'miːtɪŋ/ *noun* an annual meeting of all shareholders of a company, when the company's financial situation is presented by and discussed with the directors, when the accounts for the past year are approved and when dividends are declared and audited. Abbreviation **AGM** (NOTE: The US term is **annual meeting** or **annual stockholders' meeting**.)

annual income /ˌænjuəl 'ɪnkʌm/ *noun* money received during a calendar year

annualised /'ænjuəlaɪzd/, **annualized** *adjective* shown on an annual basis

'…he believes this may have caused the economy to grow at an annualized rate of almost 5 per cent in the final quarter of last year' [*Investors Chronicle*]

annualised percentage rate /ˌænjuəlaɪzd pə'sentɪdʒ ˌreɪt/ *noun* a yearly percentage rate, calculated by multiplying the monthly rate by twelve. Abbreviation **APR** (NOTE: The annualised percentage rate is not as accurate as the Annual Percentage Rate (APR), which includes fees and other charges.)

annually /'ænjuəli/ *adverb* each year ○ *The figures are updated annually.*

annual management charge /ˌænjuəl 'mænɪdʒmənt tʃɑːdʒ/ *noun* a charge made by the financial institution which is managing an account

annual meeting /ˌænjuəl 'miːtɪŋ/ *noun* US same as **Annual General Meeting**

Annual Percentage Rate /ˌænjuəl pə 'sentɪdʒ ˌreɪt/ *noun* a rate of interest (such as on a hire-purchase agreement) shown on an annual compound basis, and including fees and charges. Abbreviation **APR**

annual report /ˌænjuəl rɪ'pɔːt/ *noun* a report of a company's financial situation at the end of a year, sent to all the shareholders

annual return /ˌænjuəl rɪ'tɜːn/ *noun* an official report which a registered company has to make each year to the Registrar of Companies

annuitant /ə'njuːɪtənt/ *noun* a person who receives an annuity

annuity /ə'njuːɪti/ *noun* money paid each year to a retired person, usually in return for a lump-sum payment. The value of the annuity depends on how long the person lives, as it usually cannot be passed on to another person. Annuities are fixed payments, and lose their value with inflation, whereas a pension can be index-linked. ○ *to buy* or *to take out an annuity* ○ *She has a government annuity* or *an annuity from the government.*

annuity certain /əˌnjuːɪti 'sɜːtən/ *noun* an annuity that provides payments for a specific number of years, regardless of life or death of the annuitant

annuity contract /ə'njuːɪti ˌkɒntrækt/ *noun* a contract under which a person is paid a fixed sum regularly for life

antedate /ˌæntɪ'deɪt/ *verb* to put an earlier date on a document ○ *The invoice was antedated to January 1st.*

anti-dumping duty /ˌænti 'dʌmpɪŋ ˌdjuːti/ *noun* same as **countervailing duty**

anti-inflationary /ˌænti ɪn 'fleɪʃ(ə)n(ə)ri/ *adjective* restricting or trying to restrict inflation ○ *anti-inflationary measures*

anti-trust /ˌænti 'trʌst/ *adjective* attacking monopolies and encouraging competition ○ *anti-trust measures*

anti-trust laws /ˌænti 'trʌst ˌlɔːz/, **anti-trust legislation** /ˌænti 'trʌst ledʒɪ ˌsleɪʃ(ə)n/ *plural noun* laws in the United States which prevent the formation of monopolies

APB *abbreviation* **1.** Accounting Principles Board **2.** Auditing Practices Board

Appeals Commissioner *noun* a person appointed officially to supervise the collection of taxes, including income tax, capital gains tax and corporation tax, but not VAT

application /ˌæplɪ'keɪʃ(ə)n/ *noun* **1.** the act of asking for something, usually in writing, or a document in which someone asks for something, e.g. a job ○ *shares payable on application* ○ *She sent off six applications for job* or *six job applications.* **2.** effort or diligence ○ *She has shown great application in her work on the project.*

application of funds /ˌæplɪkeɪʃ(ə)n əv 'fʌndz/ *noun* details of the way in which funds have been spent during an accounting period

apportion /ə'pɔːʃ(ə)n/ *verb* to share out something, e.g. costs, funds or blame ○ *Costs are apportioned according to projected revenue.*

apportionment /ə'pɔːʃ(ə)nmənt/ *noun* the sharing out of costs

appraisal /ə'preɪz(ə)l/ *noun* a calculation of the value of someone or something

appraise /ə'preɪz/ *verb* to assess or to calculate the value of something or someone

appreciate /ə'priːʃieɪt/ *verb* (*of currency, shares, etc.*) to increase in value

appreciation /əˌpriːʃi'eɪʃ(ə)n/ *noun* **1.** an increase in value. Also called **capital appreciation 2.** the act of valuing something highly ○ *She was given a pay rise in appreciation of her excellent work.*

appropriate *verb* /ə'prəuprieɪt/ to put a sum of money aside for a special purpose ○ *to appropriate a sum of money for a capital project*

appropriation /əˌprəupri'eɪʃ(ə)n/ *noun* the act of putting money aside for a special purpose ○ *appropriation of funds to the reserve*

appropriation account /əˌprəʊpri
'eɪʃ(ə)n əˌkaʊnt/ *noun* the part of a profit
and loss account which shows how the profit
has been dealt with, e.g., how much has been
given to the shareholders as dividends and
how much is being put into the reserves

approval /ə'pruːv(ə)l/ *noun* the act of saying or thinking that something is good ○ *to
submit a budget for approval*

approve /ə'pruːv/ *verb* **1.** □ **to approve of
something** to think something is good ○
*The chairman approves of the new company
letter heading.* ○ *The sales staff do not
approve of interference from the accounts
division.* **2.** to agree to something officially
○ *to approve the terms of a contract* ○ *The
proposal was approved by the board.*

approved accounts /əˌpruːvd ə
'kaʊnts/ *plural noun* accounts that have
been formally accepted by a company's
board of directors

approved scheme /əˌpruːvd 'skiːm/
noun a pension scheme or share purchase
scheme which has been approved by the
Inland Revenue

approved securities /əˌpruːvd sɪ
'kjʊərɪtiz/ *plural noun* state bonds which
can be held by banks to form part of their
reserves (NOTE: The list of these bonds is
the 'approved list'.)

approximate /ə'prɒksɪmət/ *adjective* not
exact, but almost correct ○ *The sales division has made an approximate forecast of
expenditure.*

approximately /ə'prɒksɪmətli/ *adverb*
not quite exactly, but close to the figure
shown ○ *Expenditure on marketing is
approximately 10% down on the previous
quarter.*

approximation /əˌprɒksɪ'meɪʃ(ə)n/
noun a rough calculation ○ *Each department has been asked to provide an approximation of expenditure for next year.* ○ *The
final figure is only an approximation.*

APR *abbreviation* annualised percentage
rate

APRA *abbreviation* Australian Prudential
Regulation Authority

AR *abbreviation* accounts receivable

arbitrage /'ɑːbɪˌtrɑːʒ/ *noun* the business
of making a profit from the difference in
value of various assets, e.g. by selling foreign currencies or commodities on one market and buying on another at almost the
same time to profit from different exchange
rates, or by buying currencies forward and
selling them forward at a later date, to benefit from a difference in prices

arbitrage syndicate /'ɑːbɪtrɑːʒ
ˌsɪndɪkət/ *noun* a group of people who
together raise the capital to invest in arbitrage deals

arbitration /ˌɑːbɪ'treɪʃ(ə)n/ *noun* the settling of a dispute by an outside party agreed
on by both sides ○ *to take a dispute to arbitration* or *to go to arbitration* ○ *arbitration
in an industrial dispute* ○ *The two sides
decided to submit the dispute to arbitration*
or *to refer the question to arbitration.*

arbitrator /'ɑːbɪtreɪtə/ *noun* a person not
concerned with a dispute who is chosen by
both sides to try to settle it ○ *an industrial
arbitrator* ○ *They refused to accept* or *they
rejected the arbitrator's ruling.*

ARD *abbreviation* accounting reference
date

area manager /ˌeəriə 'mænɪdʒə/ *noun* a
manager who is responsible for a company's
work in a specific part of the country

arithmetic mean /ˌærɪθmetɪk 'miːn/
noun a simple average calculated by dividing the sum of two or more items by the
number of items

ARM *abbreviation* adjustable rate mortgage

around /ə'raʊnd/ *preposition* **1.** approximately ○ *The office costs around £2,000 a
year to heat.* ○ *Her salary is around
$85,000.* **2.** with a premium or discount

ARPS *abbreviation* adjustable rate preferred stock

ARR *abbreviation* accounting rate of return

arrangement fee /ə'reɪndʒmənt fiː/
noun a charge made by a bank to a client for
arranging credit facilities

arrears /ə'rɪəz/ *plural noun* money which
is owed, but which has not been paid at the
right time ○ *a salary with arrears effective
from January 1st* ○ *We are pressing the company to pay arrears of interest.* ○ *You must
not allow the mortgage payments to fall into
arrears.*

article /'ɑːtɪk(ə)l/ *noun* a section of a legal
agreement such as a contract or treaty ○ *See
article 8 of the contract.*

articles of association /ˌɑːtɪk(ə)lz əv
əˌsəʊsi'eɪʃ(ə)n/ *plural noun* a document
which lays down the rules for a company
regarding such matters as the issue of shares,
the conduct of meetings and the appointment of directors ○ *This procedure is not
allowed under the articles of association of
the company.* (NOTE: The US term is
bylaws)

articles of incorporation /ˌɑːtɪk(ə)lz
əv ɪnˌkɔːpə'reɪʃ(ə)n/ *plural noun US* same

as **memorandum and articles of association**

articles of partnership /ˌɑːtɪk(ə)lz əv ˈpɑːtnəʃɪp/ *plural noun* same as **partnership agreement**

ASB *abbreviation* Accounting Standards Board

ASC *abbreviation* Accounting Standards Committee

A shares /ˈeɪ ˌʃeəz/ *plural noun* ordinary shares with limited voting rights or no voting rights at all

asked price /ˈɑːskt praɪs/ *noun* a price at which a commodity or stock is offered for sale by a seller, also called 'offer price' in the UK

asking price /ˈɑːskɪŋ ˌpraɪs/ *noun* a price which the seller is hoping will be paid for the item being sold ○ *the asking price is $24,000*

as per /ˌæz ˈpɜː/ ♦ **per**

assess /əˈses/ *verb* to calculate the value of something or someone ○ *to assess damages at £1,000* ○ *to assess a property for the purposes of insurance*

assessed value /əˌsest ˈvæljuː/ *noun* a value that is the result of calculation by someone such as an auditor or investment advisor

assessment /əˈsesmənt/ *noun* a calculation of value ○ *a property assessment* ○ *a tax assessment*

asset /ˈæset/ *noun* **1.** something which belongs to a company or person, and which has a value ○ *He has an excess of assets over liabilities.* ○ *Her assets are only $640 as against liabilities of $24,000.* **2.** □ **valuation of a company on an assets basis** calculating the value of a company on the basis of the value of its assets (as opposed to a valuation on an earnings or dividend yield basis)

asset-backed securities /ˌæset bækt siˈkjʊərɪtiz/ *plural noun* bonds secured against specific assets

asset backing /ˈæset ˌbækɪŋ/ *noun* a support for a share price provided by the value of the company's assets

asset-rich company /ˌæset rɪtʃ ˈkʌmp(ə)ni/ *noun* company with valuable tangible assets, such as property, which provide firm backing for its shares

assets /ˈæsets/ *plural noun* all items of property that contribute to the value of an organisation, including tangible items such as cash, stock and real estate, as well as intangible items such as goodwill

asset stripper /ˈæset ˌstrɪpə/ *noun* a person who buys a company to sell its assets

asset stripping /ˈæset ˌstrɪpɪŋ/ *noun* the practice of buying a company at a lower price than its asset value, and then selling its assets

asset turnover /ˈæset ˌtɜːnəʊvə/ *noun* a measure of a company's efficiency that is the ratio of sales revenue to total assets

asset turnover ratio /ˌæset ˈtɜːnəʊvə ˌreɪʃiəʊ/ *noun* the number of times assets are turned over by sales during the year, calculated as turnover divided by total assets less current liabilities

asset value /ˈæset ˌvæljuː/ *noun* the value of a company calculated by adding together all its assets

assign /əˈsaɪn/ *verb* **1.** to give something to someone by means of an official legal transfer ○ *to assign a right to someone* ○ *to assign shares to someone* **2.** to give someone a job of work to do and make him or her responsible for doing it ○ *She was assigned the task of checking the sales figures.*

assignation /ˌæsɪɡˈneɪʃ(ə)n/ *noun* a legal transfer ○ *the assignation of shares to someone* ○ *the assignation of a patent*

assignee /ˌæsaɪˈniː/ *noun* a person who receives something which has been assigned to him or her

assignment /əˈsaɪnmənt/ *noun* the legal transfer of a property or right ○ *the assignment of a patent* or *of a copyright* ○ *to sign a deed of assignment*

assignor /ˌæsaɪˈnɔː/ *noun* a person who assigns something to someone

associate /əˈsəʊsiət/ *noun* **1.** a person or company linked to another in a takeover bid **2.** a title given to a junior member of a professional organisation. Senior members are usually called 'fellows'.

associate company /əˌsəʊsiət ˈkʌmp(ə)ni/ *noun* a company which is partly owned by another company

associated company /əˌsəʊsieɪtɪd ˈkʌmp(ə)ni/ *noun* a company which is partly owned by another company (though less than 50%), which exerts some management control over it or has a close trading relationship with it ○ *Smith Ltd and its associated company, Jones Brothers*

associate director /əˌsəʊsiət daɪ ˈrektə/ *noun* a director who attends board meetings, but has not been elected by the shareholders

Association of Accounting Technicians /əˌsəʊsieɪʃ(ə)n əv əˈkaʊntɪŋ ˌteknɪʃ(ə)nz/ *noun* an organisation which represents accounting technicians and grants membership to people who have passed its examinations. Abbreviation **AAT**

Association of Authorised Public Accountants /ə,səʊsieɪʃ(ə)n əv ,ɔːθəraɪzd ,pʌblɪk əˈkaʊntənts/ *noun* an organisation which represents accountants who have been authorised by the government to work as auditors. It is a subsidiary of the Association of Chartered Certified Accountants. Abbreviation **AAPA**

Association of Chartered Accountants in the United States /ə ,səʊsieɪʃ(ə)n əv ,tʃɑːtəd ə,kaʊntənts ɪn ði juː,naɪtɪd ˈsteɪts/ *noun* an organisation representing Chartered Accountants from Australia, Canada, England and Wales, Ireland, New Zealand, Scotland and South Africa who are based in the United States. Abbreviation **ACAUS**

Association of Chartered Certified Accountants /ə,səʊsieɪʃ(ə)n əv ,tʃɑːtəd ,sɜːtɪfaɪd əˈkaʊntənts/ *noun* an organisation whose members are certified accountants. Abbreviation **ACCA**

Association of Corporate Treasurers /ə,səʊsieɪʃ(ə)n əv ,kɔːp(ə)rət ˈtreʒərəz/ *noun* an organisation which groups company treasurers and awards membership to those who have passed its examinations

Association of Financial Advisers /ə ,səʊsieɪʃ(ə)n əv faɪ,nænʃ(ə)l ədˈvaɪzəz/ *noun* a trade association that represents the interests of independent financial advisers

Association of Futures Brokers and Dealers /ə,səʊsieɪʃ(ə)n əv ˈfjuːtʃəz ,brəʊkəz ən ,diːləz/ *noun* a self-regulating organisation which oversees the activities of dealers in futures and options. Abbreviation **AFBD**

assumable mortgage /ə,sjuːməb(ə)l ˈmɔːɡɪdʒ/ *noun US* a mortgage which can be passed to another person

assurance /əˈʃʊərəns/ *noun* a type of insurance which pays compensation for an event that is certain to happen at some time, especially for the death of the insured person. Also called **life assurance**, **life insurance**

assure /əˈʃʊə/ *verb* to insure someone, or someone's life, so that the insurance company will pay compensation when that person dies ○ *He has paid the premiums to have his wife's life assured.* (NOTE: **Assure**, **assurer** and **assurance** are used in Britain for insurance policies relating to something which will certainly happen (such as death);

for other types of policy (i.e. those against something which may or may not happen, such as an accident) use the terms **insure**, **insurer** and **insurance**. In the US **insure**, **insurer** and **insurance** are used for both.)

assurer /əˈʃʊərə/, **assuror** *noun* an insurer or a company which insures

AST *abbreviation* Automated Screen Trading

at call /,æt ˈkɔːl/ *adverb* immediately available

ATM *abbreviation* automated teller machine

'Swiss banks are issuing new cards which will allow cash withdrawals from ATMs in Belgium, Denmark, Spain, France, the Netherlands, Portugal and Germany' [*Banking Technology*]

'…the major supermarket operator is planning a new type of bank that would earn 90% of its revenue from fees on automated teller machine transactions. With the bank setting up ATMs at 7,000 group outlets nationwide, it would have a branch network at least 20 times larger than any of the major banks' [*Nikkei Weekly*]

at par /,æt ˈpɑː/ *phrase* equal to the face value

at sight /,æt ˈsaɪt/ *adverb* immediately, when it is presented ○ *a bill of exchange payable at sight*

attachment /əˈtætʃmənt/ *noun* the act of holding a debtor's property to prevent it being sold until debts are paid

attachment of earnings /ə,tætʃmənt əv ˈɜːnɪŋz/ *noun* a process in which a court uses its legal authority to obtain directly from a person's salary money that the person owes to the court

attachment of earnings order /ə ,tætʃmənt əv ˈɜːnɪŋz ,ɔːdə/ *noun* a court order to make an employer pay part of an employee's salary to the court to pay off debts

attachment order /əˈtætʃmənt ,ɔːdə/ *noun* an order from a court to hold a debtor's property to prevent it being sold until debts are paid

attest /əˈtest/ *noun* a formal statement, e.g. a statement by an auditor that a company's financial position is correctly stated in the company's accounts

attributable profit /ə,trɪbjʊtəb(ə)l ˈprɒfɪt/ *noun* a profit which can be shown to come from a particular area of the company's operations

auction /ˈɔːkʃən/ *noun* **1.** a method of selling goods where people who want to buy compete with each other by saying how much they will offer for something, and the item is sold to the person who makes the highest offer ○ *Their furniture will be sold in the auction rooms next week.* ○ *They announced a sale by auction of the fire-damaged stock.* ○ *The equipment was sold by auction* or *at auction.* □ **to put an item up for auction** to offer an item for sale at an auction **2.** a method of selling government stock, where all stock on issue will be sold, and the highest price offered will be accepted, as opposed to tendering ■ *verb* to sell something at an auction ○ *The factory was closed and the machinery was auctioned off.*

auctioneer /ˌɔːkʃəˈnɪə/ *noun* the person who conducts an auction

audit /ˈɔːdɪt/ *noun* the examination of the books and accounts of a company ○ *to carry out the annual audit* ■ *verb* to examine the books and accounts of a company ○ *Messrs Smith have been asked to audit the accounts.* ○ *The books have not yet been audited.* □ **to audit the stock** to carry out a stock control, in front of witnesses, so as to establish the exact quantities and value of stock

Audit Commission /ˈɔːdɪt kəˌmɪʃ(ə)n/ *noun* British government agency whose duty is to audit the accounts of ministries and other government departments (NOTE: The US term is **General Accounting Office**.)

audit committee /ˈɔːdɪt kəˌmɪti/ *noun* a committee of a company's board of directors that monitors finances, on which company executives cannot sit

audit cycle /ˈɔːdɪt ˌsaɪk(ə)l/ *noun* the interval between audits

audited accounts /ˌɔːdɪtɪd əˈkaʊnts/ *plural noun* a set of accounts that have been thoroughly scrutinised, checked and approved by a team of auditors

audit fee /ˈɔːdɪt fiː/ *noun* a fee charged by an auditor for auditing a company's accounts

auditing /ˈɔːdɪtɪŋ/ *noun* the work of examining the books and accounts of a company

Auditing Practices Board /ˌɔːdɪtɪŋ ˈpræktɪsɪz ˌbɔːd/ *noun* a body responsible for developing and issuing professional auditing standards in the United Kingdom and the Republic of Ireland. The APB was created in 1991 following an agreement between the six members of the Consultative Committee of Accountancy Bodies. Abbreviation **APB**

auditing standards /ˈɔːdɪtɪŋ ˌstændədz/ *plural noun* guidelines, established by an authoritative body, that auditors should follow when examining financial statements and other information

audit opinion /ˌɔːdɪt əˈpɪnjən/ *noun US* a report of the audit of a company's books, carried out by a certified public accountant (NOTE: The UK term is **accountant's opinion**.)

auditor /ˈɔːdɪtə/ *noun* a person who audits

auditors' fees /ˈɔːdɪtəz fiːz/ *plural noun* fees paid to a company's auditors, which are approved by the shareholders at an AGM

auditors' qualification /ˌɔːdɪtəz ˌkwɒlɪfɪˈkeɪʃ(ə)n/ *noun* a form of words in a report from the auditors of a company's accounts, stating that in their opinion the accounts are not a true reflection of the company's financial position. Also called **qualification of accounts**

auditors' report /ˈɔːdɪtəz rɪˌpɔːt/ *noun* a report written by a company's auditors after they have examined the accounts of the company. Also called **audit report** (NOTE: If the auditors are satisfied, the report certifies that, in their opinion, the accounts give a 'true and fair' view of the company's financial position.)

audit programme /ˌɔːdɪt ˈprəʊɡræm/ *noun* a listing of all the steps to be taken when auditing a company's accounts

audit regulation /ˈɔːdɪt ˌreɡjʊleɪʃ(ə)n/ *noun* the regulating of auditors by government

audit report /ˈɔːdɪt rɪˌpɔːt/ *noun* same as **auditors' report**

audit risk /ˈɔːdɪt rɪsk/ *noun* the risk that auditors may give an inappropriate audit opinion on financial statements

audit trail /ˈɔːdɪt treɪl/ *noun* the records that show all the stages of a transaction, e.g. a purchase, a sale or a customer complaint, in the order in which they happened (NOTE: An audit trail can be a useful tool for problem-solving and, in financial markets, may be used to ensure that the dealers have been fair and accurate in their proceedings.)

'…provides real-time fax monitoring and audit trail to safeguard information privacy and accuracy' [Forbes]

augend /ˈɔːɡend/ *noun* the number to which another number (the addend) is added to produce the sum

Australian Accounting Research Foundation /ɒˌstreɪliən əˌkaʊntɪŋ rɪ ˈsɜːtʃ faʊnˌdeɪʃ(ə)n/ *noun* the authority that has regulated auditing and assurance matters in Australia since 2004

Australian Prudential Regulation Authority /ɒˌstreɪliən prʊˌdenʃ(ə)l ˌreɡjʊˈleɪʃ(ə)n ɔːˌθɒrəti/ *noun* a federal government body responsible for ensuring that financial institutions are able to meet their commitments. Abbreviation **APRA**

AUT *abbreviation* authorised unit trust

authorise /ˈɔːθəraɪz/, **authorize** *verb* **1.** to give permission for something to be done ○ *to authorise payment of £10,000* **2.** to give someone the authority to do something ○ *to authorise someone to act on the company's behalf*

authorised capital /ˌɔːθəraɪzd ˈkæpɪt(ə)l/ *noun* the amount of capital which a company is allowed to have, as stated in the memorandum of association (NOTE: The US equivalent is **authorized stock**.)

authorised share capital /ˌɔːθəraɪzd ˈʃeə ˌkæpɪt(ə)l/ *noun* the amount of capital that a company is authorised to issue in the form of shares

authorised unit trust /ˌɔːθəraɪzd ˈjuːnɪt trʌst/ *noun* the official name for a unit trust which has to be managed according to EU directives. Abbreviation **AUT**

Automated Clearing House /ˌɔːtəmeɪtɪd ˈklɪərɪŋ haʊs/ *noun US* an organisation set up by the federal authorities to settle transactions carried out by computer, such as automatic mortgage payments and trade payments between businesses. Abbreviation **ACH**

Automated Screen Trading /ˌɔːtəmeɪtɪd ˈskriːn ˌtreɪdɪŋ/ *noun* a system where securities are bought, sold and matched automatically by computer. Abbreviation **AST**

automated teller machine /ˌɔːtəmeɪtɪd ˈtelə məˌʃiːn/ *noun US* same as **cash dispenser**

availability /əˌveɪləˈbɪlɪti/ *noun* the fact of being easy to obtain

AVCs *abbreviation* additional voluntary contributions

average /ˈæv(ə)rɪdʒ/ *noun* **1.** a number calculated by adding several figures together and dividing by the number of figures added ○ *the average for the last three months* or *the last three months' average* ○ *sales average* or *average of sales* **2.** the sharing of the cost of damage or loss of a ship between the insurers and the owners ■ *adjective* equal to the average of a set of figures ○ *the average increase in salaries* ○ *The average cost per unit is too high.* ○ *The average sales per representative are rising.* ■ *verb* to work out an average figure for something

'…a share with an average rating might yield 5 per cent and have a PER of about 10' [*Investors Chronicle*]

'…the average price per kilogram for this season to the end of April has been 300 cents' [*Australian Financial Review*]

average out /ˌæv(ə)rɪdʒ ˈaʊt/ *phrasal verb* to come to a figure as an average ○ *It averages out at 10% per annum.* ○ *Sales increases have averaged out at 15%.*

average cost of capital /ˌævərɪdʒ kɒst əv ˈkæpɪt(ə)l/ *noun* an average figure for the cost of borrowing or the capital raised by selling shares

average due date /ˌæv(ə)rɪdʒ ˈdjuː ˌdeɪt/ *noun* the average date when several different payments fall due

average income per capita /ˌæv(ə)rɪdʒ ˌɪnkʌm pə ˈkæpɪtə/ *noun* same as **per capita income**

avoidance /əˈvɔɪd(ə)ns/ *noun* the act of trying not to do something or not to pay something ○ *tax avoidance*

award /əˈwɔːd/ *noun* something given by a court, tribunal or other official body, especially when settling a dispute or claim ○ *an award by an industrial tribunal* ○ *The arbitrator's award was set aside on appeal.* ○ *The latest pay award has been announced.*

B

BAA *abbreviation* British Accounting Association

baby bonds /ˈbeɪbi bɒndz/ *plural noun US* bonds in small denominations which the small investor can afford to buy

back /bæk/ *adjective* referring to the past ○ *a back payment* ■ *verb* to help someone, especially financially ○ *The bank is backing us to the tune of $10,000.* ○ *She is looking for someone to back her project.*

'…the businesses we back range from start-up ventures to established companies in need of further capital for expansion' [*Times*]

back out /ˌbæk ˈaʊt/ *phrasal verb* to stop being part of a deal or an agreement ○ *The bank backed out of the contract.* ○ *We had to cancel the project when our German partners backed out.*

backdate /bækˈdeɪt/ *verb* to put an earlier date on a document such as a cheque or an invoice ○ *Backdate your invoice to April 1st.*

back duty /ˈbæk ˌdjuːti/ *noun* a duty or tax which is due but has not yet been paid

back-end loaded /ˌbæk end ˈləʊdɪd/ *adjective* referring to an insurance or investment scheme where commission is charged when the investor withdraws his or her money from the scheme. Compare **front-end loaded**

backer /ˈbækə/ *noun* a person or company that backs someone ○ *One of the company's backers has withdrawn.*

backflush costing /ˈbækflʌʃ ˌkɒstɪŋ/ *noun* a method of costing that links cost to output produced

backing /ˈbækɪŋ/ *noun* support, especially financial support ○ *She has the backing of an Australian bank.* ○ *The company will succeed only if it has sufficient backing.* ○ *She gave her backing to the proposal.*

'…the company has received the backing of a number of oil companies who are willing to pay for the results of the survey' [*Lloyd's List*]

back interest /ˈbæk ˌɪntrəst/ *noun* interest which has not yet been paid

backlog /ˈbæklɒg/ *noun* an amount of work, or of items such as orders or letters, which should have been dealt with earlier but is still waiting to be done ○ *The warehouse is trying to cope with a backlog of orders.* ○ *We're finding it hard to cope with the backlog of paperwork.*

backlog depreciation /ˈbæklɒg dɪˌpriːʃieɪʃ(ə)n/ *noun* depreciation which has not been provided in previous accounts because of an increase in the value of the asset during the current year due to inflation

back payment /ˈbæk ˌpeɪmənt/ *noun* **1.** a payment which is due but has not yet been paid **2.** the act of paying money which is owed

back rent /ˈbæk rent/ *noun* a rent due but not paid ○ *The company owes £100,000 in back rent.*

back tax /ˈbæk tæks/ *noun* tax which is owed

back-to-back loan /ˌbæk tə ˌbæk ˈləʊn/ *noun* a loan from one company to another in one currency arranged against a loan from the second company to the first in another currency. Also called **parallel loan** (NOTE: Back-to-back loans are used by international companies to get round exchange controls.)

backup withholding /ˈbækʌp wɪθ ˌhəʊldɪŋ/ *noun US* a tax retained from investment income so that the IRS is sure of getting the tax due

backwardation /ˌbækwəˈdeɪʃ(ə)n/ *noun* **1.** a penalty paid by the seller when postponing delivery of shares to the buyer **2.** a situation in which the cash price is higher than the forward price. Opposite **forwardation**

backward integration /ˌbækwəd ˌɪntɪ ˈgreɪʃ(ə)n/ *noun* a process of expansion in which a business which deals with the later stages in the production and sale of a product acquires a business that deals with an earlier stage in the same process, usually a supplier ○ *Buying up rubber plantations is part of the tyre company's backward integration policy.* Also called **vertical integration**

backwards spreading /ˌbækwədz ˈspredɪŋ/ *noun* the practice of dividing income earned in a particular accounting year into portions which are allocated to several previous accounting periods

BACS /bæks/ *noun* a company set up to organise the payment of direct debits, standing orders, salary cheques and other payments generated by computers. It operates for all the British clearing banks and several building societies; it forms part of APACS. Compare **CHAPS**

bad cheque /ˌbæd ˈtʃek/ *noun* a cheque which is returned to the drawer for any reason

bad debt /ˌbæd ˈdet/ *noun* a debt which will not be paid, usually because the debtor has gone out of business, and which has to be written off in the accounts ○ *The company has written off $30,000 in bad debts.*

bad debt expense /ˌbæd ˈdet ɪkˌspens/ *noun* an estimate of uncollectible debts which is charged to the profit and loss account

bad debt provision /ˌbæd ˈdet prə ˌvɪʒ(ə)n/ *noun* money put aside in accounts to cover potential bad debts

bad debts recovered /ˌbæd dets rɪ ˈkʌvəd/ *plural noun* money which was formerly classified as bad debts and therefore written off, but that has since been recovered either wholly or in part

badges of trade /ˌbædʒɪz əv ˈtreɪd/ *plural noun* a collection of principles established by case law to determine whether or not a person is trading. If so, he or she is taxed under different rules from non-traders.

bail out /ˌbeɪl ˈaʊt/ *phrasal verb* to rescue a company which is in financial difficulties

'…the government has decided to bail out the bank which has suffered losses to the extent that its capital has been wiped out' [*South China Morning Post*]

bailment /ˈbeɪlmənt/ *noun* a transfer of goods by someone (the 'bailor') to someone (the 'bailee') who then holds them until they have to be returned to the bailor (NOTE: Putting jewels in a bank's safe deposit box is an example of bailment.)

balance /ˈbæləns/ *noun* **1.** the amount which has to be put in one of the columns of an account to make the total debits and credits equal □ **balance brought down *or* forward** the closing balance of the previous

period used as the opening balance of the current period □ **balance carried down *or* forward** the closing balance of the current period **2.** the rest of an amount owed ○ *You can pay £100 deposit and the balance within 60 days.* ■ *verb* **1.** to be equal, i.e. the assets owned must always equal the total liabilities plus capital **2.** to calculate the amount needed to make the two sides of an account equal ○ *I have finished balancing the accounts for March.* **3.** to plan a budget so that expenditure and income are equal ○ *The president is planning for a balanced budget.*

balance off /ˌbæləns ˈɒf/ *verb* to add up and enter the totals for both sides of an account at the end of an accounting period in order to determine the balance

balanced budget /ˌbælənst ˈbʌdʒɪt/ *noun* a budget where expenditure and income are equal

balanced scorecard /ˌbælənst ˈskɔːkɑːd/ *noun* a system of measurement and assessment that uses a variety of indicators, particularly customer relations, internal efficiency, financial performance and innovation, to find out how well an organisation is doing in its attempts to achieve its main objectives

balance of payments /ˌbæləns əv ˈpeɪmənts/ *noun* a comparison between total receipts and payments arising from a country's international trade in goods, services and financial transactions. Abbreviation **BOP** □ **balance of payments capital account** items in a country's balance of payments which refer to capital investments made in or by other countries □ **balance of payments current account** record of imports and exports of goods and services and the flows of money between countries arising from investments □ **long-term balance of payments** record of movements of capital relating to overseas investments and the purchase of companies overseas

balance of payments deficit /ˌbæləns əv ˈpeɪmənts ˌdefɪsɪt/ *noun* a situation in which a country imports more than it exports

balance of payments surplus /ˌbæləns əv ˈpeɪmənts ˌsɜːpləs/ *noun* a situation in which a country exports more than it imports

balance of retained earnings /ˌbæləns əv rɪˌteɪnd ˈɜːnɪŋz/ *noun* statistics that show fluctuations in the level of income retained for reinvestment during an accounting period

balance sheet /ˈbæləns ʃiːt/ *noun* a statement of the financial position of a company at a particular time, such as the end of the financial year or the end of a quarter, showing the company's assets and liabilities ○ *Our accountant has prepared the balance sheet for the first half-year.* ○ *The company balance sheet for the last financial year shows a worse position than for the previous year.* ○ *The company balance sheet for 1984 shows a substantial loss.*

COMMENT: The balance sheet shows the state of a company's finances at a certain date. The profit and loss account shows the movements which have taken place since the end of the previous accounting period. A balance sheet must balance, with the basic equation that assets (i.e. what the company owns, including money owed to the company) must equal liabilities (i.e. what the company owes to its creditors) plus capital (i.e. what it owes to its shareholders). A balance sheet can be drawn up either in the horizontal form, with (in the UK) liabilities and capital on the left-hand side of the page (in the USA, it is the reverse) or in the vertical form, with assets at the top of the page, followed by liabilities, and capital at the bottom. Most are usually drawn up in the vertical format, as opposed to the more old-fashioned horizontal style.

balance sheet asset value /ˌbæləns ʃiːt ˈæset ˌvæljuː/ *noun* the value of a company calculated by adding together all its assets

balance sheet audit /ˌbæləns ʃiːt ˈɔːdɪt/ *noun* a limited audit of the items on a company's balance sheet in order to confirm that it complies with the relevant standards and requirements

balance sheet date /ˈbæləns ʃiːt ˌdeɪt/ *noun* the date (usually the end of a financial or accounting year) when a balance sheet is drawn up

balance sheet equation /ˈbæləns ʃiːt ɪˌkweɪʒ(ə)n/ *noun* the basis upon which all accounts are prepared, that assets = liabilities + assets

balance sheet total /ˌbæləns ʃiːt ˈtəʊt(ə)l/ *noun* in the United Kingdom, the total of assets shown at the bottom of a balance sheet and used to classify a company according to size

balancing item /ˈbælənsɪŋ ˌaɪtəm/, **balancing figure** /ˈbælənsɪŋ ˌfɪɡə/ *noun* an item introduced into a balance sheet to make the two sides balance

balloon /bəˈluːn/ *noun* a loan where the last repayment is larger than the others

balloon mortgage /bəˈluːn ˌmɔːɡɪdʒ/ *noun* a mortgage in which the final payment (called a 'balloon payment') is larger than the others

BALO *noun* a French government publication that includes financial statements of public companies. Full form **Bulletin des Annonces Légales Obligatoires**

bank /bæŋk/ *noun* a business which holds money for its clients, lends money at interest, and trades generally in money ○ *the First National Bank* ○ *the Royal Bank of Scotland* ○ *She put all her earnings into the bank.* ○ *I have had a letter from my bank telling me my account is overdrawn.* ■ *verb* to deposit money into a bank or to have an account with a bank ○ *He banked the cheque as soon as he received it.* ○ *I bank at or with Barclays.*

bankable /ˈbæŋkəb(ə)l/ *adjective* acceptable by a bank as security for a loan

bankable paper /ˌbæŋkəb(ə)l ˈpeɪpə/ *noun* a document which a bank will accept as security for a loan

bank account /ˈbæŋk əˌkaʊnt/ *noun* an account which a customer has with a bank, where the customer can deposit and withdraw money ○ *to open a bank account* ○ *to close a bank account* ○ *How much money do you have in your bank account?* ○ *If you let the balance in your bank account fall below $1,000, you have to pay bank charges.*

bank advance /ˈbæŋk ədˌvɑːns/ *noun* same as **bank loan** ○ *She asked for a bank advance to start her business.*

bank balance /ˈbæŋk ˌbæləns/ *noun* the state of a bank account at any particular time ○ *Our bank balance went into the red last month.*

bank base rate /ˌbæŋk ˈbeɪs ˌreɪt/ *noun* a basic rate of interest, on which the actual rate a bank charges on loans to its customers is calculated. Also called **base rate**

bank bill /ˈbæŋk bɪl/ *noun* **1.** a bill of exchange by one bank telling another bank, usually in another country, to pay money to someone **2.** same as **banker's bill 3.** *US* same as **banknote**

bank book /ˈbæŋk bʊk/ *noun* a book given by a bank or building society which shows money which you deposit or withdraw from your savings account or building society account. Also called **passbook**

bank borrowings /ˈbæŋk ˌbɒrəʊɪŋz/ *plural noun* money borrowed from banks

bank card /ˈbæŋk kɑːd/ *noun* a credit card or debit card issued to a customer by a bank for use instead of cash when buying goods or services (NOTE: There are internationally recognised rules that govern the authorisation of the use of bank cards and the clearing and settlement of transactions in which they are used.)

bank certificate /'bæŋk sə,tɪfɪkət/ *noun* a document, often requested during an audit, that is signed by a bank official and confirms the balances due or from a company on a specific date

bank charge /'bæŋk tʃɑːdʒ/ *noun* same as **service charge**

bank confirmation /'bæŋk ,kɒnfəmeɪʃ(ə)n/ *noun* verification of a company's balances requested by an auditor from a bank

bank credit /'bæŋk ,kredɪt/ *noun* loans or overdrafts from a bank to a customer

bank deposits /'bæŋk dɪ,pɒzɪts/ *plural noun* all money placed in banks by private or corporate customers

bank draft /'bæŋk drɑːft/ *noun* an order by one bank telling another bank, usually in another country, to pay money to someone

banker /'bæŋkə/ *noun* **1.** a person who is in an important position in a bank **2.** a bank ○ *the company's banker is Barclays*

banker's acceptance /,bæŋkəz ək 'septəns/ *noun* a bill of exchange guaranteed by a bank

Bankers' Automated Clearing Services /,bæŋkəz ,ɔːtəmeɪtɪd 'klɪərɪŋ ,sɜːvɪsɪz/ *plural noun* full form of **BACS**

banker's bill /'bæŋkəz bɪl/ *noun* an order by one bank telling another bank, usually in another country, to pay money to someone. Also called **bank bill**

banker's credit card /,bæŋkəz 'kredɪt ,kɑːd/ *noun* a credit card issued by a bank, as opposed to cards issued by stores. Typical such cards are Visa, Egg or MasterCard.

banker's draft /,bæŋkəz 'drɑːft/ *noun* a draft payable by a bank in cash on presentation. Abbreviation **B/D**

banker's lien /,bæŋkəz 'liːn/ *noun* the right of a bank to hold some property of a customer as security against payment of a debt

banker's order /'bæŋkəz ,ɔːdə/ *noun* an order written by a customer asking a bank to make a regular payment ○ *He pays his subscription by banker's order.*

banker's reference /,bæŋkəz 'ref(ə)rəns/ *noun* a written report issued by a bank regarding a particular customer's creditworthiness

bank giro /'bæŋk ,dʒaɪrəʊ/ *noun* a method used by clearing banks to transfer money rapidly from one account to another

bank holiday /,bæŋk 'hɒlɪdeɪ/ *noun* a weekday which is a public holiday when the banks are closed ○ *New Year's Day is a bank holiday.* ○ *Are we paid for bank holidays in this job?*

bank identification number /,bæŋk ,aɪdentɪfɪ'keɪʃ(ə)n ,nʌmbə/ *noun* an internationally organised six-digit number which identifies a bank for charge card purposes. Abbreviation **BIN**

banking /'bæŋkɪŋ/ *noun* the business of banks ○ *He is studying banking.* ○ *She has gone into banking.*

banking account /'bæŋkɪŋ ə,kaʊnt/ *noun* US an account which a customer has with a bank

banking covenants /'bæŋkɪŋ ,kʌvənənts/ *plural noun* a set of conditions imposed by a bank when it lends an institution a large amount of money

Banking Ombudsman /'bæŋkɪŋ ,ɒmbʊdzmən/ *noun* an official whose duty is to investigate complaints by members of the public against banks

banking products /,bæŋkɪŋ 'prɒdʌkts/ *plural noun* goods and services produced by banks for customers, e.g. statements, direct debits

bank loan /'bæŋk ləʊn/ *noun* a loan made by a bank to a customer, usually against the security of a property or asset ○ *She asked for a bank loan to start her business.* Also called **bank advance**

bank manager /'bæŋk ,mænɪdʒə/ *noun* the person in charge of a branch of a bank ○ *They asked their bank manager for a loan.*

bank mandate /'bæŋk ,mændeɪt/ *noun* a written order to a bank, asking it to open an account and allow someone to sign cheques on behalf of the account holder, and giving specimen signatures and relevant information

banknote /'bæŋk nəʊt/ *noun* **1.** a piece of printed paper money ○ *a counterfeit £20 banknote* (NOTE: The US term is **bill**.) **2.** US a non-interest bearing note, issued by a Federal Reserve Bank, which can be used as cash

Bank of England /,bæŋk əv 'ɪŋglənd/ *noun* the UK central bank, owned by the state, which, together with the Treasury, regulates the nation's finances

bank reconciliation /,bæŋk ,rekənsɪli 'eɪʃ(ə)n/ *noun* the act of making sure that the bank statements agree with the company's ledgers

bank reserves /'bæŋk rɪˌzɜːvz/ *plural noun* cash and securities held by a bank to cover deposits

bank return /'bæŋk rɪˌtɜːn/ *noun* a regular report from a bank on its financial position

bankrupt /'bæŋkrʌpt/ *noun, adjective* (a person) who has been declared by a court not to be capable of paying his or her debts and whose affairs are put into the hands of a receiver ○ *a bankrupt property developer* ○ *She was adjudicated* or *declared bankrupt.* ○ *He went bankrupt after two years in business.* ■ *verb* to make someone become bankrupt ○ *The recession bankrupted my father.*

bankruptcy /'bæŋkrʌptsi/ *noun* the state of being bankrupt ○ *The recession has caused thousands of bankruptcies.* (NOTE: The plural is **bankruptcies.**)

bankruptcy order /'bæŋkrʌptsi ˌɔːdə/ *noun* same as **declaration of bankruptcy**

bankruptcy petition /'bæŋkrʌptsi pə ˌtɪʃ(ə)n/ *noun* an application to a court asking for an order making someone bankrupt

bankruptcy proceedings /'bæŋkrʌptsi prəˌsiːdɪŋz/ *plural noun* a court case to make someone bankrupt

bank statement /'bæŋk ˌsteɪtmənt/ *noun* a written statement from a bank showing the balance of an account at a specific date

bank syndicate /'bæŋk ˌsɪndɪkət/ *noun* a group of major international banks which group together to underwrite a very large loan

bank transfer /'bæŋk ˌtrænsfɜː/ *noun* an act of moving money from a bank account to another account

bargain /'bɑːgɪn/ *noun* an agreement on the price of something ○ *to strike a bargain* or *to make a bargain* ■ *verb* to try to reach agreement about something, especially a price, usually with each person or group involved putting forward suggestions or offers which are discussed until a compromise is arrived at ○ *You will have to bargain with the dealer if you want a discount.* ○ *They spent two hours bargaining about* or *over the price.* (NOTE: You bargain **with** someone **over** or **about** or **for** something.)

barter /'bɑːtə/ *noun* a system in which goods are exchanged for other goods and not sold for money

'…under the barter agreements, Nigeria will export 175,000 barrels a day of crude oil in exchange for trucks, food, planes and chemicals' [*Wall Street Journal*]

bartering /'bɑːtərɪŋ/ *noun* the act of exchanging goods for other goods and not for money

base /beɪs/ *noun* **1.** the lowest or first position ○ *Turnover increased by 200%, but started from a low base.* **2.** a place where a company has its main office or factory, or a place where a business person's office is located ○ *The company has its base in London and branches in all the European countries.* ○ *She has an office in Madrid which she uses as a base while travelling in Southern Europe.* ■ *verb* □ **to base something on something** to calculate something using something as your starting point or basic material for the calculation ○ *We based our calculations on the forecast turnover.* □ **based on** calculating from ○ *based on last year's figures* ○ *based on population forecasts*

'…the base lending rate, or prime rate, is the rate at which banks lend to their top corporate borrowers' [*Wall Street Journal*]

'…other investments include a large stake in the Chicago-based insurance company' [*Lloyd's List*]

base currency /'beɪs ˌkʌrənsi/ *noun* a currency against which exchange rates of other currencies are quoted

base period /'beɪs ˌpɪəriəd/ *noun US* **1.** a period against which comparisons are made **2.** the time that an employee must work before becoming eligible for state unemployment insurance benefits ○ *Because she had not worked for the base period, she had to rely on the support of her family when she lost her job.* ○ *The new government shortened the base period, in order to increase social service spending.*

base rate /'beɪs reɪt/ *noun* same as **bank base rate**

base-weighted index /ˌbeɪs ˌweɪtɪd 'ɪndeks/ *noun* an index which is weighted according to the base year

base year /'beɪs jɪə/ *noun* the first year of an index, against which changes occurring in later years are measured

basic /'beɪsɪk/ *adjective* normal

basic balance /ˌbeɪsɪk 'bæləns/ *noun* the balance of current account and long-term capital accounts in a country's balance of payments

basic commodities /ˌbeɪsɪk kə 'mɒdɪtiz/ *plural noun* ordinary farm produce, produced in large quantities, e.g. corn, rice or sugar

basic discount /ˌbeɪsɪk ˈdɪskaʊnt/ *noun* a normal discount without extra percentages ○ *Our basic discount is 20%, but we offer 5% extra for rapid settlement.*

basic earnings per share /ˌbeɪsɪk ˌɜːnɪŋz pə ˈʃeə/ *noun* a figure that shows an investor how much of a company's profit belongs to each share

basic pay /ˌbeɪsɪk ˈpeɪ/ *noun* a normal salary without extra payments. Also called **basic salary**, **basic wage**

basic product /ˌbeɪsɪk ˈprɒdʌkt/ *noun* the main product made from a raw material

basic rate tax /ˈbeɪsɪk reɪt ˌtæks/ *noun* the lowest rate of income tax

basic salary /ˌbeɪsɪk ˈsæləri/, **basic wage** *noun* same as **basic pay**

basis /ˈbeɪsɪs/ *noun* **1.** a point or number from which calculations are made ○ *We forecast the turnover on the basis of a 6% price increase.* (NOTE: The plural is **bases**.) **2.** the general terms of agreement or general principles on which something is decided or done ○ *This document should form the basis for an agreement.* ○ *We have three people working on a freelance basis.* (NOTE: The plural is **bases**.) □ **on a short-term** *or* **long-term basis** for a short or long period ○ *He has been appointed on a short-term basis.*

basis of accounting /ˌbeɪsɪs əv ə ˈkaʊntɪŋ/ *noun* any of various methods of recognising income and expenditure in the preparation of accounts

basis of apportionment /ˌbeɪsɪs əv ə ˈpɔːʃənmənt/ *noun* a way in which common overhead costs are shared among various cost centres

basis of assessment /ˌbeɪsɪs əv ə ˈsesmənt/ *noun* a method of deciding in which year financial transactions should be assessed for taxation

basis period /ˈbeɪsɪs ˌpɪəriəd/ *noun* the period during which transactions occur, used for the purpose of deciding in which they should be assessed for taxation

basis point /ˈbeɪsɪs pɔɪnt/ *noun* one hundredth of a percentage point (0.01%), the basic unit used in measuring market movements or interest rates

basis swap /ˈbeɪsɪs swɒp/ *noun* the exchange of two financial instruments, each with a variable interest calculated on a different rate

basket of currencies /ˌbɑːskɪt əv ˈkʌrənsiz/ *noun* same as **currency basket**

batch /bætʃ/ *noun* **1.** a group of items which are made at one time ○ *This batch of shoes has the serial number 25–02.* **2.** a

group of documents which are processed at the same time ○ *Today's batch of invoices is ready to be mailed.* ○ *The factory is working on yesterday's batch of orders.* ○ *The accountant signed a batch of cheques.* ○ *We deal with the orders in batches of fifty at a time.* ■ *verb* to put items together in groups ○ *to batch invoices* or *cheques*

batch costing /ˈbætʃ ˌkɒstɪŋ/ *noun* a method of calculating the price of one item as part of a batch of items made at the same time

batch-level activities /ˈbætʃ ˌlev(ə)l æk.tɪvɪtiz/ *plural noun* business activities that vary as output varies

b/d *abbreviation* brought down

B/D *abbreviation* banker's draft

bear /beə/ *verb* **1.** to give interest ○ *government bonds which bear 5% interest* **2.** to have something, especially to have something written on it ○ *an envelope which bears a London postmark* ○ *a letter bearing yesterday's date* ○ *The cheque bears the signature of the company secretary.* ○ *The share certificate bears his name.* **3.** to pay costs ○ *The costs of the exhibition will be borne by the company.* ○ *The company bore the legal costs of both parties.* (NOTE: **bearing – bore – has borne**)

bearer /ˈbeərə/ *noun* a person who holds a cheque or certificate

bearer bond /ˈbeərə bɒnd/, **bearer security** /ˈbeərə sɪˌkjʊərɪti/ *noun* a bond which is payable to the bearer and does not have a name written on it

beginning inventory /bɪˈɡɪnɪŋ ˌɪnvənt(ə)ri/ *noun US* same as **opening stock**

behavioural accounting /bɪˌheɪvjərəl əˈkaʊntɪŋ/ *noun* an approach to the study of accounting that emphasises the psychological and social aspects of the profession in addition to the more technical areas

below-the-line /bɪˌləʊ ðə ˈlaɪn/ *adjective, adverb* used to describe entries in a company's profit and loss account that show how the profit is distributed, or where the funds to finance the loss originate. ◊ **above-the-line 1**

below-the-line expenditure /bɪˌləʊ ðə laɪn ɪkˈspendɪtʃə/ *noun* **1.** payments which do not arise from a company's usual activities, e.g. redundancy payments **2.** extraordinary items which are shown in the profit and loss account below net profit after taxation, as opposed to exceptional items which are included in the figure for profit before taxation

benchmark /'bentʃmɑːk/ *noun* a point or level which is important, and can be used as a reference when making evaluations or assessments

benchmark accounting policy /ˌbentʃmɑːk əˈkaʊntɪŋ ˌpɒlɪsi/ *noun* one of a choice of two possible policies within an International Accounting Standard. The other policy is marked as an 'allowed alternative', although there is no indication of preference.

benchmarking /'bentʃmɑːkɪŋ/ *noun* the practice of measuring the performance of a company against the performance of other companies in the same sector. Benchmarking is also used widely in the information technology sector to measure the performance of computer-based information systems.

beneficial interest /ˌbenɪfɪʃ(ə)l 'ɪntrəst/ *noun* a situation where someone is allowed to occupy or receive rent from a house without owning it

beneficial occupier /ˌbenɪfɪʃ(ə)l 'ɒkjʊpaɪə/ *noun* a person who occupies a property but does not own it fully

beneficiary /ˌbenɪˈfɪʃəri/ *noun* a person who gains money from something ○ *the beneficiaries of a will*

benefit /'benɪfɪt/ *verb* **1.** to make better or to improve ○ *A fall in inflation benefits the exchange rate.* **2.** □ to benefit from *or* by something to be improved by something, to gain more money because of something ○ *Exports have benefited from the fall in the exchange rate.* ○ *The employees have benefited from the profit-sharing scheme.*

'…the retail sector will also benefit from the expected influx of tourists' [*Australian Financial Review*]

benefit-cost analysis /ˌbenɪfɪt 'kɒst əˌnælɪsɪs/ *noun* same as **cost-benefit analysis**

benefit in kind /ˌbenɪfɪt ɪn 'kaɪnd/ *noun* a benefit other than money received by an employee as part of his or her total compensation package, e.g. a company car or private health insurance. Such benefits are usually subject to tax.

Benford's Law /'benfədz lɔː/ *noun* a law discovered by Dr Benford in 1938, which shows that in sets of random numbers, it is more likely that the set will begin with the number 1 than with any other number

BEP *abbreviation* break-even point

bequeath /bɪˈkwiːð/ *verb* to leave property, money, etc. (but not freehold land) to someone in a will

bequest /bɪˈkwest/ *noun* something such as property or money (but not freehold land), given to someone in a will ○ *He made several bequests to his staff.*

best practice /ˌbest 'præktɪs/ *noun* the most effective and efficient way to do something or to achieve a particular aim (NOTE: In business, best practice is often determined by benchmarking, that is by comparing the method one organisation uses to carry out a task with the methods used by other similar organisations and determining which method is most efficient and effective.)

'For the past 25 years, managers have been taught that the best practice for valuing assets…is to use a discounted-cash-flow (DCF) methodology.' [Harvard Business Review]

b/f *abbreviation* brought forward

BFH /ˌbiː ef 'aɪtʃ/ *noun* in Germany, the supreme court for issues concerning taxation. Full form **Bundesfinanzhof**

bid /bɪd/ *noun* **1.** an offer to buy something at a specific price. ◊ **takeover bid** □ to make a bid for something to offer to buy something ○ *We made a bid for the house.* ○ *The company made a bid for its rival.* □ to make a cash bid to offer to pay cash for something □ to put in *or* enter a bid for something to offer to buy something, usually in writing **2.** an offer to sell something or do a piece of work at a specific price ○ *She made the lowest bid for the job.* ■ *verb* to offer to buy □ to bid for something (*at an auction*) to offer to buy something □ he bid £1,000 for the jewels he offered to pay £1,000 for the jewels

bidder /'bɪdə/ *noun* a person who makes a bid, usually at an auction ○ *Several bidders made offers for the house.*

bidding /'bɪdɪŋ/ *noun* the act of making offers to buy, usually at an auction □ the bidding started at £1,000 the first and lowest bid was £1,000 □ the bidding stopped at £250,000 the last bid, i.e. the successful bid, was for £250,000 □ the auctioneer started the bidding at £100 the auctioneer suggested that the first bid should be £100

bid market /'bɪd ˌmɑːkɪt/ *noun* a market where there are more bids to buy than offers to sell. Opposite **offered market**

bid-offer price /ˌbɪd 'ɒfə praɪs/ *noun* a price charged by unit trusts to buyers and sellers of units, based on the bid-offer spread

bid-offer spread /ˌbɪd 'ɒfə spred/ *noun* the difference between buying and selling prices (i.e. between the bid and offer prices)

bid price /ˈbɪd praɪs/ *noun* a price at which investors sell shares or units in a unit trust (NOTE: The opposite, i.e. the buying price, is called the **offer price**; the difference between the two is the **spread**.)

bid rate /ˈbɪd reɪt/ *noun* a rate of interest offered on deposits

big business /ˌbɪg ˈbɪznɪs/ *noun* very large commercial firms

Big Four /ˌbɪg ˈfɔː/ *noun* **1.** the four large British commercial banks: Barclays, LloydsTSB, HSB and Natwest, now joined by several former building societies that have become banks **2.** the four largest international accounting companies: PricewaterhouseCoopers, Deloitte Touche Tohmatsu, Ernst & Young and KPMG **3.** the four largest Japanese securities houses: Daiwa, Nikko, Nomura and Yamaichi

bilateral clearing /baɪˌlæt(ə)rəl ˈklɪərɪŋ/ *noun* the system of annual settlements of accounts between some countries, where accounts are settled by the central banks

bilateral credit /baɪˌlæt(ə)rəl ˈkredɪt/ *noun* credit allowed by banks to other banks in a clearing system, to cover the period while cheques are being cleared

bill /bɪl/ *noun* **1.** a written list of charges to be paid ○ *The bill is made out to Smith Ltd* ○ *The sales assistant wrote out the bill.* ○ *Does the bill include VAT?* **2.** a list of charges in a restaurant ○ *Can I have the bill please?* ○ *The bill comes to £20 including service.* ○ *Does the bill include service?* Same as **check 3.** a written paper promising to pay money **4.** *US* same as **banknote** ○ *a $5 bill* **5.** a draft of a new law which will be discussed in Parliament ■ *verb* to present a bill to someone so that it can be paid ○ *The plumbers billed us for the repairs.*

bill broker /ˈbɪl ˌbrəʊkə/ *noun* a discount house, a firm which buys and sells bills of exchange for a fee

billing /ˈbɪlɪŋ/ *noun* the work of writing invoices or bills

billion /ˈbɪljən/ *noun* one thousand million (NOTE: In the US, it has always meant one thousand million, but in UK English it formerly meant one million million, and it is still sometimes used with this meaning. With figures it is usually written **bn: $5bn** say 'five billion dollars'.)

'…gross wool receipts for the selling season to end June 30 appear likely to top $2 billion' [*Australian Financial Review*]

'…at its last traded price the bank was capitalized at around $1.05 billion' [*South China Morning Post*]

bill of exchange /ˌbɪl əv ɪksˈtʃeɪndʒ/ *noun* a document, signed by the person authorising it, which tells another person or a financial institution to pay money unconditionally to a named person on a specific date (NOTE: Bills of exchange are usually used for payments in foreign currency.)

bill of lading /ˌbɪl əv ˈleɪdɪŋ/ *noun* a document listing goods that have been shipped, sent by the transporter to the seller and entered in the seller's accounts as money owed but not yet paid, and therefore as an asset

bill of materials /ˌbɪl əv məˈtɪəriəlz/ *noun* a document setting out the materials and parts required to make a product

bill of sale /ˌbɪl əv ˈseɪl/ *noun* a document which the seller gives to the buyer to show that the sale has taken place

bills payable /ˌbɪlz ˈpeɪəb(ə)l/ *plural noun* bills, especially bills of exchange, which a company will have to pay to its creditors. Abbreviation **B/P**

bills receivable /ˌbɪlz rɪˈsiːvəb(ə)l/ *plural noun* bills, especially bills of exchange, which are due to be paid by a company's debtors. Abbreviation **B/R**

BIN *abbreviation* bank identification number

binder /ˈbaɪndə/ *noun US* a temporary agreement for insurance sent before the insurance policy is issued (NOTE: The UK term is **cover note**.)

black economy /ˌblæk ɪˈkɒnəmi/ *noun* goods and services which are paid for in cash, and therefore not declared for tax. Also called **hidden economy**, **parallel economy**, **shadow economy**

black market /ˌblæk ˈmɑːkɪt/ *noun* the buying and selling of goods or currency in a way which is not allowed by law ○ *There is a flourishing black market in spare parts for cars.*

blank cheque /ˌblæŋk ˈtʃek/ *noun* a cheque with the amount of money and the payee left blank, but signed by the drawer

blanket lien /ˌblæŋkɪt ˈliːn/ *noun US* a lien on a person's property, including personal effects

blind entry /ˌblaɪnd ˈentri/ *noun* a bookkeeping entry that simply records a debit or credit but not other essential information

blind trust /ˌblaɪnd ˈtrʌst/ *noun* a trust set up to run a person's affairs without the details of any transaction being known to the person concerned (NOTE: Blind trusts are set up by politicians to avoid potential conflicts of interest.)

blocked account /ˌblɒkt əˈkaʊnt/ *noun* a bank account which cannot be used, usually because a government has forbidden its use

blocked currency /ˌblɒkt ˈkʌrənsi/ *noun* a currency which cannot be taken out of a country because of government exchange controls

blocked funds /ˌblɒkt ˈfʌndz/ *plural noun* money that cannot be transferred from one place to another, usually because of exchange controls imposed by the government of the country in which the funds are held

block trading /ˌblɒk ˈtreɪdɪŋ/ *noun* trading in very large numbers of shares

Blue Book /ˌbluː ˈbʊk/ *noun* an annual publication of national statistics of personal incomes and spending patterns

blue chip /ˈbluː tʃɪp/ *noun* a very safe investment, a risk-free share in a good company

Blue list /ˈbluː lɪst/ *noun US* a daily list of municipal bonds and their ratings, issued by Standard & Poor's

blue sky laws /ˌbluː ˈskaɪ ˌlɔːz/ *plural noun US* state laws to protect investors against fraudulent traders in securities

board /bɔːd/ *noun* **1.** same as **board of directors** ○ *He sits on the board as a representative of the bank.* ○ *Two directors were removed from the board at the AGM.* **2.** a group of people who run an organisation, trust or society **3.** □ **on board** on a ship, plane or train ■ *verb* to go on to a ship, plane or train ○ *Customs officials boarded the ship in the harbour.*

'CEOs, with their wealth of practical experience, are in great demand and can pick and choose the boards they want to serve on' [*Duns Business Month*]

Board for Actuarial Standards /ˌbɔːd fər ˌæktʃuˈeəriəl ˌstændədz/ *noun* a UK authority with responsibility for overseeing the actuarial profession and setting actuarial standards

board meeting /ˈbɔːd ˌmiːtɪŋ/ *noun* a meeting of the directors of a company

Board of Customs and Excise /ˌbɔːd əv ˌkʌstəmz ənd ˈeksaɪz/ *noun* the ruling body of the Customs and Excise

board of directors /ˌbɔːd əv daɪ ˈrektəz/ *noun* **1.** a group of directors elected by the shareholders to run a company ○ *The bank has two representatives on the board of*

directors. **2.** *US* a group of people elected by the shareholders to draw up company policy and to appoint the president and other executive officers who are responsible for managing the company

'…a proxy is the written authorization an investor sends to a stockholder meeting conveying his vote on a corporate resolution or the election of a company's board of directors' [*Barrons*]

bona fide /ˌbəʊnə ˈfaɪdi/ *adjective* trustworthy, which can be trusted

bond /bɒnd/ *noun* **1.** a contract document promising to repay money borrowed by a company or by the government on a specific date, and paying interest at regular intervals **2.** □ **goods (held) in bond** goods held by customs until duty has been paid □ **entry of goods under bond** bringing goods into a country in bond □ **to take goods out of bond** to pay duty on goods so that they can be released by customs **3.** a form of insurance fund which is linked to a unit trust, but where there is no yield because the income is automatically added to the fund

bond discount /ˈbɒnd ˌdɪskaʊnt/ *noun* the difference between the face value of a bond and the lower price at which it is issued

bonded /ˈbɒndɪd/ *adjective* held in bond

bonded warehouse /ˌbɒndɪd ˈweəhaʊs/ *noun* a warehouse where goods are stored until excise duty has been paid

bond fund /ˈbɒnd fʌnd/ *noun* a unit trust in which investments are made in the form of bonds

bondholder /ˈbɒndˌhəʊldə/ *noun* a person who holds government bonds

bond indenture /ˈbɒnd ɪnˌdentʃə/ *noun* a document that details the terms of a bond

bondised /ˈbɒndaɪzd/, **bondized** *adjective* referring to an insurance fund linked to a unit trust

bond market /ˈbɒnd ˌmaːkɪt/ *noun* a market in which government or municipal bonds are traded

bond premium /ˈbɒnd ˌpriːmiəm/ *noun* the difference between the face value of a bond and a higher price at which it is issued

bond-washing /ˈbɒnd ˌwɒʃɪŋ/ *noun* the act of selling securities cum dividend and buying them back ex dividend, or selling US Treasury bonds with the interest coupon, and buying them back ex coupon, so as to reduce tax

bond yield /ˈbɒnd jiːld/ *noun* income produced by a bond, shown as a percentage of its purchase price

bonus /ˈbəʊnəs/ *noun* an extra payment in addition to a normal payment

bonus issue /ˌbəʊnəs ˈɪʃuː/ *noun* a scrip issue or capitalisation issue, in which a company transfers money from reserves to share capital and issues free extra shares to the shareholders. The value of the company remains the same, and the total market value of shareholders' shares remains the same, the market price being adjusted to account for the new shares. Also called **share split** (NOTE: The US term is **stock split**.)

bonus share /ˈbəʊnəs ʃeə/ *noun* an extra share given to an existing shareholder

book /bʊk/ *noun* **1.** a set of sheets of paper attached together □ **a company's books** the financial records of a company **2.** a statement of a dealer's exposure to the market, i.e. the amount which he or she is due to pay or has borrowed □ **to make a book** to have a list of shares which he or she is prepared to buy or sell on behalf of clients

book inventory /ˈbʊk ˌɪnvənt(ə)ri/ *noun* the number of stock items recorded in accounts, which is verified by a physical count

bookkeeper /ˈbʊkˌkiːpə/ *noun* a person who keeps the financial records of a company or an organisation

bookkeeping /ˈbʊkˌkiːpɪŋ/ *noun* the work of keeping the financial records of a company or an organisation

bookkeeping barter /ˈbʊkkiːpɪŋ ˌbaːtə/ *noun* the direct exchange of goods between two parties without the use of money as a medium, but using monetary measures to record the transaction

bookkeeping transaction /ˈbʊkkiːpɪŋ trænˌzækʃən/ *noun* a transaction which involves changes to a company's books of accounts, but does not alter the value of the company in any way, e.g. the issue of bonus shares

book of account /ˌbʊk əv əˈkaʊnt/ *noun* an account book, a book which records financial transactions

book of prime entry /ˌbʊk əv ˌpraɪm ˈentri/, **book of original entry** *noun* a chronological record of a business's transactions arranged according to type, e.g., cash or sales. The books are then used to generate entries in a double-entry bookkeeping system.

book sales /ˈbʊk seɪlz/ *plural noun* sales as recorded in the sales book

book value /ˈbʊk ˌvæljuː/ *noun* the value of an asset as recorded in the company's balance sheet

book value per share /ˈbʊk ˌvæljuː pə ˌʃeə/ *noun* a company's own assessment of the value of its shares, which may differ considerably from the market value

boom /buːm/ *noun* a time when sales, production or business activity are increasing ○ *a period of economic boom* ○ *the boom of the 1990s*

booming /ˈbuːmɪŋ/ *adjective* expanding or becoming prosperous ○ *a booming industry or company* ○ *Technology is a booming sector of the economy.*

boost /buːst/ *noun* help given to increase something ○ *This publicity will give sales a boost.* ○ *The government hopes to give a boost to industrial development.* ■ *verb* to make something increase ○ *We expect our publicity campaign to boost sales by 25%.* ○ *The company hopes to boost its market share.* ○ *Incentive schemes are boosting production.*

'…the company expects to boost turnover this year to FFr 16bn from FFr 13.6bn last year' [*Financial Times*]

BOP *abbreviation* balance of payments

border tax adjustment /ˈbɔːdə tæks əˌdʒʌstmənt/ *noun* a deduction of indirect tax paid on goods being exported or imposition of local indirect tax on goods being imported

borrow /ˈbɒrəʊ/ *verb* **1.** to take money from someone for a time, possibly paying interest for it, and repaying it at the end of the period ○ *She borrowed £1,000 from the bank.* ○ *The company had to borrow heavily to repay its debts.* ○ *They borrowed £25,000 against the security of the factory.* **2.** to buy at spot prices and sell forward at the same time

borrower /ˈbɒrəʊə/ *noun* a person who borrows ○ *Borrowers from the bank pay 12% interest.*

borrowing /ˈbɒrəʊɪŋ/ *noun* the act of borrowing money ○ *The new factory was financed by bank borrowing.*

'…we tend to think of building societies as having the best borrowing rates and indeed many do offer excellent terms' [*Financial Times*]

borrowing costs /ˈbɒrəʊɪŋ kɒsts/ *plural noun* the interest and other charges paid on money borrowed

borrowing power /ˈbɒrəʊɪŋ ˌpaʊə/ *noun* the amount of money which a company can borrow

borrowings /ˈbɒrəʊɪŋz/ *plural noun* money borrowed ○ *The company's borrowings have doubled.*

bottleneck /'bɒt(ə)lnek/ *noun* a situation which occurs when one section of an operation cannot cope with the amount of work it has to do, which slows down the later stages of the operation and business activity in general ○ *a bottleneck in the supply system* ○ *There are serious bottlenecks in the production line.*

bottleneck activity /'bɒt(ə)lnek æk ˌtɪvɪti/ *noun* any business activity for which the work involved equals or exceeds the income generated

bottom /'bɒtəm/ *verb* to reach the lowest point □ **the market has bottomed out** the market has reached the lowest point and does not seem likely to fall further

bottom line /ˌbɒtəm 'laɪn/ *noun* **1.** the last line on a balance sheet indicating profit or loss □ **the boss is interested only in the bottom line** he is only interested in the final profit **2.** the final decision on a matter ○ *The bottom line was that the work had to com-pleted within budget.*

bottom-up budgeting /ˌbɒtəm 'ʌp ˌbʌdʒɪtɪŋ/ *noun* same as **participative budgeting**

bought day book /ˌbɔːt 'deɪ ˌbʊk/ *noun* a book used to record purchases made on credit

bought ledger /'bɔːt ˌledʒə/ *noun* a book in which purchases are recorded

bought ledger clerk /ˌbɔːt 'ledʒə ˌklɑːk/ *noun* an office employee who deals with the bought ledger or the sales ledger

bounce /baʊns/ *verb* (*of a cheque*) to be returned by the bank to the person who has tried to cash it, because there is not enough money in the payer's account to pay it ○ *She paid for the car with a cheque that bounced.*

B/P *abbreviation* bills payable

B/R *abbreviation* bills receivable

bracket /'brækɪt/ *noun* a group of items or people taken together □ **she is in the top tax bracket** she pays the highest level of tax

branch accounting /'brɑːntʃ ə ˌkaʊntɪŋ/ *noun* the fact of operating separate accounting systems for each department of an organisation

branch accounts /ˌbrɑːntʃ ə'kaʊnts/ *plural noun* accounts showing transactions belonging to the branches of a large organisation, i.e., between a branch and other branches or its head office, or other companies outside the organisation

breach /briːtʃ/ *noun* a failure to carry out the terms of an agreement

breach of contract /ˌbriːtʃ əv 'kɒntrækt/ *noun* the failure to do something which has been agreed in a contract

breach of trust /ˌbriːtʃ əv 'trʌst/ *noun* a situation where a person does not act correctly or honestly when people expect him or her to

break /breɪk/ *noun* **1.** a pause between periods of work ○ *She keyboarded for two hours without a break.* **2.** a sharp fall in share prices ■ *verb* **1.** to fail to carry out the duties of a contract ○ *The company has broken the contract* or *the agreement by selling at a lower price.* **2.** to cancel a contract ○ *The company is hoping to be able to break the contract.* (NOTE: [all verb senses] **breaking – broke – has broken**)

break down /ˌbreɪk 'daʊn/ *phrasal verb* **1.** to stop working because of mechanical failure ○ *The fax machine has broken down.* **2.** to stop ○ *Negotiations broke down after six hours.* **3.** to show all the items in a total list of costs or expenditure ○ *We broke the expenditure down into fixed and variable costs.*

break even /ˌbreɪk 'iːv(ə)n/ *verb* to balance costs and receipts, so as to make neither a profit nor a loss ○ *Last year the company only just broke even.* ○ *We broke even in our first two months of trading.*

break up /ˌbreɪk 'ʌp/ *phrasal verb* to split something large into small sections ○ *The company was broken up and separate divisions sold off.*

breakages /'breɪkɪdʒɪz/ *plural noun* breaking of items ○ *Customers are expected to pay for breakages.*

breakdown /'breɪkdaʊn/ *noun* **1.** an act of stopping working because of mechanical failure ○ *We cannot communicate with our Nigerian office because of the breakdown of the telephone lines.* **2.** an act of stopping talking ○ *a breakdown in wage negotiations* **3.** an act of showing details item by item ○ *Give me a breakdown of investment costs.*

break-even /ˌbreɪk 'iːv(ə)n/ *noun* a situation where there is neither a profit nor a loss

break-even analysis /ˌbreɪk 'iːv(ə)n ə ˌnæləsɪs/ *noun* **1.** the analysis of fixed and variable costs and sales that determines at what level of production the break-even point will be reached ○ *The break-even analysis showed that the company will only break even if it sells at least 1,000 bicycles a month.* **2.** a method of showing the point at which a company's income from sales will be equal to its production costs so that it neither makes a profit nor makes a loss (NOTE:

Break-even analysis is usually shown in the form of a chart and can be used to help companies make decisions, set prices for their products, and work out the effects of changes in production or sales volume on their costs and profits.)

break-even chart /ˈbreɪk ˌiːv(ə)n tʃɑːt/ noun a chart showing the point at which a company breaks even as the intersection between a line plotting total revenue and a line plotting total cost

break-even point /ˈbreɪkˌiːv(ə)n ˌpɔɪnt/ noun the point or level of financial activity at which expenditure equals income, or the value of an investment equals its cost so that the result is neither a profit nor a loss. Abbreviation **BEP**

break-even sales /ˈbreɪk ˌiːv(ə)n ˌseɪlz/ plural noun a level of sales that neither generates profit nor incurs loss

break-out /ˈbreɪk aʊt/ noun a movement of a share price above or below its previous trading level

break-up value /ˈbreɪk ʌp ˌvæljuː/ noun **1.** the value of the material of a fixed asset ○ What would the break-up value of our old machinery be? **2.** the value of various parts of a company taken separately

bribe /braɪb/ noun money given secretly and usually illegally to someone in authority to get them to help ○ The minister was dismissed for taking a bribe.

bricks-and-mortar /ˌbrɪks ən ˈmɔːtə/ adjective referring to the fixed assets of a company, especially its buildings

bridge finance /ˈbrɪdʒ ˌfaɪnæns/ noun loans to cover short-term needs

bridging loan /ˈbrɪdʒɪŋ ləʊn/ noun **1.** a short-term loan to help someone buy a new house when the old one has not yet been sold **2.** a short-term loan made to a company, e.g. to help in a cash-flow crisis or to fund company restructuring (NOTE: [all senses] The US term is **bridge loan**.)

bring down /ˌbrɪŋ ˈdaʊn/ phrasal verb to reduce ○ Petrol companies have brought down the price of oil.

bring forward /ˌbrɪŋ ˈfɔːwəd/ phrasal verb **1.** to make something take place earlier ○ to bring forward the date of repayment ○ The date of the next meeting has been brought forward to March. **2.** to take an account balance from the end of the previous period as the starting point for the current period ○ Balance brought forward: £365.15

bring in /ˌbrɪŋ ˈɪn/ phrasal verb to earn an amount of interest ○ The shares bring in a small amount.

British Accounting Association /ˌbrɪtɪʃ əˈkaʊntɪŋ əˌsəʊsieɪʃ(ə)n/ an organisation whose aim is to promote accounting education and research in the United Kingdom. F. Abbreviation **BAA**

broker /ˈbrəʊkə/ noun a dealer who acts as a middleman between a buyer and a seller

brokerage /ˈbrəʊkərɪdʒ/ noun **1.** same as **broker's commission 2.** same as **broking**

brokerage firm /ˈbrəʊkərɪdʒ fɜːm/, **brokerage house** /ˈbrəʊkərɪdʒ haʊs/ noun a firm which buys and sells shares for clients

broker-dealer /ˌbrəʊkə ˈdiːlə/ noun a dealer who buys shares and holds them for resale, and also deals on behalf of investor clients

broker's commission /ˌbrəʊkəz kə ˈmɪʃ(ə)n/ noun the payment to a broker for a deal which he or she has carried out. Also called **brokerage** (NOTE: Formerly, the commission charged by brokers on the London Stock Exchange was fixed, but since 1986, commissions have been variable.)

broking /ˈbrəʊkɪŋ/ noun the business of dealing in stocks and shares

brought down /ˌbrɔːt ˈdaʊn/, **brought forward** /ˌbrɔːt ˈfɔːwəd/ adjective used to describe the balance in an account from the previous period when it is taken as the starting point for the current period ○ balance brought down or forward: £365.15 Abbreviation **b/d, b/f**

B/S abbreviation balance sheet

B shares /ˈbiː ʃeəz/ plural noun ordinary shares with special voting rights, often owned by the founder of a company and his or her family. See Comment at **A shares**

buck /bʌk/ noun US a dollar (informal)

budget /ˈbʌdʒɪt/ noun **1.** a plan of expected spending and income for a period of time ○ to draw up a budget for salaries for the coming year ○ We have agreed on the budgets for next year. **2.** □ **the Budget** the annual plan of taxes and government spending ○ The minister put forward a budget aimed at boosting the economy. ■ verb to plan probable income and expenditure ○ We are budgeting for $10,000 of sales next year.

'…he budgeted for further growth of 150,000 jobs (or 2.5 per cent) in the current financial year' [Sydney Morning Herald]

'…the Federal government's budget targets for employment and growth are within reach according to the latest figures' [Australian Financial Review]

budget account /ˈbʌdʒɪt əˌkaʊnt/ noun a bank account where you plan income and expenditure to allow for periods when expenditure is high, by paying a set amount each month

budgetary /ˈbʌdʒɪt(ə)ri/ *adjective* referring to a budget

budgetary control /ˌbʌdʒɪt(ə)ri kən ˈtrəʊl/ *noun* controlled spending according to a planned budget

budgetary policy /ˌbʌdʒɪt(ə)ri ˈpɒlɪsi/ *noun* the policy of planning income and expenditure

budgetary requirements /ˌbʌdʒɪt(ə)ri rɪˈkwaɪəməntz/ *plural noun* the rate of spending or income required to meet the budget forecasts

budgetary slack /ˌbʌdʒɪt(ə)ri ˈslæk/ *noun* a deliberate underestimation of income and overestimation of costs, designed to allow for budgetary emergencies or to make targets more easily attainable

budget centre /ˌbʌdʒɪt ˈsentə/ *noun* a part of an organisation for which a separate budget is prepared

budget committee /ˈbʌdʒɪt kəˌmɪti/ *noun* the group within an organisation responsible for drawing up budgets that meet departmental requirements, ensuring they comply with policy, and then submitting them to the board of directors

budget control /ˈbʌdʒɪt kənˌtrəʊl/ *noun* the monitoring of a company's actual performance against its expected performance as detailed in a budget plan

Budget Day /ˈbʌdʒɪt deɪ/ *noun* the day when the Chancellor of the Exchequer presents the budget to Parliament. This is usually in March, but with an advance budget statement in November.

budget deficit /ˈbʌdʒɪt ˌdefɪsɪt/ *noun* **1.** a deficit in a country's planned budget, where income from taxation will not be sufficient to pay for the government's expenditure **2.** a deficit in personal finances where a household will borrow to finance large purchases which cannot be made out of income alone

budget department /ˈbʌdʒɪt dɪ ˌpɑːtmənt/ *noun* a department in a large store which sells cheaper goods

budget director /ˈbʌdʒɪt daɪˌrektə/ *noun* the person in an organisation who is responsible for running the budget system

budgeted balance sheet /ˌbʌdʒɪtɪd ˈbæləns ˌʃiːt/ *noun* a statement of company's estimated financial position at the end of a budgetary year

budgeted capacity /ˌbʌdʒɪtɪd kə ˈpæsɪti/ *noun* an organisation's available

output level for a budget period according to the budget. It may be expressed in different ways, e.g., in machine hours or standard hours.

budgeted income statement /ˌbʌdʒɪtɪd ˈɪnkʌm ˌsteɪtmənt/ *noun* a statement of a company's expected net income in a budgetary period

budgeted revenue /ˌbʌdʒɪtɪd ˈrevənjuː/ *noun* the income that an organisation expects to receive in a budget period according to the budget

budget information /ˈbʌdʒɪt ˌɪnfəmeɪʃ(ə)n/ *noun* information about a company's expected future levels of income and expenditure

budgeting /ˈbʌdʒɪtɪŋ/ *noun* the preparation of budgets to help plan expenditure and income

budgeting models /ˈbʌdʒɪtɪŋ ˌmɒd(ə)lz/ *plural noun* mathematical models used in the planning of a budget and designed to generate a profit

budget lapsing /ˈbʌdʒɪt ˌlæpsɪŋ/ *noun* withdrawal by an authority of the unspent portion of an organization's budget allowance at the time the budget period expires

budget manual /ˈbʌdʒɪt ˌmænjuəl/ *noun* a handbook or set of documents that detail budgetary procedure for a company or organisation

budget period /ˈbʌdʒɪt ˌpɪəriəd/ *noun* a period of time covered by a budget

budget planning calendar /ˈbʌdʒɪt ˌplænɪŋ ˌkælɪndə/ *noun* a schedule showing plans for the preparation of an organisation's master budget and the departmental budgets that depend on it, which usually takes several months

budget report /ˈbʌdʒɪt rɪˌpɔːt/ *noun* a report that compares a company's actual performance with its budgeted performance for a given period

budget surplus /ˌbʌdʒɪt ˈsɜːpləs/ *noun* a situation where there is more revenue than was planned for in the budget

budget variance /ˈbʌdʒɪt ˌveəriəns/ *noun* the difference between the cost as estimated for a budget and the actual cost

buffer stocks /ˈbʌfə stɒks/ *plural noun* stocks of a commodity bought by an international body when prices are low and held for resale at a time when prices have risen, with the intention of reducing sharp fluctuations in world prices of the commodity

build into /ˈbɪld ˌɪntuː/ *phrasal verb* to include something in something which is being set up ○ *You must build all the forecasts* *into the budget.*

build up /ˌbɪld ˈʌp/ *phrasal verb* **1.** to create something by adding pieces together ○ *She bought several shoe shops and gradually built up a chain.* **2.** to expand something gradually ○ *to build up a profitable business* ○ *to build up a team of sales representatives*

building and loan association /ˌbɪldɪŋ ən ˈləʊn əˌsəʊsieɪʃ(ə)n/ *noun US* same as **building society**

building society /ˈbɪldɪŋ səˌsaɪəti/ *noun* a financial institution which accepts and pays interest on deposits, and lends money to people who are buying property against the security of the property which is being bought ○ *We put our savings into a building society* or *into a building society account.* ○ *I have an account with the Nationwide Building Society.* ○ *I saw the building society manager to ask for a mortgage.* (NOTE: The US term is **savings and loan**.)

buildup /ˈbɪldʌp/ *noun* a gradual increase ○ *a buildup in sales* or *a sales buildup* ○ *There has been a buildup of complaints about customer service.*

built-in obsolescence /ˈbɪlt ɪn ɒbsəˌles(ə)ns/ *noun* a method of ensuring continuing sales of a product by making it in such a way that it will soon become obsolete

bulk buying /ˌbʌlk ˈbaɪɪŋ/ *noun* the act of buying large quantities of goods at low prices

bullet bond /ˈbʊlɪt bɒnd/ *noun US* a Eurobond which is only redeemed when it is mature (NOTE: Bullet bonds are used in payments between central banks and also act as currency backing.)

Bulletin des Annonces Légales Obligatoires /ˌbʊlətæn deɪz æˌnɒns leɪˌɡæl ɒblɪɡæˈtwɑː/ *noun* in France, an official bulletin in which companies make formal announcements to shareholders as required by law. Abbreviation **BALO**

bullet loan /ˈbʊlɪt ləʊn/ *noun US* a loan which is repaid in a single payment

bullion /ˈbʊliən/ *noun* a gold or silver bars ○ *A shipment of gold bullion was stolen from the security van.* ○ *The price of bullion is fixed daily.*

bumping /ˈbʌmpɪŋ/ *noun US* a lay-off procedure that allows an employee with greater seniority to displace a more junior employee ○ *The economic recession led to extensive bumping in companies where only the most qualified were retained for some jobs.* ○ *The trade unions strongly objected to bumping practices since they considered*

that many employees were being laid off unfairly.

Bundesfinanzhof /ˌbʊndəzfɪˈnæntshɒf/ *noun* the German Federal Finance Court

business /ˈbɪznɪs/ *noun* **1.** work in buying, selling, or doing other things to make a profit ○ *We do a lot of business with Japan.* ○ *Business is slow.* ○ *We did more business in the week before Christmas than we usually do in a month.* ○ *What's your line of business?* **2.** a commercial company ○ *He owns a small car repair business.* ○ *She runs a business from her home.* ○ *I set up in business as an insurance broker.* **3.** the affairs discussed ○ *The main business of the meeting was finished by 3 p.m.*

Business Accounting Deliberation Council /ˌbɪznɪs əˌkaʊntɪŋ dɪˌlɪbə ˈreɪʃ(ə)n ˌkaʊns(ə)l/ *noun* in Japan, a committee controlled by the Ministry of Finance that is responsible for drawing up regulations regarding the consolidated financial statements of listed companies

business address /ˈbɪznɪs əˌdres/ *noun* the details of number, street, and city or town where a company is located

business angel /ˈbɪznɪs ˌeɪndʒəl/ *noun* a wealthy entrepreneurial individual who invests money, usually less money than a venture capitalist, in a company in return for equity and some control in that company

business angel network /ˈbɪznɪs ˌeɪndʒəl ˌnetwɜːk/ *noun* a regional network of business angels

business centre /ˈbɪznɪs ˌsentə/ *noun* the part of a town where the main banks, shops and offices are located

business combination /ˌbɪznɪs ˌkɒmbɪˈneɪʃ(ə)n/ *noun* the process in which one or more businesses become subsidiaries of another business

business cycle /ˈbɪznɪs ˌsaɪk(ə)l/ *noun* the period during which trade expands, slows down and then expands again. Also called **trade cycle**

business day /ˈbɪznɪs deɪ/ *noun* a weekday when banks and stock exchanges are open for business

business entity concept /ˌbɪznɪs ˈentɪti ˌkɒnsept/ *noun* the concept that financial accounting information relates only to the activities of the business and not to the activities of its owner(s)

business expenses /ˈbɪznɪs ɪk ˌspensɪz/ *plural noun* money spent on running a business, not on stock or assets

business hours /ˈbɪznɪs ˌaʊəz/ *plural noun* the time when a business is open, usually 9.00 a.m. to 5.30 p.m.

business intelligence /ˈbɪznɪs ɪnˌtelɪdʒ(ə)ns/ *noun* information that may be useful to a business when it is planning its strategy

'…a system that enables its employees to use cell phones to access the consulting firm's business information database.' [InformationWeek]

business name /ˈbɪznɪs neɪm/ *noun* a name used by a company for trading purposes

business plan /ˈbɪznɪs plæn/ *noun* a document drawn up to show how a business is planned to work, with cash flow forecasts, sales forecasts, etc., often used when trying to raise a loan, or when setting up a new business

business property relief /ˈbɪznɪs ˌprɒpəti rɪˌliːf/ *noun* in the United Kingdom, a reduction in the amount liable to inheritance tax on certain types of business property

business ratepayer /ˈbɪznɪs ˌreɪtpeɪə/ *noun* a business which pays local taxes on a shop, office, factory, etc.

business rates /ˈbɪznɪs reɪts/ *plural noun* in the United Kingdom, a tax on businesses calculated on the value of the property occupied. Although the rate of tax is set by central government, the tax is collected the local authority.

business review /ˈbɪznɪs rɪˌvjuː/ *noun* a report on business carried out over the past year. It forms part of the directors' report.

business segment /ˈbɪznɪs ˌsegmənt/ *noun* a section of a company which can be distinguished from the rest of the company by its own revenue and expenditure

business transaction /ˈbɪznɪs trænˌzækʃən/ *noun* an act of buying or selling

business travel /ˌbɪznɪs ˈtræv(ə)l/ *noun* travel costs incurred in the course of work, as opposed to private travel or daily travel to your usual place of work

buy /baɪ/ *verb* to get something by paying money ○ *to buy wholesale and sell retail* ○ *to buy for cash* ○ *She bought 10,000 shares.* ○ *The company has been bought by its leading supplier.* (NOTE: **buying – bought**)

buy back /ˌbaɪ ˈbæk/ *phrasal verb* to buy something which you sold earlier ○ *She sold the shop last year and is now trying to buy it back.*

buy in /ˌbaɪ ˈɪn/ *phrasal verb* **1.** (*of a seller at an auction*) to buy the thing which you are trying to sell because no one will pay the price you want **2.** to buy stock to cover a position **3.** (*of a company*) to buy its own shares

buyback /ˈbaɪbæk/ *noun* **1.** a type of loan agreement to repurchase bonds or securities at a later date for the same price as they are being sold **2.** an international trading agreement where a company builds a factory in a foreign country and agrees to buy all its production

'…the corporate sector also continued to return cash to shareholders in the form of buy-backs, while raising little money in the form of new or rights issues' [*Financial Times*]

buyer /ˈbaɪə/ *noun* **1.** a person who buys **2.** a person who buys stock on behalf of a trading organisation for resale or for use in production

buyer's market /ˈbaɪəz ˌmɑːkɪt/ *noun* a market where products are sold cheaply because there are few people who want to buy them. Opposite **seller's market**

buying department /ˈbaɪɪŋ dɪˌpɑːtmənt/ *noun* the department in a company which buys raw materials or goods for use in the company (NOTE: The US term is **purchasing department**.)

buying power /ˈbaɪɪŋ ˌpaʊə/ *noun* an assessment of an individual's or organization's disposable income regarded as conferring the power to make purchases ○ *The buying power of the dollar has fallen over the last five years.*

buyout /ˈbaɪaʊt/ *noun* the purchase of a controlling interest in a company

'…we also invest in companies whose growth and profitability could be improved by a management buyout' [*Times*]

'…in a normal leveraged buyout, the acquirer raises money by borrowing against the assets or cash flow of the target company' [*Fortune*]

bylaw /ˈbaɪlɔː/ *noun* a rule made by a local authority or organisation, and not by central government

by-product /ˈbaɪ ˌprɒdʌkt/ *noun* a secondary product made as a result of manufacturing a main product which can be sold for profit

C

CA *abbreviation* chartered accountant

c/a *abbreviation* capital account

C/A *abbreviation* current account

calculate /ˈkælkjʊleɪt/ *verb* **1.** to find the answer to a problem using numbers ○ *The bank clerk calculated the rate of exchange for the dollar.* **2.** to estimate ○ *I calculate that we have six months' stock left.*

calculation /ˌkælkjʊˈleɪʃ(ə)n/ *noun* the answer to a problem in mathematics ○ *According to my calculations, we have six months' stock left.* □ **we are £20,000 out in our calculations** we have made a mistake in our calculations and arrived at a figure which is £20,000 too much or too little

calendar variance /ˈkælɪndə ˌveəriəns/ *noun* variance which occurs if a company uses calendar months for the financial accounts but uses the number of actual working days to calculate overhead expenses in the cost accounts

calendar year /ˌkælɪndə ˈjɪə/ *noun* a year from the 1st January to 31st December

call /kɔːl/ *noun* **1.** a demand for repayment of a loan by a lender **2.** a demand to pay for new shares which then become paid up ■ *verb* to ask for a loan to be repaid immediately

call in /ˌkɔːl ˈɪn/ *phrasal verb* **1.** to visit ○ *Their sales representative called in twice last week.* **2.** to ask for a debt to be paid

call up /ˌkɔːl ˈʌp/ *phrasal verb* to ask for share capital to be paid

callable bond /ˌkɔːləb(ə)l ˈbɒnd/ *noun* a bond which can be redeemed before it matures

callable capital /ˌkɔːləb(ə)l ˈkæpɪt(ə)l/ *noun* the part of a company's capital which has not been called up

call account /ˈkɔːl əˌkaʊnt/ *noun* a type of current account where money can be withdrawn without notice

call-back pay /ˈkɔːl bæk ˌpeɪ/ *noun* pay given to an employee who has been called

back to work after his or her usual working hours

called up capital /ˌkɔːld ʌp ˈkæpɪt(ə)l/ *noun* share capital in a company which has been called up. The share capital becomes fully paid when all the authorised shares have been called up.

'…a circular to shareholders highlights that the company's net assets as at August 1, amounted to £47.9 million – less than half the company's called-up share capital of £96.8 million. Accordingly, an EGM has been called for October 7' [*Times*]

call-in pay /ˈkɔːl ɪn ˌpeɪ/ *noun* payment guaranteed to employees who report for work even if there is no work for them to do ○ *Call-in pay is often necessary to ensure the attendance of employees where there is at least the possibility of work needing to be done.*

call loan /ˈkɔːl ləʊn/ *noun* a bank loan repayable at call

call money /ˈkɔːl ˌmʌni/ *noun* money loaned for which repayment can be demanded without notice. Also called **money at call**, **money on call**

call option /ˈkɔːl ˌɒpʃən/ *noun* an option to buy shares at a future date and at a specific price. Also called **call**

call price /ˈkɔːl praɪs/ *noun* a price to be paid on redemption of a US bond

call provision /ˈkɔːl prəˌvɪʒ(ə)n/ *noun* a clause that allows a bond to be redeemed before its maturity date

call purchase /ˈkɔːl ˌpɜːtʃɪs/, **call sale** /ˈkɔːl seɪl/ *noun* a transaction where the seller or purchaser can fix the price for future delivery

calls in arrear /ˌkɔːls ɪn əˈrɪə/ *plural noun* money called up for shares, but not paid at the correct time and a special calls in arrear account is set up to debit the sums owing

Canadian Institute of Chartered Accountants /kəˌneɪdiən ˌɪnstɪtjuːt əv ˌtʃɑːtəd əˈkaʊntənts/ *noun* in Canada, the principal professional accountancy body that is responsible for setting accounting standards. Abbreviation **CICA**

cap /kæp/ *noun* **1.** an upper limit placed on something, such as an interest rate. The opposite, i.e. a lower limit, is a 'floor'). **2.** same as **capitalisation** (*informal*) ○ *Last year the total market cap of all the world's gold companies fell from $71 billion to $46 billion.* ■ *verb* to place an upper limit on something ○ *to cap a department's budget* (NOTE: **capping – capped**)

CAPA *noun* a large association of accountancy bodies that operate in Asia and the Pacific Rim countries. Full form **Confederation of Asian and Pacific Accountants**

capacity /kə'pæsɪti/ *noun* **1.** the amount which can be produced, or the amount of work which can be done ○ *industrial* or *manufacturing* or *production capacity* **2.** the amount of space □ **to use up spare** *or* **excess capacity** to make use of time or space which is not fully used **3.** ability ○ *She has a particular capacity for detailed business deals with overseas companies.*

'...analysts are increasingly convinced that the industry simply has too much capacity' [*Fortune*]

capacity costs /kə'pæsɪti kɒsts/ *plural noun* costs incurred to allow a company or produce more goods or services, e.g. the purchase of machinery or buildings

capacity management /kə'pæsɪti ˌmænɪdʒmənt/ *noun* management of the cost of a company's unused capacity, which does not rightly influence pricing

capacity requirements planning /kə ˌpæsɪti rɪˌkwaɪəmənts 'plænɪŋ/ *noun* planning that determines how much machinery and equipment is needed in order to meet production targets

capacity usage variance /kə,pæsɪti 'juːsɪdʒ ˌveəriəns/ *noun* the difference in gain or loss in a given period compared to budgeted expectations, caused because the hours worked were longer or shorter than planned

capacity variance /kə'pæsɪti ˌveəriəns/ *noun* variance caused by the difference between planned and actual hours worked

Caparo case /kə'pɑːrəʊ ˌkeɪs/ *noun* in England, a court decision taken by the House of Lords in 1990 that auditors owe a duty of care to present (not prospective) shareholders as a body but not as individuals

CAPEX *abbreviation* capital expenditure

capital /'kæpɪt(ə)l/ *noun* **1.** the money, property, and assets used in a business ○ *a company with $10,000 capital* or *with a capital of $10,000* **2.** money owned by individuals or companies, which they use for investment

capital account /'kæpɪt(ə)l əˌkaʊnt/ *noun* **1.** an account that states the value of funds and assets invested in a business by the owners or shareholders **2.** the portion of a country's balance of payments that refers to investments, rather than to the buying and selling of merchandise **3.** a statement of the net worth of an organization at a given time

capital adequacy /ˌkæpɪt(ə)l 'ædɪkwəsi/, **capital adequacy ratio** /ˌkæpɪt(ə)l 'ædɪkwəsi ˌreɪʃiəʊ/ *noun* the amount of money which a bank has to have in the form of shareholders' capital, shown as a percentage of its assets. Also called **capital-to-asset ratio** (NOTE: The amount is internationally agreed at 8%.)

capital allowances /ˌkæpɪt(ə)l ə 'laʊənsɪz/ *plural noun* the allowances based on the value of fixed assets which may be deducted from a company's profits and so reduce its tax liability

capital appreciation /ˌkæpɪt(ə)l ə ˌpriːʃi'eɪʃ(ə)n/ *noun* same as **appreciation**

capital asset pricing model /ˌkæpɪt(ə)l ˌæset 'praɪsɪŋ ˌmɒd(ə)l/ *noun* an equation that shows the relationship between expected risk and expected return on an investment and serves as a model for valuing risky securities. Abbreviation **CAPM**

capital assets /ˌkæpɪt(ə)l 'æsets/ *plural noun* the property, machines, and other assets which a company owns and uses but which it does not buy and sell as part of its regular trade. Also called **fixed assets**

capital base /'kæpɪt(ə)l beɪs/ *noun* the capital structure of a company (shareholders' capital plus loans and retained profits) used as a way of assessing the company's worth

capital bonus /ˌkæpɪt(ə)l 'bəʊnəs/ *noun* an extra payment by an insurance company which is produced by a capital gain

capital budget /ˌkæpɪt(ə)l 'bʌdʒɪt/ *noun* a budget for planned purchases of fixed assets during the next budget period

capital budgeting /ˌkæpɪt(ə)l 'bʌdʒɪtɪŋ/ *noun* the process of deciding on specific investment projects, the amount of expenditure to commit to them and how the finance will be raised

capital commitments /ˌkæpɪt(ə)l kə 'mɪtmənts/ *plural noun* expenditure on assets which has been authorised by directors, but not yet spent at the end of a financial period

capital consumption /ˌkæpɪt(ə)l kən'sʌmpʃ(ə)n/ *noun* in a given period, the total depreciation of a national economy's fixed assets based on replacement costs

capital costs /ˌkæpɪt(ə)l 'kɒsts/ *plural noun* expenses on the purchase of fixed assets

capital deepening /ˈkæpɪt(ə)l ˌdiːpənɪŋ/ *noun* increased investment of capital in a business, without changing other factors of production. Also called **capital widening**

capital employed /ˌkæpɪt(ə)l ɪm'plɔɪd/ *noun* an amount of capital consisting of shareholders' funds plus the long-term debts of a business. ◊ **return on assets**

capital equipment /ˌkæpɪt(ə)l ɪ'kwɪpmənt/ *noun* equipment which a factory or office uses to work

capital expenditure /ˌkæpɪt(ə)l ɪk'spendɪtʃə/ *noun* money spent on fixed assets such as property, machines and furniture. Also called **capital investment**, **capital outlay**. Abbreviation **CAPEX**

capital expenditure budget /ˌkæpɪt(ə)l ɪk'spendɪtʃə ˌbʌdʒɪt/ *noun* a budget for planned purchases of fixed assets during the budget period

capital flight /ˌkæpɪt(ə)l 'flaɪt/ *noun* the rapid movement of capital out of a country because of lack of confidence in that country's economic future in response to political unrest, war or other conditions. Also called **flight of capital**

capital gain /ˌkæpɪt(ə)l 'geɪn/ *noun* an amount of money made by selling a fixed asset or certain other types of property, such as shares, works of art, leases etc. Opposite **capital loss**

capital gains expenses /ˌkæpɪt(ə)l 'geɪnz ɪkˌspensɪz/ *plural noun* expenses incurred in buying or selling assets, which can be deducted when calculating a capital gain or loss

capital gains tax /ˌkæpɪt(ə)l 'geɪnz tæks/ *noun* a tax on the difference between the gross acquisition cost and the net proceeds when an asset is sold. In the United Kingdom, this tax also applies when assets are given or exchanged, although each individual has an annual capital gains tax allowance that exempts gains within that tax year below a stated level. In addition, certain assets may be exempt, e.g., a person's principal private residence and transfers of assets between spouses. Abbreviation **CGT**

capital goods /ˈkæpɪt(ə)l gʊdz/ *plural noun* machinery, buildings, and raw materials which are used to make other goods

capital inflow /ˌkæpɪt(ə)l 'ɪnfləʊ/ *noun* the movement of capital into a country by buying shares in companies, buying whole companies or other forms of investment

capital-intensive industry /ˌkæpɪt(ə)l ɪn'tensɪv ˌɪndəstri/ *noun* an industry which needs a large amount of capital investment in plant to make it work

capital investment /ˌkæpɪt(ə)l ɪn'vestmənt/ *noun* same as **capital expenditure**

capital investment appraisal /ˌkæpɪt(ə)l ɪnˌvestmənt ə'preɪz(ə)l/ *noun* an analysis of the future profitability of capital purchases as an aid to good management

capitalisation /ˌkæpɪt(ə)laɪ'zeɪʃ(ə)n/, **capitalization** *noun* the value of a company calculated by multiplying the price of its shares on the stock exchange by the number of shares issued. Also called **market capitalisation**

'...she aimed to double the company's market capitalization' [*Fortune*]

capitalisation issue /ˌkæpɪtəlaɪ'zeɪʃ(ə)n ˌɪʃuː/ *noun* same as **bonus issue**

capitalisation of costs /ˌkæpɪt(ə)laɪzeɪʃ(ə)n əv 'kɒsts/ *noun* the act of including costs usually charged to the profit and loss account in the balance sheet. The effect is that profits are higher than if such costs are matched with revenues in the same accounting period.

capitalisation of earnings /ˌkæpɪtəlaɪzeɪʃ(ə)n əv 'ɜːnɪŋz/ *noun* a method of valuing a business according to its expected future profits

capitalise /ˈkæpɪt(ə)laɪz/, **capitalize** *verb* **1.** to invest money in a working company □ **the company is capitalised at £10,000** the company has a working capital of £10,000 **2.** to convert reserves or assets into capital

'...at its last traded price the bank was capitalized at around $1.05 billion with 60 per cent in the hands of the family' [*South China Morning Post*]

capitalise on *phrasal verb* to make a profit from ○ *We are seeking to capitalise on our market position.*

capitalism /ˈkæpɪt(ə)lɪz(ə)m/ *noun* the economic system in which each person has the right to invest money, to work in business, and to buy and sell, with no restrictions from the state

capitalist /ˈkæpɪt(ə)lɪst/ *adjective* working according to the principles of capitalism ○ *the capitalist system* ○ *the capitalist countries* or *world*

capitalist economy /ˌkæpɪt(ə)lɪst ɪ ˈkɒnəmi/ *noun* an economy in which each person has the right to invest money, to work in business, and to buy and sell, with no restrictions from the state

capital lease /ˈkæpɪt(ə)l liːs/ *noun* a lease that gives the lessee substantial property rights

capital levy /ˌkæpɪt(ə)l ˈlevi/ *noun* a tax on the value of a person's property and possessions

capital loss /ˌkæpɪt(ə)l ˈlɒs/ *noun* a loss made by selling assets. Opposite **capital gain**

capital maintenance concept /ˌkæpɪt(ə)l ˈmeɪntənəns ˌkɒnsept/ *noun* a concept used to determine the definition of profit, that provides the basis for different systems of inflation accounting

capital market /ˌkæpɪt(ə)l ˈmɑːkɪt/ *noun* an international market where money can be raised for investment in a business

capital outlay /ˌkæpɪt(ə)l ˈaʊtleɪ/ *noun* same as **capital expenditure**

capital profit /ˌkæpɪt(ə)l ˈprɒfɪt/ *noun* a profit made by selling an asset

capital project /ˌkæpɪt(ə)l ˈprɒdʒekt/ *noun* a large-scale and complex project, often involving construction or engineering work, in which an organisation spends part of its financial resources on creating capacity for production

capital ratio /ˈkæpɪt(ə)l ˌreɪʃiəʊ/ *noun* same as **capital adequacy**

capital rationing /ˈkæpɪt(ə)l ˌræʃ(ə)nɪŋ/ *noun* restrictions on capital investment, the result either of the internal imposition of a budget ceiling or of external limitations such as the fact that additional borrowing is not available

capital reconstruction /ˌkæpɪt(ə)l ˌriːkənˈstrʌkʃən/ *noun* the act of putting a company into voluntary liquidation and then selling its assets to another company with the same name and same shareholders, but with a larger capital base

capital redemption reserve /ˌkæpɪt(ə)l rɪˈdempʃən rɪˌzɜːv/ *noun* an account required to prevent a reduction in capital, where a company purchases or redeems its own shares out of distributable profits

capital reorganisation /ˌkæpɪt(ə)l riːˌɔːɡənaɪˈzeɪʃ(ə)n/ *noun* the process of changing the capital structure of a company by amalgamating or dividing existing shares to form shares of a higher or lower nominal value

capital reserves /ˌkæpɪt(ə)l rɪˈzɜːvz/ *plural noun* **1.** money from profits, which forms part of the capital of a company and can be used for distribution to shareholders only when a company is wound up. Also called **undistributable reserves 2.** the share capital of a company which comes from selling assets and not from their usual trading

capital shares /ˌkæpɪt(ə)l ˈʃeəz/ *plural noun* (*on the Stock Exchange*) shares in a unit trust which rise in value as the capital value of the units rises, but do not receive any income (NOTE: The other form of shares in a split-level investment trust are income shares, which receive income from the investments, but do not rise in value.)

capital stock /ˈkæpɪt(ə)l stɒk/ *noun* **1.** the amount of money raised by a company through the sale of shares, entitling holders to dividends, some rights of ownership and other benefits **2.** the face value of the share capital that a company issues

capital structure /ˌkæpɪt(ə)l ˈstrʌktʃə/ *noun* the relative proportions of equity capital and debt capital within a company's balance sheet

capital surplus /ˈkæpɪt(ə)l ˌsɜːpləs/ *noun* the total value of shares in a company that exceeds the par value

capital tax /ˈkæpɪt(ə)l tæks/ *noun* a tax levied on the capital owned by a company, rather than on its spending. ◊ **capital gains tax**

capital-to-asset ratio /ˌkæpɪt(ə)l tʊ ˈæset ˌreɪʃiəʊ/, **capital/asset ratio** *noun* same as **capital adequacy**

capital transactions /ˌkæpɪt(ə)l trænˈzækʃ(ə)nz/ *plural noun* transactions affecting non-current items such as fixed assets, long-term debt or share capital, rather than revenue transactions

capital transfer tax /ˌkæpɪt(ə)l ˈtrænsfɜː ˌtæks/ *noun* in the United Kingdom, a tax on the transfer of assets that was replaced in 1986 by inheritance tax

capital turnover ratio /ˌkæpɪt(ə)l ˈtɜːnəʊvə ˌreɪʃiəʊ/ *noun* turnover divided by average capital during the year

capital widening /ˈkæpɪt(ə)l ˌwaɪd(ə)nɪŋ/ *noun* same as **capital deepening**

CAPM *abbreviation* capital asset pricing model

capped floating rate note /ˌkæpt ˈfləʊtɪŋ reɪt ˌnəʊt/ *noun* a floating rate note which has an agreed maximum rate

captive market /ˌkæptɪv ˈmɑːkɪt/ *noun* a market where one supplier has a monopoly and the buyer has no choice over the product which he or she must purchase

carriage /ˈkærɪdʒ/ *noun* the transporting of goods from one place to another ○ *to pay for carriage*

carriage forward /ˌkærɪdʒ ˈfɔːwəd/ *noun* a deal where the customer pays for transporting the goods

carriage free /ˌkærɪdʒ ˈfriː/ *noun* a deal where the customer does not pay for the shipping

carriage inwards /ˌkærɪdʒ ˈɪnwədz/ *noun* delivery expenses incurred through the purchase of goods

carriage outwards /ˌkærɪdʒ ˈaʊtwədz/ *noun* delivery expenses incurred through the sale of goods

carriage paid /ˌkærɪdʒ ˈpeɪd/ *noun* a deal where the seller has paid for the shipping

carry /ˈkæri/ *noun* the cost of borrowing to finance a deal

carry back /ˌkæri ˈbæk/ *phrasal verb* to take back to an earlier accounting period

carry down /ˌkæri ˈdaʊn/, **carry forward** /ˌkæri ˈfɔːwəd/ *phrasal verb* to take an account balance at the end of the current period as the starting point for the next period

carry forward /ˌkæri ˈfɔːwəd/ *phrasal verb* to take an account balance at the end of the current period or page as the starting point for the next period or page

carrying cost /ˈkærɪɪŋ kɒst/ *noun* any expense associated with holding stock for a given period, e.g., from the time of delivery to the time of dispatch. Carrying costs will include storage and insurance.

carrying value /ˈkærɪɪŋ ˌvæljuː/ *noun* same as **book value**

carry-over /ˈkæri ˌəʊvə/ *noun* the stock of a commodity held at the beginning of a new financial year

cartel /kɑːˈtel/ *noun* a group of companies which try to fix the price or to regulate the supply of a product so that they can make more profit

cash /kæʃ/ *noun* **1.** money in the form of coins or notes **2.** the using of money in coins or notes ■ *verb* □ **to cash a cheque** to exchange a cheque for cash

cash in /ˌkæʃ ˈɪn/ *phrasal verb* to sell shares or other property for cash

cash in on /ˌkæʃ ˈɪn ˌɒn/ *phrasal verb* to profit from ○ *The company is cashing in on the interest in computer games.*

cash out *phrasal verb US* same as **cash up**

cash up /ˌkæʃ ˈʌp/ *phrasal verb* to add up the cash in a shop at the end of the day

cashable /ˈkæʃəb(ə)l/ *adjective* able to be cashed ○ *A crossed cheque is not cashable at any bank.*

cash account /ˈkæʃ əˌkaʊnt/ *noun* an account which records the money which is received and spent

cash accounting /ˌkæʃ əˈkaʊntɪŋ/ *noun* **1.** an accounting method in which receipts and expenses are recorded in the accounting books in the period when they actually occur **2.** in the United Kingdom, a system for Value Added Tax that enables the tax payer to account for tax paid and received during a given period, thus allowing automatic relief for bad debts

cash advance /ˌkæʃ ədˈvɑːns/ *noun* a loan in cash against a future payment

cash and carry /ˌkæʃ ən ˈkæri/ *noun* **1.** a large store selling goods at low prices, where the customer pays cash and takes the goods away immediately ○ *We get our supplies every morning from the cash and carry.* **2.** the activity of buying a commodity for cash and selling the same commodity on the futures market

'…the small independent retailer who stocks up using cash and carries could be hit hard by the loss of footfall associated with any increase in smuggled goods' [*The Grocer*]

cash at bank /ˌkæʃ ət ˈbæŋk/ *noun* the total amount of money held at the bank by an individual or company

cashback /ˈkæʃbæk/ *noun* a discount system where a purchaser receives a cash discount on the completion of the purchase

'… he mentioned BellSouth's DSL offer of $75 a month, plus a one-month cash-back rebate.' [BusinessWeek]

cash balance /ˈkæʃ ˌbæləns/ *noun* a balance that represents cash alone, as distinct from a balance that includes money owed but as yet unpaid

cash basis /ˈkæʃ ˌbeɪsɪs/ *noun* a method of preparing the accounts of a business, where receipts and payments are shown at the time when they are made, as opposed to showing debts or credits which are outstanding at the end of the accounting period. Also called **receipts and payments basis**

cash budget /ˈkæʃ ˌbʌdʒɪt/ *noun* a plan of cash income and expenditure. Also called **cash-flow budget**

cash card /ˈkæʃ kɑːd/ *noun* a plastic card used to obtain money from a cash dispenser

cash cow /ˈkæʃ kaʊ/ *noun* a product or subsidiary company that consistently generates good profits but does not provide growth

cash discount /ˌkæʃ ˈdɪskaʊnt/ *noun* a discount given for payment in cash. Also called **discount for cash**

cash dispenser /ˈkæʃ dɪˌspensə/ *noun* a machine which gives out money when a special card is inserted and instructions given

cash dividend /ˌkæʃ ˈdɪvɪdend/ *noun* a dividend paid in cash, as opposed to a dividend in the form of bonus shares

cash economy /ˌkæʃ ɪˈkɒnəmi/ *noun* a black economy, where goods and services are paid for in cash, and therefore not declared for tax

cash equivalent /ˌkæʃ ɪˈkwɪvələnt/ *noun* **1.** an amount of money that can be realised immediately by selling an asset **2.** a safe and highly liquid financial instrument such as a Treasury bill

cash equivalents /ˌkæʃ ɪˈkwɪvələnts/ *noun* short-term investments that can be converted into cash immediately and that are subject to only a limited risk. There is usually a limit on their duration, e.g., three months.

cash float /ˈkæʃ fləʊt/ *noun* cash put into the cash box at the beginning of the day or week to allow change to be given to customers

cash flow /ˈkæʃ fləʊ/ *noun* cash which comes into a company from sales (cash inflow) or the money which goes out in purchases or overhead expenditure (cash outflow)

cash-flow accounting /ˈkæʃ fləʊ əˌkaʊntɪŋ/ *noun* the practice of measuring the financial activities of a company in terms of cash receipts and payments, without recording accruals, prepayments, debtors, creditors and stocks

cash-flow budget /ˈkæʃ fləʊ ˌbʌdʒɪt/ *noun* same as **cash budget**

cash-flow forecast /ˈkæʃ fləʊ ˌfɔːkɑːst/ *noun* a forecast of when cash will be received or paid out

cash-flow ratio /ˈkæʃ fləʊ ˌreɪʃiəʊ/ *noun* a ratio that shows the level of cash in a business in relation to other assets and the use of cash in the activities of the business

cash-flow risk /ˈkæʃ fləʊ ˌrɪsk/ *noun* the risk that a company's available cash will not be sufficient to meet its financial obligations

cash-flow statement /ˈkæʃ fləʊ ˌsteɪtmənt/ *noun* a record of a company's cash inflows and cash outflows over a specific period of time, typically a year

cash-flow-to-total-debt ratio /ˌkæʃ fləʊ tə ˈdet ˌreɪʃiəʊ/ *noun* a ratio that indicates a company's ability to pay its debts, often used as an indicator of bankruptcy

cash fraction /ˌkæʃ ˈfrækʃən/ *noun* a small amount of cash paid to a shareholder to make up the full amount of part of a share which has been allocated in a share split

cash-generating unit /ˈkæʃ ˌdʒenəreɪtɪŋ ˌjuːnɪt/ *noun* the smallest identifiable group of assets that generates cash inflows and outflows that can be measured

cashier /kæˈʃɪə/ *noun* **1.** a person who takes money from customers in a shop or who deals with the money that has been paid **2.** a person who deals with customers in a bank and takes or gives cash at the counter

cashier's check /kæˌʃɪəz ˈtʃek/ *noun US* a bank's own cheque, drawn on itself and signed by a cashier or other bank official

cash inflow /ˌkæʃ ˈɪnfləʊ/ *noun* receipts of cash or cheques

cash items /ˈkæʃ ˌaɪtəmz/ *plural noun* goods sold for cash

cashless society /ˌkæʃləs səˈsaɪəti/ *noun* a society where no one uses cash, all purchases being made by credit cards, charge cards, cheques or direct transfer from one account to another

cash limit /ˈkæʃ ˌlɪmɪt/ *noun* **1.** a fixed amount of money which can be spent during some period **2.** a maximum amount someone can withdraw from an ATM using a cash card

cash offer /ˈkæʃ ˌɒfə/ *noun* an offer to pay in cash, especially an offer to pay cash when buying shares in a takeover bid

cash outflow /ˌkæʃ ˈaʊtfləʊ/ *noun* expenditure in cash or cheques

cash payment /ˈkæʃ ˌpeɪmənt/ *noun* payment in cash

cash payments journal /ˈkæʃ ˌpeɪmənts ˌdʒɜːn(ə)l/ *noun* a chronological record of all the payments that have been made from a company's bank account

cash position /ˈkæʃ pəˌzɪʃ(ə)n/ *noun* a state of the cash which a company currently has available

cash price /ˈkæʃ praɪs/ *noun* **1.** a lower price or better terms which apply if the customer pays cash **2.** same as **spot price**

cash purchase /'kæʃ ˌpɜːtʃɪs/ noun a purchase made for cash

cash receipts journal /'kæʃ rɪˌsiːts ˌdʒɜːn(ə)l/ noun a chronological record of all the receipts that have been paid into a company's bank account

cash register /'kæʃ ˌredʒɪstə/ noun a machine which shows and adds the prices of items bought, with a drawer for keeping the cash received

cash reserves /'kæʃ rɪˌzɜːvz/ plural noun a company's reserves in cash deposits or bills kept in case of urgent need ○ *The company was forced to fall back on its cash reserves.*

cash sale /'kæʃ seɪl/ noun a transaction paid for in cash

cash surrender value /ˌkæʃ səˈrendə ˌvæljuː/ noun the amount of money that an insurance company will pay a policyholder who chooses to terminate a policy before the maturity date

cash terms /'kæʃ tɜːmz/ plural noun lower terms which apply if the customer pays cash

cash-to-current-liabilities ratio /ˌkæʃ tə ˌkʌrənt ˌlaɪəˈbɪlɪtiz ˌreɪʃiəʊ/ noun a ratio that indicates a company's ability to pay its short-term debts, often used as an indicator of liquidity

cash transaction /'kæʃ trænˌzækʃən/ noun a transaction paid for in cash, as distinct from a transaction paid for by means of a transfer of a financial instrument

cash voucher /'kæʃ ˌvaʊtʃə/ noun a piece of paper which can be exchanged for cash ○ *With every $20 of purchases, the customer gets a cash voucher to the value of $2.*

casting vote /ˌkɑːstɪŋ ˈvəʊt/ noun a vote used by the chairman in the case where the votes for and against a proposal are equal ○ *The chairman has the casting vote.* ○ *She used her casting vote to block the motion.*

casual labour /ˌkæʒuəl ˈleɪbə/ noun workers who are hired for a short period

casual work /'kæʒuəl wɜːk/ noun work where the employees are hired only for a short period

casual worker /ˌkæʒuəl ˈwɜːkə/ noun an employee who can be hired for a short period

CAT abbreviation certified accounting technician

CCA abbreviation current cost accounting

CCAB abbreviation Consultative Committee of Accountancy Bodies

CD abbreviation certificate of deposit

ceiling /'siːlɪŋ/ noun the highest point that something can reach, e.g. the highest rate of a pay increase ○ *to fix a ceiling for a budget* ○ *There is a ceiling of $100,000 on deposits.* ○ *Output reached its ceiling in June and has since fallen back.* ○ *What ceiling has the government put on wage increases this year?*

central bank /ˌsentrəl ˈbæŋk/ noun the main government-controlled bank in a country, which controls that country's financial affairs by fixing main interest rates, issuing currency, supervising the commercial banks and trying to control the foreign exchange rate

central bank discount rate /ˌsentrəl bæŋk ˈdɪskaʊnt reɪt/ noun the rate at which a central bank discounts bills such as Treasury bills

central bank intervention /ˌsentrəl bæŋk ˌɪntəˈvenʃ(ə)n/ noun an action by a central bank to change base interest rates, to impose exchange controls or to buy or sell the country's own currency in an attempt to influence international money markets

central government /ˌsentrəl ˈɡʌv(ə)nmənt/ noun the main government of a country as opposed to municipal, local, provincial or state governments

centralise /'sentrəlaɪz/ verb to organise from a central point ○ *All purchasing has been centralised in our main office.* ○ *The company has become very centralised, and far more staff work at headquarters.*

central purchasing /ˌsentrəl ˈpɜːtʃɪsɪŋ/ noun purchasing organised by a central office for all branches of a company

centre /'sentə/ noun a department, area or function to which costs and/or revenues are charged (NOTE: The US spelling is **center**.)

CEO abbreviation chief executive officer

certain annuity /ˌsɜːt(ə)n əˈnjuːɪti/ noun an annuity which will be paid for a specific number of years only

certificate /səˈtɪfɪkət/ noun an official document carrying an official declaration by someone, and signed by that person

certificated bankrupt /səˌtɪfɪkeɪtɪd ˈbæŋkrʌpt/ noun a bankrupt who has been discharged from bankruptcy with a certificate to show that he or she was not at fault

certificate of approval /səˌtɪfɪkət əv ə ˈpruːv(ə)l/ noun a document showing that an item has been approved officially

certificate of deposit /səˌtɪfɪkət əv dɪ ˈpɒzɪt/ noun a document from a bank showing that money has been deposited at a guaranteed interest rate for a certain period of time. Abbreviation **CD**

'…interest rates on certificates of deposit may have little room to decline in August as demand for funds from major city banks is likely to remain strong. After delaying for months, banks are now expected to issue a large volume of CDs. If banks issue more CDs on the assumption that the official discount rate reduction will be delayed, it is very likely that CD rates will be pegged for a longer period than expected' [*Nikkei Weekly*]

certificate of incorporation /sə
ˌtɪfɪkət əv ɪnˌkɔːpəˈreɪʃ(ə)n/ *noun* a document issued by Companies House to show that a company has been legally set up and officially registered

certificate of origin /səˌtɪfɪkət əv ˈprɪdʒɪn/ *noun* a document showing where imported goods come from or were made

certificate of quality /səˌtɪfɪkət əv ˈkwɒlɪti/ *noun* a certificate showing the grade of a soft commodity

certificate of registration /səˌtɪfɪkət əv ˌredʒɪˈstreɪʃ(ə)n/ *noun* a document showing that an item has been registered

certificate to commence business /səˌtɪfɪkət tə kəˌmens ˈbɪznɪs/ *noun* a document issued by the Registrar of Companies which allows a registered company to trade

certified accountant /ˌsɜːtɪfaɪd əˈkaʊntənt/ *noun* an accountant who has passed the professional examinations and is a member of the Association of Certified Chartered Accountants (ACCA)

certified accounting technician /ˌsɜːtɪfaɪd əˌkaʊntɪŋ tekˈnɪʃ(ə)n/ *noun* a person who has passed the first stage course of the Association of Chartered Certified Accountants (ACCA). Abbreviation **CAT**

certified cheque /ˌsɜːtɪfaɪd ˈtʃek/ *noun* a cheque which a bank says is good and will be paid out of money put aside from the payer's bank account

certified public accountant /ˌsɜːtɪfaɪd ˌpʌblɪk əˈkaʊntənt/ *noun US* same as **chartered accountant**

certify /ˈsɜːtɪfaɪ/ *verb* to make an official declaration in writing ○ *I certify that this is a true copy.* ○ *The document is certified as a true copy.* (NOTE: **certifies – certifying – certified**)

cessation /seˈseɪʃ(ə)n/ *noun* the stopping of an activity or work

cession /ˈseʃ(ə)n/ *noun* the act of giving up property to someone, especially a creditor

CFO *abbreviation* chief financial officer

CGT *abbreviation* capital gains tax

CH *abbreviation* Companies House

chairman /ˈtʃeəmən/ *noun* **1.** a person who is in charge of a meeting ○ *Mr Howard was chairman* or *acted as chairman* **2.** a person who presides over the board meetings of a company ○ *the chairman of the board* or *the company chairman* □ **the chairman's report**, **the chairman's statement** an annual report from the chairman of a company to the shareholders

'…the corporation's entrepreneurial chairman seeks a dedicated but part-time president. The new president will work a three-day week' [*Globe and Mail (Toronto)*]

Chamber of Commerce /ˌtʃeɪmbər əv ˈkɒmɜːs/ *noun* an organisation of local business people who work together to promote and protect common interest in trade

Chancellor of the Exchequer /ˌtʃɑːnsələr əv ði: ɪksˈtʃekə/ *noun* the chief finance minister in the British government (NOTE: The US term is **Secretary of the Treasury**.)

change /tʃeɪndʒ/ *noun* **1.** money in coins or small notes. ◊ **exchange** □ **to give someone change for £10** to give someone coins or notes in exchange for a ten pound note **2.** money given back by the seller, when the buyer can pay only with a larger note or coin than the amount asked ○ *She gave me the wrong change.* ○ *You paid the £5.75 bill with a £10 note, so you should have £4.25 change.* **3.** an alteration of the way something is done or of the way work is carried out □ **change in accounting principles** using a method to state a company's accounts which is different from the method used in the previous accounts. This will have to be agreed with the auditors, and possibly with the Inland Revenue. ■ *verb* **1.** □ **to change a £20 note** to give someone smaller notes or coins in place of a £20 note **2.** to give one type of currency for another ○ *to change £1,000 into dollars* ○ *We want to change some traveller's cheques.*

change in accounting estimate /ˌtʃeɪndʒ ɪn əˈkaʊntɪŋ ˌestɪmət/ *noun* a change in a major assumption or forecast underpinning a set of accounts, full disclosure of which should be made in a financial statement

change machine /'tʃeɪndʒ məˌʃiːn/ *noun* a machine which gives small change for a note or larger coin

channel /'tʃæn(ə)l/ *noun* a means by which information or goods pass from one place to another

CHAPS /tʃæps/ *noun* an electronic, bank-to-bank payment system that guarantees same-day payment. Compare **BACS**

Chapter 7 /ˌtʃæptə 'sev(ə)n/ *noun* a section of the US Bankruptcy Reform Act 1978, which sets out the rules for liquidation, a choice available to individuals, partnerships and corporations

Chapter 11 /ˌtʃæptə 'ten/ *noun* a section of the US Bankruptcy Reform Act 1978, which allows a corporation to be protected from demands made by its creditors for a period of time, while it is reorganised with a view to paying its debts

Chapter 13 /ˌtʃæptə θɜːr'tiːn/ *noun* a section of the Bankruptcy Reform Act 1978, which allows a business to continue trading and to pay off its creditors by regular monthly payments over a period of time

charge /tʃɑːdʒ/ *noun* **1.** money which must be paid, or the price of a service ○ *to make no charge for delivery* ○ *to make a small charge for rental* ○ *There is no charge for this service* or *No charge is made for this service.* **2.** a guarantee of security for a loan, for which assets are pledged **3.** a sum deducted from revenue in the profit and loss account ■ *verb* **1.** to ask someone to pay for services later **2.** to ask for money to be paid ○ *to charge $5 for delivery* ○ *How much does he charge?* □ **he charges £16 an hour** he asks to be paid £16 for an hour's work **3.** to take something as guarantee for a loan **4.** to record an expense or other deduction from revenue in the profit and loss account

chargeable /'tʃɑːdʒəb(ə)l/ *adjective* able to be charged ○ *repairs chargeable to the occupier*

chargeable asset /ˌtʃɑːdʒəb(ə)l 'æset/ *noun* an asset which will produce a capital gain when sold. Assets which are not chargeable include your family home, cars, and some types of investments such as government stocks.

chargeable business asset /ˌtʃɑːdʒəb(ə)l 'bɪznɪs ˌæset/ *noun* an asset which is owned by a business and is liable to capital gains if sold

chargeable gains /ˌtʃɑːdʒəb(ə)l 'ɡeɪnz/ *plural noun* gains made by selling an asset such as shares, on which capital gains will be charged

chargeable transfer /ˌtʃɑːdʒəb(ə)l 'trænsfɜː/ *noun* in the United Kingdom, gifts that are liable to inheritance tax. Under UK legislation, individuals may gift assets to a certain value during their lifetime without incurring any liability to inheritance tax. These are regular transfers out of income that do not affect the donor's standard of living. Additionally, individuals may transfer up to £3,000 a year out of capital.

charge account /'tʃɑːdʒ əˌkaʊnt/ *noun US* same as **credit account** (NOTE: The customer will make regular monthly payments into the account and is allowed credit of a multiple of those payments.)

charge and discharge accounting /ˌtʃɑːdʒ ən 'dɪstʃɑːdʒ əˌkaʊntɪŋ/ *noun* formerly, a bookkeeping system in which a person charges himself or herself with receipts and credits himself or herself with payments. This system was used extensively in medieval times before the advent of double-entry bookkeeping.

charge by way of legal mortgage /ˌtʃɑːdʒ baɪ weɪ əv ˌliːɡ(ə)l 'mɔːɡɪdʒ/ *noun* a way of borrowing money on the security of a property, where the mortgager signs a deed which gives the mortgagee an interest in the property

charge card /'tʃɑːdʒ kɑːd/ *noun* a card issued to customers by a shop, bank or other organisation, used to charge purchases to an account for later payment. ◊ **credit card**

chargee /tʃɑː'dʒiː/ *noun* a person who has the right to force a debtor to pay

charges forward /ˌtʃɑːdʒɪz 'fɔːwəd/ *plural noun* charges which will be paid by the customer

charitable /'tʃærɪtəb(ə)l/ *adjective* benefiting the general public as a charity

charitable deductions /ˌtʃærɪtəb(ə)l dɪ'dʌkʃ(ə)nz/ *plural noun* deductions from taxable income for contributions to charity

charitable purposes /ˌtʃærɪtəb(ə)l 'pɜːpəsɪz/ *plural noun* the purpose of supporting work done by a charitable organisation, for which purpose money donated, or the value of services contributed, may be offset against tax

charitable trust /'tʃærɪtəb(ə)l trʌst/, **charitable corporation** /ˌtʃærɪtəb(ə)l ˌkɔːpə'reɪʃ(ə)n/ *noun* a trust which benefits the public as a whole, which promotes education or religion, which helps the poor or which does other useful work

charity /'tʃærɪti/ *noun* an organisation which offers free help or services to those in need ○ *Because the organisation is a charity* *it does not have to pay taxes. ○ The charity owes its success to clever marketing strategies in its fund-raising.*

charity accounts /ˌtʃærɪtɪ əˈkaʊnts/ *plural noun* the accounting records of a charitable institution, that include a statement of financial activities rather than a profit and loss account. In the United Kingdom, the accounts should conform to the requirements stipulated in the Charities Act (1993).

Charity Commissioners /ˈtʃærɪtɪ kəˌmɪʃ(ə)nəz/ *plural noun* the UK body which governs charities and sees that they follow the law and use their funds for the purposes intended

chart /tʃɑːt/ *noun* a diagram displaying information as a series of lines, blocks, etc.

charter /ˈtʃɑːtə/ *noun* **1.** a document giving special legal rights to a group ○ *a shoppers' charter* or *a customers' charter* **2.** *US* in the US, a formal document incorporating an organisation, company or educational institution

chartered /ˈtʃɑːtəd/ *adjective* **1.** in the UK, used to describe a company which has been set up by charter, and not registered under the Companies Act ○ *a chartered bank* **2.** in the US, used to describe an incorporated organisation, company or educational institution that has been set up by charter

chartered accountant /ˌtʃɑːtəd əˈkaʊntənt/ *noun* an accountant who has passed the necessary professional examinations and is a member of the Institute of Chartered Accountants. Abbreviation **CA**

Chartered Association of Certified Accountants /ˌtʃɑːtəd əˌsəʊsieɪʃ(ə)n əv ˌsɜːtɪfaɪd əˈkaʊntənts/ *noun* the former name of the Association of Chartered Certified Accountants

chartered bank /ˌtʃɑːtəd ˈbæŋk/ *noun* a bank which has been set up by government charter, formerly used in England, but now only done in the USA and Canada

chartered company /ˌtʃɑːtəd ˈkʌmp(ə)ni/ *noun* a company which has been set up by royal charter, and not registered under the Companies Act

Chartered Institute of Management Accountants /ˌtʃɑːtəd ˌɪnstɪtjuː əv ˌmænɪdʒmənt əˈkaʊntənts/ *noun* a UK organisation responsible for the education and training of management accountants who work in industry, commerce, not-for-profit and public sector organisations

Chartered Institute of Public Finance and Accountancy /ˌtʃɑːtəd ˌɪnstɪtjuːt əv ˌpʌblɪk ˌfaɪnæns ən ə ˈkaʊntənsi/ full form of **CIPFA**

Chartered Institute of Taxation /ˌtʃɑːtəd ˌɪnstɪtjuːt əv tækˈseɪʃ(ə)n/ *noun* in the United Kingdom, an organisation for professionals in the field of taxation, formerly the Institute of Taxation

charting /ˈtʃɑːtɪŋ/ *noun* the work of using charts to analyse information such as stock market trends and forecast future rises or falls

chart of accounts /ˌtʃɑːt əv əˈkaʊnts/ *noun* a detailed and ordered list of an organisation's numbered or named accounts, providing a standard list of account codes for assets, liabilities, capital, revenue and expenses

chattel mortgage /ˈtʃæt(ə)l ˌmɔːgɪdʒ/ *noun* money lent against the security of an item purchased, but not against real estate

chattels real /ˌtʃæt(ə)lz ˈrɪəl/ *plural noun* leaseholds

cheap money /ˌtʃiːp ˈmʌni/ *noun* money which can be borrowed at a low rate of interest

cheat /tʃiːt/ *verb* to trick someone so that he or she loses money ○ *He cheated the Inland Revenue out of thousands of pounds.* ○ *She was accused of cheating clients who came to ask her for advice.*

check /tʃek/ *verb* **1.** to stop or delay something ○ *to check the entry of contraband into the country* ○ *to check the flow of money out of a country* **2.** to examine or to investigate something ○ *to check that an invoice is correct* ○ *to check and sign for goods* □ **she checked the computer printout against the invoices** she examined the printout and the invoices to see if the figures were the same **3.** *US* to mark something with a sign to show that it is correct ○ *check the box marked 'R'* (NOTE: The UK term is **tick**.)

checkable /ˈtʃekəb(ə)l/ *adjective US* referring to a deposit account on which checks can be drawn

checkbook /ˈtʃekbʊk/ *noun US* same as **cheque book**

check card /ˈtʃek kɑːd/ *noun US* same as **cheque card**

checking account /ˈtʃekɪŋ əˌkaʊnt/ *noun US* same as **current account 1**

check routing symbol /ˈtʃek ˌruːtɪŋ ˌsɪmbəl/ *noun US* a number shown on a US cheque which identifies the Federal Reserve district through which the cheque will be cleared, similar to the UK 'bank sort code'

cheque /tʃek/ *noun* a note to a bank asking them to pay money from your account to the account of the person whose name is written on the note ○ *a cheque for £10* or *a £10 cheque* (NOTE: The US spelling is **check**.)

cheque account /'tʃek ə,kaʊnt/ *noun* same as **current account**

cheque book /'tʃek bʊk/ *noun* a booklet with new blank cheques (NOTE: The usual US term is **checkbook**.)

cheque card /'tʃek kɑːd/, **cheque guarantee card** /,tʃek ,gærən'tiː kɑːd/ *noun* a plastic card from a bank which guarantees payment of a cheque up to some amount, even if the user has no money in his account

cheque requisition /'tʃek ,rekwɪzɪʃ(ə)n/ *noun* an official note from a department to the company accounts staff asking for a cheque to be written

cheque stub /'tʃek stʌb/ *noun* a piece of paper left in a cheque book after a cheque has been written and taken out

cheque to bearer /,tʃek tə 'beərə/ *noun* a cheque with no name written on it, so that the person who holds it can cash it

chief executive /,tʃiːf ɪg'zekjʊtɪv/, **chief executive officer** /,tʃiːf ɪg,zekjʊtɪv 'ɒfɪsə/ *noun* the most important director in charge of a company. Abbreviation **CEO**

chief financial officer /,tʃiːf faɪ'nænʃəl ,ɒfɪsə/ *noun* an executive in charge of a company's financial operations, reporting to the CEO. Abbreviation **CFO**

chief investment officer /,tʃiːf ɪn'vestmənt ,ɒfɪsə/ *noun* a senior manager responsible for monitoring a company's investment portfolio

chief operating officer /tʃiːf 'ɒpəreɪtɪŋ ,ɒfɪsə/ *noun* a director in charge of all a company's operations (same as 'managing director'). Abbreviation **COO**

Chief Secretary to the Treasury /,tʃiːf ,sekrətri tə ðə 'treʒ(ə)ri/ *noun* a government minister responsible to the Chancellor of the Exchequer for the control of public expenditure (NOTE: In the USA, this is the responsibility of the **Director of the Budget**.)

Chinese walls /,tʃaɪniːz 'wɔːlz/ *plural noun* imaginary barriers between departments in the same organisation, set up to avoid insider dealing or conflict of interest. For example, if a merchant bank is advising on a planned takeover bid, its investment department should not know that the bid is taking place, or they would advise their clients to invest in the company being taken over.

chop /tʃɒp/ *noun* a mark made on a document to show that it has been agreed,

acknowledged, paid or that payment has been received

chose /tʃəʊz/ *phrase* a French word meaning 'item' or 'thing'

chose in action /,tʃəʊz ɪn 'ækʃən/ *noun* the legal term for a personal right which can be enforced or claimed as if it were property, e.g. a patent, copyright or debt

chose in possession /,tʃəʊz ɪn pə 'zeʃ(ə)n/ the legal term for a physical thing which can be owned, such as a piece of furniture

Christmas bonus /,krɪsməs 'bəʊnəs/ *noun* an extra payment made to staff at Christmas

chronological order /,krɒnəlɒdʒɪk(ə)l 'ɔːdə/ *noun* the arrangement of records such as files and invoices in order of their dates

CICA *abbreviation* Canadian Institute of Chartered Accountants

CIMA /'siːmə/ *abbreviation* Chartered Institute of Management Accountants

CIPFA *noun* a leading professional accountancy body in the UK, specialising in the public services. Full form **Chartered Institute of Public Finance and Accountancy**

circularisation of debtors /,sɜːkjʊləraɪzeɪʃ(ə)n əv 'detəz/ *noun* the sending of letters by a company's auditors to debtors in order to verify the existence and extent of the company's assets

circular letter of credit /,sɜːkjʊlə ,letər əv 'kredɪt/ *noun* a letter of credit sent to all branches of the bank which issues it

circulating capital /,sɜːkjʊleɪtɪŋ 'kæpɪt(ə)l/ *noun* capital in the form of cash or debtors, raw materials, finished products and work in progress which a company requires to carry on its business

circulation of capital /,sɜːkjʊleɪʃ(ə)n əv 'kæpɪt(ə)l/ *noun* a movement of capital from one investment to another

City Panel on Takeovers and Mergers /,sɪti ,pæn(ə)l ɒn ,teɪkəʊvəz ən 'mɜːdʒəz/ *noun* same as **Takeover Panel**

civil action /,sɪv(ə)l 'ækʃən/ *noun* a court case brought by a person or a company against someone who has done them wrong

claim /kleɪm/ *noun* an act of asking for something that you feel you have a right to ■ *verb* **1.** to ask for money, especially from an insurance company ○ *He claimed £100,000 damages against the cleaning firm.* ○ *She claimed for repairs to the car against her insurance policy.* **2.** to say that you have a right to something or that something is your property ○ *She is claiming possession of the house.* ○ *No one claimed the umbrella found in my office.* **3.** to state that something is a fact ○ *He claims he never received the goods.* ○ *She claims that the shares are her property.*

claim form /'kleɪm fɔːm/ *noun* a form which has to be filled in when making an insurance claim

claims department /'kleɪmz dɪ ˌpɑːtmənt/ *noun* a department of an insurance company which deals with claims

claims manager /'kleɪmz ˌmænɪdʒə/ *noun* the manager of a claims department

classical system of corporation tax /ˌklæsɪk(ə)l ˌsɪstəm əv ˌkɔːpəˈreɪʃ(ə)n ˌtæks/ *noun* a system in which companies and their owners are liable for corporation tax as separate entities. A company's taxed income is therefore paid out to shareholders who are in turn taxed again. This system operates in the United States and the Netherlands. It was replaced in the United Kingdom in 1973 by an imputation system.

classification of assets /ˌklæsɪfɪkeɪʃ(ə)n əv 'æsets/ *noun* the process of listing a company's assets under appropriate categories

classification of liabilities /ˌklæsɪfɪkeɪʃ(ə)n əv ˌlaɪəˈbɪlɪtiz/ *noun* the process of classifying liabilities by the date or period when they are due

classified stock /'klæsɪfaɪd stɒk/ *noun* a company's common stock when it is divided into categories

classify /'klæsɪfaɪ/ *verb* to put into classes or categories according to specific characteristics (NOTE: **classifies – classifying – classified**)

class of assets /ˌklɑːs əv 'æsets/ *noun* the grouping of similar assets into categories. This is done because under International Accounting Standards Committee rules, **tangible assets** and **intangible assets** cannot be revalued on an individual basis, only for a class of assets.

clause /klɔːz/ *noun* a section of a contract ○ *There are ten clauses in the contract of employment.* ○ *There is a clause in this contract concerning the employer's right to dismiss an employee.* ■ *verb* to list details of the relevant parties to a bill of exchange

claw back /ˌklɔː 'bæk/ *verb* to take back money which has been allocated ○ *Income tax claws back 25% of pensions paid out by the government.* ○ *Of the £1m allocated to the project, the government clawed back £100,000 in taxes.*

clawback /'klɔːbæk/ *noun* **1.** money taken back, especially money taken back by the government from grants or tax concessions which had previously been made **2.** the allocation of new shares to existing shareholders, so as to maintain the value of their holdings

clean float /'kliːn fləʊt/ *noun* an act of floating a currency freely on the international markets, without any interference from the government

clean opinion /ˌkliːn əˈpɪnjən/, **clean report** /ˌkliːn rɪˈpɔːt/ *noun* an auditor's report that is not qualified

clearance certificate /'klɪərəns sə ˌtɪfɪkət/ *noun* a document showing that goods have been passed by customs

clearance sale /'klɪərəns seɪl/ *noun* a sale of items at low prices to get rid of stock

clearing /'klɪərɪŋ/ *noun* **1.** □ **clearing of a debt** paying all of a debt **2.** □ **clearing of goods through customs** passing of goods through customs **3.** an act of passing of a cheque through the banking system, transferring money from one account to another

clearing account /'klɪərɪŋ əˌkaʊnt/ *noun* a temporary account containing amounts to be transferred to other accounts at a later date

clearing agency /'klɪərɪŋ ˌeɪdʒənsi/ *noun US* central office where stock exchange or commodity exchange transactions are settled (NOTE: The UK term is **clearing house**.)

clearing bank /'klɪərɪŋ bæŋk/ *noun* a bank which clears cheques, especially one of the major UK High Street banks, specialising in usual banking business for ordinary customers, such as loans, cheques, overdrafts and interest-bearing deposits

clearing house /'klɪərɪŋ haʊs/ *noun* a central office where clearing banks exchange cheques, or where stock exchange or commodity exchange transactions are settled

Clearing House Automated Payments System /ˌklɪərɪŋ haʊs ˌɔːtəmeɪtɪd 'peɪmənts ˌsɪstəm/ *noun* full form of **CHAPS**

clearing system /'klɪərɪŋ ˌsɪstəm/ *noun* the system of processing payments using phone and internet, operated in the UK by the Association for Payment Clearing Services, an organisation owned by 39 major banks and building societies

clear profit /ˌklɪə 'prɒfɪt/ *noun* a profit after all expenses have been paid ○ *We made $6,000 clear profit on the deal.*

clerical error /ˌklerɪk(ə)l 'erə/ *noun* a mistake made by someone doing office work

client /'klaɪənt/ *noun* a person with whom business is done or who pays for a service ○ *One of our major clients has defaulted on her payments.*

client account /'klaɪənt əˌkaʊnt/ *noun* a bank account opened by a solicitor or estate agent to hold money on behalf of a client

clientele /ˌkliːɒn'tel/ *noun* all the clients of a business or all the customers of a shop

close /kləʊz/ *verb* **1.** □ **to close the accounts** to come to the end of an accounting period and make up the profit and loss account **2.** to bring something to an end □ **she closed her building society account** she took all the money out and stopped using the account

close company /ˌkləʊs 'kʌmp(ə)ni/ *noun* a privately owned company controlled by a few shareholders (in the UK, fewer than five) where the public may own a small number of the shares (NOTE: The US term is **close corporation** or **closed corporation.**)

closed economy /ˌkləʊzd ɪ'kɒnəmi/ *noun* a type of economy where trade and financial dealings are tightly controlled by the government

closed-end credit /ˌkləʊzd end 'kredɪt/ *noun* a loan, plus any interest and finance charges, that is to be repaid in full by a specified future date. Loans that have property or motor vehicles as collateral are usually closed-end. ◊ **revolving credit** (NOTE: Most loans for the purchase of property or motor vehicles are closed-end credits.)

closed-end fund /ˌkləʊzd end 'fʌnd/ *noun* an investment fund shares in which can only be bought and sold on the open market

closed fund /ˌkləʊzd 'fʌnd/ *noun* a fund, such as an investment trust, where the investor buys shares in the trust and receives dividends. This is as opposed to an open-ended trust, such as a unit trust, where the investor buys units, and the investment is used to purchase further securities for the trust.

closed market /ˌkləʊzd 'mɑːkɪt/ *noun* a market where a supplier deals only with one agent or distributor and does not supply any others direct ○ *They signed a closed-market agreement with an Egyptian company.*

close-ended /ˌkləʊs 'endɪd/, **closed-end** /'kləʊzd end/ *adjective* referring to an investment which has a fixed capital, such as an investment trust

closely held /ˌkləʊsli 'held/ *adjective* referring to shares in a company which are controlled by only a few shareholders

close off /ˌkləʊz 'ɒf/ *verb* to come to the end of an accounting period and make up the profit and loss account

closing /'kləʊzɪŋ/ *adjective* **1.** final or coming at the end **2.** at the end of an accounting period ○ *At the end of the quarter the bookkeeper has to calculate the closing balance.* ■ *noun* □ **the closing of an account** the act of stopping supply to a customer on credit

closing balance /ˌkləʊzɪŋ 'bæləns/ *noun* the balance at the end of an accounting period

closing-down sale /ˌkləʊzɪŋ 'daʊn ˌseɪl/ *noun* the sale of goods when a shop is closing for ever

closing entries /ˌkləʊzɪŋ 'entriz/ *noun* in a double-entry bookkeeping system, entries made at the very end of an accounting period to balance the expense and revenue ledgers

closing out /ˌkləʊzɪŋ 'aʊt/ *noun US* the act of selling goods cheaply to try to get rid of them

closing rate /'kləʊzɪŋ reɪt/ *noun* the exchange rate of two or more currencies at the close of business of a balance sheet date, e.g. at the end of the financial year

closing-rate method /'kləʊzɪŋ reɪt ˌmeθəd/ *noun* a technique for translating the figures from a set of financial statements into a different currency using the closing rate. This method is often used for the accounts of a foreign subsidiary of a parent company.

closing stock /ˌkləʊzɪŋ 'stɒk/ *noun* a business's remaining stock at the end of an accounting period. It includes finished products, raw materials, or work in progress and is deducted from the period's costs in the balance sheets. ○ *At the end of the month the closing stock was 10% higher than at the end of the previous month.*

closure /'kləʊʒə/ *noun* the act of closing

C/N *abbreviation* credit note

CNCC *abbreviation* Compagnie Nationale des Commissaires aux Comptes

co- /kəʊ/ *prefix* working or acting together

CoCoA *abbreviation* continuously contemporary accounting

co-creditor /ˌkəʊ 'kredɪtə/ *noun* a person who is a creditor of the same company as you are

code /kəʊd/ *noun* **1.** a system of signs, numbers, or letters which mean something **2.** a set of rules

code of practice /ˌkəʊd əv ˈpræktɪs/ *noun* **1.** rules drawn up by an association which the members must follow when doing business **2.** the formally established ways in which members of a profession agree to work ○ *Advertisers have agreed to abide by the code of practice set out by the advertising council.*

codicil /ˈkəʊdɪsɪl/ *noun* a document executed in the same way as a will, making additions or changes to an existing will

coding /ˈkəʊdɪŋ/ *noun* the act of putting a code on something ○ *the coding of invoices*

coding of accounts /ˌkəʊdɪŋ əv ə ˈkaʊnts/ *noun* the practice of assigning codes to the individual accounts that make up the accounting system of a large company

co-director /ˈkəʊ daɪˌrektə/ *noun* a person who is a director of the same company as you

coefficient of variation /ˌkəʊɪfɪʃ(ə)nt əv ˌveəriˈeɪʃ(ə)n/ *noun* a measure of the spread of statistical data, which is equal to the standard deviation multiplied by 100

co-financing /ˌkəʊ ˈfaɪnænsɪŋ/ *noun* the act of arranging finance for a project from a series of sources

cold start /ˌkəʊld ˈstɑːt/ *noun* the act of beginning a new business or opening a new shop with no previous turnover to base it on

collateral /kəˈlæt(ə)rəl/ *noun* a security, such as negotiable instruments, shares or goods, used to provide a guarantee for a loan

'…examiners have come to inspect the collateral that thrifts may use in borrowing from the Fed' [*Wall Street Journal*]

collateralisation /kəˌlæt(ə)rəlaɪˈzeɪʃ(ə)n/ *noun* the act of securing a debt by selling long-term receivables to another company which secures them on the debts

collateralise /kəˈlæt(ə)rəlaɪz/, **collateralize** *verb* to secure a debt by means of a collateral

collect /kəˈlekt/ *verb* **1.** to get money which is owed to you by making the person who owes it pay **2.** to take things away from a place ○ *We have to collect the stock from the warehouse.* ■ *adverb, adjective* used to describe a phone call which the person receiving the call agrees to pay for

collectibility /kəˌlektɪˈbɪlɪti/ *noun* ability of cash owed to be collected

collecting agency /kəˈlektɪŋ ˌeɪdʒənsi/ *noun* an agency which collects money owed to other companies for a commission

collecting bank /kəˈlektɪŋ bæŋk/ *noun* a bank into which a person has deposited a cheque, and which has the duty to collect the money from the account of the writer of the cheque

collection period /kəˈlekʃən ˌpɪəriəd/ *noun* the number of days it takes a company to collect money owing

collection ratio /kəˈlekʃən ˌreɪʃiəʊ/ *noun* the average number of days it takes a firm to convert its accounts receivable into cash. Also known as **days' sales outstanding**

collections /kəˈlekʃənz/ *plural noun* money which has been collected

collective investment /kəˌlektɪv ɪnˈvestmənt/ *noun* the practice of investing money with other individuals or organisations in order to share costs and risk

collector /kəˈlektə/ *noun* a person who makes people pay money which is owed ○ *He works as a debt collector.*

column /ˈkɒləm/ *noun* a series of numbers arranged one underneath the other ○ *to add up a column of figures* ○ *Put the total at the bottom of the column.*

combined financial statement /kəmˌbaɪnd faɪˌnænʃəl ˈsteɪtmənt/ *noun* a written record covering the assets, liabilities, net worth and operating statement of two or more related or affiliated companies

comfort letter /ˈkʌmfət ˌletə/ *noun* **1.** in the United States, an accountant's statement confirming that the unaudited financial information in a prospectus follows GAAP **2.** a letter from a parent company to a lender assuring the lender that a subsidiary company that has applied for a loan will be supported by the parent in its efforts to stay in business

command economy /kəˌmɑːnd ɪˈkɒnəmi/ *noun* same as **planned economy**

commerce /ˈkɒmɜːs/ *noun* the buying and selling of goods and services

commercial /kəˈmɜːʃ(ə)l/ *adjective* **1.** referring to business **2.** profitable

commercial bank /kəˈmɜːʃ(ə)l bæŋk/ *noun* a bank which offers banking services to the public, as opposed to a merchant bank

commercial bill /kəˌmɜːʃ(ə)l ˈbɪl/ *noun* a bill of exchange issued by a company (a **trade bill**) or accepted by a bank (a **bank bill**), as opposed to a **Treasury bill**, which is issued by the government

commercial directory /kə'mɜːʃ(ə)l daɪ ˌrekt(ə)ri/ *noun* a book which lists all the businesses and business people in a town

commercial failure /kə,mɜːʃ(ə)l 'feɪljə/ *noun* financial collapse or bankruptcy

commercial law /kə,mɜːʃ(ə)l 'lɔː/ *noun* the laws regarding the conduct of businesses

commercial lawyer /kə,mɜːʃ(ə)l 'lɔːjə/ *noun* a person who specialises in company law or who advises companies on legal problems

commercial loan /kə,mɜːʃ(ə)l 'ləʊn/ *noun* a short-term renewable loan or line of credit used to finance the seasonal or cyclical working capital needs of a company

commercially /kə'mɜːʃ(ə)li/ *adverb* **1.** for the purpose of making a profit **2.** in the operation of a business

commercial paper /kə,mɜːʃ(ə)l 'peɪpə/ *noun* an IOU issued by a company to raise a short-term loan. Abbreviation **CP**

commercial property /kə,mɜːʃ(ə)l 'prɒpəti/ *noun* a building, or buildings, used as offices or shops

commercial report /kə,mɜːʃ(ə)l rɪ 'pɔːt/ *noun* an investigative report made by an organisation such as a credit bureau that specialises in obtaining information regarding a person or organisation applying for something such as credit or employment

commercial substance /kə,mɜːʃ(ə)l 'sʌbstəns/ *noun* the economic reality that underlies a transaction or arrangement, regardless of its legal or technical denomination. For example, a company may sell an office block and then immediately lease it back: the commercial substance may be that it has not been sold.

commercial year /kə,mɜːʃ(ə)l 'jɪə/ *noun* an artificial year treated as having 12 months of 30 days each, used for calculating such things as monthly sales data and inventory levels

commission /kə'mɪʃ(ə)n/ *noun* **1.** money paid to a salesperson or agent, usually a percentage of the sales made ○ *She gets 10% commission on everything she sells.* ○ *He is paid on a commission basis.* **2.** a group of people officially appointed to examine some problem ○ *He is the chairman of the government commission on export subsidies.*

commission agent /kə'mɪʃ(ə)n ˌeɪdʒənt/ *noun* an agent who is paid a percentage of sales

commissioner /kə'mɪʃ(ə)nə/ *noun* an ombudsman

Commissioner of the Inland Revenue /kə,mɪʃ(ə)nəz əv θiː ˌɪnlənd 'revənjuː/ *noun* same as **Appeals Commissioner**

commission house /kə'mɪʃ(ə)n haʊs/ *noun* a firm which buys or sells for clients, and charges a commission for this service

commission rep /kə'mɪʃ(ə)n rep/ *noun* a representative who is not paid a salary but receives a commission on sales

commit /kə'mɪt/ *verb* □ **to commit yourself to** to guarantee something, especially a loan issue, or to guarantee to do something

commitment /kə'mɪtmənt/ *noun* something which you have agreed to do ○ *to make a commitment* or *to enter into a commitment to do something* ○ *The company has a commitment to provide a cheap service.*

commitment document /kə'mɪtmənt ˌdɒkjʊmənt/ *noun* a contract, change order, purchase order or letter of intent which deals with the supply of goods and services and commits an organisation to legal, financial and other obligations

commitment fee /kə'mɪtmənt fiː/ *noun* a fee paid to a bank which has arranged a line of credit which has not been fully used

commitments basis /kə'mɪtmənts ˌbeɪsɪs/ *noun* the method of recording the expenditure of a public sector organisation at the time when it commits itself to it rather than when it actually pays for it

commitments for capital expenditure /kə,mɪtmənts fə ˌkæpɪt(ə)l ɪk 'spendɪtʃə/ *plural noun* the amount a company has committed to spend on fixed assets in the future. In the United Kingdom, companies are legally obliged to disclose this amount, and any additional commitments, in their annual report.

committed credit lines /kə,mɪtɪd 'kredɪt ˌlaɪnz/ *plural noun* a bank's agreement to provide a loan on the borrower's request, with a fee paid by the borrower for any undrawn portion of the agreed loan

Committee of European Securities Regulators /kə,mɪti əv ˌjʊərəpiːən sɪ 'kjʊərɪtiz ˌregjʊleɪtəz/ *noun* an independent organisation of securities regulators established to promote consistent supervision of the European market for financial services

Committee on Accounting Procedure /kə,mɪti ɒn ə'kaʊntɪŋ prə,siːdʒə/ *noun* in the United States, a committee of the American Institute of Certified Public Accountants that was responsible between 1939 and 1959 for issuing accounting principles, some of which are still part of the Generally Accepted Accounting Principles

commodity /kə'mɒdɪti/ *noun* something sold in very large quantities, especially a raw material such as a metal or a food such as wheat

commodity exchange /kə'mɒdɪti ɪks ˌtʃeɪndʒ/ *noun* a place where commodities are bought and sold

commodity futures /kə,mɒdɪti 'fjuːtʃəz/ *plural noun* commodities traded for delivery at a later date ○ *Silver rose 5% on the commodity futures market yesterday.*

commodity market /kə'mɒdɪti ˌmɑːkɪt/ *noun* a place where people buy and sell commodities

commodity trader /kə'mɒdɪti ˌtreɪdə/ *noun* a person whose business is buying and selling commodities

common cost /ˌkɒmən 'kɒst/ *noun* a cost which is apportioned to two or more cost centres

common ownership /ˌkɒmən 'əʊnəʃɪp/ *noun* a situation where a business is owned by the employees who work in it

common pricing /ˌkɒmən 'praɪsɪŋ/ *noun* the illegal fixing of prices by several businesses so that they all charge the same price

common stock /ˌkɒmən 'stɒk/ *noun US* same as **ordinary shares**

Compagnie Nationale des Commissaires aux Comptes /ˌkɒmpæni ˌnæʃənɑːl deɪ 'kɒmiseəz əʊ ˌkɒmt/ *noun* in France, an organisation that regulates external audit. Abbreviation **CNCC**

Companies House /ˌkʌmpəniz 'haʊs/ *noun* an official organisation where the records of companies must be deposited, so that they can be inspected by the public. The official name is the 'Companies Registration Office'.

Companies Registration Office /ˌkʌmp(ə)niz ˌredʒɪ'streɪʃ(ə)n ˌɒfɪs/ *noun* an office of the Registrar of Companies, the official organisation where the records of companies must be deposited, so that they can be inspected by the public. Abbreviation **CRO**. Also called **Companies House**

company /'kʌmp(ə)ni/ *noun* a business organisation, a group of people organised to buy, sell, or provide a service, usually for profit

company auditor /ˌkʌmp(ə)ni 'ɔːdɪtə/ *noun* the individual or firm of accountants a company appoints to audit its annual accounts

company car /ˌkʌmp(ə)ni 'kɑː/ *noun* a car which belongs to a company and is lent to an employee to use for business or other purposes

company director /ˌkʌmp(ə)ni daɪ 'rektə/ *noun* a person appointed by the shareholders to help run a company

company flat /ˌkʌmp(ə)ni 'flæt/ *noun* a flat owned by a company and used by members of staff from time to time (NOTE: The US term is **company apartment**.)

company law /ˌkʌmp(ə)ni 'lɔː/ *noun* laws which refer to the way companies work

company pension scheme /ˌkʌmp(ə)ni 'penʃən skiːm/ *noun* same as **occupational pension scheme** ○ *She decided to join the company's pension scheme.*

company promoter /ˌkʌmp(ə)ni prə 'məʊtə/ *noun* a person who organises the setting up of a new company

company registrar /ˌkʌmp(ə)ni 'redʒɪstrɑː/ *noun* the person who keeps the share register of a company

company reserves /ˌkʌmp(ə)ni rɪ 'zɜːvz/ *plural noun* same as **revenue reserves**

company secretary /ˌkʌmp(ə)ni 'sekrɪt(ə)ri/ *noun* a person who is responsible for a company's legal and financial affairs

comparability /ˌkɒmp(ə)rə'bɪlɪti/ *noun* the extent to which accurate comparisons can be made of the financial status of different companies, based on similarities in their accounting procedures, measurement concepts and other features

comparative balance sheet /kəm ˌpærətɪv 'bæləns ʃiːt/ *noun* one of two or more financial statements prepared on different financial dates that lend themselves to a comparative analysis of the financial condition of an organisation

comparative statements /kəm ˌpærətɪv 'steɪtmənts/ *plural noun* financial statements which cover different accounting periods, usually the previous accounting period, but which are prepared in the same way and therefore allow information to be fairly compared

compensate /'kɒmpənseɪt/ *verb* to give someone money to make up for a loss or injury ○ *In this case we will compensate a manager for loss of commission.* ○ *The company will compensate the employee for the burns suffered in the accident.* (NOTE: You compensate someone **for** something.)

compensating balance /ˌkɒmpənseɪtɪŋ ˈbæləns/ *noun* the amount of money which a customer has to keep in a bank account in order to get free services from the bank

compensating errors /ˌkɒmpənseɪtɪŋ ˈerəz/ *plural noun* two or more errors which are set against each other so that the accounts still balance

compensation /ˌkɒmpənˈseɪʃ(ə)n/ *noun* **1.** □ **compensation for damage** payment for damage done □ **compensation for loss of office** payment to a director who is asked to leave a company before their contract ends □ **compensation for loss of earnings** payment to someone who has stopped earning money or who is not able to earn money **2.** *US* a salary

'…compensation can also be via the magistrates courts for relatively minor injuries' [*Personnel Management*]

compensation deal /ˌkɒmpənˈseɪʃ(ə)n diːl/ *noun* a deal where an exporter is paid (at least in part) in goods from the country to which he or she is exporting

compensation fund /ˌkɒmpənˈseɪʃ(ə)n fʌnd/ *noun* a fund operated by the Stock Exchange to compensate investors for losses suffered when members of the Stock Exchange default

compensation package /ˌkɒmpən ˈseɪʃ(ə)n ˌpækɪdʒ/ *noun* the salary, pension and other benefits offered with a job

'…golden parachutes are liberal compensation packages given to executives leaving a company' [*Publishers Weekly*]

compete /kəmˈpiːt/ *verb* □ **to compete with someone** *or* **with a company** to try to do better than another person or another company ○ *We have to compete with cheap imports from the Far East.* ○ *They were competing unsuccessfully with local companies on their home territory.* □ **the two companies are competing for a market share** *or* **for a contract** each company is trying to win a larger part of the market, trying to win the contract

competition /ˌkɒmpəˈtɪʃ(ə)n/ *noun* a situation where companies or individuals are trying to do better than others, e.g. trying to win a larger share of the market, or to produce a better or cheaper product or to control the use of resources

'…profit margins in the industries most exposed to foreign competition are worse than usual' [*Sunday Times*]

'…competition is steadily increasing and could affect profit margins as the company

tries to retain its market share' [*Citizen (Ottawa)*]

competitive devaluation /kəmˌpetɪtɪv ˌdiːvæljuˈeɪʃ(ə)n/ *noun* a devaluation of a currency to make a country's goods more competitive on the international markets

competitive pricing /kəmˌpetɪtɪv ˈpraɪsɪŋ/ *noun* the practice of putting low prices on goods so as to compete with other products

competitor /kəmˈpetɪtə/ *noun* a person or company that is competing with another ○ *Two German firms are our main competitors.*

'…sterling labour costs continue to rise between 3% and 5% a year faster than in most of our competitor countries' [*Sunday Times*]

complete /kəmˈpliːt/ *verb* to sign a contract for the sale of a property and to exchange it with the other party, so making it legal

completed contract method /kəm ˌpliːtɪd ˈkɒntrækt ˌmeθəd/ *noun* a way of accounting for a particular contractual obligation, e.g., a long-term construction project, whereby the profit is not recorded until the final completion of the project, even if there has been some revenue while the project was still in progress

completion date /kəmˈpliːʃ(ə)n deɪt/ *noun* a date when something will be finished

compliance /kəmˈplaɪəns/ *noun* agreement to do what is ordered

compliance audit /kəmˈplaɪəns ˌɔːdɪt/ *noun* an audit of business activities carried out to determine whether performance matches contractual, regulatory or statutory requirements

compliance costs /kəmˈplaɪəns kɒsts/ *plural noun* expenses incurred as a result of meeting legal requirements, e.g., for safety requirements or to comply with company law

compliance department /kəmˈplaɪəns dɪˌpɑːtmənt/ *noun* a department which ensures that the company is adhering to any relevant regulations, such as FSA regulations

compliance officer /kəmˈplaɪəns ˌɒfɪsə/ *noun* an employee of a financial organisation whose job is to make sure that the organisation complies with the regulations governing its business

compliance test /kəmˈplaɪəns test/ *noun* any of various audit procedures followed to ensure that accounting procedures within a company are reasonable and comply with regulations

composition /ˌkɒmpəˈzɪʃ(ə)n/ *noun* an agreement between a debtor and creditors, where the debtor settles a debt by repaying only part of it

compound /kəmˈpaʊnd/ *verb* **1.** to agree with creditors to settle a debt by paying part of what is owed **2.** to add to ○ *The interest is compounded daily.*

compound discount /ˌkɒmpaʊnd ˈdɪskaʊnt/ *noun* the difference between the nominal amount of a particular sum in the future and its present discounted value. So, if £150 in a year's time is worth £142 now, the compound discount is £8.

compounding period /ˈkɒmpaʊndɪŋ ˌpɪəriəd/ *noun* the period over which compound interest is calculated

compound interest /ˌkɒmpaʊnd ˈɪntrəst/ *noun* interest which is added to the capital and then earns interest itself

compound journal entry /ˈkɒmpaʊnd ˌdʒɜːn(ə)l ˌentri/ *noun* an entry in a journal that comprises more than individual equally matched debit and credit items

comprehensive income /ˌkɒmprɪhensɪv ˈɪnkʌm/ *noun* a company's total income for a given accounting period, taking into account all gains and losses, not only those included in a normal income statement. In the United States, comprehensive income must be declared whereas in the United Kingdom it appears in the statement of total recognised gains and losses.

comprehensive insurance /ˌkɒmprɪhensɪv ɪnˈʃʊərəns/, **comprehensive policy** /ˌkɒmprɪhensɪv ˈpɒlɪsi/ *noun* an insurance policy which covers you against all risks which are likely to happen

comprehensive tax allocation /ˌkɒmprɪhensɪv ˈtæks ˌæləkeɪʃ(ə)n/ *noun* the setting aside of money to cover deferred tax

compromise /ˈkɒmprəmaɪz/ *noun* an agreement between two sides, where each side gives way a little ○ *Management offered £5 an hour, the union asked for £9, and a compromise of £7.50 was reached.* ■ *verb* to reach an agreement by giving way a little ○ *She asked £15 for it, I offered £7 and we compromised on £10.*

comptroller /kənˈtrəʊlə/ *noun* a financial controller

Comptroller and Auditor General /kənˌtrəʊlə ənd ˌɔːdɪtə ˈdʒen(ə)rəl/ *noun* in the United Kingdom, the head of the National Audit Office who reports back to Parliament on the audit of government departments

compulsory annuity /kəmˌpʌlsəri əˈnjuːɪti/ *noun* in the United Kingdom, the legal requirement that at least 75% of the funds built-up in a personal pension plan have to be used to purchase an annuity by the age of 75

compulsory liquidation /kəmˌpʌlsəri ˌlɪkwɪˈdeɪʃ(ə)n/ *noun* same as **compulsory winding up**

compulsory purchase /kəmˌpʌlsəri ˈpɜːtʃɪs/ *noun* the purchase of an annuity with the fund built up in a personal pension scheme

compulsory winding up /kəmˌpʌlsəri ˌwaɪndɪŋ ˈʌp/ *noun* liquidation which is ordered by a court

compulsory winding up order /kəm ˌpʌlsəri ˌwaɪndɪŋ ˈʌp ˌɔːdə/ *noun* an order from a court saying that a company must be wound up

computable /kəmˈpjuːtəb(ə)l/ *adjective* possible to calculate

computation /ˌkɒmpjʊˈteɪʃ(ə)n/ *noun* a calculation

computational error /ˌkɒmpjʊteɪʃ(ə)nəl ˈerə/ *noun* a mistake made in calculating

compute /kəmˈpjuːt/ *verb* to calculate, to do calculations

computerise /kəmˈpjuːtəraɪz/, **computerize** *verb* to change something from a manual system to one using computers ○ *We have computerised all our records.* ○ *Stock control is now completely computerised.*

concealment of assets /kənˌsiːlmənt əv ˈæsets/ *noun* the act of hiding assets so that creditors do not know they exist

concept /ˈkɒnsept/ *noun* an idea □ **concept of capital maintenance** the idea that profit is only recorded if the capital of the company, measured in terms of its net assets, increases during an accounting period. Assets can be measured at historical cost or in units of constant purchasing power. □ **concept of maintenance of operating capacity** the concept of capital maintenance measured in terms of the changes in the current values of fixed assets, stock and working capital. Profit can only be taken if the total value of these assets, called the 'net operating assets', including adjustments for changes in prices affecting these assets, increases during an accounting period.

conceptual framework /kənˌseptʃʊəl ˈfreɪmwɜːk/ *noun* a set of theoretical principles that underlies the practice and regulation of financial accounting. In the United States, this is expressed in the Statements of Financial Accounting Concepts issued by the Financial Accounting Standards Board. In the United Kingdom, it is expressed in the Statement of Principles issued by the Accounting Standards Board.

concern /kən'sɜːn/ *noun* a business or company

concession /kən'seʃ(ə)n/ *noun* **1.** the right to use someone else's property for business purposes **2.** the right to be the only seller of a product in a place ○ *She runs a jewellery concession in a department store.* **3.** an allowance, e.g. a reduction of tax or price

concessionaire /kən,seʃə'neə/ *noun* a person or business that has the right to be the only seller of a product in a place

concessionary fare /kən,seʃ(ə)nəri 'feə/ *noun* a reduced fare for some types of passenger such as pensioners, students or employees of a transport company

conciliation /kən,sɪli'eɪʃ(ə)n/ *noun* the practice of bringing together the parties in a dispute with an independent third party, so that the dispute can be settled through a series of negotiations

condition /kən'dɪʃ(ə)n/ *noun* something which has to be carried out as part of a contract or which has to be agreed before a contract becomes valid

conditional /kən'dɪʃ(ə)n(ə)l/ *adjective* provided that specific conditions are taken into account

conditionality /kən,dɪʃ(ə)'nælɪti/ *noun* the fact of having conditions attached

conditional sale /kən,dɪʃ(ə)nəl 'seɪl/ *noun* a sale which is subject to conditions, such as a hire-purchase agreement

conditions of employment /kən,dɪʃ(ə)nz əv ɪm'plɔɪmənt/ *plural noun* the terms of a contract of employment

conditions of sale /kən,dɪʃ(ə)nz əv 'seɪl/ *plural noun* special features that apply to a particular sale, e.g. discounts or credit terms

Confederation of Asian and Pacific Accountants /kən,fedəreɪʃ(ə)n əv ,eɪʒ(ə)n ən pə,sɪfɪk ə'kaʊntənts/ *noun* full form of **CAPA**

confidential report /,kɒnfɪdenʃəl rɪ'pɔːt/ *noun* a secret document which must not be shown to other people

conflict of interest /,kɒnflɪkt əv 'ɪntrəst/ *noun* a situation where a person or

firm may profit personally from decisions taken in an official capacity

conglomerate /kən'glɒmərət/ *noun* a group of subsidiary companies linked together and forming a group, each making very different types of products

connected persons /kə,nektɪd 'pɜːs(ə)nz/ *plural noun* for purposes of disclosure under the UK Companies Act, certain people who are related to or connected with members of the board of directors, including his or her spouse and children

Conseil National de la Comptabilité /kɒn,seɪ ,næʃənɑːl də æ ,kɒmtæ'bɪlɪteɪ/ *noun* in France, a committee appointed by the government that is responsible for drawing up the Plan Comptable Général (General Accounting Plan)

consensus ad idem /kən,sensəs æd 'aɪdem/ *phrase* a Latin phrase meaning 'agreement to this same thing': real agreement to a contract by both parties

conservative /kən'sɜːvətɪv/ *adjective* careful, not overestimating ○ *His forecast of expenditure was very conservative* or *She made a conservative forecast of expenditure.*

'…we are calculating our next budget income at an oil price of \$15 per barrel. We know it is a conservative projection, but we do not want to come in for a shock should prices dive at any time during the year' [*Lloyd's List*]

conservatively /kən'sɜːvətɪvli/ *adverb* not overestimating ○ *The total sales are conservatively estimated at £2.3m.*

consideration /kən,sɪdə'reɪʃ(ə)n/ *noun* **1.** serious thought ○ *We are giving consideration to moving the head office to Scotland.* **2.** something valuable exchanged as part of a contract

consign /kən'saɪn/ *verb* □ **to consign goods to someone** to send goods to someone for them to use or to sell for you

consignation /,kɒnsaɪ'neɪʃ(ə)n/ *noun* the act of consigning

consignee /,kɒnsaɪ'niː/ *noun* a person who receives goods from someone for their own use or to sell for the sender

consignment /kən'saɪnmənt/ *noun* **1.** the sending of goods to someone who will sell them for you **2.** a group of goods sent for sale ○ *A consignment of goods has arrived.* ○ *We are expecting a consignment of cars from Japan.*

'…some of the most prominent stores are gradually moving away from the traditional consignment system, under which manufacturers agree to repurchase any unsold goods, and in return dictate prices and sales strategies and even dispatch staff to sell the products' [*Nikkei Weekly*]

consignment accounts /kən'saɪnmənt ə,kaʊnts/ *plural noun* accounts kept by both consignee and consignor, showing quantities, dates of shipment, and payments for stocks held

consignment note /kən'saɪnmənt nəʊt/ *noun* a note saying that goods have been sent

consignor /kən'saɪnə/ *noun* a person who consigns goods to someone

consistency /kən'sɪstənsi/ *noun* one of the basic accounting concepts, that items in the accounts should be treated in the same way from year to year

consolidate /kən'sɒlɪdeɪt/ *verb* **1.** to include the accounts of several subsidiary companies as well as the holding company in a single set of accounts **2.** to group goods together for shipping

consolidated accounts /kən,sɒlɪdeɪtɪd ə'kaʊnts/ *plural noun* accounts where the financial position of several different companies, i.e. a holding company and its subsidiaries, are recorded together

consolidated balance sheet /kən,sɒlɪdeɪtɪd 'bæləns ʃiːt/ *noun* the balance sheets of subsidiary companies grouped together into the balance sheet of the parent company. Also called **group balance sheet**

consolidated cash flow statement /kən,sɒlɪdeɪtɪd 'kæʃ fləʊ ,steɪtmənt/ *noun* a cash flow statement for a group of enterprises and its parent company as a whole

consolidated financial statement /kən,sɒlɪdeɪtɪd faɪ,nænʃəl 'steɪtmənt/ *noun* a document that gives the main details of the financial status of a company and its subsidiaries. Also called **group financial statement**

consolidated fund /kən,sɒlɪdeɪtɪd 'fʌnd/ *noun* money in the Exchequer which comes from tax revenues and is used to pay for government expenditure

consolidated income statement /kən,sɒlɪdeɪtɪd 'ɪnkʌm ,steɪtmənt/ *noun* an income statement for a group of enterprises and its parent company as a whole

consolidated profit and loss account /kən,sɒlɪdeɪtɪd ,prɒfɪt ən 'lɒs ə ,kaʊnt/ *noun* profit and loss accounts of the holding company and its subsidiary companies, grouped together into a single profit and loss account (NOTE: The US term is

profit and loss statement or **income statement**.)

consolidation /kən,sɒlɪ'deɪʃ(ə)n/ *noun* **1.** the grouping together of goods for shipping **2.** the act of taking profits from speculative investments and investing them safely in blue-chip companies

consolidation adjustments /kən,sɒlɪ 'deɪʃ(ə)n ə,dʒʌstmənts/ *plural noun* necessary changes and deletions made to financial records when consolidating the accounts of a group of enterprises

consolidation difference /kən,sɒlɪ 'deɪʃ(ə)n ,dɪf(ə)rəns/ *noun* the difference between the price paid for a subsidiary and the value of the assets and liabilities obtained in the purchase

consols /'kɒnsɒlz/ *plural noun* government bonds which pay interest but do not have a maturity date

consortium /kən'sɔːtiəm/ *noun* a group of companies which work together ○ *A consortium of Canadian companies* or *A Canadian consortium has tendered for the job.* (NOTE: The plural is **consortia**.)

'…the consortium was one of only four bidders for the £2 billion contract to run the lines, seen as potentially the most difficult contract because of the need for huge investment' [*Times*]

constant purchasing power /,kɒnstənt 'pɜːtʃɪsɪŋ ,paʊə/ *noun* same as **current purchasing power**

constraint /kən'streɪnt/ *noun* any factor that limits the activities of a business, e.g. the capacity of a machine or the number of hours a worker can legally work

constraint-based costing /kən 'streɪnt beɪst ,kɒstɪŋ/ *noun* a costing method that takes account of restraints on capacity, e.g. the capacity of machinery

Consultative Committee of Accountancy Bodies /kən,sʌltətɪv kə ,mɪti əv ə'kaʊntənsi ,bɒdiz/ *noun* an organisation established in 1974 that represents and encourages coordination between the six professional accountancy bodies in the United Kingdom and Ireland. Abbreviation **CCAB**

consulting /kən'sʌltɪŋ/ *adjective* giving specialist advice ○ *a consulting engineer*

consulting actuary /kən,sʌltɪŋ 'æktjuəri/ *noun* an independent actuary who advises large pension funds

consumable goods /kən,sjuːməb(ə)l 'gʊdz/, **consumables** *plural noun* goods which are bought by members of the public and not by companies. Also called **consumer goods**

consumed cost /kən,sjuːmd ˈkɒst/ *noun* same as **sunk cost**

consumer /kənˈsjuːmə/ *noun* a person or company that buys and uses goods and services ○ *Gas consumers are protesting at the increase in prices.* ○ *The factory is a heavy consumer of water.*

consumer council /kən,sjuːmə ˈkaʊns(ə)l/ *noun* a group representing the interests of consumers

consumer credit /kən,sjuːmə ˈkredɪt/ *noun* credit given by shops, banks and other financial institutions to consumers so that they can buy goods (NOTE: Lenders have to be licensed under the Consumer Credit Act, 1974.)

Consumer Credit Act, 1974 /kən ,sjuːmə ˈkredɪt ækt/ *noun* an Act of Parliament which licenses lenders, and requires them to state clearly the full terms of loans which they make, including the APR

consumer goods /kən,sjuːmə ˈgʊdz/ *plural noun* same as **consumable goods**

Consumer Price Index /kən,sjuːmə ˈpraɪs ,ɪndeks/ *noun* a US index showing how prices of consumer goods have risen over a period of time, used as a way of measuring inflation and the cost of living. Abbreviation **CPI** (NOTE: The UK term is **retail prices index**.)

'…analysis of the consumer price index for the first half of the year shows that the rate of inflation went down by about 12.9 per cent' [*Business Times (Lagos)*]

consumer protection /kən,sjuːmə prə ˈtekʃən/ *noun* the activity of protecting consumers against unfair or illegal traders

consumer spending /kən,sjuːmə ˈspendɪŋ/ *noun* spending by private households on goods and services

'…companies selling in the UK market are worried about reduced consumer spending as a consequence of higher interest rates and inflation' [*Business*]

consumption tax /kənˈsʌmpʃ(ə)n tæks/ *noun* a tax used to encourage people to buy less of a particular good or service by increasing its price. This type of tax is often levied in times of national hardship.

Contact Committee /ˈkɒntækt kə,mɪti/ *noun* an advisory body, established by the European Union, that oversees the application of European accounting directives and makes recommendations to the European Commission about changes to those directives

contested takeover /kən,testɪd ˈteɪkəʊvə/ *noun* a takeover bid where the board of the target company does not recommend it to the shareholders and tries to fight it. Also called **hostile bid**

contingency fund /kənˈtɪndʒənsi fʌnd/ *noun* money set aside in case it is needed urgently

contingent expenses /kən,tɪndʒənt ɪk ˈspensɪz/ *plural noun* expenses which will be incurred only if something happens

contingent gain /kən,tɪndʒənt ˈgeɪn/ *noun* a possible gain that is conditional on the occurrence of a certain event in the future

contingent liability /kən,tɪndʒənt ,laɪə ˈbɪlɪti/ *noun* a liability which may or may not occur, but for which provision is made in a company's accounts, as opposed to 'provisions', where money is set aside for an anticipated expenditure

contingent loss /kən,tɪndʒənt ˈlɒs/ *noun* a possible loss that is conditional on the occurrence of a certain event in the future

contingent policy /kən,tɪndʒənt ˈpɒlɪsi/ *noun* an insurance policy which pays out only if something happens, such as if a person named in the policy dies before the person due to benefit

contingent reserve /kən,tɪndʒənt rɪ ˈzɜːv/ *noun* a fund set aside to meet unexpected costs, e.g. an increase in interest rates

continuing professional development /kən,tɪnjuɪŋ prə,feʃ(ə)n(ə)l dɪ ˈveləpmənt/ *noun* full form of **CPD**

continuous disclosure /kən,tɪnjuəs dɪsˈkləʊʒə/ *noun* in Canada, the practice of ensuring that complete, timely, accurate and balanced information about a public company is made available to shareholders

continuous improvement /kən ,tɪnjuəs ɪmˈpruːvmənt/ *noun* a procedure and management philosophy that focuses on looking all the time for ways in which small improvements can be made to processes and products, with the aim of increasing quality and reducing waste and cost (NOTE: Continuous improvement is one of the tools that underpin the philosophies of total quality management and lean production; in Japan it is known as kaizen.)

continuously contemporary accounting /kən,tɪnjuəsli kən ,temp(ə)rəri əˈkaʊntɪŋ/ *noun* an accounting system that measures assets and liabilities at their current cash price. Profit and loss can therefore be viewed in terms of changes in the value as all items are measured in the same way. Abbreviation **CoCoA**

contra /'kɒntrə/ *noun* an accounting term used when debits are matched with related credits in an account or set of accounts

contra account /'kɒntrə ə,kaʊnt/ *noun* an account which offsets another account, e.g. where a company's supplier is not only a creditor in that company's books but also a debtor because it has purchased goods on credit

contract *noun* /'kɒntrækt/ **1.** a legal agreement between two parties ○ *to draw up a contract* ○ *to draft a contract* ○ *to sign a contract* □ **the contract is binding on both parties** both parties signing the contract must do what is agreed □ **under contract** bound by the terms of a contract ○ *The firm is under contract to deliver the goods by November.* □ **to void a contract** to make a contract invalid **2.** □ **by private contract** by private legal agreement **3.** an agreement for the supply of a service or goods ○ *to enter into a contract to supply spare parts* ○ *to sign a contract for $10,000 worth of spare parts* **4.** (*Stock Exchange*) a deal to buy or sell shares, or an agreement to purchase options or futures ■ *verb* /kən'trækt/ to agree to do some work on the basis of a legally binding contract ○ *to contract to supply spare parts* or *to contract for the supply of spare parts*

contract costing /'kɒntrækt ,kɒstɪŋ/ *noun* a method of costing large projects, where the contracted work will run over several accounting periods

contracting party /kən,træktɪŋ 'pɑːti/ *noun* a person or company that signs a contract

contract note /'kɒntrækt nəʊt/ *noun* a note showing that shares have been bought or sold but not yet paid for, also including the commission

contract of employment /,kɒntrækt əv ɪm'plɔɪmənt/ *noun* a contract between an employer and an employee stating all the conditions of work. Also called **employment contract**

contract of service /,kɒntrækt əv 'sɜːvɪs/ *noun* a legal agreement between an employer and an employee whereby the employee will work for the employer and be directed by them, in return for payment

contractor /kən'træktə/ *noun* a person or company that does work according to a written agreement

contractual /kən'træktʃʊəl/ *adjective* according to a contract ○ *contractual conditions*

contractual liability /kən,træktʃʊəl ,laɪə'bɪlɪti/ *noun* a legal responsibility for something as stated in a contract

contractually /kən'træktjʊəli/ *adverb* according to a contract ○ *The company is contractually bound to pay our expenses.*

contractual obligation /kən,træktʃʊəl ,ɒblɪ'geɪʃ(ə)n/ *noun* something that a person is legally forced to do through having signed a contract to do □ **to fulfil your contractual obligations** to do what you have agreed to do in a contract

contract work /'kɒntrækt wɜːk/ *noun* work done according to a written agreement

contra entry /'kɒntrə ,entri/ *noun* an entry made in the opposite side of an account to make an earlier entry worthless, i.e. a debit against a credit

contribute /kən'trɪbjuːt/ *verb* to give money or add to money ○ *We agreed to contribute 10% of the profits.* ○ *They had contributed to the pension fund for 10 years.*

contribution /,kɒntrɪ'bjuːʃ(ə)n/ *noun* **1.** money paid to add to a sum **2.** the difference between sales value and the variable costs of a unit sold. This goes to cover fixed costs and provide the profit.

contribution income statement /,kɒntrɪbjuːʃ(ə)n 'ɪnkʌm ,steɪtmənt/ *noun* a way of presenting an income statement in which fixed costs are shown as a deduction from the total contribution. This format is often used as part of management accounting.

contribution margin /,kɒntrɪ'bjuːʃ(ə)n ,mɑːdʒɪn/ *noun* a way of showing how much individual products or services contribute to net profit

'The provider of rehabilitation services cited the negative impact of Part B therapy caps on estimated Contract Therapy contribution margins.' [BusinessWeek]

contribution of capital /kɒntrɪ ,bjuːʃ(ə)n əv 'kæpɪt(ə)l/ *noun* money paid to a company as additional capital

contributor of capital /kən,trɪbjʊtər əv 'kæpɪt(ə)l/ *noun* a person who contributes capital

contributory /kən'trɪbjʊt(ə)ri/ *adjective* causing or helping to cause ○ *Falling exchange rates have been a contributory factor in the company's loss of profits.*

control account /kən'trəʊl ə,kaʊnt/ *noun* an account used to record the total amounts entered in a number of different ledger accounts. It also acts as a means of checking the accuracy of the ledger accounts.

controllable variance /kən,trəʊləb(ə)l ˈveəriəns/ *noun* a difference between actual and budgeted amounts that is considered as being within the control of the budget centre manager

controlled company /kən,trəʊld ˈkʌmp(ə)ni/ *noun* company where more than 50% (or in the USA, 25%) of the shares belong to one owner

controlled economy /kən,trəʊld ɪˈkɒnəmi/ *noun* an economy where most business activity is directed by orders from the government

controller /kənˈtrəʊlə/ *noun* **1.** a person who controls something, especially the finances of a company **2.** *US* the chief accountant in a company

control limits /kənˈtrəʊl ,lɪmɪts/ *plural noun* limits on quantities or values which, if exceeded, trigger intervention from management

control period /kənˈtrəʊl ,pɪəriəd/ *noun* the fraction of the financial year, e.g., a month, for which separate totals are given in a budget

control risk /kənˈtrəʊl rɪsk/ *noun* that aspect of an audit risk that involves a client's internal control system

control totals /kənˈtrəʊl ,təʊt(ə)lz/ *plural noun* in auditing, totals calculated for important data fields, used as a check of data processing standards

conventional cost system /kən,venʃ(ə)n(ə)l ˈkɒst ,sɪstəm/ *noun* a standard system for applying overhead costs to products and services, using only unit-based cost drivers

conversion /kənˈvɜːʃ(ə)n/ *noun* the action of changing convertible loan stock into ordinary shares

conversion costs /kənˈvɜːʃ(ə)n kɒsts/ *plural noun* the cost of changing raw materials into finished or semi-finished products, including wages, other direct production costs and the production overhead

conversion of funds /kən,vɜːʃ(ə)n əv ˈfʌndz/ *noun* the act of using money which does not belong to you for a purpose for which it is not supposed to be used

conversion period /kənˈvɜːʃ(ə)n ,pɪəriəd/ *noun* a time during which convertible loan stock may be changed into ordinary shares

conversion price /kənˈvɜːʃ(ə)n praɪs/, **conversion rate** /kənˈvɜːʃ(ə)n reɪt/ *noun*

1. a price at which preference shares are converted into ordinary shares **2.** a rate at which a currency is changed into a foreign currency

conversion value /kənˈvɜːʃ(ə)n ,vælju:/ *noun* a value of convertible stock, including the extra value of the ordinary shares into which they may be converted

convert /kənˈvɜːt/ *verb* **1.** to change money of one country for money of another ○ *We converted our pounds into Swiss francs.* **2.** □ **to convert funds to your own use** to use someone else's money for yourself

convertibility /kən,vɜːtəˈbɪləti/ *noun* the ability of a currency to be exchanged for another easily

convertible currency /kən,vɜːtəb(ə)l ˈkʌrənsi/ *noun* a currency which can easily be exchanged for another

convertible debenture /kən,vɜːtəb(ə)l dɪˈbentʃə/ *noun* a debenture or loan stock which can be exchanged for ordinary shares at a later date

convertible loan stock /kən,vɜːtəb(ə)l ˈləʊn stɒk/ *noun* money lent to a company which can be converted into shares at a later date

convertibles /kənˈvɜːtəb(ə)lz/ *plural noun* corporate bonds or preference shares which can be converted into ordinary shares at a set price on set dates

conveyance /kənˈveɪəns/ *noun* a legal document which transfers a property from the seller to the buyer

conveyancer /kənˈveɪənsə/ *noun* a person who draws up a conveyance

conveyancing /kənˈveɪənsɪŋ/ *noun* the work of legally transferring a property from a seller to a buyer

COO *abbreviation* chief operating officer

cooling-off period /,ku:lɪŋ ˈɒf ,pɪəriəd/ *noun* **1.** (*during an industrial dispute*) a period when negotiations have to be carried on and no action can be taken by either side **2.** a period during which someone who is about to enter into an agreement may reflect on all aspects of the arrangement and change his or her mind if necessary ○ *New York has a three day cooling-off period for telephone sales.*

cooperative society /kəʊˈɒp(ə)rətɪv sə,saɪəti/ *noun* an organisation where customers and employees are partners and share the profits

cooperative store /kəʊˈɒp(ə)rətɪv stɔː/ *noun* a store owned by those who shop there as well as by its workers

coproperty /ˌkəʊˈprɒpəti/ *noun* the ownership of property by two or more people together

coproprietor /ˌkəʊprəˈpraɪətə/ *noun* a person who owns a property with another person or several other people

copyright /ˈkɒpiraɪt/ *noun* an author's legal right to publish his or her own work and not to have it copied, lasting seventy years after the author's death ▪ *verb* to confirm the copyright of a written work by inserting a copyright notice and publishing the work

Copyright Act /ˈkɒpiraɪt ækt/ *noun* an Act of Parliament making copyright legal, and controlling the copying of copyright material

copyright deposit /ˌkɒpiraɪt dɪˈpɒzɪt/ *noun* the act of depositing a copy of a published work in a copyright library, which is part of the formal copyrighting of copyright material

copyright holder /ˈkɒpiraɪt ˌhəʊldə/ *noun* a person who owns a copyright and who can expect to receive royalties from it

copyright law /ˈkɒpiraɪt lɔː/ *noun* laws concerning the protection of copyright

copyright notice /ˈkɒpiraɪt ˌnəʊtɪs/ *noun* a note in a book showing who owns the copyright and the date of ownership

corporate /ˈkɔːp(ə)rət/ *adjective* referring to corporations or companies, or to a particular company as a whole

'…the prime rate is the rate at which banks lend to their top corporate borrowers' [*Wall Street Journal*]

'…if corporate forecasts are met, sales will exceed $50 million next year' [*Citizen (Ottawa)*]

corporate bond /ˈkɔːp(ə)rət bɒnd/ *noun* a loan stock officially issued by a company to raise capital, usually against the security of some of its assets (NOTE: The company promises to pay an amount of interest on a set date every year until the redemption date, when it repays the loan.)

corporate finance /ˌkɔːp(ə)rət ˈfaɪnæns/ *noun* the financial affairs of companies

corporate governance /ˌkɔːp(ə)rət ˈɡʌv(ə)nəns/ *noun* the way a company or other organisation is run, including the powers of the board of directors, audit committees, ethics, environmental impact, treatment of workers, directors' salaries and internal control

corporate loan /ˌkɔːp(ə)rət ˈləʊn/ *noun* a loan issued by a corporation

corporate name /ˌkɔːp(ə)rət ˈneɪm/ *noun* the name of a large corporation

corporate plan /ˌkɔːp(ə)rət ˈplæn/ *noun* a plan for the future work of a whole company

corporate planning /ˌkɔːp(ə)rət ˈplænɪŋ/ *noun* **1.** the process of planning the future work of a whole company **2.** planning the future financial state of a group of companies

corporate profits /ˌkɔːp(ə)rət ˈprɒfɪts/ *plural noun* the profits of a corporation

'…corporate profits for the first quarter showed a 4 per cent drop from last year' [*Financial Times*]

corporate raider /ˌkɔːp(ə)rət ˈreɪdə/ *noun* a person or company which buys a stake in another company before making a hostile takeover bid

corporation /ˌkɔːpəˈreɪʃ(ə)n/ *noun* **1.** a large company **2.** *US* a company which is incorporated in the United States **3.** a municipal authority

corporation income tax /ˌkɔːpəreɪʃ(ə)n ˈɪnkʌm tæks/ *noun* a tax on profits made by incorporated companies

corporation loan /ˌkɔːpəˈreɪʃ(ə)n ləʊn/ *noun* a loan issued by a local authority

corporation tax /ˌkɔːpəˈreɪʃ(ə)n tæks/ *noun* a tax on profits and capital gains made by companies, calculated before dividends are paid. Abbreviation **CT**

correcting entry /kəˌrektɪŋ ˈentri/ *noun* an entry made in accounts to make something right which was previously wrong

correlation /ˌkɒrəˈleɪʃ(ə)n/ *noun* the degree to which there is a relationship between two sets of data ○ *Is there any correlation between people's incomes and the amount they spend on clothing?*

COSA *abbreviation* cost of sales adjustment

cost /kɒst/ *noun* the amount of money paid to acquire, produce or maintain something, e.g. the money paid for materials, labour and overheads in the manufacture of a product produced and sold by a business ○ *Computer costs are falling each year.* ○ *We cannot afford the cost of two cars.* ▪ *verb* **1.** to cause money to be spent or lost **2.** to determine the cost of something □ **to cost a product** to calculate how much money will be needed to make a product, and so work out its selling price

cost absorption /ˈkɒst əbˌzɔːpʃən/ *noun* any system in which costs are assigned to units produced

cost accountant /'kɒst ə,kaʊntənt/ *noun* an accountant who gives managers information about their business costs

cost accounting /'kɒst ə,kaʊntɪŋ/ *noun* the process of preparing special accounts of manufacturing and sales costs

cost accumulation /,kɒst ə,kjuːmjʊ 'leɪʃ(ə)n/ *noun* a system of presenting costs in an account

cost allocation /'kɒst ,æləkeɪʃ(ə)n/ *noun* the way in which overhead expenses are related to various cost centres

cost analysis /'kɒst ə,næləsɪs/ *noun* the process of calculating in advance what a new product will cost

cost apportionment /'kɒst ə ,pɔːʃ(ə)nmənt/ *noun* the sharing out of common overhead costs among various cost centres

cost assignment path /,kɒst ə 'saɪnmənt ,pɑːθ/ *noun* a link between a cost and its cost object

cost-based price /'kɒst beɪst ,praɪs/ *noun* a price for a particular product or service based on that portion of overall costs assigned to it

cost behaviour pattern /,kɒst bɪ 'heɪvjə ,pæt(ə)n/ *noun* the extent to which a cost will change as the level of activity of a business changes

cost-benefit analysis /,kɒst 'benɪfɪt ə ,næləsɪs/ *noun* the process of comparing the costs and benefits of various possible ways of using available resources. Also called **benefit-cost analysis**

cost centre /'kɒst ,sentə/ *noun* **1.** a person or group whose costs can be itemised and to which costs can be allocated in accounts **2.** a unit, a process or an individual that provides a service needed by another part of an organisation and whose cost is therefore accepted as an overhead of the business

cost (at cost) concept /,kɒst ət 'kɒst ,kɒnsept/ *noun* the practice of valuing assets with reference to their acquisition cost

cost control /'kɒst kən,trəʊl/ *noun* the process of ensuring that a business's actual costs do not exceed predetermined acceptable limits

cost-cutting /'kɒst ,kʌtɪŋ/ *adjective* intended to reduce costs ○ *We have taken out the second telephone line as a cost-cutting exercise.* ■ *noun* the process of reducing costs ○ *As a result of cost-cutting, we have had to make three staff redundant.*

cost driver /'kɒst ,draɪvə/ *noun* a factor that determines how much it costs to carry out a particular task or project, e.g. the amount of resources needed for it, or the activities involved in completing it

cost-effective /,kɒstɪ 'fektɪv/ *adjective* giving good value when compared with the original cost ○ *We find advertising in the Sunday newspapers very cost-effective.*

cost-effectiveness /,kɒst ɪ'fektɪvnəs/, **cost efficiency** /,kɒst ɪ'fɪʃənsi/ *noun* the quality of being cost-effective ○ *Can we calculate the cost-effectiveness of air freight against shipping by sea?*

cost element /'kɒst ,elɪmənt/ *noun* a single element of a total cost, e.g. the cost of depreciation of an item or the cost of warehousing the item

cost estimation /'kɒst ,estɪmeɪʃ(ə)n/ *noun* the process of determining cost behaviour patterns

cost factor /'kɒst ,fæktə/ *noun* any activity or item of material, equipment or personnel that incurs a cost

cost function /kɒst 'fʌŋkʃ(ə)n/ *noun* a mathematical function that links a company's total costs to its output and factor costs

cost hierarchy /'kɒst ,haɪərɑːki/ *noun* a system for classifying a company's activities according to the costs they incur

costing /'kɒstɪŋ/ *noun* a calculation of the manufacturing costs, and so the selling price, of a product ○ *The costings give us a retail price of $2.95.* ○ *We cannot do the costing until we have details of all the production expenditure.*

costly /'kɒstli/ *adjective* costing a lot of money, or costing too much money ○ *Defending the court case was a costly process.* ○ *The mistakes were time-consuming and costly.*

cost management /'kɒst ,mænɪdʒmənt/ *noun* the application of management accounting concepts, methods of data collection, analysis and presentation, in order to provide the information required to enable costs to be planned, monitored and controlled

cost management function /'kɒst ,mænɪdʒmənt ,fʌŋkʃ(ə)n/ *noun* the management of those activities that help determine accurate costs

cost modelling /'kɒst ,mɒd(ə)lɪŋ/ *noun* the use of a costing system to give a clear view of the costs and profitability of a product or service

cost object /ˈkɒst ˌɒbdʒɪkt/ *noun* any aspect of a company's business for which a costing can be produced, e.g. employees' salaries and factory overheads

cost of borrowing /ˌkɒst əv ˈbɒrəʊɪŋ/ *noun* an interest rate paid on borrowed money

cost of capital /ˌkɒst əv ˈkæpɪt(ə)l/ *noun* interest paid on the capital used in operating a business

cost of goods sold /ˌkɒst əv ˌgʊdz ˈsəʊld/ *noun* same as **cost of sales**

cost of living /ˌkɒst əv ˈlɪvɪŋ/ *noun* money which has to be paid for basic items such as food, heating or rent ○ *to allow for the cost of living in the salary adjustments*

cost-of-living adjustment /ˌkɒst əv ˈlɪvɪŋ əˌdʒʌstmənt/ *noun* an increase in wages or salary that compensates for an increase in the cost of living

cost-of-living allowance /ˌkɒst əv ˈlɪvɪŋ əˌlaʊəns/ *noun* an addition to normal salary to cover increases in the cost of living

cost-of-living bonus /ˌkɒst əv ˈlɪvɪŋ ˌbəʊnəs/ *noun* money paid to meet an increase in the cost of living

cost-of-living increase /ˌkɒst əv ˈlɪvɪŋ ˌɪnkriːs/ *noun* an increase in salary to allow it to keep up with the increased cost of living

cost-of-living index /ˌkɒst əv ˈlɪvɪŋ ˌɪndeks/ *noun* a way of measuring the cost of living which is shown as a percentage increase on the figure for the previous year. It is similar to the consumer price index, but includes other items such as the interest on mortgages.

cost of replacement /ˌkɒst əv rɪ ˈpleɪsmənt/ *noun* same as **replacement cost**

cost of sales /ˌkɒst əv ˈseɪlz/ *noun* all the costs of a product sold, including manufacturing costs and the staff costs of the production department, before general overheads are calculated. Also called **cost of goods sold**

cost of sales adjustment /ˌkɒst əv ˈseɪlz əˌdʒʌstmənt/ *noun* an adjustment made in current cost accounting to a company's historical cost profit figure to take into account the effect of inflation on the value of materials used in production during the accounting period. If prices are rising, the COSA will reduce historical cost profit. Abbreviation **COSA**

cost plus /ˌkɒst ˈplʌs/ *noun* a system of calculating a price, by taking the cost of production of goods or services and adding a percentage to cover the supplier's overheads and margin ○ *We are charging for the work on a cost plus basis.*

cost pool /ˈkɒst puːl/ *noun* a grouping of individual costs, e.g. by department or by type of job

cost price /ˈkɒst praɪs/ *noun* a selling price that is the same as the price paid by the seller, which results in no profit being made

cost reduction programme /ˈkɒst rɪ ˌdʌkʃən ˌprəʊgræm/ *noun* a programme of cutting costs in order to improve profitability

costs /kɒsts/ *plural noun* the expenses involved in a court case ○ *The judge awarded costs to the defendant.* ○ *Costs of the case will be borne by the prosecution.*

costs of nonconformance /ˌkɒsts əv ˌnɒnkənˈfɔːməns/ *plural noun* costs incurred by a company in rectifying defects in products or services sold

costs of quality /ˌkɒsts əv ˈkwɒləti/ *plural noun* costs incurred in applying quality control standards

cost summary schedule /ˌkɒst ˈsʌməri ˌʃedjuːl/ *noun* a method of determining the cost to be transferred to a department's finished goods inventory account

cost-volume-profit analysis /ˌkɒst ˌvɒljuːm ˈprɒfɪt əˌnæləsɪs/ *noun* an analysis of the relationship between gross profit and costs of production at different selling prices and output volumes. Also called **CVP analysis**

coterminous period ends /ˌkəʊtɜːmɪnəs ˈpɪəriəd ˌendz/ *plural noun* a point in time that marks the end of the accounting period for separate and related accounts that cover the same period

council tax /ˈkaʊnsəl tæks/ *noun* a tax paid by individuals or companies to a local authority. Introduced in April 1993 as a replacement for the much maligned community charge, or 'poll tax', council tax depends on the value of the residential or commercial property occupied.

count /kaʊnt/ *verb* **1.** to add figures together to make a total ○ *She counted up the sales for the six months to December.* **2.** to include something ○ *Did you count my trip to New York as part of my sales expenses?*

counterbid /ˈkaʊntəbɪd/ *noun* a higher bid in reply to a previous bid ○ *When I bid $20 she put in a counterbid of $25.*

counter-claim /ˈkaʊntə kleɪm/ *noun* a claim for damages made in reply to a previous claim ○ *Jones claimed £25,000 in dam-*

ages against Smith, and Smith entered a counter-claim of £50,000 for loss of office.

counterfeit /ˈkaʊntəfɪt/ *adjective* referring to false or imitation money ○ *Shops in the area have been asked to look out for counterfeit £20 notes.* ■ *verb* to make imitation money

counterfoil /ˈkaʊntəfɔɪl/ *noun* a slip of paper kept after writing a cheque, an invoice or a receipt, as a record of the deal which has taken place

countermand /ˌkaʊntəˈmɑːnd/ *verb* to say that an order must not be carried out ○ *to countermand an order* □ **to countermand an order** to say that an order must not be carried out

counter-offer /ˈkaʊntər ˌɒfə/ *noun* a higher or lower offer made in reply to another offer ○ *Smith Ltd made an offer of $1m for the property, and Blacks replied with a counter-offer of $1.4m.*

'...the company set about paring costs and improving the design of its product. It came up with a price cut of 14%, but its counter-offer – for an order that was to have provided 8% of its workload next year – was too late and too expensive' [*Wall Street Journal*]

counterparty /ˈkaʊntəpɑːti/ *noun* each of the other parties to a contract, considered from the viewpoint of a particular party

counterpurchase /ˈkaʊntəpɜːtʃɪs/ *noun* an international trading deal, where a company agrees to use money received on a sale to purchase goods in the country where the sale was made

countersign /ˈkaʊntəsaɪn/ *verb* to sign a document which has already been signed by someone else ○ *All our cheques have to be countersigned by the finance director.* ○ *The sales director countersigns all my orders.*

countertrade /ˈkaʊntətreɪd/ *noun* a trade which does not involve payment of money, but something such as a barter or a buy-back deal instead

countervailing duty /ˈkaʊntəveɪlɪŋ ˌdjuːti/ *noun* a duty imposed by a country on imported goods, where the price of the goods includes a subsidy from the government in the country of origin. Also called **anti-dumping duty**

counting house /ˈkaʊntɪŋ haʊs/ *noun* a department dealing with cash (*dated*)

country risk /ˈkʌntri rɪsk/ *noun* the risk associated with undertaking transactions with, or holding assets in, a particular country. Sources of risk might be political, economic or regulatory instability affecting overseas taxation, repatriation of profits, nationalisation, currency instability, etc.

coupon /ˈkuːpɒn/ *noun* **1.** a piece of paper used in place of money **2.** a slip of paper attached to a government bond certificate which can be cashed to provide the annual interest

coupon rate /ˈkuːpɒn reɪt/ *noun* the percentage fixed interest rate on a government bond or a debenture

coupon security /ˈkuːpɒn sɪˌkjʊəriti/ *noun* a government security which carries a coupon and pays interest, as opposed to one which pays no interest but is sold at a discount to its face value

covenant /ˈkʌvənənt/ *noun* a legal contract ■ *verb* to agree to pay annually a specified sum of money to a person or organisation by contract. When payments are made under covenant to a charity, the charity can reclaim the tax paid by the donee. ○ *to covenant to pay £10 per annum*

cover /ˈkʌvə/ *noun* an amount of money large enough to guarantee that something can be paid for ○ *Do you have sufficient cover for this loan?* ■ *verb* **1.** to provide protection by insurance against something ○ *The insurance covers fire, theft and loss of work.* □ **to cover a risk** to be protected by insurance against a risk **2.** to earn enough money to pay for costs, expenses, etc. ○ *We do not make enough sales to cover the expense of running the shop.* ○ *Break-even point is reached when sales cover all costs.* **3.** to ask for security against a loan which you are making

'...three export credit agencies have agreed to provide cover for large projects in Nigeria' [*Business Times (Lagos)*]

coverage /ˈkʌv(ə)rɪdʒ/ *noun US* protection guaranteed by insurance ○ *Do you have coverage against fire damage?*

'...from a PR point of view it is easier to get press coverage when you are selling an industry and not a brand' [*PR Week*]

covered option /ˈkʌvəd ˌɒpʃ(ə)n/ *noun* an option the owner of which is also the owner of the shares for the option

cover note /ˈkʌvə nəʊt/ *noun* a letter from an insurance company giving details of an insurance policy and confirming that the policy exists

CP *abbreviation* commercial paper

CPA *abbreviation* certified public accountant

CPD /ˌsiː piː diː/ *noun* training and education that continues throughout a person's career in order to improve the skills and knowledge they use to do a job or succession of jobs. Full form **continuing professional development**

CPI *abbreviation* Consumer Price Index

creative accountancy /kri,eɪtɪv əˈkaʊntənsi/, **creative accounting** /kri,eɪtɪv əˈkaʊntɪŋ/ *noun* an adaptation of a company's figures to present a better picture than is correct, usually intended to make a company more attractive to a potential buyer, or done for some other reason which may not be strictly legal

credit /ˈkredɪt/ *noun* **1.** a period of time allowed before a customer has to pay a debt incurred for goods or services ○ *to give someone six months' credit* ○ *to sell on good credit terms* **2.** an amount entered in accounts to show a decrease in assets or expenses or an increase in liabilities, revenue or capital. In accounts, credits are entered in the right-hand column. ○ *to enter $100 to someone's credit* ○ *to pay in $100 to the credit of Mr Smith* Compare **debit** ■ *verb* to put money into someone's account, or to note money received in an account ○ *to credit an account with £100* or *to credit £100 to an account*

credit account /ˈkredɪt əˌkaʊnt/ *noun* an account which a customer has with a shop which allows him or her to buy goods and pay for them later

credit agency /ˈkredɪt ˌeɪdʒənsi/ *noun* a company which reports on the creditworthiness of customers to show whether they should be allowed credit. Also called **credit bureau**

credit agreement /ˈkredɪt əˌgriːmənt/ *noun* a document that sets out the terms under which credit is made available, or the agreement enshrined in such a document

credit analysis /ˈkredɪt əˌnæləsɪs/ *noun* the process of assessing a potential borrower's creditworthiness

credit balance /ˈkredɪt ˌbæləns/ *noun* a balance in an account showing that more money has been received than is owed ○ *The account has a credit balance of £100.*

credit bank /ˈkredɪt bæŋk/ *noun* a bank which lends money

credit bureau /ˈkredɪt ˌbjʊərəʊ/ *noun US* same as **credit agency**

credit card /ˈkredɪt kɑːd/ *noun* a plastic card which allows someone to borrow money and to buy goods up to a certain limit without paying for them immediately, but only after a period of grace of about 25–30 days. ◊ **charge card**

credit card holder /ˈkredɪt kɑːd ˌhəʊldə/ *noun* a person who has a credit card

credit column /ˈkredɪt ˌkɒləm/ *noun* the right-hand column in accounts showing money received

credit control /ˈkredɪt kənˌtrəʊl/ *noun* a check that customers pay on time and do not owe more than their credit limit

credit controller /ˈkredɪt kənˌtrəʊlə/ *noun* a member of staff whose job is to try to get payment of overdue invoices

credit entry /ˈkredɪt ˌentri/ *noun* an entry on the credit side of an account

credit facilities /ˈkredɪt fəˌsɪlɪtiz/ *plural noun* an arrangement with a bank or supplier to have credit so as to buy goods

credit freeze /ˈkredɪt friːz/ *noun* a period when lending by banks is restricted by the government

credit limit /ˈkredɪt ˌlɪmɪt/ *noun* the largest amount of money which a customer can borrow

credit line /ˈkredɪt laɪn/ *noun* an overdraft, the amount by which a person can draw money from an account with no funds, with the agreement of the bank

credit note /ˈkredɪt nəʊt/ *noun* a note showing that money is owed to a customer ○ *The company sent the wrong order and so had to issue a credit note.* Abbreviation **C/N**

creditor /ˈkredɪtə/ *noun* a person or company that is owed money, i.e. a company's creditors are its liabilities

creditor days /ˈkredɪtə deɪz/ *plural noun* the number of days on average that a company requires to pay its creditors. ◊ **debtor days**

creditors /ˈkredɪtəz/ *plural noun* a list of all liabilities in a set of accounts, including overdrafts, amounts owing to other companies in the group, trade creditors, payments received on account for goods not yet supplied, etc.

creditors' meeting /ˈkredɪtəz ˌmiːtɪŋ/ *noun* a meeting of all the people to whom an insolvent company owes money, to decide how to obtain the money owed

credit rating /ˈkredɪt ˌreɪtɪŋ/ *noun* an amount which a credit agency feels a customer will be able to repay

credit reference /ˌkredɪt ˈref(ə)rəns/ *noun* a credit rating or other indication of the creditworthiness of a company or individual

credit-reference agency /ˈkredɪt ˌrefər(ə)ns ˌeɪdʒənsi/ *noun* same as **credit agency**

credit report /ˌkredɪt rɪˈpɔːt/ *noun* information about an individual or entity relevant to a decision to grant credit

credit risk /ˈkredɪt rɪsk/ *noun* a risk that a borrower may not be able to repay a loan

credit side /ˈkredɪt saɪd/ *noun* the right-hand column of accounts showing money received

credit squeeze /ˈkredɪt skwiːz/ *noun* a period when lending by the banks is restricted by the government

credit union /ˈkredɪt ˌjuːnjən/ *noun* a group of people who pay in regular deposits or subscriptions which earn interest and are used to make loans to other members of the group

creditworthiness /ˈkredɪtˌwɜːðinəs/ *noun* the extent to which an individual or organisation is creditworthy

creditworthy /ˈkredɪtwɜːði/ *adjective* judged as likely to be able to repay money borrowed, either, in the case of an individual, by a credit reference agency, or, in the case of an organisation, by a credit rating agency ○ *We will do some checks on her to see if she is creditworthy.*

crisis /ˈkraɪsɪs/ *noun* a serious economic situation where decisions have to be taken rapidly ○ *a banking crisis* ○ *The government stepped in to try to resolve the international crisis.* ○ *Withdrawals from the bank have reached crisis level.*

crisis management /ˈkraɪsɪs ˌmænɪdʒmənt/ *noun* **1.** management of a business or a country's economy during a period of crisis **2.** actions taken by an organisation to protect itself when unexpected events or situations occur that could threaten its success or continued operation (NOTE: Crisis situations may result from external factors such as the development of a new product by a competitor or changes in legislation, or from internal factors such as a product failure or faulty decision-making, and often involve the need to make quick decisions on the basis of uncertain or incomplete information.)

critical-path method /ˌkrɪtɪk(ə)l ˈpɑːθ ˌmeθəd/ *noun* a technique used in project management to identify the activities within a project that are critical to its success, usually by showing on a diagram or flow chart the order in which activities must be carried out so that the project can be completed in the shortest time and at the least cost

'…need initial project designs to be more complex or need to generate Critical Path Method charts or PERT reports.' [InformationWeek]

CRO *abbreviation* Companies Registration Office

cross-border /ˌkrɒs ˈbɔːdə/ *adjective* from one country to another, covering several countries

cross-border services /ˌkrɒs ˌbɔːdə ˈsɜːvɪsɪz/ *plural noun* accountancy services provided by an accountancy firm in one country for a client in another country

crossed cheque /ˌkrɒst ˈtʃek/ *noun* a cheque with two lines across it showing that it can only be deposited at a bank and not exchanged for cash

cross holdings /ˈkrɒs ˌhəʊldɪŋz/ *plural noun* a situation where two companies own shares in each other in order to stop either from being taken over ○ *The two companies have protected themselves from takeover by a system of cross holdings.*

cross rate /ˈkrɒs reɪt/ *noun* an exchange rate between two currencies expressed in a third currency

cross-subsidy /ˌkrɒs ˈsʌbsɪdi/ *noun* the process of deliberately assigning costs to items in an account in such a way that some items are undercosted and some overcosted

crown jewels /ˌkraʊn ˈdʒuːəlz/ *plural noun* the most valuable assets of a company, the reason why other companies may want to make takeover bids

crystallise /ˈkrɪstəlaɪz/, **crystallize** *verb* to become chargeable on an asset ○ *a deferred gain is crystallised when you realise the gain by selling the asset*

CT *abbreviation* corporation tax

cum /kʌm/ *preposition* with

cum all /ˌkʌm ˈɔːl/ *adverb* including all entitlements

cum coupon /ˌkʌm ˈkuːpɒn/ *adverb* with a coupon attached or before interest due on a security is paid

cum dividend /ˌkʌm ˈdɪvɪdend/, **cum div** *adverb* including the next dividend still to be paid

cum rights /ˌkʌm ˈraɪts/ *adverb* sold with the right to purchase new shares in a rights issue

cumulative /ˈkjuːmjʊlətɪv/ *adjective* added to regularly over a period of time

cumulative interest /ˌkjuːmjʊlətɪv ˈɪntrəst/ *noun* the total amount of interest that has been charged on a loan up to a given point

cumulative preference share /ˌkjuːmjʊlətɪv ˈpref(ə)rəns ʃeə/ *noun* a preference share which will have the dividend paid at a later date even if the company is not able to pay a dividend in the current year (NOTE: The US term is **cumulative preferred stock**.)

cumulative weighted average cost /ˌkjuːmjʊlətɪv ˌweɪtɪd ˈæv(ə)rɪdʒ kɒst/, **cumulative weighted average price** /ˌkjuːmjʊlətɪv ˌweɪtɪd ˈæv(ə)rɪdʒ praɪs/ *noun* the average price per unit of stock delivered in a period calculated each time a new delivery is received. Compare **periodic weighted average cost**

currency /ˈkʌrənsi/ *noun* **1.** money in coins and notes which is used in a particular country **2.** foreign currency, the currency of another country (NOTE: **Currency** has no plural when it refers to the money of one country: *He was arrested trying to take currency out of the country.*)

'...today's wide daily variations in exchange rates show the instability of a system based on a single currency, namely the dollar' [*Economist*]

'...the level of currency in circulation increased to N4.9 billion in the month of August' [*Business Times (Lagos)*]

currency backing /ˈkʌrənsi ˌbækɪŋ/ *noun* gold or government securities which maintain the strength of a currency

currency band /ˈkʌrənsi bænd/ *noun* the exchange rate levels between which a currency is allowed to move without full devaluation

currency basket /ˈkʌrənsi ˌbɑːskɪt/ *noun* a group of currencies, each of which is weighted, calculated together as a single unit against which another currency can be measured

currency clause /ˈkʌrənsi klɔːz/ *noun* a clause in a contract which avoids problems of payment caused by changes in exchange rates, by fixing the exchange rate for the various transactions covered by the contract

currency futures /ˈkʌrənsi ˌfjuːtʃəz/ *plural noun* purchases of foreign currency for delivery at a future date

currency hedging /ˈkʌrənsi ˌhedʒɪŋ/ *noun* a method of reducing exchange rate risk by diversifying currency holdings and adjusting them according to changes in exchange rates

currency mismatching /ˈkʌrənsi ˌmɪsmætʃɪŋ/ *noun* the activity of borrowing money in the currency of a country where interest rates are low and depositing it in the currency of a country with higher interest rates. The potential profit from the interest rate margin may be offset by changes in the exchange rates which increase the value of the loan in the company's balance sheet.

currency movements /ˈkʌrənsi ˌmuːvmənts/ *plural noun* fluctuations in the value of the world's currencies that occur as they are traded

currency note /ˈkʌrənsi nəʊt/ *noun* a bank note

currency reserves /ˈkʌrənsi rɪˌzɜːvz/ *plural noun* foreign money held by a government to support its own currency and to pay its debts

currency swap /ˈkʌrənsi swɒp/ *noun* **1.** an agreement to use a certain currency for payments under a contract in exchange for another currency (the two companies involved can each buy one of the currencies at a more favourable rate than the other) **2.** the buying or selling of a fixed amount of a foreign currency on the spot market, and the selling or buying of the same amount of the same currency on the forward market

current account /ˈkʌrənt əˌkaʊnt/ *noun* **1.** an account in an bank from which the customer can withdraw money when he or she wants. Current accounts do not always pay interest. ○ *to pay money into a current account* Also called **cheque account** (NOTE: The US term is **checking account**.) **2.** an account of the balance of payments of a country relating to the sale or purchase of raw materials, goods and invisibles

current assets /ˌkʌrənt ˈæsets/ *plural noun* the assets used by a company in its ordinary work, e.g. materials, finished goods, cash and monies due, and which are held for a short time only

current cost /ˌkʌrənt ˈkɒst/ *noun* the amount it would cost to replace an asset at current prices

current cost accounting /ˌkʌrənt ˈkɒst əˌkaʊntɪŋ/ *noun* a method of accounting in which assets are valued at the amount it would cost to replace them, rather than at the original cost. Abbreviation **CCA**. Also called **replacement cost accounting**

current liabilities /ˌkʌrənt ˌlaɪəˈbɪlɪtiz/ *plural noun* the debts which a company has to pay within the next accounting period. In a company's annual accounts, these would be debts which must be paid within the year and are usually payments for goods or services received.

current purchasing power /ˌkʌrənt ˈpɜːtʃɪsɪŋ ˌpaʊə/ *noun* a method of accounting which takes inflation into account by using constant monetary units (actual amounts multiplied by a general price index). Also called **constant purchasing power**

current ratio /ˌkʌrənt ˈreɪʃiəʊ/ *noun* a ratio of current assets to current liabilities showing if a company may not be able to meet its immediate debts

current value /ˈkʌrənt ˌvæljuː/ *noun* a figure that represents the amount by which current assets are greater than current liabilities

current value accounting /ˌkʌrənt ˈvæljuː əˌkaʊntɪŋ/ *noun* a reassessment of the value of assets and liabilities

current year /ˌkʌrənt ˈjɪə/ *noun* the year in which an accounting period falls ○ *Under self-assessment, income is taxed on a current year basis – i.e. it is taxed in the year in which it is received.*

current yield /ˌkʌrənt ˈjiːld/ *noun* a dividend calculated as a percentage of the current price of a share on the stock market

curve /kɜːv/ *noun* a line which is not straight, e.g. a line on a graph ○ *The graph shows an upward curve.*

cushion /ˈkʊʃ(ə)n/ *noun* money which allows a company to pay interest on its borrowings or to survive a loss ○ *We have sums on deposit which are a useful cushion when cash flow is tight.*

custodian /kʌˈstəʊdiən/ *noun* a bank whose principal function is to maintain and grow the assets contained in a trust

custom /ˈkʌstəm/ *noun* the use of a shop by regular shoppers

customer /ˈkʌstəmə/ *noun* a person or company that buys goods ○ *The shop was full of customers.* ○ *Can you serve this customer first please?* ○ *She's a regular customer of ours.* (NOTE: The customer may not be the consumer or end user of the product.)

'…unless advertising and promotion is done in the context of an overall customer orientation, it cannot seriously be thought of as marketing' [*Quarterly Review of Marketing*]

customer profitability /ˌkʌstəmə ˌprɒfɪtəˈbɪliti/ *noun* the amount of profit generated by each individual customer. Usually a small percentage of customers generate the most profit.

customer profitability analysis /ˌkʌstəm ˌprɒfɪtəˈbɪliti əˌnælɪsɪs/ *noun* analysis of the revenues and costs associated with particular customers

customer service department /ˌkʌstəmə ˈsɜːvɪs dɪˌpɑːtmənt/ *noun* a department which deals with customers and their complaints and orders

customise /ˈkʌstəmaɪz/, **customize** *verb* to change something to fit the special needs of a customer ○ *We use customised computer terminals.*

customs /ˈkʌstəmz/ *plural noun* the government department which organises the collection of taxes on imports, or an office of this department at a port or airport ○ *He was stopped by customs.* ○ *Her car was searched by customs.*

Customs and Excise /ˌkʌstəmz ən ˈeksaɪz/ *noun* a former UK government department which organised the collection of taxes on imports and also collected VAT. It merged with the Inland Revenue to form HM Revenue & Customs in 2005.

customs barrier /ˈkʌstəmz ˌbæriə/ *noun* any provision intended to make trade more difficult, e.g. a high level of duty

customs broker /ˈkʌstəmz ˌbrəʊkə/ *noun* a person or company that takes goods through customs for a shipping company

customs clearance /ˈkʌstəmz ˌklɪərəns/ *noun* **1.** the act of passing goods through customs so that they can enter or leave the country **2.** a document given by customs to a shipper to show that customs duty has been paid and the goods can be shipped ○ *to wait for customs clearance*

customs declaration /ˈkʌstəmz dekləˌreɪʃ(ə)n/ *noun* a statement showing goods being imported on which duty will have to be paid ○ *to fill in a customs declaration form*

customs duty /ˈkʌstəmz ˌdjuːti/ *noun* a tax on goods imported into a country

customs entry point /ˌkʌstəmz ˈentri pɔɪnt/ *noun* a place at a border between two countries where goods are declared to customs

customs examination /ˈkʌstəmz ɪgˌzæmɪneɪʃ(ə)n/ *noun* the inspection of goods or baggage by customs officials

customs formalities /ˈkʌstəmz fɔːˌmælɪtiz/ *plural noun* a declaration of goods by the shipper and examination of them by customs

customs officer /ˈkʌstəmz ˌɒfɪsə/ *noun* a person working for the customs department of a country

customs seal /ˈkʌstəmz siːl/ *noun* a seal attached by a customs officer to a box, to show that the contents have not passed through customs

customs tariff /ˈkʌstəmz ˌtærɪf/ *noun* a list of taxes to be paid on imported goods

customs union /ˈkʌstəmz ˌjuːnjən/ *noun* an agreement between several countries that goods can travel between them, without paying duty, while goods from other countries have to pay special duties

cut /kʌt/ *noun* **1.** the sudden lowering of a price, salary or the number of jobs ○ *price cuts* or *cuts in prices* □ **he took a cut in salary, he took a salary cut** he accepted a lower salary **2.** a share in a payment ○ *She introduces new customers and gets a cut of the sales rep's commission.* ■ *verb* **1.** to lower something suddenly ○ *We are cutting prices on all our models.* ○ *We have taken out the second telephone line in order to try to cut costs.* **2.** to reduce the number of something

'…state-owned banks cut their prime rates a percentage point to 11%' [*Wall Street Journal*]

'…the US bank announced a cut in its prime from 10½ per cent to 10 per cent' [*Financial Times*]

'Opec has on average cut production by one third since 1979' [*Economist*]

cut down (on) *phrasal verb* to reduce suddenly the amount of something used ○ *The government is cutting down on welfare expenditure.* ○ *The office is trying to cut down on electricity consumption.* ○ *We have installed networked computers to cut down on paperwork.*

cutback /ˈkʌtbæk/ *noun* a reduction ○ *cutbacks in government spending*

cut-off /ˈkʌt ɒf/ *noun* a date and procedure for isolating the flow of cash and goods, stocktaking and the related documentation, to ensure that all aspects of a transaction are dealt with in the same financial period

CVP analysis /ˌsiː viː ˈpiː əˌnælɪsɪs/ *noun* same as **cost-volume-profit analysis**

cycle /ˈsaɪk(ə)l/ *noun* a set of events which happen in a regularly repeated sequence

cyclical /ˈsɪklɪk(ə)l/ *adjective* happening in cycles

cyclical factors /ˌsɪklɪk(ə)l ˈfæktəz/ *plural noun* the way in which a trade cycle affects businesses

D

D/A *abbreviation* deposit account

damages /'dæmɪdʒɪz/ *plural noun* money claimed as compensation for harm done ○ *to claim £1000 in damages* ○ *to be liable for damages* ○ *to pay £25,000 in damages*

D & B *abbreviation* Dun & Bradstreet

danger money /'deɪndʒə ˌmʌni/ *noun* extra money paid to employees in dangerous jobs ○ *The workforce has stopped work and asked for danger money.* ○ *He decided to go to work on an oil rig because of the danger money offered as an incentive.*

Datastream /'deɪtəstriːm/ *noun* a data system available online, giving information about securities, prices, stock exchange transactions, etc.

date of bill /ˌdeɪt əv 'bɪl/ *noun* a date when a bill will mature

date of maturity /ˌdeɪt əv mə'tjʊərɪti/ *noun* same as **maturity date**

date of record /ˌdeɪt əv 'rekɔːd/ *noun* the date when a shareholder must be registered to qualify for a dividend

date stamp /'deɪt stæmp/ *noun* a stamp with rubber figures which can be moved, used for marking the date on documents

dawn raid /dɔːn 'reɪd/ *noun* a sudden planned purchase of a large number of a company's shares at the beginning of a day's trading (NOTE: Up to 15% of a company's shares may be bought in this way, and the purchaser must wait for seven days before purchasing any more shares. Sometimes a dawn raid is the first step towards a takeover of the target company.)

day book /'deɪ bʊk/ *noun* a book with an account of sales and purchases made each day

DCF *abbreviation* discounted cash flow

DD *abbreviation* direct debit

dead account /ˌded ə'kaʊnt/ *noun* an account which is no longer used

dead loss /ˌded 'lɒs/ *noun* a total loss ○ *The car was written off as a dead loss.*

dead money /ˌded 'mʌni/ *noun* money which is not invested to make a profit

deal /diːl/ *noun* a business agreement, affair or contract ○ *The sales director set up a deal with a Russian bank.* ○ *The deal will be signed tomorrow.* ○ *They did a deal with an American airline.* ■ *verb* to buy and sell □ **to deal in leather** *or* **options** to buy and sell leather or options

dealer /'diːlə/ *noun* **1.** a person who buys and sells ○ *a used-car dealer* **2.** a person or firm that buys or sells on their own account, not on behalf of clients

dealing /'diːlɪŋ/ *noun* **1.** the business of buying and selling on the Stock Exchange, commodity markets or currency markets □ **dealing for** *or* **within the account** buying shares and selling the same shares during an account, which means that the dealer has only to pay the difference between the price of the shares bought and the price obtained for them when they are sold **2.** the business of buying and selling goods

dear money /'dɪə ˌmʌni/ *noun* money which has to be borrowed at a high interest rate, and so restricts expenditure by companies. Also called **tight money**

death benefit /'deθ ˌbenɪfɪt/ *noun* insurance benefit paid to the family of someone who dies in an accident at work

death duty /'deθ ˌdjuːti/ *noun* same as **inheritance tax**

death in service /ˌdeθ ɪn 'sɜːvɪs/ *noun* an insurance benefit or pension paid when someone dies while employed by a company

death tax /'deθ tæks/ *noun* same as **inheritance tax**

debenture /dɪ'bentʃə/ *noun* agreement to repay a debt with fixed interest using the company's assets as security ○ *The bank holds a debenture on the company.*

debenture bond /dɪ'bentʃə bɒnd/ *noun* US **1.** a certificate showing that a debenture has been issued **2.** an unsecured loan

debenture capital /dɪˈbentʃə ˌkæpɪt(ə)l/ *noun* capital borrowed by a company, using its fixed assets as security

debenture holder /dɪˈbentʃə ˌhəʊldə/ *noun* a person who holds a debenture for money lent

debenture issue /dɪˈbentʃə ˌɪʃuː/ *noun* the activity of borrowing money against the security of the company's assets

debenture stock /dɪˈbentʃə stɒk/ *noun* a form of debt instrument in which a company guarantees payments on a fixed schedule or at a fixed rate of interest

debit /ˈdebɪt/ *noun* an amount entered in accounts which shows an increase in assets or expenses or a decrease in liabilities, revenue or capital. In accounts, debits are entered in the left-hand column. Compare **credit**

debitable /ˈdebɪtəb(ə)l/ *adjective* able to be debited

debit balance /ˈdebɪt ˌbæləns/ *noun* a balance in an account showing that more money is owed than has been received ○ *Because of large payments to suppliers, the account has a debit balance of £1,000.*

debit card /ˈdebɪt kɑːd/ *noun* a plastic card, similar to a credit card, but which debits the holder's account immediately through an EPOS system

debit column /ˈdebɪt ˌkɒləm/ *noun* the left-hand column in accounts showing the money paid or owed to others

debit entry /ˈdebɪt ˌentri/ *noun* an entry on the debit side of an account

debit note /ˈdebɪt nəʊt/ *noun* a note showing that a customer owes money ○ *We undercharged Mr Smith and had to send him a debit note for the extra amount.*

debits and credits /ˌdebɪts ən ˈkredɪts/ *plural noun* money which a company owes and money it receives, or figures which are entered in the accounts to record increases or decreases in assets, expenses, liabilities, revenue or capital

debit side /ˈdebɪt saɪd/ *noun* a left-hand column of accounts showing money owed or paid to others

debt /det/ *noun* money owed for goods or services ○ *The company stopped trading with debts of over £1 million.* □ **he is in debt to the tune of £250,000** he owes £250,000

debt collection /ˈdet kəˌlekʃən/ *noun* the act of collecting money which is owed

debt collection agency /ˈdet kə ˌlekʃən ˌeɪdʒənsi/ *noun* a company which collects debts for other companies for a commission

debt collector /ˈdet kəˌlektə/ *noun* a person who collects debts

debt-convertible bond /ˌdet kən ˌvɜːtɪb(ə)l ˈbɒnd/ *noun* a floating-rate bond which can be converted to a fixed rate of interest. ◊ **droplock bond**

debt counselling /ˈdet ˌkaʊnsəlɪŋ/ *noun* the work of advising people who are in debt of the best ways to arrange their finances so as to pay off their debts

debt-equity ratio /ˌdet ˈekwɪti ˌreɪʃiəʊ/ *noun* a measure of a company's ability to repay its creditors, equal to its total long term debt divided by the total of shareholders' equity. ◊ **gearing**

debt factoring /ˈdet ˌfæktərɪŋ/ *noun* the business of buying debts at a discount. A factor collects a company's debts when due, and pays the creditor in advance part of the sum to be collected, so 'buying' the debt.

debtor /ˈdetə/ *noun* a person who owes money

debtor days /ˈdetə deɪz/ *plural noun* the number of days on average that it takes a company to receive payment for what it sells. ◊ **creditor days**

debtors /ˈdetəz/ *noun* all money owed to a company as shown in the accounts

debtors control account /ˈdetəz kən ˌtrəʊl əˌkaʊnt/ *noun* an account used to summarise the balances on the individual sales ledger accounts

debtor side /ˈdetə saɪd/ *noun* the debit side of an account

debtors ledger /ˈdetəz ˌledʒə/ *noun* same as **sales ledger**

debtors turnover ratio /ˌdetəz ˈtɜːnəʊvə ˌreɪʃiəʊ/ *noun* the average time which debtors take to pay

debt ratio /ˈdet ˌreɪʃiəʊ/ *noun* the debts of a company shown as a percentage of its equity plus loan capital

debt rescheduling /ˈdet riːˌʃedjuːlɪŋ/ *noun* the process of reorganising the way in which debts are repaid. Debt rescheduling may be necessary if a company is unable to pay its debts and may involve postponing debt payments, postponing payment of interest, or negotiating a new loan.

decile /ˈdesaɪl/ *noun* one of a series of nine figures below which one tenth or several tenths of the total fall

decimalisation /ˌdesɪm(ə)laɪˈzeɪʃ(ə)n/, **decimalization** *noun* the process of changing to a decimal system

decimalise /'desɪm(ə)laɪz/, **decimalize** *verb* to change something to a decimal system

decimal point /ˌdesɪm(ə)l 'pɔɪnt/ *noun* a dot which indicates the division between the whole unit and its smaller parts, e.g. 4.75

decimal system /'desɪm(ə)l ˌsɪstəm/ *noun* a system of mathematics based on the number 10

decision support system /dɪ'sɪʒ(ə)n səˌpɔːt ˌsɪstəm/ *noun* a computer-based system which presents auditor judgments in a structured way and can be used to create audit programmes or document the assessment of business risk

decision theory /dɪ'sɪʒ(ə)n ˌθɪəri/ *noun* the mathematical methods for weighing the various factors in making decisions ○ *In practice it is difficult to apply decision theory to our planning.* ○ *Students study decision theory to help them suggest strategies in case-studies.*

decision tree /dɪ'sɪʒ(ə)n triː/ *noun* a model for decision-making, showing the possible outcomes of different decisions ○ *This computer programme incorporates a decision tree.*

declaration /ˌdeklə'reɪʃ(ə)n/ *noun* an official statement

declaration date /ˌdeklə'reɪʃ(ə)n deɪt/ *noun US* the date on which a board of directors declares the dividend to be paid

declaration of bankruptcy /ˌdekləreɪʃ(ə)n əv 'bæŋkrʌptsi/ *noun* an official statement that someone is bankrupt

declaration of income /ˌdekləreɪʃ(ə)n əv 'ɪnkʌm/ *noun* same as **income tax return**

declaration of solvency /ˌdekləreɪʃ(ə)n əv 'sɒlv(ə)nsi/ *noun* a document, lodged with the Registrar of Companies, that lists the assets and liabilities of a company seeking voluntary liquidation to show that the company is capable of repaying its debts within 12months

declare /dɪ'kleə/ *verb* to make an official statement of something, or announce something to the public ○ *to declare someone bankrupt* ○ *The company declared an interim dividend of 10p per share.*

declared /dɪ'kleəd/ *adjective* having been made public or officially stated

declared value /dɪˌkleəd 'væljuː/ *noun* the value of goods entered on a customs declaration

decline /dɪ'klaɪn/ *verb* to fall slowly or decrease ○ *Shares declined in a weak market.* ○ *New job applications have declined over the last year.* ○ *The economy declined during the last government.* ○ *The purchasing power of the pound declined over the decade.*

'Saudi oil production has declined by three quarters to around 2.5m barrels a day' [*Economist*]

'…this gives an average monthly decline of 2.15 per cent during the period' [*Business Times (Lagos)*]

'…share prices disclosed a weak tendency right from the onset of business and declined further, showing losses over a broad front' [*The Hindu*]

declining balance method /dɪˌklaɪnɪŋ 'bæləns ˌmeθəd/ *noun US* same as **reducing balance method**

decrease /dɪ'kriːs/ *verb* to fall or to become less ○ *Imports are decreasing.* ○ *The value of the pound has decreased by 5%.*

deduct /dɪ'dʌkt/ *verb* to take money away from a total ○ *to deduct £3 from the price* ○ *to deduct a sum for expenses* ○ *After deducting costs the gross margin is only 23%.* ○ *Expenses are still to be deducted.*

deductible /dɪ'dʌktɪb(ə)l/ *adjective* possible to deduct

deduction /dɪ'dʌkʃən/ *noun* the removing of money from a total, or the amount of money removed from a total ○ *Net salary is salary after deduction of tax and social security.* ○ *The deduction from her wages represented the cost of repairing the damage she had caused to the machinery.* □ **deductions from salary**, **salary deductions**, **deductions at source** money which a company removes from salaries to give to the government as tax, National Insurance contributions, etc.

deed /diːd/ *noun* a legal document or written agreement

deed of arrangement /ˌdiːd əv ə'reɪndʒmənt/ *noun* an agreement made between a debtor and creditors whereby the creditors accept an agreed sum in settlement of their claim rather than make the debtor bankrupt

deed of assignment /ˌdiːd əv ə'saɪnmənt/ *noun* a document which legally transfers a property from a debtor to a creditor

deed of covenant /ˌdiːd əv 'kʌvənənt/ *noun* a legal document in which a person or organisation promises to pay a third party a sum of money on an annual basis. In certain countries this arrangement may have tax advantages. For example, in the United

Kingdom, it is often used for making regular payments to a charity.

deed of partnership /ˌdiːd əv ˈpɑːtnəʃɪp/ *noun* agreement which sets up a partnership

deed of transfer /ˌdiːd əv ˈtrænsfɜː/ *noun* a document which transfers the ownership of shares

deep pocket /ˌdiːp ˈpɒkɪt/ *noun* a company which provides finance for another

defalcation /ˌdiːfælˈkeɪʃ(ə)n/ *noun* the illegal use of money by someone who is not the owner but who has been trusted to look after it

default /dɪˈfɔːlt/ *noun* a failure to carry out the terms of a contract, especially failure to pay back a debt ■ *verb* to fail to carry out the terms of a contract, especially to fail to pay back a debt ○ *There was a major financial crisis when the bank defaulted.*

defaulter /dɪˈfɔːltə/ *noun* a person who defaults

default notice /dɪˈfɔːlt ˌnəʊtɪs/ *noun* a formal notice to a borrower stating that he or she has defaulted on the loan and legal action may be taken to recover the money. Also called **notice of default** (NOTE: The US term is **notice of default**.)

defer /dɪˈfɜː/ *verb* to put back to a later date, to postpone ○ *We will have to defer payment until January.* ○ *The decision has been deferred until the next meeting.* (NOTE: **deferring – deferred**)

deferment /dɪˈfɜːmənt/ *noun* the act of leaving until a later date ○ *deferment of payment* ○ *deferment of a decision*

deferred annuity /dɪˌfɜːd əˈnjuːəti/ *noun* an investment that does not pay out until at least one year after the final premium has been paid

deferred consideration /dɪˌfɜːd kənˌsɪdəˈreɪʃ(ə)n/ *noun* instalment payments for the acquisition of new subsidiaries usually made in the form of cash and shares, where the balance due after the initial deposit depends on the performance of the business acquired

deferred cost /dɪˈfɜːd kɒst/ *noun* a cost with future benefit that extends beyond the current accounting period

deferred credit /dɪˌfɜːd ˈkredɪt/ *noun* income received but not yet entered in accounts as income

deferred creditor /dɪˌfɜːd ˈkredɪtə/ *noun* a person who is owed money by a bankrupt but who is paid only after all other creditors

deferred expenditure /dɪˌfɜːd ɪkˈspendɪtʃə/ *noun* expenditure incurred now but reflected in the accounts of future years

deferred maintenance /dɪˌfɜːd ˈmeɪntənəns/ *noun* a failure to carry out maintenance, e.g. to machinery, that adversely affects its value, recorded in accounts

deferred payment /dɪˌfɜːd ˈpeɪmənt/ *noun* **1.** money paid later than the agreed date **2.** payment for goods by instalments over a long period

deferred revenue /dɪˌfɜːd ˈrevənjuː/ *noun* revenue carried forward to future accounting periods

deferred tax /dɪˌfɜːd ˈtæks/ *noun* a tax which may become payable at some later date

deficiency /dɪˈfɪʃ(ə)nsi/ *noun* a lack of something, or the amount by which something, e.g. a sum of money, is less than it should be ○ *There is a £10 deficiency in the petty cash.*

deficit /ˈdefɪsɪt/ *noun* the amount by which spending is higher than income

deficit financing /ˈdefɪsɪt ˌfaɪnænsɪŋ/ *noun* a type of financial planning by a government in which it borrows money to cover the difference between its tax income and its expenditure

deflation /diːˈfleɪʃ(ə)n/ *noun* a general reduction in economic activity as a result of a reduced supply of money and credit, leading to lower prices ○ *The oil crisis resulted in worldwide deflation.* Opposite **inflation**

'...the reluctance of people to spend is one of the main reasons behind 26 consecutive months of price deflation, a key economic ill that has led to price wars, depressed the profit margins of state enterprises and hit incomes among the rural population' [*Financial Times*]

deflationary /diːˈfleɪʃ(ə)n(ə)ri/ *adjective* causing deflation ○ *The government has introduced some deflationary measures in the budget.*

deflator /diːˈfleɪtə/ *noun* the amount by which a country's GNP is reduced to take inflation into account

degearing /diːˈɡɪərɪŋ/ *noun* a reduction in gearing, reducing a company's loan capital in relation to the value of its ordinary shares

del credere /ˌdel ˈkreɪdəri/ *noun* an amount added to a charge to cover the possibility of not being paid

del credere agent /ˌdel ˈkreɪdəri ˌeɪdʒənt/ *noun* an agent who receives a high commission because he or she guarantees payment by customers

delinquency /dɪˈlɪŋkwənsi/ *noun US* the fact of being overdue in payment of an account, an interest payment, etc.

delinquent /dɪˈlɪŋkwənt/ *adjective US* referring to an account or payment of tax which is overdue

deliver /dɪˈlɪvə/ *verb* to transport goods to a customer □ **goods delivered free** *or* **free delivered goods** goods transported to the customer's address at a price which includes transport costs □ **goods delivered on board** goods transported free to the ship or plane but not to the customer's warehouse

delivered price /dɪˈlɪvəd praɪs/ *noun* a price which includes packing and transport

delivery /dɪˈlɪv(ə)ri/ *noun* **1.** a consignment of goods being delivered □ *We take in three deliveries a day.* ○ *There were four items missing in the last delivery.* **2.** the transport of a commodity to a purchaser **3.** the transfer of a bill of exchange or other negotiable instrument to the bank which is due to make payment

delivery cycle time /dɪˈlɪv(ə)ri ˌsaɪk(ə)l ˌtaɪm/ *noun* the interval between the time of accepting an order and the time of making the final delivery

delivery month /dɪˈlɪv(ə)ri mʌnθ/ *noun* a month in a futures contract when actual delivery will take place

delivery note /dɪˈlɪv(ə)ri nəʊt/ *noun* a list of goods being delivered, given to the customer with the goods

delivery of goods /dɪˌlɪv(ə)ri əv ˈɡʊdz/ *noun* the transport of goods to a customer's address

delivery order /dɪˈlɪv(ə)ri ˌɔːdə/ *noun* the instructions given by the customer to the person holding her goods, to tell her where and when to deliver them

delivery time /dɪˈlɪv(ə)ri taɪm/ *noun* the number of days before something will be delivered

demand /dɪˈmɑːnd/ *noun* **1.** an act of asking for payment **2.** an act of asking for something and insisting on getting it ○ *The management refused to give in to union demands for a meeting.* ■ *verb* **1.** the need that customers have for a product or their eagerness to buy it ○ *There was an active demand for oil shares on the stock market.* ○ *The factory had to cut production when demand slackened.* ○ *The office cleaning company cannot keep up with the demand for its services.* □ **to meet** *or* **fill a demand** to supply what is needed ○ *The factory had to increase pro-*

duction to meet the extra demand. **2.** to ask for something and expect to get it ○ *She demanded a refund.* ○ *The suppliers are demanding immediate payment of their outstanding invoices.*

'…spot prices are now relatively stable in the run-up to the winter's peak demand' [*Economist*]

'…the demand for the company's products remained strong throughout the first six months of the year with production and sales showing significant increases' [*Business Times (Lagos)*]

'…growth in demand is still coming from the private rather than the public sector' [*Lloyd's List*]

demand bill /dɪˈmɑːnd bɪl/ *noun* a bill of exchange which must be paid when payment is asked for

demand price /dɪˈmɑːnd praɪs/ *noun* the price at which a quantity of goods will be bought

demerge /diːˈmɜːdʒ/ *verb* to separate a company into several separate parts

demerger /diːˈmɜːdʒə/ *noun* the separation of a company into several separate parts, especially used of companies which have grown by acquisition

demise /dɪˈmaɪz/ *noun* **1.** a death ○ *On his demise the estate passed to his daughter.* **2.** the act of granting a property on a lease ■ *verb* to grant property on a lease

demonetisation /diːˌmʌnɪtaɪˈzeɪʃ(ə)n/, **demonetization** *noun* the act of stopping a coin or note being used as money

demonetise /diːˈmʌnɪtaɪz/, **demonetize** *verb* to stop a coin or note being used as money

demurrage /dɪˈmʌrɪdʒ/ *noun* money paid to a customer when a shipment is delayed at a port or by customs

demutualisation /diːˌmjuːtjuəlaɪˈzeɪʃ(ə)n/, **demutualization** *noun* the process by which a mutual society, such as a building society, becomes a publicly owned corporation

demutualise /diːˈmjuːtjuəlaɪz/, **demutualize** /diːˈmjuːtʃuəˌlaɪz/ *verb* to stop having mutual status and become a publicly owned corporation by selling shares to the general public on the stock market

denomination /dɪˌnɒmɪˈneɪʃ(ə)n/ *noun* a unit of money on a coin, banknote or stamp ○ *We collect coins of all denominations for charity.* ○ *Small denomination notes are not often counterfeited.*

departmental accounts /ˌdiːpɑːtˈment(ə)l əˈkaʊnts/ *plural noun* accounts which analyse the sales of different departments or products of a company

Department for Education and Skills /dɪˌpɑːtmənt fər edjʊˌkeɪʃ(ə)n ən 'skɪlz/ *noun* a British government department responsible for education and training. Abbreviation **DFES**

Department of Trade and Industry /dɪˌpɑːtmənt əv ˌtreɪd ənd 'ɪndəstri/ *noun* a British government department which deals with areas such as commerce, international trade and the stock exchange. Abbreviation **DTI**

dependent variable /dɪˌpendənt 'veəriəb(ə)l/ *noun* a variable or factor which changes as a result of a change in another (the 'independent variable') ○ *We are trying to understand the effects of several independent variables on one dependent variable, in this case, sales.*

deposit /dɪ'pɒzɪt/ *noun* **1.** money placed in a bank for safe keeping or to earn interest **2.** money given in advance so that the thing which you want to buy will not be sold to someone else ○ *to pay a deposit on a watch* ○ *to leave £10 as deposit* ■ *verb* **1.** to put documents somewhere for safe keeping ○ *to deposit shares with a bank* ○ *We have deposited the deeds of the house with the bank.* ○ *He deposited his will with his solicitor.* **2.** to put money into a bank account ○ *to deposit £100 in a current account*

deposit account /dɪ'pɒzɪt əˌkaʊnt/ *noun* a bank account which pays interest but on which notice has to be given to withdraw money. Abbreviation **D/A**

depositary /dɪ'pɒzɪtəri/ *noun US* a person or corporation which can place money or documents for safekeeping with a depositary. ◊ **American Depositary Receipt** (NOTE: Do not confuse with **depository**.)

depositor /dɪ'pɒzɪtə/ *noun* a person who deposits money in a bank, building society, etc.

depository /dɪ'pɒzɪt(ə)ri/ *noun* a person or company with whom money or documents can be deposited (NOTE: Do not confuse with **depositary**.)

deposit slip /dɪ'pɒzɪt slɪp/ *noun US* same as **paying-in slip**

deposit-taking institution /dɪˌpɒzɪt ˌteɪkɪŋ ˌɪnstɪ'tjuːʃ(ə)n/, **depository institution** /dɪˌpɒzɪtri ˌɪnstɪ'tjuːʃ(ə)n/ *noun* an institution which is licensed to receive money on deposit from private individuals and to pay interest on it, e.g. a building society, bank or friendly society

depreciable /dɪ'priːʃiəb(ə)l/ *adjective* possible to depreciate

depreciable asset /dɪˌpriːʃiəb(ə)l 'æset/ *noun* an asset which will be used over more than one accounting period, but which has a limited life and so can be depreciated

depreciable cost /dɪ'priːʃiəb(ə)l kɒst/ *noun* a cost that can be applied to more than one accounting period

depreciable life /dɪˌpriːʃiəb(ə)l 'laɪf/ *noun* the period over which the cost of an asset may be spread

depreciate /dɪ'priːʃieɪt/ *verb* **1.** to make an allowance in accounts for the loss of value of an asset over time ○ *We depreciate our company cars over three years.* **2.** to lose value ○ *a share that has depreciated by 10% over the year* ○ *The pound has depreciated by 5% against the dollar.*

depreciation /dɪˌpriːʃi'eɪʃ(ə)n/ *noun* **1.** a loss of value ○ *a share that has shown a depreciation of 10% over the year* ○ *the depreciation of the pound against the dollar* **2.** the loss of value of an asset over time, which is recorded in accounts as an expense

depreciation accounting /dɪˌpriːʃi 'eɪʃ(ə)n əˌkaʊntɪŋ/ *noun* the process of spreading the cost of an asset over its useful life

depreciation provision /dɪˌpriːʃi 'eɪʃ(ə)n prəˌvɪʒ(ə)n/ *noun* the amount of depreciation, in relation to a particular asset, that has been charged cumulatively to an account since the asset was acquired

depreciation rate /dɪˌpriːʃi'eɪʃ(ə)n reɪt/ *noun* the rate at which an asset is depreciated each year in the company accounts

depress /dɪ'pres/ *verb* to reduce something ○ *Reducing the money supply has the effect of depressing demand for consumer goods.*

depressed market /dɪˌprest 'mɑːkɪt/ *noun* a market where there are more goods than customers

deregulate /diː'regjʊleɪt/ *verb* to remove government controls from an industry ○ *The US government deregulated the banking sector in the 1980s.*

deregulation /diːˌregjʊ'leɪʃ(ə)n/ *noun* the reduction of government control over an industry ○ *the deregulation of the airlines*

'…after the slump in receipts last year that followed liner shipping deregulation in the US, carriers are probably still losing money on their transatlantic services. But with a possible contraction in capacity and healthy trade growth, this year has begun in a much more promising fashion than last' [*Lloyd's List*]

derivative instruments /dɪˌrɪvətɪv ˈɪnstrʊmənts/, **derivatives** /dɪˈrɪvətɪvz/ *plural noun* any forms of traded security such as option contracts, which are derived from ordinary bonds and shares, exchange rates or stock market indices

designated account /ˌdezɪgneɪtɪd əˈkaʊnt/ *noun* an account opened and held in one person's name, but which also features another person's name for extra identification purposes

detailed audit /ˌdiːteɪld ˈɔːdɪt/ *noun* an audit that involves examining all or most of a company's transactions, rather than a sample of them

devaluation /ˌdiːvæljuˈeɪʃ(ə)n/ *noun* a reduction in the value of a currency against other currencies ○ *the devaluation of the rand*

devalue /diːˈvæljuː/ *verb* to reduce the value of a currency against other currencies ○ *The pound has been devalued by 7%.*

development costs /dɪˈveləpmənt kɒsts/ *plural noun* costs of developing new or improved products, sometimes also incorporating a portion of standard overhead costs

devise /dɪˈvaɪz/ *noun* the act of giving freehold land to someone in a will ■ *verb* to give freehold property to someone in a will

devisee /dɪvaɪˈziː/ *noun* a person who receives freehold property in a will

DFES *abbreviation* Department for Education and Skills

differential tariffs /ˌdɪfərenʃəl ˈtærɪfs/ *plural noun* different tariffs for different classes of goods as, e.g., when imports from some countries are taxed more heavily than similar imports from other countries

digit /ˈdɪdʒɪt/ *noun* a single number ○ *a seven-digit phone number*

digital analysis /ˌdɪdʒɪt(ə)l əˈnæləsɪs/ *noun* auditing techniques that investigate the digits in accounting numbers to reveal fraud and error

diluted earnings per share /daɪˌluːtɪd ˌɜːnɪŋz pə ˈʃeə/ *noun* a hypothetical measure of the quality of a company's earnings per share that assumes all convertible securities are exercised

dilution of shareholding /daɪˌluːʃ(ə)n əv ˈʃeəhəʊldɪŋ/ *noun* a situation where the ordinary share capital of a company has been increased, but without an increase in the assets so that each share is worth less than before

diminish /dɪˈmɪnɪʃ/ *verb* to become smaller ○ *Our share of the market has diminished over the last few years.*

direct allocation method /ˌdaɪrekt ˌæləˈkeɪʃ(ə)n ˌmeθəd/, **direct method** /daɪˈrekt ˌmeθəd/ *noun* a method of relating the costs incurred by service departments of a company to the production departments

direct cost /daɪˌrekt ˈkɒst/ *noun* a cost which can be directly related to the making of a product, i.e. its production cost

direct cost variance /daɪˌrekt kɒst ˈveəriəns/ *noun* the difference between the planned direct costs for a product and the actual direct costs

direct debit /daɪˌrekt ˈdebɪt/ *noun* a system where a customer allows a company to charge costs to his or her bank account automatically and where the amount charged can be increased or decreased with the agreement of the customer ○ *I pay my electricity bill by direct debit.* Abbreviation **DD**

direct expenses /daɪˌrekt ɪkˈspensɪz/ *plural noun* expenses excluding materials, labour or purchase of stock for resale which are incurred in making a product

directional testing /daɪˌrekʃən(ə)l ˈtestɪŋ/ *noun* an auditing technique by which work is reduced by testing debits only for overstatement and credits only for understatement

directive /daɪˈrektɪv/ *noun* an order or command to someone to do something ○ *The Commission issued a directive on food prices.* (NOTE: Directives from the European Union are binding, but member states can implement them as they wish. A directive is binding as to the result to be achieved, but leaves to the national authorities the choice of form and method.)

direct labour costs /daɪˌrekt ˈleɪbə ˌkɒsts/ *plural noun* the cost of employing those workers directly involved in producing a particular product, not including materials or overheads

direct materials cost /daɪˌrekt məˈtɪəriəlz ˌkɒst/ *noun* the cost of the materials used in producing a particular product

director /daɪˈrektə/ *noun* a senior employee appointed by the shareholders to help run a company, who is usually in charge of one or other of its main functions, e.g. sales or human relations, and usually, but not always, a member of the board of directors

'…the research director will manage and direct a team of business analysts reporting on the latest developments in retail distribution throughout the UK' [*Times*]

directorate /daɪˈrekt(ə)rət/ *noun* a group of directors

Director of the Budget /daɪˌrektər əv ðə ˈbʌdʒɪt/ *noun* the member of a government in charge of the preparation of the budget

director's fees /daɪˈrektəz fiːz/ *plural noun* money paid to a director for attendance at board meetings

directorship /daɪˈrektəʃɪp/ *noun* the post of director ○ *She was offered a directorship with Smith Ltd*

directors' report /daɪˈrektəz rɪˌpɔːt/ *noun* the annual report from the board of directors to the shareholders

direct product profitability /daɪˌrekt ˌprɒdʌkt ˌprɒfɪtəˈbɪlɪti/ *noun* an assessment of the net profit generated by a particular product, which considers costs such as distribution, warehousing and retailing but not the original purchase price. Abbreviation **DPP**

direct share ownership /daɪˌrekt ˈʃeə ˌəʊnəʃɪp/ *noun* the ownership of shares by private individuals, buying or selling through brokers, and not via holdings in unit trusts

direct tax /daɪˌrekt ˈtæks/ *noun* a tax that is paid directly to the government, e.g. income tax, as distinct from a tax such as VAT that is paid indirectly

direct taxation /daɪˌrekt tækˈseɪʃ(ə)n/ *noun* the process in which a government raises revenue in the form of direct taxes ○ *The government raises more money by direct taxation than by indirect.*

dirty float /ˈdɜːti fləʊt/ *noun* the process of floating a currency, in which the government intervenes to regulate the exchange rate

disallow /ˌdɪsəˈlaʊ/ *verb* not to accept a claim for insurance ○ *She claimed £2,000 for fire damage, but the claim was disallowed.*

disallowable /ˌdɪsəˈlaʊəb(ə)l/ *adjective* not able to be allowed for tax relief ○ *The use of a car for private travel is a disallowable expense.* Opposite **allowable**

disburse /dɪsˈbɜːs/ *verb* to pay money

disbursement /dɪsˈbɜːsmənt/ *noun* the payment of money

discharge /dɪsˈtʃɑːdʒ/ *noun* /ˈdɪstʃɑːdʒ/ **1.** the act of paying a debt □ **in full discharge of a debt** as full payment of a debt **2.** □ **in discharge of her duties as director** while carrying out her duties as director ■ *verb* **1.** to pay a debt □ **to discharge a bank-**

rupt to release someone from bankruptcy because they have has paid their debts **2.** □ **to discharge a debt, to discharge your liabilities** to pay a debt or your liabilities in full **3.** to dismiss an employee ○ *to discharge an employee for negligence*

discharged bankrupt /dɪsˌtʃɑːdʒd ˈbæŋkrʌpt/ *noun* a person who has been released from being bankrupt because his or her debts have been paid

disclaimer /dɪsˈkleɪmə/ *noun* a legal refusal to accept responsibility

disclose /dɪsˈkləʊz/ *verb* to tell something that was previously unknown to other people or secret ○ *The bank has no right to disclose details of my account to the tax office.*

disclosure /dɪsˈkləʊʒə/ *noun* the act of telling something that was previously unknown to other people or secret ○ *The disclosure of the takeover bid raised the price of the shares.*

disclosure of shareholding /dɪs ˌkləʊʒər əv ˈʃeəhəʊldɪŋ/ *noun* the act of making public the fact that someone owns shares in a company

discount *noun* /ˈdɪskaʊnt/ **1.** the percentage by which the seller reduces the full price for the buyer ○ *to give a discount on bulk purchases* □ **to sell goods at a discount** *or* **at a discount price** to sell goods below the normal price □ **10% discount for cash, 10% cash discount** you pay 10% less if you pay in cash **2.** the amount by which something is sold for less than its value ■ *verb* /dɪsˈkaʊnt/ **1.** to reduce prices to increase sales **2.** □ **to discount bills of exchange** to buy or sell bills of exchange for less than the value written on them in order to cash them later **3.** to react to something which may happen in the future, such as a possible takeover bid or currency devaluation **4.** to calculate the value of future income or expenditure in present value terms

discountable /ˈdɪskaʊntəb(ə)l/ *adjective* possible to discount ○ *These bills are not discountable.*

discounted cash flow /ˌdɪskaʊntɪd ˈkæʃ fləʊ/ *noun* the calculation of the forecast return on capital investment by discounting future cash flows from the investment, usually at a rate equivalent to the company's minimum required rate of return. Abbreviation **DCF**

discounted value /ˌdɪskaʊntɪd ˈvæljuː/ *noun* the difference between the face value of a share and its lower market price

discounter /'dɪskaʊntə/ *noun* a person or company that discounts bills or invoices, or sells goods at a discount

discount for cash /ˌdɪskaʊnt fə 'kæʃ/ *noun* same as **cash discount**

discount house /'dɪskaʊnt haʊs/ *noun* a financial company which specialises in discounting bills

discount rate /'dɪskaʊnt reɪt/ *noun* the rate charged by a central bank on any loans it makes to other banks

discrepancy /dɪ'skrepənsi/ *noun* a lack of agreement between figures in invoices or accounts

discretion /dɪ'skreʃ(ə)n/ *noun* the ability to decide what should be done

discretionary account /dɪˌskreʃ(ə)n(ə)ri ə'kaʊnt/ *noun* a client's account with a stockbroker, where the broker invests and sells at his or her own discretion without the client needing to give him specific instructions

discretionary client /dɪˌskreʃ(ə)n(ə)ri 'klaɪənt/ *noun* a client whose funds are managed on a discretionary basis

discretionary cost /dɪˌskreʃ(ə)n(ə)ri 'kɒst/ *noun* a cost that can vary greatly within an accounting period and is determined by the appropriate budget holder

discretionary funds /dɪˌskreʃ(ə)n(ə)ri 'fʌndz/ *plural noun* funds managed on a discretionary basis

discretionary trust /dɪˌskreʃ(ə)n(ə)ri 'trʌst/ *noun* a trust where the trustees decide how to invest the income and when and how much income should be paid to the beneficiaries

diseconomies of scale /dɪsɪˌkɒnəmiz əv 'skeɪl/ *plural noun* a situation where increased production leads to a higher production cost per unit or average production cost

disequilibrium /ˌdɪsiːkwɪ'lɪbriəm/ *noun* an imbalance in the economy when supply does not equal demand

dishonoured cheque /dɪsˌɒnəd 'tʃek/ *noun* a cheque which the bank will not pay because there is not enough money in the account to pay it

disinvest /ˌdɪsɪn'vest/ *verb* to reduce investment by not replacing capital assets when they wear out

disinvestment /ˌdɪsɪn'vestmənt/ *noun* a reduction in capital assets by not replacing them when they wear out

dispensation /ˌdɪspen'seɪʃ(ə)n/ *noun* arrangement between an employer and the Inland Revenue by which business expenses paid to an employee are not declared for tax

disposable personal income /dɪˌspəʊzəb(ə)l ˌpɜːs(ə)nəl 'ɪnkʌm/ *noun* the income left after tax and National Insurance have been deducted. Also called **take-home pay**

disposal /dɪ'spəʊz(ə)l/ *noun* a sale ○ *a disposal of securities* ○ *The company has started a systematic disposal of its property portfolio.* □ **lease *or* business for disposal** a lease or business for sale

disposals /dɪ'spəʊz(ə)lz/ *plural noun* assets which have been sold or scrapped

disqualification /dɪsˌkwɒlɪfɪ'keɪʃ(ə)n/ *noun* **1.** the act of making someone disqualified to do something **2.** a court order which forbids a person from being a director of a company. A variety of offences, even those termed as 'administrative', can result in some being disqualified for up to five years.

disqualify /dɪs'kwɒlɪfaɪ/ *verb* to make a person unqualified to do something, such as to be a director of a company

dissolution /ˌdɪsə'luːʃ(ə)n/ *noun* the ending of a partnership

dissolve /dɪ'zɒlv/ *verb* to bring to an end ○ *to dissolve a partnership*

distrain /dɪ'streɪn/ *verb* to seize goods to pay for debts

distress /dɪ'stres/ *noun* the act of taking someone's goods to pay for debts

distress merchandise /dɪ'stres ˌmɜːtʃəndaɪs/ *noun US* goods sold cheaply to pay a company's debts

distress sale /dɪ'stres seɪl/ *noun* a sale of goods at low prices to pay a company's debts

distributable /dɪs'trɪbjʊtəb(ə)l/ *adjective* possible to distribute

distributable profits /dɪsˌtrɪbjʊtəb(ə)l 'prɒfɪts/ *plural noun* profits which can be distributed to shareholders as dividends if the directors decide to do so

distributable reserve /dɪˌstrɪbjʊtb(ə)l rɪ'zɜːv/ *noun* a reserve fund that is able to be distributed to shareholders in the form of dividends

distribute /dɪ'strɪbjuːt/ *verb* **1.** to share out dividends ○ *Profits were distributed among the shareholders.* **2.** to send out goods from a manufacturer's warehouse to retail shops ○ *Smith Ltd distributes for several smaller companies.* ○ *All orders are distributed from our warehouse near Oxford.*

distributed profits /dɪˌstrɪbjʊtɪd ˈprɒfɪts/ *plural noun* profits passed to shareholders in the form of dividends

distribution /ˌdɪstrɪˈbjuːʃ(ə)n/ *noun* the act of sending goods from the manufacturer to the wholesaler and then to retailers ○ *Stock is held in a distribution centre which deals with all order processing.* ○ *Distribution costs have risen sharply over the last 18 months.* ○ *She has several years' experience as distribution manager.*

'British distribution companies are poised to capture a major share of the European market' [*Management News*]

distribution cost /ˌdɪstrɪˈbjuːʃ(ə)n ˌkɒst/, **distribution expense** /ˌdɪstrɪ ˈbjuːʃ(ə)n ɪkˌspens/, **distribution overhead** /ˌdɪstrɪˈbjuːʃ(ə)n ˌəʊvəhed/ *noun* expenditure involved in warehousing, packing and sending products for sale

distribution network /ˌdɪstrɪˈbjuːʃ(ə)n ˌnetwɜːk/ *noun* a series of points or small warehouses from which goods are sent all over a country

distribution of income /ˌdɪstrɪbjuːʃ(ə)n əv ˈɪnkʌm/ *noun* the payment of dividends to shareholders

distributor /dɪˈstrɪbjʊtə/ *noun* a company which sells goods for another company which makes them

distributorship /dɪˈstrɪbjʊtəʃɪp/ *noun* the position of being a distributor for a company

District Bank /ˌdɪstrɪkt ˈbæŋk/ *noun* one of the 12 US banks that make up the Federal Reserve System. Each District Bank is responsible for all banking activity in its area.

diversification /daɪˌvɜːsɪfɪˈkeɪʃ(ə)n/ *noun* the process in which a company begins to engage in a new and different type of business

diversify /daɪˈvɜːsɪfaɪ/ *verb* **1.** to add new types of business to existing ones ○ *The company is planning to diversify into new products.* **2.** to invest in different types of shares or savings so as to spread the risk of loss

divestiture /daɪˈvestɪtʃə/ *noun* the sale of an asset

dividend /ˈdɪvɪdend/ *noun* **1.** a percentage of profits paid to shareholders □ **to raise** *or* **increase the dividend** to pay out a higher dividend than in the previous year □ **to omit** *or* **pass the dividend** to pay no dividend **2.** a number or quantity that is to be divided by another number or quantity

dividend check /ˈdɪvɪdend tʃek/ *noun* US same as **dividend warrant**

dividend cover /ˈdɪvɪdend ˌkʌvə/ *noun* the ratio of profits to dividends paid to shareholders

dividend forecast /ˈdɪvɪdend ˌfɔːkɑːst/ *noun* a forecast of the amount of an expected dividend

dividend growth model /ˌdɪvɪdend grəʊθ ˈmɒd(ə)l/ *noun* a financial model that assesses the value of a company using figures for its current and assumed future dividend payments

dividend mandate /ˈdɪvɪdend ˌmændeɪt/ *noun* authorisation by a shareholder to the company, to pay his or her dividends directly into a bank account

dividend payout /ˈdɪvɪdend ˌpeɪaʊt/ *noun* money paid as dividends to shareholders

dividend per share /ˌdɪvɪdend pə ˈʃeə/ *noun* an amount of money paid as dividend for each share held

dividend warrant /ˈdɪvɪdend ˌwɒrənt/ *noun* a cheque which makes payment of a dividend (NOTE: The US term is **dividend check**.)

dividend yield /ˈdɪvɪdend jiːld/ *noun* a dividend expressed as a percentage of the current market price of a share

dividend yield basis /ˈdɪvɪdend jiːld ˌbeɪsɪs/ *noun* a method of valuing shares in a company, by which the dividend per share is divided by the expected dividend yield

divisional headquarters /dɪˌvɪʒ(ə)nəl hedˈkwɔːtəz/ *plural noun* the main office of a division of a company

divisor /dɪˈvaɪzə/ *noun* a number divided into another number

document /ˈdɒkjʊmənt/ *noun* a paper, especially an official paper, with written information on it ○ *He left a file of documents in the taxi.* ○ *She asked to see the documents relating to the case.*

documentary /ˌdɒkjʊˈment(ə)ri/ *adjective* in the form of documents ○ *documentary evidence*

documentary credit /ˌdɒkjʊment(ə)ri ˈkredɪt/ *noun* a credit document used in export trade, when a bank issues a letter of credit against shipping documents

documentation /ˌdɒkjʊmenˈteɪʃ(ə)n/ *noun* all the documents referring to something ○ *Please send me the complete documentation concerning the sale.*

dollar /ˈdɒlə/ *noun* a unit of currency used in the US and other countries such as Australia, Bahamas, Barbados, Bermuda, Brunei, Canada, Fiji, Hong Kong, Jamaica, New Zealand, Singapore and Zimbabwe ○ *The US dollar rose 2%.* ○ *They sent a cheque for fifty Canadian dollars.* ○ *It costs six Australian dollars.*

dollar area /ˈdɒlər ˌeəriə/ *noun* an area of the world where the US dollar is the main trading currency

dollar balances /ˈdɒlə ˌbælənsɪz/ *plural noun* a country's trade balances expressed in US dollars

dollar-cost averaging /ˌdɒlər kɒst ˈæv(ə)rɪdʒɪŋ/ *noun* ♦ **pound-cost averaging**

dollar crisis /ˈdɒlə ˌkraɪsɪs/ *noun* a fall in the exchange rate for the US dollar

dollar gap /ˌdɒlə ˈgæp/ *noun* a situation where the supply of US dollars is not enough to satisfy the demand for them from overseas buyers

dollar millionaire /ˌdɒlə ˌmɪljəˈneə/ *noun* a person who has more than one million dollars

dollar stocks /ˌdɒlə ˈstɒks/ *plural noun* shares in US companies

domestic production /dəˌmestɪk prə ˈdʌkʃən/ *noun* the production of goods for use in the home country

domicile /ˈdɒmɪsaɪl/ *noun* the country where someone lives or where a company's office is registered ■ *verb* □ **she is domiciled in Denmark** she lives in Denmark officially

donation /dəʊˈneɪʃ(ə)n/ *noun* a gift, especially to a charity

donee /ˌdəʊˈniː/ *noun* a person who receives a gift from a donor

donor /ˈdəʊnə/ *noun* a person who gives, especially someone who gives money

dormant /ˈdɔːmənt/ *adjective* no longer active or no longer operating

dormant account /ˌdɔːmənt əˈkaʊnt/ *noun* a bank account which is no longer used

dormant company /ˌdɔːmənt ˈkʌmp(ə)ni/ *noun* company which has not made any transactions during an accounting period

dot.com /ˌdɒt ˈkɒm/, **dot-com** /ˌdɒt ˈkɒm/ *noun* a business that markets its products through the Internet, rather than by using traditional marketing channels

double-entry bookkeeping /ˌdʌb(ə)l ˌentri ˈbʊkiːpɪŋ/ *noun* the most commonly used system of bookkeeping, based on the principle that every financial transac-

tion is accounted for on both the credit and debit side of an account

double taxation /ˌdʌb(ə)l tækˈseɪʃ(ə)n/ *noun* the act of taxing the same income twice

double taxation agreement /ˌdʌb(ə)l tækˈseɪʃ(ə)n əˌgriːmənt/, **double taxation treaty** /ˌdʌb(ə)l tækˈseɪʃ(ə)n ˌtriːti/ *noun* an agreement between two countries that a person living in one country shall not be taxed in both countries on the income earned in the other country

double taxation relief /ˌdʌb(ə)l tæk ˈseɪʃ(ə)n rɪˌliːf/ *noun* a reduction of tax payable in one country by the amount of tax on income, profits or capital gains already paid in another country

doubtful /ˈdaʊtf(ə)l/ *adjective* □ **doubtful debt** a debt which may never be paid □ **doubtful loan** a loan which may never be repaid

doubtful debt provision /ˌdaʊtf(ə)l ˈdet prəˌvɪʒ(ə)n/ *noun* ♦ **bad debt provision**

doubtful loan /ˌdaʊtf(ə)l ˈləʊn/ *noun* a loan which may never be repaid

downgrade /ˈdaʊngreɪd/ *verb* **1.** to reduce the status of an employee or position ○ *The post was downgraded in the company reorganisation.* **2.** to revise an earlier assessment of a company's future financial position, or of the return on an investment, to give a less favourable likely outcome

down payment /ˌdaʊn ˈpeɪmənt/ *noun* part of a total payment made in advance ○ *We made a down payment of $100.*

downside factor /ˈdaʊnsaɪd ˌfæktə/, **downside potential** /ˌdaʊnsaɪd pə ˈtenʃ(ə)l/ *noun* the possibility of making a loss in an investment

downside risk /ˈdaʊnsaɪd rɪsk/ *noun* the risk that an investment will fall in value. Opposite **upside potential**

down time /ˈdaʊn taɪm/ *noun* the time when a machine is not working or not available because it is broken or being mended

downturn /ˈdaʊntɜːn/ *noun* a downward trend in sales or profits ○ *a downturn in the market price* ○ *The last quarter saw a downturn in the economy.*

DPP *abbreviation* direct profit profitability

draft /drɑːft/ *noun* **1.** an order for money to be paid by a bank ○ *We asked for payment by banker's draft.* **2.** a first rough plan or document which has not been finished ○ *The finance depart* ○ *A draft of the contract* or *The draft contract is waiting for the MD's comments.* ○ *He drew up the draft agree-*

ment on the back of an envelope. ■ *verb* to make a first rough plan of a document ○ *to draft a letter* ○ *to draft a contract* ○ *The contract is still being drafted* or *is still in the drafting stage.*

drafting /'drɑːftɪŋ/ *noun* an act of preparing the draft of a document ○ *The drafting of the contract took six weeks.*

drain /dreɪn/ *noun* a gradual loss of money flowing away ○ *The costs of the London office are a continual drain on our resources.* ■ *verb* to remove something gradually ○ *The expansion plan has drained all our profits.* ○ *The company's capital resources have drained away.*

draw /drɔː/ *verb* **1.** to take money away ○ *to draw money out of an account* **2.** to write a cheque ○ *She paid the invoice with a cheque drawn on an Egyptian bank.* (NOTE: **drawing – drew – has drawn**)

draw up *phrasal verb* to write a legal document ○ *to draw up a contract* or *an agreement* ○ *to draw up a company's articles of association*

drawback /'drɔːbæk/ *noun* **1.** something which is not convenient or which is likely to cause problems ○ *One of the main drawbacks of the scheme is that it will take six years to complete.* **2.** a rebate on customs duty for imported goods when these are then used in producing exports

drawdown /'drɔːdaʊn/ *noun* the act of drawing money which is available under a credit agreement

drawee /drɔː'iː/ *noun* the person or bank asked to make a payment by a drawer

drawer /'drɔːə/ *noun* the person who writes a cheque or a bill asking a drawee to pay money to a payee

drawing account /'drɔːɪŋ ə,kaʊnt/ *noun* a current account, or any account from which the customer may take money when he or she wants

drawings /'drɔːɪŋz/ *plural noun* money or trading stock taken by a partner from a partnership, or by a sole trader from his or her business

drawings account /'drɔːɪŋz ə,kaʊnt/ *noun* an account showing amounts drawn by partners in a partnership

drop /drɒp/ *noun* a fall ○ *a drop in sales* ○ *Sales show a drop of 10%.* ○ *The drop in prices resulted in no significant increase in sales.* ■ *verb* to fall ○ *Sales have dropped by 10%* or *have dropped 10%.* ○ *The pound dropped three points against the dollar.*

'…while unemployment dropped by 1.6 per cent in the rural areas, it rose by 1.9 per

cent in urban areas during the period under review' [*Business Times (Lagos)*]

'…corporate profits for the first quarter showed a 4 per cent drop from last year's final three months' [*Financial Times*]

'…since last summer American interest rates have dropped by between three and four percentage points' [*Sunday Times*]

droplock bond /'drɒplɒk bɒnd/ *noun* a floating rate bond which will convert to a fixed rate of interest if interest rates fall to some level. ◊ **debt-convertible bond**

dry goods /,draɪ 'ɡʊdz/ *plural noun* cloth, clothes and household goods

DTI *abbreviation* Department of Trade and Industry

dual currency bond /,djuːəl 'kʌrənsi bɒnd/ *noun* a bond which is paid for in one currency but which is repayable in another on redemption

dual listing /,djuːəl 'lɪstɪŋ/ *noun* the listing of a share on two stock exchanges

dual pricing /,djuːəl 'praɪsɪŋ/ *noun* the practice of setting different prices for a given product in the different market in which it is sold

dual resident /,djuːəl 'rezɪd(ə)nt/ *noun* a person who is legally resident in two countries

dud /dʌd/ *noun, adjective* referring to a coin or banknote that is false or not good, or something that does not do what it is supposed to do (*informal*) ○ *The £50 note was a dud.*

dud cheque /,dʌd 'tʃek/ *noun* a cheque which cannot be cashed because the person writing it does not have enough money in the account to pay it

due /djuː/ *adjective* owed ○ *a sum due from a debtor* □ **to fall** *or* **become due** to be ready for payment

'…many expect the US economic indicators for April, due out this Thursday, to show faster economic growth' [*Australian Financial Review*]

due date /'djuː deɪt/ *noun* the date on which a debt is required to be paid

due diligence /,djuː 'dɪlɪdʒəns/ *noun* the examination of a company's accounts prior to a potential takeover by another organisation. This assessment is often undertaken by an independent third party.

dues /djuːz/ *plural noun* orders taken but not supplied until new stock arrives

dumping /'dʌmpɪŋ/ *noun* the act of getting rid of excess goods cheaply in an overseas market ○ *The government has passed* *anti-dumping legislation.* ○ *Dumping of goods on the European market is banned.*

Dun & Bradstreet /ˌdʌn ən ˈbrædstriːt/ *noun* an organisation which produces reports on the financial rating of companies, and also acts as a debt collection agency. Abbreviation **D&B**

duty /ˈdjuːti/ *noun* a tax that has to be paid ○ *Traders are asking the government to take the duty off alcohol* or *to put a duty on cigarettes.*

'Canadian and European negotiators agreed to a deal under which Canada could lower its import duties on $150 million worth of European goods' [*Globe and Mail (Toronto)*]

'…the Department of Customs and Excise collected a total of N79m under the new advance duty payment scheme' [*Business Times (Lagos)*]

duty-free /ˌdjuːti ˈfriː/ *adjective, adverb* sold with no duty to be paid ○ *She bought duty-free perfume at the airport.* ○ *He bought the watch duty-free.*

duty-paid goods /ˌdjuːti ˈpeɪd gʊdz/ *plural noun* goods where the duty has been paid

E

e- /iː/ *prefix* referring to electronics or the Internet

EAA *abbreviation* European Accounting Association

e. & o.e. *abbreviation* errors and omissions excepted

early withdrawal /ˌɜːli wɪð'drɔːəl/ *noun* the act of withdrawing money from a deposit account before the due date ○ *Early withdrawal usually incurs a penalty.*

earmark /'ɪəmɑːk/ *verb* to reserve for a special purpose ○ *to earmark funds for a project* ○ *The grant is earmarked for computer systems development.*

earn /ɜːn/ *verb* **1.** to be paid money for working ○ *to earn £100 a week* ○ *How much do you earn in your new job?* **2.** to produce interest or dividends ○ *a building society account which earns interest at 10%* ○ *What level of dividend do these shares earn?*

earned income /ˌɜːnd 'ɪnkʌm/ *noun* income from wages, salaries, pensions, fees, rental income, etc., as opposed to 'unearned' income from investments

earnest /'ɜːnɪst/ *noun* money paid as an initial payment by a buyer to a seller, to show commitment to the contract of sale

earning capacity /'ɜːnɪŋ kəˌpæsɪti/, **earning power** /'ɜːnɪŋ ˌpaʊə/ *noun* the amount of money someone should be able to earn

earning potential /'ɜːnɪŋ pəˌtenʃəl/ *noun* **1.** the amount of money a person should be able to earn in his or her professional capacity **2.** the amount of dividend which a share is capable of earning

earning power /'ɜːnɪŋ ˌpaʊə/ *noun* the amount of money someone should be able to earn ○ *She is such a fine designer that her earning power is very large.*

earnings /'ɜːnɪŋz/ *plural noun* **1.** salary, wages, dividends or interest received ○ *High earnings in top management reflect the heavy responsibilities involved.* ○ *The cal-*

culation is based on average earnings over three years. **2.** the profit made by a company

'…the US now accounts for more than half of our world-wide sales. It has made a huge contribution to our earnings turnaround' [*Duns Business Month*]

'…last fiscal year the chain reported a 116% jump in earnings, to $6.4 million or $1.10 a share' [*Barrons*]

earnings before interest, taxes, depreciation and amortisation /ˌɜːnɪŋz bɪˌfɔː ˌɪntrəst ˌtæksɪz dɪ ˌpriːʃieɪʃ(ə)n ənd əˌmɔːtaɪ'zeɪʃ(ə)n/ *plural noun* the earnings generated by a business's fundamental operating performance, frequently used in accounting ratios for comparison with other companies. Interest on borrowings, tax payable on those profits, depreciation, and amortisation are excluded on the basis that they can distort the underlying performance. Abbreviation **EBITDA**

earnings before interest and tax /ˌɜːnɪŋz bɪˌfɔː 'ɪntrəst ən tæks/ *noun* the amount earned by a business before deductions are made for tax and interest payments. Abbreviation **EBIT**

earnings cap /'ɜːnɪŋz kæp/ *noun* the upper limit on the amount of salary that can be taken into account when calculating pensions

earnings growth /'ɜːnɪŋz grəʊθ/ *noun* an increase in profit per share

earnings performance /'ɜːnɪŋz pə ˌfɔːməns/ *noun* a way in which shares earn dividends

earnings per share /ˌɜːnɪŋz pə 'ʃeə/ *plural noun* the money earned in dividends per share, shown as a percentage of the market price of one share. Abbreviation **EPS**

earnings-related contributions /ˌɜːnɪŋz rɪˌleɪtɪd ˌkɒntrɪ'bjuːʃ(ə)nz/ *plural noun* contributions to social security which rise as the employee's earnings rise

earnings-related pension /ˌɜːnɪŋz rɪ ˌleɪtɪd 'penʃən/ *noun* a pension which is linked to the size of a person's salary

earnings surprises /'ɜːnɪŋz sə‚praɪzɪz/ *plural noun* an announced income level for a company that is significantly higher or lower than that forecast by analysts

earnings yield /'ɜːnɪŋz jiːld/ *noun* the money earned in dividends per share as a percentage of the current market price of the share

ease /iːz/ *verb* to fall a little ○ *The share index eased slightly today.*

easy market /‚iːzi 'mɑːkɪt/ *noun* a market where few people are buying, so prices are lower than they were before

easy money /‚iːzi 'mʌni/ *noun* **1.** money which can be earned with no difficulty **2.** a loan available on easy repayment terms

easy money policy /‚iːzi 'mʌni ‚pɒlɪsi/ *noun* a government policy of expanding the economy by making money more easily available, e.g. through lower interest rates and easy access to credit

easy terms /‚iːzi 'tɜːmz/ *plural noun* financial terms which are not difficult to accept ○ *The shop is let on very easy terms.*

EBIT /'iːbɪt/ *abbreviation* earnings before interest and tax

EBITDA /'iːbɪt‚dɑː/ *abbreviation* earnings before interest, taxes, depreciation and amortisation

EBRD *abbreviation* European Bank for Reconstruction and Development

e-business /'iː ‚bɪznɪs/ *noun* a general term that refers to any type of business activity on the Internet, including marketing, branding and research ○ *E-business is a rising part of the economy.*

'…the enormous potential of e-business is that it can automate the link between suppliers and customers' [*Investors Chronicle*]

ECB *abbreviation* European Central Bank

ECGD *abbreviation* Export Credit Guarantee Department

e-commerce /‚iː 'kɒmɜːs/ *noun* a general term that is usually used to refer to the process of buying and selling goods over the Internet

'…the problem is that if e-commerce takes just a 3 per cent slice of the market that would be enough to reduce margins to ribbons' [*Investors Chronicle*]

'…the new economy requires new company structures. He believes that other blue-chip organizations are going to find that new set-ups would be needed to attract and retain the best talent for e-commerce' [*Times*]

econometrics /ɪ‚kɒnə'metrɪks/ *noun* the study of the statistics of economics, using computers to analyse these statistics and make forecasts using mathematical models

economic /‚iːkə'nɒmɪk/ *adjective* **1.** providing enough money to make a profit ○ *The flat is let at an economic rent.* ○ *It is hardly economic for the company to run its own warehouse.* **2.** referring to the financial state of a country ○ *economic trends* ○ *Economic planners are expecting a consumer-led boom.* ○ *The economic situation is getting worse.* ○ *The country's economic system needs more regulation.*

'…each of the major issues on the agenda at this week's meeting is important to the government's success in overall economic management' [*Australian Financial Review*]

economical /‚iːkə'nɒmɪk(ə)l/ *adjective* saving money or materials or being less expensive ○ *This car is very economical.* □ **an economical use of resources** the fact of using resources as carefully as possible

Economic and Monetary Union /‚iːkənɒmɪk ən ‚mʌnɪt(ə)ri 'juːnjən/ *noun* same as **European Monetary Union**

economic crisis /‚iːkənɒmɪk 'kraɪsɪs/, **economic depression** /‚iːkənɒmɪk dɪ'preʃ(ə)n/ *noun* a situation where a country is in financial collapse ○ *The government has introduced import controls to solve the current economic crisis.*

economic cycle /‚iːkənɒmɪk 'saɪk(ə)l/ *noun* a period during which trade expands, then slows down and then expands again

economic development /‚iːkənɒmɪk dɪ'veləpmənt/ *noun* improvements in the living standards and wealth of the citizens of a country ○ *The government has offered tax incentives to speed up the economic development of the region.* ○ *Economic development has been relatively slow in the north, compared with the rest of the country.*

economic forecaster /‚iːkənɒmɪk 'fɔːkɑːstə/ *noun* a person who says how he or she thinks a country's economy will perform in the future

economic growth /‚iːkənɒmɪk 'grəʊθ/ *noun* the rate at which a country's national income grows

economic life /‚iːkənɒmɪk 'laɪf/ *noun* the extent of trade and manufacturing in a country, regarded as a measure of its relative prosperity

economic model /‚iːkənɒmɪk 'mɒd(ə)l/ *noun* a computerised plan of a country's economic system, used for forecasting economic trends

economic order quantity /ˌiːkənɒmɪk ˈɔːdə ˌkwɒntɪti/ *noun* the quantity of stocks which a company should hold, calculated on the basis of the costs of warehousing, of lower unit costs because of higher quantities purchased, the rate at which stocks are used, and the time it takes for suppliers to deliver new orders. Abbreviation **EOQ**

economic planning /ˌiːkənɒmɪk ˈplænɪŋ/ *noun* plans made by a government for the future financial state of a country

economics /ˌiːkəˈnɒmɪks/ *noun* the study of the production, distribution, selling and use of goods and services ■ *plural noun* the study of financial structures to show how a product or service is costed and what returns it produces ○ *I do not understand the economics of the coal industry.* (NOTE: [all senses] takes a singular verb)

economic sanctions /ˌiːkənɒmɪk ˈsæŋkʃ(ə)nz/ *plural noun* restrictions on trade that foreign governments impose with the aim of influencing the political situation of a country ○ *to impose economic sanctions on a country*

economic stagnation /ˌiːkənɒmɪk stægˈneɪʃ(ə)n/ *noun* a lack of expansion in the economy

economic value added /ˌiːkənɒmɪk ˌvæljuː ˈædɪd/ *noun* a way of judging financial performance by measuring the amount by which the earnings of a project, an operation or a company exceed or fall short of the total amount of capital that was originally invested by its owners. Abbreviation **EVA**

economies of scale /ɪˌkɒnəmiz əv ˈskeɪl/ *plural noun* the cost advantages of a company producing a product in larger quantities so that each unit costs less to make. Compare **diseconomies of scale**

economies of scope /ɪˌkɒnəmiz əv ˈskəʊp/ *plural noun* the cost advantages of a company producing a number of products or engaging in a number of profitable activities that use the same technology

economist /ɪˈkɒnəmɪst/ *noun* a person who specialises in the study of economics ○ *Government economists are forecasting a growth rate of 3% next year.* ○ *An agricultural economist studies the economics of the agriculture industry.*

economy /ɪˈkɒnəmi/ *noun* **1.** an action which is intended to stop money or materials from being wasted, or the quality of being careful not to waste money or materials □ **to**

introduce economies *or* **economy measures into the system** to start using methods to save money or materials **2.** the financial state of a country, or the way in which a country makes and uses its money ○ *The country's economy is in ruins.*

economy drive /ɪˈkɒnəmi draɪv/ *noun* a vigorous effort to save money or materials

ECP *abbreviation* Eurocommercial paper

ecu /ˈekjuː/, **ECU** *abbreviation* European Currency Unit

ED *abbreviation* exposure draft

EDI *abbreviation* electronic data interchange

EEA *abbreviation* European Economic Area

effect /ɪˈfekt/ *noun* **1.** a result ○ *The effect of the pay increase was to raise productivity levels.* **2.** an operation □ **terms of a contract which take effect** *or* **come into effect from January 1st** terms which start to operate on January 1st **3.** meaning □ **a clause to the effect that** a clause which means that ■ *verb* to carry out

effective /ɪˈfektɪv/ *adjective* **1.** actual, as opposed to theoretical **2.** □ **a clause effective as from January 1st** a clause which starts to be applied on January 1st **3.** producing results ○ *Advertising in the Sunday papers is the most effective way of selling.* ○ *She is an effective marketing manager.* ◊ **cost-effective**

effective annual rate /ɪˌfektɪv ˌænjuəl ˈreɪt/ *noun* the average interest rate paid on a deposit for a period of a year. It is the total interest received over 12 months expressed as a percentage of the principal at the beginning of the period.

effective date /ɪˈfektɪv deɪt/ *noun* the date on which a rule or contract starts to be applied, or on which a transaction takes place

effective demand /ɪˌfektɪv dɪˈmɑːnd/ *noun* demand for a product made by individuals and institutions with sufficient wealth pay for it

effective exchange rate /ɪˌfektɪv ɪks ˈtʃeɪndʒ ˌreɪt/ *noun* a rate of exchange for a currency calculated against a basket of currencies

effective price /ɪˌfektɪv ˈpraɪs/ *noun* a share price which has been adjusted to allow for a rights issue

effective rate /ɪˌfektɪv ˈreɪt/ *noun* the real interest rate on a loan or deposit, i.e., the APR

effective tax rate /ɪˌfektɪv 'tæks ˌreɪt/ *noun* the average tax rate applicable to a given transaction, whether it is income from work undertaken, the sale of an asset, or a gift, taking into account personal allowances and scales of tax. It is the amount of money generated by the transaction divided by the additional tax payable because of it.

effective yield /ɪˌfektɪv 'jiːld/ *noun* actual yield shown as a percentage of the price paid after adjustments have been made

efficiency ratio /ɪ'fɪʃ(ə)nsi 'reɪʃiəʊ/ *noun* a measure of the efficiency of a business, expressed as expenditure divided by revenue

efficiency variance /ɪ'fɪʃ(ə)nsi ˌveəriəns/ *noun* the discrepancy between the actual cost of making a product and the standard cost

Efficient Market Hypothesis /ɪˌfɪʃ(ə)nt 'mɑːkɪt haɪˌpɒθəsɪs/, **Efficient Markets Hypothesis** /ɪˌfɪʃ(ə)nt 'mɑːkɪts haɪˌpɒθəsɪs/ *noun* the hypothesis that all relevant information is immediately reflected in the price of a security. Abbreviation **EMH**

EFT *abbreviation* electronic funds transfer

EFTA *abbreviation* European Free Trade Association

EFTPOS /'eftpɒz/ *abbreviation* electronic funds transfer at point of sale

EIB *abbreviation* European Investment Bank

eighty/twenty law /ˌeɪti 'twenti ruːl/, **80/20 law** *noun* the rule that a small percentage of customers may account for a large percentage of sales. ◊ **Pareto's Law**

EIS *abbreviation* Enterprise Investment Scheme

elastic /ɪ'læstɪk/ *adjective* able to expand or contract easily because of small changes in price

elasticity /ˌɪlæ'stɪsɪti/ *noun* the ability to change easily in response to a change in circumstances

eldercare /'eldəkeə/ *noun* assurance services sold to elderly people and their families

-elect /ɪlekt/ *suffix* referring to a person who has been elected but has not yet started the term of office

electronic banking /ˌelektrɒnɪk 'bæŋkɪŋ/ *noun* the use of computers to carry out banking transactions such as withdrawals through cash dispensers or transfer of funds at point of sale

electronic data interchange /ˌelektrɒnɪk 'deɪtə ˌɪntətʃeɪndʒ/ *noun* a standard format used when business documents such as invoices and purchase orders are exchanged over electronic networks such as the Internet. Abbreviation **EDI**

electronic funds transfer /ˌelektrɒnɪk 'fʌndz ˌtrænsfɜː/ *noun* the system used by banking organisations for the movement of funds between accounts and for the provision of services to the customer. Abbreviation **EFT**

electronic funds transfer at point of sale /ˌelektrɒnɪk ˌfʌndz ˌtrænsfɜː ət ˌpɔɪnt əv 'seɪl/ *noun* the payment for goods or services by a bank customer using a card that is swiped through an electronic reader on the till, thereby transferring the cash from the customer's account to the retailer's or service provider's account. Abbreviation **EFTPOS**

Electronic Lodgement Service /ˌelektrɒnɪk 'lɒdʒmənt ˌsɜːvɪs/ *noun* a British system for filing your tax return electronically. Abbreviation **ELS**

electronic point of sale /ˌelektrɒnɪk ˌpɔɪnt əv 'seɪl/ *noun* a system where sales are charged automatically to a customer's credit card and stock is controlled by the shop's computer. Abbreviation **EPOS**

electronic version of the tax return /ˌelektrɒnɪk ˌvɜːʃ(ə)n əv ðə 'tæks rɪˌtɜːn/ *noun* a method of making an individual's tax return using email. Abbreviation **EVR**

ELS *abbreviation* Electronic Lodgement Service

email /'iːmeɪl/, **e-mail** *noun* **1.** a system of sending messages from one computer terminal to another, using a modem and telephone lines ○ *You can contact me by phone or email if you want.* **2.** a message sent electronically ○ *I had six emails from him today.* ■ *verb* to send a message from one computer to another, using a modem and telephone lines ○ *She emailed her order to the warehouse.* ○ *I emailed him about the meeting.*

embargo /ɪm'bɑːgəʊ/ *noun* **1.** a government order which stops a type of trade □ **to impose** *or* **put an embargo on trade with a country** to say that trade with a country must not take place ○ *The government has put an embargo on the export of computer equipment.* **2.** a period of time during which specific information in a press release must not be published (NOTE: The plural is **embargoes**.) ■ *verb* **1.** to stop trade, or not to allow something to be traded ○ *The government has embargoed trade with countries that are in breach of international agreements.* **2.** not to allow publication of information for a period of time ○ *The news of the merger has been embargoed until next Wednesday.*

embezzle /ɪm'bez(ə)l/ *verb* to use illegally money which is not yours, or which you are looking after for someone ○ *He was sent to prison for six months for embezzling his clients' money.*

embezzlement /ɪm'bez(ə)lmənt/ *noun* the act of embezzling ○ *He was sent to prison for six months for embezzlement.*

embezzler /ɪm'bez(ə)lə/ *noun* a person who embezzles

EMH *abbreviation* Efficient Market Hypothesis

emoluments /ɪ'mɒljʊmənts/ *plural noun* pay, salary or fees, or the earnings of directors who are not employees (NOTE: US English uses the singular **emolument**.)

employed /ɪm'plɔɪd/ *adjective* **1.** in regular paid work **2.** referring to money used profitably ■ *plural noun* people who are working ○ *the employers and the employed*

employee /ɪm'plɔɪiː/ *noun* a person employed by another ○ *Employees of the firm are eligible to join a profit-sharing scheme.* ○ *Relations between management and employees are good.* ○ *The company has decided to take on new employees.*

'…companies introducing robotics think it important to involve individual employees in planning their introduction' [*Economist*]

employee contribution /ɪm,plɔɪiː ,kɒntrɪ'bjuːʃ(ə)n/ *noun* a contribution paid by an employee towards his or her pension

employee share ownership plan /ɪm ,plɔɪiː 'ʃeər ,əʊnəʃɪp ,plæn/, **employee share ownership programme** /ɪm,plɔɪiː 'ʃeər ,əʊnəʃɪp ,prəʊgræm/, **employee share scheme** /ɪm,plɔɪiː 'ʃeə ,skiːm/ *noun* a plan which allows employees to obtain shares in the company for which they work, though tax may be payable if the shares are sold to employees at a price which is lower than the current market price. Abbreviation **ESOP**

employer /ɪm'plɔɪə/ *noun* a person or company that has regular employees and pays them

employer's contribution /ɪm,plɔɪəz ,kɒntrɪ'bjuːʃ(ə)n/ *noun* money paid by an employer towards an employee's pension

employers' liability insurance /ɪm ,plɔɪəz ,laɪə'bɪlɪti ɪn,ʃʊərəns/ *noun* insurance to cover accidents which may happen at work, and for which the company may be responsible

employment contract /ɪm,plɔɪmənt 'kɒntrækt/ *noun* same as **contract of employment**

employment income /ɪm'plɔɪmənt ,ɪnkʌm/ *noun* money received from an employer, e.g. salary, fees, commission, bonus, fringe benefits

EMS *abbreviation* European Monetary System

EMU *abbreviation* **1.** Economic and Monetary Union **2.** European Monetary Union

encash /ɪn'kæʃ/ *verb* to cash a cheque, to exchange a cheque for cash

encashable /ɪn'kæʃəb(ə)l/ *adjective* possible to cash

encashment /ɪn'kæʃmənt/ *noun* an act of exchanging something for cash

encumbrance /ɪn'kʌmbrəns/ *noun* a liability which is attached usually to a property or land, e.g. a mortgage or charge

endorse /ɪn'dɔːs/ *verb* to say that a product is good □ **to endorse a bill** *or* **a cheque** to sign a bill or cheque on the back to show that you accept it

endorsee /,endɔː'siː/ *noun* a person whose name is written on a bill or cheque as having the right to cash it

endorsement /ɪn'dɔːsmənt/ *noun* **1.** the act of endorsing **2.** a signature on a document which endorses it **3.** a note on an insurance policy which adds conditions to the policy

endorser /ɪn'dɔːsə/ *noun* a person who endorses a bill or cheque which is then paid to him or her

endowment /ɪn'daʊmənt/ *noun* the act of giving money to provide a regular income

endowment assurance /ɪn'daʊmənt ə ,ʃʊərəns/, **endowment insurance** /ɪn 'daʊmənt ɪn,ʃʊərəns/ *noun* an insurance policy where a sum of money is paid to the insured person on a specific date or to his heirs if he dies before that date

endowment mortgage /ɪn'daʊmənt ,mɔːgɪdʒ/ *noun* a mortgage in which the initial sum borrowed is repaid at the end of the loan term by the proceeds of an insurance policy linked to it

endowment policy /ɪn'daʊmənt ,pɒlɪsi/ *noun* same as **endowment assurance**

end product /,end 'prɒdʌkt/ *noun* a manufactured product resulting from a production process

energy costs /'enədʒi kɒsts/ *plural noun* costs of gas, electricity, etc., as shown in accounts

enforce /ɪnˈfɔːs/ *verb* to make sure something is done or that a rule is obeyed ○ *to enforce the terms of a contract*

enforcement /ɪnˈfɔːsmənt/ *noun* the act of making sure that something is obeyed ○ *enforcement of the terms of a contract*

engagement /ɪnˈgeɪdʒmənt/ *noun* an agreement to do something

engagement letter /ɪnˈgeɪdʒmənt ˌletə/ *noun* a letter, usually required by professional standards, sent by an accountant to a client setting out the work the accountant is to do and further administrative matters, such as any limit on the accountant's liability

entail /ɪnˈteɪl/ *noun* a legal condition which passes ownership of a property only to some specific persons

enterprise /ˈentəpraɪz/ *noun* **1.** a system of carrying on a business **2.** a business

enterprise accounting /ˈentəpraɪz əˌkaʊntɪŋ/ *noun* accounts prepared for the whole of a business, not merely for a department or other subdivisions

Enterprise Investment Scheme /ˌentəpraɪz ɪnˈvestmənt skiːm/ *noun* a scheme which provides income and capital gains tax relief for people prepared to risk investing in a single unquoted or AIM-listed trading company. Abbreviation **EIS**

enterprise resource planning /ˈentəpraɪz rɪˌzɔːs ˌplænɪŋ/ *noun* a sophisticated computerised management system that connects multiple business operations, e.g. personnel, the financial accounting system, production and distribution, and can also connect the business with its suppliers and customers. Abbreviation **ERP**

enterprise zone /ˈentəpraɪz zəʊn/ *noun* an area of the country where businesses are encouraged to develop by offering special conditions such as easy planning permission for buildings or a reduction in the business rate

entertainment allowance /ˌentəˈteɪnmənt əˌlaʊəns/ *noun* an amount of money set aside by a company for entertaining clients and visitors

entertainment expenses /ˌentəˈteɪnmənt ɪkˌspensɪz/ *plural noun* money spent on giving meals to business visitors

entitle /ɪnˈtaɪt(ə)l/ *verb* to give the right to someone to have something ○ *After one year's service the employee is entitled to four weeks' holiday.*

entitlement /ɪnˈtaɪt(ə)lmənt/ *noun* a person's right to something

entity /ˈentɪti/ *noun* a single separate body or organisation

entity accounting /ˈentɪti əˌkaʊntɪŋ/ *noun* a form of accounting in which accounts are prepared for an entity which is smaller than or distinct from a company, e.g. for a branch or a particular activity

entrepreneur /ˌɒntrəprəˈnɜː/ *noun* a person who is willing to take commercial risks by starting or financing commercial enterprises

entrepreneurial /ˌɒntrəprəˈnɜːriəl/ *adjective* taking commercial risks ○ *an entrepreneurial decision*

entry /ˈentri/ *noun* **1.** an item of written information put in an accounts ledger (NOTE: The plural is **entries**.) **2.** an act of going in or the place where you can go in ○ *to pass a customs entry point* ○ *entry of goods under bond*

entry price /ˈentri praɪs/ *noun* the replacement cost of an asset recorded in an account

entry value /ˈentri ˌvæljuː/ *noun* replacement cost, the cost of replacing an asset already bought or a service already received and accounted for

environmental accounting /ɪnˌvaɪrənment(ə)l əˈkaʊntɪŋ/ *noun* the practice of including the indirect costs and benefits of a product or activity, e.g. its environmental effects on health and the economy, along with its direct costs when making business decisions

environmental reporting /ɪnˌvaɪrən ˈment(ə)l rɪˌpɔːtɪŋ/ *noun* the process in which a UK company reports on its use of resources and its generation and disposal of waste to the Department for Environment, Food and Rural Affairs

EOQ *abbreviation* economic order quantity

epos /ˈiːpɒs/, **EPOS**, **EPoS** *abbreviation* electronic point of sale

EPS *abbreviation* earnings per share

equal /ˈiːkwəl/ *adjective* exactly the same ○ *Male and female employees have equal pay.* ■ *verb* to be the same as ○ *Production this month has equalled our best month ever.* (NOTE: **equalling – equalled**. The US spelling is **equaling – equaled**.)

equalise /ˈiːkwəlaɪz/, **equalize** *verb* to make equal ○ *to equalise dividends*

equally /ˈiːkwəli/ *adverb* so that each has or pays the same, or to the same degree ○ *Costs will be shared equally between the two parties.* ○ *They were both equally responsible for the disastrous launch.*

equate /ɪ'kweɪt/ *verb* to reduce to a standard value

equation /ɪ'kweɪʒ(ə)n/ *noun* a set of mathematical rules applied to solve a problem ○ *The basic accounting equation is that assets equal liabilities plus equity.*

equilibrium /ˌiːkwɪ'lɪbriəm/ *noun* the state of balance in the economy where supply equals demand or a country's balance of payments is neither in deficit nor in excess

equities /'ekwɪtiz/ *plural noun* ordinary shares

'…in the past three years commercial property has seriously underperformed equities and dropped out of favour as a result' [*Investors Chronicle*]

equity /'ekwɪti/ *noun* **1.** the right to receive dividends from the profit of a company in which shares are owned **2.** the value of a company that is the property of its shareholders, calculated as the value of the company's assets minus the value of its liabilities, not including the ordinary share capital **3.** the value of an asset minus any loans outstanding on it **4.** a fair system of laws, the system of British law which developed in parallel with the common law to make the common law fairer, summarised in the maxim 'equity does not suffer a wrong to be without a remedy'

equity accounting /'ekwɪti əˌkaʊntɪŋ/ *noun* a method of accounting which puts part of the profits of a subsidiary into the parent company's books

equity capital /'ekwɪti ˌkæpɪt(ə)l/ *noun* the nominal value of the shares owned by the ordinary shareholders of a company (NOTE: Preference shares are not equity capital. If the company were wound up, none of the equity capital would be distributed to preference shareholders.)

equity dividend cover /ˌekwɪti 'dɪvɪdend ˌkʌvə/ *noun* an accounting ratio, calculated by dividing the distributable profits during a given period by the actual dividend paid in that period, that indicates the likelihood of the dividend being maintained in future years. ◊ **capital reserves**

equity finance /'ekwɪti ˌfaɪnæns/ *noun* finance for a company in the form of ordinary shares paid for by shareholders

equity gearing /'ekwɪti ˌgɪərɪŋ/ *noun* the ratio between a company's borrowings at interest and its ordinary share capital

equity kicker /'ekwɪti ˌkɪkə/ *noun US* an incentive given to people to lend a company money, in the form of a warrant to share in future earnings (NOTE: The UK term is **equity sweetener**.)

equity share capital /ˌekwɪti 'ʃeə ˌkæpɪt(ə)l/ *noun* a company's issued share capital less capital which carries preferential rights. Equity share capital normally comprises ordinary shares.

equity sweetener /'ekwɪti ˌswiːt(ə)nə/ *noun* an incentive to encourage people to lend a company money, in the form of a warrant giving the right to buy shares at a later date and at an agreed price

equivalence /ɪ'kwɪvələns/ *noun* the condition of having the same value or of being the same

equivalent /ɪ'kwɪvələnt/ *noun* a person who is the equal of someone else

equivalent production /ɪˌkwɪvələnt prə'dʌkʃən/ *noun* a way of measuring units produced by a company that combines parts of units produced into whole-unit equivalents

equivalent taxable yield /ɪˌkwɪvələnt ˌtæksəb(ə)l 'jiːld/ *noun* the level of taxable investment required to provide the same return as some other form of investment

equivalent unit /ɪˌkwɪvələnt 'juːnɪt/ *noun* a unit of unfinished production calculated for valuation purposes when work started during the period is not finished at the end of the period, or when work started during the previous period is finished during the current period

ERP *abbreviation* enterprise resource planning

errors and omissions excepted /ˌerəz ənd əʊˌmɪʃ(ə)nz ɪk'septɪd/ *phrase* words written on an invoice to show that the company has no responsibility for mistakes in the invoice. Abbreviation **e. & o.e.**

ESC *abbreviation* European Social Charter

escalate /'eskəleɪt/ *verb* to increase steadily

escalator clause /'eskəleɪtə klɔːz/, **escalation clause** *noun* a clause in a contract allowing for regular price increases because of increased costs, or regular wage increases because of the increased cost of living

escape clause /ɪ'skeɪp klɔːz/ *noun* a clause in a contract which allows one of the parties to avoid carrying out the terms of the contract under conditions

escrow /'eskrəʊ/ *noun US* an agreement between two parties that something should be held by a third party until conditions are fulfilled

escrow account /ˈeskrəʊ əˌkaʊnt/ *noun US* an account where money is held in escrow until a contract is signed or until goods are delivered

ESOP *abbreviation* employee share ownership plan

establishment /ɪˈstæblɪʃmənt/ *noun* **1.** a commercial business ○ *He runs an important printing establishment.* **2.** the number of people working in a company

establishment charges /ɪˈstæblɪʃmənt ˌtʃɑːdʒɪz/ *plural noun* the cost of people and property in a company's accounts

estate /ɪˈsteɪt/ *noun* property left by a dead person

estate accounting /ɪˈsteɪt əˌkaʊntɪŋ/ *noun* the preparation of financial accounts by the person administering the estate of someone deceased

estate duty /ɪˈsteɪt ˌdjuːti/ *noun* a tax paid on the property left by a dead person (NOTE: now called **inheritance tax**)

estate tax /ɪˈsteɪt tæks/ *noun US* a tax paid on the right to pass property on to heirs, based on the value of the property and paid before it is passed to the heirs

estimate *noun* /ˈestɪmət/ **1.** a calculation of the probable cost, size or time of something ○ *Can you give me an estimate of how much time was spent on the job?* **2.** a calculation by a contractor or seller of a service of how much something is likely to cost, given to a client in advance of an order ○ *You should ask for an estimate before committing yourselves.* ○ *Before we can give the grant we must have an estimate of the total costs involved.* ○ *Unfortunately the final bill was quite different from the estimate.* ■ *verb* /ˈestɪmeɪt/ to calculate the probable cost, size, or time of something ○ *to estimate that it will cost £1m* or *to estimate costs at £1m* ○ *We estimate current sales at only 60% of last year.*

estimated /ˈestɪmeɪtɪd/ *adjective* calculated approximately ○ *estimated sales* ○ *Costs were slightly more than the estimated figure.*

estimated cost /ˈestɪmeɪtɪd kɒst/ *noun* necessary future expenditure that the purchase of something entails, e.g. future running costs or future repairs

estimated liability /ˌestɪmeɪtɪd ˌlaɪə-ˈbɪlɪti/ *noun* a liability that exists but has a cost that can only be estimated as yet, as can any future tax liability

estimation /ˌestɪˈmeɪʃ(ə)n/ *noun* an approximate calculation

estimator /ˈestɪmeɪtə/ *noun* a person whose job is to calculate estimates for carrying out work

EU *abbreviation* European Union ○ *EU ministers met today in Brussels.* ○ *The US is increasing its trade with the EU.*

euro /ˈjʊərəʊ/ *noun* a unit of currency adopted by several European countries for electronic payments in 1999 and then as legal tender from January 1st, 2002 ○ *Many articles are priced in euros.* ○ *What's the exchange rate for the euro?* (NOTE: The plural is **euro** or **euros**. Written **€** before numbers: *€250:* say: 'two hundred and fifty euros'.)

'…cross-border mergers in the European Union have shot up since the introduction of the euro' [*Investors Chronicle*]

Euro- /ˈjʊərəʊ/ *prefix* referring to Europe or the European Union

euro account /ˈjʊərəʊ əˌkaʊnt/ *noun* a bank account in euros

Eurobond /ˈjʊərəʊbɒnd/ *noun* a long-term bearer bond issued by an international corporation or government outside its country of origin and sold to purchasers who pay in a Eurocurrency, sold on the Eurobond market

Eurocheque /ˈjʊərəʊtʃek/ *noun* a cheque which can be cashed in any European bank. The Eurocheque system is based in Brussels.

Eurocommercial paper /ˌjʊərəʊkəmɜːʃ(ə)l ˈpeɪpə/ *noun* a form of short-term borrowing in Eurocurrencies. Abbreviation **ECP**

eurocredit /ˈjʊərəʊˌkredɪt/ *noun* a large bank loan in a Eurocurrency, usually provided by a group of banks to a large commercial undertaking

Eurocurrency /ˈjʊərəʊkʌrənsi/ *noun* any currency used for trade within Europe but outside its country of origin, the Eurodollar being the most important ○ *a Eurocurrency loan* ○ *the Eurocurrency market*

eurodeposit /ˈjʊərəʊdɪˌpɒzɪt/ *noun* a deposit of Eurodollars in a bank outside the US

Eurodollar /ˈjʊərəʊdɒlə/ *noun* a US dollar deposited in a bank outside the US, used mainly for trade within Europe ○ *a Eurodollar loan* ○ *the Eurodollar markets*

euroequity /ˈjʊərəʊˌekwɪti/ *noun* a share in an international company traded on European stock markets outside its country of origin

Euroland /ˈjʊərəʊlænd/ *noun* same as **Eurozone**

euronote /ˈjʊərəʊˌnəʊt/ *noun* a short-term Eurocurrency bearer note

euro-option /ˈjʊərəʊ ˌɒpʃ(ə)n/ *noun* an option to buy European bonds at a later date

Europe /ˈjʊərəp/ *noun* **1.** the continent of Europe, the part of the world to the west of Asia, from Russia to Ireland ○ *Most of the countries of Western Europe are members of the EU.* ○ *Poland is in eastern Europe, and Greece, Spain and Portugal are in southern Europe.* **2.** the European Union, including the UK ○ *Canadian exports to Europe have risen by 25%.*

European /ˌjʊərəˈpiːən/ *adjective* referring to Europe ○ *They do business with several European countries.*

European Accounting Association /ˌjʊərəpiːən əˈkaʊntɪŋ əˌsəʊsieɪʃ(ə)n/ *noun* an organisation for teachers and researchers in accountancy, founded in 1977 and based in Brussels, that aims to be a forum for European research in the subject. Abbreviation **EAA**

European Bank for Reconstruction and Development /ˌjʊərəpiːən bæŋk fə riːkənˌstrʌktʃ(ə)n ən dɪˈveləpmənt/ *noun* a bank, based in London, which channels aid from the EU to Eastern European and Central Asian countries. Abbreviation **EBRD**

European Central Bank /ˌjʊərəpiːən ˌsentrəl ˈbæŋk/ *noun* the central bank for most of the countries in the European Union, those which have accepted European Monetary Union and have the euro as their common currency. Abbreviation **ECB**

'…the ECB begins with some $300 billion of foreign exchange reserves, far more than any other central bank' [*Investors Chronicle*]

'…any change in the European bank's statutes must be agreed and ratified by all EU member nations' [*The Times*]

European Currency Unit /ˌjʊərəpiːən ˈkʌrənsi ˌjuːnɪt/ *noun* the official monetary unit of the European Union from 1979 to 1999. Abbreviation **ECU**

European Economic Area /ˌjʊərəpiːən ˌiːkənɒmɪk ˈeərɪə/ an area comprising the countries of the EU and the members of EFTA, formed by an agreement on trade between the two organisations. Abbreviation **EEA**

European Federation of Accountants /ˌjʊərəpiːən ˌfedəreɪʃ(ə)n əv əˈkaʊntənts/ *noun* the representative organisation for the accountancy profession in Europe

European Financial Reporting Advisory Group /ˌjʊərəˈpiːən faɪˈnænʃ(ə)l rɪˈpɔːtɪŋ/ *noun* a group that advises on the technical assessment of accounting standards in Europe

European Free Trade Association /ˌjʊərəpiːən friː ˈtreɪd əˌsəʊsieɪʃ(ə)n/ *noun* a group of countries (Iceland, Liechtenstein, Norway and Switzerland) formed to encourage freedom of trade between its members, and linked with the EU in the European Economic Area. Abbreviation **EFTA**

European Investment Bank /ˌjʊərəpiːən ɪnˈvestmənt bæŋk/ *noun* a financial institution whose main task is to facilitate regional development within the EU by financing capital projects, modernising or converting undertakings, and developing new activities. Abbreviation **EIB**

European Monetary System /ˌjʊərəpiːən ˈmʌnɪt(ə)ri ˌsɪstəm/ *noun* the first stage of economic and monetary union of the EU, which came into force in March 1979, giving stable, but adjustable, exchange rates. Abbreviation **EMS**

European Monetary Union /ˌjʊərəpiːən ˈmʌnɪt(ə)ri ˌjuːnjən/ *noun* the process by which some of the member states of the EU joined together to adopt the euro as their common currency on 1st January 1999. The euro became legal tender for these member states from 2002. Abbreviation **EMU**

European Social Charter /ˌjʊərəpiːən ˌsəʊʃ(ə)l ˈtʃɑːtə/ *noun* a charter for employees, drawn up by the EU in 1989, by which employees have the right to a fair wage, and to equal treatment for men and women, a safe work environment, training, freedom of association and collective bargaining, provision for disabled workers, freedom of movement from country to country, guaranteed standards of living both for the working population and for retired people. Abbreviation **ESC**. Also called **Social Charter**

European Union /ˌjʊərəpiːən ˈjuːnjən/ *noun* a group of European countries linked together by the Treaty of Rome. Abbreviation **EU**

euroyen /ˈjʊərəʊˌjen/ *noun* a Japanese yen deposited in a European bank and used for trade within Europe

Eurozone /ˈjʊərəʊzəʊn/ *noun* the European countries which use the euro as a common currency, seen as a group. Also called **Euroland**

'…the European Central Bank left the door open yesterday for a cut in Eurozone interest rates' [*Financial Times*]

'…a sustained recovery in the euro will require either a sharp slowdown in US growth or a rise in inflation and interest rates in the Eurozone beyond that already discounted' [*Investors Chronicle*]

EVA *abbreviation* economic value added

evade /ɪ'veɪd/ *verb* to try to avoid something □ **to evade tax** to try illegally to avoid paying tax

evaluate /ɪ'væljueɪt/ *verb* to calculate a value for something ○ *to evaluate costs* ○ *We will evaluate jobs on the basis of their contribution to the organisation as a whole.* ○ *We need to evaluate the experience and qualifications of all the candidates.*

evaluation /ɪ,vælju'eɪʃ(ə)n/ *noun* the process of calculating the value of an asset

evasion /ɪ'veɪʒ(ə)n/ *noun* the act of avoiding something

EVR *abbreviation* electronic version of the tax return

ex /eks/ *prefix* out of or from ■ *adverb* without

exact /ɪg'zækt/ *adjective* strictly correct, not varying in any way from, e.g. not any more or less than, what is stated ○ *The exact time is 10.27.* ○ *The salesgirl asked me if I had the exact sum, since the shop had no change.*

exact interest /ɪg,zækt 'ɪntrəst/ *noun* annual interest calculated on the basis of 365 days, as opposed to ordinary interest which is calculated on 360 days

exactly /ɪg'zæktli/ *adverb* not varying in any way from, e.g. not any more or less than, what is stated ○ *The total cost was exactly £6,500.*

ex-all /,eks 'ɔːl/ *adjective* referring to a share price where the share is sold without the dividend, rights issue or any other current issue. Abbreviation **xa**

ex ante /,eks 'ænti/ *adverb* a Latin phrase meaning 'before the event'. Compare **ex post** (NOTE: An ex ante budget, or standard, is set before a period of activity commences, and is based on the best information available at that time on expected levels of cost, performance, etc.)

exceed /ɪk'siːd/ *verb* to be more than ○ *a discount not exceeding 15%* ○ *Last year costs exceeded 20% of income for the first time.*

exceptional items /ɪk,sepʃən(ə)l 'aɪtəmz/ *plural noun* **1.** items which arise from normal trading but which are unusual because of their size or nature (NOTE: Such items are shown separately in a note to the company's accounts but not on the face of the P & L account unless they are profits or losses on the sale or termination of an operation, or costs of a fundamental reorganisation or restructuring which have a material effect on the nature and focus of the reporting entity's operations, or profits or losses on the disposal of fixed assets.) **2.** items in a balance sheet which do not appear there each year and which are included in the accounts before the pre-tax profit is calculated, as opposed to extraordinary items which are calculated after the pre-tax profit

exception report /ɪk'sepʃən rɪ,pɔːt/ *noun* a report which flags discrepancies between a company's actual and expected performance, used to identify issues which then need investigating

excess /'ekses/; /ɪk'ses/ *noun, adjective* an amount which is more than what is allowed ○ *an excess of expenditure over revenue* ○ *Excess costs have caused us considerable problems.*

excess capacity /,ekses kə'pæsɪti/ *noun* spare capacity which is not being used

excess profit /,ekses 'prɒfɪt/ *noun* a level of profit that is higher than a level regarded as normal

excess profits tax /,ekses 'prɒfɪts tæks/ *noun* a tax on excess profit

excess reserves /ɪk,ses rɪ'zɜːvz/ *plural noun* US reserves held by a financial institution that are higher than those required by the regulatory authorities. As such reserves may indicate that demand for loans is low, banks often sell their excess reserves to other institutions. Compare **required reserves**

exchange /ɪks'tʃeɪndʒ/ *noun* **1.** the act of giving one thing for another **2.** a market for shares, commodities, futures, etc. ■ *verb* **1.** □ **to exchange something (for something else)** to give one thing in place of something else ○ *He exchanged his motorcycle for a car.* ○ *Goods can be exchanged only on production of the sales slip.* **2.** to change money of one country for money of another ○ *to exchange euros for pounds*

'…under the barter agreements, Nigeria will export crude oil in exchange for trucks, food, planes and chemicals' [*Wall Street Journal*]

exchangeable /ɪks'tʃeɪndʒəb(ə)l/ *adjective* possible to exchange

exchange controls /ɪks'tʃeɪndʒ kən,trəʊlz/ *plural noun* government restrictions on changing the local currency into foreign currency ○ *The government had to impose exchange controls to stop the rush to buy dollars.* ○ *They say the government is going to lift exchange controls.*

exchange cross rates /ɪksˌtʃeɪndʒ 'krɒs reɪts/ *plural noun* rates of exchange for two currencies, shown against each other, but in terms of a third currency, often the US dollar

exchange dealer /ɪks'tʃeɪndʒ ˌdiːlə/ *noun* a person who buys and sells foreign currency

exchange dealings /ɪks'tʃeɪndʒ ˌdiːlɪŋz/ *plural noun* the buying and selling of foreign currency

exchange gain /ɪks'tʃeɪndʒ ɡeɪn/, **exchange loss** /ɪks'tʃeɪndʒ lɒs/ *noun* a gain or loss made from changes in the exchange rate which take place during the period of the transaction

exchange premium /ɪks'tʃeɪndʒ ˌpriːmiəm/ *noun* an extra cost above the usual rate for buying a foreign currency

exchanger /ɪks'tʃeɪndʒə/ *noun* a person who buys and sells foreign currency

exchange rate /ɪks'tʃeɪndʒ reɪt/ *noun* **1.** a rate at which one currency is exchanged for another. Also called **rate of exchange 2.** a figure that expresses how much a unit of one country's currency is worth in terms of the currency of another country

exchange rate mechanism /ɪks 'tʃeɪndʒ reɪt ˌmekənɪz(ə)m/ *noun* a former method of stabilising exchange rates within the European Monetary System, where currencies could only move up or down within a narrow band (usually 2.25% either way, but for some currencies widened to 6%) without involving a realignment of all the currencies in the system

exchange rate parity /ɪks'tʃeɪndʒ reɪt ˌpærɪti/ *noun* the existence of uniform exchange rate levels between a group of countries, such that a basket of goods costs the same in the currencies of these countries

exchange transaction /ɪks'tʃeɪndʒ trænˌzækʃən/ *noun* a purchase or sale of foreign currency

Exchequer /ɪks'tʃekə/ ◇ **the Exchequer 1.** the fund of all money received by the government of the UK from taxes and other revenues **2.** the British government's account with the Bank of England **3.** the British government department dealing with public revenue

Exchequer stocks /ɪks'tʃekə stɒks/ *plural noun* same as **Treasury stocks**

excise duty /'eksaɪz ˌdjuːti/ *noun* a tax on goods such as alcohol and petrol which are produced in the country

excise tax /'ɪksaɪz tæks/ *noun US* a tax levied for a particular purpose

exclude /ɪk'skluːd/ *verb* to keep out, or not to include ○ *The interest charges have been excluded from the document.* ○ *Damage by fire is excluded from the policy.*

exclusion clause /ɪk'skluːʒ(ə)n klɔːz/ *noun* a clause in an insurance policy or warranty which says which items or events are not covered

exclusive agreement /ɪkˌskluːsɪv ə 'ɡriːmənt/ *noun* an agreement where a person is made sole agent for a product in a market

exclusive of tax /ɪkˌskluːsɪv əv 'tæks/ *adjective* not including tax ○ *All payments are exclusive of tax.*

exclusivity /ˌekskluː'sɪvɪti/ *noun* the exclusive right to market a product

ex coupon /ˌeks 'kuːpɒn/ *adverb* without the interest coupons or after interest has been paid

ex dividend /ˌeks 'dɪvɪdend/, **ex div** /ˌeks 'dɪv/ *adjective* used to describe a share that does not have the right to receive the next dividend ○ *The shares went ex dividend yesterday.* Abbreviation **xd**

execute /'eksɪkjuːt/ *verb* to carry out an order ○ *Failure to execute orders may lead to dismissal.* ○ *There were many practical difficulties in executing the managing director's instructions.*

execution /ˌeksɪ'kjuːʃ(ə)n/ *noun* the carrying out of a commercial order or contract

executive /ɪɡ'zekjʊtɪv/ *adjective* putting decisions into action

executive director /ɪɡˌzekjʊtɪv daɪ 'rektə/ *noun* **1.** a director who works full-time in the company. Compare **non-executive director 2.** a senior employee of an organisation who is usually in charge of one or other of its main functions, e.g. sales or human relations, and is usually, but not always, a member of the board of directors

executive power /ɪɡˌzekjʊtɪv 'paʊə/ *noun* the right to act as director or to put decisions into action

executive share option scheme /ɪɡ ˌzekjʊtɪv 'ʃeər ɒpʃən ˌskiːm/ *noun* a scheme under which senior managers are given the opportunity to buy shares in their company at a preferential fixed price at a later date

executor /ɪgˈzekjʊtə/ *noun* a person or firm that sees that the terms of a will are carried out ○ *She was named executor of her brother's will.*

executrix /ɪgˈzekjʊtrɪks/ *noun* a female executor

exempt /ɪgˈzempt/ *adjective* not forced to do something, especially not forced to obey a particular law or rule, or not forced to pay something ○ *Anyone over 65 is exempt from charges* □ **exempt from tax** not required to pay tax ○ *As a non-profit-making organisation we are exempt from tax.*

'Companies with sales under $500,000 a year will be exempt from the minimum-wage requirements' [*Nation's Business*]

exempt assets /ɪgˌzempt ˈæsets/ *plural noun* assets such as cars which are not subject to capital gains tax when sold

exempt gift /ɪgˌzempt ˈgɪft/ *noun* a gift that is not subject to US gift tax

exempt investment fund /ɪgˌzempt ɪn ˈvestmənt fʌnd/ *noun* in the United Kingdom, a collective investment, usually a unit trust, for investors who have certain tax privileges, e.g., charities or contributors to pension plans

exemption /ɪgˈzempʃ(ə)n/ *noun* the act of exempting something from a contract or from a tax □ **exemption from tax, tax exemption** the fact of being free from having to pay tax ○ *As a non-profit-making organisation you can claim tax exemption.*

exempt supplies /ɪgˌzempt səˈplaɪz/ *plural noun* products or services on which the supplier does not have to charge VAT, e.g., the purchase of, or rent on, property and financial services

exercise /ˈeksəsaɪz/ *noun* **1.** the use of something **2.** a financial year ○ *during the current exercise* ■ *verb* to use ○ *The chairwoman exercised her veto to block the motion.*

exercise date /ˈeksəsaɪz deɪt/ *noun* the date when an option can be put into effect

exercise price /ˈeksəsaɪz praɪs/ *noun* the price at which an option will be put into effect

ex gratia /ˌeks ˈgreɪʃə/ *adjective* as an act of favour, without obligation

exit /ˈeksɪt/ *noun* the way in which an investor can realise their investment, e.g. by selling the company they have invested in

exit charge /ˈeksɪt tʃɑːdʒ/, **exit fee** /ˈeksɪt fiː/ *noun* a charge sometimes made by a trust when selling units in a unit trust or when selling out of an investment such as an ISA

exit price /ˈeksɪt praɪs/ *noun* the price at which an investor sells an investment or at which a firm sells up and leaves a market

exit value /ˈeksɪt ˌvæljuː/ *noun* income that would be received if an asset or a business were sold

ex officio /ˌeks əˈfɪʃiəʊ/ *adjective, adverb* because of an office held ○ *The treasurer is ex officio a member or an ex officio member of the finance committee.*

expand /ɪkˈspænd/ *verb* to get bigger, or make something bigger ○ *an expanding economy* ○ *The company is expanding fast.* ○ *We have had to expand our sales force.*

expansion /ɪkˈspænʃən/ *noun* an increase in size ○ *The expansion of the domestic market.* ○ *The company had difficulty in financing its current expansion programme.*

'…inflation-adjusted GNP moved up at a 1.3% annual rate, its worst performance since the economic expansion began' [*Fortune*]

'…the businesses we back range from start-up ventures to established businesses in need of further capital for expansion' [*Times*]

'…the group is undergoing a period of rapid expansion and this has created an exciting opportunity for a qualified accountant' [*Financial Times*]

ex parte /ˌeks ˈpɑːti/ *phrase* a Latin phrase meaning 'on behalf of'

expected annual activity /ɪkˌspektɪd ˌænjʊəl ækˈtɪvɪti/ *noun* a company's anticipated level of activity or production for a given year

expected value /ɪkˌspektɪd ˈvæljuː/ *noun* the future value of a course of action, weighted according to the probability that the course of action will actually occur. If the possible course of action produces income of £10,000 and has a 10% chance of occurring, its expected value is 10% of £10,000 or £1,000.

expenditure /ɪkˈspendɪtʃə/ *noun* the amount of money spent

expense /ɪkˈspens/ *noun* money spent ○ *The expense is too much for my bank balance.* ○ *The likely profits do not justify the expense of setting up the project.*

expense account /ɪkˈspens əˌkaʊnt/ *noun* an allowance of money which a business pays for an employee to spend on travelling and entertaining clients in connection with that business ○ *I'll put this lunch on my expense account.*

expenses /ɪkˈspensɪz/ *plural noun* money paid to cover the costs incurred by someone when doing something ○ *The salary offered is £10,000 plus expenses.* ○ *She has a high salary and all her travel expenses are paid by the company.*

expert system /ˈekspɜːt ˌsɪstəm/ *noun* software that applies the knowledge, advice and rules defined by experts in a particular field to a user's data to help solve a problem

expiration /ˌekspəˈreɪʃ(ə)n/ *noun* the act of coming to an end ○ *the expiration of an insurance policy* ○ *to repay before the expiration of the stated period*

expiration date /ˌekspəˈreɪʃ(ə)n deɪt/ *noun US* same as **expiry date**

expire /ɪkˈspaɪə/ *verb* to come to an end ○ *The lease expires in 2010.*

expiry /ɪkˈspaɪəri/ *noun* the act of coming to an end ○ *the expiry of an insurance policy*

expiry date /ɪkˈspaɪəri deɪt/ *noun* a date when something will end

exponent /ɪkˈspəʊnənt/ *noun* a number or variable placed to the upper right of a number or mathematical expression that indicates the number of times the number or expression is to be multiplied by itself, as in 2^3, which equals 8

exponential smoothing /ekspə ˌnenʃ(ə)l ˈsmuːðɪŋ/ *noun* a technique for working out averages while allowing for recent changes in values by moving forward the period under consideration at regular intervals

export *noun* /ˈekspɔːt/ the practice or business of sending goods to foreign countries to be sold ○ *50% of the company's profits come from the export trade* or *the export market.* ◊ **exports** ■ *verb* /ɪkˈspɔːt/ to send goods to foreign countries for sale ○ *50% of our production is exported.* ○ *The company imports raw materials and exports the finished products.*

exportation /ˌekspɔːˈteɪʃ(ə)n/ *noun* the act of sending goods to foreign countries for sale

Export Credit Guarantee Department /ˌekspɔːt ˌkredɪt ˌɡærənˈtiː dɪ ˌpɑːtmənt/ *noun* a British government department which insures sellers of exports sold on credit against the possibility of non-payment by the purchasers. Abbreviation **ECGD**

export department /ˈekspɔːt dɪ ˌpɑːtmənt/ *noun* the section of a company which deals in sales to foreign countries

export duty /ˈekspɔːt ˌdjuːti/ *noun* a tax paid on goods sent out of a country for sale

exporter /ɪkˈspɔːtə/ *noun* a person, company, or country that sells goods in foreign countries ○ *a major furniture exporter* ○ *Canada is an important exporter of oil* or *an important oil exporter.*

export house /ˈekspɔːt haʊs/ *noun* a company which specialises in the export of goods manufactured by other companies

export licence /ˈekspɔːt ˌlaɪs(ə)ns/ *noun* a government permit allowing something to be exported ○ *The government has refused an export licence for computer parts.*

export manager /ˈekspɔːt ˌmænɪdʒə/ *noun* the person in charge of an export department in a company ○ *The export manager planned to set up a sales force in Southern Europe.* ○ *Sales managers from all export markets report to our export manager.*

exports /ˈekspɔːts/ *plural noun* goods sent to a foreign country to be sold ○ *Exports to Africa have increased by 25%.* ◊ **export** (NOTE: Usually used in the plural, but the singular form is used before a noun.)

ex post /ˌeks ˈpəʊst/ *adverb* a Latin phrase meaning 'after the event'. Compare **ex ante** (NOTE: An ex post budget, or standard, is set after the end of a period of activity, when it can represent the optimum achievable level of performance in the conditions which were experienced. Thus the budget can be flexed, and standards can reflect factors such as unanticipated changes in technology and in price levels.)

exposure /ɪkˈspəʊʒə/ *noun* **1.** publicity given to an organisation or product ○ *Our company has achieved more exposure since we decided to advertise nationally.* **2.** the amount of risk which a lender or investor runs ○ *He is trying to limit his exposure in the property market.*

'…it attributed the poor result to the bank's high exposure to residential mortgages, which showed a significant slow-down in the past few months' [*South China Morning Post*]

exposure draft /ɪkˈspəʊʒə drɑːft/ *noun* a document produced by a body before a new authoritative pronouncement is published. It invites accountants and other interested parties to comment on matters raised by the draft. Abbreviation **ED**

expressly /ɪkˈspresli/ *adverb* clearly in words ○ *The contract expressly forbids sales to the United States.*

ex-rights /ˌeks ˈraɪts/ *adjective* referring to a share price where the share is sold without a recent rights issue. Abbreviation **xr**

extend /ɪkˈstend/ *verb* **1.** to offer something ○ *to extend credit to a customer* **2.** to make something longer ○ *Her contract of employment was extended for two years.* ○ *We have extended the deadline for making the appointment by two weeks.*

extended credit /ɪkˌstendɪd ˈkredɪt/ *noun* **1.** credit allowing the borrower a very long time to pay ○ *We sell to Australia on extended credit.* **2.** *US* an extra long credit used by commercial banks borrowing from the Federal Reserve

Extensible Business Reporting Language /ɪkˌstensɪb(ə)l ˌbɪznɪs rɪ ˈpɔːtɪŋ ˌlæŋgwɪdʒ/ *noun* full form of **XBRL**

extension /ɪkˈstenʃən/ *noun* an additional period of time allowed for something, e.g. the repayment of a debt

extensive /ɪkˈstensɪv/ *adjective* very large or covering a wide area ○ *an extensive network of sales outlets* ○ *an extensive recruitment drive*

external /ɪkˈstɜːn(ə)l/ *adjective* **1.** outside a country. Opposite **internal 2.** outside a company

external account /ɪkˌstɜːn(ə)l əˈkaʊnt/ *noun* an account in a British bank belonging to someone who is living in another country

external audit /ɪkˌstɜːn(ə)l ˈɔːdɪt/ *noun* **1.** an audit carried out by an independent auditor who is not employed by the company **2.** an evaluation of the effectiveness of a company's public relations carried out by an outside agency

external auditing /ɪkˌstɜːn(ə)l ˈɔːdɪtɪŋ/ *noun* an action of auditing a set of accounts by an external auditor

external auditor /ɪkˌstɜːn(ə)l ˈɔːdɪtə/ *noun* an independent person who audits the company's accounts

external debt /ɪkˌstɜːn(ə)l ˈdet/ *noun* money which a company has borrowed from outside sources such as a bank, as opposed to money raised from shareholders. Also called **external funds**

external failure costs /ɪkˌstɜːn(ə)l ˈfeɪljə ˌkɒsts/ *plural noun* costs incurred as a result of products proving faulty, e.g. the cost of replacements and lost sales

external funds /ɪkˌstɜːn(ə)l ˈfʌndz/ *plural noun* same as **external debt**

external growth /ɪkˌstɜːn(ə)l ˈgrəʊθ/ *noun* the growth of a firm by buying other companies, rather than by expanding existing sales or products. Opposite **internal growth**

external liabilities /ɪkˌstɜːn(ə)l ˌlaɪə ˈbɪlɪtiz/ *plural noun* money owed to lenders and other creditors outside a company

external trade /ɪkˌstɜːn(ə)l ˈtreɪd/ *noun* trade with foreign countries. Opposite **internal trade**

extract /ˈekstrækt/ *noun* a printed document which is part of a larger document ○ *He sent me an extract of the accounts.*

extraordinary item /ɪkˈstrɔːd(ə)n(ə)ri ˌaɪtəm/ *noun* a large item of income or expenditure entered into accounts that is unusual in nature and also occurs very infrequently

F

face value /ˌfeɪs ˈvæljuː/ *noun* the value written on a coin, banknote or share certificate

'…travellers cheques cost 1% of their face value – some banks charge more for small amounts' [*Sunday Times*]

facility /fəˈsɪlɪti/ *noun* the total amount of credit which a lender will allow a borrower

facility fee /fəˈsɪlɪti fiː/ *noun* a charge made to a borrower by a bank for arranging credit facilities

facility-sustaining activities /fəˌsɪlɪti səˌsteɪnɪŋ ækˈtɪvɪtiz/ *plural noun* activities undertaken to support the organisation as a whole, which cannot be logically linked to individual units of output. Accounting is a facility-sustaining activity. ◊ **hierarchy of activities**

factor /ˈfæktə/ *noun* **1.** something which is important, or which is taken into account when making a decision ○ *The drop in sales is an important factor in the company's lower profits.* ○ *Motivation was an important factor in drawing up the new pay scheme.* **2.** a number used in multiplication to produce another number □ **by a factor of ten** ten times **3.** a person or company which is responsible for collecting debts for companies, by buying debts at a discount on their face value **4.** a person who sells for a business or another person and earns a commission ■ *verb* to buy debts from a company at a discount

'…factors 'buy' invoices from a company, which then gets an immediate cash advance representing most of their value. The balance is paid when the debt is met. The client company is charged a fee as well as interest on the cash advanced' [*Times*]

factorial /fækˈtɔːriəl/ *noun* the product of all the numbers below a number ○ *example: 4 factorial = 1x2x3x4 = 24* (NOTE: **4 factorial** is written **4!**)

factoring /ˈfæktərɪŋ/ *noun* the business of buying debts from a firm at a discount and then enforcing the payment of the debt

factoring charges /ˈfæktərɪŋ ˌtʃɑːdʒɪz/ *plural noun* the cost of selling debts to a factor for a commission

factors of production /ˌfæktəz əv prəˈdʌkʃən/ *plural noun* land, labour and capital, i.e. the three things needed to produce a product

factory gate price /ˌfækt(ə)ri ˈɡeɪt praɪs/ *noun* the actual cost of manufacturing goods before any mark-up is added to give profit (NOTE: The factory gate price includes direct costs such as labour, raw materials and energy, and indirect costs such as interest on loans, plant maintenance or rent.)

factory overhead /ˈfækt(ə)ri ˌəʊvəhed/ *noun* same as **production overhead**

FAE *abbreviation* Final Admitting Exam

fail /feɪl/ *verb* to be unsuccessful ○ *The prototype failed its first test.*

failure /ˈfeɪljə/ *noun* an act of breaking down or stopping ○ *the failure of the negotiations*

failure costs /ˈfeɪljə kɒsts/ *plural noun* costs that include external failure costs as well as associated costs, e.g. the cost of running a complaints department

fair /feə/ *adjective* reasonable, with equal treatment

fair dealing /ˌfeə ˈdiːlɪŋ/ *noun* the legal buying and selling of shares

fair market value /ˌfeə ˌmɑːkɪt ˈvæljuː/ *noun* same as **fair value**

fair price /ˌfeə ˈpraɪs/ *noun* a good price for both buyer and seller

fair trade /ˌfeə ˈtreɪd/ *noun* an international business system where countries agree not to charge import duties on some items imported from their trading partners

fair value /ˌfeə ˈvæljuː/ *noun* **1.** a price paid by a buyer who knows the value of what he or she is buying, to a seller who also knows the value of what is being sold, i.e., neither is cheating the other **2.** a method of valuing the assets and liabilities of a business based on the amount for which they could be sold to independent parties at the time of valuation

fair wear and tear /ˌfeə weər ən 'teə/ *noun* acceptable damage caused by normal use ○ *The insurance policy covers most damage but not fair wear and tear to the machine.*

fall /fɔːl/ *noun* a sudden reduction or loss of value ○ *a fall in the exchange rate* ○ *a fall in the price of gold* ○ *a fall on the Stock Exchange* ○ *Profits showed a 10% fall.* ■ *verb* **1.** to be reduced suddenly to a lower price or value ○ *Shares fell on the market today.* ○ *Gold shares fell 10% or fell 45 cents on the Stock Exchange.* ○ *The price of gold fell for the second day running.* ○ *The pound fell against the euro.* **2.** to happen or to take place ○ *The public holiday falls on a Tuesday.*

'…market analysts described the falls in the second half of last week as a technical correction to the market' [*Australian Financial Review*]

'…for the first time since mortgage rates began falling in March a financial institution has raised charges on homeowner loans' [*Globe and Mail (Toronto)*]

'…interest rates were still falling as late as June, and underlying inflation remains below the government's target of 2.5 per cent' [*Financial Times*]

fall behind *phrasal verb* to be late in doing something ○ *They fell behind with their mortgage repayments.*

falling /ˈfɔːlɪŋ/ *adjective* becoming smaller or dropping in price

'…falling profitability means falling share prices' [*Investors Chronicle*]

false /fɔːls/ *adjective* not true or not correct ○ *to make a false claim for a product* ○ *to make a false entry in the balance sheet*

false accounting /ˌfɔːls əˈkaʊntɪŋ/ *noun* the criminal offence of changing, destroying or hiding accounting records for a dishonest purpose

false market /ˌfɔːls 'mɑːkɪt/ *noun* a market in shares caused by persons or companies conspiring to buy or sell and so influence the share price to their advantage

falsification /ˌfɔːlsɪfɪˈkeɪʃ(ə)n/ *noun* the act of making false entries in accounts

falsify /ˈfɔːlsɪfaɪ/ *verb* to change something to make it wrong ○ *They were accused of falsifying the accounts.*

family company /ˈfæm(ə)li ˌkʌmp(ə)ni/ *noun* a company in which most of the shares are owned by members of a family

f. & f. *abbreviation* fixtures and fittings

FASB *abbreviation* Financial Accounting Standards Board

favourable trade balance /ˌfeɪv(ə)rəb(ə)l 'treɪd ˌbæləns/ *noun* a situation where a country exports more than it imports ○ *The country has had an adverse balance of trade for the second month running.*

favourable variance /ˌfeɪv(ə)rəb(ə)l 'veəriəns/ *noun* variance which shows that the actual result is better than expected

fax /fæks/ *noun* a system for sending the exact copy of a document via telephone lines ○ *Can you confirm the booking by fax?* ■ *verb* to send a message by fax ○ *The details of the offer were faxed to the brokers this morning.* ○ *I've faxed the documents to our New York office.*

FCA *abbreviation* Fellow of the Institute of Chartered Accountants in England and Wales

FCCA *abbreviation* Fellow of the Association of Chartered Certified Accountants

FCR *abbreviation* full cost recovery

FD *abbreviation* financial director

feasibility study /ˌfiːzə'bɪlɪti ˌstʌdi/ *noun* the careful investigation of a project to see whether it is worth undertaking ○ *We will carry out a feasibility study to decide whether it is worth setting up an agency in North America.*

federal /ˈfed(ə)rəl/ *adjective* **1.** referring to a system of government where a group of states are linked together in a federation **2.** referring to the central government of the United States ○ *Most federal offices are in Washington.*

'…federal examiners will determine which of the privately-insured savings and loans qualify for federal insurance' [*Wall Street Journal*]

'…since 1978 America has freed many of its industries from federal rules that set prices and controlled the entry of new companies' [*Economist*]

Federal Funds /ˌfed(ə)rəl 'fʌndz/ *plural noun* deposits by commercial banks with the Federal Reserve Banks, which can be used for short-term loans to other banks

Federal Reserve /ˌfed(ə)rəl rɪ'zɜːv/, **Federal Reserve System** /ˌfed(ə)rəl rɪ 'zɜːv ˌsɪstəm/ *noun* the system of federal government control of the US banks, where the Federal Reserve Board regulates money supply, prints money, fixes the discount rate and issues government bonds

Federal Reserve Bank /ˌfed(ə)rəl rɪ'zɜːv ˌbæŋk/ *noun* any one of the twelve federally-owned regional banks in the US, which are directed by the Federal Reserve Board. Abbreviation **FRB**

Federal Reserve Board /ˌfed(ə)rəl rɪ'zɜːv bɔːd/ *noun* a government organisation which runs the central banks in the US. Abbreviation **FRB**

'...pressure on the Federal Reserve Board to ease monetary policy mounted yesterday with the release of a set of pessimistic economic statistics' [*Financial Times*]

federation /ˌfedə'reɪʃ(ə)n/ *noun* a group of societies, companies or organisations which have a central organisation which represents them and looks after their common interests ○ *a federation of trades unions* ○ *the employers' federation*

Fédération des Experts-Comptables Européen *noun* same as **European Federation of Accountants**

Fed Funds /ˈfed fʌndz/ *plural noun US* same as **Federal Funds** (*informal*)

fed funds rate /ˈfed fʌndz ˌreɪt/ *noun* the rate charged by banks for lending money deposited with the Federal Reserve to other banks

fee /fiː/ *noun* money paid for work carried out by a professional person such as an accountant, a doctor or a lawyer ○ *We charge a small fee for our services.* ○ *The consultant's fee was much higher than we expected.*

fee work /ˈfiː wɜːk/ *noun* any work on a project carried out by independent workers or contractors, rather than by the organisation's employees

fellow /ˈfeləʊ/ *noun* a title given to senior members of a professional association. Junior members are usually called 'associates'.

fiat money /ˈfiːæt ˌmʌni/ *noun* coins or notes which are not worth much as paper or metal, but are said by the government to have a value and are recognised as legal tender

fictitious assets /fɪkˌtɪʃəs 'æsets/ *plural noun* assets which do not really exist, but are entered as assets to balance the accounts

fiddle /ˈfɪd(ə)l/ (*informal*) *noun* an act of cheating ○ *It's all a fiddle.* ■ *verb* to cheat ○ *He tried to fiddle his tax returns.* ○ *The salesman was caught fiddling his expense account.*

fiduciary /fɪ'djuːʃjəri/ *noun, adjective* (a person) in a position of trust ○ *Directors have fiduciary duty to act in the best interests of the company.*

fiduciary deposits /fɪˌdjuːʃəri dɪ'pɒzɪtz/ *plural noun* bank deposits which are managed for the depositor by the bank

FIFO /ˈfaɪfəʊ/ *abbreviation* first in first out

fifty-fifty /ˌfɪfti 'fɪfti/ *adjective, adverb* half

figure /ˈfɪɡə/ *noun* **1.** a number, or a cost written in numbers ○ *The figure in the accounts for heating is very high.* **2.** □ **his income runs into six figures** *or* **he has a six-figure income** his income is more than £100,000

figures /ˈfɪɡəz/ *plural noun* **1.** written numbers **2.** the results for a company ○ *the figures for last year* or *last year's figures*

file /faɪl/ *noun* **1.** documents kept for reference **2.** a section of data on a computer, e.g. payroll, address list, customer accounts ○ *How can we protect our computer files?* ■ *verb* **1.** to make an official request **2.** to register something officially ○ *to file an application for a patent* ○ *to file a return to the tax office*

file copy /ˈfaɪl ˌkɒpi/ *noun* a copy of a document which is kept for reference in an office

filing date /ˈfaɪlɪŋ deɪt/ *noun* the date by which income tax returned must be filed with the Inland Revenue

final accounts /ˌfaɪn(ə)l ə'kaʊnts/ *plural noun* the accounts produced at the end of an accounting period, including the balance sheet and profit and loss account

Final Admitting Exam /ˌfaɪn(ə)l əd'mɪtɪŋ ɪɡˌzæm/ *noun* a final examination set by the ICAEW to admit student accountants as chartered accountants. Abbreviation **FAE**

final closing date /ˌfaɪn(ə)l 'kləʊzɪŋ deɪt/ *noun* the last date for acceptance of a takeover bid, when the bidder has to announce how many shareholders have accepted his or her offer

final demand /ˌfaɪn(ə)l dɪ'mɑːnd/ *noun* a last reminder that payment of a debt is due, after which a supplier normally sues for payment

final discharge /ˌfaɪn(ə)l 'dɪstʃɑːdʒ/ *noun* a final payment the completes the repayment of a debt

final dividend /ˌfaɪn(ə)l 'dɪvɪdend/ *noun* a dividend paid at the end of a year's trading, which has to be approved by the shareholders at an AGM

finalise /'faɪnəlaɪz/, **finalize** *verb* to agree final details ○ *We hope to finalise the agreement tomorrow.* ○ *After six weeks of negotiations the loan was finalised yesterday.*

final settlement /ˌfaɪn(ə)l 'set(ə)lmənt/ *noun* the last payment which settles a debt

finance /'faɪnæns/ *noun* **1.** money used by a company, provided by the shareholders or by loans ○ *Where will they get the necessary finance for the project?* (NOTE: The US term is **financing**) **2.** money (used by a club, local authority, etc.) ○ *She is the secretary of the local authority finance committee.* ■ *verb* to provide money to pay for something ○ *They plan to finance the operation with short-term loans.*

'…an official said that the company began to experience a sharp increase in demand for longer-term mortgages at a time when the flow of money used to finance these loans diminished' [*Globe and Mail*]

Finance Act /'faɪnæns ækt/ *noun* an annual Act of Parliament which gives the government the power to obtain money from taxes as proposed in the Budget

Finance and Tax Tribunals /ˌfaɪnæns ən 'tæks ˌtraɪbjuːn(ə)lz/ *plural noun* a collective name for four tribunals established in 2006 to hear appeals against decisions of HM Customs and Excise and the Inland Revenue and to adjudicate on matters relating to certain decisions of the Financial Services Authority and the Pensions Regulator

Finance Bill /'faɪnæns bɪl/ *noun* **1.** a bill that lists the proposals in a Chancellor's budget and that is debated before being voted into law as the Finance Act **2.** *US* a short-term bill of exchange which provides credit for a corporation so that it can continue trading

finance controller /'faɪnæns kən ˌtrəʊlə/ *noun* an accountant whose main task is to manage the company's monetary resources

finance lease /'faɪnæns liːs/ *noun* a lease which requires the lessee company to show the asset acquired under the lease in its balance sheet and to depreciate it in the usual way

finance leasing /'faɪnæns ˌliːsɪŋ/ *noun* leasing a property under a finance lease

finance market /'faɪnæns ˌmɑːkɪt/ *noun* a place where large sums of money can be lent or borrowed

finances /'faɪnænsɪz/ *plural noun* money or cash which is available ○ *the bad state of the company's finances*

financial /faɪ'nænʃəl/ *adjective* relating to money

Financial Accountant /faɪˌnænʃ(ə)l ə 'kaʊntənt/ *noun* a qualified accountant, a member of the Institute of Financial Accountants, who advises on accounting matters or who works as the financial director of a company

financial accounting /faɪˌnænʃ(ə)l ə 'kaʊntɪŋ/, **financial accountancy** /faɪ ˌnænʃ(ə)l ə'kaʊntənsi/ *noun* **1.** the form of accounting in which financial reports are produced to provide investors or other external parties with information on a company's financial status. Compare **management accounting 2.** the process of classifying and recording a company's transactions and presenting them in the form of profit and loss accounts, balance sheets and cash flow statements for a given accounting period

Financial Accounting Standards Board /faɪˌnænʃ(ə)l əˌkaʊntɪŋ 'stændədz ˌbɔːd/ *noun* the body which regulates accounting standards in the USA. Abbreviation **FASB**

financial adviser /faɪˌnænʃəl əd'vaɪzə/ *noun* a person or company that gives financial advice to clients for a fee

financial aid /faɪˌnænʃəl 'eɪd/ *noun* monetary assistance given to an individual, organisation or nation. International financial aid, that is from one country to another, is often used to fund educational, health-related or other humanitarian activities.

financial analysis software /faɪ ˌnænʃəl ə'næləsɪs ˌsɒftweə/ *noun* software that can produce information on trends and calculate ratios using information from an online database

financial assistance /faɪˌnænʃəl ə 'sɪstəns/ *noun* help in the form of money

financial calendar /faɪˌnænʃəl 'kælɪndə/ *noun* a list of significant events and dates in a company's financial reporting year

financial correspondent /faɪˌnænʃəl ˌkɒrɪs'pɒndənt/ *noun* a journalist who writes articles on money matters for a newspaper

financial director /faɪ'nænʃəl daɪ ˌrektə/ *noun* the member of a board of directors who is responsible for a company's financial operations. Abbreviation **FD**

financial engineering /faɪˌnænʃəl ˌendʒɪ'nɪərɪŋ/ *noun* the act of converting one type of financial instrument into another

financial futures /faɪˌnænʃəl 'fjuːtʃəz/, **financial futures contract** /faɪˌnænʃəl 'fjuːtʃəz ˌkɒntrækt/ *noun* a contract for the purchase of gilt-edged securities for delivery at a date in the future. Also called **financials**

financial futures market /faɪˌnænʃəl 'fjuːtʃəz ˌmɑːkɪt/ *noun* the market in gilt-edged securities for delivery at a date in the future

financial information system /faɪˌnænʃəl ˌɪnfəˈmeɪʃ(ə)n ˌsɪstəm/ *noun* a computer-based system that analyses and gathers financial information for use in running a business

financial institution /faɪˌnænʃəl ˌɪnstɪˈtjuːʃ(ə)n/ *noun* a bank, investment trust or insurance company whose work involves lending or investing large sums of money

financial instrument /faɪˌnænʃəl 'ɪnstrʊmənt/ *noun* **1.** a document showing that money has been lent or borrowed, invested or passed from one account to another, e.g. a bill of exchange, share certificate, certificate of deposit or IOU **2.** any form of investment in the stock market or in other financial markets, e.g. shares, government stocks, certificates of deposit or bills of exchange

financial intermediary /faɪˌnænʃəl ˌɪntəˈmiːdiəri/ *noun* an institution which takes deposits or loans from individuals and lends money to clients

financial leverage /faɪˌnænʃəl 'levərɪdʒ/ *noun* ▸ **gearing**

financially /fɪˈnænʃəli/ *adverb* regarding money □ **a company which is financially sound** a company which is profitable and has strong assets

financial management /faɪˌnænʃəl 'mænɪdʒmənt/ *noun* the management of the acquisition and use of long- and short-term capital by a business

financial position /faɪˌnænʃəl pə 'zɪʃ(ə)n/ *noun* the state of a person's or company's bank balance in terms of assets and debts

financial projection /faɪˌnænʃəl prə 'dʒekʃən/ *noun* business planning that deals with budgets and estimates of future financing needs

financial report /faɪˌnænʃəl rɪˈpɔːt/ *noun* a document which gives the financial position of a company or of a club, etc.

Financial Reporting Council /faɪ ˌnænʃ(ə)l rɪˈpɔːtɪŋ ˌkaʊns(ə)l/ *noun* the UK's independent regulator for corporate reporting and governance

Financial Reporting Review Panel /faɪˌnænʃ(ə)l rɪˌpɔːtɪŋ rɪˈvjuː ˌpæn(ə)l/ *noun* a UK body that receives and investigates complaints about the annual accounts of companies in which it is claimed that the accounting requirements of the Companies Act have not been fulfilled. Abbreviation **FRRP**

Financial Reporting Standards /faɪ ˌnænʃ(ə)l rɪˈpɔːtɪŋ ˌstændədz/ *plural noun* a series of accounting standards issued by the Accounting Standards Board outlining common accounting practice. Abbreviation **FRSs**

financial resources /faɪˌnænʃəl rɪ 'zɔːsɪz/ *plural noun* the supply of money for something ○ *a company with strong financial resources*

financial review /faɪˌnænʃəl rɪˈvjuː/ *noun* an examination of an organisation's finances

financial risk /faɪˌnænʃəl 'rɪsk/ *noun* the possibility of losing money ○ *The company is taking a considerable financial risk in manufacturing 25 million units without doing any market research.* ○ *There is always some financial risk in selling on credit.*

financials /faɪˈnænʃəlz/ *plural noun* same as **financial futures**

financial services /faɪˌnænʃəl 'sɜːvɪsɪz/ *plural noun* services such as banking and insurance the main business of which is the management and transfer of money

Financial Services Act /faɪˌnænʃəl 'sɜːvɪsɪz ækt/ *noun* an Act of the British Parliament which regulates the offering of financial services to the general public and to private investors

Financial Services Authority /faɪ ˌnænʃ(ə)l 'sɜːvɪsɪz ɔːˌθɒrəti/ *noun* an independent non-governmental body formed in 1997 as a result of reforms in the regulation of financial services in the United Kingdom. The Securities and Investments Board (SIB) became responsible for the supervision of banking and investment services and changed its name to become the Financial Services Authority. The FSA's four statutory objectives were specified by the Financial Services and Markets Act 2000: maintaining market confidence; increasing public knowledge of the finance system; ensuring appropriate protection for consumers; and reducing financial crime. Abbreviation **FSA**

financial statement /faɪˌnænʃəl 'steɪtmənt/ *noun* a document which shows the financial situation of a company ○ *The* *accounts department has prepared a financial statement for the shareholders.*

financial statement analysis /faɪˌnænʃəl ˈsteɪtmənt əˌnæləsɪs/ *noun* any of various methods used for evaluating the past, current and projected performance of a company

financial supermarket /faɪˌnænʃəl ˈsuːpəmɑːkɪt/ *noun* a company which offers a range of financial services, e.g. a bank offering loans, mortgages, pensions and insurance as well as the usual personal banking services

Financial Times /faɪˌnænʃ(ə)l ˈtaɪmz/ *noun* an important British financial daily newspaper (printed on pink paper). Abbreviation **FT**

financial year /faɪˌnænʃəl ˈjɪə/ *noun* the twelve-month period for which a company produces accounts. A financial year is not necessarily the same as a calendar year.

financier /faɪˈnænsɪə/ *noun* a person who lends large amounts of money to companies or who buys shares in companies as an investment

financing /ˈfaɪnænsɪŋ/ *noun* the act of providing money for a project ○ *The financing of the project was done by two international banks.*

finder's fee /ˈfaɪndəz fiː/ *noun* a fee paid to a person who finds a client for another, e.g., someone who introduces a client to a stockbroking firm

fine /faɪn/ *noun* money paid because of something wrong which has been done ○ *She was asked to pay a $25,000 fine.* ○ *We had to pay a £50 parking fine.*

fine-tuning /ˌfaɪn ˈtjuːnɪŋ/ *noun* the act of making of small adjustments in areas such as interest rates, tax bands or the money supply, to improve a nation's economy

finished goods /ˌfɪnɪʃt ˈɡʊdz/ *plural noun* manufactured goods which are ready to be sold

fire insurance /ˈfaɪər ɪnˌʃʊərəns/ *noun* insurance against damage by fire

firm /fɜːm/ *noun* a company, business or partnership ○ *a manufacturing firm* ○ *an important publishing firm* ○ *She is a partner in a law firm.* ■ *adjective* **1.** unchangeable ○ *to make a firm offer for something* ○ *to place a firm order for two aircraft* **2.** not dropping in price and possibly going to rise ○ *Sterling was firmer on the foreign exchange markets.* ○ *Shares remained firm.* ■ *verb* to remain at a price and seem likely to rise ○ *The shares firmed at £1.50.*

'…some profit-taking was noted, but underlying sentiment remained firm' [*Financial Times*]

firm up *phrasal verb* to agree on the final details of something ○ *We expect to firm up the deal at the next trade fair.*

firmness /ˈfɜːmnəs/ *noun* the fact of being steady at a particular price, or likely to rise ○ *the firmness of the dollar on foreign exchanges*

'Toronto failed to mirror New York's firmness as a drop in gold shares on a falling bullion price left the market closing on a mixed note' [*Financial Times*]

firm price /ˌfɜːm ˈpraɪs/ *noun* a price which will not change ○ *They are quoting a firm price of $1.23 a unit.*

firm sale /ˌfɜːm ˈseɪl/ *noun* a sale which does not allow the purchaser to return the goods

first in first out /ˌfɜːst ɪn ˌfɜːst ˈaʊt/ *phrase* an accounting policy in which it is assumed that stocks in hand were purchased last, and that stocks sold during the period were purchased first. Abbreviation **FIFO**. Compare **last in first out**

first option /ˌfɜːst ˈɒpʃən/ *noun* allowing someone to be the first to have the possibility of deciding something

first quarter /ˌfɜːst ˈkwɔːtə/ *noun* the period of three months from January to the end of March ○ *The first quarter's rent is payable in advance.*

first year allowance /ˌfɜːst jɪər ə ˈlaʊəns/ *noun* an allowance which can be claimed on capital expenditure by a business or self-employed person during the year in which the purchase was made. After the first year, the written-down allowance (WDA) applies. Abbreviation **FYA**

fiscal /ˈfɪskəl/ *adjective* referring to tax or to government revenues

fiscal drag /ˌfɪskəl ˈdræɡ/ *noun* **1.** the effect of inflation on a government's tax revenues. As inflation increases so do prices and wages, and tax revenues rise proportionately. Even if inflation is low, increased earnings will give the government increased revenues anyway. **2.** the negative effect of higher personal taxation on an individual's work performance

fiscal measures /ˌfɪskəl ˈmeʒəz/ *plural noun* tax changes made by a government to improve the working of the economy

fiscal year /ˌfɪskəl ˈjɪə/ *noun* a twelve-month period on which taxes are calculated. In the UK this is April 6th to April 5th.

'…last fiscal year the chain reported a 116% jump in earnings' [*Barron's*]

fittings /'fɪtɪŋz/ *plural noun* items which are sold with a property but are not permanently fixed, e.g. carpets or shelves. ◊ **fixtures**

fixed assets /ˌfɪkst 'æsets/ *plural noun* property or machinery which a company owns and uses, but which the company does not buy or sell as part of its regular trade, including the company's investments in shares of other companies

fixed asset turnover /ˌfɪkst 'æset ˌtɜːnəʊvə/ *noun* a measure of how efficient a company's property and equipment is in generating revenue

fixed asset unit /ˌfɪkst 'æset ˌjuːnɪt/ *noun* a single item of the fixed assets of a company, e.g. a specific piece of equipment

fixed budget /ˌfɪkst 'bʌdʒɪt/ *noun* a budget which refers to a specific level of business, i.e., a sales turnover which produces a specific level of profit

fixed capital /ˌfɪkst 'kæpɪt(ə)l/ *noun* capital in the form of buildings and machinery

fixed charge /ˌfɪkst 'tʃɑːdʒ/ *noun* a charge over a particular asset or property

fixed costs /ˌfɪkst 'kɒsts/ *plural noun* business costs which do not change with the quantity of the product made

fixed deduction /ˌfɪkst dɪ'dʌkʃən/ *noun* a deduction agreed by the Inland Revenue and a group of employees, such as a trade union, which covers general expenditure on clothes or tools used in the course of employment

fixed deposit /ˌfɪkst dɪ'pɒzɪt/ *noun* a deposit which pays a stated interest over a set period

fixed exchange rate /ˌfɪkst ɪks'tʃeɪndʒ ˌreɪt/ *noun* a rate of exchange of one currency against another which cannot fluctuate, and can only be changed by devaluation or revaluation

fixed expenses /ˌfɪkst ɪk'spensɪz/ *plural noun* expenses which do not vary with different levels of production, e.g. rent, staff salaries and insurance

fixed income /ˌfɪkst 'ɪnkʌm/ *noun* income which does not change from year to year, as from an annuity

fixed-interest /ˌfɪkst 'ɪntrəst/ *adjective* having an interest rate which does not vary

fixed-interest investments /ˌfɪkst ˌɪntrəst ɪn'vestmənts/ *plural noun* investments producing a level of interest which does not change

fixed-interest securities /ˌfɪkst ˌɪntrəst sɪ'kjʊərɪtiz/ *plural noun* securities such as government bonds which produce a level of interest which does not change

fixed-price /ˌfɪkst 'praɪs/ *adjective* having a price which cannot be changed

fixed-price agreement /ˌfɪkst 'praɪs əˌgriːmənt/ *noun* an agreement where a company provides a service or a product at a price which stays the same for the whole period of the agreement

fixed rate /ˌfɪkst 'reɪt/ *noun* a rate, e.g. an exchange rate, which does not change

fixed rate loan /ˌfɪkst reɪt 'ləʊn/ *noun* a loan on which the rate of interest stays the same for the duration of the loan

fixed scale of charges /ˌfɪkst skeɪl əv 'tʃɑːdʒɪz/ *noun* a set of charges that do not vary according to individual circumstances but are applied consistently in all cases of a particular kind

fixed yield /ˌfɪkst 'jiːld/ *noun* a percentage return which does not change

fixtures /'fɪkstʃəz/ *plural noun* items in a property which are permanently attached to it, e.g. sinks and lavatories

fixtures and fittings /ˌfɪkstʃəz ən 'fɪtɪŋz/ *plural noun* objects in a property which are sold with the property, both those which cannot be removed and those which can. Abbreviation **f. & f.**

flash report /'flæʃ rɪˌpɔːt/ *noun* an interim financial report produced before the full accounts have been drawn up, and used to identify or resolve potential problems

flat /flæt/ *adjective* **1.** used to describe market prices which do not fall or rise, because of low demand ○ *The market was flat today.* **2.** not changing in response to different conditions ○ *a flat rate*

'…the government revised its earlier reports for July and August. Originally reported as flat in July and declining by 0.2% in August, industrial production is now seen to have risen by 0.2% and 0.1% respectively in those months' [*Sunday Times*]

flat rate /ˌflæt 'reɪt/ *noun* a charge which always stays the same ○ *a flat-rate increase of 10%* ○ *We pay a flat rate for electricity each quarter.*

flat tax /ˌflæt 'tæks/ *noun* a tax levied at one fixed rate whatever an individual's income

flat yield /ˌflæt ˈjiːld/ *noun* an interest rate as a percentage of the price paid for fixed-interest stock

flex /fleks/ *verb* to adjust figures in order to reflect changes in circumstances since the original figures were produced ○ *flexing a budget*

flexibility /ˌfleksɪˈbɪlɪti/ *noun* the ability to be easily changed ○ *There is no flexibility in the company's pricing policy.*

'...they calculate interest on their 'flexible' mortgage on an annual basis rather than daily. Charging annual interest makes a nonsense of the whole idea of flexibility which is supposed to help you pay off your mortgage more quickly' [*Financial Times*]

flexible /ˈfleksɪb(ə)l/ *adjective* possible to alter or change ○ *We try to be flexible where the advertising budget is concerned.* ○ *The company has adopted a flexible pricing policy.*

flexible budget /ˌfleksɪb(ə)l ˈbʌdʒɪt/ *noun* a budget which changes in response to changes in sales turnover or output

flight of capital /ˌflaɪt əv ˈkæpɪt(ə)l/ *noun* a rapid movement of capital out of one country because of lack of confidence in that country's economic future

flight to quality /ˌflaɪt tə ˈkwɒlɪti/ *noun* a tendency of investors to buy safe blue-chip securities when the economic outlook is uncertain

float /fləʊt/ *noun* **1.** cash taken from a central supply and used for running expenses ○ *The sales reps have a float of £100 each.* **2.** the process of starting a new company by selling shares in it on the Stock Exchange ○ *The float of the new company was a complete failure.* **3.** the process of allowing a currency to settle at its own exchange rate, without any government intervention **4.** the period between the presentation of a cheque as payment and the actual payment to the payee, or the financial advantage provided by this period to the drawer of a cheque ■ *verb* to let a currency settle at its own exchange rate on the international markets and not be fixed ○ *The government has let sterling float.* ○ *The government has decided to float the pound.*

floating /ˈfləʊtɪŋ/ *adjective* not fixed ○ *floating exchange rates* ○ *the floating pound*

'...in a world of floating exchange rates the dollar is strong because of capital inflows rather than weak because of the nation's trade deficit' [*Duns Business Month*]

floating capital /ˌfləʊtɪŋ ˈkæpɪt(ə)l/ *noun* the portion of capital invested in current assets, as distinct from that invested in fixed assets or capital assets

floating charge /ˈfləʊtɪŋ tʃɑːdʒ/ *noun* a charge linked to any of the company's assets in a category, but not to any specific item

floating rate /ˈfləʊtɪŋ reɪt/ *noun* **1.** same as **variable rate 2.** an exchange rate for a currency, which can vary according to market demand, and is not fixed by the government

floating-rate notes /ˌfləʊtɪŋ reɪt ˈnəʊts/ *plural noun* Eurocurrency loans arranged by a bank which are not at a fixed rate of interest. Abbreviation **FRNs**

floor /flɔː/ *noun* the bottom level of something, e.g. the lowest exchange rate which a government will accept for its currency or the lower limit imposed on an interest rate ○ *The government will impose a floor on wages to protect the poor.*

floor price /ˈflɔː praɪs/ *noun* the lowest price, a price which cannot go any lower

floor space /ˈflɔː speɪs/ *noun* an area of floor in an office or warehouse ○ *We have 3,500 square metres of floor space to let.*

flop /flɒp/ *noun* a failure, or something which has not been successful ○ *The new model was a flop.*

flow chart /ˈfləʊ tʃɑːt/, **flow diagram** /ˈfləʊ ˌdaɪəgræm/ *noun* a chart which shows the arrangement of work processes in a series

fluctuate /ˈflʌktʃueɪt/ *verb* to move up and down ○ *Prices fluctuated between £1.10 and £1.25.* ○ *The pound fluctuated all day on the foreign exchange markets.*

fluctuation /ˌflʌktʃuˈeɪʃ(ə)n/ *noun* an up and down movement ○ *the fluctuations of the yen* ○ *the fluctuations of the exchange rate*

FOB, f.o.b. *abbreviation* free on board

folio /ˈfəʊliəʊ/ *noun* a page with a number, especially two facing pages in an account book which have the same number ■ *verb* to put a number on a page

forced sale /ˌfɔːst ˈseɪl/ *noun* a sale which takes place because a court orders it or because it is the only way to avoid a financial crisis

force majeure /ˌfɔːs mæˈʒɜː/ *noun* something which happens which is out of the control of the parties who have signed a contract, e.g. a strike, war, or storm

forecast /ˈfɔːkɑːst/ *noun* a description or calculation of what will probably happen in the future ○ *The chairman did not believe the sales director's forecast of higher turnover.*

forecast dividend /ˌfɔːkɑːst 'dɪvɪdend/ *noun* a dividend which a company expects to pay at the end of the current year. Also called **prospective dividend**

forecaster /'fɔːkɑːstə/ *noun* a person who says what he or she thinks will happen in the future

forecasting /'fɔːkɑːstɪŋ/ *noun* the process of calculating what will probably happen in the future ○ *Manpower planning will depend on forecasting the future levels of production.*

foreclose /fɔː'kləʊz/ *verb* to sell a property because the owner cannot repay money which he or she has borrowed, using the property as security ○ *to foreclose on a mortgaged property*

foreclosure /fɔː'kləʊʒə/ *noun* an act of foreclosing

foreign banks /ˌfɒrɪn 'bæŋks/ *plural noun* banks from other countries which have branches in a country

foreign branch /ˌfɒrɪn 'brɑːntʃ/ *noun* a branch of a company in another country. The accounts of foreign branches may cause problems because of varying exchange rates.

foreign company /ˌfɒrɪn 'kʌmp(ə)ni/ *noun* a company that is registered in a foreign country

foreign currency /ˌfɒrɪn 'kʌrənsi/ *noun* money of another country

foreign currency account /ˌfɒrɪn 'kʌrənsi əˌkaʊnt/ *noun* a bank account in the currency of another country, e.g. a dollar account in a UK bank

foreign currency reserves /ˌfɒrɪn 'kʌrənsi rɪˌzɜːvz/ *plural noun* foreign money held by a government to support its own currency and pay its debts. Also called **foreign exchange reserves**, **international reserves**

'…the treasury says it needs the cash to rebuild its foreign reserves which have fallen from $19 billion when the government took office to $7 billion in August' [*Economist*]

foreign earnings /ˌfɒrɪn 'ɜːnɪŋz/ *plural noun* earnings received from employment in a foreign country

foreign entity /ˌfɒrɪn 'entɪti/ *noun* a person or incorporated company based in a foreign country

foreign exchange /ˌfɒrɪn ɪks'tʃeɪndʒ/ *noun* **1.** the business of exchanging the money of one country for that of another **2.** foreign currencies

'…the dollar recovered a little lost ground on the foreign exchanges yesterday' [*Financial Times*]

foreign exchange broker /ˌfɒrɪn ɪks'tʃeɪndʒ ˌbrəʊkə/, **foreign exchange dealer** /ˌfɒrɪn ɪks'tʃeɪndʒ ˌdiːlə/ *noun* a person who deals on the foreign exchange market

foreign exchange dealing /ˌfɒrɪn ɪks'tʃeɪndʒ ˌdiːlɪŋ/ *noun* the business of buying and selling foreign currencies

foreign exchange market /ˌfɒrɪn ɪks'tʃeɪndʒ ˌmɑːkɪt/ *noun* **1.** a market where people buy and sell foreign currencies ○ *She trades on the foreign exchange market.* **2.** dealings in foreign currencies ○ *Foreign exchange markets were very active after the dollar devalued.*

foreign exchange reserves /ˌfɒrɪn ɪks'tʃeɪndʒ rɪˌzɜːvz/ *plural noun* same as **foreign currency reserves**

foreign exchange transfer /ˌfɒrɪn ɪks'tʃeɪndʒ ˌtrænsfɜː/ *noun* the sending of money from one country to another

foreign income /ˌfɒrɪn 'ɪnkʌm/ *noun* income derived from sources in a foreign country

foreign investments /ˌfɒrɪn ɪn'vestmənts/ *plural noun* money invested in other countries

foreign money order /ˌfɒrɪn 'mʌni ˌɔːdə/ *noun* a money order in a foreign currency which is payable to someone living in a foreign country

foreign tax credit /ˌfɒrɪn 'tæks ˌkredɪt/ *noun* a tax advantage that applies in the case of taxes paid to or in another country

foreign trade /ˌfɒrɪn 'treɪd/ *noun* a trade with other countries

forensic /fə'rensɪk/ *adjective* referring to the courts or to the law in general

forensic accounting /fəˌrensɪk ə'kaʊntɪŋ/ *noun* the scrutinisation of an entity's past financial activities in order to discover whether illegal practices have been used at any time

forensic partner /fəˌrensɪk 'pɑːtnə/ *noun* a partner in an accountancy firm who deals with litigation

foreseeable loss /fɔːˌsiːəb(ə)l 'lɒs/ *noun* a loss which is expected to occur during a long-term contract

forfaiting /'fɔːfɪtɪŋ/ *noun* the action of providing finance for exporters, where an agent or forfaiter accepts a bill of exchange from an overseas customer; he or she buys the bill at a discount, and collects the payments from the customer in due course

forfeit /'fɔːfɪt/ *verb* to have something taken away as a punishment □ **to forfeit shares** to be forced to give back shares if money called up is not paid on time

forfeit clause /'fɔːfɪt klɔːz/ *noun* a clause in a contract which says that goods or a deposit will be taken away if the contract is not obeyed

forfeiture /'fɔːfɪtʃə/ *noun* the act of forfeiting a property

form /fɔːm/ *noun* **1.** □ **form of words** words correctly laid out for a legal document □ **receipt in due form** a correctly written receipt **2.** an official printed paper with blank spaces which have to be filled in with information ○ *a pad of order forms* ○ *You have to fill in form A20.* ○ *Each passenger was given a customs declaration form.* ○ *The reps carry pads of order forms.*

formal /'fɔːm(ə)l/ *adjective* clearly and legally written ○ *to make a formal application* ○ *to send a formal order* ○ *Is this a formal job offer?* ○ *The factory is prepared for the formal inspection by the government inspector.*

formal documents /ˌfɔːm(ə)l 'dɒkjʊmənts/ *plural noun* documents giving full details of a takeover bid

formality /fɔː'mælɪti/ *noun* something which has to be done to obey the law

form letter /'fɔːm ˌletə/ *noun* a letter which can be sent without any change to several correspondents, e.g. a letter chasing payment

forward /'fɔːwəd/ *adjective* in advance or to be paid at a later date

forward accounting /'fɔːwəd ə ˌkaʊntɪŋ/ *noun* the practice of using accounting procedures to forecast a business's future performance

forwardation /ˌfɔːwəd'eɪʃ(ə)n/ *noun* a situation in which the cash price is lower than the forward price (NOTE: The opposite is **backwardation.**)

forward contract /'fɔːwəd ˌkɒntrækt/ *noun* a one-off agreement to buy currency, shares or commodities for delivery at a later date at a specific price

forward cover /'fɔːwəd ˌkʌvə/ *noun* an arrangement to cover the risks on a forward contract

forward delivery /ˌfɔːwəd dɪ'lɪv(ə)ri/ *noun* a delivery at some date in the future which has been agreed between the buyer and seller

forward exchange rate /ˌfɔːwəd ɪks 'tʃeɪndʒ reɪt/ *noun* a rate for purchase of foreign currency at a fixed price for delivery at a later date ○ *What are the forward rates for the pound?* Also called **forward rate**

forward financial statement /ˌfɔːwəd faɪˌnænʃ(ə)l 'steɪtmənt/ *noun* an estimate of a company's future financial position

forwarding agent /'fɔːwədɪŋ ˌeɪdʒənt/ *noun* a person or company which arranges shipping and customs documents

forward integration /ˌfɔːwəd ˌɪntə 'greɪʃ(ə)n/ *noun* a process of expansion in which a company becomes its own distributor or takes over a company in the same line of business as itself ○ *Forward integration will give the company greater control over its selling.* ○ *Forward integration has brought the company closer to its consumers and has made it aware of their buying habits.* Compare **backward integration**

forward margin /ˌfɔːwəd 'mɑːdʒɪn/ *noun* the difference between the current price and the forward price

forward market /ˌfɔːwəd 'mɑːkɪt/ *noun* a market for purchasing foreign currency, oil or commodities for delivery at a later date

forward price /'fɔːwəd praɪs/ *noun* a price of goods which are to be delivered in the future

forward rate /'fɔːwəd reɪt/ *noun* same as **forward exchange rate**

forward sales /'fɔːwəd seɪlz/ *plural noun* sales of shares, commodities or foreign exchange for delivery at a later date

forwards spreading /ˌfɔːwədz 'spredɪŋ/ *noun* the act of spreading lump sum income over several years in the future

forward trading /'fɔːwəd ˌtreɪdɪŋ/ *noun* the activity of buying or selling commodities for delivery at a later date

founder /'faʊndə/ *noun* a person who starts a company

401(k) plan /ˌfɔː əʊ wʌn 'keɪ plæn/ *noun* US a personal pension plan arranged by an employer for a member of staff, invested in bonds, mutual funds or stock (the employee contributes a proportion of salary, on which tax is deferred; the employer can also make contributions)

fourth quarter /ˌfɔːθ 'kwɔːtə/ *noun* a period of three months from 1st October to the end of the year

fraction /'frækʃən/ *noun* a very small amount ○ *Only a fraction of the new share issue was subscribed.*

fractional /ˈfrækʃənəl/ *adjective* very small

fractional certificate /ˈfrækʃənəl səˈtɪfɪkət/ *noun* a certificate for part of a share

franc /fræŋk/ *noun* **1.** a former unit of currency in France and Belgium ○ *French francs* or *Belgian francs* **2.** a unit of currency in Switzerland and several other currencies ○ *It costs twenty-five Swiss francs.*

franchise /ˈfræntʃaɪz/ *noun* a licence to trade using a brand name and paying a royalty for it ○ *He's bought a printing franchise* or *a pizza franchise.* ■ *verb* to sell licences for people to trade using a brand name and paying a royalty ○ *His sandwich bar was so successful that he decided to franchise it.*

'…many new types of franchised businesses will join the ranks of the giant chains of fast-food restaurants, hotels and motels and rental car agencies' [*Franchising Opportunities*]

franchisee /ˌfræntʃaɪˈziː/ *noun* a person who runs a franchise

franchiser /ˈfræntʃaɪzə/ *noun* a person who licenses a franchise

franchising /ˈfræntʃaɪzɪŋ/ *noun* the act of selling a licence to trade as a franchise ○ *She runs her sandwich chain as a franchising operation.*

franco /ˈfræŋkəʊ/ *adverb* free

franked /fræŋkd/ *adjective* on which tax has already been paid

fraud /frɔːd/ *noun* the act of making money by making people believe something which is not true ○ *He got possession of the property by fraud.* ○ *She was accused of frauds relating to foreign currency.*

fraudulent /ˈfrɔːdjʊlənt/ *adjective* not honest, or aiming to cheat people ○ *a fraudulent transaction*

fraudulently /ˈfrɔːdjʊləntli/ *adverb* not honestly ○ *goods imported fraudulently*

fraudulent misrepresentation /ˌfrɔːdjʊlənt mɪsˌreprɪzenˈteɪʃ(ə)n/ *noun* the act of making a false statement with the intention of tricking a customer

fraudulent trading /ˌfrɔːdjʊlənt ˈtreɪdɪŋ/ *noun* the process of carrying on the business of a company, knowing that the company is insolvent

FRB *abbreviation* **1.** Federal Reserve Bank **2.** Federal Reserve Board

free /friː/ *adjective, adverb* **1.** not costing any money ○ *I have been given a free ticket to the exhibition.* ○ *The price includes free delivery.* ○ *All goods in the store are delivered free.* ○ *A catalogue will be sent free on request.* **2.** with no restrictions □ **free of tax** with no tax having to be paid ○ *Interest is paid free of tax.* □ **free of duty** with no duty to be paid ○ *to import wine free of duty* ■ *verb* to make something available or easy ○ *The government's decision has freed millions of pounds for investment.*

'American business as a whole is increasingly free from heavy dependence on manufacturing' [*Sunday Times*]

free cash flow /ˌfriː ˈkæʃ ˌfləʊ/ *noun* the level of cash flow after the deduction of interest payments, tax payments, dividends and ongoing capital expenditure

free competition /ˌfriː ˌkɒmpəˈtɪʃ(ə)n/ *noun* the fact of being free to compete without government interference

free currency /ˌfriː ˈkʌrənsi/ *noun* a currency which is allowed by the government to be bought and sold without restriction

free enterprise /ˌfriː ˈentəpraɪz/ *noun* a system of business free from government interference

freeholder /ˈfriːhəʊldə/ *noun* a person who owns a freehold property

freehold property /ˈfriːhəʊld ˌprɒpəti/ *noun* property which the owner holds for ever and on which no rent is paid

free issue /ˌfriː ˈɪʃuː/ *noun* same as **bonus issue**

free market /ˌfriː ˈmɑːkɪt/ *noun* a market in which there is no government control of supply and demand, and the rights of individuals and organisations to physical and intellectual property are upheld

free market economy /ˌfriː ˌmɑːkɪt ɪ ˈkɒnəmi/ *noun* an economic system where the government does not interfere in business activity in any way

free on board /ˌfriː ɒn ˈbɔːd/ *adjective* **1.** including in the price all the seller's costs until the goods are on the ship for transportation. Abbreviation **f.o.b. 2.** including in the price all the seller's costs until the goods are delivered to a place

free reserves /ˌfriː rɪˈzɜːvz/ *plural noun* the part of a bank's reserves which are above the statutory level and so can be used for various purposes as the bank wishes

free-standing additional voluntary contribution /ˌfriː ˌstændɪŋ əˌdɪʃ(ə)nəl ˌvɒlənt(ə)ri ˌkɒntrɪˈbjuːʃ(ə)n/ *noun* a payment made by an individual into an independent pension fund to supplement an occupational pension scheme. The anticipated benefits from the two schemes together must be less than the maximum permitted under the rules laid down by the Inland Revenue. Abbreviation **FSAVC**

free trade /ˌfriː ˈtreɪd/ *noun* a system where goods can go from one country to another without any restrictions

free trade area /ˌfriː ˈtreɪd ˌeəriə/ *noun* a group of countries practising free trade

free trader /ˌfriː ˈtreɪdə/ *noun* a person who is in favour of free trade

free trade zone /ˌfriː ˈtreɪd ˌzəʊn/ *noun* an area where there are no customs duties

freeze /friːz/ *noun* □ **a freeze on wages and prices** period when wages and prices are not allowed to be increased ■ *verb* to keep something such as money or costs at their present level and not allow them to rise ○ *to freeze wages and prices* ○ *to freeze credits* ○ *to freeze company dividends* ○ *We have frozen expenditure at last year's level.* (NOTE: **freezing – froze – frozen**)

freight /freɪt/ *noun* the cost of transporting goods by air, sea, or land ○ *At an auction, the buyer pays the freight.*

freightage /ˈfreɪtɪdʒ/ *noun* the cost of transporting goods

freight costs /ˈfreɪt kɒsts/ *plural noun* money paid to transport goods

freight forward /ˌfreɪt ˈfɔːwəd/ *noun* a deal where the customer pays for transporting the goods

friendly society /ˈfrendli səˌsaɪəti/ *noun* a group of people who pay regular subscriptions which are used to help members of the group when they are ill or in financial difficulties

fringe benefit /ˈfrɪndʒ ˌbenɪfɪt/ *noun* an extra item given by a company to employees in addition to a salary, e.g. company cars or private health insurance ○ *The fringe benefits make up for the poor pay.* ○ *Use of the company recreation facilities is one of the fringe benefits of the job.*

FRNs *abbreviation* floating-rate notes

front /frʌnt/ *noun* □ **money up front** payment in advance ○ *They are asking for £10,000 up front before they will consider the deal.* ○ *He had to put money up front before he could clinch the deal.*

front-end /ˌfrʌnt ˈend/ *adjective* referring to the start of an investment or insurance

front-end loaded /ˈfrʌnt end ˌlaʊdɪd/ *adjective* used to describe an insurance or investment scheme in which most of the management charges are incurred in the first year of the investment or insurance, and are not spread out over the whole period. Compare **back-end loaded**

front-end loading /ˈfrʌnt end ˌlaʊdɪŋ/ *noun* the practice of deducting commission and administrative costs relating to an investment or insurance plan from the early payments the customer makes

frozen /ˈfrəʊz(ə)n/ *adjective* not allowed to be changed or used ○ *Wages have been frozen at last year's rates.*

frozen account /ˈfrəʊz(ə)n əˌkaʊnt/ *noun* a bank account where the money cannot be moved or used because of a court order

frozen assets /ˌfrəʊz(ə)n ˈæsets/ *plural noun* a company's assets which by law cannot be sold because someone has a claim against them

frozen credits /ˌfrəʊz(ə)n ˈkredɪts/ *plural noun* credits in an account which cannot be moved

FRRP *abbreviation* Financial Reporting Review Panel

FRSs *abbreviation* Financial Reporting Standards

frustrate /frʌˈstreɪt/ *verb* to prevent something, especially the terms of a contract, being fulfilled

FSA *abbreviation* Financial Services Authority

FSAVC *abbreviation* free-standing additional voluntary contribution

FT *abbreviation* Financial Times

FTASI *abbreviation* FTSE Actuaries Share Indices

FTSE 100 /ˌfʊtsi wʌn ˈhʌndrəd/ *noun* an index based on the prices of one hundred leading companies (this is the main London index)

'…the benchmark FTSE 100 index ended the session up 94.3 points' [*Times*]

FTSE Actuaries Share Indices /ˌfʊtsi ˌæktjʊəriz ˈʃeə ˌɪndɪsiz/ *plural noun* several indices based on prices on the London Stock Exchange, which are calculated by and published in the Financial Times in conjunction with the Actuaries Investment Research Committee. Abbreviation **FTASI**.
◊ **Financial Times**

full /fʊl/ *adjective* **1.** with as much inside it as possible ○ *The train was full of commuters.* ○ *Is the container full yet?* ○ *We sent a lorry full of spare parts to our warehouse.* ○ *When the disk is full, don't forget to make a backup copy.* **2.** complete, including everything

'…a tax-free lump sum can be taken partly in lieu of a full pension' [*Investors Chronicle*]

full cost recovery /ˌfʊl 'kɒst rɪˌkʌvəri/ noun the practice by which organisations such as charities seek enough funding to cover all their costs, including overheads. Abbreviation **FCR**

full cover /ˌfʊl 'kʌvə/ noun insurance cover against a wide range of risks

full employment /ˌfʊl ɪm'plɔɪmənt/ noun a situation where all the people who can work have jobs

full price /ˌfʊl 'praɪs/ noun a price with no discount ○ She bought a full-price ticket.

full production costs /ˌfʊl prə'dʌkʃən ˌkɒsts/ plural noun all the costs of manufacturing a product, including both fixed and variable costs

full rate /ˌfʊl 'reɪt/ noun the standard charge for a service, with no special discounts applied

full repairing lease /ˌfʊl rɪ'peərɪŋ ˌliːs/ noun a lease where the tenant has to pay for all repairs to the property

full-service banking /ˌfʊl ˌsɜːvɪs 'bæŋkɪŋ/ noun banking that offers a whole range of services including mortgages, loans, pensions, etc.

full-time /'fʊl taɪm/ adjective, adverb working all the usual working time, i.e. about eight hours a day, five days a week ○ She's in full-time work or She works full-time or She's in full-time employment. ○ He is one of our full-time staff.

fully diluted earnings per share /ˌfʊli daɪˌluːtɪd ˌɜːnɪŋz pə 'ʃeə/, **fully diluted EPS** /ˌfʊli ˌdaɪluːtɪd ˌiː piː 'es/ plural noun earnings per share calculated over the whole number of shares assuming that convertible shares have been converted to ordinary shares

fully paid-up capital /ˌfʊli peɪd ʌp 'kæpɪt(ə)l/ noun all money paid for the issued capital shares

function /'fʌŋkʃən/ noun a mathematical formula, where a result is dependent upon several other numbers

functional accounting /'fʌŋkʃən(ə)l əˌkaʊntɪŋ/ noun a form of accounting that classifies accountancy items according to the function they perform in an organisation

functional budget /ˌfʌŋkʃən(ə)l 'bʌdʒɪt/ noun a budget relating to a specific function such as marketing or personnel

functional reporting of expenses /ˌfʌŋkʃən(ə)l rɪˌpɔːtɪŋ əv ɪk'spensɪz/ noun the element of functional accounting that deals with expenses

function cost /'fʌŋkʃən kɒst/ noun the category of item for which costs are incurred

fund /fʌnd/ noun **1.** money set aside for a special purpose **2.** money invested in an investment trust as part of a unit trust, or given to a financial adviser to invest on behalf of a client. ◊ **funds** ■ verb to provide money for a purpose ○ The company does not have enough resources to fund its expansion programme.

'…the S&L funded all borrowers' development costs, including accrued interest' [Barrons]

fund accounting /'fʌnd əˌkaʊntɪŋ/ noun the preparation of financial statements for an entity such as a non-profitmaking organisation, in order to show how money has been spent rather than how much profit has been made

fundamental analysis /ˌfʌndəment(ə)l ə'næləsɪs/ noun an assessment of how the external and internal influences on a company's activities should affect investment decisions

fundamental assumptions /ˌfʌndəment(ə)l ə'sʌmpʃ(ə)ns/ plural noun the basic assumptions on which the preparation of accounts depends (NOTE: These assumptions are: that the company is a going concern, that the principles on which the accounts are prepared do not change from year to year, that revenues and costs are accrued (i.e., they are written into the accounts when they occur, not when they are received or paid).)

fundamental issues /ˌfʌndəment(ə)l 'ɪʃuːz/ plural noun matters relating to a company's profits or assets

fundamental research /ˌfʌndəment(ə)l rɪ'sɜːtʃ/, **fundamental analysis** /ˌfʌndəment(ə)l ə'næləsɪs/ noun an examination of the basic factors which affect a market

fundamentals /ˌfʌndə'ment(ə)lz/ plural noun the basic realities of a stock market or of a company, e.g. its assets, profitability and dividends

funded /'fʌndɪd/ adjective backed by long-term loans ○ long-term funded capital

funded scheme /ˌfʌndɪd 'skiːm/ noun a pension scheme where money is invested in securities to create a fund from which the pension is later paid

funding /'fʌndɪŋ/ noun **1.** money for spending ○ The bank is providing the funding for the new product launch. **2.** the act of changing a short-term debt into a long-term loan ○ *The capital expenditure programme requires long-term funding.*

fund management /'fʌnd ˌmænɪdʒmənt/ *noun* the business of dealing with the investment of sums of money on behalf of clients

funds /fʌndz/ *plural noun* **1.** money which is available for spending ○ *The company has no funds to pay for the research programme.* ◊ **non-sufficient funds** □ **to convert funds to your own use** to use someone else's money for yourself **2.** □ **the Funds** government stocks and securities. ◊ **Federal Funds**

'…small innovative companies have been hampered for lack of funds' [*Sunday Times*]

'…the company was set up with funds totalling NorKr 145m' [*Lloyd's List*]

funds flow /'fʌndz fləʊ/ *noun* □ **budgeted funds flow statement** a plan of anticipated incoming funds and the use to which they will be put □ **funds flow method of budgeting** preparing a budget of funds flow, as opposed to a budget of expenditure □ **funds flow statement** a statement which shows the amount of funds (cash and working capital) which have come into a business during the last financial period, the sources of these funds, and the use made of the funds (see FRS1, formerly SSAP10)

fungibility /ˌfʌndʒə'bɪlɪti/ *noun* a measure of how easily an asset can be exchanged for something similar

fungible /'fʌndʒəb(ə)l/ *adjective* referring to a security which can be exchanged for another of the same type

funny money /'fʌni ˌmʌni/ *noun* an unusual type of financial instrument created by a company

future delivery /ˌfjuːtʃə dɪ'lɪv(ə)ri/ *noun* delivery at a later date

futures /'fjuːtʃəz/ *plural noun* shares, currency or commodities that are bought or sold for now for delivery at a later date ○ *Gold rose 5% on the commodity futures market yesterday.*

'…cocoa futures plummeted in November to their lowest levels in seven years' [*Business in Africa*]

futures contract /'fjuːtʃəz ˌkɒntrækt/ *noun* a contract for the purchase of commodities for delivery at a date in the future

futures exchange /'fjuːtʃəz ɪks ˌtʃeɪndʒ/ *noun* a commodity market which only deals in futures

future value /ˌfjuːtʃə 'væljuː/ *noun* the value to which a sum of money will increase if invested for a certain period of time at some rate of interest. Abbreviation **FV**

FV *abbreviation* future value

FYA *abbreviation* first year allowance

G

GAAP *abbreviation* Generally Accepted Accounting Principles

gain /geɪn/ *noun* **1.** an increase, or the act of becoming larger **2.** an increase in profit, price, or value ○ *Oil shares showed gains on the Stock Exchange.* ○ *Property shares put on gains of 10%-15%.* **3.** money made by a company which is not from the company's usual trading ■ *verb* **1.** to get or to obtain ○ *She gained some useful experience working in a bank.* □ **to gain control of a business** to buy more than 50% of the shares so that you can direct the business **2.** to rise in value ○ *The dollar gained six points on the foreign exchange markets.*

galloping inflation /ˌɡæləpɪŋ ɪnˈfleɪʃ(ə)n/ *noun* very rapid inflation which is almost impossible to reduce

gap analysis /ˈɡæp əˌnæləsɪs/ *noun* analysis of a market to try to find a particular area that is not at present being satisfied ○ *Gap analysis showed that there was a whole area of the market we were not exploiting.*

gap financing /ˈɡæp ˌfaɪnænsɪŋ/ *noun* the process of arranging extra loans such as a bridging loan to cover a purchase not covered by an existing loan

garnishee /ˌɡɑːnɪˈʃiː/ *noun* a person who owes money to a creditor and is ordered by a court to pay that money to a creditor of the creditor, and not to the creditor himself

garnishee order /ˌɡɑːnɪˈʃiː ˌɔːdə/ *noun* a court order, making a garnishee pay money not to the debtor, but to a third party

GAS *abbreviation* Government Accountancy Service

GDP *abbreviation* gross domestic product

gear /ɡɪə/ *verb* to link something to something else

gearing /ˈɡɪərɪŋ/ *noun* **1.** the ratio of capital borrowed by a company at a fixed rate of interest to the company's total capital. Also called **leverage 2.** the act of borrowing money at fixed interest which is then used to produce more money than the interest paid

gearing ratio /ˈɡɪərɪŋ ˌreɪʃiəʊ/ *noun* any ratio that compares equity to borrowing

general audit /ˌdʒen(ə)rəl ˈɔːdɪt/ *noun* the process of examining all the books and accounts of a company

general average /ˌdʒen(ə)rəl ˈæv(ə)rɪdʒ/ *noun* a process by which the cost of lost goods is shared by all parties to an insurance policy, such as in cases where some goods have been lost in an attempt to save the rest of the cargo

general balance sheet /ˌdʒen(ə)rəl ˈbæləns ˌʃiːt/ *noun* the standard form of balance sheet used by non-commercial organisations such as charities and government departments

General Commissioners /ˌdʒen(ə)rəl kəˈmɪʃ(ə)nəz/ *plural noun* a body of unpaid individuals appointed by the Lord Chancellor in England, Wales and Northern Ireland, and the Secretary of State for Scotland in Scotland, to hear appeals on tax matters

general damages /ˌdʒen(ə)rəl ˈdæmɪdʒɪz/ *plural noun* damages awarded by court to compensate for a loss which cannot be calculated, such as an injury

general expenses /ˌdʒen(ə)rəl ɪkˈspensɪz/ *plural noun* minor expenses of various kinds incurred in the running of a business

general fund /ˈdʒen(ə)rəl fʌnd/ *noun* a unit trust with investments in a variety of stocks

general insurance /ˌdʒen(ə)rəl ɪnˈʃʊərəns/ *noun* insurance relating to various potential losses, e.g. theft or damage, but excluding life insurance

general ledger /ˈdʒen(ə)rəl ˌledʒə/ *noun* a book which records a company's income and expenditure in general

general lien /ˌdʒen(ə)rəl ˈliːən/ *noun* **1.** a right to hold goods or property until a debt has been paid **2.** a lien against the personal possessions of a borrower, but not against his or her house or land. ◊ **banker's lien**

Generally Accepted Accounting Principles /ˌdʒen(ə)rəli əkˌseptɪd ə'kaʊntɪŋ ˌprɪnsɪp(ə)lz/ *plural noun US* a summary of best practice in respect of the form and content of financial statements and auditor's reports, and of accounting policies and disclosures adopted for the preparation of financial information. GAAP does not have any statutory or regulatory authority in the United Kingdom, unlike in a number of other countries where the term is in use, such as the United States, Canada. Abbreviation **GAAP**

generally accepted auditing standards /ˌdʒen(ə)rəli əkˌseptɪd 'ɔːdɪtɪŋ ˌstændədz/ *plural noun* guidelines that are designed to inform the work of auditors and set out the auditor's responsibilities

general manager /ˌdʒen(ə)rəl 'mænɪdʒə/ *noun* a manager in charge of the administration of a company

general meeting /ˌdʒen(ə)rəl 'miːtɪŋ/ *noun* a meeting of all the shareholders of a company or of all the members of a society

general partner /ˌdʒen(ə)rəl 'pɑːtnə/ *noun* a partner in a business whose responsibility for its debts is not limited and, therefore, whose personal assets may be at risk if the company's assets are not sufficient to discharge its debts

general partnership /ˌdʒen(ə)rəl 'pɑːtnəʃɪp/ *noun* the relationship of a general partner to his or her company

general undertaking /ˌdʒen(ə)rəl ˌʌndə'teɪkɪŋ/ *noun* an undertaking signed by the directors of a company applying for a Stock Exchange listing, promising to work within the regulations of the Stock Exchange

gift aid /'ɡɪft eɪd/ *noun* payment above some limit made to a registered charity, meaning that the charity is able to reclaim the basic rate tax which you have paid on the gift

gift inter vivos /ˌɡɪft ɪntə 'viːvəʊs/ *noun* a gift given to another living person. Abbreviation **GIV**

gift tax /'ɡɪft tæks/ *noun* a tax on gifts. Only gifts between husband and wife are exempt.

gilt-edged /'ɡɪlt edʒd/ *adjective* used to describe an investment which is very safe

gilt-edged securities /ˌɡɪlt edʒd sɪ'kjʊərɪtiz/ *plural noun* investments in British government stock

gilts /ɡɪlts/ *plural noun* same as **government bonds**

giro /'dʒaɪrəʊ/ *noun* same as **bank giro**

GIV *abbreviation* gift inter vivos

GM *abbreviation* gross margin

GNP *abbreviation* gross national product

goal congruence /'ɡəʊl ˌkɒŋɡruəns/ *noun* a situation that leads individuals or companies to take actions which are in their own best interests

go-go fund /'ɡəʊ ɡəʊ ˌfʌnd/ *noun* a fund which aims to give very high returns because it is invested in speculative stocks

going concern /ˌɡəʊɪŋ kən'sɜːn/ *noun* a company that is actively trading and making a profit

going concern value /ˌɡəʊɪŋ kən'sɜːn ˌvæljuː/ *noun* the value of a company as it continues trading as opposed to its break-up value

gold bullion /ˌɡəʊld 'bʊliən/ *noun* bars of gold

gold card /'ɡəʊld kɑːd/ *noun* a credit card issued to important customers, i.e., those with a high income, which gives certain privileges such as a higher spending limit than ordinary credit cards

golden handcuffs /ˌɡəʊld(ə)n 'hændkʌfs/ *plural noun* a contractual arrangement to make sure that a valued member of staff stays in their job, by which they are offered special financial advantages if they stay and heavy penalties if they leave

golden handshake /ˌɡəʊld(ə)n 'hændʃeɪk/ *noun* a large, usually tax-free, sum of money given to a director who retires from a company before the end of his or her service contract ○ *The retiring director received a golden handshake of £250,000.*

golden parachute agreement /ˌɡəʊld(ə)n 'pærəˌʃuːt əˌɡriːmənt/ *noun* a contract that gives a senior manager very generous monetary compensation if his or job is lost as a result of a merger or acquisition

golden share /ˌɡəʊld(ə)n 'ʃeə/ *noun* a share in a privatised company which is retained by the government and carries special privileges such as the right to veto foreign takeover bids

goldmine /'ɡəʊldmaɪn/ *noun* a mine which produces gold

gold point /'ɡəʊld pɔɪnt/ *noun* an amount by which a currency which is linked to gold can vary in price

gold reserves /'ɡəʊld rɪˌzɜːvz/ *plural noun* the country's store of gold kept to pay international debts

goods /gʊdz/ *plural noun* items which can be moved and are for sale □ **goods received** goods which have been sent by a seller and received by a purchaser during an accounting period □ **goods received note** an internal note within a company which shows the date when goods were received, by whom and in what quantities

'…profit margins are lower in the industries most exposed to foreign competition – machinery, transportation equipment and electrical goods' [*Sunday Times*]

'…the minister wants people buying goods ranging from washing machines to houses to demand facts on energy costs' [*Times*]

goods and chattels /ˌgʊdz ən ˈtʃæt(ə)lz/ *plural noun* movable personal possessions

Goods and Services Tax /ˌgʊdz ən ˈsɜːvɪsɪz tæks/ *noun* a Canadian tax on the sale of goods or the provision of services, similar to VAT. Abbreviation **GST**

goodwill /gʊdˈwɪl/ *noun* the good reputation of a business, which can be calculated as part of a company's asset value, though separate from its tangible asset value ○ *He paid £10,000 for the goodwill of the shop and £4,000 for the stock.* (NOTE: The goodwill can include the trading reputation, the patents, the trade names used, the value of a 'good site', etc., and is very difficult to establish accurately.)

go private /ˌgəʊ ˈpraɪvət/ *verb* to become a private company again, by concentrating all its shares in the hands of one or a few shareholders and removing its stock exchange listing

go public /ˌgəʊ ˈpʌblɪk/ *phrasal verb* to become a public company by placing some of its shares for sale on the stock market so that anyone can buy them

govern /ˈgʌv(ə)n/ *verb* to rule a country ○ *The country is governed by a group of military leaders.*

governance /ˈgʌv(ə)nəns/ *noun* the process of managing a company, especially with respect to the soundness or otherwise of its management

'…the chairman has committed the cardinal sin in corporate governance – he acted against the wishes and interests of the shareholders' [*Investors Chronicle*]

'…in two significant decisions, the Securities and Exchange Board of India today allowed trading of shares through the Internet and set a deadline for companies to conform to norms for good corporate governance' [*The Hindu*]

Government Accountancy Service /ˌgʌv(ə)nmənt əˈkaʊntənsi ˌsɜːvɪs/ *noun* part of HM Treasury, a service whose remit it is to ensure that best accounting practice is observed and conducted across the whole of the Civil Service. Abbreviation **GAS**

governmental /ˌgʌv(ə)nˈment(ə)l/ *adjective* referring to a government

government-backed /ˈgʌv(ə)nmənt ˌbækt/ *adjective* backed by the government

government bonds /ˌgʌv(ə)nmənt ˈbɒndz/ *plural noun* bonds or other securities issued by the government on a regular basis as a method of borrowing money for government expenditure

government contractor /ˌgʌv(ə)nmənt kənˈtræktə/ *noun* a company which supplies the government with goods by contract

government-controlled /ˈgʌv(ə)nmənt kənˌtrəʊld/ *adjective* under the direct control of the government ○ *Advertisements cannot be placed in the government-controlled newspapers.*

government economic indicators /ˌgʌv(ə)nmənt ˌiːkənɒmɪk ˈɪndɪkeɪtəz/ *plural noun* statistics which show how the country's economy is going to perform in the short or long term

government grant /ˌgʌv(ə)nmənt ˈgrɑːnt/ *noun* a grant of money or assets given by a central government, a local government or a government agency ○ *The laboratory has a government grant to cover the cost of the development programme*

government loan /ˌgʌv(ə)nmənt ˈləʊn/ *noun* money lent by the government

government-regulated /ˈgʌv(ə)nmənt ˌregjʊleɪtɪd/ *adjective* of which the affairs are subject to government regulation

government sector /ˌgʌv(ə)nmənt ˈsektə/ *noun* same as **public sector**

government securities /ˌgʌv(ə)nmənt sɪˈkjʊərɪtiz/ *plural noun* same as **government bonds**

government-sponsored /ˈgʌv(ə)nmənt ˌspɒnsəd/ *adjective* encouraged by the government and backed by government money ○ *She is working in a government-sponsored scheme to help small businesses.*

government stock /ˌgʌv(ə)nmənt ˈstɒk/ *noun* same as **government bonds**

government support /ˌgʌv(ə)nmənt səˈpɔːt/ *noun* a financial help given by the government ○ *The aircraft industry relies on government support.*

governor /ˈgʌv(ə)nə/ *noun* **1.** a person in charge of an important institution **2.** *US* one of the members of the Federal Reserve Board

grace /greɪs/ *noun* a favour shown by granting a delay ○ *to give a creditor a period of grace* or *two weeks' grace*

graduate /ˈgrædʒuət/ *noun* a person who has obtained a degree

graduated /ˈgrædʒueɪtɪd/ *adjective* changing in small regular stages

graduated income tax /ˌgrædʒueɪtɪd ˈɪnkʌm tæks/ *noun* a tax which rises in steps, with those having the highest income paying the highest percentage of tax

graduated pension scheme /ˌgrædʒueɪtɪd ˈpenʃən skiːm/ *noun* a pension scheme where the benefit is calculated as a percentage of the salary of each person in the scheme

graduated taxation /ˌgrædʒueɪtɪd tæk ˈseɪʃ(ə)n/ *noun* same as **progressive taxation**

grand /grænd/ *noun* one thousand pounds or dollars (*informal*) ○ *They offered him fifty grand for the information.* ○ *She's earning fifty grand plus car and expenses.*

grand total /ˌgrænd ˈtəʊt(ə)l/ *noun* the final total made by adding several subtotals

grant /grɑːnt/ *noun* money given by the government to help pay for something ○ *The laboratory has a government grant to cover the cost of the development programme.* ○ *The government has allocated grants towards the costs of the scheme.* ■ *verb* to agree to give someone something ○ *to grant someone a loan* or *a subsidy* ○ *to grant someone three weeks' leave of absence* ○ *The local authority granted the company an interest-free loan to start up the new factory.*

'…the budget grants a tax exemption for $500,000 in capital gains' [*Toronto Star*]

grantor /grɑːnˈtɔː/ *noun* a person who grants a property to another

graph /grɑːf/ *noun* a diagram which shows the relationship between two sets of quantities or values, each of which is represented on an axis ○ *A graph was used to show salary increases in relation to increases in output.* ○ *According to the graph, as average salaries have risen so has absenteeism.*

gratis /ˈgrætɪs/ *adverb* free or not costing anything ○ *We got into the exhibition gratis.*

greenback /ˈgriːnbæk/ *noun US* a dollar bill (*informal*)

'…gold's drop this year is of the same magnitude as the greenback's 8.5% rise' [*Business Week*]

green card /ˌgriːn ˈkɑːd/ *noun* **1.** a special British insurance certificate to prove that a car is insured for travel abroad **2.** an identity card and work permit for a person going to live in the US

green currency /ˌgriːn ˈkʌrənsiː/ *noun* formerly, a currency used in the EU for calculating agricultural payments. Each country had an exchange rate fixed by the Commission, so there were 'green pounds', 'green francs', 'green marks', etc.

greenmail /ˈgriːnmeɪl/ *noun* the practice of making a profit by buying a large number of shares in a company, threatening to take the company over, and then selling the shares back to the company at a higher price

'…he proposes that there should be a limit on greenmail, perhaps permitting payment of a 20% premium on a maximum of 8% of the stock' [*Duns Business Month*]

Green Paper /ˌgriːn ˈpeɪpə/ *noun* a report from the British government on proposals for a new law to be discussed in Parliament. Compare **White Paper**

green pound /ˌgriːn ˈpaʊnd/ *noun* a value for the British pound used in calculating agricultural prices and subsidies in the EU

green report /ˈgriːn rɪˌpɔːt/ *noun* a part of a company's annual report dealing with ecological matters

grey market /ˈgreɪ ˌmɑːkɪt/ *noun* an unofficial market run by dealers, where new issues of shares are bought and sold before they officially become available for trading on the Stock Exchange even before the share allocations are known

gross /grəʊs/ *noun* twelve dozen (144) ○ *He ordered four gross of pens.* (NOTE: no plural) ■ *adjective* total, with no deductions ■ *adverb* with no deductions ○ *My salary is paid gross.*

'…gross wool receipts for the selling season to end June appear likely to top $2 billion' [*Australian Financial Review*]

gross domestic product /ˌgrəʊs də ˌmestɪk ˈprɒdʌkt/ *noun* the annual value of goods and services paid for inside a country. Abbreviation **GDP**

gross earnings /ˌgrəʊs ˈɜːnɪŋz/ *plural noun* total earnings before tax and other deductions

gross income /ˌgrəʊs ˈɪnkʌm/ *noun* a salary before tax is deducted

gross interest /ˌɡrəʊs ˈɪntrəst/ *noun* the interest earned on a deposit or security before the deduction of tax. ◊ **net interest**

gross margin /ˌɡrəʊs ˈmɑːdʒɪn/ *noun* the percentage difference between the received price and the unit manufacturing cost or purchase price of goods for resale. Abbreviation **GM**

gross margin pricing /ˌɡrəʊs ˈmɑːdʒɪn ˌpraɪsɪŋ/ *noun* pricing that takes into account the total production costs of a product

gross margin ratio /ˌɡrəʊs ˈmɑːdʒɪn ˌreɪʃiəʊ/ *noun* same as **gross profit margin**

gross national product /ˌɡrəʊs ˌnæʃ(ə)nəl ˈprɒdʌkt/ *noun* the annual value of goods and services in a country including income from other countries. Abbreviation **GNP**

gross profit /ˌɡrəʊs ˈprɒfɪt/ *noun* a profit calculated as sales income less the cost of the goods sold, i.e. without deducting any other expenses

gross profit analysis /ˌɡrəʊs ˈprɒfɪt ə ˌnæləsɪs/ *noun* analysis of the discrepancy between actual profit and budgeted profit or previous year's profit

gross profit margin /ˌɡrəʊs ˈprɒfɪt ˌmɑːdʒɪn/ *noun* the percentage of each pound of income from sales that remains after goods sold have been paid for by the producer or retailer

gross profit method /ˌɡrəʊs ˈprɒfɪt ˌmeθəd/ *noun* a method of estimating inventory at the point of preparing an interim report

gross receipts /ˌɡrəʊs rɪˈsiːts/ *plural noun* the total amount of money received before expenses are deducted

gross salary /ˌɡrəʊs ˈsæləri/ *noun* same as **gross income**

gross sales /ˌɡrəʊs ˈseɪlz/ *plural noun* money received from sales before deductions for goods returned, special discounts, etc. ○ *Gross sales are impressive since many buyers seem to be ordering more than they will eventually need.*

gross turnover /ˌɡrəʊs ˈtɜːnəʊvə/ *noun* the total turnover including VAT and discounts

gross yield /ˌɡrəʊs ˈjiːld/ *noun* a profit from investments before tax is deducted

ground landlord /ˈɡraʊnd ˌlændlɔːd/ *noun* a person or company that owns the freehold of a property which is then let and sublet ○ *Our ground landlord is an insurance company.*

ground rent /ˈɡraʊnd rent/ *noun* a rent paid by the main tenant to the ground landlord

group /ɡruːp/ *noun* **1.** several things or people together ○ *A group of managers has sent a memo to the chairman complaining about noise in the office.* ○ *The respondents were interviewed in groups of three or four, and then singly.* **2.** several companies linked together in the same organisation ○ *the group chairman* or *the chairman of the group* ○ *group turnover* or *turnover for the group* ○ *the Granada Group*

group accounts /ˈɡruːp əˌkaʊnts/ *plural noun* accounts for a holding company and its subsidiaries

group balance sheet /ˌɡruːp ˈbæləns ˌʃiːt/ *noun* same as **consolidated balance sheet**

group depreciation /ˌɡruːp dɪˌpriːʃi ˈeɪʃ(ə)n/ *noun* a way of calculating depreciation for multiple assets that are similar in nature and have a similar useful life

group financial statement /ˌɡruːp faɪ ˈnænʃ(ə)l ˌsteɪtmənt/ *noun* same as **consolidated financial statement**

group results /ˌɡruːp rɪˈzʌlts/ *plural noun* the end-of-year financial statements and accounts of a group of companies

growth /ɡrəʊθ/ *noun* the fact of becoming larger or increasing

'…a general price freeze succeeded in slowing the growth in consumer prices' [*Financial Times*]

'…growth in demand is still coming from the private rather than the public sector' [*Lloyd's List*]

'…population growth in the south-west is again reflected by the level of rental values' [*Lloyd's List*]

growth index /ˈɡrəʊθ ˌɪndeks/ *noun* an index showing the growth in a company's revenues, earnings, dividends or other figures

growth prospects /ˈɡrəʊθ ˌprɒspekts/ *plural noun* potential for growth in a share

growth rate /ˈɡrəʊθ reɪt/ *noun* the speed at which something grows

GST *abbreviation* Goods and Services Tax

'…because the GST is applied only to fees for brokerage and appraisal services, the new tax does not appreciably increase the price of a resale home' [*Toronto Globe & Mail*]

guarantee /ˌɡærənˈtiː/ *noun* **1.** a legal document in which the producer agrees to compensate the buyer if the product is faulty or becomes faulty before a specific date after purchase ○ *a certificate of guarantee* or *a guarantee certificate* ○ *The guarantee lasts for two years.* ○ *It is sold with a twelve-month guarantee.* **2.** a promise that someone will pay another person's debts □ **company limited by guarantee** company where each member stated in the memorandum of association how much money he will contribute to the company if it becomes insolvent (as opposed to a company limited by shares) **3.** something given as a security ○ *to leave share certificates as a guarantee* ■ *verb* to give a promise that something will happen

guaranteed bond /ˌgærən'tiːd ˌbɒnd/ *noun* in the United States, a bond or stock on which the principal and interest are guaranteed by a company that is not the issuing company

guaranteed wage /ˌgærəntiːd 'weɪdʒ/ *noun* a wage which a company promises will not fall below a specific figure

guarantor /ˌgærən'tɔː/ *noun* a person who promises to pay another person's debts if he or she should fail to ○ *She stood guarantor for her brother.*

H

half-year /ˌhɑːf ˈjiə/ *noun* six months of an accounting period

half-yearly /ˌhɑːf ˈjiəli/ *adjective* happening every six months, or referring to a period of six months ○ *half-yearly accounts* ○ *half-yearly payment* ○ *half-yearly statement* ○ *a half-yearly meeting* ■ *adverb* every six months ○ *We pay the account half-yearly.*

handling charge /ˈhændlɪŋ tʃɑːdʒ/ *noun* money to be paid for packing, invoicing and dealing with goods which are being shipped

hard cash /ˌhɑːd ˈkæʃ/ *noun* money in notes and coins, as opposed to cheques or credit cards

hard currency /ˌhɑːd ˈkʌrənsi/ *noun* the currency of a country which has a strong economy, and which can be changed into other currencies easily ○ *to pay for imports in hard currency* ○ *to sell raw materials to earn hard currency* Also called **scarce currency**

hardening /ˈhɑːd(ə)nɪŋ/ *adjective* (*of a market*) slowly moving upwards

hard landing /ˌhɑːd ˈlændɪŋ/ *noun* a change in economic strategy to counteract inflation which has serious results for the population such as high unemployment, rising interest rates, etc.

head and shoulders /ˌhed ən ˈʃəʊldəz/ *noun* a term used by chartists showing a share price which rises to a peak, then falls slightly, then rises to a much higher peak, then falls sharply and rises to a lower peak before falling again, looking similar to a person's head and shoulders when shown on a graph

headlease /ˈhedliːs/ *noun* a lease from the freehold owner to a tenant

headline inflation rate /ˌhedlaɪn ɪn ˈfleɪʃ(ə)n ˌreɪt/ *noun* a British inflation figure which includes items such as mortgage interest and local taxes, which are not included in the inflation figures for other countries. Compare **underlying inflation rate**

head office /ˌhed ˈɒfɪs/ *noun* an office building where the board of directors works and meets

headquarters /hedˈkwɔːtəz/ *plural noun* the main office, where the board of directors meets and works ○ *The company's headquarters are in New York.*

heads of agreement /ˌhedz əv ə ˈɡriːmənt/ *plural noun* **1.** a draft agreement with not all the details complete **2.** the most important parts of a commercial agreement

health insurance /ˈhelθ ɪnˌʃʊərəns/ *noun* insurance which pays the cost of treatment for illness, especially when travelling abroad

healthy /ˈhelθi/ *adjective* □ **a healthy balance sheet** a balance sheet which shows a good profit

heavy industry /ˌhevi ˈɪndəstri/ *noun* an industry which deals in heavy raw materials such as coal or makes large products such as ships or engines

hedge /hedʒ/ *noun* a protection against a possible loss, which involves taking an action which is the opposite of an action taken earlier ■ *verb* to protect against the risk of a loss □ **to hedge your bets** to make investments in several areas so as to be protected against loss in one of them □ **to hedge against inflation** to buy investments which will rise in value faster than the increase in the rate of inflation

'…during the 1970s commercial property was regarded by investors as an alternative to equities, with many of the same inflation-hedge qualities' [*Investors Chronicle*]

'…the move saved it from having to pay its creditors an estimated $270 million owed in connection with hedge contracts which began working against the company when the price of gold rose unexpectedly during September' [*Business in Africa*]

hedge fund /ˈhedʒ fʌnd/ *noun* a partnership open to a small number of rich investors, which invests in equities, currency futures and derivatives and may produce high returns but carries a very high risk

'…much of what was described as near hysteria was the hedge funds trying to liquidate bonds to repay bank debts after losing multi-million dollar bets on speculations that the yen would fall against the dollar' [*Times*]

'…hedge funds generally have in common an ability to sell short (that is, sell stocks you do not own), and to increase growth prospects – and risk – by borrowing to enhance the fund's assets' [*Money Observer*]

'…the stock is a hedge fund – limited by the Securities and Exchange Commission to only wealthy individuals and qualified institutions' [*Smart Money*]

hedging /'hedʒɪŋ/ *noun* the act of buying investments at a fixed price for delivery later, so as to protect against possible loss

hereditament /ˌherɪ'dɪtəmənt/ *noun* a property, including land and buildings

hidden asset /ˌhɪd(ə)n 'æset/ *noun* an asset which is valued much less in the company's accounts than its true market value

hidden economy /ˌhɪd(ə)n ɪ'kɒnəmi/ *noun* same as **black economy**

hidden reserves /ˌhɪd(ə)n rɪ'zɜːvz/ *plural noun* **1.** reserves which are not easy to identify in the company's balance sheet. Reserves which are illegally kept hidden are called 'secret reserves'. **2.** illegal reserves which are not declared in the company's balance sheet

hidden tax /'hɪd(ə)n tæks/ *noun* a tax that is not immediately apparent. For example, while a consumer may be aware of a tax on retail purchases, a tax imposed at the wholesale level, which consequently increases the cost of items to the retailer, will not be apparent.

hierarchy of activities /ˌhaɪərɑːki əv æk'tɪvɪtiz/ *noun* a diagrammatic representation of the relative importance of activities undertaken in the running of a business

high /haɪ/ *adjective* large, not low ○ *High overhead costs increase the unit price.* ○ *They are budgeting for a high level of expenditure.* ○ *High interest rates are crippling small businesses.* ■ *noun* a point where prices or sales are very large ○ *Prices have dropped by 10% since the high of January 2nd.*

'American interest rates remain exceptionally high in relation to likely inflation rates' [*Sunday Times*]

'…in a leveraged buyout the acquirer raises money by selling high-yielding debentures to private investors' [*Fortune*]

higher-rate tax /ˌhaɪə reɪt 'tæks/ *noun* in the United Kingdom, the highest of the three bands of income tax. Most countries have bands of income tax with different rates applicable to income within each band.

high finance /ˌhaɪ 'faɪnæns/ *noun* the lending, investing and borrowing of very large sums of money organised by financiers

high gearing /ˌhaɪ 'ɡɪərɪŋ/ *noun* a situation where a company has a high level of borrowing compared to its share price

high-income /ˌhaɪ 'ɪnkʌm/ *adjective* used for referring to a fund that yields a high rate of return ○ *high-income shares* ○ *a high-income portfolio*

highly-geared company /ˌhaɪli ɡɪəd 'kʌmp(ə)ni/ *noun* a company which has a high proportion of its funds from fixed-interest borrowings

highly-paid /ˌhaɪli 'peɪd/ *adjective* earning a large salary

high yield /ˌhaɪ 'jiːld/ *noun* a dividend yield which is higher than is usual for the type of company

hike /haɪk/ *noun* an increase ■ *verb* to increase

hire /'haɪə/ *noun* an arrangement whereby customers pay money to be able to use a car, boat or piece of equipment owned by someone else for a time (NOTE: The more usual term in the US is **rent**)

hire purchase /ˌhaɪə 'pɜːtʃɪs/ *noun* a system of buying something by paying a sum regularly each month ○ *to buy a refrigerator on hire purchase* (NOTE: The US term is **installment credit**, **installment plan** or **installment sale**.)

hire purchase agreement /ˌhaɪə 'pɜːtʃɪs əˌɡriːmənt/ *noun* a contract to pay for something by instalments

hire-purchase company /ˌhaɪə 'pɜːtʃɪs ˌkʌmp(ə)ni/ *noun* a company which provides money for hire purchase

historical cost /hɪˌstɒrɪk(ə)l 'kɒst/, **historic cost** /hɪˌstɒrɪk 'kɒst/ *noun* the actual cost of purchasing something which was bought some time ago

historical cost accounting /hɪˌstɒrɪk(ə)l 'kɒst əˌkaʊntɪŋ/ *noun* the preparation of accounts on the basis of historical cost, with assets valued at their original cost of purchase. Compare **current cost accounting**

historical cost concept /hɪˌstɒrɪk(ə)l kɒst 'kɒnsept/, **historical cost conven-**

tion /hɪˌstɒrɪk(ə)l kɒst kənˈvenʃən/ *noun* a basis for the treatment of assets in financial statements where they are recorded at their historical cost, without adjustment for inflation or other price variations (NOTE: Use 'historical cost convention' not 'historic cost convention'.)

historical cost depreciation /hɪ ˌstɒrɪk(ə)l ˈkɒst dɪˌpriːʃieɪʃ(ə)n/ *noun* depreciation based on the original cost of the asset

historical figures /hɪˌstɒrɪk(ə)l ˈfɪgəz/ *plural noun* figures that were correct at the time of purchase or payment, as distinct from, e.g., a current saleable value or market value

historical pricing /hɪˌstɒrɪk(ə)l ˈpraɪsɪŋ/ *noun* a method of setting prices for a good or service that is based on prices previously set. Sometimes revised prices may take into account the effects of inflation.

historical summary /hɪˌstɒrɪk(ə)l ˈsʌməri/ *noun* in the United Kingdom, an optional synopsis of a company's results over a period of time, often five or ten years, featured in the annual accounts

historical trading range /hɪˌstɒrɪk(ə)l ˈtreɪdɪŋ reɪndʒ/ *noun* the difference between the highest and lowest price for a share or bond over a period of time

hive /haɪv/ *verb*

hive off *phrasal verb* to split off part of a large company to form a smaller subsidiary ○ *The new managing director hived off the retail sections of the company.*

HM Revenue & Customs /ˌeɪtʃ ˌem ˌrevənjuː ən ˈkʌstəmz/ *noun* a UK government department which deals with taxes on imports and on products such as alcohol produced in the country. It also deals with VAT and tax credits. Abbreviation **HMRC**

HM Treasury /ˌeɪtʃ ˌem ˈtreʒəri/ *noun* the UK government department responsible for managing the country's public revenues. The department is run on a day-to-day basis by the Chancellor of the Exchequer.

hoard /hɔːd/ *verb* to buy and store goods in case of need

hoarder /ˈhɔːdə/ *noun* a person who buys and stores goods in case of need

hold /həʊld/ *noun* **1.** the bottom part of a ship or aircraft, in which cargo is carried **2.** the action of keeping something ■ *verb* **1.** to own or to keep something ○ *She holds 10% of the company's shares.* **2.** to make something happen ○ *The receiver will hold an auction of the company's assets.* **3.** not to

sell ○ *You should hold these shares – they look likely to rise.*

'…as of last night, the bank's shareholders no longer hold any rights to the bank's shares' [*South China Morning Post*]

hold down *phrasal verb* to keep at a low level ○ *We are cutting margins to hold our prices down.*

'…real wages have been held down; they have risen at an annual rate of only 1% in the last two years' [*Sunday Times*]

hold up *phrasal verb* **1.** to stay at a high level ○ *Share prices have held up well.* ○ *Sales held up during the tourist season.* **2.** to delay something ○ *The shipment has been held up at customs.* ○ *Payment will be held up until the contract has been signed.*

holder /ˈhəʊldə/ *noun* **1.** a person who owns or keeps something ○ *holders of government bonds* or *bondholders* ○ *holder of stock* or *of shares in a company* ○ *holder of an insurance policy* or *policy holder* **2.** a thing which keeps something, which protects something

holders of record /ˌhəʊldəz əv ˈrekɔːd/ *plural noun* the owners of a company's shares

hold harmless letter /ˌhəʊld ˈhɑːmləs ˌletə/ *noun* a letter issued by parties to a business deal to reporting accountants stating that the accountants will not be held responsible for any losses suffered on the deal

holding /ˈhəʊldɪŋ/ *noun* a group of shares owned ○ *She has sold all her holdings in the Far East.* ○ *The company has holdings in German manufacturing companies.*

holding company /ˈhəʊldɪŋ ˌkʌmp(ə)ni/ *noun* **1.** a company which owns more than 50% of the shares in another company. ◊ **subsidiary company 2.** a company which exists only or mainly to own shares in subsidiary companies. ◊ **subsidiary**

holding cost /ˈhəʊldɪŋ kɒst/ *noun* the cost of keeping items of stock including warehousing and handling costs, insurance, losses through deterioration, wastage, theft, etc. and the cost of capital used to acquire the stock measured in terms of the interest lost on the money which was spent on purchasing the stock in the first place or the interest paid on the loans which were needed to finance the purchase of the stock

home banking /ˌhəʊm ˈbæŋkɪŋ/ *noun* a system of banking using a personal computer in your own home to carry out various financial transactions such as paying invoices or checking your bank account

home loan /ˈhəʊm ləʊn/ *noun* a loan by a bank or building society to help someone buy a house

home trade /ˌhəʊm ˈtreɪd/ *noun* trade in the country where a company is based

honorarium /ˌɒnəˈreəriəm/ *noun* money paid to a professional person such as an accountant or a lawyer when a specific fee has not been requested (NOTE: The plural is **honoraria**.)

honorary /ˈɒnərəri/ *adjective* not paid a salary for the work done for an organisation ○ *He is honorary president of the translators' association.*

honorary   secretary   /ˌɒnərəri ˈsekrət(ə)ri/ *noun* a person who keeps the minutes and official documents of a committee or club, but is not paid a salary

honorary treasurer /ˌɒnərəri ˈtreʒərə/ *noun* a treasurer who does not receive any fee

honour /ˈɒnə/ *verb* to pay something because it is owed and is correct ○ *to honour a bill* (NOTE: The US spelling is **honor**.)

horizontal integration /ˌhɒrɪzɒnt(ə)l ˌɪntɪˈgreɪʃ(ə)n/ *noun* the process of joining similar companies or taking over a company in the same line of business as yourself

hostile bid /ˌhɒstaɪl ˈbɪd/ *noun* same as **contested takeover**

hot money /ˌhɒt ˈmʌni/ *noun* **1.** money which is moved from country to country to get the best returns **2.** money that has been obtained by dishonest means. ◊ **money laundering**

hour /aʊə/ *noun* **1.** a period of time lasting sixty minutes **2.** sixty minutes of work ○ *She earns £14 an hour.* ○ *We pay £16 an hour.*

house /haʊs/ *noun* a company ○ *the largest London finance house* ○ *a brokerage house* ○ *a publishing house*

household goods /ˌhaʊshəʊld ˈgʊdz/ *plural noun* items which are used in the home

human capital accounting /ˌhjuːmən ˈkæpɪt(ə)l əˌkaʊntɪŋ/ *noun* an attempt to place a financial value on the knowledge and skills possessed by the employees of an organisation. Also called **human asset accounting, human resource accounting**

hurdle rate /ˈhɜːd(ə)l reɪt/ *noun* a minimum rate of return needed by a bank to fund a loan, the rate below which a loan is not profitable for the bank

hybrid /ˈhaɪbrɪd/ *noun* a combination of financial instruments, e.g., a bond with warrants attached, or a range of cash and derivative instruments designed to mirror the performance of a financial market

hyper- /haɪpə/ *prefix* very large

hyperinflation   /ˌhaɪpərɪnˈfleɪʃ(ə)n/ *noun* inflation which is at such a high percentage rate that it is almost impossible to reduce

hypothecation /haɪˌpɒθəˈkeɪʃ(ə)n/ *noun* **1.** an arrangement in which property such as securities is used as collateral for a loan but without transferring legal ownership to the lender, as opposed to a mortgage, where the lender holds the title to the property **2.** an action of earmarking money derived from specific sources for related expenditure, as when investing taxes from private cars or petrol sales solely on public transport

I

IAASB *abbreviation* International Auditing and Assurance Standards Board

IAS *abbreviation* International Accounting Standards

IASB *abbreviation* International Accounting Standards Board

IASC *abbreviation* International Accounting Standards Committee

IBRD *abbreviation* International Bank for Reconstruction and Development (the World Bank)

ICAEW *abbreviation* Institute of Chartered Accountants in England and Wales

ICAI *abbreviation* Institute of Chartered Accountants in Ireland

ICANZ *abbreviation* Institute of Chartered Accountants of New Zealand

ICAS *abbreviation* Institute of Chartered Accountants in Scotland

ICSID *abbreviation* International Centre for Settlement of Investment Disputes

ICTA *abbreviation* Income and Corporation Taxes Act

ideal capacity /aɪˈdɪəl kəˌpæsɪti/ *noun* the greatest volume of output possible, which would be produced only in ideal conditions in which optimum capacity was maintained constantly

idle capacity /ˈaɪd(ə)l kəˌpæsɪti/ *noun* **1.** the existence of unused capacity **2.** a situation in which a given market will not absorb all of the goods produced in that sector

idle capacity variance /ˌaɪd(ə)l kə ˈpæsɪti ˌveəriəns/ *noun* a level of capacity that is lower than that forecast or budgeted for

idle capital /ˌaɪd(ə)l ˈkæpɪt(ə)l/ *noun* capital which is not being used productively

idle time /ˈaɪd(ə)l taɪm/ *noun* the time for which employees are paid although they are unable to work because of factors beyond their control ○ *Idle time in January was attributed to the temporary closing down of one of the company's factories.* ○ *Workers were laid off to avoid excessive idle time.*

IFA *abbreviation* **1.** independent financial adviser **2.** Institute of Financial Accountants

IFAC *abbreviation* International Federation of Accountants

IFRIC *abbreviation* International Financial Reporting Interpretations Committee

IFRS *abbreviation* International Financial Reporting Standards

IHT *abbreviation* inheritance tax

illegal /ɪˈliːg(ə)l/ *adjective* not legal or against the law

illegality /ˌɪliːˈgælɪti/ *noun* the fact of being illegal

illegally /ɪˈliːgəli/ *adverb* against the law ○ *He was accused of illegally laundering money.*

illicit /ɪˈlɪsɪt/ *adjective* not legal or not permitted ○ *the illicit sale of alcohol*

illiquid /ɪˈlɪkwɪd/ *adjective* **1.** referring to an asset which is not easy to change into cash **2.** used to describe a person or business that lacks cash or assets such as securities that can readily be converted into cash

IMA *abbreviation* **1.** Institute of Management Accountants **2.** Investment Management Association

IMF *abbreviation* International Monetary Fund

immovable /ɪˈmuːvəb(ə)l/ *adjective* impossible to move

immovable property /ɪˌmuːvəb(ə)l ˈprɒpəti/ *noun* houses and other buildings on land

impact /ˈɪmpækt/ *noun* a shock or strong effect ○ *the impact of new technology on the cotton trade* ○ *The new design has made little impact on the buying public.*

impact statement /ˈɪmpækt ˌsteɪtmənt/ *noun* a written statement outlining the effects of something on an individual or company

impairment of capital /ɪmˌpeəmənt əv ˈkæpɪt(ə)l/ *noun* the extent to which the value of a company is less than the par value of its shares

impairment of value /ɪm,peəmənt əv 'væljuː/ *noun* a decline in the value of an asset such that its original cost can never be recovered

impersonal account /ɪm,pɜːs(ə)n(ə)l ə 'kaʊnt/ *noun* any account other than a personal account, being classified as either a real account, in which property is recorded, or a nominal account, in which income, expenses and capital are recorded. ◊ **account, personal account**

implement /'ɪmplɪ,ment/ *verb* to put into action ○ *to implement an agreement* ○ *to implement a decision*

implementation /,ɪmplɪmən'teɪʃ(ə)n/ *noun* the process of putting something into action ○ *the implementation of new rules*

import /ɪm'pɔːt/ *verb* to bring goods from abroad into a country for sale ○ *The company imports television sets from Japan.* ○ *This car was imported from France.*

importation /,ɪmpɔː'teɪʃ(ə)n/ *noun* the act of importing ○ *The importation of arms is forbidden.* ○ *The importation of livestock is subject to very strict controls.*

import ban /'ɪmpɔːt bæn/ *noun* a government order forbidding imports of a particular kind or from a particular country ○ *The government has imposed an import ban on arms.*

import duty /'ɪmpɔːt ,djuːti/ *noun* a tax on goods imported into a country

importer /ɪm'pɔːtə/ *noun* a person or company that imports goods ○ *a cigar importer* ○ *The company is a big importer of foreign cars.*

import-export /,ɪmpɔːt 'ekspɔːt/ *adjective, noun* referring to business which deals with both bringing foreign goods into a country and sending locally made goods abroad ○ *Rotterdam is an important centre for the import-export trade.* ○ *She works in import-export.*

import levy /'ɪmpɔːt ,levi/ *noun* a tax on imports, especially in the EU a tax on imports of farm produce from outside the EU

import quota /'ɪmpɔːt ,kwəʊtə/ *noun* a fixed quantity of a particular type of goods which the government allows to be imported ○ *The government has imposed a import quota on cars.*

import restrictions /'ɪmpɔːt rɪ ,strɪkʃ(ə)nz/ *plural noun* actions taken by a government to reduce the level of imports by imposing quotas, duties, etc.

imports /'ɪmpɔːts/ *plural noun* goods brought into a country from abroad for sale

○ *Imports from Poland have risen to $1m a year.* (NOTE: Usually used in the plural, but the singular is used before a noun.)

import surcharge /'ɪmpɔːt ,sɜːtʃɑːdʒ/ *noun* the extra duty charged on imported goods, to try to stop them from being imported and to encourage local manufacture

impose /ɪm'pəʊz/ *verb* to give orders for something regarded as unpleasant or unwanted, such as a tax or a ban ○ *to impose a tax on bicycles* ○ *They tried to impose a ban on smoking.* ○ *The government imposed a special duty on oil.*

imposition /,ɪmpə'zɪʃ(ə)n/ *noun* the act of imposing something

impound /ɪm'paʊnd/ *verb* to take something away and keep it until a tax is paid ○ *Customs impounded the whole cargo.*

impounding /ɪm'paʊndɪŋ/ *noun* an act of taking something and keeping it until a tax is paid

imprest account /'ɪmprest ə,kaʊnt/ *noun* a UK term for a record of the transactions of a type of petty cash system. An employee is given an advance of money, an imprest, for incidental expenses and when most of it has been spent, he or she presents receipts for the expenses to the accounts department and is then reimbursed with cash to the total value of the receipts.

imprest system /'ɪmprest ,sɪstəm/ *noun* a system of controlling petty cash, where cash is paid out against a written receipt and the receipt is used to get more cash to bring the float to the original level

improved offer /ɪm,pruːvd 'ɒfə/ *noun* an offer which is larger or has better terms than the previous offer

imputation system /,ɪmpjuː'teɪʃ(ə)n ,sɪstəm/ *noun* a former system of taxation of dividends, where the company paid Advance Corporation Tax on the dividends it paid to its shareholders, and the shareholders paid no tax on the dividends received, assuming that they paid tax at the standard rate

inactive account /ɪn,æktɪv ə'kaʊnt/ *noun* a bank account which is not used over a period of time

inactive market /ɪn,æktɪv 'mɑːkɪt/ *noun* a stock market with few buyers or sellers

incentive /ɪn'sentɪv/ *noun* something which encourages a customer to buy, or employees to work better

'…some further profit-taking was seen yesterday as investors continued to lack fresh incentives to renew buying activity' [*Financial Times*]

'…a well-designed plan can help companies retain talented employees and offer enticing performance incentives – all at an affordable cost' [*Fortune*]

'…the right incentives can work when used strategically' [*Management Today*]

'…an additional incentive is that the Japanese are prepared to give rewards where they are due' [*Management Today*]

incentive bonus /ɪnˈsentɪv ˌbəʊnəs/, **incentive payment** /ɪnˈsentɪv ˌpeɪmənt/ *noun* an extra payment offered to employees to make them work better

incentive scheme /ɪnˈsentɪv skiːm/ *noun* a plan to encourage better work by paying higher commission or bonuses ○ *Incentive schemes are boosting production.*

incentive stock option /ɪnˌsentɪv ˈstɒk ˌɒpʃən/ *noun* (*in the United States*) a plan that gives each qualifying employee the right to purchase a specific number of the corporation's shares at a set price during a specific time period (NOTE: Tax is only payable when the shares are sold.)

inchoate /ɪnˈkəʊət/ *adjective* referring to an instrument which is incomplete

incidence of tax /ˌɪnsɪd(ə)ns əv ˈtæks/ *noun* the point at which a tax is ultimately paid. For example, although a retailer pays any sales tax to the tax collecting authority, the tax itself is ultimately paid by the customer.

incidental expenses /ˌɪnsɪdent(ə)l ɪkˈspensɪz/ *plural noun* small amounts of money spent at various times in addition to larger amounts

include /ɪnˈkluːd/ *verb* to count something along with other things ○ *The charge includes VAT.* ○ *The total is £140 not including insurance and freight.* ○ *The account covers services up to and including the month of June.*

inclusive /ɪnˈkluːsɪv/ *adjective* counting something in with other things ○ *inclusive of tax* ○ *not inclusive of VAT*

income /ˈɪnkʌm/ *noun* **1.** money which a person receives as salary or dividends □ **lower income bracket**, **upper income bracket** the groups of people who earn low or high salaries considered for tax purposes **2.** money which an organisation receives as gifts or from investments ○ *The hospital has a large income from gifts.*

'…there is no risk-free way of taking regular income from your money much

higher than the rate of inflation' [*Guardian*]

income account /ˈɪnkʌm əˌkaʊnt/ *noun* an account that lists revenue and expenses, as distinct from a balance sheet account

income bond /ˈɪnkʌm bɒnd/ *noun* a bond that pays a rate of return in proportion to the issuer's income

income distribution /ˈɪnkʌm dɪstrɪˌbjuːʃ(ə)n/ *noun* the UK term for the payment to investors of the income generated by a collective investment, less management charges, tax and expenses. It is distributed in proportion to the number of units or shares held by each investor.

income gearing /ˈɪnkʌm ˌɡɪərɪŋ/ *noun* the ratio of the interest a company pays on its borrowing shown as a percentage of its pretax profits before the interest is paid

income per head /ˌɪnkʌm pə ˈhed/, **income per capita** *noun* same as **per capita income**

income recognition /ˈɪnkʌm ˌrekəɡnɪʃ(ə)n/ *noun* the policy under which income is shown in an account

income shares /ˈɪnkʌm ʃeəz/ *plural noun* shares in an investment trust that receive income from the investments, but do not benefit from any rise in capital value of the investments

income smoothing /ˈɪnkʌm ˌsmuːðɪŋ/ *noun* a UK term for a form of creative accounting that involves the manipulation of a company's financial statements to show steady annual profits rather than large fluctuations

income summary /ˈɪnkʌm ˌsʌməri/ *noun* a summary showing a company's net profit or net loss for the year

income support /ˈɪnkʌm səˌpɔːt/ *noun* a government benefit paid to low-income earners who are working less than 16 hours per week, provided they can show that they are actively looking for jobs. Abbreviation **IS**

income tax /ˈɪnkʌm tæks/ *noun* **1.** the tax on a person's income, both earned and unearned **2.** the tax on the profits of a corporation

income tax form /ˈɪnkʌm tæks ˌfɔːm/ *noun* a form to be completed which declares all income to the tax office

income tax return /ˈɪnkʌm tæks rɪˌtɜːn/ *noun* a completed tax form, with details of income and allowances. Also called **declaration of income**, **tax return**

income units /ˈɪnkʌm ˌjuːnɪts/ *plural noun* units in a unit trust, from which the investor receives dividends in the form of income

incomplete records /ˌɪnkəmpliːt 'rekɔːdz/ *plural noun* an accounting system which is not double-entry bookkeeping. Various degrees of incompleteness can occur, e.g., **single-entry bookkeeping**, in which usually only a cash book is maintained.

inconvertible /ˌɪnkən'vɜːtɪb(ə)l/ *adjective* referring to currency which cannot be easily converted into other currencies

incorporate /ɪn'kɔːpəreɪt/ *verb* **1.** to bring something in to form part of a main group ○ *Income from the 1998 acquisition is incorporated into the accounts.* **2.** to form a registered company ○ *a company incorporated in the US* ○ *an incorporated company* ○ *J. Doe Incorporated*

incorporation /ɪnˌkɔːpə'reɪʃ(ə)n/ *noun* an act of incorporating a company

increase *noun* /'ɪnkriːs/ **1.** an act of becoming larger ○ *There have been several increases in tax* or *tax increases in the last few years.* ○ *There is an automatic 5% increase in price* or *price increase on January 1st.* ○ *Profits showed a 10% increase* or *an increase of 10% on last year.* **2.** a higher salary ○ *increase in pay* or *pay increase* ○ *The government hopes to hold salary increases to 3%.* □ **she had two increases last year** her salary went up twice ■ *verb* /ɪn'kriːs/ **1.** to grow bigger or higher ○ *Profits have increased faster than the increase in the rate of inflation.* ○ *Exports to Africa have increased by more than 25%.* ○ *The price of oil has increased twice in the past week.* □ **to increase in size** *or* **value** to become larger or more valuable **2.** to make something bigger or higher □ **the company increased her salary to £50,000** the company gave her a rise in salary to £50,000

'…turnover has the potential to be increased to over 1 million dollars with energetic management and very little capital' [*Australian Financial Review*]

'…competition is steadily increasing and could affect profit margins as the company tries to retain its market share' [*Citizen (Ottawa)*]

increment /'ɪnkrɪmənt/ *noun* a regular automatic increase in salary ○ *an annual increment* □ **salary which rises in annual increments of £1000** each year the salary is increased by £1000

incremental /ˌɪnkrɪ'ment(ə)l/ *adjective* rising automatically in stages

incremental analysis /ˌɪnkrɪment(ə)l ə'næləsɪs/ *noun* analysis of the changes in costs and revenues that occur when business activity changes

incremental budgeting /ˌɪnkrɪment(ə)l 'bʌdʒɪtɪŋ/ *noun* a method of setting budgets in which the prior period budget is used as a base for the current budget, which is set by adjusting the prior period budget to take account of any anticipated changes

incremental cost /ˌɪnkrɪment(ə)l 'kɒst/ *noun* the cost of making extra units above the number already planned. This may then include further fixed costs.

incremental increase /ˌɪnkrɪment(ə)l 'ɪnkriːs/ *noun* an increase in salary according to an agreed annual increment

incremental scale /ˌɪnkrɪment(ə)l 'skeɪl/ *noun* a salary scale with regular annual salary increases

incur /ɪn'kɜː/ *verb* to make yourself liable to something

'…the company blames fiercely competitive market conditions in Europe for a £14m operating loss last year, incurred despite a record turnover' [*Financial Times*]

indebted /ɪn'detɪd/ *adjective* owing money to someone ○ *to be indebted to a property company*

indemnification /ɪnˌdemnɪfɪ'keɪʃən/ *noun* payment for damage

indemnify /ɪn'demnɪfaɪ/ *verb* to pay for damage ○ *to indemnify someone for a loss*

indemnity /ɪn'demnɪti/ *noun* **1.** a guarantee of payment after a loss ○ *She had to pay an indemnity of £100.* **2.** compensation paid after a loss

indent /'ɪndent/ *noun* an order placed by an importer for goods from overseas ○ *They put in an indent for a new stock of soap.*

indenture /ɪn'dentʃə/ *noun US* a formal agreement showing the terms of a bond issue

independent company /ˌɪndɪpendənt 'kʌmp(ə)ni/ *noun* a company which is not controlled by another company

independent financial adviser /ˌɪndɪpendənt faɪˌnænʃ(ə)l əd'vaɪzə/ *noun* a person who gives impartial advice on financial matters, who is not connected with any financial institution. Abbreviation **IFA**

independent variable /ˌɪndɪpendənt 'veərɪəb(ə)l/ *noun* a factor whose value, when it changes, influences one or more other variables called 'dependent variables' ○ *In this model personal income is the independent variable and expenditure the dependent variable.*

index /ˈɪndeks/ *noun* **1.** a list of items classified into groups or put in alphabetical order **2.** a regular statistical report which shows rises and falls in prices, values, or levels **3.** a figure based on the current market price of shares on a stock exchange (NOTE: [all noun senses] The plural is **indexes** or **indices**.) ■ *verb* to link a payment to an index ○ *salaries indexed to the cost of living*

'…the index of industrial production sank 0.2 per cent for the latest month after rising 0.3 per cent in March' [*Financial Times*]

'…an analysis of the consumer price index for the first half of the year shows that the rate of inflation went down by 12.9 per cent' [*Business Times (Lagos)*]

indexation /ˌɪndekˈseɪʃ(ə)n/ *noun* the linking of something to an index

indexed portfolio /ˌɪndekst ˈpɔːt ˈfəʊliəʊ/ *noun* a portfolio of shares in all the companies which form the basis of a stock exchange index

index fund /ˈɪndeks fʌnd/ *noun* an investment fund consisting of shares in all the companies which are used to calculate a Stock Exchange index

index-linked /ˈɪndeks ˌlɪŋkt/ *adjective* rising automatically by the percentage increase in the cost of living ○ *index-linked government bonds* ○ *Inflation did not affect her as she has an index-linked pension.*

'…two-year index-linked savings certificates now pay 3 per cent a year tax free, in addition to index-linking' [*Financial Times*]

index number /ˈɪndeks ˌnʌmbə/ *noun* a number showing the percentage rise of something over a period

index tracker /ˈɪndeks ˌtrækə/ *noun* an investor or fund manager who tracks an index

index-tracking /ˈɪndeks ˌtrækɪŋ/ *adjective* adjusted to follow changes in a particular index, e.g. the Bank of England's base rate

indicator /ˈɪndɪkeɪtə/ *noun* a factor of a situation that gives an indication of a general trend

'…it reduces this month's growth in the key M3 indicator from about 19% to 12%' [*Sunday Times*]

'…we may expect the US leading economic indicators for April to show faster economic growth' [*Australian Financial Review*]

'…other indicators, such as high real interest rates, suggest that monetary conditions are extremely tight' [*Economist*]

indirect costs /ˌɪndaɪrekt ˈkɒsts/, **indirect expenses** /ˌɪndaɪrekt ɪkˈspensɪz/ *plural noun* costs which are not directly related to the making of a product, e.g. cleaning, rent or administration

indirect labour costs /ˌɪndaɪrekt ˈleɪbə ˌkɒsts/ *plural noun* the cost of paying employees not directly involved in making a product, such as cleaners or administrative staff. Such costs cannot be allocated to a cost centre.

indirect liability /ˌɪndaɪrekt ˌlaɪəˈbɪlɪti/ *noun* an obligation that may arise in future, as, e.g., if a lawsuit is brought against the company

indirect material cost /ˌɪndaɪrekt məˈtɪəriəl ˌkɒst/, **indirect materials cost** /ˌɪndaɪrekt məˈtɪəriəlz ˌkɒst/ *noun* the cost of materials which cannot be allocated to the production of a particular product

indirect tax /ˌɪndaɪrekt ˈtæks/ *noun* a tax such as VAT paid to someone who then pays it to the government

indirect taxation /ˌɪndaɪrekt tækˈseɪʃ(ə)n/ *noun* taxes which are not paid direct to the government, e.g. sales tax ○ *The government raises more money by indirect taxation than by direct.*

Individual Retirement Account /ˌɪndɪvɪdʒuəl rɪˈtaɪəmənt əˌkaʊnt/ *noun* *US* a tax-deferred pension scheme, that allows individuals to make contributions to a personal retirement fund. Abbreviation **IRA**

Individual Savings Account /ˌɪndɪvɪdʒuəl ˈseɪvɪŋz əˌkaʊnt/ *noun* a British scheme by which individuals can invest by putting a limited amount of money each year in a tax-free account. Abbreviation **ISA**

Individual Voluntary Arrangement /ˌɪndɪvɪdʒuəl ˌvɒlənt(ə)ri əˈreɪndʒmənt/ *noun* a legally binding arrangement between a debtor and creditors by which the debtor offers the creditors the best deal he or she can afford by realising his assets, and so the expense of bankruptcy proceedings is avoided. Abbreviation **IVA**

inducement /ɪnˈdjuːsmənt/ *noun* something which helps to persuade someone to do something ○ *They offered her a company car as an inducement to stay.*

industrial arbitration tribunal /ɪnˌdʌstriəl ˌɑːbɪˈtreɪʃ(ə)n traɪˌbjuːn(ə)l/ *noun* a court which decides in industrial disputes

industrial tribunal /ɪnˌdʌstriəl traɪˈbjuːn(ə)l/ *noun* a court which can decide in disputes about employment

'ACAS has a legal obligation to try and solve industrial grievances before they reach industrial tribunals' [*Personnel Today*]

inflation /ɪnˈfleɪʃ(ə)n/ *noun* a greater increase in the supply of money or credit than in the production of goods and services, resulting in higher prices and a fall in the purchasing power of money ○ *to take measures to reduce inflation* ○ *High interest rates tend to increase inflation.* □ **we have 3% inflation** *or* **inflation is running at 3%** prices are 3% higher than at the same time last year

inflation accounting /ɪnˈfleɪʃ(ə)n əˌkaʊntɪŋ/ *noun* an accounting system in which inflation is taken into account when calculating the value of assets and the preparation of accounts

inflationary /ɪnˈfleɪʃ(ə)n(ə)ri/ *adjective* tending to increase inflation ○ *inflationary trends in the economy*

'…inflationary expectations fell somewhat this month, but remained a long way above the actual inflation rate, according to figures released yesterday. The annual rate of inflation measured by the consumer price index has been below 2 per cent for over 18 months' [*Australian Financial Review*]

inflation-proof /ɪnˈfleɪʃ(ə)n pruːf/ *adjective* referring to a pension, etc. which is index-linked, so that its value is preserved in times of inflation

inflow /ˈɪnfləʊ/ *noun* the act of coming in or being brought in

'…the dollar is strong because of capital inflows rather than weak because of the trade deficit' [*Duns Business Month*]

influx /ˈɪnflʌks/ *noun* an inflow, especially one where people or things come in in large quantities ○ *an influx of foreign currency into the country* ○ *an influx of cheap labour into the cities*

'…the retail sector will also benefit from the expected influx of tourists' [*Australian Financial Review*]

inherit /ɪnˈherɪt/ *verb* to get something from a person who has died ○ *When her father died she inherited the shop.* ○ *He inherited £10,000 from his grandfather.*

inheritance /ɪnˈherɪt(ə)ns/ *noun* property which is received from a dead person

inheritance tax /ɪnˈherɪt(ə)ns tæks/ *noun* tax payable on wealth or property worth above a certain amount and inherited after the death of someone. The current threshold is £285,000, and the estate is liable for 40% tax on the excess amount. Abbreviation **IHT**. Also called **death duty**

in-house /ˌɪn ˈhaʊs/ *adverb, adjective* done by someone employed by a company on their premises, not by an outside contractor ○ *the in-house staff* ○ *We do all our data processing in-house.*

initial capital /ɪˌnɪʃ(ə)l ˈkæpɪt(ə)l/ *noun* capital which is used to start a business

initial public offering /ɪˌnɪʃ(ə)l ˌpʌblɪk ˈɒf(ə)rɪŋ/ *noun US* the process of offering shares in a corporation for sale to the public for the first time. Abbreviation **IPO** (NOTE: The UK term is **offer for sale**.)

initial sales /ɪˌnɪʃ(ə)l ˈseɪlz/ *plural noun* the first sales of a new product

initial yield /ɪˌnɪʃ(ə)l ˈjiːld/ *noun* the estimated yield of an investment fund at the time when it is launched

initiate /ɪˈnɪʃieɪt/ *verb* to start ○ *to initiate discussions*

injection /ɪnˈdʒekʃən/ *noun* □ **a capital injection of £100,000** *or* **an injection of £100,000 capital** putting £100,000 into an existing business

injunction /ɪnˈdʒʌŋkʃ(ə)n/ *noun* a court order telling someone not to do something ○ *He got an injunction preventing the company from selling his car.*

inland /ˈɪnlənd/ *adjective* inside a country

inland freight charges /ˌɪnlənd ˈfreɪt ˌtʃɑːdʒɪz/ *plural noun* charges for carrying goods from one part of the country to another

inland postage /ˌɪnlənd ˈpəʊstɪdʒ/ *noun* postage for a letter to another part of the same country

Inland Revenue /ˌɪnlənd ˈrevənjuː/ *noun* a former UK government department which dealt with taxes such as income tax, corporation tax, capital gains tax and inheritance tax, but not duties such as Value Added Tax. It merged with the Customs and Excise to form HM Revenue & Customs in 2005. ○ *He received a letter from the Inland Revenue.* (NOTE: The US term is **Internal Revenue Service** or **IRS**.)

Inland Revenue Commissioner /ˌɪnlænd ˈrevənjuː kəˌmɪʃ(ə)nə/ *noun* a person appointed officially to supervise the collection of taxes, including income tax, capital gains tax and corporation tax, but not VAT. Abbreviation **IRC**

input cost /ˈɪnpʊt kɒst/ *noun* the cost of overhead items such as labour and material used in the production of goods or services

inputs /'ɪnpʊts/ *plural noun* goods or services bought by a company and which may be liable to VAT

input tax /'ɪnpʊt tæks/ *noun* VAT which is paid by a company on goods or services bought

insider /ɪn'saɪdə/ *noun* a person who works in an organisation and therefore knows its secrets

insider trading /ɪn,saɪdə 'treɪdɪŋ/, **insider buying** /,ɪnsaɪdə 'baɪɪŋ/, **insider dealing** /ɪn,saɪdə 'diːlɪŋ/ *noun* the illegal buying or selling of shares by staff of a company or other persons who have secret information about the company's plans

insolvency /ɪn'sɒlvənsi/ *noun* the fact of not being able to pay debts. Opposite **solvency** (NOTE: A company is insolvent when its liabilities are higher than its assets: if this happens it must cease trading. Note that insolvency is a general term, but is usually applied to companies; individuals or partners are usually described as bankrupt once they have been declared so by a court.)

'…hundreds of thrifts found themselves on the brink of insolvency after a deregulation programme prompted them to enter dangerous financial waters' [*Times*]

insolvency practitioner /ɪn'sɒlvənsi præk,tɪʃ(ə)nə/ *noun* a person who advises insolvent companies

insolvent /ɪn'sɒlvənt/ *adjective* not able to pay debts ○ *The company was declared insolvent.* (NOTE: see note at **insolvency**)

inspect /ɪn'spekt/ *verb* to examine in detail ○ *to inspect a machine* or *an installation* ○ *Officials from the DTI have come to inspect the accounts.*

inspection /ɪn'spekʃ(ə)n/ *noun* the close examination of something ○ *to make an inspection* or *to carry out an inspection of a machine* or *an installation*

inspector /ɪn'spektə/ *noun* an official who inspects ○ *The inspectors will soon be round to make sure the building is safe.*

inspectorate /ɪn'spekt(ə)rət/ *noun* an authority to which inspectors are responsible

inspector of taxes /ɪn,spektər əv 'tæksɪz/ *noun* in the United Kingdom, an official who reports to HM Revenue & Customs and is responsible for issuing tax returns and assessments, agreeing tax liabilities and conducting appeals on matters of tax

inspector of weights and measures /ɪn,spektər əv ,weɪts ən 'meʒəz/ *noun* a government official who inspects weighing machines and goods sold in shops to see if the quantities and weights are correct

instalment /ɪn'stɔːlmənt/ *noun* a part of a payment which is paid regularly until the total amount is paid ○ *The first instalment is payable on signature of the agreement.* (NOTE: The US spelling is **installment**.) □ **to pay £25 down and monthly instalments of £20** to pay a first payment of £25 and the rest in payments of £20 each month

institute /'ɪnstɪtjuːt/ *noun* a society or organisation which represents a particular profession or activity ○ *the Institute of Chartered Accountants*

Institute of Chartered Accountants in England and Wales /,ɪnstɪtjuːt əv ,tʃɑːtəd ə,kaʊntənts ɪn ,ɪŋglənd ən 'weɪlz/ *noun* the largest professional accountancy body in Europe, providing qualification by examinations, ensuring high standards of education and training, and supervising professional conduct. Abbreviation **ICAEW**

Institute of Chartered Accountants in Ireland /,ɪnstɪtjuːt əv ,tʃɑːtəd ə ,kaʊntənts ɪn 'aɪələnd/ *noun* the oldest and largest professional body for accountants in Ireland, founded in 1888 with the aims of in promoting best practice in chartered accountancy and maintaining high standards of professionalism among its members. Abbreviation **ICAI**

Institute of Chartered Accountants in Scotland /,ɪnstɪtjuːt əv ,tʃɑːtəd ə ,kaʊntənts ɪn 'skɒtlənd/ *noun* the world's oldest professional body for accountants, based in Edinburgh. Abbreviation **ICAS**

Institute of Chartered Accountants of New Zealand /,ɪnstɪtjuːt əv ,tʃɑːtəd ə,kaʊntənts əv njuː 'ziːlənd/ *noun* the only professional accounting body in New Zealand, representing over 26,000 members in that country and abroad. Abbreviation **ICANZ**

Institute of Financial Accountants /,ɪnstɪtjuːt əv faɪ,nænʃ(ə)l ə'kaʊntənts/ *noun* a professional body, established in 1916, which aims to set technical and ethical standards in UK financial accountancy. Abbreviation **IFA**

institution /,ɪnstɪ'tjuːʃ(ə)n/ *noun* an organisation or society set up for a particular purpose. ◊ **financial institution**

institutional /,ɪnstɪ'tjuːʃ(ə)n(ə)l/ *adjective* relating to an institution, especially a financial institution

'…during the 1970s commercial property was regarded by big institutional investors as an alternative to equities' [*Investors Chronicle*]

institutional investor /ˌɪnstɪtjuːʃ(ə)n(ə)l ɪnˈvestə/ *noun* **1.** a financial institution which invests money in securities **2.** an organisation (such as a pension fund or insurance company) with large sums of money to invest

instruction /ɪnˈstrʌkʃən/ *noun* an order which tells what should be done or how something is to be used ○ *She gave instructions to his stockbroker to sell the shares immediately.*

instrument /ˈɪnstrʊmənt/ *noun* **1.** a tool or piece of equipment ○ *The technician brought instruments to measure the output of electricity.* **2.** a legal document

insufficient funds /ˌɪnsəfɪʃ(ə)nt ˈfʌndz/ *plural noun US* same as **non-sufficient funds**

insurable /ɪnˈʃʊərəb(ə)l/ *adjective* possible to insure

insurable interest /ɪnˌʃʊərəb(ə)l ˈɪntrəst/ *noun* the value of the thing insured which is attributed to the person who is taking out the insurance

insurance /ɪnˈʃʊərəns/ *noun* an agreement that in return for regular payments called 'premiums', a company will pay compensation for loss, damage, injury or death ○ *to take out insurance* ○ *Repairs will be paid for by the insurance.*

insurance adjuster /ɪnˈʃʊərəns əˌdʒʌstə/ *noun US* same as **loss adjuster**

insurance agent /ɪnˈʃʊərəns ˌeɪdʒənt/, **insurance broker** /ɪnˈʃʊərəns ˌbrəʊkə/ *noun* a person who arranges insurance for clients

insurance claim /ɪnˈʃʊərəns kleɪm/ *noun* a request to an insurance company to pay compensation for damage or loss

insurance company /ɪnˈʃʊərəns ˌkʌmp(ə)ni/ *noun* a company whose business is insurance

insurance contract /ɪnˈʃʊərəns ˌkɒntrækt/ *noun* an agreement by an insurance company to insure

insurance cover /ɪnˈʃʊərəns ˌkʌvə/ *noun* protection guaranteed by an insurance policy

insurance policy /ɪnˈʃʊərəns ˌpɒlɪsi/ *noun* a document which shows the conditions of an insurance contract

insurance premium /ɪnˈʃʊərəns ˌpriːmiəm/ *noun* an annual payment made by a person or a company to an insurance company

insurance premium tax /ɪnˈʃʊərəns ˌpriːmiəm ˌtæks/ *noun* a tax on household, motor vehicle, travel and other general insurance

insurance rates /ɪnˈʃʊərəns reɪts/ *plural noun* the amount of premium which has to be paid per £1000 of insurance

insure /ɪnˈʃʊə/ *verb* to have a contract with a company whereby, if regular small payments are made, the company will pay compensation for loss, damage, injury or death ○ *to insure a house against fire* ○ *to insure someone's life* ○ *to insure against loss of earnings* ○ *She was insured for £100,000.*

insurer /ɪnˈʃʊərə/ *noun* a company which insures (NOTE: For life insurance, UK English prefers to use **assurer**.)

intangible /ɪnˈtændʒɪb(ə)l/ *adjective* not possible to touch

intangible assets /ɪnˌtændʒɪb(ə)l ˈæsets/, **intangible fixed assets** /ɪnˌtændʒɪb(ə)l fɪkst ˈæsets/, **intangibles** /ɪnˈtændʒɪb(ə)lz/ *plural noun* assets that have a value but which cannot be seen, e.g. goodwill or a trademark

intangible value /ɪnˈtændʒɪb(ə)l ˌvæljuː/ *noun* a value of an organisation equal to its total value minus the value of its tangible assets

integrate /ˈɪntɪɡreɪt/ *verb* to link things together to form one whole group

integrated accounts /ˌɪntɪɡreɪtɪd əˈkaʊnts/ *plural noun* accounting records that show both financial and cost accounts

integration /ˌɪntɪˈɡreɪʃ(ə)n/ *noun* the act of bringing several businesses together under a central control

inter-bank /ˌɪntə ˈbæŋk/ *adjective* between banks

inter-bank loan /ˌɪntə bæŋk ˈləʊn/ *noun* a loan from one bank to another

intercompany account /ˌɪntə ˌkʌmp(ə)ni əˈkaʊnt/ *noun* an account that records transactions between companies that are affiliated to each other

inter-company dealings /ˌɪntə ˌkʌmp(ə)ni ˈdiːlɪŋz/, **inter-company transactions** /ˌɪntə ˌkʌmp(ə)ni træn ˈzækʃ(ə)nz/ *plural noun* dealings or transactions between two companies in the same group

intercompany profit /ˌɪntəˌkʌmp(ə)ni ˈprɒfɪt/ *noun* the profit on services provided to a related company

interest /'ɪntrəst/ *noun* **1.** payment made by a borrower for the use of money, calculated as a percentage of the capital borrowed □ **high interest, low interest** interest at a high or low percentage **2.** money paid as income on investments or loans ○ *to receive interest at 5%* ○ *deposit which yields* or *gives* or *produces* or *bears 5% interest* ○ *account which earns interest at 10%* or *which earns 10% interest* ○ *The bank pays 10% interest on deposits.* ○ *The loan pays 5% interest.* **3.** a part of the ownership of something, e.g. if you invest money in a company you acquire a financial share or interest in it

interest-bearing deposits /ˌɪntrəst ˌbeərɪŋ dɪ'pɒzɪts/ *plural noun* a deposit of money with a financial institution that pays interest on the deposit

interest charges /'ɪntrəst ˌtʃɑːdʒɪz/ *plural noun* money paid as interest on a loan

interest coupon /'ɪntrəst ˌkuːpɒn/ *noun* a slip of paper attached to a government bond certificate which can be cashed to provide the annual interest

interest cover /'ɪntrəst ˌkʌvə/ *noun* the ability to pay interest payments on a loan

interested party /ˌɪntrestɪd 'pɑːti/ *noun* a person or company with a financial interest in a company

interest expense /'ɪntrəst ɪk,spens/ *noun* the cost of the interest payments on borrowed money

interest-free credit /ˌɪntrəst friː 'kredɪt/ *noun* a credit or loan where no interest is paid by the borrower ○ *The company gives its staff interest-free loans.*

interest rate /'ɪntrəst reɪt/ *noun* a figure which shows the percentage of the capital sum borrowed or deposited which is to be paid as interest. Also called **rate of interest**

interest rate margin /'ɪntrəst reɪt ˌmɑːdʒɪn/ *noun* the difference between the interest a bank pays on deposits and the interest it charges on loans

interest rate swap /'ɪntrəst reɪt ˌswɒp/ *noun* an agreement between two companies to exchange borrowings. A company with fixed-interest borrowings might swap them for variable interest borrowings of another company. Also called **plain vanilla swap**

interest sensitive /ˌɪntrəst 'sensɪtɪv/ *adjective* used to describe assets, generally purchased with credit, that are in demand when interest rates fall but considered less attractive when interest rates rise

interest yield /'ɪntrəst jiːld/ *noun* a yield on a fixed-interest investment

interim /'ɪntərɪm/ *adjective* made, measured or happening in the middle of a period, such as the financial year, and before the final result for the period is available ■ *noun* a statement of interim profits or dividends

'…the company plans to keep its annual dividend unchanged at 7.5 per share, which includes a 3.75 interim payout' [*Financial Times*]

interim audit /'ɪntərɪm ˌɔːdɪt/ *noun* an audit carried out for a period within a full accounting year, often for a half year

interim dividend /ˌɪntərɪm 'dɪvɪdend/ *noun* a dividend paid at the end of a half-year

interim financial statement /ˌɪntərɪm faɪˌnænʃəl 'steɪtmənt/ *noun* a financial statement that covers a period other than a full financial year. Although UK companies are not legally obliged to publish interim financial statements, those listed on the London Stock Exchange are obliged to publish a half-yearly report of their activities and a profit and loss account which may either be sent to shareholders or published in a national newspaper. In the United States, the practice is to issue quarterly financial statement.

interim payment /ˌɪntərɪm 'peɪmənt/ *noun* a payment of part of a dividend

interim receiver /ˌɪntərɪm rɪ'siːvə/ *noun* a receiver appointed to deal with a person's affairs until a bankruptcy order is made

intermediate debt /ˌɪntə'miːdiət det/ *noun* a form of debt which has to be repaid between four and ten years' time

internal /ɪn'tɜːn(ə)l/ *adjective* **1.** inside a company **2.** inside a country or a region

internal audit /ɪnˌtɜːn(ə)l 'ɔːdɪt/ *noun* an audit carried out by a department inside the company

internal auditor /ɪnˌtɜːn(ə)l 'ɔːdɪtə/ *noun* a member of staff who audits a company's accounts

internal control /ɪnˌtɜːn(ə)l kən'trəʊl/ *noun* a system set up by the management of a company to monitor and control the company's activities

internal growth /ɪnˌtɜːn(ə)l 'grəʊθ/ *noun* the development of a company by growing its existing business with its own finances, as opposed to acquiring other businesses. Also called **organic growth**

internal rate of return /ɪnˌtɜːn(ə)l reɪt əv rɪ'tɜːn/ *noun* an average annual yield of an investment, where the interest earned over a period of time is the same as the original cost of the investment. Abbreviation **IRR**

internal reporting /ɪnˌtɜːn(ə)l rɪˈpɔːtɪŋ/ *noun* financial information gathered and communicated within a company

Internal Revenue Service /ɪnˌtɜːn(ə)l ˈrevənjuː ˌsɜːvɪs/ *noun* in the United States, the branch of the federal government charged with collecting the majority of federal taxes. Abbreviation **IRS**

internal trade /ɪnˌtɜːn(ə)l ˈtreɪd/ *noun* trade between various parts of a country. Opposite **external trade**

International Accounting Standards /ˌɪntənæʃ(ə)nəl əˈkaʊntɪŋ ˌstændədz/ *plural noun* standards of accounting procedure set and monitored, since 2001, by the International Accounting Standards Board

International Accounting Standards Board /ˌɪntənæʃ(ə)nəl əˌkaʊntɪŋ ˈstændədz ˌbɔːd/ *noun* a London-based independent organisation established to set international standards fro accounting procedures. Abbreviation **IASB**

International Accounting Standards Committee /ˌɪntənæʃ(ə)nəl əˌkaʊntɪŋ ˈstændədz kəˌmɪti/ *noun* formerly, an organisation based in London that worked towards achieving global agreement on accounting standards. It was made part of the International Accounting Standards Board in 2001. Abbreviation **IASC**

International Bank for Reconstruction and Development /ˌɪntənæʃ(ə)nəl bæŋk fə ˌriːkənstrʌkʃ(ə)n ən dɪˈveləpmənt/ *noun* the official name of the World Bank. Abbreviation **IBRD**

International Centre for Settlement of Investment Disputes /ˌɪntənæʃ(ə)nəl ˌsentə fə ˌset(ə)lmənt əv ɪnˈvestmənt dɪˌspjuːts/ *noun* one of the five institutions that comprises the World Bank Group. It was established in 1966 to undertake the role previously undertaken in a personal capacity by the President of the World Bank in assisting in mediation or conciliation of investment disputes between governments and private foreign investors. The overriding consideration in its establishment was that a specialist institution could help to promote increased flows of international investment. Although ICSID has close links to the World Bank, it is an autonomous organisation. Abbreviation **ICSID**

International Federation of Accountants /ˌɪntənæʃ(ə)nəl ˌfedəreɪʃ(ə)n əv əˈkaʊntənts/ *noun* a glo-

bal organisation for the accountancy profession that seeks to protect the public interest by encouraging high quality practices by the world's accountants

International Financial Reporting Standards /ˌɪntənæʃ(ə)nəl faɪˌnænʃ(ə)l rɪˈpɔːtɪŋ ˌstændədz/ *plural noun* an internationally agreed set of high-quality, understandable and enforceable global standards for financial reporting

International Monetary Fund /ˌɪntənæʃ(ə)nəl ˈmʌnɪt(ə)ri ˌfʌnd/ *noun* a type of bank which is part of the United Nations and helps member states in financial difficulties, gives financial advice to members and encourages world trade. Abbreviation **IMF**

international money markets /ˌɪntənæʃ(ə)nəl ˈmʌni ˌmɑːkɪts/ *plural noun* markets such as the Euromarket, the international market for lending or borrowing in Eurocurrencies

international reserves /ˌɪntənæʃ(ə)nəl rɪˈzɜːvz/ *plural noun* same as **foreign currency reserves**

international trade /ˌɪntənæʃ(ə)nəl ˈtreɪd/ *noun* trade between different countries

Internet /ˈɪntənet/ *noun* an international network linking thousands of computers using telephone, cable and satellite links ○ *He searched the Internet for information on cheap tickets to the US* ○ *Much of our business is done on the Internet.* ○ *Internet sales form an important part of our turnover.*

‘…they predict a tenfold increase in sales via internet or TV between 1999 and 2004’ [*Investors Chronicle*]

‘…in two significant decisions, the Securities and Exchange Board of India today allowed trading of shares through the Internet and set a deadline for companies to conform to norms for good corporate governance’ [*The Hindu*]

Internet banking /ˌɪntənet ˈbæŋkɪŋ/ *noun* the operation of a bank account over the Internet

interpolation /ɪnˌtɜːpəˈleɪʃ(ə)n/ *noun* a method of estimating a value between two established values

intervene /ˌɪntəˈviːn/ *verb* to try to make a change in a situation in which you have not been involved before

intervention /ˌɪntəˈvenʃən/ *noun* the act of becoming involved in a situation in order to change it ○ *the central bank's intervention in the banking crisis*

intervention mechanism /ˌɪntə 'venʃən ˌmekənɪz(ə)m/ *noun* a method used by central banks in maintaining exchange rate parities, e.g. buying or selling foreign currency

inter vivos /ˌɪntə 'viːvəʊs/ *phrase* a Latin phrase, 'between living people'

inter vivos trust /ˌɪntə 'viːvəʊs trʌst/ *noun* a trust set up by one person for another living person

intestacy /ɪn'testəsi/ *noun* the state of having died without having made a will

intestate /ɪn'testət/ *adjective* □ **to die intestate** to die without having made a will

intrinsic value /ɪnˌtrɪnsɪk 'væljuː/ *noun* the material value of something ○ *These objects have sentimental value, but no intrinsic value at all.* ○ *The intrinsic value of jewellery makes it a good investment.*

introduction /ˌɪntrə'dʌkʃ(ə)n/ *noun* the act of bringing an established company to the Stock Exchange (i.e., getting permission for the shares to be traded on the Stock Exchange, used when a company is formed by a demerger from an existing larger company, and no new shares are being offered for sale)

invalid /ɪn'vælɪd/ *adjective* not valid or not legal ○ *This permit is invalid.* ○ *The claim has been declared invalid.*

invalidate /ɪn'vælɪdeɪt/ *verb* to make something invalid ○ *Because the company has been taken over, the contract has been invalidated.*

invalidation /ɪnˌvælɪ'deɪʃən/ *noun* the act of making invalid

invalidity /ˌɪnvə'lɪdɪti/ *noun* the fact of being invalid ○ *the invalidity of the contract*

inventory /'ɪnvənt(ə)ri/ *noun* **1.** *especially US* all the stock or goods in a warehouse or shop ○ *to carry a high inventory* ○ *to aim to reduce inventory* Also called **stock** **2.** a list of the contents of a building such as a house for sale or an office for rent ○ *to draw up an inventory of fixtures and fittings* ■ *verb* to make a list of stock or contents

inventory control /'ɪnvənt(ə)ri kən ˌtrəʊl/ *noun US* same as **stock control**

inventory financing /'ɪnvənt(ə)ri ˌfaɪnænsɪŋ/ *noun especially US* the use of money from working capital to purchase stock for resale

inventory turnover /'ɪnvənt(ə)ri ˌtɜːnəʊvə/ *noun especially US* the total value of stock sold during a year, divided by the value of the goods remaining in stock

invest /ɪn'vest/ *verb* **1.** to put money into shares, bonds, a building society, etc., hoping that it will produce interest and increase in value ○ *He invested all his money in unit trusts.* ○ *She was advised to invest in real estate* or *in government bonds.* **2.** to spend money on something which you believe will be useful ○ *to invest money in new machinery* ○ *to invest capital in a new factory*

'...we have substantial venture capital to invest in good projects' [*Times*]

investment /ɪn'vestmənt/ *noun* **1.** the placing of money so that it will produce interest and increase in value ○ *They called for more government investment in new industries.* ○ *She was advised to make investments in oil companies.* **2.** a share, bond or piece of property bought in the hope that it will produce more money than was used to buy it

'...investment trusts, like unit trusts, consist of portfolios of shares and therefore provide a spread of investments' [*Investors Chronicle*]

'...investment companies took the view that prices had reached rock bottom and could only go up' [*Lloyd's List*]

investment analyst /ɪn'vestmənt ˌænəlɪst/ *noun* a person working for a stockbroking firm, who analyses the performance of companies in a sector of the market, or the performance of a market sector as a whole, or economic trends in general

investment appraisal /ɪnˌvestmənt ə 'preɪz(ə)l/ *noun* the analysis of the future profitability of capital purchases as an aid to good management

investment bank /ɪn'vestmənt bæŋk/ *noun US* a bank which deals with the underwriting of new issues, and advises corporations on their financial affairs (NOTE: The UK term is **issuing house**.)

investment company /ɪn'vestmənt ˌkʌmp(ə)ni/ *noun* company whose shares can be bought on the Stock Exchange, and whose business is to make money by buying and selling stocks and shares

investment grant /ɪn'vestmənt grɑːnt/ *noun* a government grant to a company to help it to invest in new machinery

investment income /ɪn'vestmənt ˌɪnkʌm/ *noun* income from investments, e.g. interest and dividends. Compare **earned income**

Investment Management Association /ɪnˌvestmənt 'mænɪdʒmənt ə ˌsəʊsieɪʃ(ə)n/ *noun* the trade body for the UK investment industry, formed in February

2002 following the merger of the Association of Unit Trusts and Investment Funds (AUTIF) and the Fund Manager's Association. Abbreviation **IMA**

investment property /ɪnˈvestmənt ˌprɒpəti/ *noun* property which is held for letting

investment revaluation reserve /ɪn ˈvestmənt riːˌvæljueɪʃən rɪˌzɜːv/ *noun* the capital reserve where changes in the value of a business's investment properties are disclosed when they are revalued

investment trust /ɪnˈvestmənt trʌst/ *noun* a company whose shares can be bought on the Stock Exchange and whose business is to make money by buying and selling stocks and shares

investment turnover /ɪnˈvestmənt ˌtɜːnəʊvə/ *noun* income earned on capital invested in a business

investor /ɪnˈvestə/ *noun* a person who invests money

investor protection /ɪnˈvestə prəˌtekʃ(ə)n/ *noun* legislation to protect small investors from unscrupulous investment brokers and advisers

Investors in Industry /ɪnˌvestəz ɪn ˈɪndəstri/ *plural noun* a finance group partly owned by the big British High Street banks, providing finance especially to smaller companies. Abbreviation **3i**

invisible assets /ɪnˌvɪzɪb(ə)l ˈæsets/ *plural noun US* same as **intangible assets**

invisible earnings /ɪnˌvɪzɪb(ə)l ˈɜːnɪŋz/ *plural noun* foreign currency earned by a country by providing services, receiving interests or dividends, but not by selling goods

invisible exports /ɪnˌvɪzɪb(ə)l ˈekspɔːts/ *plural noun* services, e.g. banking, insurance and tourism, that are provided to customers overseas and paid for in foreign currency. Opposite **visible exports**

invisible imports /ɪnˌvɪzɪb(ə)l ˈɪmpɔːts/ *plural noun* services that overseas companies provide to domestic customers who pay for them in local currency. Opposite **visible imports**

invisibles /ɪnˈvɪzɪb(ə)lz/ *plural noun* invisible imports and exports

invisible trade /ɪnˌvɪzɪb(ə)l ˈtreɪd/ *noun* trade involving invisible imports and exports. Opposite **visible trade**

invoice /ˈɪnvɔɪs/ *noun* a note asking for payment for goods or services supplied ○ *your invoice dated November 10th* ○ *to make out an invoice for £250* ○ *to settle* or

to pay an invoice ○ *They sent in their invoice six weeks late.* ■ *verb* to send an invoice to someone ○ *to invoice a customer*

invoice discounting /ˈɪnvɔɪs ˌdɪskaʊntɪŋ/ *noun* a method of obtaining early payment of invoices by selling them at a discount to a company which will receive payment of the invoices when they are paid. The debtor is not informed of this arrangement, as opposed to factoring, where the debtor is informed.

invoice price /ˈɪnvɔɪs praɪs/ *noun* the price as given on an invoice, including any discount and VAT

invoice register /ˈɪnvɔɪs ˌredʒɪstə/ *noun* a list of purchase invoices recording the date of receipt of the invoice, the supplier, the invoice value and the person to whom the invoice has been passed to ensure that all invoices are processed by the accounting system

invoicing /ˈɪnvɔɪsɪŋ/ *noun* the work of sending invoices ○ *All our invoicing is done by computer.*

invoicing department /ˈɪnvɔɪsɪŋ dɪˌpɑːtmənt/ *noun* the department in a company which deals with preparing and sending invoices

involuntary bankruptcy /ɪnˌvɒlənt(ə)ri ˈbæŋkrʌptsi/ *noun US* an application by creditors to have a person or corporation made bankrupt (NOTE: The UK term is **compulsory winding up**.)

inward /ˈɪnwəd/ *adjective* towards the home country

inward bill /ˌɪnwəd ˈbɪl/ *noun* a bill of lading for goods arriving in a country

IOU /ˌaɪ əʊ ˈjuː/ *noun* 'I owe you', a signed document promising that you will pay back money borrowed ○ *to pay a pile of IOUs* ○ *I have a pile of IOUs which need paying.*

IPO *abbreviation* initial public offering

IRA /ˈaɪrə/ *abbreviation US* Individual Retirement Account

IRC *abbreviation* Inland Revenue Commissioner

IRR *abbreviation* internal rate of return

irrecoverable debt /ɪrɪˌkʌv(ə)rəb(ə)l ˈdet/ *noun* a debt which will never be paid

irredeemable bond /ɪrɪˌdiːməb(ə)l ˈbɒnd/ *noun* a government bond which has no date of maturity and which therefore provides interest but can never be redeemed at full value

irrevocable /ɪˈrevəkəb(ə)l/ *adjective* unchangeable

irrevocable letter of credit /ɪ ˌrevəkəb(ə)l ˌletər əv ˈkredɪt/ *noun* a letter of credit which cannot be cancelled or changed, except if agreed between the two parties involved

IRS *abbreviation US* Internal Revenue Service

IS *abbreviation* income support

ISA /ˈaɪsə/ *abbreviation* Individual Savings Account

issue /ˈɪʃuː/ *noun* an act of offering new shares for sale

'…the company said that its recent issue of 10.5 per cent convertible preference shares at A\$8.50 a share has been oversubscribed' [*Financial Times*]

issued capital /ˌɪʃuːd ˈkæpɪt(ə)l/ *noun* an amount of capital which is given out as shares to shareholders

issued price /ˌɪʃuːd ˈpraɪs/, **issue price** /ˈɪʃuː praɪs/ *noun* the price of shares in a new company when they are offered for sale for the first time

issuer /ˈɪʃuə/ *noun* a financial institution that issues credit and debit cards and maintains the systems for billing and payment

issuing /ˈɪʃuɪŋ/ *adjective* organising an issue of shares

itemise /ˈaɪtəmaɪz/, **itemize** *verb* to make a detailed list of things ○ *Itemising the sales figures will take about two days.*

IVA *abbreviation* Individual Voluntary Arrangement

J

J curve /'dʒeɪ 'kɜːv/ *noun* a line on a graph shaped like a letter 'J', with an initial short fall, followed by a longer rise, used to describe the effect of a falling exchange rate on a country's balance of trade

JIT *abbreviation* just-in-time

job card /'dʒɒb kɑːd/ *noun* a record card relating to a job and giving details of the time taken to do a piece of work and the materials used. This is used to allocate direct labour and materials costs.

job costing /'dʒɒb ˌkɒstɪŋ/ *noun* the process of calculating the cost of a single job or batch of work. Also called **specific order costing**

job order /'dʒɒb ˌɔːdə/ *noun* an authorised order for the production of goods or services

job order costing /'dʒɒb ˌɔːdə ˌkɒstɪŋ/ *noun* the accumulation of costs incurred by fulfilling specific orders for goods or services

joint /dʒɔɪnt/ *adjective* **1.** carried out or produced together with others ○ *a joint undertaking* **2.** one of two or more people who work together or who are linked ○ *They are joint beneficiaries of the will.* ○ *The two countries are joint signatories of the treaty.*

joint account /'dʒɔɪnt əˌkaʊnt/ *noun* a bank or building society account shared by two people ○ *Many married couples have joint accounts so that they can pay for household expenses.*

joint and several liability /ˌdʒɔɪnt ən ˌsev(ə)rəl ˌlaɪə'bɪlɪti/ *noun* a situation where someone who has a claim against a group of people can sue them separately or together as a group

joint cost /ˌdʒɔɪnt 'kɒst/ *noun* the cost of which can be allocated to more than one product, project or service

joint-life annuity /'dʒɔɪnt laɪf əˌnjuəti/ *noun* an annuity that continues until both parties have died. They are attractive to married couples as they ensure that the survivor has an income for the rest of his or her life.

jointly /'dʒɔɪntli/ *adverb* together with one or more other people ○ *to own a property jointly* ○ *to manage a company jointly* ○ *They are jointly liable for damages.*

joint management /ˌdʒɔɪnt 'mænɪdʒmənt/ *noun* management done by two or more people

joint ownership /ˌdʒɔɪnt 'əʊnəʃɪp/ *noun* the owning of a property by several owners

joint products /ˌdʒɔɪnt 'prɒdʌkts/ *plural noun* two or more products that are produced as a unit but are sold separately and each have a saleable value high enough for them to be regarded as a main product

joint return /ˌdʒɔɪnt rɪ'tɜːn/ *noun* a tax return that is filed jointly by a husband and wife

joint-stock bank /ˌdʒɔɪnt 'stɒk ˌbæŋk/ *noun* a bank which is a public company quoted on the Stock Exchange

joint-stock company /'dʒɔɪnt stɒk ˌkʌmp(ə)ni/ *noun* formerly, a public company in the UK whose shares were owned by very many people. Now called a Public Limited Company or Plc.

joint venture /ˌdʒɔɪnt 'ventʃə/ *noun* a situation where two or more companies join together for one specific large business project

journal /'dʒɜːn(ə)l/ *noun* a book with the account of sales and purchases made each day

journal entry /'dʒɜːn(ə)l ˌentri/ *noun* a record of the accounting information for a business transaction, made at first in a journal and later transferred to a ledger

judgment /'dʒʌdʒmənt/, **judgement** *noun* a legal decision or official decision of a court □ **to pronounce judgment, to give your judgment on something** to give an official or legal decision about something

judgment creditor /'dʒʌdʒmənt ˌkredɪtə/ *noun* a person who has been given a court order making a debtor pay him a debt

judgment debtor /'dʒʌdʒmənt ˌdetə/ *noun* a debtor who has been ordered by a court to pay a debt

junior capital /ˌdʒuːniə 'kæpɪt(ə)l/ *noun* capital in the form of shareholders' equity, which is repaid only after secured loans called 'senior capital' have been paid if the firm goes into liquidation

junior mortgage /ˌdʒuːniə 'mɔːɡɪdʒ/ *noun* a second mortgage

junior partner /ˌdʒuːniə 'pɑːtnə/ *noun* a person who has a small part of the shares in a partnership

junior security /ˌdʒuːniə sɪ'kjʊərɪti/ *noun* a security which is repaid after other securities

just-in-time /ˌdʒʌst ɪn 'taɪm/ *noun* a system in which goods are made or purchased just before they are needed, so as to avoid carrying high levels of stock. Abbreviation **JIT**

K

K *abbreviation* one thousand □ **'salary: £20K+'** salary more than £20,000 per annum

Keogh plan /ˈkiːəʊ ˌplæn/ *noun US* a private pension plan allowing self-employed businesspeople and professionals to set up pension and retirement plans for themselves

key-person insurance /ˈkiː pɜːs(ə)n ɪn ˌʃʊərəns/ *noun* an insurance policy taken out to cover the costs of replacing an employee who is particularly important to an organisation if he or she dies or is ill for a long time

key rate /ˈkiː reɪt/ *noun* an interest rate which gives the basic rate on which other rates are calculated, e.g. the former bank base rate in the UK, or the Federal Reserve's discount rate in the USA

kickback /ˈkɪkbæk/ *noun* an illegal commission paid to someone, especially a government official, who helps in a business deal

kicker /ˈkɪkə/ *noun* a special inducement to buy a bond, e.g. making it convertible to shares at a preferential rate (*informal*)

kite /kaɪt/ *verb* **1.** *US* to write cheques on one account which may not be able to honour them and deposit them in another, withdrawing money from the second account before the cheques are cleared **2.** to use stolen credit cards or cheque books

kitty /ˈkɪti/ *noun* money which has been collected by a group of people to be used later, such as for an office party ○ *We each put £5 into the kitty.*

Know How Fund /ˈnəʊ haʊ ˌfʌnd/ *noun* formerly, a fund created by the UK government to provide technical training and advice to countries of Eastern Europe. This function is now carried out by the Department for International Development.

knowledge management /ˈnɒlɪdʒ ˌmænɪdʒmənt/ *noun* the task of co-ordinating the specialist knowledge possessed by employees so that it can be exploited to create benefits and competitive advantage for the organisation

L

labour /ˈleɪbə/ *noun* **1.** heavy work (NOTE: The US spelling is **labor.**) □ **labour is charged at £15 an hour** each hour of work costs £15 **2.** workers, the workforce ○ *We will need to employ more labour if production is to be increased.* ○ *The costs of labour are rising in line with inflation.* (NOTE: The US spelling is **labor.**)

'…the possibility that British goods will price themselves back into world markets is doubtful as long as sterling labour costs continue to rise faster than in competitor countries' [*Sunday Times*]

labour costs /ˈleɪbə kɒsts/ *plural noun* the cost of the employees employed to make a product, not including materials or overheads

labour efficiency variance /ˈleɪbə ɪˈfɪʃ(ə)nsi ˌveəriəns/ *noun* the discrepancy between the usual or expected labour time used to produce something and the actual time used

labour force /ˈleɪbə fɔːs/ *noun* all the employees in a company or in an area ○ *The management has made an increased offer to the labour force.* ○ *We are opening a new factory in the Far East because of the cheap local labour force.*

'70 per cent of Australia's labour force is employed in service activity' [*Australian Financial Review*]

labour market /ˈleɪbə ˌmɑːkɪt/ *noun* the number of people who are available for work ○ *25,000 school-leavers have just come on to the labour market.*

labour rate (price) variance /ˈleɪbə reɪt ˌpraɪs ˌveəriəns/ *noun* any change to the normal hourly rate paid to workers

labour relations /ˈleɪbə rɪˌleɪʃ(ə)nz/ *plural noun* relations between management and employees ○ *The company has a history of bad labour relations.*

labour turnover /ˈleɪbə ˌtɜːnəʊvə/ *noun* the movement of employees with some leaving their jobs and others joining. Also called **turnover of labour**

labour variance /ˈleɪbə ˌveəriəns/ *noun* any discrepancy between the actual cost of labour in an organisation and the standard industry cost

Laffer curve /ˈlæfə kɜːv/ *noun* a chart showing that cuts in tax rates increase output in the economy. Alternatively, increases in tax rates initially produce more revenue and then less as the economy slows down.

lag /læg/ *verb* to be behind or to be slower than something

lagging indicator /ˈlægɪŋ ˌɪndɪkeɪtə/ *noun* an indicator which shows a change in economic trends later than other indicators, e.g. the gross national product. Opposite **leading indicator**

landlord /ˈlændlɔːd/ *noun* a person or company which owns a property which is let

land register /ˈlænd ˌredʒɪstə/ *noun* a list of pieces of land, showing who owns each and what buildings are on it

land registration /ˈlænd redʒɪˌstreɪʃ(ə)n/ *noun* a system of registering land and its owners

Land Registry /ˈlænd ˌredʒɪstri/ *noun* a government office where details of land ownership and sales are kept

land tax /ˈlænd tæks/ *noun* a tax on the amount of land owned

lapse /læps/ *verb* to stop being valid, or to stop being active ○ *The guarantee has lapsed.*

lapsed option /ˌlæpst ˈɒpʃən/ *noun* an option which has not been taken up, and now has expired

last in first out /ˌlɑːst ɪn ˌfɜːst ˈaʊt/ *phrase* an accounting method where stock is valued at the price of the earliest purchases. Abbreviation **LIFO.** Compare **first in first out**

last quarter /ˌlɑːst ˈkwɔːtə/ *noun* a period of three months at the end of the financial year

last will and testament /ˌlɑːst ˌwɪl ən ˈtestəmənt/ *noun* a will, a document by which a person says what he or she wants to happen to their property when they die

launder /ˈlɔːndə/ *verb* to pass illegal profits, money from selling drugs, money which has not been taxed, etc., into the banking system ○ *to launder money through an offshore bank*

'…it has since emerged that the bank was being used to launder drug money and some of its executives have been given lengthy jail sentences' [*Times*]

LAUTRO /ˈlaʊtrəʊ/ *abbreviation* Life Assurance and Unit Trust Regulatory Organisation

law /lɔː/ *noun* **1.** ♦ **laws 2.** □ **inside** *or* **within the law** obeying the laws of a country □ **against** *or* **outside the law** not according to the laws of a country ○ *The company is possibly operating outside the law.* □ **to break the law** to do something which is not allowed by law ○ *He is breaking the law by trading without a licence.* **3.** a rule governing some aspect of human activity made and enforced by the state

lawful /ˈlɔːf(ə)l/ *adjective* acting within the law

law of supply and demand /ˌlɔː əv sə ˌplaɪ ən dɪˈmɑːnd/ *noun* a general rule that the amount of a product which is available is related to the needs of potential customers

laws /lɔːz/ *plural noun* rules by which a country is governed and the activities of people and organisations controlled

lay out *phrasal verb* to spend money ○ *We had to lay out half our cash budget on equipping the new factory.*

LBO *abbreviation* leveraged buyout

L/C *abbreviation* letter of credit

LCM *abbreviation* lower of cost or market

LDT *abbreviation* licensed deposit-taker

lead bank /ˌliːd ˈbæŋk/ *noun* the main bank in a loan syndicate

leading indicator /ˌliːdɪŋ ˈɪndɪkeɪtə/ *noun* an indicator such as manufacturing order books which shows a change in economic trends earlier than other indicators. Opposite **lagging indicator**

lead manager /ˌliːd ˈmænɪdʒə/ *noun* a person who organises a syndicate of underwriters for a new issue of securities

leads and lags /ˌliːdz ən ˈlægz/ *plural noun* in businesses that deal in foreign currencies, the practice of speeding up the receipt of payments (leads) if a currency is going to weaken, and slowing down the payment of costs (lags) if a currency is thought to be about to strengthen, in order to maximise gains and reduce losses

lead time /ˈliːd taɪm/ *noun* the time between deciding to place an order and receiving the product ○ *The lead time on this item is more than six weeks.*

lead underwriter /ˌliːd ˈʌndəraɪtə/ *noun* an underwriting firm which organises the underwriting of a share issue (NOTE: The US term is **managing underwriter**.)

learning curve /ˈlɜːnɪŋ kɜːv/ *noun* **1.** a process of learning something that starts slowly and then becomes faster **2.** a line on a graph which shows the relationship between experience in doing something and competence at carrying it out **3.** a diagram or graph that represents the way in which people gain knowledge or experience over time (NOTE: A steep learning curve represents a situation where people learn a great deal in a short time; a shallow curve represents a slower learning process. The curve eventually levels out, representing the time when the knowledge gained is being consolidated.) **4.** the decrease in the effort required to produce each single item when the total number of items produced is doubled (NOTE: The concept of the learning curve has its origin in productivity research in the aircraft industry of the 1930s, when it was discovered that the time and effort needed to assemble an aircraft decreased by 20% each time the total number produced doubled.)

lease /liːs/ *noun* a written contract for letting or renting a building, a piece of land or a piece of equipment for a period against payment of a fee ○ *to rent office space on a twenty-year lease* □ **the lease expires next year** *or* **the lease runs out next year** the lease comes to an end next year ■ *verb* **1.** to let or rent offices, land or machinery for a period ○ *to lease offices to small firms* ○ *to lease equipment* **2.** to use an office, land or machinery for a time and pay a fee ○ *to lease an office from an insurance company* ○ *All our company cars are leased.*

lease back *phrasal verb* to sell a property or machinery to a company and then take it back on a lease ○ *They sold the office building to raise cash, and then leased it back on a twenty-five year lease.*

leasehold /ˈliːshəʊld/ *noun, adjective* possessing property on a lease, for a fixed time ○ *to buy a property leasehold* ○ *We are currently occupying a leasehold property.* ○ *The company has some valuable leaseholds.* ■ *noun* a property held on a lease from a freeholder ○ *The company has some valuable leaseholds.*

leaseholder /'liːʃhəʊldə/ *noun* a person who holds a property on a lease

leasing /'liːsɪŋ/ *noun* the use of a lease or of equipment under a lease ○ *an equipment-leasing company* ○ *The company has branched out into car leasing.* ◊ **lessee**

leasing agreement /ˌliːsɪŋ ə'griːmənt/ *noun* a contract between an owner and a lessee, by which the lessee has the exclusive use of a piece of equipment for a period of time, against payment of a fee

ledger /'ledʒə/ *noun* a book in which accounts are written

legacy /'legəsi/ *noun* a piece of property given by someone to someone else in a will

legal /'liːg(ə)l/ *adjective* **1.** according to the law or allowed by the law ○ *The company's action in sacking the accountant was completely legal.* **2.** referring to the law

legal capital /ˌliːg(ə)l 'kæpɪt(ə)l/ *noun* the amount of shareholders' equity in a company that is not reduced when dividends are paid

legal charge /ˌliːg(ə)l 'tʃɑːdʒ/ *noun* a legal document held by the Land Registry showing who has a claim on a property

legal claim /'liːg(ə)l kleɪm/ *noun* a statement that someone owns something legally ○ *He has no legal claim to the property.*

legal costs /'liːg(ə)l kɒsts/, **legal charges** /'liːg(ə)l ˌtʃɑːdʒɪz/, **legal expenses** /'liːg(ə)l ɪkˌspensɪz/ *plural noun* money spent on fees to lawyers ○ *The clerk could not afford the legal expenses involved in suing her boss.*

legal currency /ˌliːg(ə)l 'kʌrənsi/ *noun* money which is legally used in a country

legal tender /ˌliːg(ə)l 'tendə/ *noun* coins or notes which can be legally used to pay a debt

legatee /ˌlegə'tiː/ *noun* a person who receives property from someone who has died

lend /lend/ *verb* to allow someone to use something for a period ○ *to lend something to someone* or *to lend someone something* ○ *to lend money against security* ○ *He lent the company money* or *He lent money to the company.* ○ *The bank lent her £50,000 to start her business.* (NOTE: **lending – lent**)

lender /'lendə/ *noun* a person who lends money

lender of the last resort /ˌlendə əv ðə ˌlɑːst rɪ'zɔːt/ *noun* a central bank which lends money to commercial banks

lending limit /'lendɪŋ ˌlɪmɪt/ *noun* a restriction on the amount of money a bank can lend

lending margin /'lendɪŋ ˌmɑːdʒɪn/ *noun* an agreed spread for lending, based on the LIBOR

less /les/ *adjective* smaller than, of a smaller size or of a smaller value ○ *We do not grant credit for sums of less than £100.* ○ *He sold it for less than he had paid for it.* ■ *preposition* minus, with a sum removed ○ *purchase price less 15% discount* ○ *interest less service charges* ■ *adverb* not as much

lessee /le'siː/ *noun* a person who has a lease or who pays money for a property he or she leases

lessor /le'sɔː/ *noun* a person who grants a lease on a property

let /let/ *verb* to allow the use of a house, an office or a farm to someone for the payment of rent (NOTE: The US term is **rent**.)

letter of acknowledgement /ˌletər əv ək'nɒlɪdʒmənt/ *noun* a letter which says that something has been received

letter of credit /ˌletər əv 'kredɪt/ *noun* a document issued by a bank on behalf of a customer authorising payment to a supplier when the conditions specified in the document are met. Abbreviation **L/C**

letter of indemnity /ˌletər əv ɪn'demnɪti/ *noun* a letter promising payment as compensation for a loss

letter of intent /ˌletər əv ɪn'tent/ *noun* a letter which states what a company intends to do if something happens

letter of licence /ˌletər əv 'laɪs(ə)ns/ *noun* a letter from a creditor to a debtor who is having problems repaying money owed, giving the debtor a certain period of time to raise the money and an undertaking not to bring legal proceedings to recover the debt during that period

letters patent /ˌletəz 'peɪtənt/ *plural noun* the official term for a patent

level /'lev(ə)l/ *verb* □ **to level off** *or* **to level out** to stop rising or falling ○ *Profits have levelled off over the last few years.* ○ *Prices are levelling out.*

leverage /'levərɪdʒ/ *noun* **1.** same as **gearing 2.** the act of borrowing money at fixed interest which is then used to produce more money than the interest paid

leveraged /'liːvərɪdʒ/ *adjective* borrowing relatively large sums of money in order to finance assets

leveraged buyout /ˌliːvərɪdʒd 'baɪaʊt/, **leveraged takeover** /ˌliːvərɪdʒd 'teɪkəʊvə/ *noun* an act of buying all the shares in a company by borrowing money against the security of the shares to be bought. Abbreviation **LBO**

'...the offer came after management had offered to take the company private through a leveraged buyout for $825 million' [*Fortune*]

levy /'levi/ *noun* money which is demanded and collected by the government

'...royalties have been levied at a rate of 12.5% of full production' [*Lloyd's List*]

liabilities /ˌlaɪəˈbɪlɪtiz/ *plural noun* the debts of a business, including dividends owed to shareholders ○ *The balance sheet shows the company's assets and liabilities.* □ **to discharge your liabilities in full** to pay everything which you owe

liability /ˌlaɪəˈbɪlɪti/ *noun* **1.** a legal responsibility for damage, loss or harm ○ *The two partners took out insurance to cover employers' liability.* **2.** responsibility for a payment such as the repayment of a loan

LIBOR /'laɪbɔː/ *abbreviation* London Interbank Offered Rate

licensed deposit-taker /ˌlaɪs(ə)nst dɪˈpɒzɪt ˌteɪkə/, **licensed institution** /ˌlaɪs(ə)nst ˌɪnstɪˈtjuːʃ(ə)n/ *noun* a deposit-taking institution which is licensed to receive money on deposit from private individuals and to pay interest on it, e.g. a building society, bank or friendly society. Abbreviation **LDT**

lien /'liːən/ *noun* the legal right to hold someone's goods and keep them until a debt has been paid

life assurance /'laɪf əˌʃʊərəns/ *noun* insurance which pays a sum of money when someone dies, or at an agreed date if they are still alive

Life Assurance and Unit Trust Regulatory Organisation /ˌlaɪf əˌʃɔːrəns ən ˌjuːnɪt trʌst ˈregjʊlət(ə)ri ˌɔːgənaɪzeɪʃ(ə)n/ *noun* an organisation set up to regulate the operations of life assurance companies and unit trusts, now replaced by the FSA. Abbreviation **LAUTRO**

life assurance company /'laɪf əˌʃɔːrəns ˌkʌmp(ə)ni/ *noun* a company providing life assurance, but usually also providing other services such as investment advice

life-cycle costing /'laɪf ˌsaɪk(ə)l ˌkɒstɪŋ/ *noun* an estimate of the likely revenue generated by, and costs incurred by, a product over its life cycle

life expectancy /'laɪf ɪkˌspektənsi/ *noun* the number of years a person is likely to live

life insurance /'laɪf ɪnˌʃʊərəns/ *noun* US same as **life assurance**

life interest /ˌlaɪf ˈɪntrəst/ *noun* a situation where someone benefits from a property as long as he or she is alive

life tables /'laɪf ˌteɪb(ə)lz/ *plural noun* same as **actuarial tables**

LIFO /'laɪfəʊ/ *abbreviation* last in first out

limit /'lɪmɪt/ *noun* the point at which something ends or the point where you can go no further ■ *verb* **1.** to stop something from going beyond a specific point, to restrict the number or amount of something **2.** to restrict the number or amount of something

'...the biggest surprise of 1999 was the rebound in the price of oil. In the early months of the year commentators were talking about a fall to $5 a barrel but for the first time in two decades, the oil exporting countries got their act together, limited production and succeeded in pushing prices up' [*Financial Times*]

limitation /ˌlɪmɪˈteɪʃ(ə)n/ *noun* the act of allowing only a specific quantity of something ○ *The contract imposes limitations on the number of cars which can be imported.*

limited company /ˌlɪmɪtɪd ˈkʌmp(ə)ni/ *noun* a company in which each shareholder is responsible for the company's debts only to the amount that he or she has invested in the company. Limited companies must be formed by at least two directors. Abbreviation **Ltd**. Also called **limited liability company**

limited liability /ˌlɪmɪtɪd ˌlaɪəˈbɪlɪti/ *noun* a situation where someone's liability for debt is limited by law

limited liability company /ˌlɪmɪtɪd ˌlaɪəbɪlɪti ˈkʌmp(ə)ni/ *noun* same as **limited company**

limited partner /ˌlɪmɪtɪd ˈpɑːtnə/ *noun* a partner who is responsible for the debts of the firm only up to the amount of money which he or she has provided to the business

limited partnership /ˌlɪmɪtɪd ˈpɑːtnəʃɪp/ *noun* a registered business where the liability of the partners is limited to the amount of capital they have each provided to the business and where the partners may not take part in the running of the business

limiting factor /ˌlɪmɪtɪŋ ˈfæktə/ *noun* a factor which limits a company's ability to achieve its goals, e.g. sales demand being too low for the company to make enough profit ○ *The short holiday season is a limiting factor on the hotel trade.*

line item budget /ˌlaɪn ˌaɪtəm ˈbʌdʒɪt/ *noun* a well-established budget layout that shows the costs of a cost object analysed by their nature in a line-by-line format

line of credit /ˌlaɪn əv ˈkredɪt/ *noun* **1.** the amount of money made available to a customer by a bank as an overdraft □ **to open a line of credit** *or* **a credit line** to make credit available to someone **2.** the borrowing limit on a credit card

link /lɪŋk/ *verb* to join or to attach to something else ○ *to link pensions to inflation* ○ *to link bonus payments to productivity* ○ *His salary is linked to the cost of living.* ♢ **index-linked**

liquid /ˈlɪkwɪd/ *adjective* easily converted to cash, or containing a large amount of cash

liquid assets /ˌlɪkwɪd ˈæsets/ *plural noun* cash, or investments which can be quickly converted into cash

liquidation /ˌlɪkwɪˈdeɪʃ(ə)n/ *noun* **1.** the sale of assets for cash, usually in order to pay debts □ **liquidation of a debt** payment of a debt **2.** the winding up or closing of a company and selling of its assets □ **the company went into liquidation** the company was closed and its assets sold

liquidation value /ˌlɪkwɪˈdeɪʃ(ə)n ˌvælju:/ *noun* the amount of money that would be yielded by a quick sale of all of a company's assets

liquidator /ˈlɪkwɪdeɪtə/ *noun* a person named to supervise the closing of a company which is in liquidation

liquidity /lɪˈkwɪdɪti/ *noun* cash, or the fact of having cash or assets which can be changed into cash

liquidity ratio /lɪˈkwɪdɪti ˌreɪʃɪəʊ/ *noun* an accounting ratio used to measure an organisation's liquidity. It is calculated by taking the business's current assets, minus its stocks, divided by its current liabilities. Also called **acid test ratio, quick ratio**

listed company /ˌlɪstɪd ˈkʌmp(ə)ni/ *noun* a company whose shares can be bought or sold on the Stock Exchange

listed securities /ˌlɪstɪd sɪˈkjʊərɪtiz/ *plural noun* shares which can be bought or sold on the Stock Exchange, shares which appear on the official Stock Exchange list

Listing Agreement /ˈlɪstɪŋ əˌgri:mənt/ *noun* a document which a company signs when being listed on the Stock Exchange, in which it promises to abide by stock exchange regulations

listing details /ˈlɪstɪŋ ˌdi:teɪlz/ *plural noun* details of a company which are published when the company applies for a stock exchange listing (the US equivalent is the 'registration statement')

listing particulars /ˈlɪstɪŋ pəˌtɪkjʊləz/ *plural noun* same as **listing details**

listing requirements /ˈlɪstɪŋ rɪ ˌkwaɪəmənts/ *plural noun* the conditions which must be met by a corporation before its stock can be listed on the New York Stock Exchange

litigation /ˌlɪtɪˈgeɪʃ(ə)n/ *noun* the bringing of a lawsuit against someone

loan /ləʊn/ *noun* money which has been lent

'…over the last few weeks, companies raising new loans from international banks have been forced to pay more, and an unusually high number of attempts to syndicate loans among banks has failed' [*Financial Times*]

loan capital /ˈləʊn ˌkæpɪt(ə)l/ *noun* a part of a company's capital which is a loan to be repaid at a later date

loan stock /ˈləʊn stɒk/ *noun* stock issued to an organisation in return for a loan. Loan stock earns interest.

local /ˈləʊk(ə)l/ *adjective* located in or providing a service for a restricted area

'…each cheque can be made out for the local equivalent of £100 rounded up to a convenient figure' [*Sunday Times*]

'…the business agent for Local 414 of the Store Union said his committee will recommend that the membership ratify the agreement' [*Toronto Star*]

'EC regulations insist that customers can buy cars anywhere in the EC at the local pre-tax price' [*Financial Times*]

local authority /ˌləʊk(ə)l ɔːˈθɒrɪti/ *noun* an elected section of government which runs a small area of the country

local currency /ˌləʊk(ə)l ˈkʌrənsi/ *noun* the currency of a particular country where a transaction is being carried out ○ *Because of the weakness of the local currency, all payments are in dollars.*

local government /ˌləʊk(ə)l ˈgʌv(ə)nmənt/ *noun* elected authorities and administrative organisations which deal with the affairs of small areas of a country

lock into /ˌlɒk ˈɪntə/, **lock in** /ˌlɒk ˈɪn/ *verb* to be fixed to an interest rate or exchange rate ○ *By buying francs forward the company is in effect locking itself into a pound-franc exchange rate of 10.06.*

London Interbank Offered Rate /ˌlʌndən ˌɪntəbæŋk 'ɒfəd reɪt/ *noun* the rate at which banks offer to lend Eurodollars to other banks. Abbreviation **LIBOR**

long /lɒŋ/ *adjective* for a large period of time

long bond /'lɒŋ bɒnd/, **long coupon bond** /'lɒŋ ˌkuːpɒn ˌbɒnd/ *noun* a bond which will mature in more than ten years' time

long credit /ˌlɒŋ 'kredɪt/ *noun* credit terms which allow the borrower a long time to pay

long-dated bill /ˌlɒŋ ˌdeɪtɪd 'bɪl/ *noun* a bill which is payable in more than three months' time

long-dated stocks /ˌlɒŋ ˌdeɪtɪd 'stɒks/ *plural noun* same as **longs**

long lease /ˌlɒŋ 'liːs/ *noun* a lease which runs for fifty years or more ○ *to take an office building on a long lease*

long position /ˌlɒŋ pə'zɪʃ(ə)n/ *noun* a situation where an investor sells long, i.e. sells forward shares which he or she owns. Compare **short position**

long-range /ˌlɒŋ 'reɪndʒ/ *adjective* for a long period of time in the future

longs /lɒŋz/ *plural noun* government stocks which will mature in over fifteen years' time. Also called **long-dated stocks**

long-term /ˌlɒŋ 'tɜːm/ *adjective* relating to a long time into the future ○ *The management projections are made on a long-term basis.* ○ *Sound long-term planning will give the company more direction.*

long-term borrowings /ˌlɒŋ tɜːm 'bɒrəʊɪŋz/ *plural noun* borrowings which do not have to be repaid for some years

long-term debt /ˌlɒŋ tɜːm 'det/ *noun* loans that are not repaid within a year

loose change /ˌluːs 'tʃeɪndʒ/ *noun* money in coins

lose /luːz/ *verb* **1.** not to have something any more **2.** to have less money ○ *He lost £25,000 in his father's computer company.*

loss /lɒs/ *noun* **1.** the state or process of not having something any more **2.** the state of having less money than before or of not making a profit □ **the car was written off as a dead loss** *or* **a total loss** the car was so badly damaged that the insurers said it had no value □ **to cut your losses** to stop doing something which is losing money

'…against losses of FFr 7.7m two years ago, the company made a net profit of FFr 300,000 last year' [*Financial Times*]

loss adjuster /'lɒs əˌdʒʌstə/ *noun* a person who calculates how much insurance should be paid on a claim

loss carryback /'lɒs ˌkæribæk/ *noun* the process of applying a net operating loss to a previous accounting year

loss carryforward /'lɒs ˌkærifɔːwəd/ *noun* the process of applying a net operating loss to a following accounting year

loss relief /'lɒs rɪˌliːf/ *noun* an amount of tax not to be paid on one year's profit to off-set a loss in the previous year

lot /lɒt/ *noun* **1.** a group of items sold together at an auction ○ *to bid for lot 23* ○ *At the end of the auction half the lots were unsold.* **2.** a group of shares which are sold ○ *to sell a lot of shares* ○ *to sell shares in small lots*

lottery /'lɒtəri/ *noun* a game where numbered tickets are sold and prizes given for some of the numbers

lower of cost or market /ˌləʊər əv kɒst ɔː 'mɑːkɪt/ *noun* a stock-accounting method in which a manufacturing or supply firm values items of stock either at their original cost or the current market price, whichever is lower. Abbreviation **LCM**

low gearing /ˌləʊ 'ɡɪərɪŋ/ *noun* the fact of not having much borrowing in proportion to your capital

low yield /ˌləʊ 'jiːld/ *noun* a yield on the share price which is low for the sector, suggesting that investors anticipate that the company will grow fast, and have pushed up the share price in expectation of growth

loyalty bonus /'lɔɪəlti ˌbəʊnəs/ *noun* a special privilege given to shareholders who keep their shares for a long period of time, used especially to attract investors to privatisation issues

Ltd *abbreviation* limited company

lump sum /ˌlʌmp 'sʌm/ *noun* money paid in one single amount, not in several small sums ○ *When he retired he was given a lump-sum bonus.* ○ *She sold her house and invested the money as a lump sum.*

luncheon voucher /'lʌnʃtən ˌvaʊtʃə/ *noun* a ticket given by an employer to an employee in addition to their wages, which can be exchanged for food in a restaurant

luxury tax /'lʌkʃəri tæks/ *noun* a tax on goods or services that are considered non-essential

M

machine hour rate /mə,ʃiːn 'aʊə ˌreɪt/ *noun* a method of calculating production overhead absorption rate, where the number of hours the machines are expected to work is divided into the budgeted production overhead to give a rate per hour

macro- /mækrəʊ/ *prefix* very large, covering a wide area

macroeconomics /ˌmækrəʊiːkə'nɒmɪks/ *plural noun* a study of the economics of a whole area, a whole industry, a whole group of the population or a whole country, in order to help in economic planning. Compare **microeconomics** (NOTE: takes a singular verb)

majority shareholder /mə,dʒɒrəti 'ʃeəhəʊldə/ *noun* a person who owns more than half the shares in a company

majority shareholding /mə,dʒɒrəti 'ʃeəhəʊldɪŋ/ *noun* a group of shares which are more than half the total

majority vote /mə'dʒɒrɪti vəʊt/, **majority decision** /mə'dʒɒrɪti dɪ,sɪʒ(ə)n/ *noun* a decision which represents the wishes of the largest group as shown by a vote

make /meɪk/ *verb* **1.** to produce or to manufacture ○ *The factory makes three hundred cars a day.* **2.** to earn money ○ *He makes £50,000 a year* or *£25 an hour.* **3.** to increase in value ○ *The shares made $2.92 in today's trading.* **4.** □ **to make a profit** to have more money after a deal □ **to make a loss** to have less money after a deal □ **to make a killing** to make a very large profit

make over *phrasal verb* to transfer property legally ○ *to make over the house to your children*

make up *phrasal verb* to compensate for something □ **to make up a loss** *or* **difference** to pay extra so that the loss or difference is covered

make-or-buy decision /,meɪk ɔː 'baɪ dɪ,sɪʒ(ə)n/ *noun* a choice between manufacturing a product or component and buying it in

maladministration /,mæləd,mɪnɪ'streɪʃ(ə)n/ *noun* incompetent administration

manage /'mænɪdʒ/ *verb* to direct or to be in charge of something ○ *to manage a branch office* ○ *A competent and motivated person is required to manage an important department in the company.*

'…the research director will manage and direct a team of graduate business analysts reporting on consumer behaviour throughout the UK' [*Times*]

managed earnings /,mænɪdʒ 'ɜːnɪŋz/ *plural noun* the use of any of various accounting devices to make profits appear higher or lower than they actually were in a given accounting period

managed fund /'mænɪdʒd fʌnd/ *noun* a unit trust fund which is invested in specialist funds within the group and can be switched from one specialised investment area to another. Also called **managed unit trust**

managed rate /'mænɪdʒd reɪt/ *noun* a rate of interest charged by a financial institution for borrowing that is not prescribed as a margin over base rate but is set from time to time by the institution

managed unit trust /,mænɪdʒd 'juːnɪt trʌst/ *noun* same as **managed fund**

management /'mænɪdʒmənt/ *noun* **1.** the process of directing or running a business ○ *a management graduate* or *a graduate in management* ○ *Good management* or *efficient management is essential in a large organisation.* ○ *Bad management* or *inefficient management can ruin a business.* **2.** a group of managers or directors ○ *The management has decided to give everyone a pay increase.* (NOTE: Where **management** refers to a group of people it is sometimes followed by a plural verb.)

'…the management says that the rate of loss-making has come down and it expects further improvement in the next few years' [*Financial Times*]

management accountant /'mænɪdʒmənt ə,kaʊntənt/ *noun* an accountant who prepares financial information for managers so that they can take decisions

management accounting /'mænɪdʒmənt ə,kaʊntɪŋ/, **management accountancy** /,mænɪdʒmənt ə'kaʊntənsi/ *noun* the providing of information to managers, which helps them to plan, to control their businesses and to take decisions which will make them run their businesses more efficiently. Compare **financial accounting**

management accounts /'mænɪdʒmənt ə,kaʊnts/ *plural noun* financial information prepared for a manager so that decisions can be made, including monthly or quarterly financial statements, often in great detail, with analysis of actual performance against the budget

management audit /'mænɪdʒmənt ,ɔːdɪt/ *noun* a listing of all the managers in an organisation with information about their skills and experience ○ *The management audit helped determine how many more managers needed to be recruited.*

management buyin /,mænɪdʒmənt 'baɪɪn/ *noun* the purchase of a subsidiary company by a group of outside directors. Abbreviation **MBI**

management buyout /,mænɪdʒmənt 'baɪaʊt/ *noun* the takeover of a company by a group of employees, usually senior managers and directors. Abbreviation **MBO**

management charge /'mænɪdʒmənt tʃɑːdʒ/ *noun* same as **annual management charge**

management consultant /'mænɪdʒmənt kən,sʌltənt/ *noun* a person who gives advice on how to manage a business

management control system /'mænɪdʒmənt kən,trəʊl ,sɪstəm/ *noun* a comprehensive plan designed to ensure that an organisation's resources are used effectively

management decision cycle /,mænɪdʒmənt dɪ'sɪʒ(ə)n ,saɪk(ə)l/ *noun* a model for efficiency in business decision-making, following the process from the identification of a need or problem to an accountant's analysis of the effect of the decisions taken

management information system /,mænɪdʒmənt ,ɪnfə'meɪʃ(ə)n ,sɪstəm/ *noun* a computer-based information system that is specially designed to assist with management tasks and decision-making. Abbreviation **MIS**

management review /'mænɪdʒmənt rɪ,vjuː/ *noun* an external auditor's evaluation of the performance of the managers of an organisation. Also called **management letter**

management team /'mænɪdʒmənt tiːm/ *noun* all the managers who work in a particular company

manager /'mænɪdʒə/ *noun* **1.** the head of a department in a company ○ *She's a department manager in an engineering company.* ○ *Go and see the human resources manager if you have a problem.* ○ *The production manager has been with the company for only two weeks.* **2.** the person in charge of a branch or shop ○ *Mr Smith is the manager of our local Lloyds Bank.* ○ *The manager of our Lagos branch is in London for a series of meetings.*

'…the No. 1 managerial productivity problem in America is managers who are out of touch with their people and out of touch with their customers' [*Fortune*]

managing director /,mænədʒɪŋ daɪ'rektə/ *noun* the director who is in charge of a whole company. Abbreviation **MD**

mandate /'mændeɪt/ *noun* an order which allows something to take place

mandatory bid /,mændət(ə)ri 'bɪd/ *noun* an offer to purchase the shares of a company which has to be made when a shareholder acquires 30% of that company's shares

manipulate /mə'nɪpjʊleɪt/ *verb* □ **to manipulate the accounts** to make false accounts so that the company seems profitable

manpower forecasting /'mænpaʊə ,fɔːkɑːstɪŋ/ *noun* the process of calculating how many employees will be needed in the future, and how many will actually be available

manpower planning /'mænpaʊə ,plænɪŋ/ *noun* the process of planning to obtain the right number of employees in each job

manufacturing /,mænjʊ'fæktʃərɪŋ/ *noun* the production of machine-made products for sale ○ *We must try to reduce the manufacturing overheads.* ○ *Manufacturing processes are continually being updated.*

manufacturing profit /,mænjʊ 'fæktʃərɪŋ ,prɒfɪt/ *noun* the difference between the cost of buying a product from another supplier and the cost to the company of manufacturing it itself

manufacturing resource planning /ˌmænjʊ'fæktʃərɪŋ rɪˌzɔːs ˌplænɪŋ/ *noun* an integrated computerised information system that integrates all aspects of a company's manufacturing business

margin /'mɑːdʒɪn/ *noun* **1.** the difference between the money received when selling a product and the money paid for it **2.** extra space or time allowed **3.** the difference between interest paid to depositors and interest charged to borrowers by a bank, building society, etc. **4.** a deposit paid when purchasing a futures contract

'...profit margins in the industries most exposed to foreign competition – machinery, transportation equipment and electrical goods – are significantly worse than usual' [*Australian Financial Review*]

marginal /'mɑːdʒɪn(ə)l/ *adjective* hardly worth the money paid

marginal analysis /ˌmɑːdʒɪn(ə)l ə'næləsɪs/ *noun* an assessment of the impact of minor changes on a company, industry or economy

marginal cost /ˌmɑːdʒɪn(ə)l 'kɒst/ *noun* the cost of making a single extra unit above the number already planned

marginal costing /ˌmɑːdʒɪn(ə)l 'kɒstɪŋ/ *noun* the costing of a product on the basis of its variable costs only, excluding fixed costs

marginal pricing /ˌmɑːdʒɪn(ə)l 'praɪsɪŋ/ *noun* **1.** the practice of basing the selling price of a product on its variable costs of production plus a margin, but excluding fixed costs **2.** the practice of making the selling price the same as the cost of a single extra unit above the number already planned

marginal rate of tax /ˌmɑːdʒɪn(ə)l reɪt əv 'tæks/, **marginal rate of taxation** /ˌmɑːdʒɪn(ə)l reɪt əv tæks'eɪʃ(ə)n/ *noun* the percentage of tax which a taxpayer pays at the top rate, which he or she therefore pays on every further pound or dollar he or she earns. Also called **marginal tax rate**

'...pensioner groups claim that pensioners have the highest marginal rates of tax. Income earned by pensioners above $30 a week is taxed at 62.5 per cent, more than the highest marginal rate' [*Australian Financial Review*]

marginal revenue /ˌmɑːdʒɪn(ə)l 'revenjuː/ *noun* the income from selling a single extra unit above the number already sold

marginal tax rate /ˌmɑːdʒɪn(ə)l 'tæks reɪt/ *noun* same as **marginal rate of tax**

margin call /'mɑːdʒɪn kɔːl/ *noun* a request for a purchaser of a futures contract or an option to pay more margin, since the fall in the price of the securities or commodity has removed the value of the original margin deposited

margin of safety /ˌmɑːdʒɪn əv 'seɪfti/ *noun* the units produced or sales of such units which are above the breakeven point

mark down *phrasal verb* to make the price of something lower

mark up *phrasal verb* to make the price of something higher

mark-down /'mɑːk daʊn/ *noun* **1.** a reduction of the price of something to less than its usual price **2.** the percentage amount by which a price has been lowered ○ *There has been a 30% mark-down on all goods in the sale.*

market /'mɑːkɪt/ *noun* **1.** an area where a product might be sold or the group of people who might buy a product ○ *There is no market for this product.* ○ *Our share of the Far eastern market has gone down.* **2.** the possible sales of a specific product or demand for a specific product ○ *There's no market for word processors* ○ *The market for home computers has fallen sharply.* ○ *We have 20% of the UK car market.* **3.** a place where money or commodities are traded **4.** □ **sell at the market** an instruction to stockbroker to sell shares at the best price possible **5.** □ **to put something on the market** to start to offer something for sale ○ *They put their house on the market.* ○ *I hear the company has been put on the market.* □ **the company has priced itself out of the market** the company has raised its prices so high that its products do not sell

'...market analysts described the falls in the second half of last week as a technical correction to a market which had been pushed by demand to over the 900 index level' [*Australian Financial Review*]

marketability /ˌmɑːkɪtə'bɪlɪti/ *noun* the fact of being able to be sold easily ○ *the marketability of shares in electronic companies*

marketable /'mɑːkɪtəb(ə)l/ *adjective* easily sold

market analysis /ˌmɑːkɪt ə'næləsɪs/ *noun* the detailed examination and report of a market

market capitalisation /ˌmɑːkɪt ˌkæpɪtəlaɪ'zeɪʃ(ə)n/ *noun* the total market value of a company, calculated by multiplying the price of its shares on the Stock

Exchange by the number of shares outstanding ○ *company with a £1m capitalisation*

market economist /ˌmɑːkɪt ɪˈkɒnəmɪst/ *noun* a person who specialises in the study of financial structures and the return on investments in the stock market

market forces /ˌmɑːkɪt ˈfɔːsɪz/ *plural noun* the influences on the sales of a product which bring about a change in prices

marketing /ˈmɑːkɪtɪŋ/ *noun* the business of presenting and promoting goods or services in such a way as to make customers want to buy them

'…reporting to the marketing director, the successful applicant will be responsible for the development of a training programme for the new sales force' [*Times*]

marketing agreement /ˈmɑːkɪtɪŋ əˌɡriːmənt/ *noun* a contract by which one company will market another company's products

marketing cost /ˈmɑːkɪtɪŋ kɒst/ *noun* the cost of selling a product, including advertising, packaging, etc.

marketing department /ˈmɑːkɪtɪŋ dɪˌpɑːtmənt/ *noun* the section of a company dealing with marketing and sales

marketing manager /ˈmɑːkɪtɪŋ ˌmænɪdʒə/ *noun* a person in charge of a marketing department ○ *The marketing manager has decided to start a new advertising campaign.*

market leader /ˌmɑːkɪt ˈliːdə/ *noun* **1.** a product which sells most in a market **2.** the company with the largest market share ○ *We are the market leader in home computers.*

'…market leaders may benefit from scale economies or other cost advantages; they may enjoy a reputation for quality simply by being at the top, or they may actually produce a superior product that gives them both a large market share and high profits' [*Accountancy*]

marketmaker /ˈmɑːkɪtmeɪkə/ *noun* a person or firm that buys and sells shares on the stock market and offers to do so (NOTE: Marketmakers list the securities they are willing to buy or sell and their bid and offer prices. If the prices are met, they immediately buy or sell and make their money by charging a commission on each transaction. Marketmakers play an important part in maintaining an orderly market.)

market opportunities /ˌmɑːkɪt ɒpəˈtjuːnɪtiz/ *plural noun* the possibility of finding new sales in a market

market price /ˈmɑːkɪt praɪs/ *noun* **1.** the price at which a product can be sold **2.** the price at which a share stands in a stock market

market rate /ˌmɑːkɪt ˈreɪt/ *noun* the usual price in the market ○ *We pay the market rate for temporary staff* or *We pay temporary staff the market rate.*

'…after the prime rate cut yesterday, there was a further fall in short-term market rates' [*Financial Times*]

market research /ˌmɑːkɪt rɪˈsɜːtʃ/ *noun* the process of examining the possible sales of a product and the possible customers for it before it is put on the market

market risk premium /ˈmɑːkɪt rɪsk ˌpriːmiəm/ *noun* the extra return required from a high-risk share to compensate for its higher-than-average risk

market trends /ˌmɑːkɪt ˈtrendz/ *plural noun* gradual changes taking place in a market

market value /ˌmɑːkɪt ˈvæljuː/ *noun* the value of an asset, a share, a product or a company if sold today

mark-up /ˈmɑːk ʌp/ *noun* **1.** an increase in price ○ *We put into effect a 10% mark-up of all prices in June.* ○ *Since I was last in the store they have put at least a 5% mark-up on the whole range of items.* **2.** the difference between the cost of a product or service and its selling price □ **we work to a 3.5 times mark-up** *or* **to a 350% mark-up** we take the unit cost and multiply by 3.5 to give the selling price

mass production /ˌmæs prəˈdʌkʃən/ *noun* the manufacture of large quantities of identical products

master budget /ˈmɑːstə ˌbʌdʒɪt/ *noun* a plan that assesses an organisation's proposed activities in terms of assets, equities, revenues and costs

matching /ˈmætʃɪŋ/ *noun* the process of comparing costs to sales in order to calculate profits during an accounting period

matching concept /ˈmætʃɪŋ ˌkɒnsept/, **matching convention** /ˈmætʃɪŋ kənˌvenʃən/ *noun* the basis for preparing accounts which says that profits can only be recognised if sales are fully matched with costs accrued during the same period

material facts /məˌtɪəriəl ˈfækts/ *plural noun* **1.** in an insurance contract, information that the insured has to reveal at the time that the policy is taken out, e.g., that a house is located on the edge of a crumbling cliff. Failure to reveal material facts can result in the contract being declared void. **2.** information that has to be disclosed in a prospectus. ◊ **listing requirements**

materiality /məˌtɪəriˈælɪti/ *noun* the seriousness of an omission or misstatement in accounts

material news /məˌtɪəriəl ˈnjuːz/ *plural noun* price sensitive developments in a company, e.g., proposed acquisitions, mergers, profit warnings and the resignation of directors, that most stock exchanges require a company to announce immediately to the exchange (NOTE: The US term is **material information**.)

material requirement planning /mə ˈtɪəriəl rɪˌkwaɪəmənt ˌplænɪŋ/ a computer-based system that deals with the ordering and processing of component parts and materials. Abbreviation **MRP**

materials price variance /məˈtɪəriəlz praɪs ˌveəriəns/ *noun* the discrepancy between the price actually paid for materials and the price that it was expected would be paid

materials quantity (usage) variance /məˈtɪəriəlz ˌkwɒntɪti ˌveəriəns/ *noun* the discrepancy between the actual quantity of materials used in production and the quantity of materials normally allowed

materials variance /məˈtɪəriəlz ˌveəriəns/ *noun* a combination of materials price variance and materials quantity (usage) variance

maternity benefit /məˈtɜːnɪti ˌbenɪfɪt/ *noun* money paid by the National Insurance to a mother when she has her child

maternity pay period /məˈtɜːnɪti peɪ ˌpɪəriəd/ *noun* a period of eighteen weeks when statutory maternity pay is paid. Abbreviation **MPP**

maturity /məˈtʃʊərɪti/ *noun* the time at which something becomes due for payment or repayment

maturity date /məˈtʃʊərɪti deɪt/ *noun* a date when a government stock, an assurance policy or a debenture will become due for payment. Also called **date of maturity**

maturity value /məˈtʃʊərɪti ˌvæljuː/ *noun* the amount payable when a bond or other financial instrument matures

maxi ISA /ˈmæksi ˌaɪsə/ *noun* an ISA that offers the opportunity to invest on the stock market, with a limit on combined cash and stock market investments of £7000 per year. ◊ **mini ISA**

maximisation /ˌmæksɪmaɪˈzeɪʃ(ə)n/, **maximization** *noun* the process of making something as large as possible ○ *profit maximisation* or *maximisation of profit*

maximise /ˈmæksɪmaɪz/, **maximize** *verb* to make something as large as possible ○ *Our aim is to maximise profits.* ○ *She is paid on results, and so has to work flat out to maximise her earnings.*

maximum /ˈmæksɪməm/ *noun* the largest possible number, price or quantity ○ *It is the maximum the insurance company will pay.* (NOTE: The plural is **maxima** or **maximums**.) □ **up to a maximum of £10** no more than £10 ■ *adjective* largest possible ○ *40% is the maximum income tax rate* or *the maximum rate of tax.* ○ *The maximum load for the truck is one ton.* ○ *Maximum production levels were reached last week.*

MBI *abbreviation* management buyin

MBO *abbreviation* management buyout

MD *abbreviation* managing director ○ *She was appointed MD of a property company.*

mean /miːn/ *adjective* average ○ *The mean annual increase in sales is 3.20%.* ■ *noun* the average or number calculated by adding several quantities together and dividing by the number of quantities added ○ *Unit sales are over the mean for the first quarter* or *above the first-quarter mean.*

means /miːnz/ *noun* a way of doing something ○ *Do we have any means of copying all these documents quickly?* ○ *Bank transfer is the easiest means of payment.* (NOTE: The plural is **means**.) ■ *plural noun* money or resources ○ *The company has the means to launch the new product.* ○ *Such a level of investment is beyond the means of a small private company.*

means test /ˈmiːnz test/ *noun* an inquiry into how much money someone earns to see if they are eligible for state benefits

means-test /ˈmiːnz test/ *verb* to find out how much money someone has in savings and assets ○ *All applicants will be means-tested.*

measure /ˈmeʒə/ *noun* **1.** a way of calculating size or quantity **2.** a type of action ■ *verb* □ **to measure a company's performance** to judge how well a company is doing

measurement of profitability /ˌmeʒəmənt əv ˌprɒfɪtəˈbɪlɪti/ *noun* a way of calculating how profitable something is

median /ˈmiːdiən/ *noun* the middle number in a list of numbers

medical insurance /ˈmedɪk(ə)l ɪnˌʃʊərəns/ *noun* insurance which pays the cost of medical treatment, especially when someone is travelling abroad

medium of exchange /ˌmiːdiəm əv ɪks ˈtʃeɪndʒ/ *noun* anything that is used to pay for goods. Nowadays, this usually takes the form of money (banknotes and coins), but in ancient societies, it included anything from cattle to shells.

mediums /ˈmiːdiəmz/ *plural noun* government stocks which mature in seven to fifteen years' time

medium-sized company /ˌmiːdiəm saɪzd ˈkʌmp(ə)ni/ *noun* a company which has an annual turnover of less than £22.8m and does not employ more than 250 staff ○ *a medium-sized engineering company*

medium-term bond /ˌmiːdiəm tɜːm ˈbɒnd/ *noun* a bond which matures within five to fifteen years

member /ˈmembə/ *noun* **1.** a person who belongs to a group, society or organisation ○ *Committee members voted on the proposal.* ○ *They were elected members of the board.* ○ *Every employer is a member of the employers' federation.* **2.** a shareholder in a company **3.** an organisation which belongs to a larger organisation ○ *the member states of the EU* ○ *the members of the United Nations* ○ *the member companies of a trade association*

'…it will be the first opportunity for party members and trade union members to express their views on the tax package' [*Australian Financial Review*]

member bank /ˌmembə ˈbæŋk/ *noun* a bank which is part of the Federal Reserve system

member firm /ˌmembə ˈfɜːm/ *noun* a stockbroking firm which is a member of a stock exchange

membership /ˈmembəʃɪp/ *noun* **1.** the fact of belonging to a group, society or organisation ○ *membership qualifications* ○ *conditions of membership* ○ *membership of the EU* **2.** all the members of a group ○ *The membership was asked to vote for the new president.*

'…the bargaining committee will recommend that its membership ratify the agreement at a meeting called for June' [*Toronto Star*]

members' voluntary winding up /ˌmembəz ˌvɒlənt(ə)ri ˌwaɪndɪŋ ˈʌp/ *noun* the winding up of a company by the shareholders themselves

memorandum and articles of association /memə,rændəm ənd ˌɑːtɪk(ə)lz əv ə,səʊsiˈeɪʃ(ə)n/, **memorandum of association** /ˌmemərændəm əv ə,səʊsi ˈeɪʃ(ə)n/ *noun* the legal documents which set up a limited company and give details of its name, aims, authorised share capital, conduct of meetings, appointment of directors and registered office

merchant /ˈmɜːtʃənt/ *noun* **1.** a businessperson who buys and sells, especially one who buys imported goods in bulk for retail sale ○ *a coal merchant* ○ *a wine merchant* **2.** a company, shop or other business which accepts a credit card for purchases

merchant bank /ˈmɜːtʃənt bæŋk/ *noun* **1.** a bank which arranges loans to companies, deals in international finance, buys and sells shares and launches new companies on the Stock Exchange, but does not provide banking services to the general public **2.** *US* a bank which operates a credit card system, accepting payment on credit cards from retailers or 'merchants'

merchant banker /ˌmɜːtʃənt ˈbæŋkə/ *noun* a person who has a high position in a merchant bank

merchant number /ˈmɜːtʃənt ˌnʌmbə/ *noun* a number of the merchant, printed at the top of the report slip when depositing credit card payments

merge /mɜːdʒ/ *verb* to join together ○ *The two companies have merged.* ○ *The firm merged with its main competitor.*

merger /ˈmɜːdʒə/ *noun* the joining together of two or more companies ○ *As a result of the merger, the company is now the largest in the field.*

merger accounting /ˈmɜːdʒə əˌkaʊntɪŋ/ *noun* a way of presenting the accounts of a newly acquired company within the group accounts, so as to show it in the best possible light

mezzanine finance /ˈmetsəniːn ˌfaɪnæns/ *noun* finance provided to a company after it has received start-up finance

micro- /maɪkrəʊ/ *prefix* very small

microeconomics /ˈmaɪkrəʊ iːkə ˌnɒmɪks/ *plural noun* the study of the economics of people or single companies. Compare **macroeconomics** (NOTE: takes a singular verb)

middle management /ˌmɪd(ə)l ˈmænɪdʒmənt/ *noun* department managers in a company, who carry out the policy set by the directors and organise the work of a group of employees

middle price /ˈmɪd(ə)l praɪs/ *noun* a price between the buying and selling price, usually shown in indices

mid-month /ˌmɪd ˈmʌnθ/ *adjective* happening in the middle of the month ○ *mid-month accounts*

mid-week /ˌmɪd ˈwiːk/ *adjective* happening in the middle of a week ○ *the mid-week lull in sales*

millionaire /ˌmɪljəˈneə/ *noun* a person who has more than one million pounds or dollars

mini ISA /ˈmɪni ˌaɪsə/ *noun* an ISA in which either up to £4000 can be invested in stocks and shares, or up to £3000 cash can be invested, in a given year. ◊ **maxi ISA**

minimisation /ˌmɪnɪmaɪˈzeɪʃ(ə)n/ *noun* making as small as possible

minimum /ˈmɪnɪməm/ *noun* the smallest possible quantity, price or number ○ *to keep expenses to a minimum* ○ *to reduce the risk of a loss to a minimum* (NOTE: The plural is **minima** or **minimums**.) ■ *adjective* smallest possible

minimum cash balance /ˌmɪnɪməm ˈkæʃ ˌbæləns/ *noun* a reserve cash fund held to offset unexpected cash shortages

minimum lending rate /ˌmɪnɪməm ˈlendɪŋ reɪt/ *noun* the lowest rate of interest formerly charged by the Bank of England to discount houses, now replaced by the base rate

minimum reserves /ˌmɪnɪməm rɪ ˈzɜːvz/ *plural noun* the smallest amount of reserves which a commercial bank must hold with a central bank

minimum wage /ˌmɪnɪməm ˈweɪdʒ/ *noun* the lowest hourly wage which a company can legally pay its employees

minority interest /maɪˈnɒrəti ˌɪntrəst/ *noun* the nominal value of those shares in a subsidiary company that are held by members other than the parent company or its nominees

minority shareholder /maɪˈnɒrəti ˈʃeəhəʊldə/ *noun* a person who owns a group of shares but less than half of the shares in a company

minority shareholding /maɪˈnɒrəti ˈʃeəhəʊldɪŋ/ *noun* a group of shares which are less than half the total ○ *He acquired a minority shareholding in the company.*

minus /ˈmaɪnəs/ *preposition, adverb* less, without ○ *Net salary is gross salary minus tax and National Insurance deductions.* ○ *Gross profit is sales minus production costs.*

minus factor /ˈmaɪnəs ˌfæktə/ *noun* a factor that is unfavourable in some way, e.g. because it reduces profitability ○ *To have lost sales in the best quarter of the year is a minus factor for the sales team.*

MIS *abbreviation* management information system

misappropriate /ˌmɪsəˈprəʊprieɪt/ *verb* to use illegally money which is not yours, but with which you have been trusted

misappropriation /ˌmɪsəprəʊpri ˈeɪʃ(ə)n/ *noun* the illegal use of money by someone who is not the owner but who has been trusted to look after it

miscalculate /mɪsˈkælkjʊleɪt/ *verb* to calculate wrongly, or to make a mistake in calculating something ○ *The salesman miscalculated the discount, so we hardly broke even on the deal.*

miscalculation /mɪsˌkælkjʊˈleɪʃ(ə)n/ *noun* a mistake in calculating

miscount *noun* /ˈmɪskaʊnt/ a mistake in counting ■ *verb* /mɪsˈkaʊnt/ to count wrongly, or to make a mistake in counting something

mismanage /mɪsˈmænɪdʒ/ *verb* to manage something badly ○ *The company had been badly mismanaged under the previous MD.*

mismanagement /mɪsˈmænɪdʒmənt/ *noun* bad management ○ *The company failed because of the chairman's mismanagement.*

misrepresent /ˌmɪsreprɪˈzent/ *verb* to report facts or what someone says wrongly ○ *Our spokesman was totally misrepresented in the Sunday papers.*

misrepresentation /ˌmɪsˌreprɪzen ˈteɪʃ(ə)n/ *noun* the act of making a wrong statement in order to persuade someone to enter into a contract such as one for buying a product or service

misuse *noun* /mɪsˈjuːs/ the act of using something, e.g. invested money, for a wrong purpose ○ *the misuse of funds* or *of assets* ■ *verb* /mɪsˈjuːz/ □ **to misuse funds** to use funds in a wrong way (especially funds which do not belong to you)

mixed /mɪkst/ *adjective* **1.** made up of different sorts or of different types of things together **2.** neither good nor bad

'…prices closed on a mixed note after a moderately active trading session' [*Financial Times*]

mixed economy /ˌmɪkst ɪˈkɒnəmi/ *noun* a system which contains both nationalised industries and private enterprise

modified accounts /ˌmɒdɪfaɪd ə ˈkaʊnts/ *plural noun* ♦ **abbreviated accounts**

monetarism /ˈmʌnɪtəˌrɪz(ə)m/ *noun* a theory that the amount of money in the economy affects the level of prices, so that inflation can be controlled by regulating money supply

monetarist /ˈmʌnɪtərɪst/ *noun* a person who believes in monetarism and acts accordingly ■ *adjective* according to monetarism ○ *monetarist theories*

monetary /'mʌnɪt(ə)ri/ *adjective* referring to money or currency

'...the decision by the government to tighten monetary policy will push the annual inflation rate above the year's previous high' [*Financial Times*]

'...it is not surprising that the Fed started to ease monetary policy some months ago' [*Sunday Times*]

'...a draft report on changes in the international monetary system' [*Wall Street Journal*]

monetary assets /ˌmʌnɪt(ə)ri 'æsets/ *plural noun* assets, principally accounts receivable, cash and bank balances, that are realisable at the amount stated in the accounts. Other assets, e.g., facilities and machinery, inventories, and marketable securities will not necessarily realise the sum stated in a business's balance sheet.

monetary items /ˌmʌnɪt(ə)ri 'aɪtəmz/ *plural noun* monetary assets such as cash or debtors, and monetary liabilities such as an overdraft or creditors, whose values stay the same in spite of inflation

monetary standard /ˌmʌnɪt(ə)ri 'stændəd/ *noun* a fixed exchange rate for a currency

monetary targets /ˌmʌnɪt(ə)ri 'tɑːgɪts/ *plural noun* figures which are given as targets by the government when setting out its budget for the forthcoming year, e.g. the money supply or the PSBR

monetary unit /'mʌnɪt(ə)ri ˌjuːnɪt/ *noun* a main item of currency of a country

money /'mʌni/ *noun* coins and notes used for buying and selling □ **money up front** payment in advance ○ *They are asking for £10,000 up front before they will consider the deal.* ○ *He had to put money up front before he could clinch the deal.*

money at call /ˌmʌni ət 'kɔːl/ *noun* same as **call money**

money at call and short notice /ˌmʌni ət kɔːl ən ʃɔːt 'nəʊtɪs/ *noun* in the United Kingdom, balances in an account that are either available upon demand (call) or within 14 days (short notice)

money broker /'mʌni ˌbrəʊkə/ *noun* a dealer operating in the interbank and foreign exchange markets

money laundering /'mʌni ˌlɔːndərɪŋ/ *noun* the act of passing illegal money into the banking system

moneylender /'mʌniˌlendə/ *noun* a person who lends money at interest

money lying idle /ˌmʌni ˌlaɪɪŋ 'aɪd(ə)l/ *noun* money which is not being used to produce interest, which is not invested in business

money-making /'mʌni ˌmeɪkɪŋ/ *adjective* able to turn over a profit ○ *a money-making plan*

money market fund /'mʌni ˌmɑːkɪt fʌnd/ *noun* an investment fund, which only invests in money market instruments

money market instruments /'mʌni ˌmɑːkɪt ˌɪnstrʊmənts/ *plural noun* short-term investments which can be easily turned into cash and are traded on the money markets, e.g. CDs

money on call /ˌmʌni ɒn 'kɔːl/ *noun* same as **call money**

money order /'mʌni ˌɔːdə/ *noun* a document which can be bought as a way of sending money through the post

money rates /'mʌni reɪts/ *plural noun* rates of interest for borrowers or lenders

money supply /'mʌni səˌplaɪ/ *noun* the amount of money in a country's economy, consisting mainly of the money in circulation and that held in savings and cheque accounts

monies /'mʌniz/ *plural noun* sums of money ○ *monies owing to the company* ○ *to collect monies due*

monopoly /məˈnɒpəli/ *noun* a situation where one person or company is the only supplier of a particular product or service ○ *to be in a monopoly situation* ○ *The company has the monopoly of imports of Brazilian wine.* ○ *The factory has the absolute monopoly of jobs in the town.*

Monte Carlo method /ˌmɒnti 'kɑːləʊ ˌmeθəd/ *noun* a statistical analysis technique for calculating an unknown quantity which has an exact value by using an extended series of random trials (NOTE: The name refers to the fact that a roulette wheel in a casino, as in Monte Carlo, continually generates random numbers.)

month /mʌnθ/ *noun* one of twelve periods which make a year ○ *bills due at the end of the current month* ○ *The company pays him £1600 a month.* ○ *She earns£2,000 a month.*

month end /ˌmʌnθ 'end/ *noun* the end of a calendar month, when accounts have to be drawn up ○ *The accounts department are working on the month-end accounts.*

monthly /'mʌnθli/ *adjective* happening every month or which is received every month ○ *We get a monthly statement from the bank.* ○ *She makes monthly payments to the credit card company.* ○ *He is paying for* *his car by monthly instalments.* ○ *My monthly salary cheque is late.* □ **monthly statement** a statement sent to a customer at the end of each month, itemising transactions which have taken place in his or her account ■ *adverb* every month ○ *She asked if she could pay monthly by direct debit.* ○ *The account is credited monthly.*

moonlight /ˈmuːnlaɪt/ *verb* to do a second job for cash, often in the evening, as well as a regular job (*informal*)

moral hazard /ˌmɒrəl ˈhæzəd/ *noun* a risk that someone will behave immorally because insurance, the law or some other agency protects them against loss that the immoral behaviour might otherwise cause

moratorium /ˌmɒrəˈtɔːriəm/ *noun* a temporary stop to repayments of interest on loans or capital owed ○ *The banks called for a moratorium on payments.* (NOTE: The plural is **moratoria** or **moratoriums**.)

mortality tables /mɔːˈtæləti ˌteɪb(ə)lz/ *plural noun* same as **actuarial tables**

mortgage /ˈmɔːɡɪdʒ/ *noun* a legal agreement where someone lends money to another person so that he or she can buy a property, the property being the security ○ *to take out a mortgage on a house*

'…mortgage payments account for just 20 per cent of the average first-time buyer's gross earnings against an average of 24 per cent during the past 15 years' [*Times*]

'…mortgage money is becoming tighter. Applications for mortgages are running at a high level and some building societies are introducing quotas' [*Times*]

'…for the first time since mortgage rates began falling a financial institution has raised charges on homeowner loans' [*Globe and Mail (Toronto)*]

mortgage bond /ˈmɔːɡɪdʒ bɒnd/ *noun* a certificate showing that a mortgage exists and that property is security for it

mortgage debenture /ˈmɔːɡɪdʒ dɪˌbentʃə/ *noun* a debenture where the lender can be repaid by selling the company's property

mortgagee /mɔːɡəˈdʒiː/ *noun* a person or company which lends money for someone to buy a property

mortgage famine /ˈmɔːɡɪdʒ ˌfæmɪn/ *noun* a situation where there is not enough money available to offer mortgages to house buyers

mortgager /ˈmɔːɡɪdʒə/, **mortgagor** *noun* a person who borrows money to buy a property

movable /ˈmuːvəb(ə)l/, **moveable** *adjective* possible to move ○ *All the movable property has been seized by the bailiffs.*

movable property /ˌmuːvəb(ə)l ˈprɒpəti/ *noun* chattels and other objects which can be moved, as opposed to land

movables /ˈmuːvəb(ə)lz/, **moveables** *plural noun* movable property

moving average /ˌmuːvɪŋ ˈæv(ə)rɪdʒ/ *noun* an average of share prices on a stock market, where the calculation is made over a period which moves forward regularly

MPP *abbreviation* maternity pay period

MRP *abbreviation* material requirement planning

multi- /mʌlti/ *prefix* referring to many things or many of one thing

multicurrency /ˌmʌltiˈkʌrənsi/ *adjective* in several currencies

multifunctional card /ˌmʌltɪfʌnkʃən(ə)l ˈkɑːd/ *noun* a plastic card that may be used for two or more purposes, e.g., as a cash card, a cheque card and a debit card

multilateral /ˌmʌltiˈlæt(ə)rəl/ *adjective* between several organisations or countries ○ *a multilateral agreement*

multilateral netting /ˌmʌltilæt(ə)rəl ˈnetɪŋ/ *noun* a method of putting together sums from various sources into one currency, used by groups of banks trading in several currencies at the same time

multimillion /ˌmʌltiˈmɪljən/ *adjective* referring to several million pounds or dollars ○ *They signed a multimillion pound deal.*

multimillionaire /ˌmʌltimɪljəˈneə/ *noun* a person who owns property or investments worth several million pounds or dollars

multiple exchange rate /ˌmʌltɪp(ə)l ɪksˈtʃeɪndʒ reɪt/ *noun* a two-tier rate of exchange used in certain countries where the more advantageous rate may be for tourists or for businesses proposing to build a factory

multiple ownership /ˌmʌltɪp(ə)l ˈəʊnəʃɪp/ *noun* a situation where something is owned by several parties jointly

multiplication sign /ˌmʌltɪplɪˈkeɪʃ(ə)n saɪn/ *noun* a sign (x) used to show that a number is being multiplied by another

multiplier /ˈmʌltɪplaɪə/ *noun* **1.** a number which multiplies another, or a factor which tends to multiply something, as the effect of new expenditure on total income and reserves **2.** same as **uniform business rate**

multiply /ˈmʌltɪplaɪ/ *verb* **1.** to calculate the sum of various numbers added together a particular number of times ○ *If you multiply twelve by three you get thirty-six.* ○ *Square measurements are calculated by multiplying length by width.* **2.** to grow or to increase ○ *Profits multiplied in the boom years.*

municipal bond /mjuː,nɪsɪp(ə)l ˈbɒnd/ *noun US* a bond issued by a town or district (NOTE: The UK term is **local authority bond**.)

mutual /ˈmjuːtʃuəl/ *adjective* owned by members, not by shareholders ■ *noun* any commercial organisation that is owned by its members, rather than by shareholders

mutual fund /ˈmjuːtʃuəl fʌnd/ *noun US* same as **unit trust**

N

naked /'neɪkɪd/ *adjective* used for describing investment that is not protected from risks inherent in a particular position or market

named /neɪmd/ *adjective* □ **the person named in the policy** the person whose name is given on an insurance policy as the person insured

NAO *abbreviation* National Audit Office

narration /nə'reɪʃ(ə)n/, **narrative** /'nærətɪv/ *noun* a series of notes and explanations relating to transactions in the accounts

national /'næʃ(ə)nəl/ *adjective* referring to the whole of a particular country

National Audit Office /,næʃ(ə)nəl 'ɔːdɪt ,ɒfɪs/ *noun* a body which investigates the use of public money by central government departments. It acts on behalf of the Parliamentary Public Accounts Committee. Abbreviation **NAO**

national bank /'næʃ(ə)nəl bæŋk/ *noun* in the US, a bank which is chartered by the federal government and is part of the Federal Reserve system. Compare **state bank**

national income /,næʃ(ə)nəl 'ɪnkʌm/ *noun* the value of income from the sales of goods and services in a country

national income accounts /,næʃ(ə)nəl 'ɪnkʌm ə,kaʊnts/ *plural noun* economic statistics that show the state of a nation's economy over a given period of time, usually a year. ◊ **gross domestic product**, **gross national product**

National Insurance /,næʃ(ə)nəl ɪn 'ʃʊərəns/ *noun* state insurance in the United Kingdom, organised by the government, which pays for medical care, hospitals, unemployment benefits, etc. Abbreviation **NI**

National Insurance contribution /,næʃ(ə)nəl ɪn'ʃʊərəns kɒntrɪ,bjuːʃ(ə)n/ *noun* a proportion of income paid each month by an employee and the employee's company to the National Insurance scheme, which pays for medical care, hospitals,

unemployment benefits, etc. Abbreviation **NIC**

National Insurance number /,næʃ(ə)nəl ɪn'ʃʊərəns ,nʌmbə/ *noun* a number given to each British citizen, which is the number by which he or she is known to the social security services

National Savings and Investments /,næʃ(ə)nəl ,seɪvɪŋz ənd ɪn'vestmənts/ *noun* a part of the Exchequer, a savings scheme for small investors including savings certificates and premium bonds. Abbreviation **NS&I**

National Savings Bank /,næʃ(ə)nəl 'seɪvɪŋz ,bæŋk/ *noun* in the United Kingdom, a savings scheme established in 1861 as the Post Office Savings Bank and now operated by National Savings and Investments. Abbreviation **NSB**

National Savings certificates /,næʃ(ə)nəl 'seɪvɪŋz sə,tɪfɪkəts/ *plural noun* certificates showing that someone has invested in National Savings and Investments. The NS&I issues certificates with stated interest rates and stated maturity dates, usually five or ten years.

National Savings Stock Register /,næʃ(ə)nəl ,seɪvɪŋz 'stɒk ,redʒɪstə/ *noun* an organisation, run by National Savings and Investments, which gives private individuals the opportunity to buy British government stocks by post without going through a stockbroker

NAV *abbreviation* net asset value

NBV *abbreviation* net book value

negative carry /,negətɪv 'kæri/ *noun* a deal where the cost of finance is more than the return on the capital used

negative cash flow /,negətɪv 'kæʃ fləʊ/ *noun* a situation where more money is going out of a company than is coming in

negative confirmation /,negətɪv ,kɒnfə'meɪʃən/ *noun* an auditor's request to have financial information confirmed as accurate, to which a reply need only be sent in the case of a discrepancy

negative equity /ˌnegətɪv 'ekwɪtɪ/ *noun* a situation where a house bought with a mortgage becomes less valuable than the money borrowed to buy it because of falling house prices

negative goodwill /ˌnegətɪv gʊd'wɪl/ *noun* the position of a company that has assets with a market value that is greater than the price the company paid for them

negative yield curve /ˌnegətɪv 'jiːld kɜːv/ *noun* a situation where the yield on a long-term investment is less than that on a short-term investment

negligence /'neglɪdʒəns/ *noun* a lack of proper care or failure to carry out a duty (with the result that a person or property is harmed)

negotiable instrument /nɪˌgəʊʃiəb(ə)l 'ɪnstrʊmənt/ *noun* a document which can be exchanged for cash, e.g. a bill of exchange or a cheque

negotiable paper /nɪˌgəʊʃiəb(ə)l 'peɪpə/ *noun* a document which can be transferred from one owner to another for cash

negotiate /nɪ'gəʊʃieɪt/ *verb* **1.** □ **to negotiate terms and conditions** *or* **a contract** to discuss and agree the terms of a contract □ **he negotiated a £250,000 loan with the bank** he came to an agreement with the bank for a loan of £250,000 **2.** to transfer financial instruments, e.g. bearer securities, bills of exchange, cheques and promissory notes, to another person in return for a consideration

negotiation /nɪˌgəʊʃi'eɪʃ(ə)n/ *noun* the discussion of terms and conditions in order to reach an agreement □ **to enter into** *or* **to start negotiations** to start discussing a problem

'…after three days of tough negotiations, the company reached agreement with its 1,200 unionized workers' [*Toronto Star*]

nest egg /'nest eg/ *noun* money which someone has saved over a period of time, usually kept in an interest-bearing account and intended for use after retirement

net /net/ *adjective* referring to a price, weight, pay, etc., after all deductions have been made ■ *verb* to make a true profit ○ *to net a profit of £10,000* (NOTE: **netting – netted**)

'…out of its earnings a company will pay a dividend. When shareholders receive this it will be net, that is it will have had tax deducted at 30 per cent' [*Investors Chronicle*]

expected cash flows minus the cost of a

net assets /ˌnet 'æsets/ *plural noun* the amount by which the value of a company's assets is greater than its liabilities

net asset value /ˌnet 'æset ˌvæljuː/ *noun* the total value of a company after deducting the money owed by it (it is the value of shareholders' capital plus reserves and any money retained from profits). Abbreviation **NAV**. Also called **net worth**

net asset value per share /ˌnet ˌæset ˌvæljuː pə 'ʃeə/ *noun* the value of a company calculated by dividing the shareholders' funds by the number of shares issued

net book value /ˌnet 'bʊk ˌvæljuː/ *noun* the historical cost of an asset less any accumulated depreciation or other provision for diminution in value, e.g. reduction to net realisable value, or asset value which has been revalued downwards to reflect market conditions. Abbreviation **NBV**. Also called **written-down value**

net borrowings /ˌnet 'bɒrəʊɪŋz/ *plural noun* a company's borrowings, less any cash the company is holding in its bank accounts

net cash flow /ˌnet 'kæʃ ˌfləʊ/ *noun* the difference between the money coming in and the money going out of a firm

net cash inflow /ˌnet 'kæʃ ˌɪnfləʊ/ *noun* a situation in which cash receipts exceed cash payments

net current assets /ˌnet ˌkʌrənt 'æsets/ *plural noun* the current assets of a company, i.e. cash and stocks, less any liabilities. Also called **net working capital**

net current liabilities /ˌnet ˌkʌrənt ˌlaɪə'bɪlɪtiz/ *plural noun* current liabilities of a company less its current assets

net dividend per share /ˌnet ˌdɪvɪdend pə 'ʃeə/ *noun* the dividend per share after deduction of personal income tax

net income /ˌnet 'ɪnkʌm/ *noun* a person's or organisation's income which is left after taking away tax and other deductions

net interest /ˌnet 'ɪntrəst/ *noun* a figure equal to gross interest minus tax paid on it

net liquid funds /ˌnet ˌlɪkwɪd 'fʌndz/ *plural noun* an organisation's cash plus its marketable investments less its short-term borrowings, such as overdrafts and loans

net loss /ˌnet 'lɒs/ *noun* an actual loss, after deducting overheads

net margin /ˌnet 'mɑːdʒɪn/ *noun* the percentage difference between received price and all costs, including overheads

net present value /ˌnet ˌprezənt 'væljuː/ *noun* the present value of the project. Abbreviation **NPV**

net price /ˌnet ˈpraɪs/ *noun* the price of goods or services which cannot be reduced by a discount

net price method /ˈnet praɪs ˌmeθəd/ *noun* an approach that records the cost of purchases after discounts have been deducted

net proceeds /ˈnet ˌprəʊsiːdz/ *plural noun* a figure equal to the amount realised from a transaction minus the cost of making the transaction

net profit /ˌnet ˈprɒfɪt/ *noun* the amount by which income from sales is larger than all expenditure. Also called **profit after tax**

net profit ratio /ˌnet ˈprɒfɪt ˌreɪʃiəʊ/ *noun* the ratio of an organisation's net profit to its total net sales. Comparing the net profit ratios of companies in the same sector shows which are the most efficient.

net realisable value /ˌnet ˌriːəlaɪzəb(ə)l ˈvæljuː/ *noun* the price at which goods in stock could be sold, less any costs incurred in making the sale. Abbreviation **NRV**

net receipts /ˌnet rɪˈsiːts/ *plural noun* receipts after deducting commission, tax, discounts, etc.

net relevant earnings /ˌnet ˌreləv(ə)nt ˈɜːnɪŋz/ *plural noun* earnings which qualify for calculating pension contributions and against which relief against tax can be claimed. Such earnings can be income from employment which is not pensionable, profits of a self-employed sole trader, etc.

net residual value /ˌnet rɪˌzɪdjuəl ˈvæljuː/ *noun* the anticipated proceeds of an asset at the end of its useful life, less the costs of selling it, e.g., transport and commission. It is used when calculating the annual charge for the straight-line method of depreciation. Abbreviation **NRV**

net return /ˌnet rɪˈtɜːn/ *noun* a return on an investment after tax has been paid

net salary /ˌnet ˈsæləri/ *noun* the salary which is left after deducting tax and National Insurance contributions

net sales /ˌnet ˈseɪlz/ *plural noun* the total amount of sales less damaged or returned items and discounts to retailers

net turnover /ˌnet ˈtɜːnˌəʊvə/ *noun* turnover before VAT and after trade discounts have been deducted

net working capital /ˌnet ˌwɜːkɪŋ ˈkæpɪt(ə)l/ *noun* same as **net current assets**

net worth /ˌnet ˈwɜːθ/ *noun* the value of all the property of a person or company after taking away what the person or company owes ○ *The upmarket product is targeted at individuals of high net worth.*

net yield /ˌnet ˈjiːld/ *noun* the profit from investments after deduction of tax

new issue /ˌnjuː ˈɪʃuː/ *noun* an issue of new shares to raise finance for a company

new issues department /ˌnjuː ˈɪʃuːz dɪˌpɑːtmənt/ *noun* the section of a bank which deals with issues of new shares

NI *abbreviation* National Insurance

NIC *abbreviation* National Insurance contribution

NIF *abbreviation* note issuance facility

night safe /ˈnaɪt seɪf/ *noun* a safe in the outside wall of a bank, where money and documents can be deposited at night, using a special door

nil /nɪl/ *noun* zero or nothing ○ *The advertising budget has been cut to nil.*

nil paid shares /ˌnɪl peɪd ˈʃeəz/ *plural noun* new shares which have not yet been paid for

nil return /ˌnɪl rɪˈtɜːn/ *noun* a report showing no sales, income, tax, etc.

no-claims bonus /ˌnəʊ ˈkleɪmz ˌbəʊnəs/ *noun* **1.** a reduction of premiums on an insurance policy because no claims have been made **2.** a lower premium paid because no claims have been made against the insurance policy

nominal /ˈnɒmɪn(ə)l/ *adjective* (*of a payment*) very small ○ *They are paying a nominal rent.* ○ *The employment agency makes a nominal charge for its services.*

nominal account /ˈnɒmɪn(ə)l əˌkaʊnt/ *noun* an account for recording transactions relating to a particular type of expense or receipt

nominal capital /ˌnɒmɪn(ə)l ˈkæpɪt(ə)l/ *noun* the total of the face value of all the shares which a company is authorised to issue

nominal interest rate /ˌnɒmɪn(ə)l ˈɪntrəst reɪt/ *noun* an interest rate expressed as a percentage of the face value of a bond, not on its market value

nominal ledger /ˌnɒmɪn(ə)l ˈledʒə/ *noun* a book which records a company's transactions in the various accounts

nominal share capital /ˌnɒmɪn(ə)l ˈʃeə ˌkæpɪt(ə)l/ *noun* the total of the face value of all the shares which a company is authorised to issue according to its memorandum of association

nominal value /ˌnɒmɪn(ə)l ˈvæljuː/ *noun* same as **face value**

nominee /ˌnɒmɪˈniː/ *noun* a person who is nominated, especially someone who is appointed to deal with financial matters on your behalf

nominee account /ˌnɒmɪˈniː əˌkaʊnt/ *noun* an account held on behalf of someone

non-acceptance /ˌnɒn əkˈseptəns/ *noun* a situation in which the person who is to pay a bill of exchange does not accept it

noncash items /ˌnɒn kæʃ ˈaɪtəmz/ *plural noun* cheques, drafts and similar items which are not in the form of cash

noncontrollable cost /ˌnɒnkəntrəʊləb(ə)l ˈkɒst/ *noun* a business cost that the management team cannot influence, e.g. the level of rent payable on buildings occupied

non-coterminous period ends /ˌnɒnkəʊtɜːmɪnəs ˈpɪəriəd ˌendz/ *noun* a point at which separate and related accounts cease to cover different accounting periods and begin to run coterminously

non-cumulative preference share /ˌnɒn ˌkjuːmjʊlətɪv ˈpref(ə)rəns ˌʃeə/ *noun* a preference share where, if the dividend is not paid in the current year, it is lost

non-current assets /ˌnɒn ˌkʌrənt ˈæsets/ *plural noun* ♦ **fixed assets**

non-executive director /nɒn ɪg ˌzekjʊtɪv daɪˈrektə/ *noun* a director who attends board meetings and gives advice, but does not work full-time for the company. Also called **outside director**

non-historic /ˌnɒn hɪˈstɒrɪk/ *adjective* not calculated on a historical cost basis

non-monetary /ˌnɒn ˈmʌnɪt(ə)ri/ *adjective* used for describing items or assets that are not money and can be valued at a higher value than their original purchase price

non-negotiable instrument /ˌnɒn nɪ ˌgəʊʃəb(ə)l ˈɪnstrʊmənt/ *noun* a document which cannot be exchanged for cash, e.g. a crossed cheque

non-performing loan /ˌnɒn pɜːˌfɔːmɪŋ ˈləʊn/ *noun US* a loan where the borrower is not likely to pay any interest nor to repay the principal, as in the case of loans to Third World countries by western banks

nonproductive capacity /ˌnɒnprə ˈdʌktɪv kəˌpæsɪti/ *noun* capacity that produces no net production, e.g. because production needs to be repeated owing to defects in earlier products

nonprofit accounting /nɒnˈprɒfɪt ə ˌkaʊntɪŋ/ *noun* the accounting policies and methods employed by nonprofit organisations such as charities

non-profit-making organisation /ˌnɒn ˌprɒfɪtmeɪkɪŋ ˌɔːgənaɪˈzeɪʃən/ *noun* an organisation which is not allowed by law to make a profit ○ *Non-profit-making organisations are exempted from tax.* (NOTE: Non-profit-making organisations include charities, professional associations, trade unions, and religious, arts, community, research, and campaigning bodies. The US term is **nonprofit organization**.)

non-recurring items /ˌnɒn rɪˌkɜːrɪŋ ˈaɪtəmz/ *plural noun* items in an income statement that are unusual in nature or do not occur regularly

non-refundable /ˌnɒn rɪˈfʌndəb(ə)l/ *adjective* not refunded in normal circumstances ○ *You will be asked to make a non-refundable deposit.*

non-resident /ˌnɒn ˈrezɪd(ə)nt/ *noun, adjective* a person who is not considered a resident of a country for tax purposes ○ *He has a non-resident bank account.*

non-sufficient funds /ˌnɒn səˌfɪʃənt ˈfʌndz/ *noun US* a lack of enough money in a bank account to pay a cheque drawn on that account. Abbreviation **NSF**. Also called **insufficient funds**, **not sufficient funds**

non-tariff barriers /ˌnɒn ˈtærɪf ˌbæriəz/ *plural noun* barriers to international trade other than tariffs. They include over-complicated documentation, verification of goods for health and safety reasons and blocked deposits payable by importers to obtain foreign currency. Abbreviation **NTBs**

non-taxable /ˌnɒn ˈtæksəb(ə)l/ *adjective* not subject to tax ○ *non-taxable income* ○ *Lottery prizes are non-taxable.*

non-trade creditor /ˌnɒn ˈtreɪd ˌkredɪtə/ *noun* a creditor who is not owed money in the normal trade of a business, e.g. a debenture holder or the Inland Revenue

non-voting shares /ˌnɒn ˌvəʊtɪŋ ˈʃeəz/ *plural noun* shares which do not allow the shareholder to vote at meetings. ♦ **A shares**

normal absorption costing /ˌnɔːm(ə)l əbˈzɔːpʃən ˌkɒstɪŋ/ *noun* a method of product costing that averages out fluctuations in overhead costs

normal costs /ˈnɔːm(ə)l kɒsts/ *plural noun* annual product costs averaged out to give a monthly figure, as distinct from a monthly figure that records seasonal fluctuations in costs

normalise /ˈnɔːməlaɪz/, **normalize** *verb* to store and represent numbers in a pre-agreed form, usually to provide maximum precision

normal loss /ˌnɔːm(ə)l ˈlɒs/ *noun* loss which is usual in the type of business being carried on, e.g. the loss of small quantities of materials during the manufacturing process

normal spoilage /ˌnɔːm(ə)l ˈspɔɪlɪdʒ/ *noun* the deterioration of products that will always take place, even under the best operating conditions

notary public /ˌnəʊtəri ˈpʌblɪk/ *noun* a lawyer who has the authority to witness documents and spoken statements, making them official (NOTE: The plural is **notaries public**.)

note /nəʊt/ *noun* **1.** ○ *to send someone a note* ○ *I left a note on her desk.* □ **notes to the accounts** notes attached to a company's accounts by the auditors to explain items in the accounts or to explain the principles of accounting used **2.** paper showing that money has been borrowed

note issuance facility /ˈnəʊt ˌɪʃuəns fə ˌsɪlɪti/ *noun* a credit facility where a company obtains a loan underwritten by banks and can issue a series of short-term Eurocurrency notes to replace others which have expired. Abbreviation **NIF**

note of hand /ˌnəʊt əv ˈhænd/ *noun* a document stating that someone promises to pay an amount of money on an agreed date

note payable /ˌnəʊt ˈpeɪəb(ə)l/ *noun* a document that gives a guarantee to pay money at a future date

note receivable /ˌnəʊt rɪˈsiːvəb(ə)l/ *noun* a document that gives a guarantee to receive money at a future date

notice of coding /ˌnəʊtɪs əv ˈkɒdɪŋ/ *noun* an official notice from a tax authority of someone's tax code, which indicates the level of tax allowance he or she is entitled to receive

notice of default /ˌnəʊtɪs əv dɪˈfɔːlt/ *noun* US same as **default notice**

notional /ˈnəʊʃ(ə)n(ə)l/ *adjective* probable but not known exactly or not quantifiable

notional income /ˌnəʊʃ(ə)n(ə)l ˈɪnkʌm/ *noun* an invisible benefit which is not money or goods and services

notional rent /ˌnəʊʃ(ə)n(ə)l ˈrent/ *noun* a sum put into accounts as rent where the company owns the building it is occupying and so does not pay an actual rent

not negotiable /ˌnɒt nɪˈɡəʊʃiəb(ə)l/ *phrase* used for referring to a cheque that must be deposited in an account and cannot therefore be immediately exchanged for cash. ◊ **crossed cheque, negotiable instrument**

novation /nəʊˈveɪʃ(ə)n/ *noun* an agreement to change a contract by substituting a third party for one of the two original parties

NPV *abbreviation* net present value

NRV *abbreviation* **1.** net realisable value **2.** net residual value

NS&I *abbreviation* National Savings and Investments

NSB *abbreviation* National Savings Bank

NSF *abbreviation* not sufficient funds *or* non-sufficient funds

NTBs *abbreviation* non-tariff barriers

number /ˈnʌmbə/ *noun* **1.** a quantity of things or people ○ *The number of persons on the payroll has increased over the last year.* ○ *The number of days lost through strikes has fallen.* **2.** a printed or written figure that identifies a particular thing ○ *Please write your account number on the back of the cheque.* ○ *If you have a complaint to make, always quote the batch number.* ○ *She noted the cheque number in the ledger.* ■ *verb* to put a figure on a document ○ *to number an order* ○ *I refer to your invoice numbered 1234.*

numbered account /ˌnʌmbəd əˈkaʊnt/ *noun* a bank account, usually in Switzerland, which is referred to only by a number, the name of the person holding it being kept secret

numeral /ˈnjuːm(ə)rəl/ *noun* a character or symbol which represents a number

O

O & M *abbreviation* organisation and methods

OAP *abbreviation* old age pensioner

objectivity /ˌɒbdʒek'tɪvɪti/ *noun* the fact that an accounting item can be verified by supporting evidence, e.g. by a voucher of some kind

obligation /ˌɒblɪ'geɪʃ(ə)n/ *noun* **1.** a duty to do something ○ *There is no obligation to help out in another department* ○ *There is no obligation to buy.* □ **to fulfil your contractual obligations** to do what is stated in a contract **2.** a debt □ **to meet your obligations** to pay your debts

obsolescence /ˌɒbsə'les(ə)ns/ *noun* the process of a product going out of date because of progress in design or technology, and therefore becoming less useful or valuable

obsolete /'ɒbsəliːt/ *adjective* no longer used ○ *Computer technology changes so fast that hardware soon becomes obsolete.*

occupational pension /ˌɒkjʊpeɪʃ(ə)nəl 'penʃə/ *noun* a pension which is paid by the company by which an employee has been employed

occupational pension scheme /ˌɒkjʊpeɪʃ(ə)nəl 'penʃən skiːm/ *noun* a pension scheme where the employee gets a pension from a fund set up by the company he or she has worked for, which is related to the salary he or she was earning. Also called **company pension scheme**

occupier /'ɒkjʊpaɪə/ *noun* a person who lives in a property

O/D *abbreviation* overdraft

odd lot /ˌɒd 'lɒt/ *noun* **1.** a group of miscellaneous items for sale at an auction **2.** *US* a group of less than 100 shares of stock bought or sold together

OEIC /ɔɪk/ *abbreviation* open-ended investment company

off /ɒf/ *adjective* not working or not in operation ○ *to take three days off* ○ *The agreement is off.* ○ *They called the strike off.* ○ *We give the staff four days off at Christmas.* ■ *adverb* **1.** taken away from a price ○ *We give 5% off for quick settlement.* **2.** lower than a previous price ○ *The shares closed 2% off.* ■ *preposition* **1.** subtracted from ○ *to take £25 off the price* ○ *We give 10% off our usual prices.* **2.** not included □ **items off balance sheet** *or* **off balance sheet assets** financial items which do not appear in a company's balance sheet as assets, such as equipment acquired under an operating lease

'…its stock closed Monday at $21.875 a share in NYSE composite trading, off 56% from its high last July' [*Wall Street Journal*]

off-balance sheet asset /ˌɒf 'bæləns ʃiːt ˌæset/ *noun* an item that is a valuable resource but does not feature on the balance sheet, e.g. an expected rebate of some sort

off-balance-sheet financing /ˌɒf 'bæləns ʃiːt ˌfaɪnænsɪŋ/ *noun* a way of raising finance through a long-term lease that does not qualify as a capital lease and therefore does not appear on the balance sheet

off-balance sheet liability /ˌɒf 'bæləns ʃiːt laɪə,bɪlɪti/ *noun* a potential liability that does not feature on the balance sheet

offer /'ɒfə/ *noun* **1.** a statement that you are willing to give or do something, especially to pay a specific amount of money to buy something ○ *to make an offer for a company* ○ *We made an offer of £10 a share.* □ **or near offer** *US*, **or best offer** or an offer of a price which is slightly less than the price asked ○ *The car is for sale at £2,000 or near offer.* **2.** a statement that you are willing to sell something **3.** a statement that you are willing to employ someone □ **she received six offers of jobs** *or* **six job offers** six companies told her she could have a job with them **4.** a statement that a company is prepared to buy another company's shares and take the company over ■ *verb* **1.** to say that you are willing to pay a specific amount of money for something ○ *to offer someone*

£100,000 for their house ○ She offered £10 a share. **2.** to say that you are willing to sell something ○ They are offering special prices on winter holidays in the US ○ We offered the house for sale.

offer document /ˈɒfə ˌdɒkjʊmənt/ noun a formal document where a company offers to buy shares at some price as part of a take-over bid

offered market /ˌɒfəd ˈmɑːkɪt/ noun a market where there are more sellers than buyers

offer for sale /ˌɒfə fə ˈseɪl/ noun a situation in which a company advertises new shares for sale to the public as a way of launching itself on the Stock Exchange (NOTE: The other ways of launching a company are a 'tender' or a 'placing.')

offering circular /ˈɒf(ə)rɪŋ ˌsɜːkjʊlə/ noun a document which gives information about a company whose shares are being sold to the public for the first time

offeror /ˈɒfərə/ noun a person who makes an offer

offer period /ˈɒfə ˌpɪəriəd/ noun a time during which a takeover bid for a company is open

offer price /ˈɒfə praɪs/ noun the price at which investors buy new shares or units in a unit trust. The opposite, i.e. the selling price, is called the 'bid price', the difference between the two is the 'spread'.

Office of Fair Trading /ˌɒfɪs əv feə ˈtreɪdɪŋ/ noun a department of the UK government that protects consumers against unfair or illegal business. Abbreviation **OFT**

Office of Management and Budget /ˌɒfɪs əv ˌmænɪdʒmənt ən ˈbʌdʒɪt/ noun US the department of the US government that prepares the federal budget. Abbreviation **OMB**

Office of Thrift Supervision /ˌɒfɪs əv ˈθrɪft suːpəˌvɪʒ(ə)n/ noun US a department of the US government which regulates the savings and loan associations. Abbreviation **OTS**

official books of account /əˌfɪʃ(ə)l bʊks əv əˈkaʊnt/ plural noun the official financial records of an institution

Official List /əˌfɪʃ(ə)l ˈlɪst/ noun a daily publication by the London Stock Exchange of the highest and lowest prices recorded for each share during the trading session

official receiver /əˌfɪʃ(ə)l rɪˈsiːvə/ noun a government official who is appointed to run a company which is in financial difficulties, to pay off its debts as far as possible and to close it down ○ The company is in the hands of the official receiver. Also called **receiver**

official return /əˌfɪʃ(ə)l rɪˈtɜːn/ noun an official report

offload /ɒfˈləʊd/ verb to pass something which you do not want to someone else

offset /ɒfˈset/ verb to balance one thing against another so that they cancel each other out ○ to offset losses against tax ○ Foreign exchange losses more than offset profits in the domestic market. (NOTE: **offsetting – offset**)

offset account /ˈɒfset əˌkaʊnt/ noun an account established to allow the gross amount of another account to be reduced

offsetting error /ˈɒfsetɪŋ ˌerə/ noun an accounting error that cancels out another error

offshore /ˈɒfʃɔː/ adjective, adverb **1.** on an island or in the sea near to land ○ an offshore oil field ○ an offshore oil platform **2.** on an island which is a tax haven **3.** based outside a country, especially in a tax haven

offshore banking /ˌɒfʃɔː ˈbæŋkɪŋ/ noun banking in a tax haven

offshore finance subsidiary /ˌɒfʃɔː ˈfaɪnæns səbˌsɪdiəri/ noun a company created in another country to handle financial transactions, giving the owning company certain tax and legal advantages in its home country (NOTE: The US term is **offshore financial subsidiary**.)

offshore financial centre /ˌɒfʃɔː faɪ ˈnænʃəl ˌsentə/ noun a country or other political unit that has banking laws intended to attract business from industrialised nations

offshore fund /ˌɒfʃɔː ˈfʌnd/ noun a fund that is based overseas, usually in a country that has less strict taxation regulations

off-the-shelf company /ˌɒf ðə ˌʃelf ˈkʌmp(ə)ni/ noun a company which has already been registered by an accountant or lawyer, and which is ready for sale to someone who wants to set up a new company quickly

OFT abbreviation Office of Fair Trading

old age pension /ˌəʊld eɪdʒ ˈpenʃən/ noun a state pension given to people over some age (currently to a man who is 65 or to a woman who is 60)

old age pensioner /ˌəʊld eɪdʒ ˈpenʃ(ə)nə/ noun a person who receives the retirement pension. Abbreviation **OAP**

OMB abbreviation Office of Management and Budget

ombudsman /ˈɒmbʊdzmən/ *noun* an official who investigates complaints by the public against government departments or other large organisations (NOTE: The plural is **ombudsmen**.)

'…radical changes to the disciplinary system, including appointing an ombudsman to review cases where complainants are not satisfied with the outcome, are proposed in a consultative paper the Institute of Chartered Accountants issued last month' [*Accountancy*]

on account *phrase* paid in part in advance

oncosts /ˈɒnkɒsts/ *plural noun* business costs that cannot be charged directly to a particular good or service and must be apportioned across the business

on demand /ˌɒn dɪˈmɑːnd/ *adjective* used to describe an account from which withdrawals may be made without giving a period of notice

one-man business /ˌwʌn mæn ˈbɪznɪs/, **one-man firm** /ˌwʌn mæn ˈfɜːm/, **one-man company** /ˌwʌn mæn ˈkʌmp(ə)ni/ *noun* a business run by one person alone with no staff or partners

one-off /ˌwʌn ˈɒf/ *adjective* done or made only once ○ *one-off item* ○ *one-off deal* ○ *one-off payment*

one-sided /ˌwʌn ˈsaɪdɪd/ *adjective* favouring one side and not the other in a negotiation

one-year money /ˌwʌn jɪə ˈmʌni/ *noun* money invested for one year

open /ˈəʊpən/ *adjective* **1.** at work, not closed ○ *The store is open on Sunday mornings.* ○ *Our offices are open from 9 to 6.* ○ *They are open for business every day of the week.* **2.** ready to accept something ■ *verb* **1.** to start a new business ○ *She has opened a shop in the High Street.* ○ *We have opened a branch in London.* **2.** to start work, to be at work ○ *The office opens at 9 a.m.* ○ *We open for business on Sundays.* **3.** to begin something **4.** to set something up or make something available ○ *to open a bank account* ○ *to open a line of credit* ○ *to open a loan* **5.** □ **shares opened lower** share prices were lower at the beginning of the day's trading

'…after opening at 79.1 the index touched a peak of 79.2 and then drifted to a low of 78.8' [*Financial Times*]

open account /ˌəʊpən əˈkaʊnt/ *noun* an account where the supplier offers the purchaser credit without security

open book management /ˌəʊpən ˈbʊk ˌmænɪdʒmənt/ *noun* a management method that gives staff open access to financial and operational information, with the aim of giving everyone a stake in increasing production

open cheque /ˌəʊpən ˈtʃek/ *noun* same as **uncrossed cheque**

open credit /ˌəʊpən ˈkredɪt/ *noun* credit given to good customers without security

open-ended /ˌəʊpən ˈendɪd/ *adjective* with no fixed limit or with some items not specified ○ *They signed an open-ended agreement.* ○ *The candidate was offered an open-ended contract with a good career plan.* (NOTE: The US term is **open-end**.)

open-ended credit /ˌəʊpən ˌendɪd ˈkredɪt/ *noun* same as **revolving credit**

open-ended fund /ˌəʊpən ˈendɪd ˌfʌnd/ *noun* a fund such as a unit trust where investors buy units, the money paid being invested in a range of securities. This is as opposed to a closed fund, such as an investment trust, where the investor buys shares in the trust company, and receives dividends.

open-ended investment company /ˌəʊpən ˌendɪd ɪnˈvestmənt ˌkʌmp(ə)ni/ *noun* a form of unit trust, in which the investor purchases shares at a single price, as opposed to the bid-offer pricing system used by ordinary unit trusts. Abbreviation **OEIC**

open-ended management company /ˌəʊpən ˌendɪd ˈmænɪdʒmənt ˌkʌmp(ə)ni/ *noun* a company that sells unit trusts (NOTE: The US term is **open-end management company.**)

open-ended trust /ˌəʊpən ˈendɪd ˌtrʌst/ *noun* a fund in which investors can freely buy and sell units at any time

opening balance /ˈəʊp(ə)nɪŋ ˌbæləns/ *noun* a balance at the beginning of an accounting period

opening balance sheet /ˌəʊp(ə)nɪŋ ˈbæləns ˌʃiːt/ *noun* an account showing an organisation's opening balances

opening entry /ˈəʊp(ə)nɪŋ ˌentri/ *noun* the first entry in an account

opening price /ˌəʊp(ə)nɪŋ ˈpraɪs/ *noun* a price at the start of a day's trading

opening stock /ˌəʊp(ə)nɪŋ ˈstɒk/ *noun* on a balance sheet, the closing stock at the end of one accounting period that is transferred forward and becomes the opening stock in the one that follows (NOTE: The US term is **beginning inventory**.)

open market /ˌəʊpən ˈmɑːkɪt/ *noun* a market where anyone can buy or sell

open-market value /ˌəʊpən ˈmɑːkɪt ˌvæljuː/ *noun* the price that an asset or security would realise if it was offered on a market open to all

operate /'ɒpəreɪt/ *verb* to be in force ○ *The new terms of service will operate from January 1st.* ○ *The rules operate on inland postal services only.*

'…the company gets valuable restaurant locations which will be converted to the family-style restaurant chain that it operates and franchises throughout most parts of the US' [*Fortune*]

operating /'ɒpəreɪtɪŋ/ *noun* the general running of a business or of a machine

'…the company blamed over-capacity and competitive market conditions in Europe for a £14m operating loss last year' [*Financial Times*]

operating activities /'ɒpəreɪtɪŋ æk ˌtɪvɪtiz/ *plural noun* those activities that a business engages in by reason of its being the type of business it is, as opposed to non-operating activities such as investment

operating budget /'ɒpəreɪtɪŋ ˌbʌdʒɪt/ *noun* a forecast of income and expenditure over a period of time

operating budget sequence /'ɒpəreɪtɪŋ ˌbʌdʒɪt ˌsiːkwəns/ *noun* a part of a master budget that records the acquisition and use of resources

operating costing /'ɒpəreɪtɪŋ ˌkɒstɪŋ/ *noun* costing which is based on the costs of services provided

operating costs /'ɒpəreɪtɪŋ kɒsts/ *plural noun* the costs of the day-to-day activities of a company. Also called **operating expenses**, **running costs**

operating cycle /'ɒpəreɪtɪŋ ˌsaɪk(ə)l/ *noun* the time it takes for purchases of materials for production to generate revenue from sales

operating expenses /'ɒpəreɪtɪŋ ɪk ˌspensɪz/ *plural noun* same as **operating costs**

operating lease /'ɒpəreɪtɪŋ liːs/ *noun* a lease which does not require the lessee company to show the asset acquired under the lease in its balance sheet, but the annual rental charge for such assets must be disclosed in a note to the accounts

operating leverage /'ɒpəreɪtɪŋ ˌlevərɪdʒ/ *noun* the ratio of a business's fixed costs to its total costs. As the fixed costs have to be paid regardless of output, the higher the ratio, the higher the risk of losses in an economic downturn.

operating loss /'ɒpəreɪtɪŋ lɒs/ *noun* a loss made by a company in its usual business

operating margin /'ɒpəreɪtɪŋ ˌmɑːdʒɪn/ *noun* a measurement of the proportion of a company's revenue that is left over after variable costs of production have been met

operating performance ratio /'ɒpəreɪtɪŋ pəˌfɔːməns ˌreɪʃiəʊ/ *noun* a ratio of profitability to sales

operating profit /'ɒpəreɪtɪŋ ˌprɒfɪt/ *noun* the difference between a company's revenues and any related costs and expenses, not including income or expenses from any sources other than its normal methods of providing goods or a service

operating revenue /'ɒpəreɪtɪŋ ˌrevənjuː/ *noun* the amount of income generated as a result of a company's normal business operations

operating risk /'ɒpəreɪtɪŋ rɪsk/ *noun* the risk of having a high operating leverage

operating statement /'ɒpəreɪtɪŋ ˌsteɪtmənt/ *noun* a financial statement which shows a company's expenditure and income, and consequently its final profit or loss ○ *The operating statement shows unexpected electricity costs.* ○ *Let's look at the operating statement to find last month's expenditure.*

operation /ˌɒpəˈreɪʃ(ə)n/ *noun* **1.** an activity or a piece of work, or the task of running something ○ *the company's operations in West Africa* ○ *He heads up the operations in Northern Europe.* **2.** □ **in operation** working or being used ○ *The system will be in operation by June.* ○ *The new system came into operation on January 1st.*

'…a leading manufacturer of business, industrial and commercial products requires a branch manager to head up its mid-western Canada operations based in Winnipeg' [*Globe and Mail (Toronto)*]

operational /ˌɒpəˈreɪʃ(ə)nəl/ *adjective* referring to the day-to-day activities of a business or to the way in which something is run

operational audit /ˌɒpəreɪʃ(ə)nəl 'ɔːdɪt/ *noun* a systematic review of the systems and procedures used in an organisation in order to assess whether they are being carried out efficiently and effectively. Also known as **management audit**, **operations audit**

operational budget /ˌɒpəreɪʃ(ə)nəl 'bʌdʒɪt/ *noun* same as **operating budget**

operational costs /ˌɒpəreɪʃ(ə)nəl 'kɒsts/ *plural noun* the costs of running a business

operational gearing /ˌɒpəreɪʃ(ə)nəl ˈɡɪərɪŋ/ *noun* a situation where a company has high fixed costs which are funded by borrowings

operational planning /ˌɒpəreɪʃ(ə)nəl ˈplænɪŋ/ *noun* the planning of how a business is to be run

operational research /ˌɒpəreɪʃ(ə)nəl rɪ ˈsɜːtʃ/ *noun* a study of a company's way of working to see if it can be made more efficient and profitable

operations review /ˌɒpəˈreɪʃ(ə)nz rɪ ˌvjuː/ *noun* an act of examining the way in which a company or department works to see how it can be made more efficient and profitable

operation time /ˌɒpəˈreɪʃ(ə)n taɪm/ *noun* the time taken for a business operation to be completed

opinion /əˈpɪnjən/ *noun* a piece of expert advice ○ *the lawyers gave their opinion* ○ *to ask an adviser for his opinion on a case*

opportunity cost /ˌɒpəˈtjuːnɪti kɒst/ *noun* **1.** the cost of a business initiative in terms of profits that could have been gained through an alternative plan ○ *It's a good investment plan and we will not be deterred by the opportunity cost.* Also called **alternative cost 2.** the value of another method of investment which could have been used, instead of the one adopted

opportunity cost approach /ˌɒpə ˈtjuːnɪti kɒst əˌprəʊtʃ/ *noun* the use of the concept of opportunity cost in business decision-making

optimal capital structure /ˌɒptɪm(ə)l ˌkæpɪt(ə)l ˈstrʌktʃə/ *noun* the optimal range for a company's capital structure

optimise /ˈɒptɪmaɪz/, **optimize** *verb* to allocate such things as resources or capital as efficiently as possible

optimum /ˈɒptɪməm/ *adjective* best ○ *The market offers optimum conditions for sales.*

option /ˈɒpʃən/ *noun* the opportunity to buy or sell something, such as a security, within a fixed period of time at a fixed price □ **to take up an option** *or* **to exercise an option** to accept the option which has been offered and to put it into action ○ *They exercised their option* or *they took up their option to acquire sole marketing rights to the product.*

option contract /ˈɒpʃən ˌkɒntrækt/ *noun* a right to buy or sell a specific number of shares at a fixed price

option dealing /ˈɒpʃən ˌdiːlɪŋ/ *noun* the activity of buying and selling share options

option trading /ˈɒpʃən ˌtreɪdɪŋ/ *noun* the business of buying and selling share options

order /ˈɔːdə/ *noun* **1.** the way in which records such as filing cards or invoices are arranged ○ *in alphabetical or numerical order* **2.** an official request for goods to be supplied ○ *to give someone an order* or *to place an order with someone for twenty filing cabinets* ○ *The management ordered the workforce to leave the factory.* □ **to fill an order, to fulfil an order** to supply items which have been ordered ○ *We are so understaffed we cannot fulfil any more orders before Christmas.* □ **items available to order only** items which will be manufactured only if someone orders them □ **on order** ordered but not delivered ○ *This item is out of stock, but is on order.* **3.** a document which allows money to be paid to someone ○ *She sent us an order on the Chartered Bank.* **4.** (*Stock Exchange*) an instruction to a broker to buy or sell **5.** □ **pay to Mr Smith or order** pay money to Mr Smith or as he orders □ **pay to the order of Mr Smith** pay money directly to Mr Smith or to his account ■ *verb* to ask for goods to be supplied ○ *They ordered a new Rolls Royce for the managing director.*

order book /ˈɔːdə bʊk/ *noun* a book which records orders received

order-driven system /ˈɔːdə ˌdrɪv(ə)n ˌsɪstəm/, **order-driven market** /ˌɔːdə ˌdrɪv(ə)n ˈmɑːkɪt/ *noun* a price system on a stock exchange where prices vary according to the level of orders. Compare **quote-driven system**

order entry /ˈɔːdə ˌentri/ *noun* the process of entering information on orders into a processing system

order fulfilment /ˈɔːdə fʊlˌfɪlmənt/ *noun* the process of supplying items which have been ordered

ordering costs /ˈɔːdərɪŋ kɒsts/ *plural noun* the total of the costs involved in making a purchase order, including telephone and stationery costs

order processing /ˈɔːdə ˌprəʊsesɪŋ/ *noun* the work of dealing with orders

order receipt time /ˌɔːdə rɪˈsiːt ˌtaɪm/ *noun* the interval between the receipt of an order and the point at which it is ready to be despatched

ordinarily resident /ˌɔːd(ə)n(ə)rɪli ˈrezɪd(ə)nt/ *adjective* normally living in a country ○ *Mr Schmidt is ordinarily resident in Canada*

ordinary activities /ˌɔːd(ə)n(ə)ri æk
'tɪvɪtiz/ *plural noun* the usual trading of a
company, that is, what the company usually
does

ordinary interest /ˌɔːd(ə)n(ə)ri 'ɪntrəst/
noun annual interest calculated on the basis
of 360 days, as opposed to 'exact interest'
which is calculated on 365 days

ordinary resolution /ˌɔːd(ə)n(ə)ri ˌrezə
'luːʃ(ə)n/ *noun* a resolution put before an
AGM, usually referring to some general procedural matter, and which requires a simple
majority of votes to be accepted

ordinary share capital /ˌɔːd(ə)n(ə)ri
'ʃeə ˌkæpɪt(ə)l/ *noun* the capital of a company in the form of money paid for ordinary
shares

ordinary shareholder /ˌɔːd(ə)n(ə)ri
'ʃeəhəʊldə/ *noun* a person who owns ordinary shares in a company

ordinary shares /'ɔːd(ə)n(ə)ri ʃeəz/ *plural noun* shares that entitle the holder to
receive a dividend after the dividend on preference shares has been paid (NOTE: The US
term is **common stock**.)

ordinary stock *noun* same as **ordinary
shares**

organic growth /ɔːˌgænɪk 'grəʊθ/ *noun*
same as **internal growth**

organisation /ˌɔːgənaɪ'zeɪʃ(ə)n/,
organization *noun* **1.** a way of arranging
something so that it works efficiently ○ *the
organisation of the head office into departments* ○ *The chairman handles the organisation of the AGM.* ○ *The organisation of
the group is too centralised to be efficient.* **2.**
a group or institution which is arranged for
efficient work

'…working with a client base which
includes many major commercial organizations and nationalized industries'
[*Times*]

organisational /ˌɔːgənaɪ'zeɪʃ(ə)n(ə)l/,
organizational *adjective* referring to the
way in which something is organised ○ *The
paper gives a diagram of the company's
organisational structure.*

organisational chart /ˌɔːgənaɪ
'zeɪʃ(ə)n(ə)l tʃɑːt/ *noun* a chart that shows
the relationships of people in an organisation in terms of their areas of authority and
responsibility

organisation and methods
/ˌɔːgənaɪzeɪʃ(ə)n ən 'meθədz/ *noun* a
process of examining how an office works,
and suggesting how it can be made more
efficient. Abbreviation **O & M**

organisation chart /ˌɔːgənaɪ'zeɪʃ(ə)n
tʃɑːt/ *noun* same as **organisational chart**

organisation costs /ˌɔːgənaɪ'zeɪʃ(ə)n
ˌkɒsts/ *plural noun* the costs associated with
setting up a business, e.g. legal fees and
business filing fees

organise /'ɔːgənaɪz/, **organize** *verb* **1.** to
set up a system for doing something ○ *The
company is organised into six profit centres.*
○ *The group is organised by sales areas.* **2.**
to arrange something so that it works

'…we organize a rate with importers who
have large orders and guarantee them
space at a fixed rate so that they can plan
their costs' [*Lloyd's List*]

original cost /əˌrɪdʒən(ə)l 'kɒst/ *noun*
the total cost of acquiring an asset

original entry /əˌrɪdʒən(ə)l 'entri/ *noun*
the act of recording a transaction in a journal

other capital /ˌʌðə 'kæpɪt(ə)l/ *noun* capital that is not listed in specific categories

other long-term capital /ˌʌðə ˌlɒŋ tɜːm
'kæpɪt(ə)l/ *noun* long-term capital that is
not listed in specific categories

other long-term liabilities /ˌʌðə ˌlɒŋ
tɜːm ˌlaɪə'bɪlɪtiz/ *plural noun* obligations
with terms greater than one year on which
there is no charge for interest in the next year

other short-term capital /ˌʌðə ˌʃɔːt
tɜːm 'kæpɪt(ə)l/ *noun* short-term capital
that is not listed in specific categories

OTS *abbreviation* Office of Thrift Supervision

out /aʊt/ *adverb* □ **we are £20,000 out in
our calculations** we have £20,000 too much
or too little

outgoings /'aʊtgəʊɪŋz/ *plural noun*
money which is paid out

outlay /'aʊtleɪ/ *noun* money spent,
expenditure

outlook /'aʊtlʊk/ *noun* a view of what is
going to happen in the future ○ *The economic outlook is not good.* ○ *The stock market outlook is worrying.*

'American demand has transformed the
profit outlook for many European manufacturers' [*Duns Business Month*]

out-of-date cheque /ˌaʊt əv deɪt 'tʃek/
noun a cheque which has not been cleared
because its date is too old, normally more
than six months

out of pocket /ˌaʊt əv 'pɒkɪt/ *adjective,
adverb* having paid out money personally ○
The deal has left me out of pocket.

out-of-pocket expenses /ˌaʊt əv
ˌpɒkɪt ɪk'spensɪz/ *plural noun* an amount
of money paid back to an employee who has

spent his or her personal money on company business

output /'aʊtpʊt/ *noun* the amount which a company, person, or machine produces ○ *Output has increased by 10%.* ○ *25% of our output is exported.*

'…crude oil output plunged during the last month and is likely to remain near its present level for the near future' [*Wall Street Journal*]

output per hour /,aʊtpʊt pər 'aʊə/ *noun* the amount of something produced in one hour

output tax /'aʊtpʊt tæks/ *noun* VAT charged by a company on goods or services sold, and which the company pays to the government

outright /,aʊt'raɪt/ *adverb, adjective* completely

outside director /,aʊtsaɪd daɪ'rektə/ *noun* same as **non-executive director**

outsource /'aʊtsɔːs/ *verb* to use a source outside a company or business to do the work that is needed

'The services unit won outsourcing contracts from the Environmental Protection Agency and NASA, which the company says played a significant part in the increase.' [InformationWeek]

outsourcing /'aʊtsɔːsɪŋ/ *noun* **1.** the practice of obtaining services from specialist bureaux or other companies, rather than employing full-time staff members to provide them **2.** the transfer of work previously done by employees of an organisation to another organisation, usually one that specialises in that type of work (NOTE: Things that have usually been outsourced in the past include legal services, transport, catering, and security, but nowadays IT services, training, and public relations are often added to the list.)

'…organizations in the public and private sectors are increasingly buying in specialist services – or outsourcing – allowing them to cut costs and concentrate on their core business activities' [*Financial Times*]

outstanding /aʊt'stændɪŋ/ *adjective* not yet paid or completed

outstanding cheque /aʊt,stændɪŋ 'tʃek/ *noun* a cheque which has been written and therefore has been entered in the company's ledgers, but which has not been presented for payment and so has not been debited from the company's bank account

overabsorbed /,əʊvərəbzɔːbd/

overabsorbed overhead /,əʊvərəbzɔːbd 'əʊvəhed/ *noun* an absorbed overhead which ends up by being higher than the actual overhead incurred

overabsorption /,əʊvərəb'zɔːpʃ(ə)n/ *noun* a situation where the actual overhead incurred is less than the absorbed overhead. Opposite **underabsorption**

overall /,əʊvər'ɔːl/ *adjective* covering or including everything □ **the company reported an overall fall in profits** the company reported a general fall in profits

overall balance of payments /,əʊvərɔːl ,bæləns əv 'peɪmənts/ *noun* the total of current and long-term balance of payments

overall capitalisation rate /,əʊvərɔːl ,kæpɪt(ə)laɪ'zeɪʃ(ə)n ,reɪt/ *noun* net operating income, other than debt service, divided by value

overall return /,əʊvərɔːl rɪ'tɜːn/ *noun* the aggregate of all the dividends received over an investment's life together with its capital gain or loss at the date of its realisation, calculated either before or after tax. It is one of the ways an investor can look at the performance of an investment.

overborrowed /,əʊvə'bɒrəʊd/ *adjective* referring to a company which has very high borrowings compared to its assets, and has difficulty in meeting its interest payments

overcapitalised /,əʊvə'kæpɪtəlaɪzd/, **overcapitalized** *adjective* referring to a company with more capital than it needs

overcharge *noun* /'əʊvətʃɑːdʒ/ a charge which is higher than it should be ○ *to pay back an overcharge* ■ *verb* /,əʊvə'tʃɑːdʒ/ to ask someone for too much money ○ *They overcharged us for our meals.* ○ *We asked for a refund because we'd been overcharged.*

overdraft /'əʊvədrɑːft/ *noun* **1.** an amount of money which a company or person can withdraw from a bank account, with the bank's permission, despite the fact that the account is empty ○ *The bank has allowed me an overdraft of £5,000.* Abbreviation **O/D** (NOTE: The US term is **overdraft protection.**) □ **we have exceeded our overdraft facilities** we have taken out more than the overdraft allowed by the bank **2.** a negative amount of money in an account, i.e. a situation where a cheque is more than the money in the account on which it is drawn

overdraw /,əʊvə'drɔː/ *verb* to take out more money from a bank account than there is in it

overdue /,əʊvə'djuː/ *adjective* having not been paid on time

overdue account /ˌəʊvədjuː əˈkaʊnt/ *noun* an account whose holder owes money that should have been paid earlier

overestimate /ˌəʊvərˈestɪmeɪt/ *verb* to think something is larger or worse than it really is ○ *She overestimated the amount of time needed to fit out the factory.* ○ *They overestimated the costs of moving the offices to central London.*

overgeared /ˌəʊvəˈɡɪəd/ *adjective* referring to a company which has high borrowings in comparison to its assets

overhang /ˈəʊvəhæŋ/ *noun* a large quantity of shares or of a commodity or of unsold stock available for sale, which has the effect of depressing the market price

overhead absorption rate /ˌəʊvəhed əbˈzɔːpʃən reɪt/ *noun* a rate at which production costs are increased to absorb higher overhead costs

overhead budget /ˌəʊvəhed ˈbʌdʒɪt/ *noun* a plan of probable overhead costs

overhead cost variance /ˌəʊvəhed kɒst ˈveəriəns/ *noun* the difference between the overhead cost absorbed and the actual overhead costs incurred, both fixed and variable

overhead expenditure variance /ˌəʊvəhed ɪkˈspendɪtʃə ˌveəriəns/ *noun* the difference between the budgeted overhead costs and the actual expenditure

overheads /ˈəʊvəhedz/ *plural noun* the indirect costs of the day-to-day running of a business, i.e. not money spent of producing goods, but money spent on such things as renting or maintaining buildings and machinery ○ *The sales revenue covers the manufacturing costs but not the overheads.* (NOTE: The US term is **overhead**.)

overlap profit /ˌəʊvəlæp ˈprɒfɪt/ *noun* a profit which occurs in two accounting periods, i.e. when two accounting periods overlap, and on which overlap relief can be claimed

overpaid /ˌəʊvəˈpeɪd/ *adjective* paid too much ○ *Our staff are overpaid and underworked.*

overpay /ˌəʊvəˈpeɪ/ *verb* to pay too much to someone or for something ○ *We overpaid the invoice by $245.*

overpayment /ˌəʊvəˈpeɪmənt/ *noun* an act of paying too much

overrider /ˈəʊvəraɪdə/, **overriding commission** /ˌəʊvəraɪdɪŋ kəˈmɪʃ(ə)n/ *noun* a special extra commission which is above all other commissions

overseas /ˈəʊvəsiːz/; /ˌəʊvəˈsiːz/ *noun* foreign countries ○ *The profits from overseas are far higher than those of the home division.*

overseas division /ˌəʊvəsiːz dɪˈvɪʒ(ə)n/ *noun* the section of a company dealing with trade with other countries

overseas funds /ˌəʊvəˈsiːz fʌndz/ *plural noun* investment funds based in other countries

overseas markets /ˌəʊvəsiːz ˈmɑːkɪts/ *plural noun* markets in foreign countries

overseas taxation /ˌəʊvəsiːz tækˈseɪʃ(ə)n/ *noun* ♦ **double taxation**, **double taxation agreement**

overseas trade /ˌəʊvəsiːz ˈtreɪd/ *noun* same as **foreign trade**

overspend /ˌəʊvəˈspend/ *verb* to spend too much □ **to overspend your budget** to spend more money than is allowed in your budget

overspending /ˌəʊvəˈspendɪŋ/ *noun* the act of spending more than is allowed ○ *The board decided to limit the overspending by the production departments.*

overstate /ˌəʊvəˈsteɪt/ *verb* to enter in an account a figure that is higher than the actual figure ○ *the company accounts overstate the real profit*

overstatement /ˌəʊvəˈsteɪtmənt/ *noun* the fact of entering in an account a figure that is higher than the actual figure

overstock /ˌəʊvəˈstɒk/ *verb* to have a bigger stock of something than is needed

'Cash paid for your stock: any quantity, any products, overstocked lines, factory seconds' [*Australian Financial Review*]

overstocks /ˈəʊvəstɒks/ *plural noun US* a surplus of stock ○ *We will have to sell off the overstocks to make room in the warehouse.*

over-the-counter market /ˌəʊvə ðə ˈkaʊntə ˌmɑːkɪt/ *noun* a secondary market in shares which are not listed on the main Stock Exchange

over-the-counter sales /ˌəʊvə ðə ˈkaʊntə ˌseɪlz/ *plural noun* the legal selling of shares that are not listed in the official Stock Exchange list, usually carried out by telephone

overtime /ˈəʊvətaɪm/ *noun* hours worked in addition to your usual working hours ○ *to work six hours' overtime* ○ *The overtime rate is one and a half times normal pay.*

overtime pay /ˈəʊvətaɪm peɪ/ *noun* pay for extra time worked

overtrading /ˌəʊvəˈtreɪdɪŋ/ *noun* a situation where a company increases sales and production too much and too quickly, so that it runs short of cash

overvalue /ˌəʊvə'væljuː/ *verb* to give a higher value to something or someone than is right □ **these shares are overvalued at £1.25** the shares are worth less than the £1.25 for which they are selling

'…the fact that sterling has been overvalued for the past three years shows that currencies can remain above their fair value for very long periods' [*Investors Chronicle*]

owe /əʊ/ *verb* to have to pay money ○ *He owes the bank £250,000.* □ **they still owe the company for the stock they purchased last year** they have still not paid for the stock

owner-occupier /ˌəʊnər 'ɒkjʊpaɪə/ *noun* a person who owns the property in which he or she lives

owners' equity /ˌəʊnəz 'ekwɪti/ *noun* the value of the shares in a company owned by the owners of the company

P

package deal /ˈpækɪdʒ ˌdiːl/ *noun* an agreement which covers several different things at the same time ○ *They agreed a package deal which involves the construction of the factory, training of staff, and purchase of the product.*

paid /peɪd/ *adjective* **1.** for which money has been given ○ *The invoice is marked 'paid'.* **2.** referring to an amount which has been settled ○ *The order was sent carriage paid.*

paid-in capital /ˌpeɪd ɪn ˈkæpɪt(ə)l/ *noun* capital in a business which has been provided by its shareholders, usually in the form of payments for shares above their par value

paid-up shares /ˌpeɪd ʌp ˈʃeəz/ *noun* shares which have been completely paid for by the shareholders

paper /ˈpeɪpə/ *noun* **1.** a document which can represent money, e.g. a bill of exchange or a promissory note **2.** shares in the form of share certificates

paper gain /ˌpeɪpə ˈgeɪn/ *noun* same as **paper profit**

'…the profits were tax-free and the interest on the loans they incurred qualified for income tax relief; the paper gains were rarely changed into spending money' [*Investors Chronicle*]

paper loss /ˌpeɪpə ˈlɒs/ *noun* a loss made when an asset has fallen in value but has not been sold. Also called **unrealised loss**

paper millionaire /ˌpeɪpə ˌmɪljəˈneə/ *noun* a person who owns shares which, if sold, would be worth one million pounds or dollars

paper money /ˌpeɪpə ˈmʌni/ *noun* payments in paper form, e.g., cheques

paper offer /ˌpeɪpə ˈɒfə/ *noun* a takeover bid where the purchasing company offers its shares in exchange for shares in the company being taken over, as opposed to a cash offer

paper profit /ˌpeɪpə ˈprɒfɪt/ *noun* a profit on an asset which has increased in price but has not been sold ○ *He is showing a paper profit of £25,000 on his investment.* Also called **paper gain**, **unrealised profit**

par /pɑː/ *adjective* equal, at the same price

parallel economy /ˌpærəlel ɪˈkɒnəmi/ *noun* same as **black economy**

parallel loan /ˌpærəlel ˈləʊn/ *noun* same as **back-to-back loan**

parameter /pəˈræmɪtə/ *noun* a fixed limit ○ *The budget parameters are fixed by the finance director.* ○ *Spending by each department has to fall within agreed parameters.*

parcel of shares /ˌpɑːs(ə)l əv ˈʃeəz/ *noun* a fixed number of shares which are sold as a group ○ *The shares are on offer in parcels of 50.*

parent company /ˈpeərənt ˌkʌmp(ə)ni/ *noun* a company which owns more than 50% of the shares of another company

Pareto's Law /pəˈriːtəʊz lɔː/, **Pareto Effect** /pəˈriːtəʊ ɪˌfekt/ *noun* the theory that incomes are distributed in the same way in all countries, whatever tax regime is in force, and that a small percentage of a total is responsible for a large proportion of value or resources. Also called **eighty/twenty law**

pari passu /ˌpæri ˈpæsuː/ *adverb* a Latin phrase meaning 'equally' ○ *The new shares will rank pari passu with the existing ones.*

parity /ˈpærɪti/ *noun* **1.** the state of being equal □ **the pound fell to parity with the dollar** the pound fell to a point where one pound equalled one dollar **2.** a situation when the price of a commodity, foreign currency or security is the same in different markets

'…the draft report on changes in the international monetary system casts doubt about any return to fixed exchange-rate parities' [*Wall Street Journal*]

Parliamentary Public Accounts Committee /ˌpɑːləmənt(ə)ri ˌpʌblɪk ə ˈkaʊnts kəˌmɪti/ *noun* a UK parliamentary committee established in 1961 to examine that the sums of money agreed by Parliament for public spending are properly spent

part exchange /ˌpɑːt ɪksˈtʃeɪndʒ/ *noun* the act of giving an old product as part of the payment for a new one ○ *to take a car in part exchange*

partial /ˈpɑːʃ(ə)l/ *adjective* not complete

participate /pɑːˈtɪsɪpeɪt/ *verb* to take part in an activity or enterprise ○ *The staff are encouraged to participate actively in the company's decision-making processes.*

participating preference shares /pɑːˌtɪsɪpeɪtɪŋ ˈpref(ə)rəns ʃeəz/, **participating preferred stock** /pɑːˌtɪsɪpeɪtɪŋ prɪˌfɜːd ˈstɒk/ *plural noun* preference shares which get an extra bonus dividend if company profits reach a high level

participative budgeting /pɑːˌtɪsɪpətɪv ˈbʌdʒɪtɪŋ/ *noun* a budgeting system in which all budget holders are given the opportunity to participate in setting their own budgets. Also called **bottom-up budgeting**

partly-paid capital /ˌpɑːtli peɪd ˈkæpɪt(ə)l/ *noun* a capital which represents partly-paid shares

partly-paid up shares /ˌpɑːtli peɪd ʌp ˈʃeəz/, **partly-paid shares** /ˌpɑːtli peɪd ˈʃeəz/ *plural noun* shares in which the shareholders have not paid the full face value

partner /ˈpɑːtnə/ *noun* a person who works in a business and has an equal share in it with other partners ○ *I became a partner in a firm of solicitors.*

partnership /ˈpɑːtnəʃɪp/ *noun* an unregistered business where two or more people (but not more than twenty) share the risks and profits according to a partnership agreement ○ *to go into partnership with someone* ○ *to join with someone to form a partnership*

partnership accounts /ˈpɑːtnəʃɪp əˌkaʊnts/ *plural noun* the capital and current accounts of each partner in a partnership, or the accounts recording the partnership's business activities

partnership agreement /ˈpɑːtnəʃɪp əˌgriːmənt/ *noun* a document setting up a partnership, giving the details of the business and the amount each partner is contributing to it. Also called **articles of partnership**

part-owner /ˌpɑːt ˈəʊnə/ *noun* a person who owns something jointly with one or more other people ○ *I am part-owner of the restaurant.*

part-ownership /ˌpɑːt ˈəʊnəʃɪp/ *noun* a situation where two or more persons own the same property

part payment /ˌpɑːt ˈpeɪmənt/ *noun* a partial payment that leaves a balance to pay at some future time ○ *I gave him £250 as part payment for the car.*

part-time /ˌpɑːt ˈtaɪm/ *adjective, adverb* not working for the whole working week ○ *a part-time employee*

party /ˈpɑːti/ *noun* a person or organisation involved in a legal dispute or legal agreement ○ *How many parties are there to the contract?* ○ *The company is not a party to the agreement.*

par value /ˌpɑː ˈvæljuː/ *noun* same as **face value**

passbook /ˈpɑːsbʊk/ *noun* same as **bank book**

'…instead of customers having transactions recorded in their passbooks, they will present plastic cards and have the transactions printed out on a receipt' [*Australian Financial Review*]

patent /ˈpeɪtənt, ˈpætənt/ *noun* an official document showing that a person has the exclusive right to make and sell an invention ○ *to take out a patent for a new type of light bulb* ○ *to apply for a patent for a new invention* □ **'patent applied for'**, **'patent pending'** words on a product showing that the inventor has applied for a patent for it

patent agent /ˈpeɪtənt ˌeɪdʒənt/ *noun* a person who advises on patents and applies for patents on behalf of clients

patent office /ˈpeɪtənt ˌɒfɪs/ *noun* a government office which grants patents and supervises them

patent rights /ˈpeɪtənt raɪts/ *plural noun* the rights which an inventor holds because of a patent

paternity leave /pəˈtɜːnɪti liːv/ *noun* a short period of leave given to a father to be away from work when his partner has a baby

pathfinder prospectus /ˈpɑːθfaɪndə prəˌspektəs/ *noun* a preliminary prospectus about a company which is going to be launched on the Stock Exchange, sent to potential major investors before the issue date, giving details of the company's background, but not giving the price at which shares will be sold

pay /peɪ/ *noun* a salary or wages, money given to someone for regular work ■ *verb* **1.** to give money to buy an item or a service ○ *to pay £1,000 for a car* ○ *How much did you pay to have the office cleaned?* (NOTE: **paying – paid**) □ **'pay cash'** words written on a crossed cheque to show that it can be paid in cash if necessary **2.** to produce or distribute money (NOTE: **paying – paid**) **3.** to give an employee money for work done ○ *The workforce has not been paid for three weeks.* ○ *We pay good wages for skilled workers.* ○ *How much do they pay you per hour?* (NOTE: **paying – paid**) □ **to be paid at piecework rates** to get money for each piece of work finished **4.** to give money which is owed or which has to be paid ○ *He was late paying the bill.* ○ *We phoned to ask when they were going to pay the invoice.* ○ *You will have to pay duty on these imports.* ○ *She pays tax at the highest rate.* (NOTE: **paying – paid**) □ **please pay the sum of £10** please give £10 in cash or by cheque

'…recession encourages communication not because it makes redundancies easier, but because it makes low or zero pay increases easier to accept' [*Economist*]

'…the yield figure means that if you buy the shares at their current price you will be getting 5% before tax on your money if the company pays the same dividend as in its last financial year' [*Investors Chronicle*]

pay back *phrasal verb* to give money back to someone ○ *Banks are warning students not to take out loans which they cannot pay back.* ○ *I lent him £50 and he promised to pay me back in a month.* ○ *She has never paid me back the money she borrowed.*

pay off *phrasal verb* **1.** to finish paying money which is owed for something ○ *He won the lottery and paid off his mortgage.* ○ *She is trying to pay off the loan by monthly instalments.* **2.** to terminate somebody's employment and pay all wages that are due ○ *When the company was taken over the factory was closed and all the employees were paid off.*

pay out *phrasal verb* to give money ○ *The company pays out thousands of pounds in legal fees.* ○ *We have paid out half our profits in dividends.*

pay up *phrasal verb* to give money which is owed ○ *The company only paid up when we sent them a letter from our solicitor.* ○ *She finally paid up six months late.*

payable /ˈpeɪəb(ə)l/ *adjective* due to be paid

payable to order /ˌpeɪəb(ə)l tə ˈɔːdə/ *adjective* words written on a bill of exchange or cheque to indicate that it may be transferred

payback /ˈpeɪbæk/ *noun* **1.** the act of paying back money which has been borrowed **2.** the time required for the cash inflows from a capital investment project to equal the cash outflows

payback clause /ˈpeɪbæk klɔːz/ *noun* a clause in a contract which states the terms for repaying a loan

payback period /ˈpeɪbæk ˌpɪəriəd/ *noun* **1.** a period of time over which a loan is to be repaid or an investment is to pay for itself **2.** the length of time it will take to earn back the money invested in a project

pay day /ˈpeɪ deɪ/ *noun* a day on which wages are paid to employees, usually Friday for employees paid once a week and during the last week of the month for employees who are paid once a month

pay differentials /ˈpeɪ dɪfəˌrenʃəlz/ *plural noun* the difference in salary between employees in similar types of jobs. Also called **salary differentials**, **wage differentials**

paydown /ˈpeɪdaʊn/ *noun* a repayment of part of a sum which has been borrowed

payee /peɪˈiː/ *noun* a person who receives money from someone, or the person whose name is on a cheque

payer /ˈpeɪə/ *noun* a person who gives money to someone

pay hike /ˈpeɪ haɪk/ *noun* an increase in salary

paying /ˈpeɪɪŋ/ *adjective* **1.** making a profit ○ *It is a paying business.* **2.** producing money, source of money ■ *noun* the act of giving money

paying agent /ˈpeɪɪŋ ˌeɪdʒənt/ *noun* a bank which pays dividend or interest to a bondholder

paying-in book /ˌpeɪɪŋ ˈɪn bʊk/ *noun* a book of forms for paying money into a bank account or a building society account

paying-in slip /ˌpeɪɪŋ ˈɪn slɪp/ *noun* a printed form which is filled in when money is being deposited in a bank (NOTE: The US term is **deposit slip**.)

paymaster /ˈpeɪmɑːstə/ *noun* the person responsible for paying an organisation's employees

payment /ˈpeɪmənt/ *noun* **1.** the act of giving money in exchange for goods or a service ○ *We always ask for payment in cash* or *cash payment and not payment by cheque.* ○ *The payment of interest* or *the interest payment should be made on the 22nd of each month.* **2.** money paid

payment terms /ˈpeɪmənt tɜːmz/ *plural noun* the conditions laid down by a business regarding when it should be paid for goods or services that it supplies, e.g. cash with order, payment on delivery, or payment within a particular number of days of the invoice date

pay negotiations /ˈpeɪ nɪɡəʊʃi ˌeɪʃ(ə)nz/, **pay talks** /ˈpeɪ tɔːks/ *plural noun* discussions between management and employees about pay increases

payoff /ˈpeɪɒf/ *noun* money paid to finish paying something which is owed, such as money paid to an employee when his or her employment is terminated

'…the finance director of the group is to receive a payoff of about £300,000 after deciding to leave the company and pursue other business opportunities' [*Times*]

payout /ˈpeɪaʊt/ *noun* money paid to help a company or person in difficulties, a subsidy ○ *The company only exists on payouts from the government.*

'…after a period of recession followed by a rapid boost in incomes, many tax payers embarked upon some tax planning to minimize their payouts' [*Australian Financial Review*]

payout ratio /ˈpeɪaʊt ˌreɪʃiəʊ/ *noun* the percentage of a company's earnings that it pays out in dividends (NOTE: The opposite is **dividend cover**.)

pay packet /ˈpeɪ ˌpækɪt/ *noun* wages or salary, or an envelope containing cash wages and a pay slip

pay review /ˈpeɪ rɪˌvjuː/ *noun* an occasion when an employee's salary is considered and usually increased ○ *I'm soon due for a pay review and hope to get a rise.*

pay rise /ˈpeɪ raɪz/ *noun* an increase in pay

payroll /ˈpeɪrəʊl/ *noun* **1.** the list of people employed and paid by a company ○ *The company has 250 on the payroll.* **2.** the money paid by a company in salaries ○ *The office has a weekly payroll of £10,000.*

payroll costs /ˈpeɪrəʊl kɒsts/ *plural noun* the running costs of payroll administration, as well as the actual salaries themselves

payroll giving scheme /ˌpeɪrəʊl ˈɡɪvɪŋ ˌskiːm/ *noun* a scheme by which an employee pays money to a charity directly out of his or her salary. The money is deducted by the employer and paid to the charity; the employee gets tax relief on such donations.

payroll ledger /ˈpeɪrəʊl ˌledʒə/ *noun* a list of staff and their salaries

payroll register /ˈpeɪrəʊl ˌredʒɪstə/ *noun* a central register of payroll information

payroll tax /ˈpeɪrəʊl tæks/ *noun* a tax on the people employed by a company

pay scale /ˈpeɪ skeɪl/ *noun* a hierarchy of wage levels, typically varying according to job title, salary or length of service. Also called **salary scale**, **wage scale**

pay slip /ˈpeɪ slɪp/, **pay statement** /ˈpeɪ ˌsteɪtmənt/ *noun* a piece of paper showing the full amount of an employee's pay, and the money deducted as tax, pension and National Insurance contributions

pay threshold /ˈpeɪ ˌθreʃhəʊld/ *noun* a point at which pay increases because of a threshold agreement

PBIT *abbreviation* profit before interest and tax

P/C *abbreviation* petty cash

P/E *abbreviation* price/earnings

pecuniary /pɪˈkjuːniəri/ *adjective* referring to money

peg /peɡ/ *verb* to maintain or fix something at a specific level

penalise /ˈpiːnəlaɪz/, **penalize** *verb* to punish or fine someone ○ *to penalise a supplier for late deliveries* ○ *They were penalised for bad time-keeping.*

penalty /ˈpen(ə)lti/ *noun* **1.** a punishment, often a fine, which is imposed if something is not done or is done incorrectly or illegally **2.** an arbitrary pre-arranged sum that becomes payable if one party breaks a term of a contract or an undertaking. The most common penalty is a high rate of interest on an unauthorised overdraft.

penetration pricing /ˌpenɪˈtreɪʃ(ə)n ˌpraɪsɪŋ/ *noun* the practice of pricing a product low enough to achieve market penetration ○ *Penetration pricing is helping us acquire a bigger market share at the expense of short-term profits.*

pension /ˈpenʃən/ *noun* money paid regularly to someone who no longer works

pensionable /ˈpenʃənəb(ə)l/ *adjective* able to receive a pension

pensionable earnings /ˌpenʃənəb(ə)l ˈɜːnɪŋz/ *plural noun* earnings being received at the moment of retirement, on which the pension is calculated

pension contributions /ˈpenʃən kɒntrɪˌbjuːʃ(ə)nz/ *plural noun* money paid by a company or employee into a pension fund

pension entitlement /ˈpenʃən ɪnˌtaɪt(ə)lmənt/ *noun* the amount of pension which someone has the right to receive when he or she retires

pensioner /ˈpenʃənə/ *noun* a person who receives a pension

pension fund /ˈpenʃən fʌnd/ *noun* a large sum of money made up of contributions from employees and their employer which provides pensions for retired employees

pension funds /'penʃən fʌndz/ *plural noun* investments managed by pension companies to produce pensions for investors

pension income /'penʃən ˌɪnkʌm/ *noun* income which you receive from a pension scheme

pension scheme /'penʃən skiːm/, **pension plan** /'penʃən plæn/ *noun* an arrangement by which an employer and, usually, an employee pay into a fund that is invested to provide the employee with a pension on retirement

PEP *abbreviation* Personal Equity Plan

per /pɜː, pə/ *preposition* **1.** □ **as per** according to **2.** for each □ **we pay £10 per hour** we pay £10 for each hour worked □ **the earnings per share** the dividend received for each share □ **the average sales per representative** the average sales achieved by one representative

'...a 100,000 square-foot warehouse generates $600 in sales per square foot of space' [*Duns Business Month*]

PER *abbreviation* price/earnings ratio

per annum /pər 'ænəm/ *adverb* in a year ○ *What is their turnover per annum?* ○ *What is his total income per annum?* ○ *She earns over £100,000 per annum.*

P/E ratio /ˌpiː 'iː ˌreɪʃiəʊ/ *noun* same as **price/earnings ratio**

per capita /pə 'kæpɪtə/ *adjective, adverb* for each person

per capita income /pə ˌkæpɪtə 'ɪnkʌm/ *noun* **1.** the average income of one person. Also called **income per capita**, **income per head 2.** the average income of each member of a particular group of people, e.g., the citizens of a country

per cent /pə 'sent/ *adjective, adverb* out of each hundred, or for each hundred

'...this would represent an 18 per cent growth rate – a slight slackening of the 25 per cent turnover rise in the first half' [*Financial Times*]

'...buildings are depreciated at two per cent per annum on the estimated cost of construction' [*Hongkong Standard*]

percentage /pə'sentɪdʒ/ *noun* an amount shown as part of one hundred

'...state-owned banks cut their prime rates a percentage point to 11%' [*Wall Street Journal*]

'...a good percentage of the excess stock was taken up during the last quarter' [*Australian Financial Review*]

'...the Federal Reserve Board, signalling its concern about the weakening American economy, cut the discount rate by one-half percentage point to 6.5%' [*Wall Street Journal*]

percentage discount /pəˌsentɪdʒ 'dɪskaʊnt/ *noun* a discount calculated at an amount per hundred

percentage increase /pəˌsentɪdʒ 'ɪnkriːs/ *noun* an increase calculated on the basis of a rate for one hundred

percentage point /pə'sentɪdʒ pɔɪnt/ *noun* 1 per cent

percentile /pə'sentaɪl/ *noun* one of a series of ninety-nine figures below which a percentage of the total falls

per day /pə 'deɪ/, **per diem** /ˌpɜː 'diːem/ *adverb* for each day

perform /pə'fɔːm/ *verb* to do well or badly

performance /pə'fɔːməns/ *noun* **1.** the way in which someone or something acts ○ *Last year saw a dip in the company's performance.* □ **performance of staff against objectives** how staff have worked, measured against the objectives set **2.** the way in which a share increases in value

'...inflation-adjusted GNP edged up at a 1.3% annual rate, its worst performance since the economic expansion began' [*Fortune*]

performance audit /pə'fɔːməns ˌɔːdɪt/ *noun* an investigation into the efficiency of a particular area of an organisation, or of the organisation as a whole

performance rating /pə'fɔːməns ˌreɪtɪŋ/ *noun* a judgment of how well a share or a company has performed

performance report /pə'fɔːməns rɪˌpɔːt/ *noun* a report of the findings of a performance audit

per head /pə 'hed/ *adverb* for each person ○ *Allow £15 per head for expenses.* ○ *Representatives cost on average £50,000 per head per annum.*

period bill /'pɪəriəd bɪl/ *noun* a bill of exchange payable on a certain date rather than on demand. Also known as **term bill**

period cost /'pɪəriəd kɒst/ *noun* a fixed cost, such as rent or insurance, which is related to a period of time

period end /'pɪəriəd end/ *noun* the date which marks the end of a particular accounting period, e.g. the end of the financial year

periodicity concept /ˌpɪəriə'dɪsɪti ˌkɒnsept/ *noun* a legal requirement that states that entities must produce required financial documentation at agreed times

periodic stock check /ˌpɪəriɒdɪk 'stɒk ˌtʃek/ *noun* the counting of stock at some point in time, usually at the end of an accounting period

periodic weighted average cost /ˌpɪəriɒdɪk ˌweɪtɪd ˌæv(ə)rɪdʒ 'kɒst/, **periodic weighted average price** /ˌpɪəriɒdɪk ˌweɪtɪd ˌæv(ə)rɪdʒ 'praɪs/ *noun* the average price per unit of stock delivered in a period calculated at the end of the period. Compare **cumulative weighted average cost**

period of account /ˌpɪəriəd əv ə'kaʊnt/ *noun* the period usually covered by a firm's accounts

period of qualification /ˌpɪəriəd əv ˌkwɒlɪfɪ'keɪʃ(ə)n/ *noun* the time which has to pass before someone qualifies for something

perk /pɜːk/ *noun* an extra item given by a company to employees in addition to their salaries, e.g. company cars or private health insurance (*informal*) ○ *She earns a good salary and in addition has all sorts of perks.*

perpetual inventory system /pɜː ˌpetjʊəl 'ɪnventəri ˌsɪstəm/ *noun* a stock control system by which the stock is continually counted as it moves into and out of the warehouse, so avoiding having to close the warehouse for annual stock checks. Abbreviation **PIS**

perpetuity /ˌpɜːpɪt'juːɪti/ *noun* same as **annuity**

perquisite /'pɜːkwɪzɪt/ *noun* same as **perk**

personal /'pɜːs(ə)n(ə)l/ *adjective* referring to one person □ **apart from the family shares, she has a personal shareholding in the company** apart from shares belonging to her family as a group, she has shares which she owns herself

personal account /'pɜːs(ə)n(ə)l ə ˌkaʊnt/ *noun* an account for recording amounts receivable from or payable to a person or an entity. ◊ **impersonal account**

personal allowance /ˌpɜːs(ə)n(ə)l ə 'laʊəns/ *noun* a part of a person's income which is not taxed

personal assets /ˌpɜːs(ə)n(ə)l 'æsets/ *plural noun* movable assets which belong to a person

Personal Equity Plan /ˌpɜːs(ə)nəl 'ekwɪti plæn/ *noun* a share-based investment replaced by the ISA in 1999. Abbreviation **PEP**

personal financial planning /ˌpɜːs(ə)n(ə)l faɪˌnænʃəl 'plænɪŋ/ *noun* short- and long-term financial planning by

an individual, either independently or with the assistance of a professional adviser. It will include the use of tax efficient schemes such as Individual Savings Accounts, ensuring adequate provisions are being made for retirement, and examining short- and long-term borrowing requirements such as overdrafts and mortgages.

Personal Identification Number /ˌpɜːs(ə)n(ə)l aɪˌdentɪfɪ'keɪʃ(ə)n ˌnʌmbə/ *noun* a unique number allocated to the holder of a cash card or credit card, by which he or she can enter an automatic banking system, as e.g., to withdraw cash from a cash machine or to pay in a store. Abbreviation **PIN**

personal income /ˌpɜːs(ə)n(ə)l 'ɪnkʌm/ *noun* the income received by an individual person before tax is paid

Personal Investment Authority /ˌpɜːs(ə)nəl ɪn'vestmənt ɔːˌθɒrəti/ *noun* a self-regulatory body which regulates the activities of financial advisers, insurance brokers and others who give financial advice or arrange financial services for small clients. Abbreviation **PIA**

personal loan /ˌpɜːs(ə)nəl 'ləʊn/ *noun* a loan to a person for household or other personal use, not for business use

personal pension plan /ˌpɜːs(ə)n(ə)l 'penʃən ˌplæn/ *noun* a pension plan which applies to one employee only, usually a self-employed person, not to a group. Abbreviation **PPP**

personal property /ˌpɜːs(ə)n(ə)l 'prɒpəti/ *noun* things which belong to a person ○ *The fire caused considerable damage to personal property.*

personal representative /ˌpɜːs(ə)n(ə)l ˌreprɪ'zentətɪv/ *noun* a person who is the executor of a will or the administrator of the estate of a deceased person

PERT /pɜːt/ *abbreviation* programme evaluation and review technique

petroleum revenues /pə'trəʊliəm ˌrevənjuːz/ *plural noun* income from selling oil

petroleum revenue tax /pəˌtrəʊliəm 'revənjuː ˌtæks/ *noun* a British tax on revenues from companies extracting oil from the North Sea. Abbreviation **PRT**

petty cash /ˌpeti 'kæʃ/ *noun* a small amount of money kept in an office to pay small debts. Abbreviation **P/C**

petty cash voucher /ˌpeti 'kæʃ ˌvaʊtʃə/ *noun* a piece of paper on which cash expenditure is noted so that an employee can be reimbursed for what he or she has spent on company business

petty expenses /ˌpeti ɪkˈspensɪz/ *plural noun* small sums of money spent

phase /feɪz/ *noun* a period or part of something which takes place ○ *the first phase of the expansion programme*

phase in *phrasal verb* to bring something in gradually ○ *The new invoicing system will be phased in over the next two months.*

'…the budget grants a tax exemption for $500,000 in capital gains, phased in over the next six years' [*Toronto Star*]

phase out *phrasal verb* to remove something gradually ○ *Smith Ltd will be phased out as a supplier of spare parts.*

phoenix company /ˈfiːnɪks ˌkʌmp(ə)ni/ *noun* a company formed by the directors of a company which has gone into receivership, which trades in the same way as the first company, and in most respects (except its name) seems to be exactly the same as the first company

'…the prosecution follows recent calls for a reform of insolvency legislation to prevent directors from leaving behind a trail of debt while continuing to trade in phoenix companies – businesses which fold only to rise again, often under a slightly different name in the hands of the same directors and management' [*Financial Times*]

physical asset /ˌfɪzɪk(ə)l ˈæset/ *noun* an asset that is a physically existing thing, as opposed to cash or securities

physical inventory /ˌfɪzɪk(ə)l ˈɪnvənt(ə)ri/ *noun US* same as **physical stock**

physical market /ˌfɪzɪk(ə)l ˈmɑːkɪt/ *noun* a commodity market where purchasers actually buy the commodities, as opposed to the futures market, where they buy and sell the right to purchase commodities at a future date

physical price /ˌfɪzɪk(ə)l ˈpraɪs/ *noun* a current cash price for a commodity for immediate delivery

physicals /ˈfɪzɪk(ə)lz/ *plural noun* actual commodities which are sold on the current market, as opposed to futures

physical stock /ˌfɪzɪk(ə)l ˈstɒk/ *noun* the actual items of stock held in a warehouse

PIA *abbreviation* Personal Investment Authority

piece rate /ˈpiːs reɪt/ *noun* a rate of pay calculated as an amount for each product produced or for each piece of work done,

and not as an amount for each hour worked ○ *to earn piece rates*

piecework /ˈpiːswɜːk/ *noun* work for which employees are paid in accordance with the number of products produced or pieces of work done and not at an hourly rate

pie chart /ˈpaɪ tʃɑːt/ *noun* a diagram where information is shown as a circle cut up into sections of different sizes

pilferage /ˈpɪlfərɪdʒ/, **pilfering** /ˈpɪlfərɪŋ/ *noun* the stealing of small amounts of money or small items from an office or shop

PIN /pɪn/ *abbreviation* Personal Identification Number

PIS *abbreviation* perpetual inventory system

placement /ˈpleɪsmənt/ *noun* **1.** the act of finding work for someone ○ *The bureau specialises in the placement of former executives.* **2.** *US* the act of finding buyers for an issue of new shares (NOTE: The UK term is **placing.**)

placing /ˈpleɪsɪŋ/ *noun* the act of finding a single buyer or a group of institutional buyers for a large number of shares in a new company or a company that is going public

plain vanilla swap /ˌpleɪn vəˌnɪlə ˈswɒp/ *noun* same as **interest rate swap**

plan /plæn/ *noun* **1.** an organised way of doing something ○ *an investment plan* ○ *a pension plan* ○ *a savings plan* **2.** a way of saving or investing money ■ *verb* to organise carefully how something should be done in the future

'…the benefits package is attractive and the compensation plan includes base, incentive and car allowance totalling $50,000+' [*Globe and Mail (Toronto)*]

plan comptable /ˌplɒn kɒmˈtɑːblə/ *noun* in France, a uniformly structured and detailed bookkeeping system that companies are required to comply with

planned economy /ˌplænd ɪˈkɒnəmi/ *noun* a system where the government plans all business activity, regulates supply, sets production targets and itemises work to be done. Also called **command economy**, **central planning**

planned obsolescence /ˌplænd ˌɒbsəˈles(ə)ns/ *noun* same as **built-in obsolescence** ○ *Planned obsolescence was condemned by the consumer organisation as a cynical marketing ploy.*

plant and machinery /ˌplɑːnt ən məˈʃiːnəri/ *noun* equipment used to help someone trade such as trucks, tools, office furniture, computers, ladders, etc.

plant asset /'plɑːnt ˌæset/ *noun* any fixed asset such as machinery

plant ledger /'plɑːnt ˌledʒə/ *noun* a ledger that records information relating to specific items of plant, including information on replacements and repairs

plastic /'plæstɪk/ *noun* credit cards and charge cards (*informal*)

Plc, PLC, plc *abbreviation* public limited company

plus /plʌs/ *preposition* added to ○ *Her salary plus commission comes to more than £45,000.* ○ *Production costs plus overheads are higher than revenue.* ■ *adverb* more than □ **houses valued at £100,000 plus** houses valued at over £100,000

pocket /'pɒkɪt/ *noun* □ **to be £25 in pocket** to have made a profit of £25 □ **to be £25 out of pocket** to have lost £25

point /pɔɪnt/ *noun* **1.** a place or position **2.** a unit for calculations □ **government stocks rose by one point** they rose by £1

poison pill /ˌpɔɪz(ə)n 'pɪl/ *noun* an action taken by a company to make itself less attractive to a potential takeover bid

policy cost /'pɒlɪsi kɒst/ *noun* a fixed cost, such as advertising cost, which is governed by the management's policy on the amount of advertising to be done

portable pension /ˌpɔːtəb(ə)l 'penʃən/, **portable pension plan** /ˌpɔːtəb(ə)l 'penʃən plæn/ *noun* a pension entitlement which can be moved from one company to another without loss as an employee changes jobs

portfolio investments /pɔːtˌfəʊliəʊ ɪn 'vestmənts/ *plural noun* investments in shares and government stocks, as opposed to investments in property, etc.

portfolio management /pɔːt'fəʊliəʊ ˌmænɪdʒmənt/ *noun* the systematic buying and selling shares in order to make the highest-possible profits for a single investor

portfolio theory /pɔːt'fəʊliəʊ ˌθɪəri/ *noun* a basis for managing a portfolio of investments, i.e. a mix of safe stocks and more risky ones

position /pə'zɪʃ(ə)n/ *noun* **1.** a situation or state of affairs **2.** a point of view **3.** a job or paid work in a company ○ *to apply for a position as manager* ○ *We have several positions vacant.* **4.** the state of a person's current financial holding in a stock

position audit /pə'zɪʃ(ə)n ˌɔːdɪt/ *noun* part of the planning process which examines the current state of an entity in respect of the following: resources of tangible and intangible assets and finance; products, brands and

markets; operating systems such as production and distribution; internal organisation; current results; and returns to stockholders

positive carry /ˌpɒzɪtɪv 'kæri/ *noun* a situation in which the cost of financing an investment is less than the return obtained from it

positive cash flow /ˌpɒzɪtɪv 'kæʃ fləʊ/ *noun* a situation in which more money is coming into a company than is going out

positive confirmation /ˌpɒzɪtɪv ˌkɒnfə 'meɪʃ(ə)n/ *noun* an auditor's request to have financial information confirmed as accurate, to which a reply must be sent, not only in the case of a discrepancy

positive goodwill /ˌpɒzɪtɪv gʊd'wɪl/ *noun* the position of a company that has assets for which the acquisition costs exceed the values of the identifiable assets and liabilities

positive yield curve /ˌpɒzɪtɪv 'jiːld ˌkɜːv/ *noun* a situation where the yield on a short-term investment is less than that on a long-term investment

possess /pə'zes/ *verb* to own something ○ *The company possesses property in the centre of the town.* ○ *He lost all he possessed in the collapse of his company.* Compare **repossess**

possession /pə'zeʃ(ə)n/ *noun* the fact of owning or having something

possessions /pə'zeʃ(ə)nz/ *plural noun* property, things owned ○ *They lost all their possessions in the fire.* Compare **repossession**

post-acquisition /pəʊst ˌækwɪ'zɪʃ(ə)n/ *adjective* taking place after a company has been acquired

post-acquisition profit /ˌpəʊst ˌækwɪ ˌzɪʃ(ə)n 'prɒfɪt/ *noun* a profit of a subsidiary company in the period after it has been acquired, which is treated as revenue and transferred to the consolidated reserves of the holding company

post a credit /ˌpəʊst ə 'kredɪt/ *verb* to enter a credit item in a ledger

post-balance sheet event /ˌpəʊst ˌbæləns ʃiːt ɪ'vent/ *noun* something which happens after the date when the balance sheet is drawn up, and before the time when the balance sheet is officially approved by the directors, which affects a company's financial position

post balance-sheet review /ˌpəʊst 'bæləns ʃiːt rɪˌvjuː/ *noun* those procedures of an audit that relate to the interval between the date of the financial statements and the completion date of the audit fieldwork

postdate /ˌpəʊstˈdeɪt/ *verb* to put a later date on a document ○ *He sent us a postdated cheque.* ○ *Her cheque was postdated to June.*

post-purchase costs /ˌpəʊst ˈpɜːtʃɪs ˌkɒsts/ *plural noun* costs incurred after a capital expenditure decision has been implemented and facilities acquired. These costs may include training, maintenance and the cost of upgrades.

pound /paʊnd/ *noun* **1.** a measure of weight (= 0.45 kilos) ○ *to sell oranges by the pound* ○ *a pound of oranges* ○ *Oranges cost 50p a pound.* (NOTE: Usually written **lb** after a figure: **25lb**. Note also that the pound is now no longer officially used in the UK) **2.** a unit of currency used in the UK and many other countries including Cyprus, Egypt, Lebanon, Malta, Sudan, Syria and, before the euro, Ireland

poundage /ˈpaʊndɪdʒ/ *noun* a rate charged per pound in weight

pound-cost averaging /ˌpaʊnd kɒst ˈæv(ə)rɪdʒɪŋ/ *noun* the practice of buying securities at different times, but always spending the same amount of money

pound sterling /ˌpaʊnd ˈstɜːlɪŋ/ *noun* the official term for the UK currency

power /ˈpaʊə/ *noun* **1.** strength or ability **2.** a force or legal right **3.** a mathematical term describing the number of times a number is to be multiplied by itself ○ *5 to the power 2 is equal to 25* (NOTE: written as small figures in superscript: **10^5**. Say: 'ten to the power five')

power of attorney /ˌpaʊər əv əˈtɜːni/ *noun* a legal document which gives someone the right to act on someone's behalf in legal matters

PPI *abbreviation* producers' price index

PPP *abbreviation* personal pension plan

pre-acquisition profits /ˌpriː ˌækwɪzɪʃən ˈprɒfɪts/ *plural noun* profits of a company in the part of its accounting period before it was acquired by another company. Under acquisition accounting methods, the holding company deducts these profits from the combined reserves of the group.

pre-acquisition write-down /ˌpriː ˌækwɪzɪʃən ˈraɪt ˌdaʊn/ *noun* a reduction in the fair value of a new subsidiary in the balance sheet of a holding company against the potential future costs or the possible revaluation of the subsidiary's assets after acquisition

prebilling /priːˈbɪlɪŋ/ *noun* the practice of submitting a bill for a product or service before it has actually been delivered

preceding year /prɪˌsiːdɪŋ ˈjɪə/ *noun* the year before the accounting year in question □ **taxed on a preceding year basis** tax on income or capital gains arising in the previous year is payable in the current year

pre-emption right /priːˈempʃən raɪt/ *noun* the right of an existing shareholder to be first to buy a new stock issue

pre-emptive /ˌpriː ˈemptɪv/ *adjective* done before anyone else takes action in order to stop something happening

preference dividend /ˈpref(ə)rəns ˌdɪvɪdend/ *noun* a dividend paid on preference shares

preference shares /ˈpref(ə)rəns ʃeəz/ *plural noun* shares, often with no voting rights, which receive their dividend before all other shares and are repaid first at face value if the company goes into liquidation (NOTE: The US term is **preferred stock**.)

preferential creditor /ˌprefərenʃ(ə)l ˈkredɪtə/ *noun* a creditor who must be paid first if a company is in liquidation. Also called **preferred creditor**

preferential debt /ˌprefərenʃ(ə)l ˈdet/ *noun* a debt which is paid before all others

preferential payment /ˌprefərenʃəl ˈpeɪmənt/ *noun* a payment to a preferential creditor

preferential shares /ˌprefəˈrenʃ(ə)l ʃeəz/ *plural noun* shares which are part of a new issue and are set aside for the employees of the company

preferred creditor /prɪˌfɜːd ˈkredɪtə/ *noun* same as **preferential creditor**

preferred shares /prɪˌfɜːd ˈʃeəz/, **preferred stock** /prɪˌfɜːd ˈstɒk/ *plural noun* same as **preference shares**

pre-financing /ˌpriː ˈfaɪnænsɪŋ/ *noun* money paid in advance by customers to help finance a project the future products of which the customer contracts to buy by making additional payments

preliminary announcement /prɪˌlɪmɪn(ə)ri əˈnaʊnsmənt/ *noun* an announcement of a company's full-year results, given out to the press before the detailed annual report is released

preliminary audit /prɪˌlɪmɪn(ə)ri ˈɔːdɪt/ *noun* audit fieldwork carried out before the end of the accounting period in question

preliminary prospectus /prɪˌlɪmɪn(ə)ri prəˈspektəs/ *noun* same as **pathfinder prospectus**

premium /'pri:miəm/ *noun* **1.** a regular payment made to an insurance company for the protection provided by an insurance policy **2.** an amount to be paid to a landlord or a tenant for the right to take over a lease ○ *flat to let with a premium of £10,000 ○ annual rent: £8,500, premium: £25,000* **3.** an extra sum of money in addition to a usual charge, wage, price or other amount **4.** a gift, discount or other incentive to encourage someone to buy

premium bond /'pri:miəm bɒnd/ *noun* a government bond, part of the National Savings and Investment scheme, which pays no interest, but gives the owner the chance to win a weekly or monthly prize

premium income /ˌpri:miəm 'ɪnkʌm/ *noun* income which an insurance company derives from premiums paid by insured persons

premium on redemption /ˌpri:miəm ɒn rɪ'dempʃən/ *noun* an extra amount above the nominal value of a share or debenture paid to the holder by a company buying back its share or loan stock

prepaid expenses /pri:ˌpeɪd ɪk 'spensɪz/ *plural noun* expenditure on items such as rent, which is made in one accounting period but covers part of the next period also

prepaid interest /pri:ˌpeɪd 'ɪntrəst/ *noun* interest paid in advance of its due date

prepay /pri:'peɪ/ *verb* to pay something in advance (NOTE: **prepaying – prepaid**)

prepayment /pri:'peɪmənt/ *noun* **1.** a payment in advance, or the act of paying in advance **2.** *US* the repayment of the principal of a loan before it is due

prepayment penalty /pri:'peɪmənt ˌpen(ə)lti/ *noun US* a charge levied on someone who repays a loan such as a mortgage before it is due

present value /ˌprez(ə)nt 'vælju:/ *noun* **1.** the value something has now ○ *In 1984 the pound was worth five times its present value.* **2.** the value now of a specified sum of money to be received in the future, if invested at current interest rates. Abbreviation **PV 3.** a price which a share must reach in the future to be the equivalent of today's price, taking inflation into account

preservation of capital /ˌprezəveɪʃ(ə)n əv 'kæpɪt(ə)l/ *noun* an approach to financial management that protects a person's or company's capital by arranging additional forms of finance

pretax /'pri:tæks/, **pre-tax** *adjective* before tax has been deducted or paid

'...the company's goals are a growth in sales of up to 40 per cent, a rise in pre-tax earnings of nearly 35 per cent and a rise in after-tax earnings of more than 25 per cent' [*Citizen (Ottawa)*]

'EC regulations which came into effect in July insist that customers can buy cars anywhere in the EC at the local pre-tax price' [*Financial Times*]

pretax profit /ˌpri:tæks 'prɒfɪt/ *noun* the amount of profit a company makes before taxes are deducted ○ *The dividend paid is equivalent to one quarter of the pretax profit.* Also called **profit before tax**, **profit on ordinary activities before tax**

pretax profit margin /ˌpri:tæks 'prɒfɪt ˌmɑ:dʒɪn/ *noun* the pretax profit shown as a percentage of turnover in a profit and loss account

preventive costs /prɪ'ventɪv kɒsts/ *plural noun* those costs incurred in seeking to prevent defects in products and services supplied, e.g. the cost of training programmes

previous balance /ˌpri:viəs 'bæləns/ *noun* a balance in an account at the end of the accounting period before the current one

price /praɪs/ *noun* money which has to be paid to buy something □ **cars in the £18–19,000 price range** cars of different makes, selling for between £18,000 and £19,000 ■ *verb* to give a price to a product ○ *We have two used cars for sale, both priced at £5,000.*

price ceiling /'praɪs ˌsi:lɪŋ/ *noun* a limit beyond which prices will not or cannot rise

price change /'praɪs tʃeɪndʒ/ *noun* an amount by which the price of a share moves during a day's trading

price controls /'praɪs kənˌtrəʊlz/ *plural noun* legal measures to prevent prices rising too fast

price cutting /'praɪs ˌkʌtɪŋ/ *noun* a sudden lowering of prices

'...in today's circumstances, price-cutting is inevitable in an attempt to build up market share' [*Marketing Week*]

price-cutting war /'praɪs ˌkʌtɪŋ wɔ:/ *noun* same as **price war**

price differential /'praɪs dɪfəˌrenʃəl/ *noun* the difference in price between products in a range

price/earnings ratio /ˌpraɪs 'ɜ:nɪŋz ˌreɪʃiəʊ/ *noun* a ratio between the current market price of a share of stock and the earnings per share (the current dividend it produces), calculated by dividing the market price by the earnings per share ○ *These* *shares sell at a P/E ratio of 7* Also called **P/E ratio**. Abbreviation **PER**

price fixing /'praɪs ˌfɪksɪŋ/ *noun* an illegal agreement between companies to charge the same price for competing products

price-insensitive /ˌpraɪs ɪn'sensətɪv/ *adjective* used to describe a good or service for which sales remain constant no matter what its price because it is essential to buyers

price range /'praɪs reɪndʒ/ *noun* a series of prices for similar products from different suppliers

price-to-sales ratio /ˌpraɪs tə 'seɪlz ˌreɪʃiəʊ/ *noun* the ratio of the total value of a company's shares to its sales for the previous twelve months

price variance /'praɪs ˌveəriəns/ *noun* the discrepancy between the actual price of a unit produced and the standard price

price war /'praɪs wɔː/ *noun* a competition between companies to get a larger market share by cutting prices. Also called **price-cutting war**

pricing /'praɪsɪŋ/ *noun* the act of giving a price to a product

pricing model /'praɪsɪŋ ˌmɒd(ə)l/ *noun* a computerised system for calculating a price, based on costs, anticipated margins, etc.

pricing policy /'praɪsɪŋ ˌpɒlisi/ *noun* a company's policy in giving prices to its products ○ *Our pricing policy aims at producing a 35% gross margin.*

primary commodities /ˌpraɪməri kə 'mɒdɪtiz/ *plural noun* farm produce grown in large quantities, e.g. corn, rice or cotton

primary industry /ˌpraɪməri 'ɪndəstri/ *noun* an industry dealing with basic raw materials such as coal, wood, or farm produce

prime /praɪm/ *adjective* **1.** most important **2.** basic ■ *noun* same as **prime rate**

prime bills /ˌpraɪm 'bɪlz/ *plural noun* bills of exchange which do not involve any risk

prime cost /ˌpraɪm 'kɒst/ *noun* the cost involved in producing a product, excluding overheads

prime rate /'praɪm reɪt/ *noun US* the best rate of interest at which a bank lends to its customers. Also called **prime**

prime sites /ˌpraɪm 'saɪts/ *plural noun* the most valuable commercial sites, i.e. in main shopping streets. Compare **secondary sites**

priming /'praɪmɪŋ/ *noun* ♦ **pump priming**

principal /'prɪnsɪp(ə)l/ *noun* **1.** a person or company that is represented by an agent ○ *The agent has come to London to see his principals.* **2.** a person acting for him or herself, such as a marketmaker buying securities on his or her own account **3.** money invested or borrowed on which interest is paid ○ *to repay principal and interest* ○ *We try to repay part of principal each month.* (NOTE: Do not confuse with **principle**.) ■ *adjective* most important ○ *The principal shareholders asked for a meeting.* ○ *The country's principal products are paper and wood.* ○ *The company's principal asset is its design staff.*

'…the company was set up with funds totalling NorKr 145m with the principal aim of making capital gains on the second-hand market' [*Lloyd's List*]

prior charge percentage /ˌpraɪə 'tʃɑːdʒ pəˌsentɪdʒ/ *noun* same as **priority percentage**

priority /praɪ'ɒriti/ *noun* □ **to have priority over** *or* **to take priority over something** to be more important than something ○ *Reducing overheads takes priority over increasing turnover.* ○ *Debenture holders have priority over ordinary shareholders.*

priority percentage /praɪˌɒriti pə 'sentɪdʒ/ *noun* the proportion of a business's net profit that is paid in interest to preference shareholders and holders of debt capital. Also called **prior charge percentage**

prior period adjustment /'praɪə ˌpɪəriəd əˌdʒʌstmənt/ *noun* a change in the revenue or expenses for a previous accounting period, introduced in order to correct an error or to apply a new accounting policy

prior year adjustments /ˌpraɪə jɪər ə 'dʒʌstmənts/ *plural noun* adjustments made to accounts for previous years, because of changes in accounting policies or because of errors

private /'praɪvət/ *adjective* belonging to a single person or to individual people, not to a company or the state □ **a letter marked 'private and confidential'** a letter which must not be opened by anyone other than the person it is addressed to □ **to sell (a house) by private treaty** to sell (a house) to another person not by auction

private bank /ˌpraɪvət 'bæŋk/ *noun* **1.** a bank that is owned by a single person or a limited number of private shareholders **2.** a bank that provides banking facilities to high net worth individuals. ◊ **private banking**

private banking /ˌpraɪvət ˈbæŋkɪŋ/ *noun* a service offered by certain financial institutions to high net worth individuals. In addition to standard banking services, it will typically include portfolio management and advisory services on taxation, including estate planning.

private company /ˌpraɪvət ˈkʌmp(ə)ni/ *noun* a registered company whose shares are not offered for sale to the public

private debt /ˌpraɪvət ˈdet/ *noun* money owed by individuals and organisations other than governments

private enterprise /ˌpraɪvət ˈentəpraɪz/ *noun* businesses that are owned privately, not nationalised ○ *The project is completely funded by private enterprise.*

private income /ˌpraɪvət ˈɪnkʌm/ *noun* income from dividends, interest or rent which is not part of a salary

private investor /ˌpraɪvət ɪnˈvestə/ *noun* an ordinary person with money to invest

private limited company /ˌpraɪvət ˌlɪmɪtɪd ˈkʌmp(ə)ni/ *noun* **1.** a company with a small number of shareholders, whose shares are not traded on the Stock Exchange **2.** a subsidiary company whose shares are not listed on the Stock Exchange, while those of its parent company are ▶ abbreviation **Pty Ltd**

privately held company /ˌpraɪvətli held ˈkʌmp(ə)ni/ *noun US* company controlled by a few shareholders or its directors. Also called **closed corporation**

private ownership /ˌpraɪvət ˈəʊnəʃɪp/ *noun* a situation in which a company is owned by private shareholders

private placement /ˌpraɪvət ˈpleɪsmənt/ *noun* the sale of securities for the purpose of investment, not for resale

private placing /ˌpraɪvət ˈpleɪsɪŋ/, **private placement** /ˌpraɪvət ˈpleɪsmənt/ *noun* the act of placing a new issue of shares with a group of selected financial institutions

private practice /ˌpraɪvət ˈpræktɪs/ *noun* accounting services offered to clients, as opposed to accounting work carried out as an employee of a company

private property /ˌpraɪvət ˈprɒpəti/ *noun* property which belongs to a private person, not to the public

private sector /ˈpraɪvət ˌsektə/ *noun* one of the parts of the economy of a country, which itself is made up of the corporate sector (firms owned by private shareholders), the personal sector (individuals and their income and expenditure), and the financial sector (banks and other institutions dealing in money) ○ *The expansion is completely funded by the private sector.* ○ *Salaries in the private sector have increased faster than in the public sector.*

'…in the private sector the total number of new house starts was 3 per cent higher than in the corresponding period last year, while public sector starts were 23 per cent lower' [*Financial Times*]

private treaty /ˌpraɪvət ˈtriːti/ *noun* an agreement between individual persons

probability /ˌprɒbəˈbɪlɪti/ *noun* the likelihood that something will happen, expressed mathematically

probability distribution /ˌprɒbəˈbɪləti ˌdɪstrɪbjuːʃ(ə)n/ *noun* a mathematical formula that shows the probability for each value of a variable in a statistical study

probate /ˈprəʊbeɪt/ *noun* legal acceptance that a document, especially a will, is valid □ **the executor was granted probate** *or* **obtained a grant of probate** the executor was told officially that the will was valid

procedural audit /prəˈsiːdʒərəl ˌɔːdɪt/ *noun* the process of evaluating all policies, controls and other procedures of a business

procedure /prəˈsiːdʒə/ *noun* a way in which something is done ○ *The inquiry found that the company had not followed the approved procedures.*

'…this was a serious breach of disciplinary procedure and the dismissal was unfair' [*Personnel Management*]

proceeds /ˈprəʊsiːdz/ *plural noun* money received from selling something

process /ˈprəʊses/ *verb* to deal with something in the usual routine way ○ *It usually takes at least two weeks to process an insurance claim.* ○ *Orders are processed in our warehouse.*

process costing /ˈprəʊses ˌkɒstɪŋ/ *noun* a method of costing something which is manufactured from a series of continuous processes, where the total costs of those processes are divided by the number of units produced

process cost report /ˈprəʊses kɒst rɪ ˌpɔːt/ *noun* a set of schedules that managers use to track costs in a process costing system

processing /ˈprəʊsesɪŋ/ *noun* the act of sorting information ○ *the processing of information* or *of statistics by a computer*

producer /prəˈdjuːsə/ *noun* same as **supplier** ○ *a country which is a producer of high-quality watches* ○ *The company is a major car producer.*

producers' price index /prə,djuːsə 'praɪs ˌɪndeks/ *noun US* a measure of the annual increase in the prices of goods and services charged by producers which is used to indicate the rate of inflation in the US economy. Abbreviation **PPI**

product /'prɒdʌkt/ *noun* **1.** something which is made or manufactured **2.** a manufactured item for sale

product advertising /'prɒdʌkt ˌædvətaɪzɪŋ/ *noun* the advertising of a particular named product, not the company which makes it

product analysis /'prɒdʌkt ə,næləsɪs/ *noun* an examination of each separate product in a company's range to find out why it sells, who buys it, etc.

product cost /'prɒdʌkt kɒst/ *noun* the total cost of goods produced but not yet sold

product costing system /'prɒdʌkt ˌkɒstɪŋ ˌsɪstəm/ *noun* a set of procedures that provides information on unit cost

product design /'prɒdʌkt dɪ,zaɪn/ *noun* the design of consumer products

product development /'prɒdʌkt dɪ,veləpmənt/ *noun* the process of improving an existing product line to meet the needs of the market

production /prə'dʌkʃən/ *noun* **1.** the act of showing something **2.** the work of making or manufacturing goods for sale ○ *We are hoping to speed up production by installing new machinery.* ○ *Higher production is rewarded with higher pay.*

production budget /prə'dʌkʃən ˌbʌdʒɪt/ *noun* a plan of the level of manufacturing required to satisfy budgeted sales and inventory expectations

production cost /prə'dʌkʃən kɒst/ *noun* the cost of making a product

production department /prə'dʌkʃən dɪ,pɑːtmənt/ *noun* the section of a company which deals with the making of the company's products

production line /prə'dʌkʃən laɪn/ *noun* a system of making a product, where each item such as a car moves slowly through the factory with new sections added to it as it goes along ○ *He works on the production line.* ○ *She is a production-line employee.*

production manager /prə'dʌkʃən ˌmænɪdʒə/ *noun* the person in charge of the production department

production overhead /prə'dʌkʃən ˌəʊvəhed/ *noun* the indirect costs of production which are absorbed into the cost of goods produced. Also called **factory overhead**

production target /prə'dʌkʃən ˌtɑːgɪt/ *noun* the number of units a business is expected to produce

production unit /prə'dʌkʃən ˌjuːnɪt/ *noun* a separate small group of employees producing a product

production yield variance /prə'dʌkʃən jiːld ˌveərɪəns/ *noun* a discrepancy between expected levels of productivity and actual levels, for a given amount of input

productive capital /prə,dʌktɪv 'kæpɪt(ə)l/ *noun* capital which is invested to give interest

productivity /,prɒdʌk'tɪvɪti/ *noun* the rate of output per employee, or per item of equipment, in a business ○ *Bonus payments are linked to productivity.* ○ *The company is aiming to increase productivity.* ○ *Productivity has fallen or risen since the company was taken over.*

'…though there has been productivity growth, the absolute productivity gap between many British firms and their foreign rivals remains' [*Sunday Times*]

productivity agreement /,prɒdʌk'tɪvɪti ə,griːmənt/ *noun* an agreement to pay a productivity bonus

productivity bonus /,prɒdʌk'tɪvɪti ,bəʊnəs/ *noun* an extra payment made to employees because of increased production per employee

productivity drive /,prɒdʌk'tɪvɪti draɪv/ *noun* an extra effort to increase productivity

product life cycle /,prɒdʌkt 'laɪf ,saɪk(ə)l/ *noun* stages in the life of a product in terms of sales and profitability, from its launch to its decline ○ *Growth is the first stage in the product life cycle.* ○ *The machine has reached a point in its product life cycle where we should be thinking about a replacement for it.*

product management /'prɒdʌkt ˌmænɪdʒmənt/ *noun* the process of overseeing the making and selling of a product as an independent item

product mix /'prɒdʌkt mɪks/ *noun* the range of different products which a company has for sale

product mix decisions /'prɒdʌkt mɪks dɪ,sɪʒ(ə)nz/ *plural noun* decisions about which products or services to concentrate on in order to maximise total profits

product unit cost /,prɒdʌkt 'juːnɪt ,kɒst/ *noun* the cost of manufacturing a single unit of product

profession /prə'feʃ(ə)n/ *noun* **1.** an occupation for which official qualifications are needed and which is often made a lifelong career ○ *The managing director is an accountant by profession.* ○ *HR management is now more widely recognised as a profession.* **2.** a group of specialised workers ○ *the accounting profession* ○ *the legal profession*

'…one of the key advantages of an accountancy qualification is its worldwide marketability. Other professions are not so lucky: lawyers, for example, are much more limited in where they can work' [*Accountancy*]

professional /prə'feʃ(ə)nəl/ *adjective* referring to one of the professions ○ *The accountant sent in his bill for professional services.* ○ *We had to ask our lawyer for professional advice on the contract.* □ **professional man**, **professional woman** a man or woman who works in one of the professions such as a lawyer, doctor or accountant

professional fees /prə,feʃ(ə)nəl 'fiːz/ *plural noun* fees paid to lawyers, accountants, architects, etc.

profit /'prɒfɪt/ *noun* money gained from a sale which is more than the money spent on making the item sold or on providing the service offered □ **to take your profit** to sell shares at a higher price than was paid for them, and so realise the profit, rather than to keep them as an investment □ **to make a profit** to have more money as a result of a deal

profitability /,prɒfɪtə'bɪlɪti/ *noun* **1.** the ability to make a profit ○ *We doubt the profitability of the project.* **2.** the amount of profit made as a percentage of costs

profitability index /,prɒfɪtə'bɪlɪti ,ɪndeks/ *noun* a figure that is the current estimated final value of an investment divided by the amount of the original investment

profitable /'prɒfɪtəb(ə)l/ *adjective* making a profit ○ *She runs a very profitable employment agency.*

profitably /'prɒfɪtəbli/ *adverb* making a profit ○ *The aim of every company must be to trade profitably.*

profit after tax /,prɒfɪt ɑːftə 'tæks/ *noun* same as **net profit**

profit and loss account /,prɒfɪt ənd 'lɒs ,steɪtmənt/ *noun* the accounts for a company showing expenditure and income over a period of time, usually one calendar year, balanced to show a final profit or loss.

Also called **consolidated profit and loss account**, **P&L statement**

profit before interest and tax /,prɒfɪt bɪ,fɔː ,ɪntrəst ən 'tæks/ *noun* operating profit shown before deducting interest on borrowings and tax due to the Inland Revenue. Abbreviation **PBIT**

profit before tax /,prɒfɪt bɪfɔː 'tæks/ *noun* same as **pretax profit**

profit centre /'prɒfɪt ,sentə/ *noun* a person, unit or department within an organisation which is considered separately for the purposes of calculating a profit ○ *We count the kitchen equipment division as a single profit centre.*

profit distribution /'prɒfɪt ,dɪstrɪbjuːʃ(ə)n/ *noun* the allocation of profits to different recipients such as shareholders and owners, or for different purposes such as research or investment

profiteer /,prɒfɪ'tɪə/ *noun* a person who makes too much profit, especially when goods are rationed or in short supply

profiteering /,prɒfɪ'tɪərɪŋ/ *noun* the practice of making too much profit

profit from ordinary activities /,prɒfɪt frəm ,ɔːd(ə)n(ə)ri æk'tɪvɪtiz/ *noun* profits earned in the normal course of business, as opposed to profits from extraordinary sources such as windfall payments

profit-making /'prɒfɪt ,meɪkɪŋ/ *adjective* making a profit, or operated with the primary objective of making a profit ○ *The whole project was expected to be profit-making by 2001 but it still hasn't broken even.* ○ *It is hoped to make it into a profit-making concern.*

profit margin /'prɒfɪt ,mɑːdʒɪn/ *noun* the percentage difference between sales income and the cost of sales

profit maximisation /'prɒfɪt ,mæksɪmaɪzeɪʃ(ə)n/ *noun* the notion that the aim of a business is to maximise profits

profit on ordinary activities before tax /,prɒfɪt ɒn ,ɔːd(ə)n(ə)ri æk,tɪvɪtiz bɪ ,fɔː 'tæks/ *noun* same as **pretax profit**

profit planning /'prɒfɪt ,plænɪŋ/ *noun* the process of developing a plan that outlines revenue and expenses for a given period

profit-related /'prɒfɪt rɪ,leɪtɪd/ *adjective* linked to profit

profit-related bonus /,prɒfɪt rɪ,leɪtɪd 'bəʊnəs/ *noun* a bonus paid which is related to the amount of profit a company makes

profit-related pay /ˌprɒfɪt rɪˌleɪtɪd ˈpeɪ/ noun pay including bonuses which is linked to profit

profit retained for the year /ˌprɒfɪt rɪˈteɪnɪd fə ðə ˌjɪə/ noun same as **retained earnings**

profit-sharing /ˈprɒfɪt ˌʃeərɪŋ/ noun **1.** an arrangement whereby employees get a share of the profits of the company they work for ○ *The company runs a profit-sharing scheme.* **2.** the practice of dividing profits among employees

profit squeeze /ˈprɒfɪt skwiːz/ noun a strict control of the amount of profits which companies can pay out as dividend

profit-taking /ˈprɒfɪt ˌteɪkɪŋ/ noun the act of selling investments to realise the profit, rather than keeping them ○ *Share prices fell under continued profit-taking.*

'…some profit-taking was seen yesterday as investors continued to lack fresh incentives to renew buying activity' [*Financial Times*]

profit variance /ˈprɒfɪt ˌveərɪəns/ noun a discrepancy between actual profit and budgeted profit

profit-volume chart /ˌprɒfɪt ˈvɒljuːm ˌtʃɑːt/ noun a chart that shows how profit varies with changes in volume of production

profit warning noun an announced income level for a company that is significantly lower than that forecast by analysts

pro forma /ˌprəʊ ˈfɔːmə/ verb to issue a pro forma invoice ○ *Can you pro forma this order?*

pro-forma financial statement /prəʊ ˌfɔːmə faɪˌnænʃəl ˈsteɪtmənt/ noun a projection showing a business's financial statements after the completion of a planned transaction

pro forma invoice /ˌprəʊ ˌfɔːmə ˈɪnvɔɪs/, **pro forma** /ˌprəʊ ˈfɔːmə/ noun an invoice sent to a buyer before the goods are sent, so that payment can be made or so that goods can be sent to a consignee who is not the buyer ○ *They sent us a pro forma invoice.* ○ *We only supply that account on pro forma.*

programme evaluation and review technique /ˌprəʊɡræm ɪˌvæljuˌeɪʃ(ə)n ən rɪˈvjuː tekˌniːk/ noun a way of planning and controlling a large project, concentrating on scheduling and completion on time. Abbreviation **PERT**

progress noun /ˈprəʊɡres/ the movement of work towards completion ○ *to report on the progress of the work* or *of the negotiations* ■ verb /prəʊˈɡres/ to move forward, to go ahead ○ *The contract is progressing through various departments.*

progressive /prəˈɡresɪv/ adjective moving forward in stages

progressive tax /prəˈɡresɪv tæks/ noun a tax with a rate that increases as income increases

progressive taxation /prəˌɡresɪv tækˈseɪʃ(ə)n/ noun a taxation system where tax levels increase as the income is higher. Also called **graduated taxation**

prohibitive /prəˈhɪbɪtɪv/ adjective with a price so high that you cannot afford to pay it ○ *The cost of redesigning the product is prohibitive.*

project /ˈprɒdʒekt/ noun **1.** a plan ○ *She has drawn up a project for developing new markets in Europe.* **2.** a particular job of work which follows a plan ○ *We are just completing an engineering project in North Africa.* ○ *The company will start work on the project next month.*

project accounting /ˈprɒdʒekt əˌkaʊntɪŋ/ noun the form of accounting in which financial reports are produced in order to track costs on individual projects

project costing /ˈprɒdʒekt ˌkɒstɪŋ/ noun a system used for collecting information on the costs of a specific business activity or project

projected /prəˈdʒektɪd/ adjective planned or expected

project finance /ˌprɒdʒekt ˈfaɪnæns/ noun money raised for a specific undertaking, usually a construction or development project

projection /prəˈdʒekʃən/ noun a forecast of something which will happen in the future ○ *Projection of profits for the next three years.* ○ *The sales manager was asked to draw up sales projections for the next three years.*

project planning /ˈprɒdʒekt ˌplænɪŋ/ noun the process of making decisions about major, long-term capital investments

promise /ˈprɒmɪs/ noun an act of saying that you will do something ■ verb to say that you will do something ○ *They promised to pay the last instalment next week.*

promissory note /ˈprɒmɪsəri ˌnəʊt/ noun a document stating that someone promises to pay an amount of money on a specific date

promote /prəˈməʊt/ verb **1.** to give someone a more important job or to move someone to a higher grade ○ *He was promoted from salesman to sales manager.* **2.** to advertise a product

promotion /prə'məʊʃ(ə)n/ *noun* the fact of being moved up to a more important job ○ *I ruined my chances of promotion when I argued with the managing director.* ○ *The job offers good promotion chances* or *promotion prospects.*

'...finding the right promotion to appeal to children is no easy task' [*Marketing*]

'...you have to study the profiles and people involved very carefully and tailor the promotion to fill those needs' [*Marketing Week*]

prompt /prɒmpt/ *adjective* rapid or done immediately ○ *We got very prompt service at the complaints desk.* ○ *Thank you for your prompt reply to my letter.*

proof /pruːf/ *noun* evidence which shows that something is true

-proof /pruːf/ *suffix* protected from the negative effect of something ○ *an inflation-proof pension*

property /'prɒpəti/ *noun* **1.** land and buildings ○ *Property taxes are higher in the inner city.* ○ *They are assessing damage to property* or *property damage after the storm.* ○ *The commercial property market is booming.* **2.** a building ○ *We have several properties for sale in the centre of the town.*

property bond /'prɒpəti bɒnd/ *noun* an investment in a fund invested in properties or in property companies

property company /'prɒpəti ˌkʌmp(ə)ni/ *noun* a company which buys buildings to lease them

proportion /prə'pɔːʃ(ə)n/ *noun* a part of a total ○ *A proportion of the pre-tax profit is set aside for contingencies.* ○ *Only a small proportion of our sales comes from retail shops.*

proportional /prə'pɔːʃ(ə)nəl/ *adjective* increasing or decreasing at the same rate as something else ○ *The increase in profit is proportional to the reduction in overheads.*

proportionally /prə'pɔːʃ(ə)nəli/ *adverb* in a way that is proportional

proportional taxation /prəˌpɔːʃ(ə)nəl tækˈseɪʃ(ə)n/ *noun* a tax system in which the tax collected is in constant proportion to the income being taxed, i.e. as income rises so tax rises proportionately

proprietary /prə'praɪət(ə)ri/ *noun, adjective* a product, e.g. a medicine which is made and owned by a company

proprietary company /prəˌpraɪət(ə)ri 'kʌmp(ə)ni/ *noun US* a company formed to invest in stock of other companies so as to control them. Abbreviation **pty**

proprietary drug /prəˌpraɪət(ə)ri 'drʌg/ *noun* a drug which is made by a particular company and marketed under a brand name

proprietor /prə'praɪətə/ *noun* the owner of a business, especially in the hospitality industry ○ *She is the proprietor of a hotel* or *a hotel proprietor.* ○ *The restaurant has a new proprietor.*

proprietors' interest /prəˌpraɪətəz 'ɪntrəst/ *noun* the amount which the owners of a business have invested in the business

pro rata /ˌprəʊ 'rɑːtə/ *adjective, adverb* at a rate which varies according to the size or importance of something ○ *When part of the shipment was destroyed we received a pro rata payment.* ○ *The full-time pay is £800 a week and the part-timers are paid pro rata.*

prospect /'prɒspekt/ *noun* a chance or possibility that something will happen in the future □ **her job prospects are good** she is very likely to find a job

prospective /prə'spektɪv/ *adjective* possibly happening in the future

prospective dividend /prəˌspektɪv 'dɪvɪdend/ *noun* same as **forecast dividend**

prospective P/E ratio /prəˌspektɪv ˌpiː 'iː ˌreɪʃɪəʊ/ *noun* a P/E ratio expected in the future on the basis of forecast dividends

prospects /'prɒspekts/ *plural noun* the possibilities for the future

prospectus /prə'spektəs/ *noun* a document which gives information to attract buyers or customers ○ *The restaurant has people handing out prospectuses in the street.*

'...when the prospectus emerges, existing shareholders and any prospective new investors can find out more by calling the free share information line; they will be sent a leaflet. Non-shareholders who register in this way will receive a prospectus when it is published; existing shareholders will be sent one automatically' [*Financial Times*]

protectionism /prə'tekʃənɪz(ə)m/ *noun* the practice of protecting producers in the home country against foreign competitors by banning or taxing imports or by imposing import quotas

protective tariff /prəˌtektɪv 'tærɪf/ *noun* a tariff which tries to ban imports to stop them competing with local products

pro tem /ˌprəʊ 'tem/ *adverb* temporarily, for a time

protest /'prəʊtest/ *noun* an official document which proves that a bill of exchange has not been paid

provide /prə'vaɪd/ *verb* **1.** to give or supply something **2.** to put money aside in accounts to cover expenditure or loss in the future ○ *£25,000 is provided against bad debts.*

provident /'prɒvɪd(ə)nt/ *adjective* providing benefits in case of illness, old age or other cases of need ○ *a provident fund* ○ *a provident society*

provider of capital /prə,vaɪdər əv 'kæpɪt(ə)l/ *noun* a person or company which provides capital to a business, usually by being a shareholder

provision /prə'vɪʒ(ə)n/ *noun* an amount of money put aside in accounts for anticipated expenditure where the timing or amount of expenditure is uncertain, often for doubtful debts ○ *The bank has made a £2m provision for bad debts* or *a $5bn provision against Third World loans.*

'…landlords can create short lets of dwellings which will be free from the normal security of tenure provisions' [*Times*]

provisional /prə'vɪʒ(ə)n(ə)l/ *adjective* temporary, not final or permanent ○ *The sales department has been asked to make a provisional forecast of sales.* ○ *The provisional budget has been drawn up for each department.*

provisionally /prə'vɪʒ(ə)nəli/ *adverb* not finally ○ *The contract has been accepted provisionally.*

provisions /prə'vɪʒ(ə)nz/ *plural noun* money put aside in accounts for anticipated expenditure where the timing or amount of expenditure is uncertain. If the expenditure is not certain to occur at all, then the money set aside is called a 'contingent liability'.

proxy /'prɒksi/ *noun* **1.** a document which gives someone the power to act on behalf of someone else ○ *to sign by proxy* **2.** a person who acts on behalf of someone else ○ *She asked the chairman to act as proxy for her.*

proxy form /'prɒksi fɔːm/, **proxy card** /'prɒksi kɑːd/ *noun* a form that shareholders receive with their invitations to attend an AGM, and that they fill in if they want to appoint a proxy to vote for them on a resolution

proxy statement /'prɒksi ,steɪtmənt/ *noun* a document, filed with the SEC, outlining executive pay packages, option grants and other perks, and also giving details of dealings by executives in shares of the company

proxy vote /'prɒksi vəʊt/ *noun* a vote made on behalf of someone who is not present ○ *The proxy votes were all in favour of the board's recommendation.*

PRT *abbreviation* petroleum revenue tax

prudence /'pruːdəns/ *noun* an accounting approach that, in cases where there are alternative procedures or values, favours choosing the one that results in a lower profit, a lower asset value and a higher liability value

prudent /'pruːdənt/ *adjective* careful, not taking any risks

prudential ratio /pru,denʃ(ə)l 'reɪʃiəʊ/ *noun* a ratio of capital to assets which a bank feels it is prudent to have, according to EU regulations

PSBR *abbreviation* Public Sector Borrowing Requirement

Pty *abbreviation* proprietary company

Pty Ltd *abbreviation* private limited company

public /'pʌblɪk/ *adjective* **1.** referring to all the people in general **2.** referring to the government or the state

Public Accounts Committee /,pʌblɪk ə'kaʊnts kə,mɪti/ *noun* a committee of the House of Commons which examines the spending of each department and ministry

public company /,pʌblɪk 'kʌmp(ə)ni/ *noun* same as **public limited company**

public debt /,pʌblɪk 'det/ *noun* the money that a government or a set of governments owes

public deposits /,pʌblɪk dɪ'pɒzɪts/ *plural noun* in the United Kingdom, the government's credit monies held at the Bank of England

public expenditure /,pʌblɪk ɪk'spendɪtʃə/ *noun* money spent by the local or central government

public finance /,pʌblɪk 'faɪnæns/ *noun* the raising of money by governments by taxes or borrowing, and the spending of it

public funds /,pʌblɪk 'fʌndz/ *plural noun* government money available for expenditure

publicity budget /pʌ'blɪsɪti ,bʌdʒɪt/ *noun* money allowed for expenditure on publicity

public limited company /,pʌblɪk ,lɪmɪtɪd 'kʌmp(ə)ni/ *noun* a company whose shares can be bought on the Stock Exchange. Abbreviation **Plc**, **PLC**, **plc**. Also called **public company**

publicly held company /,pʌblɪkli held 'kʌmp(ə)ni/ *noun US* a company controlled by a few shareholders or its directors, but which is quoted on the Stock Exchange and which allows the public to hold a few shares

public offering /ˌpʌblɪk ˈɒf(ə)rɪŋ/ *noun* an offering of new shares in a corporation for sale to the public as a way of launching the corporation on the Stock Exchange

public ownership /ˌpʌblɪk ˈəʊnəʃɪp/ *noun* a situation in which the government owns a business, i.e. where an industry is nationalised

public placing /ˌpʌblɪk ˈpleɪsɪŋ/, **public placement** /ˌpʌblɪk ˈpleɪsmənt/ *noun* an act of offering a new issue of shares to investing institutions, though not to private investors in general

public sector /ˈpʌblɪk ˌsektə/ *noun* nationalised industries and services ○ *a report on wage rises in the public sector* or *on public-sector wage settlements* Also called **government sector**

Public Sector Borrowing Requirement /ˌpʌblɪk ˌsektə ˈbɒrəʊɪŋ rɪ ˌkwaɪəmənt/ *noun* the amount of money which a government has to borrow to pay for its own spending. Abbreviation **PSBR**

public spending /ˌpʌblɪk ˈspendɪŋ/ *noun* spending by the government or by local authorities

Public Trustee /ˌpʌblɪk ˌtrʌˈstiː/ *noun* an official who is appointed as a trustee of an individual's property

published accounts /ˌpʌblɪʃt ə ˈkaʊnts/ *plural noun* the accounts of a company which have been prepared and audited and then must be published by sending to the shareholders and other interested parties

pump priming /ˈpʌmp ˌpraɪmɪŋ/ *noun* government investment in new projects which it hopes will benefit the economy

purchase book /ˈpɜːtʃɪs bʊk/ *noun* a book in which purchases are recorded

purchase daybook /ˈpɜːtʃɪs ˌdeɪbʊk/, **purchases daybook** /ˈpɜːtʃɪsɪz ˌdeɪbʊk/ *noun* a book which records the purchases made each day

purchase invoice /ˌpɜːtʃɪs ˈɪnvɔɪs/ *noun* an invoice received by a purchaser from a seller

purchase ledger /ˈpɜːtʃɪs ˌledʒə/ *noun* a book in which purchases are recorded

purchase order /ˈpɜːtʃɪs ˌɔːdə/ *noun* an official order made out by a purchasing department for goods which a company wants to buy ○ *We cannot supply you without a purchase order number.*

purchase order lead time /ˌpɜːtʃɪs ˌɔːdə ˈliːd ˌtaɪm/ *noun* the interval between the placing of an order for raw materials or parts and their being delivered

purchase price /ˈpɜːtʃɪs praɪs/ *noun* a price paid for something

purchase requisition /ˌpɜːtʃɪs ˌrekwɪ ˈzɪʃ(ə)n/ *noun* an instruction from a department within an organisation to its purchasing department to buy goods or services, stating the kind and quantity required, and forming the basis of a purchase order

purchase tax /ˈpɜːtʃɪs tæks/ *noun* a tax paid on things which are bought

purchasing department /ˈpɜːtʃɪsɪŋ dɪ ˌpɑːtmənt/ *noun* the section of a company which deals with the buying of stock, raw materials, equipment, etc.

purchasing manager /ˈpɜːtʃɪsɪŋ ˌmænɪdʒə/ *noun* the head of a purchasing department

purchasing officer /ˈpɜːtʃɪsɪŋ ˌɒfɪsə/ *noun* a person in a company or organisation who is responsible for buying stock, raw materials, equipment, etc.

purchasing power /ˈpɜːtʃɪsɪŋ ˌpaʊə/ *noun* the quantity of goods which can be bought by a particular group of people or with a particular sum of money ○ *the purchasing power of the school market* ○ *The purchasing power of the pound has fallen over the last five years.*

pure endowment /ˌpjʊər ɪnˈdaʊmənt/ *noun* a monetary gift the use of which is strictly prescribed by the donor

put down *phrasal verb* **1.** to make a deposit ○ *to put down money on a house* **2.** to write an item in a ledger or an account book ○ *to put down a figure for expenses*

put up *phrasal verb* **1.** □ **who put up the money for the shop?** who provided the investment money for the shop to start? □ **to put something up for sale** to advertise that something is for sale ○ *When he retired he decided to put his town flat up for sale.* **2.** to increase something, to make something higher ○ *The shop has put up all its prices by 5%.*

put option /ˈpʊt ˌɒpʃən/ *noun* an option to sell a specified number of shares at a specified price within a specified period of time. Also called **put**

PV *abbreviation* present value

pyramid selling /ˈpɪrəmɪd ˌselɪŋ/ *noun* an illegal way of selling goods or investments to the public, where each selling agent pays for the franchise to sell the product or service, and sells that right on to other agents together with stock, so that in the end the person who makes the most money is the original franchiser, and sub-agents or investors may lose all their investments

'...much of the population had committed their life savings to get-rich-quick pyramid investment schemes – where newcomers pay the original investors until the money runs out – which inevitably collapsed' [*Times*]

Q

qualification /ˌkwɒlɪfɪˈkeɪʃ(ə)n/ *noun* a document or some other formal proof of the fact that someone has successfully completed a specialised course of study or has acquired a skill ○ *You must have the right qualifications for the job.* ○ *Job-hunting is difficult if you have no qualifications.*

'…personnel management is not an activity that can ever have just one set of qualifications as a requirement for entry into it' [*Personnel Management*]

qualification of accounts /ˌkwɒlɪfɪkeɪʃ(ə)n əv əˈkaʊnts/ *noun* same as **auditors' qualification**

qualified /ˈkwɒlɪfaɪd/ *adjective* **1.** having passed special examinations in a subject ○ *She is a qualified accountant.* ○ *We have appointed a qualified designer to supervise the decorating of the new reception area.* **2.** with some reservations or conditions ○ *qualified acceptance of a contract* ○ *The plan received qualified approval from the board.*

'…applicants will be professionally qualified and ideally have a degree in Commerce and postgraduate management qualifications' [*Australian Financial Review*]

qualified acceptance of a bill /ˌkwɒlɪfaɪd əkˌseptəns əv ə ˈbɪl/ *noun* an agreement to pay a bill of exchange provided that certain conditions are met

qualified accounts /ˌkwɒlɪfaɪd əˈkaʊnts/ *plural noun* accounts which have been noted by the auditors because they contain something with which the auditors do not agree

qualified domestic trust /ˌkwɒlɪfaɪd dəˈmestɪk trʌst/ *noun* a trust for the non-citizen spouse of a US citizen, affording tax advantages at the time of the citizen's death

qualified valuer /ˌkwɒlɪfaɪd ˈvæljʊə/ *noun* a person conducting a valuation who holds a recognised and relevant professional qualification and has recent post-qualification experience, and sufficient knowledge of the state of the market, with reference to the location and category of the tangible fixed asset being valued

qualifying distribution /ˌkwɒlɪfaɪɪŋ ˌdɪstrɪˈbjuːʃ(ə)n/ *noun* a payment of a dividend, or other distribution of profits, that was subject, in the UK, to advance corporation tax before it was scrapped in 1999

qualifying period /ˈkwɒlɪfaɪɪŋ ˌpɪərɪəd/ *noun* a time which has to pass before something or someone qualifies for something, e.g. a grant or subsidy ○ *There is a six-month qualifying period before you can get a grant from the local authority.*

qualifying shares /ˌkwɒlɪfaɪɪŋ ˈʃeəz/ *plural noun* the number of shares you need to earn to get a bonus issue or to be a director of the company, etc.

qualitative factors /ˈkwɒlɪtətɪv ˌfæktəz/ *plural noun* factors that inform a business decision but cannot be expressed numerically

quality assurance /ˈkwɒlɪti əˌʃʊərəns/ *noun* the procedures that a company uses to ensure compliance with a quality standard

quality control /ˈkwɒlɪti kənˌtrəʊl/ *noun* the process of making sure that the quality of a product is good

quality costs /ˈkwɒlɪti kɒsts/ *plural noun* costs incurred when goods produced or services delivered fail to meet quality standards

quango /ˈkwæŋɡəʊ/ *noun* an official body, set up by a government to investigate or deal with a special problem (NOTE: The plural is **quangos**.)

quantifiable /ˈkwɒntɪfaɪəb(ə)l/ *adjective* possible to quantify ○ *The effect of the change in the discount structure is not quantifiable.*

quantitative factors /ˈkwɒntɪtətɪv ˌfæktəz/ *plural noun* factors that inform a business decision but cannot be expressed numerically

quantity discount /ˌkwɒntɪti ˈdɪskaʊnt/ *noun* a discount given to people who buy large quantities

quantum meruit /ˌkwæntʊm ˈmeruɪt/ *phrase* a Latin phrase meaning 'as much as has been earned'

quarter /ˈkwɔːtə/ *noun* **1.** one of four equal parts (25%) ○ *She paid only a quarter of the list price.* **2.** a period of three months ○ *The instalments are payable at the end of each quarter.*

'...corporate profits for the first quarter showed a 4 per cent drop from last year's final three months' [*Financial Times*]

'...economists believe the economy is picking up this quarter and will do better still in the second half of the year' [*Sunday Times*]

quarter day /ˈkwɔːtə deɪ/ *noun* a day at the end of a quarter, when rents, fees etc. should be paid

quarterly /ˈkwɔːtəli/ *adjective, adverb* happening once every three months ○ *There is a quarterly charge for electricity.* ○ *The bank sends us a quarterly statement.* ○ *We agreed to pay the rent quarterly* or *on a quarterly basis.*

quarterly report /ˌkwɔːtəli rɪˈpɔːt/ *noun* the results of a corporation, produced each quarter

quartile /ˈkwɔːtaɪl/ *noun* one of a series of three figures below which 25%, 50% or 75% of the total falls

quasi- /kweɪzaɪ/ *prefix* almost or which seems like ○ *a quasi-official body*

quasi-loan /ˌkweɪzaɪ ˈləʊn/ *noun* an agreement between two parties where one agrees to pay the other's debts, provided that the second party agrees to reimburse the first at some later date

quasi-public corporation /ˌkweɪzaɪ ˌpʌblɪk ˌkɔːpəˈreɪʃ(ə)n/ *noun* a US institution which is privately owned, but which serves a public function, such as the Federal National Mortgage Association

queue /kjuː/ *noun* **1.** a line of people waiting one behind the other ○ *to form a queue* or *to join a queue* ○ *Queues formed at the doors of the bank when the news spread about its possible collapse.* (NOTE: The US term is **line**.) **2.** a series of documents such as orders or application forms which are dealt with in order ■ *verb* to form a line one after the other for something ○ *When food was rationed, people had to queue for bread.* ○ *We queued for hours to get tickets.* ○ *A list of companies queueing to be launched on the Stock Exchange.* ○ *The candidates queued outside the interviewing room.*

quick asset /ˈkwɪk ˌæset/ *noun* an asset that can be converted into cash relatively quickly

quick ratio /ˌkwɪk ˈreɪʃiəʊ/ *noun* same as **liquidity ratio**

quid /kwɪd/ *noun* one pound Sterling (*slang*)

quid pro quo /ˌkwɪd prəʊ ˈkwəʊ/ *noun* money paid or an action carried out in return for something ○ *She agreed to repay the loan early, and as a quid pro quo the bank released the collateral.*

quorum /ˈkwɔːrəm/ *noun* a minimum number of people who have to be present at a meeting to make it valid

quota /ˈkwəʊtə/ *noun* a limited amount of something which is allowed to be produced, imported, etc.

'Canada agreed to a new duty-free quota of 600,000 tonnes a year' [*Globe and Mail (Toronto)*]

quota system /ˈkwəʊtə ˌsɪstəm/ *noun* **1.** a system where imports or supplies are regulated by fixed maximum amounts **2.** an arrangement for distribution which allows each distributor only a specific number of items

quotation /kwəʊˈteɪʃ(ə)n/ *noun* an estimate of how much something will cost ○ *They sent in their quotation for the job.* ○ *Our quotation was much lower than all the others.* ○ *We accepted the lowest quotation.*

quote /kwəʊt/ *verb* **1.** to repeat words or a reference number used by someone else ○ *He quoted figures from the annual report.* ○ *She replied, quoting the number of the account.* **2.** to estimate what a cost or price is likely to be ○ *to quote a price for supplying stationery* ○ *Their prices are always quoted in dollars.* ○ *He quoted me a price of £1,026.* ■ *noun* an estimate of how much something will cost (*informal*) ○ *to give someone a quote for supplying computers* ○ *We have asked for quotes for refitting the shop.* ○ *Her quote was the lowest of three.*

quoted company /ˌkwəʊtɪd ˈkʌmp(ə)ni/ *noun* a company whose shares can be bought or sold on the Stock Exchange

quoted investments /ˌkwəʊtɪd ɪnˈvestmənts/ *plural noun* investments which are listed on a stock exchange

quote-driven system /ˈkwəʊt ˌdrɪv(ə)n ˌsɪstəm/ *noun* a system of working a stock market, where marketmakers quote a price for a stock. Compare **order-driven system**

quoted shares /ˌkwəʊtɪd ˈʃeəz/, **quoted stocks** *plural noun* shares which can be bought or sold on the Stock Exchange

R

racket /'rækɪt/ *noun* an illegal deal which makes a lot of money ○ *She runs a cut-price ticket racket.*

rack rent /'ræk rent/ *noun* a very high rent

raise /reɪz/ *noun US* an increase in salary ○ *He asked the boss for a raise.* ○ *She got her raise last month.* (NOTE: The UK term is **rise.**) ■ *verb* **1.** to increase or to make higher ○ *The government has raised the tax levels.* ○ *The company raised its dividend by 10%.* ○ *This increase in production will raise the standard of living in the area.* **2.** to obtain money or to organise a loan ○ *The company is trying to raise the capital to fund its expansion programme.* ○ *The government raises more money by indirect taxation than by direct.*

'…the company said yesterday that its recent share issue has been oversubscribed, raising A\$225.5m' [*Financial Times*]

'…investment trusts can raise capital, but this has to be done as a company does, by a rights issue of equity' [*Investors Chronicle*]

'…over the past few weeks, companies raising new loans from international banks have been forced to pay more' [*Financial Times*]

rally /'ræli/ *noun* a rise in price when the trend has been downwards ○ *Shares staged a rally on the Stock Exchange.* ○ *After a brief rally shares fell back to a new low.* ■ *verb* to rise in price, when the trend has been downwards ○ *Shares rallied on the news of the latest government figures.*

'…when Japan rallied, it had no difficulty in surpassing its previous all-time high, and this really stretched the price-earnings ratios into the stratosphere' [*Money Observer*]

'…bad news for the US economy ultimately may have been the cause of a late rally in stock prices yesterday' [*Wall Street Journal*]

R&D *abbreviation* research and development

random check /ˌrændəm 'tʃek/ *noun* a check on items taken from a group without any special selection

random sample /ˌrændəm 'sɑːmpəl/ *noun* a sample taken without any selection

range /reɪndʒ/ *noun* **1.** a series of items ○ *Their range of products* or *product range is too narrow.* ○ *There are a whole range of alternatives for the new salary scheme.* **2.** a scale of items from a low point to a high one □ **range of prices** the difference between the highest and lowest price for a share or bond over a period of time

rank /ræŋk/ *noun* a position in a company or an organisation, especially one which shows how important someone is relative to others ○ *All managers are of equal rank.* ○ *Promotion means moving up from a lower rank.* ■ *verb* **1.** to classify in order of importance ○ *Candidates are ranked in order of their test results.* **2.** to be in a position ○ *The non-voting shares rank equally with the voting shares.* ○ *Deferred ordinary shares do not rank for dividend.*

rate /reɪt/ *noun* **1.** the money charged for time worked or work completed **2.** an amount of money paid, e.g. as interest or dividend, shown as a percentage **3.** the value of one currency against another ○ *What is today's rate* or *the current rate for the dollar?* **4.** an amount, number or speed compared with something else ○ *the rate of increase in redundancies* ○ *The rate of absenteeism* or *The absenteeism rate always increases in fine weather.*

rateable value /ˌreɪtəb(ə)l 'væljuː/ *noun* the value of a property as a basis for calculating local taxes

rate of exchange /ˌreɪt əv ɪksˈtʃeɪndʒ/ *noun* same as **exchange rate** ○ *The current rate of exchange is \$1.60 to the pound.*

rate of interest /ˌreɪt əv 'ɪntrəst/ *noun* same as **interest rate**

rate of return /ˌreɪt əv rɪˈtɜːn/ *noun* the amount of interest or dividend which comes from an investment, shown as a percentage of the money invested

rate of sales /ˌreɪt əv ˈseɪlz/ *noun* the speed at which units are sold

rates /reɪts/ *plural noun* local UK taxes formerly levied on property in the UK and now replaced by the council tax

rating /ˈreɪtɪŋ/ *noun* **1.** the act of giving something a value, or the value given **2.** the valuing of property for local taxes

rating agency /ˈreɪtɪŋ ˌeɪdʒənsi/ *noun* an organisation which gives a rating to companies or other organisations issuing bonds

rating officer /ˈreɪtɪŋ ˌɒfɪsə/ *noun* an official in a local authority who decides the rateable value of a commercial property

ratio /ˈreɪʃiəʊ/ *noun* a proportion or quantity of something compared to something else ○ *the ratio of successes to failures* ○ *Our product outsells theirs by a ratio of two to one.* ○ *With less manual work available, the ratio of employees to managers is decreasing.*

ratio analysis /ˈreɪʃiəʊ əˌnæləsɪs/ *noun* a method of analysing the performance of a company by showing the figures in its accounts as ratios and comparing them with those of other companies

raw materials /ˌrɔː məˈtɪəriəlz/ *plural noun* basic materials which have to be treated or processed in some way before they can be used, e.g. wood, iron ore or crude petroleum

R/D *abbreviation* refer to drawer

RDPR *abbreviation* refer to drawer please represent

readjust /ˌriːəˈdʒʌst/ *verb* to adjust something again or in a new way, or to change in response to new conditions ○ *to readjust prices to take account of the rise in the costs of raw materials* ○ *to readjust salary scales* ○ *Share prices readjusted quickly to the news of the devaluation.*

readjustment /ˌriːəˈdʒʌstmənt/ *noun* an act of readjusting ○ *a readjustment in pricing* ○ *After the devaluation there was a period of readjustment in the exchange rates.*

ready cash /ˌredi ˈkæʃ/ *noun* money which is immediately available for payment

ready money /ˌredi ˈmʌni/ *noun* cash or money which is immediately available

real asset /ˌrɪəl ˈæset/ *noun* a non-movable asset such as land or a building

real earnings /ˌrɪəl ˈɜːnɪŋz/ *plural noun* income which is available for spending after tax and other contributions have been deducted, corrected for inflation. Also called **real income**, **real wages**

real estate /ˈrɪəl ɪˌsteɪt/ *noun* property in the form of land or buildings

'…on top of the cost of real estate, the investment in inventory and equipment to open a typical warehouse comes to around \$5 million' [*Duns Business Month*]

real estate agent /ˈrɪəl ɪˌsteɪt ˌeɪdʒənt/, **real estate broker** *noun US* a person who sells property for customers

real estate investment trust /ˌrɪəl ɪˌsteɪt ɪnˈvestmənt trʌst/ *noun* a public trust company which invests only in property. Abbreviation **REIT**

real exchange rate /ˌrɪəl ɪksˈtʃeɪndʒ ˌreɪt/ *noun* an exchange rate that has been adjusted for inflation

real income /ˌrɪəl ˈɪnkʌm/ *noun* same as **real earnings**

real interest rate /ˌrɪəl ˈɪntrəst ˌreɪt/ *noun* an interest rate after taking inflation into account

real investment /ˌrɪəl ɪnˈvestmənt/ *noun* the purchase of assets such as land, property, and plant and machinery as opposed to the acquisition of securities

realisation /ˌrɪəlaɪˈzeɪʃ(ə)n/, **realization** *noun* the act of making real □ **the realisation of a project** putting a project into action ○ *The plan moved a stage nearer realisation when the contracts were signed.*

realisation concept /ˌrɪəlaɪˈzeɪʃ(ə)n ˌkɒnsept/ *noun* the principle that increases in value should only be recognised when the assets in question are realised by being sold to an independent purchaser

realise /ˈrɪəlaɪz/, **realize** *verb* **1.** to make something become real □ **to realise a project** *or* **a plan** to put a project or a plan into action **2.** to sell for money ○ *The company was running out of cash, so the board decided to realise some property* or *assets.* ○ *The sale realised £100,000.* □ **realised gain** *or* **loss** a gain or loss made when assets are sold

realised profit /ˌrɪəlaɪzd ˈprɒfɪt/ *noun* an actual profit made when something is sold, as opposed to paper profit

real rate of return /ˌrɪəl ˌreɪt əv rɪˈtɜːn/ *noun* an actual rate of return, calculated after taking inflation into account

real return after tax /ˌrɪəl rɪˌtɜːn ˌɑːftə ˈtæks/ *noun* the return calculated after deducting tax and inflation

realty /ˈrɪəlti/ *noun* property or real estate

real value /ˌrɪəl ˈvæljuː/ *noun* a value of an investment which is kept the same, e.g. by index-linking

real wages /ˌrɪəl ˈweɪdʒɪz/ *plural noun* same as **real earnings**

reassess /ˌriːəˈses/ *verb* to assess again ○ *The manager was asked to reassess the department staff, after the assessments were badly done by the supervisors.*

reassessment /ˌriːəˈsesmənt/ *noun* a new assessment

rebate /ˈriːbeɪt/ *noun* **1.** a reduction in the amount of money to be paid ○ *We are offering a 10% rebate on selected goods.* **2.** money returned to someone because they have paid too much ○ *She got a tax rebate at the end of the year.*

recapitalisation /riːˌkæpɪt(ə)laɪ ˈzeɪʃ(ə)n/ *noun* a change in the capital structure of a company as when new shares are issued, especially when undertaken to avoid the company going into liquidation

receipt /rɪˈsiːt/ *noun* **1.** a piece of paper showing that money has been paid or that something has been received ○ *He kept the customs receipt to show that he had paid duty on the goods.* ○ *She lost her taxi receipt.* ○ *Keep the receipt for items purchased in case you need to change them later.* **2.** the act of receiving something ○ *Goods will be supplied within thirty days of receipt of order.* ○ *Invoices are payable within thirty days of receipt.* ○ *On receipt of the notification, the company lodged an appeal.* ■ *verb* to stamp or to sign a document to show that it has been received, or to stamp an invoice to show that it has been paid ○ *Receipted invoices are filed in the ring binder.*

receipts /rɪˈsiːts/ *plural noun* money taken in sales ○ *to itemise receipts and expenditure* ○ *Receipts are down against the same period of last year.*

'…the public sector borrowing requirement is kept low by treating the receipts from selling public assets as a reduction in borrowing' [*Economist*]

'…gross wool receipts for the selling season to end June appear likely to top $2 billion' [*Australian Financial Review*]

receipts and payments account /rɪ ˌsiːts ən ˈpeɪmənts əˌkaʊnt/ *noun* a report of cash transactions during a period. It is used in place of an income and expenditure account when it is not considered appropriate to distinguish between capital and revenue transactions or to include accruals.

receipts and payments basis /rɪˌsiːts ən ˈpeɪmənts ˌbeɪsɪs/ *noun* an accounting method in which receipts and payments are accounted for when the money is actually received or paid out, not necessarily when they are entered in the books. Also called **cash basis**

receivable /rɪˈsiːvəb(ə)l/ *adjective* able to be received

receivables /rɪˈsiːvəb(ə)lz/ *plural noun* money which is owed to a company

receive /rɪˈsiːv/ *verb* to get something which is given or delivered to you ○ *We received the payment ten days ago.* ○ *The employees have not received any salary for six months.*

receiver /rɪˈsiːvə/ *noun* same as **official receiver**

Receiver of Revenue /rɪˌsiːvə əv ˈrevənjuː/ *noun* an informal term for the South African Revenue Service as a whole

receiving /rɪˈsiːvɪŋ/ *noun* an act of getting something which has been delivered

receiving clerk /rɪˈsiːvɪŋ klɑːk/ *noun* an official who works in a receiving office

receiving department /rɪˈsiːvɪŋ dɪ ˌpɑːtmənt/ *noun* a section of a company which deals with incoming goods or payments

receiving office /rɪˈsiːvɪŋ ˌɒfɪs/ *noun* an office where goods or payments are received

receiving order /rɪˈsiːvɪŋ ˌɔːdə/ *noun* an order from a court appointing an official receiver to a company

recession /rɪˈseʃ(ə)n/ *noun* a period where there is a decline in trade or in the economy ○ *The recession has reduced profits in many companies.* ○ *Several firms have closed factories because of the recession.*

reciprocal /rɪˈsɪprək(ə)l/ *adjective* done by one person, company, or country to another one, which does the same thing in return ○ *We signed a reciprocal agreement* or *a reciprocal contract with a Russian company.*

reciprocal allocation method /rɪ ˌsɪprək(ə)l ˌæləˈkeɪʃ(ə)n ˌmeθəd/ *noun* a method by which service department costs are allocated to production departments

reciprocal holdings /rɪˌsɪprək(ə)l ˈhəʊldɪŋz/ *plural noun* a situation in which two companies own shares in each other to prevent takeover bids

reciprocal trade /rɪˌsɪprək(ə)l ˈtreɪd/ *noun* trade between two countries

reciprocate /rɪˈsɪprəkeɪt/ *verb* to do the same thing for someone as that person has done for you ○ *They offered us an exclusive agency for their cars and we reciprocated with an offer of the agency for our buses.*

reckon /'rekən/ *verb* to calculate something ○ *to reckon the costs at £25,000* ○ *We reckon the loss to be over £1m.* ○ *They reckon the insurance costs to be too high.*

recognise /'rekəgnaɪz/ *verb* to record an item in an account or other financial statement □ **statement of total recognised gains and losses** financial statement showing changes in shareholders' equity during an accounting period (see FRS 3)

recognised professional body /ˌrekəgnaɪzd prə,feʃ(ə)nəl 'bɒdi/ *noun* a professional body which is in charge of the regulation of the conduct of its members and is recognised by the FSA. Abbreviation **RPB**

recognised qualification /ˌrekəgnaɪzd ˌkwɒlɪfɪ'keɪʃ(ə)n/ *noun* a qualification that employers and professional bodies accept as worthwhile and valid

reconcile /'rekənsaɪl/ *verb* to make two financial accounts or statements agree ○ *She is trying to reconcile one account with another* or *to reconcile the two accounts.*

reconciliation /ˌrekənsɪli'eɪʃ(ə)n/, **reconcilement** /'rekənsaɪlmənt/ *noun* the act of making two accounts or statements agree

reconciliation statement /ˌrekənsɪli 'eɪʃ(ə)n ˌsteɪtmənt/ *noun* a statement which explains how two accounts can be made to agree

reconstruction /ˌriːkən'strʌkʃən/ *noun* **1.** the process of building again ○ *The economic reconstruction of an area after a disaster.* **2.** new way of organising

record /'rekɔːd/ *noun* **1.** a report of something which has happened ○ *The chairman signed the minutes as a true record of the last meeting.* ○ *She has a very poor timekeeping record.* □ **for the record** *or* **to keep the record straight** in order that everyone knows what the real facts of the matter are ○ *For the record, I should like to say that these sales figures have not yet been checked by the sales department.* **2.** a description of what has happened in the past ○ *the salesperson's record of service* or *service record* ○ *the company's record in industrial relations* **3.** a success which is better than anything before ○ *Last year was a record year for the company.* ○ *Our top sales rep has set a new record for sales per call.*

record book /'rekɔːd bʊk/ *noun* a book in which minutes of meetings are kept

record date /'rekɔːd deɪt/ *noun* same as **date of record**

recording /rɪ'kɔːdɪŋ/ *noun* the act of making a note of something ○ *the recording of an order* or *of a complaint*

records /'rekɔːdz/ *plural noun* documents which give information ○ *The names of customers are kept in the company's records.* ○ *We find from our records that our invoice number 1234 has not been paid.*

recoup /rɪ'kuːp/ *verb* □ **to recoup your losses** to get back money which you thought you had lost

recourse /rɪ'kɔːs/ *noun* a right of a lender to compel a borrower to repay money borrowed

recover /rɪ'kʌvə/ *verb* **1.** to get back something which has been lost ○ *to recover damages from the driver of the car* ○ *to start a court action to recover property* ○ *He never recovered his money.* ○ *The initial investment was never recovered.* **2.** to get better, to rise ○ *The market has not recovered from the rise in oil prices.* ○ *The stock market fell in the morning, but recovered during the afternoon.*

recoverable amount /rɪ,kʌv(ə)rəb(ə)l ə'maʊnt/ *noun* the value of an asset, either the price it would fetch if sold, or its value to the company when used, whichever is the larger figure

recovery /rɪ'kʌv(ə)ri/ *noun* **1.** the act of getting back something which has been lost ○ *to start an action for recovery of property* ○ *We are aiming for the complete recovery of the money invested.* **2.** a movement upwards of shares or of the economy ○ *signs of recovery after a slump* ○ *The economy staged a recovery.*

rectification /ˌrektɪfɪ'keɪʃ(ə)n/ *noun* correction

rectify /'rektɪfaɪ/ *verb* to correct something, to make something right ○ *to rectify an entry* (NOTE: **rectifies – rectifying – rectified**)

recurrent /rɪ'kʌrənt/ *adjective* happening again and again ○ *a recurrent item of expenditure* ○ *There is a recurrent problem in supplying this part.*

recurring payments /rɪ,kɜːrɪŋ 'peɪmənts/ *plural noun* payments, such as mortgage interest or payments on a hire purchase agreement, which are made each month

recycle /riː'saɪk(ə)l/ *verb* to take waste material and process it so that it can be used again

red /red/ *noun* the colour of debit or overdrawn balances in some bank statements □ **in the red** showing a debit or loss ○ *My bank account is in the red.* ○ *The company went into the red in 1998.* ○ *The company is out of the red for the first time since 1990.*

Red Book /ˈred bʊk/ *noun* a document published on Budget Day, with the text of the Chancellor of the Exchequer's financial statement and budget

redeem /rɪˈdiːm/ *verb* to pay off a loan or a debt ○ *to redeem a mortgage* ○ *to redeem a debt*

redeemable /rɪˈdiːməb(ə)l/ *adjective* referring to a bond which can be sold for cash

redeemable government stock /rɪ ˌdiːməb(ə)l ˌɡʌv(ə)nmənt ˈstɒk/ *noun* stock which can be redeemed for cash at some time in the future. In the UK, only the War Loan is irredeemable.

redeemable preference share /rɪ ˌdiːməb(ə)l ˈpref(ə)rəns ʃeə/ *noun* a preference share which must be bought back by the company at an agreed date and for an agreed price

redeemable security /rɪˌdiːməb(ə)l sɪ ˈkjʊərɪti/ *noun* a security which can be redeemed at its face value at a specific date in the future

redemption /rɪˈdempʃən/ *noun* the repayment of a loan

redemption date /rɪˈdempʃən deɪt/ *noun* a date on which a loan or debt is due to be repaid

redemption value /rɪˈdempʃən ˌvæljuː/ *noun* the value of a security when redeemed

redemption yield /rɪˈdempʃən jiːld/ *noun* a yield on a security including interest and its redemption value

redistribute /ˌriːdɪˈstrɪbjuːt/ *verb* to move items, work or money to different areas or people ○ *The government aims to redistribute wealth by taxing the rich and giving grants to the poor.* ○ *The orders have been redistributed among the company's factories.*

redistributed cost /ˌriːdɪˈstrɪbjʊtɪd kɒst/ *noun* a cost that has been reassigned to a different department within an organisation

redistribution of wealth /ˌriːdɪstrɪbjuːʃən əv ˈwelθ/ *noun* the process of sharing wealth among the whole population

reduce /rɪˈdjuːs/ *verb* to make something smaller or lower ○ *They have reduced prices in all departments.* ○ *We were expecting the* government to reduce taxes not to increase them. ○ *The company reduced output because of a fall in demand.* ○ *The government's policy is to reduce inflation to 5%.*

reduced /rɪˈdjuːst/ *adjective* lower ○ *Reduced prices have increased unit sales.* ○ *Prices have fallen due to a reduced demand for the goods.*

reducing balance method /rɪˌdjuːsɪŋ ˈbæləns ˌmeθəd/ *noun* a method of depreciating assets, where the asset is depreciated at a constant percentage of its cost each year. Also called **declining balance method**

redundancy /rɪˈdʌndənsi/ *noun* the dismissal of a person whose job no longer needs to be done

redundancy payment /rɪˈdʌndənsi ˌpeɪmənt/ *noun* a payment made to an employee to compensate for losing his or her job

redundancy rebate /rɪˈdʌndənsi ˌriːbeɪt/ *noun* a payment made to a company to compensate for redundancy payments made

redundant /rɪˈdʌndənt/ *adjective* more than is needed, useless ○ *a redundant clause in a contract* ○ *The new legislation has made clause 6 redundant.* ○ *Retraining can help employees whose old skills have become redundant.*

redundant staff /rɪˌdʌndənt ˈstɑːf/ *noun* staff who have lost their jobs because they are not needed any more

re-export /ˌriːekˈspɔːt/ *verb* to export something which has been imported

re-exportation /ˌriː ekspɔːˈteɪʃ(ə)n/ *noun* the exporting of goods which have been imported

refer /rɪˈfɜː/ *verb* □ **'refer to drawer'** words written on a cheque which a bank refuses to pay and returns it to the person who wrote it. Abbreviation **R/D**

reference /ˈref(ə)rəns/ *noun* **1.** the process of mentioning or dealing with something ○ *with reference to your letter of May 25th* **2.** a series of numbers or letters which make it possible to find a document which has been filed ○ *our reference: PC/MS 1234* ○ *Thank you for your letter (reference 1234).* **3.** a written report on someone's character or ability ○ *to write someone a reference* or *to give someone a reference* ○ *to ask applicants to supply references* □ **to ask a company for trade references** or **for bank references** to ask for reports from traders or a bank on the company's financial status and reputation

referral /rɪ'fɜːrəl/ *noun* an action of referring or recommending someone to someone

refer to drawer please represent /rɪ ˌfɜː tə ˌdrɔːə pliːz ˌriːprɪ'zent/ *noun* in the United Kingdom, written on a cheque by the paying banker to indicate that there are currently insufficient funds to meet the payment, but that the bank believes sufficient funds will be available shortly. ◊ **'refer to drawer'**. Abbreviation **RDPR**

refinance /ˌriː'faɪnæns/ *verb* to replace one source of finance with another

refund *noun* /'riːfʌnd/ money paid back ○ *The shoes don't fit – I'm going to ask for a refund.* ○ *She got a refund after complaining to the manager.* ■ *verb* /rɪ'fʌnd/ **1.** to pay back money ○ *to refund the cost of postage* ○ *All money will be refunded if the goods are not satisfactory.* **2.** to borrow money to repay a previous debt

refundable /rɪ'fʌndəb(ə)l/ *adjective* possible to pay back ○ *We ask for a refundable deposit of £20.*

register /'redʒɪstə/ *noun* an official list ○ *to enter something in a register* ○ *to keep a register up to date* ○ *people on the register of electors* ■ *verb* **1.** to write something in an official list ○ *to register a fall in the numbers of unemployed teenagers* ○ *To register a company you must pay a fee to Companies House.* ○ *When a property is sold, the sale is registered at the Land Registry.* **2.** to send a letter by registered post ○ *I registered the letter, because it contained some money.*

registered /'redʒɪstəd/ *adjective* having been noted on an official list ○ *a registered share transaction*

registered cheque /ˌredʒɪstəd 'tʃek/ *noun* a cheque written on a bank account on behalf of a client who does not have a bank account

registered company /ˌredʒɪstəd 'kʌmp(ə)ni/ *noun* a company which has been officially set up and registered with the Registrar of Companies

registered office /ˌredʒɪstəd 'ɒfɪs/ *noun* the office address of a company which is officially registered with the Companies' Registrar

registered security /ˌredʒɪstəd sɪ'kjʊərɪti/ *noun* a security such as a share in a quoted company which is registered with Companies House and whose holder is listed in the company's share register

registered trademark /ˌredʒɪstəd 'treɪdmɑːk/ *noun* a name, design or symbol which has been registered by the manufacturer and which cannot be used by other

manufacturers. It is an intangible asset. ○ *You can't call your beds 'Softn'kumfi' – it is a registered trademark.*

register of companies /ˌredʒɪstər əv 'kʌmp(ə)niz/ *noun* in the United Kingdom, the list of companies maintained at Companies House

register of directors /ˌredʒɪstər əv daɪ'rektəz/ *noun* an official list of the directors of a company which has to be sent to the Registrar of Companies

registrant /'redʒɪstrənt/ *noun US* company applying to register with the Securities and Exchange Commission

registrar /ˌredʒɪ'strɑː/ *noun* a person who keeps official records

Registrar of Companies /ˌredʒɪstrɑː əv 'kʌmp(ə)niz/ *noun* a government official whose duty is to ensure that companies are properly registered, and that, when registered, they file accounts and other information correctly

registration /ˌredʒɪ'streɪʃ(ə)n/ *noun* the act of having something noted on an official list ○ *the registration of a trademark* or *of a share transaction*

registration fee /ˌredʒɪ'streɪʃ(ə)n fiː/ *noun* **1.** money paid to have something registered **2.** money paid to attend a conference

registration statement /ˌredʒɪ 'streɪʃ(ə)n ˌsteɪtmənt/ *noun US* a document which gives information about a company when it is registered and listed on a stock exchange (NOTE: The UK term is **listing particulars**.)

regression analysis /rɪ'greʃ(ə)n ə ˌnæləsɪs/, **regression model** /rɪ'greʃ(ə)n ˌmɒd(ə)l/ *noun* **1.** a method of discovering the ratio of one dependent variable and one or more independent variables, so as to give a value to the dependent variable **2.** a forecasting technique that identifies trends by establishing the relationship between quantifiable variables

regressive tax /rɪˌgresɪv 'tæk/ *noun* a tax with a rate that decreases as income, or the value of the taxed item, rises

regressive taxation /rɪˌgresɪv tæk 'seɪʃ(ə)n/ *noun* a system of taxation in which tax gets progressively less as income rises. Compare **progressive taxation**

regular income /ˌregjʊlər 'ɪnkʌm/ *noun* an income which comes in every week or month ○ *She works freelance so she does not have a regular income.*

regulate /'regjʊleɪt/ *verb* **1.** to adjust something so that it works well or is correct **2.** to change or maintain something by law

regulated consumer credit agreement /ˌreɡjʊleɪtɪd kənˌsjuːmə ˈkredɪt əˌɡriːmənt/ *noun* a credit agreement as defined by the Consumer Credit Act

regulation /ˌreɡjʊˈleɪʃ(ə)n/ *noun* **1.** a law or rule ○ *the new government regulations on housing standards* ○ *Regulations concerning imports and exports are set out in this leaflet.* **2.** the use of laws or rules stipulated by a government or regulatory body, such as the FSA, to provide orderly procedures and to protect consumers and investors ○ *government regulation of trading practices*

'EC regulations which came into effect in July insist that customers can buy cars anywhere in the EC at the local pre-tax price' [*Financial Times*]

'…a unit trust is established under the regulations of the Department of Trade, with a trustee, a management company and a stock of units' [*Investors Chronicle*]

'…fear of audit regulation, as much as financial pressures, is a major factor behind the increasing number of small accountancy firms deciding to sell their practices or merge with another firm' [*Accountancy*]

Regulation S-X /ˌreɡjʊleɪʃ(ə)n es ˈeks/ *noun* the rule of the US Securities and Exchange Commission which regulates annual reports from companies

regulator /ˈreɡjʊleɪtə/ *noun* a person whose job it is to see that regulations are followed

'…the regulators have sought to protect investors and other market participants from the impact of a firm collapsing' [*Banking Technology*]

regulatory body /ˈreɡjʊlət(ə)ri ˌbɒdi/ *noun* an independent organisation, usually established by a government, that makes rules and sets standards for an industry and oversees the activities of companies within it

'Management of PharmaPlus is facing opposition from the regulatory body of pharmacists, which has authority over a pharmacy's operations and the stakeholders in the current industry structure.' [Harvard Business Review]

regulatory powers /ˈreɡjʊlət(ə)ri ˌpaʊəz/ *noun* powers to enforce government regulations

reimburse /ˌriːɪmˈbɜːs/ *verb* □ **to reimburse someone their expenses** to pay someone back for money which they have spent ○ *You will be reimbursed for your expenses* or *Your expenses will be reimbursed.*

reimbursement /ˌriːɪmˈbɜːsmənt/ *noun* the act of paying back money ○ *reimbursement of expenses*

reinvest /ˌriːɪnˈvest/ *verb* to invest money again ○ *She sold her shares and reinvested the money in government stocks.*

reinvestment /ˌriːɪnˈvestmənt/ *noun* **1.** the act of investing money again in the same securities **2.** the act of investing a company's earnings in its own business by using them to create new products for sale

'…many large US corporations offer shareholders the option of reinvesting their cash dividend payments in additional company stock at a discount to the market price. But to some big securities firms these discount reinvestment programs are an opportunity to turn a quick profit' [*Wall Street Journal*]

REIT *abbreviation US* real estate investment trust

reject /rɪˈdʒekt/ *verb* to refuse to accept something, or to say that something is not satisfactory ○ *The board rejected the draft budget.*

related company /rɪˌleɪtɪd ˈkʌmp(ə)ni/ *noun* a company in which another company makes a long-term capital investment in order to gain control or influence

related party /rɪˌleɪtɪd ˈpɑːti/ *noun* any person or company which controls or participates in the policy decisions of an accounting entity

relative error /ˌrelətɪv ˈerə/ *noun* the difference between an estimate and its correct value

release /rɪˈliːs/ *noun* the act of setting someone free or of making something or someone no longer subject to an obligation or restriction ○ *release from a contract* ○ *the release of goods from customs* ○ *She was offered early release so that she could take up her new job.*

'…pressure to ease monetary policy mounted yesterday with the release of a set of pessimistic economic statistics' [*Financial Times*]

'…the national accounts for the March quarter released by the Australian Bureau of Statistics showed a real increase in GDP' [*Australian Financial Review*]

relevant benefits /ˌreləv(ə)nt ˈbenɪfɪts/ *plural noun* benefits such as pension, endowment insurance, etc. provided by a pension scheme

relevant range /ˈreləv(ə)nt reɪndʒ/ *noun* the levels of business activity within which assumptions about cost behaviour remain valid

relocation /ˌriːləʊˈkeɪʃ(ə)n/ *noun* the act of moving to a different place ○ *We will pay all the staff relocation costs.*

relocation package /ˌriːləʊˈkeɪʃ(ə)n ˌpækɪdʒ/ *noun* payments made by an employer to an employee when the employee is asked to move to a new area in order to work. Payments up to a minimum level are exempt from tax.

reminder /rɪˈmaɪndə/ *noun* a letter to remind a customer that he or she has not paid an invoice ○ *to send someone a reminder*

remission of taxes /rɪˌmɪʃ(ə)n əv ˈtæksɪz/ *noun* a refund of taxes which have been overpaid

remit /rɪˈmɪt/ *verb* to send money ○ *to remit by cheque* (NOTE: **remitting – remitted**)

remittance /rɪˈmɪt(ə)ns/ *noun* money which is sent to pay back a debt or to pay an invoice ○ *Please send remittances to the treasurer.* ○ *The family lives on a weekly remittance from their father in the United States.*

remittance advice /rɪˈmɪt(ə)ns əd ˌvaɪs/, **remittance slip** /rɪˈmɪt(ə)ns slɪp/ *noun* an advice note sent with payment, showing why it is being made, i.e. quoting the invoice number or a reference number

remitting bank /rɪˈmɪtɪŋ bæŋk/ *verb* a bank into which a person has deposited a cheque, and which has the duty to collect the money from the account of the writer of the cheque

remortgage /riːˈmɔːɡɪdʒ/ *verb* to mortgage a property which is already mortgaged ○ *The bank offered him better terms than the building society, so he decided to remortgage the house.*

remunerate /rɪˈmjuːnəreɪt/ *verb* to pay someone for doing something ○ *The company refused to remunerate them for their services.*

remuneration /rɪˌmjuːnəˈreɪʃ(ə)n/ *noun* payment for services ○ *The job is interesting but the remuneration is low.* ○ *She receives a small remuneration of £400 a month.*

renegotiate /ˌriːnɪˈɡəʊʃieɪt/ *verb* to negotiate something again ○ *The company was forced to renegotiate the terms of the loan.*

renew /rɪˈnjuː/ *verb* to continue something for a further period of time ○ *We have asked the bank to renew the bill of exchange.* ○

Her contract was renewed for a further three years.

renewal /rɪˈnjuːəl/ *noun* the act of renewing ○ *renewal of a lease* or *of a subscription* or *of a bill* ○ *Her contract is up for renewal* ○ *When is the renewal date of the bill?*

renewal notice /rɪˈnjuːəl ˌnəʊtɪs/ *noun* a note sent by an insurance company asking the insured person to renew the insurance

renewal premium /rɪˈnjuːəl ˌpriːmiəm/ *noun* a premium to be paid to renew an insurance

rent /rent/ *noun* money paid to use an office, house or factory for a period of time
■ *verb* **1.** to pay money to hire an office, house, factory or piece of equipment for a period of time ○ *to rent an office* or *a car* ○ *He rents an office in the centre of town.* ○ *They were driving a rented car when they were stopped by the police.* **2.** *US* same as **let** □ **rent a room** a scheme by which a tax-payer can let a room in his or her house and be exempt from tax on the rental income below a certain level

rental /ˈrent(ə)l/ *noun* money paid to use an office, house, factory, car, piece of equipment, etc., for a period of time ○ *The car rental bill comes to over £1000 a quarter.*

'…top quality office furniture: short or long-term rental 50% cheaper than any other rental company' [*Australian Financial Review*]

'…until the vast acres of empty office space start to fill up with rent-paying tenants, rentals will continue to fall and so will values. Despite the very sluggish economic recovery under way, it is still difficult to see where the new tenants will come from' [*Australian Financial Review*]

rental value /ˈrent(ə)l ˌvæljuː/ *noun* a full value of the rent for a property if it were charged at the current market rate, i.e. calculated between rent reviews

rent control /ˈrent kənˌtrəʊl/ *noun* government regulation of rents

rent review /ˈrent rɪˌvjuː/ *noun* an increase in rents which is carried out during the term of a lease. Most leases allow for rents to be reviewed every three or five years.

rent tribunal /ˈrent traɪˌbjuːn(ə)l/ *noun* a court which can decide if a rent is too high or low

renunciation /rɪˌnʌnsiˈeɪʃ(ə)n/ *noun* an act of giving up ownership of shares

reorder /riːˈɔːdə/ *noun* a further order for something which has been ordered before ○ *The product has only been on the market ten* *days and we are already getting reorders.* ■ *verb* to place a new order for something ○ *We must reorder these items because stock is getting low.*

reorder level /riː'ɔːdə ˌlev(ə)l/ *noun* a minimum amount of an item which a company holds in stock, such that, when stock falls to this amount, the item must be reordered

reorder quantity /riː'ɔːdə ˌkwɒntəti/ *noun* a quantity of a product which is reordered, especially the economic order quantity (EOQ)

reorganisation /riːˌɔːɡənaɪ'zeɪʃ(ə)n/, **reorganization** *noun* the process of organising a company in a different way, as in the US when a bankrupt company applies to be treated under Chapter 11 to be protected from its creditors while it is being reorganised

repay /rɪ'peɪ/ *verb* to pay something back, or to pay back money to someone ○ *to repay money owed* ○ *The company had to cut back on expenditure in order to repay its debts.*

repayable /rɪ'peɪəb(ə)l/ *adjective* possible to pay back ○ *loan which is repayable over ten years*

repayment /rɪ'peɪmənt/ *noun* the act of paying money back or money which is paid back ○ *The loan is due for repayment next year.*

repayment mortgage /rɪ'peɪmənt ˌmɔːɡɪdʒ/ *noun* a mortgage where the borrower pays back both interest and capital over the period of the mortgage. This is opposed to an endowment mortgage, where only the interest is repaid, and an insurance is taken out to repay the capital at the end of the term of the mortgage.

replacement cost /rɪ'pleɪsmənt kɒst/ *noun* the cost of an item to replace an existing asset. Also called **cost of replacement**

replacement cost accounting /rɪ'pleɪsmənt kɒst əˌkaʊntɪŋ/ *noun* same as **current cost accounting**. Compare **historical cost accounting**

replacement cost depreciation /rɪ'pleɪsmənt kɒst dɪˌpriːʃieɪʃ(ə)n/ *noun* depreciation based on the actual cost of replacing the asset in the current year

replacement price /rɪ'pleɪsmənt praɪs/ *noun* a price at which the replacement for an asset would have to be bought

replacement value /rɪ'pleɪsmənt ˌvæljuː/ *noun* the value of something for insurance purposes if it were to be replaced ○ *The computer is insured at its replacement value.*

report /rɪ'pɔːt/ *noun* a statement describing what has happened or describing a state of affairs ○ *to make a report* or *to present a report* or *to send in a report on market opportunities in the Far East* ○ *The accountants are drafting a report on salary scales.* ■ *verb* **1.** to make a statement describing something ○ *The sales force reported an increased demand for the product.* ○ *He reported the damage to the insurance company.* ○ *We asked the bank to report on his financial status.* **2.** to publish the results of a company for a period and declare the dividend

'…a draft report on changes in the international monetary system' [*Wall Street Journal*]

'…responsibilities include the production of premium quality business reports' [*Times*]

'…the research director will manage a team of business analysts monitoring and reporting on the latest development in retail distribution' [*Times*]

'…the successful candidate will report to the area director for profit responsibility for sales of leading brands' [*Times*]

report form /rɪ'pɔːt fɔːm/ *noun* a balance sheet laid out in vertical form. It is the opposite of 'account' or 'horizontal' form. Also called **vertical form**

reporting entity /rɪ'pɔːtɪŋ ˌentɪti/ *noun* any organisation, such as a limited company, which reports its accounts to its shareholders

reporting period /rɪ'pɔːtɪŋ ˌpɪəriəd/ *noun* the amount of time covered by a particular financial report, be it a whole financial year or a shorter amount of time

repossess /ˌriːpə'zes/ *verb* to take back an item which someone is buying under a hire-purchase agreement, or a property which someone is buying under a mortgage, because the purchaser cannot continue the payments

repossession /ˌriːpə'zeʃ(ə)n/ *noun* an act of repossessing ○ *Repossessions are increasing as people find it difficult to meet mortgage repayments.*

reprice /riː'praɪs/ *verb* to change the price on an item, usually to increase it

reproduction cost /ˌriːprə'dʌkʃ(ə)n ˌkɒst/ *noun* the cost of duplicating an asset exactly, as distinct from replacing it

repudiation /rɪˌpjuːdi'eɪʃ(ə)n/ *noun* a refusal to accept something such as a debt

repurchase /riː'pɜːtʃɪs/ *verb* to buy something again, especially something which you have recently bought and then sold

require /rɪˈkwaɪə/ *verb* to ask for or to demand something ○ *to require a full explanation of expenditure* ○ *The law requires you to submit all income to the tax authorities.*

required rate of return /rɪˌkwaɪəd reɪt əv rɪˈtɜːn/ *noun* the minimum return for a proposed project investment to be acceptable. ◊ **discounted cash flow**

required reserves /rɪˌkwaɪəd rɪˈzɜːvz/ *plural noun* reserves which a US bank is required to hold in cash in its vaults or as deposit with the Federal Reserve. Compare **excess reserves**

resale /ˈriːseɪl/ *noun* the selling of goods which have been bought ○ *to purchase something for resale* ○ *The contract forbids resale of the goods to the US*

resale price maintenance /ˌriːseɪl ˈpraɪs ˌmeɪntənəns/ *noun* a system in which the price for an item is fixed by the manufacturer, and the retailer is not allowed to sell it at a lower price. Abbreviation **RPM**

reschedule /riːˈʃedjuːl/ *verb* **1.** to arrange a new timetable for something ○ *She missed her plane, and all the meetings had to be rescheduled.* **2.** to arrange new credit terms for the repayment of a loan ○ *Companies which are unable to keep up the interest payments on their loans have asked for their loans to be rescheduled.*

rescind /rɪˈsɪnd/ *verb* to annul or to cancel something ○ *to rescind a contract* or *an agreement*

research and development /rɪˌsɜːtʃ ən dɪˈveləpmənt/ *noun* activities that are designed to produce new knowledge and ideas and to develop ways in which these can be commercially exploited by a business (NOTE: Research and development activities are often grouped together to form a separate division or department within an organisation.)

research and development expenditure /rɪˌsɜːtʃ ən dɪˈveləpmənt ɪkˌspendɪtʃə/ *noun* money spent on R & D

resell /riːˈsel/ *verb* to sell something which has just been bought ○ *The car was sold in June and the buyer resold it to an dealer two months later.* (NOTE: **reselling – resold**)

reserve currency /rɪˈzɜːv ˌkʌrənsi/ *noun* a strong currency used in international finance, held by other countries to support their own weaker currencies

reserve for fluctuations /rɪˌzɜːv fə ˌflʌktʃuˈeɪʃ(ə)nz/ *noun* money set aside to allow for changes in the values of currencies

reserve fund /rɪˈzɜːv fʌnd/ *noun* profits in a business which have not been paid out as dividend but have been ploughed back into the business

reserve price /rɪˈzɜːv praɪs/ *noun* the lowest price which a seller will accept, e.g. at an auction or when selling securities through a broker ○ *The painting was withdrawn when it failed to reach its reserve price.*

reserves /rɪˈzɜːvz/ *plural noun* money from profits not paid as dividend, but kept back by a company in case it is needed for a special purpose

residence /ˈrezɪd(ə)ns/ *noun* **1.** a house or flat where someone lives ○ *He has a country residence where he spends his weekends.* **2.** the fact of living or operating officially in a country

residence permit /ˈrezɪd(ə)ns ˌpɜːmɪt/ *noun* an official document allowing a foreigner to live in a country ○ *He has applied for a residence permit.* ○ *She was granted a residence permit for one year* or *a one-year residence permit.*

resident /ˈrezɪd(ə)nt/ *noun, adjective* a person or company considered to be living or operating in a country for official or tax purposes ○ *The company is resident in France.*

residential property /ˌrezɪdenʃ(ə)l ˈprɒpəti/ *noun* houses or flats owned or occupied by individual residents

residual /rɪˈzɪdjuəl/ *adjective* remaining after everything else has gone

residual income /rɪˌzɪdjuəl ˈɪnkʌm/ *noun* a performance measure for businesses, calculated as net operating income minus a figure equal to minimum return on investment times operating assets

residual value /rɪˌzɪdjuəl ˈvæljuː/ *noun* a value of an asset after it has been depreciated in the company's accounts

residue /ˈrezɪdjuː/ *noun* money left over ○ *After paying various bequests the residue of his estate was split between his children.*

resource cost assignment /rɪˈzɔːs kɒst əˌsaɪnmənt/ *noun* the process of assigning costs to business activities

resource costs /rɪˈzɔːs kɒsts/ *plural noun* the costs of all elements used to carry out business activities, including such elements as workers' salaries and the cost of materials

resource driver /rɪˈzɔːs ˌdraɪvə/, **resource cost driver** /rɪˈzɔːs kɒst ˌdraɪvə/ *noun* a type of cost driver which is used to quantify the resources involved in creating a product or service

responsibility accounting /rɪˌspɒnsɪˈbɪlɪti əˌkaʊntɪŋ/ *noun* the keeping of financial records with an emphasis on who is responsible for each item

responsibility centre /rɪˈspɒnsɪˈbɪlɪti ˌsentə/ *noun* a department of an organisation with responsibility for a particular financial aspect of business, e.g. costs, revenues or investment funds

restated balance sheet /ˌriːsteɪtd ˈbæləns ʃiːt/ *noun* a balance sheet with information presented in a way that serves a particular purpose, such as highlighting depreciation on assets

restatement /riːˈsteɪtmənt/ *noun* a revision of an earlier financial statement

restrict /rɪˈstrɪkt/ *verb* to limit something or to impose controls on something ○ *to restrict credit* ○ *to restrict the flow of trade* or *to restrict imports*

restricted fund /rɪˈstrɪktɪd fʌnd/ *noun* in a not-for-profit organisation, a fund whose assets can only be used for those purposes designated by donors

restrictive /rɪˈstrɪktɪv/ *adjective* not allowing something to go beyond a point

restrictive covenant /rɪˌstrɪktɪv ˈkʌvənənt/ *noun* a clause in a contract which prevents someone from doing something

restructure /riːˈstrʌktʃə/ *verb* to reorganise the financial basis of a company

restructuring /riːˈstrʌktʃərɪŋ/ *noun* the process of reorganising the financial basis of a company

result /rɪˈzʌlt/ *noun* **1.** a profit or loss account for a company at the end of a trading period ○ *The company's results for last year were an improvement on those of the previous year.* **2.** something which happens because of something else ○ *What was the result of the price investigation?* ○ *The company doubled its sales force with the result that the sales rose by 26%.*

'…the company has received the backing of a number of oil companies who are willing to pay for the results of the survey' [*Lloyd's List*]

'…some profit-taking was noted, but underlying sentiment remained firm in a steady stream of strong corporate results' [*Financial Times*]

retail /ˈriːteɪl/ *noun* the sale of small quantities of goods to the general public □ **the goods in stock have a retail value of £1m** the value of the goods if sold to the public is £1m, before discounts and other factors are taken into account ■ *adverb* □ **he buys wholesale and sells retail** he buys goods in bulk at a wholesale discount and sells in small quantities to the public ■ *verb* to sell for a price □ **these items retail at *or* for £2.50** the retail price of these items is £2.50

retail banking /ˈriːteɪl ˌbæŋkɪŋ/ *noun* services provided by commercial banks to individuals as opposed to business customers, e.g. current accounts, deposit and savings accounts, as well as credit cards, mortgages and investments. Compare **wholesale banking** (NOTE: In the United Kingdom, although this service was traditionally provided by high street banks, separate organisations are now providing Internet and telephone banking services.)

retail deposit /ˈriːteɪl dɪˌpɒzɪt/ *noun* a deposit placed by an individual with a bank

retailer /ˈriːteɪlə/ *noun* a person who runs a retail business, selling goods direct to the public

retailing /ˈriːteɪlɪŋ/ *noun* the selling of full-price goods to the public ○ *From car retailing the company branched out into car leasing.*

retail investor /ˈriːteɪl ɪnˌvestə/ *noun* a private investor, as opposed to institutional investors

retail price /ˈriːteɪl ˌpraɪs/ *noun* the price at which the retailer sells to the final customer

retail price index /ˌriːteɪl ˈpraɪs ˌɪndeks/, **retail prices index** /ˌriːteɪl ˈpraɪsɪz ˌɪndeks/ *noun* an index which shows how prices of consumer goods have increased or decreased over a period of time. Abbreviation **RPI** (NOTE: The US term is **Consumer Price Index.**)

retain /rɪˈteɪn/ *verb* to keep something or someone ○ *measures to retain experienced staff* ○ *Out of the profits, the company has retained £50,000 as provision against bad debts.*

retained earnings /rɪˌteɪnd ˈɜːnɪŋz/ *plural noun* an amount of profit after tax which a company does not pay out as dividend to the shareholders, but which is kept to be used for the further development of the business. Also called **retentions**

retained income /rɪˌteɪnd ˈɪnkʌm/, **retained profit** /rɪˌteɪnd ˈprɒfɪt/ *noun* same as **retained earnings**

retainer /rɪ'teɪnə/ *noun* money paid in advance to someone so that they will work for you and not for someone else ○ *We pay them a retainer of £1,000.*

retentions /rɪ'tenʃənz/ *plural noun* same as **retained earnings**

retiral /rɪ'taɪərəl/ *noun* same as **retirement**

retire /rɪ'taɪə/ *verb* **1.** to stop work and take a pension ○ *She retired with a £15,000 pension.* ○ *The founder of the company retired at the age of 85.* **2.** to make an employee stop work and take a pension ○ *They decided to retire all staff over 50.*

retirement /rɪ'taɪəmənt/ *noun* the act of retiring from work ○ *I am looking forward to my retirement.* ○ *Older staff are planning what they will do in retirement.*

retirement age /rɪ'taɪəmənt eɪdʒ/ *noun* the age at which people retire. In the UK this is usually 65 for men and 60 (but soon to become 65) for women.

retirement annuity /rɪ'taɪəmənt ə ˌnjuːɪti/ *noun* an annuity bought when someone retires, using part of the sum put into a personal pension plan

retirement benefits /rɪ'taɪəmənt 'benɪfɪts/ *plural noun* benefits which are payable by a pension scheme to a person on retirement

retirement pension /rɪ'taɪəmənt ˌpenʃən/ *noun* a state pension given to a man who is over 65 or and woman who is over 60

retroactive /ˌretrəʊ'æktɪv/ *adjective* which takes effect from a time in the past ○ *They got a pay rise retroactive to last January.*

'The salary increases, retroactive from April of the current year, reflect the marginal rise in private sector salaries' [*Nikkei Weekly*]

retroactively /ˌretrəʊ'æktɪvli/ *adverb* going back to a time in the past

return /rɪ'tɜːn/ *noun* **1.** a profit or income from money invested ○ *We are buying technology shares because they bring in a quick return.* ○ *What is the gross return on this line?* **2.** an official statement or form that has to be sent in to the authorities ■ *verb* to make a statement ○ *to return income of £15,000 to the tax authorities*

'…with interest rates running well above inflation, investors want something that offers a return for their money' [*Business Week*]

'Section 363 of the Companies Act 1985 requires companies to deliver an annual return to the Companies Registration Office. Failure to do so before the end of the period of 28 days after the company's return date could lead to directors and other officers in default being fined up to £2000' [*Accountancy*]

return date /rɪ'tɜːn deɪt/ *noun* a date by which a company's annual return has to be made to the Registrar of Companies

return on assets /rɪˌtɜːn ɒn 'æsets/, **return on capital employed** /rɪˌtɜːn ɒn ˌkæpɪt(ə)l ɪm'plɔɪd/, **return on equity** /rɪ ˌtɜːn ɒn 'ekwɪti/ *noun* a profit shown as a percentage of the capital or money invested in a business. Abbreviation **ROA, ROCE, ROE**

return on investment /rɪˌtɜːn ɒn ɪn 'vestmənt/ *noun* a ratio of the profit made in a financial year as a percentage of an investment. Abbreviation **ROI**

return on net assets /rɪˌtɜːn ɒn net 'æsets/ *noun* a ratio of the profit made in a financial year as a percentage of the assets of a company

returns /rɪ'tɜːnz/ *plural noun* profits or income from investment ○ *The company is looking for quick returns on its investment.*

revaluation /riːˌvæljʊ'eɪʃən/ *noun* an act of revaluing ○ *The balance sheet takes into account the revaluation of the company's properties.*

revaluation method /riːˌvæljʊ'eɪʃən ˌmeθəd/ *noun* a method of calculating the depreciation of assets, by which the asset is depreciated by the difference in its value at the end of the year over its value at the beginning of the year

revaluation reserve /riːˌvæljʊ'eɪʃən rɪ ˌzɜːv/ *noun* money set aside to account for the fact that the value of assets may vary as a result of accounting in different currencies

revalue /riː'væljuː/ *verb* to value something again, usually setting a higher value on it than before ○ *The company's properties have been revalued.* ○ *The dollar has been revalued against all world currencies.*

revenue /'revənjuː/ *noun* **1.** money received ○ *revenue from advertising* or *advertising revenue* ○ *Oil revenues have risen with the rise in the dollar.* **2.** money received by a government in tax

revenue accounts /'revənjuː əˌkaʊnts/ *plural noun* accounts of a business which record money received as sales, commission, etc.

revenue centre /'revənjuː ˌsentə/ *noun* a department of an organisation with responsibility for maximising revenue

revenue expenditure /ˈrevənjuː ɪkˌspendɪtʃə/ *noun* expenditure on purchasing stock but not capital items, which is then sold during the current accounting period

revenue ledger /ˈrevənjuː ˌledʒə/ *noun* a record of all the income received by an organisation

revenue officer /ˈrevənjuː ˌɒfɪsə/ *noun* a person working in the government tax offices

revenue recognition /ˈrevənjuː ˌrekəgnɪʃ(ə)n/ *noun* the process of recording revenue in accounts

revenue reserves /ˈrevənjuː rɪˌzɜːvz/ *plural noun* retained earnings which are shown in the company's balance sheet as part of the shareholders' funds. Also called **company reserves**

revenue sharing /ˈrevənjuː ˌʃeərɪŋ/ *noun* the distribution of income within limited partnerships

reverse /rɪˈvɜːs/ *adjective* opposite or in the opposite direction ■ *verb* to change a decision to the opposite ○ *The committee reversed its decision on import quotas.*

'…the trade balance sank $17 billion, reversing last fall's brief improvement' [*Fortune*]

reverse leverage /rɪˌvɜːs ˈlevərɪdʒ/ *noun* the borrowing of money at a rate of interest higher than the expected rate of return on investing the money borrowed

reverse takeover /rɪˌvɜːs ˈteɪkəʊvə/ *noun* a takeover in which the company that has been taken over ends up owning the company which has taken it over. The acquiring company's shareholders give up their shares in exchange for shares in the target company.

reverse yield gap /rɪˌvɜːs ˈjiːld ˌgæp/ *noun* the amount by which bond yield exceeds equity yield, or interest rates on loans exceed rental values as a percentage of the costs of properties

reversing entry /rɪˈvɜːsɪŋ ˌentri/ *noun* an entry in a set of accounts which reverses an entry in the preceding accounts

reversion /rɪˈvɜːʃ(ə)n/ *noun* the return of property to its original owner

reversionary /rɪˈvɜːʃ(ə)n(ə)ri/ *adjective* referring to property which passes to another owner on the death of the present one

reversionary annuity /rɪˌvɜːʃ(ə)n(ə)ri əˈnjuːɪti/ *noun* an annuity paid to someone on the death of another person

reversionary bonus /rɪˌvɜːʃ(ə)n(ə)ri ˈbəʊnəs/ *noun* an annual bonus on a life assurance policy, declared by the insurer

review /rɪˈvjuː/ *noun* a general examination ○ *to conduct a review of distributors* ■ *verb* to examine something generally

revise /rɪˈvaɪz/ *verb* to change something which has been calculated or planned ○ *Sales forecasts are revised annually.*

revolving credit /rɪˌvɒlvɪŋ ˈkredɪt/ *noun* a system where someone can borrow money at any time up to an agreed amount, and continue to borrow while still paying off the original loan. Also called **open-ended credit**

revolving loan /rɪˌvɒlvɪŋ ˈləʊn/ *noun* a loan facility whereby the borrower can choose the number and timing of withdrawals against their bank loan and any money repaid may be reborrowed at a future date. Such loans are available both to businesses and personal customers.

rider /ˈraɪdə/ *noun* an additional clause ○ *to add a rider to a contract*

right /raɪt/ *noun* a legal entitlement to something ○ *There is no automatic right of renewal to this contract.* ○ *She has a right to the property.*

rights issue /ˈraɪts ˌɪʃuː/ *noun* an arrangement which gives shareholders the right to buy more shares at a lower price (NOTE: The US term is **rights offering**.)

rights offering /ˈraɪts ˌɒfərɪŋ/ *noun* an occasion when a rights issue is offered for sale

ring fence /ˈrɪŋ fens/ *verb* **1.** to separate valuable assets or profitable businesses from others in a group which are unprofitable and may make the whole group collapse **2.** to identify money from certain sources and only use it in certain areas ○ *The grant has been ring-fenced for use in local authority education projects only.* ◊ **hypothecation**

rise /raɪz/ *noun* **1.** an increase ○ *a rise in the price of raw materials* ○ *Oil price rises brought about a recession in world trade.* ○ *The recent rise in interest rates has made mortgages dearer.* ○ *There needs to be an increase in salaries to keep up with the rise in the cost of living.* **2.** an increase in pay ○ *She asked her boss for a rise.* ○ *He had a 6% rise in January.* (NOTE: The US term is **raise**.) ■ *verb* to move upwards or to become higher ○ *Prices or Salaries are rising faster than inflation.* ○ *Interest rates have risen to 15%.* (NOTE: **rising – rose – risen**)

risk /rɪsk/ *noun* possible harm or a chance of danger

'…remember, risk isn't volatility. Risk is the chance that a company's earnings power will erode – either because of a change in the industry or a change in the business that will make the company significantly less profitable in the long term' [*Fortune*]

risk-adjusted return on capital /ˌrɪsk əˌdʒʌstɪd rɪˌtɜːn ɒn 'kæpɪt(ə)l/ *noun* a figure for capital calculated in a way that takes into account the risks associated with income

risk arbitrage /'rɪsk ˌɑːbɪtrɑːʒ/ *noun* the business of buying shares in companies which are likely to be taken over and so rise in price

risk arbitrageur /'rɪsk ˌɑːbɪtrɑːʒɜː/ *noun* a person whose business is risk arbitrage

risk asset ratio /ˌrɪsk ˌæset 'reɪʃiəʊ/ *noun* a proportion of a bank's capital which is in risk assets

risk capital /'rɪsk ˌkæpɪt(ə)l/ *noun* same as **venture capital**

risk-free /ˌrɪsk 'friː/, **riskless** /'rɪskləs/ *adjective* with no risk involved ○ *a risk-free investment*

'…there is no risk-free way of taking regular income from your money higher than the rate of inflation and still preserving its value' [*Guardian*]

'…many small investors have also preferred to put their spare cash with risk-free investments such as building societies rather than take chances on the stock market. The returns on a host of risk-free investments have been well into double figures' [*Money Observer*]

risk management /'rɪsk ˌmænɪdʒmənt/ *noun* the work of managing a company's exposure to risk from its credit terms or exposure to interest rate or exchange rate fluctuations

risk premium /'rɪsk ˌpriːmiəm/ *noun* an extra payment, e.g. increased dividend or higher than usual profits, for taking risks

risk-weighted assets /ˌrɪsk ˌweɪtɪd 'æsets/ *plural noun* assets which include off-balance sheet items for insurance purposes

risky /'rɪski/ *adjective* dangerous or which may cause harm ○ *We lost all our money in some risky ventures in South America.*

'…while the bank has scaled back some of its more risky trading operations, it has

retained its status as a top-rate advisory house' [*Times*]

ROA *abbreviation* return on assets

ROCE *abbreviation* return on capital employed

ROE *abbreviation* return on equity

ROI *abbreviation* return on investment

roll over *phrasal verb* □ **to roll over a credit** to make credit available over a continuing period □ **to roll over a debt** to allow a debt to stand after the repayment date

'…at the IMF in Washington, officials are worried that Japanese and US banks might decline to roll over the principal of loans made in the 1980s to Southeast Asian and other developing countries' [*Far Eastern Economic Review*]

roll up /ˌrəʊl 'ʌp/ *phrasal verb* to extend a loan, by adding the interest due to be paid to the capital

rolled-up coupons /ˌrəʊld ʌp 'kuːpɒnz/ *plural noun* interest coupons on securities, which are not paid out, but added to the capital value of the security

rolling budget /ˌrəʊlɪŋ 'bʌdʒɪt/ *noun* a budget which moves forward on a regular basis, such as a budget covering a twelve-month period which moves forward each month or quarter

rollover /'rəʊləʊvə/ *noun* an extension of credit or of the period of a loan, though not necessarily on the same terms as previously

rollover relief /'rəʊləʊvə rɪˌliːf/ *noun* tax relief where profit on the sale of an asset is not taxed if the money realised is used to acquire another asset. The profit on the eventual sale of this second asset will be taxed unless the proceeds of the second sale are also invested in new assets.

Romalpa clause /rəʊ'mɒlpə ˌklɔːz/ *noun* a clause in a contract whereby the seller provides that title to the goods does not pass to the buyer until the buyer has paid for them

root /ruːt/ *noun* a fractional power of a number

root cause analysis /ˌruːt 'kɔːz əˌnælɪsɪs/ *noun* a problem-solving technique that seeks to identify the underlying cause of a problem

rough /rʌf/ *adjective* approximate, not very accurate

rough out *phrasal verb* to make a draft or a general design of something, which may be changed later ○ *The finance director roughed out a plan of investment.*

round off /ˌraʊnd 'ɒf/ *phrasal verb* to reduce the digits in a decimal number by removing the final zeros

round down *phrasal verb* to decrease a fractional figure to the nearest full figure

round up *phrasal verb* to increase a fractional figure to the nearest full figure ○ *to round up the figures to the nearest pound*

'…each cheque can be made out for the local equivalent of œ100 rounded up to a convenient figure' [*Sunday Times*]

round figures /ˌraʊnd ˈfɪɡəz/ *plural noun* figures that have been adjusted up or down to the nearest 10, 100, 1,000, and so on

royalty /ˈrɔɪəlti/ *noun* money paid to an inventor, writer, or the owner of land for the right to use their property, usually a specific percentage of sales, or a specific amount per sale ○ *The country will benefit from rising oil royalties.* ○ *He is still receiving substantial royalties from his invention.*

RPB *abbreviation* recognised professional body

RPI *abbreviation* retail price index

RPM *abbreviation* resale price maintenance

rubber check /ˌrʌbə ˈtʃek/ *noun US* a cheque which cannot be cashed because the person writing it does not have enough money in the account to pay it (NOTE: The UK term is **bouncing cheque**.)

rule /ruːl/ *noun* a statement that directs how people should behave ○ *It is a company rule that smoking is not allowed in the offices.* ○ *The rules of the organisation are explained during the induction sessions.* ■ *verb* **1.** to give an official decision ○ *The commission of inquiry ruled that the company was in breach of contract.* ○ *The judge ruled that the documents had to be deposited with the court.* **2.** to be in force or to be current ○ *The current ruling agreement is being redrafted.*

rulebook /ˈruːlbʊk/ *noun* a set of rules by which the members of a self-regulatory organisation must operate

rule of 72 /ˌruːl əv ˌsev(ə)nti ˈtuː/ *noun* a calculation that an investment will double in value at compound interest after a period shown as 72 divided by the interest percent-

age, so interest at 10% compound will double the capital invested in 7.2 years

rule of 78 /ˌruːl əv ˌsev(ə)nti ˈeɪt/ *noun* a method used to calculate the rebate on a loan with front-loaded interest that has been repaid early. It takes into account the fact that as the loan is repaid, the share of each monthly payment related to interest decreases, while the share related to repayment increases.

run /rʌn/ *noun* a rush to buy something ○ *The Post Office reported a run on the new stamps.* □ **a run on the bank** a rush by customers to take deposits out of a bank which they think may close down ■ *verb* **1.** to be in force ○ *The lease runs for twenty years.* ○ *The lease has only six months to run.* **2.** to amount to ○ *The costs ran into thousands of pounds.*

'…applications for mortgages are running at a high level' [*Times*]

'…with interest rates running well above inflation, investors want something that offers a return for their money' [*Business Week*]

run into *phrasal verb* to amount to ○ *Costs have run into thousands of pounds.* □ **he has an income running into five figures** he earns more than £10,000

run up *phrasal verb* to make debts or costs go up quickly ○ *He quickly ran up a bill for £250.*

running account credit /ˌrʌnɪŋ ə ˌkaʊnt ˈkredɪt/ *noun* an overdraft facility, credit card or similar system that allows customers to borrow up to a specific limit and reborrow sums previously repaid by either writing a cheque or using their card

running costs /ˈrʌnɪŋ kɒsts/ *plural noun* same as **operating costs**

running total /ˌrʌnɪŋ ˈtəʊt(ə)l/ *noun* the total carried from one column of figures to the next

running yield /ˈrʌnɪŋ jiːld/ *noun* a yield on fixed interest securities, where the interest is shown as a percentage of the price paid

S

safe deposit /ˈseɪf dɪˌpɒzɪt/ *noun* a bank safe where you can leave jewellery or documents

safe deposit box /ˌseɪf dɪˈpɒzɪt ˌbɒks/ *noun* a small box which you can rent to keep jewellery or documents in a bank's safe

safeguarding of assets /ˌseɪfɡɑːdɪŋ əv ˈæsets/ *noun* the practice of guarding against loss of assets

safe investment /ˌseɪf ɪnˈvestmənt/ *noun* something, e.g. a share, which is not likely to fall in value

safety /ˈseɪfti/ *noun* the fact of being free from danger or risk □ **to take safety precautions** *or* **safety measures** to act to make sure something is safe

salaried /ˈsælərɪd/ *adjective* earning a salary ○ *The company has 250 salaried staff.*

salaried partner /ˌsælərɪd ˈpɑːtnə/ *noun* a partner, often a junior one, who receives a regular salary in accordance with the partnership agreement

salary /ˈsælərɪ/ *noun* **1.** a regular payment for work done, made to an employee usually as a cheque at the end of each month ○ *The company froze all salaries for a six-month period.* ○ *The salary may be low, but the fringe benefits attached to the job are good.* ○ *She got a salary increase in June.* **2.** the amount paid to an employee, shown as a monthly, quarterly or yearly total (NOTE: The plural is **salaries**.)

salary cheque /ˈsælərɪ tʃek/ *noun* a monthly cheque by which an employee is paid

salary cut /ˈsælərɪ kʌt/ *noun* a sudden reduction in salary

salary deductions /ˈsælərɪ dɪˌdʌkʃənz/ *plural noun* money which a company removes from salaries to pay to the government as tax, National Insurance contributions, etc.

salary differentials /ˈsælərɪ dɪfəˌrenʃəlz/ *plural noun* same as **pay differentials**

salary review /ˈsælərɪ rɪˌvjuː/ *noun* same as **pay review** ○ *She had a salary review last April* or *Her salary was reviewed last April.*

salary scale /ˈsælərɪ skeɪl/ *noun* same as **pay scale** ○ *He was appointed at the top end of the salary scale.*

sale /seɪl/ *noun* **1.** an act of giving an item or doing a service in exchange for money, or for the promise that money will be paid □ **to offer something for sale** *or* **to put something up for sale** to announce that something is ready to be sold ○ *They put the factory up for sale.* ○ *His shop is for sale.* ○ *These items are not for sale to the general public.* **2.** an act of selling goods at specially low prices ○ *The shop is having a sale to clear old stock.* ○ *The sale price is 50% of the usual price.*

'…the latest car sales for April show a 1.8 per cent dip from last year's total' [*Investors Chronicle*]

sale and lease-back /ˌseɪl ən ˈliːs bæk/ *noun* **1.** a situation where a company sells a property to raise cash and then leases it back from the purchaser **2.** the sale of an asset, usually a building, to somebody else who then leases it back to the original owner

sales /seɪlz/ *plural noun* money received for selling something ○ *Sales have risen over the first quarter.*

sales analysis /ˈseɪlz əˌnæləsɪs/ *noun* an examination of the reports of sales to see why items have or have not sold well

sales book /ˈseɪlz bʊk/ *noun* a record of sales

sales budget /ˈseɪlz ˌbʌdʒɪt/ *noun* a plan of probable sales

sales department /ˈseɪlz dɪˌpɑːtmənt/ *noun* the section of a company which deals with selling the company's products or services

sales figures /ˈseɪlz ˌfɪɡəz/ *plural noun* total sales

sales force /ˈseɪlz fɔːs/ *noun* a group of sales staff

sales forecast /'seɪlz ˌfɔːkɑːst/ *noun* an estimate of future sales

sales invoice /'seɪlz ˌɪnvɔɪs/ *noun* an invoice relating to a sale

sales journal /'seɪlz ˌdʒɜːn(ə)l/ *noun* the book in which non-cash sales are recorded with details of customer, invoice, amount and date. These details are later posted to each customer's account in the sales ledger.

sales ledger /'seɪlz ˌledʒə/ *noun* a book in which sales to each customer are entered. Also called **debtors ledger**

sales ledger clerk /'seɪlz ˌledʒə ˌklɑːk/ *noun* an office employee who deals with the sales ledger

sales manager /'seɪlz ˌmænɪdʒə/ *noun* a person in charge of a sales department

sales mix /'seɪlz mɪks/ *noun* the sales and profitability of a wide range of products sold by a single company

sales mix profit variance /ˌseɪlz mɪks 'prɒfɪt ˌveəriəns/ *noun* the differing profitability of different products within a product range

sales mix variance /'seɪlz mɪks ˌveəriəns/ *noun* a discrepancy between the actual mix of products produced and sold and the budgeted mix

sales price variance /ˌseɪlz praɪs 'veəriəns/ *noun* the difference between expected revenue from actual sales and actual revenue

sales return /'seɪlz rɪˌtɜːn/ *noun* a report of sales made each day or week or quarter

sales revenue /'seɪlz ˌrevənjuː/ *noun* US the income from sales of goods or services

sales target /'seɪlz ˌtɑːgɪt/ *noun* the amount of sales a sales representative is expected to achieve

sales tax /'seɪlz tæks/ *noun* US same as **VAT**

sales value /'seɪlz ˌvæljuː/ *noun* the amount of money which would be received if something is sold

sales volume /'seɪlz ˌvɒljuːm/ *noun* the number of units sold (NOTE: The UK term is **turnover**.)

sales volume profit variance /ˌseɪlz ˌvɒljuːm 'prɒfɪt ˌveəriəns/ *noun* the difference between the profit on the number of units actually sold and the forecast figure

sales volume variance /'seɪlz ˌvɒljuːm ˌveəriəns/ *noun* a discrepancy between the actual volume of sales and the budgeted volume

salvage /'sælvɪdʒ/ *noun* **1.** the work of saving a ship or a cargo from being destroyed **2.** goods saved from a wrecked ship, from a fire or from some other accident ○ *a sale of flood salvage items* (NOTE: no plural) ■ *verb* **1.** to save goods or a ship from being destroyed ○ *We are selling off a warehouse full of salvaged goods.* **2.** to save something from loss ○ *The company is trying to salvage its reputation after the managing director was sent to prison for fraud.* ○ *The receiver managed to salvage something from the collapse of the company.*

salvage value /'sælvɪdʒ ˌvæljuː/ *noun* the value of an asset if sold for scrap

S&L *abbreviation* savings and loan

Sarbanes-Oxley Act /ˌsɑːbæn 'ɒksli ˌækt/ *noun* an act of the US Congress designed to protect investors from fraudulent accounting activities

SAS *abbreviation* Statement of Auditing Standards

save /seɪv/ *verb* to choose not to spend money ○ *He is trying to save money by walking to work.* ○ *She is saving to buy a house.*

save-as-you-earn /ˌseɪv əz juː 'ɜːn/ *noun* a savings-related scheme set up by an employer that gives employees a right to buy a certain number of shares in the company at a fixed price at a particular time. Abbreviation **SAYE**

saver /'seɪvə/ *noun* a person who saves money

savings /'seɪvɪŋz/ *plural noun* money saved (i.e. money which is not spent) ○ *She put all her savings into a deposit account.*

savings account /'seɪvɪŋz əˌkaʊnt/ *noun* an account where you put money in regularly and which pays interest, often at a higher rate than a deposit account

savings and loan /ˌseɪvɪŋz ən 'ləʊn/, **savings and loan association** /ˌseɪvɪŋz ən 'ləʊn əˌsəʊsieɪʃ(ə)n/ *noun* US same as **building society**

savings bank /'seɪvɪŋz bæŋk/ *noun* a bank where you can deposit money and receive interest on it

savings certificate /'seɪvɪŋz səˌtɪfɪkət/ *noun* a document showing that you have invested money in a government savings scheme

savings income /'seɪvɪŋz ˌɪnkʌm/ *noun* income in the form of interest on deposits with banks and building societies, government bonds, etc., but not income from dividends or rental income from property

savings-related share option scheme /ˌseɪvɪŋz rɪˌleɪtɪd ˈʃeər ˌɒpʃən ˌskiːm/ *noun* a scheme which allows employees of a company to buy shares with money which they have contributed to a savings scheme

SAYE *abbreviation* save-as-you-earn

SBA *abbreviation* Small Business Administration

scale /skeɪl/ *noun* a system which is graded into various levels □ **scale of charges** *or* **scale of prices** a list showing various prices □ **scale of salaries** a list of salaries showing different levels of pay in different jobs in the same company

scarce currency /ˌskeəs ˈkʌrənsi/ *noun* same as **hard currency**

schedule /ˈʃedjuːl/ *noun* **1.** a timetable, a plan of how time should be spent, drawn up in advance ○ *The managing director has a busy schedule of appointments.* ○ *Her assistant tried to fit us into her schedule.* **2.** a list, especially a list forming an additional document attached to a contract ○ *the schedule of territories to which a contract applies* ○ *Please find enclosed our schedule of charges.* ○ *See the attached schedule* or *as per the attached schedule.* **3.** a list of interest rates

Schedule A /ˌʃedjuːl ˈeɪ/ *noun* a schedule under which tax is charged on income from land or buildings

Schedule B /ˌʃedjuːl ˈbiː/ *noun* a schedule under which tax was formerly charged on income from woodlands

Schedule C /ˌʃedjuːl ˈsiː/ *noun* a schedule under which tax is charged on profits from government stock

Schedule D /ˌʃedjuːl ˈdiː/ *noun* a schedule under which tax is charged on income from trades or professions, interest and other earnings not derived from being employed

Schedule E /ˌʃedjuːl ˈiː/ *noun* a schedule under which tax is charged on income from salaries, wages or pensions

Schedule F /ˌʃedjuːl ˈef/ *noun* a schedule under which tax is charged on income from dividends

scheme /skiːm/ *noun* a plan, arrangement or way of working ○ *Under the bonus scheme all employees get 10% of their annual pay as a Christmas bonus.* ○ *She has joined the company pension scheme.* ○ *We operate a profit-sharing scheme for managers.*

scheme of arrangement /ˌskiːm əv ə ˈreɪndʒmənt/ *noun* a scheme drawn up by an individual or company to offer ways of paying debts, so as to avoid bankruptcy proceedings. Also called **voluntary arrangement**

scope limitation /ˈskəʊp ˌlɪmɪteɪʃ(ə)n/ *noun* the fact that the scope of audit is limited in some way, e.g. owing to restrictions beyond the client's control

scorched earth policy /ˌskɔːtʃt ˈɜːθ ˌpɒlɪsi/ *noun* a way of combating a takeover bid, where the target company sells valuable assets or purchases unattractive assets. ◊ **poison pill**

scrap /skræp/ *noun* material left over after an industrial process, and which still has some value, as opposed to waste, which has no value ○ *to sell a ship for scrap*

scrap value /ˈskræp ˌvæljuː/ *noun* the value of an asset if sold for scrap ○ *Its scrap value is £2,500.*

scrip /skrɪp/ *noun* a security, e.g. a share, bond, or the certificate issued to show that someone has been allotted a share or bond

'…under the rule, brokers who fail to deliver stock within four days of a transaction are to be fined 1% of the transaction value for each day of missing scrip' [*Far Eastern Economic Review*]

scrip dividend /ˈskrɪp ˌdɪvɪdend/ *noun* a dividend which takes the form of new shares in the company, as opposed to cash

scrip issue /ˈskrɪp ˌɪʃuː/ *noun* same as **bonus issue**

SDRs *abbreviation* special drawing rights

seal /siːl/ *noun* **1.** a special symbol, often one stamped on a piece of wax, which is used to show that a document is officially approved by the organisation that uses the symbol **2.** a piece of paper, metal, or wax attached to close something, so that it can be opened only if the paper, metal, or wax is removed or broken ■ *verb* **1.** to close something tightly ○ *The computer disks were sent in a sealed container.* **2.** to attach a seal, to stamp something with a seal ○ *Customs sealed the shipment.*

seasonal /ˈsiːz(ə)n(ə)l/ *adjective* which lasts for a season or which only happens during a particular season ○ *seasonal variations in sales patterns* ○ *The demand for this item is very seasonal.*

seasonal adjustment /ˌsiːz(ə)n(ə)l ə ˈdʒʌstmənt/ *noun* an adjustment made to accounts to allow for any short-term seasonal factors, such as Christmas sales, that may distort the figures

seasonal business /ˌsiːz(ə)n(ə)l ˈbɪznɪs/ *noun* trade that varies depending on the time of the year, e.g. trade in goods such as suntan products or Christmas trees

seasonality /ˌsiːzəˈnælɪti/ *noun* variations in production or sales that occur at different but predictable times of the year

SEC *abbreviation* Securities and Exchange Commission

second /ˈsekənd/ *noun, adjective* the thing which comes after the first ■ *verb* **1.** □ **to second a motion** to be the first person to support a proposal put forward by someone else ○ *Mrs Smith seconded the motion* or *The motion was seconded by Mrs Smith.* **2.** /sɪˈkɒnd/ to lend a member of staff to another company, organisation or department for a fixed period of time ○ *He was seconded to the Department of Trade for two years.*

secondary buyout /ˈsekənd(ə)ri ˌbaɪaʊt/ *noun* a situation in which an investor such as a private equity company sells its investment in a company to another investor, as a means of realising their investment

secondary industry /ˈsekənd(ə)ri ˌɪndəstri/ *noun* an industry which uses basic raw materials to produce manufactured goods

secondary sites /ˈsekənd(ə)ri saɪts/ *plural noun* less valuable commercial sites. Compare **prime sites**

second half /ˌsekənd ˈhɑːf/ *noun* the period of six months from 1st July to 31st December ○ *The figures for the second half are up on those for the first part of the year.*

second half-year /ˌsekənd ˈhɑːf jɪə/ *noun* the six-month period from July to the end of December

secondment /sɪˈkɒndmənt/ *noun* the fact or period of being seconded to another job for a period ○ *She is on three years' secondment to an Australian college.*

second mortgage /ˌsekənd ˈmɔːɡɪdʒ/ *noun* a further mortgage on a property which is already mortgaged

second quarter /ˌsekənd ˈkwɔːtə/ *noun* the period of three months from April to the end of June

secretary /ˈsekrət(ə)ri/ *noun* an official of a company or society whose job is to keep records and write letters

Secretary of the Treasury /ˌsekrət(ə)ri əv ðə ˈtreʒəri/ *noun US* a senior member of the government in charge of financial affairs

secret reserves /ˌsiːkrət rɪˈzɜːvz/ *plural noun* reserves which are illegally kept hidden in a company's balance sheet, as

opposed to 'hidden reserves' which are simply not easy to identify

section /ˈsekʃən/ *noun* one of the parts of an Act of Parliament

secure /sɪˈkjʊə/ *adjective* safe, which cannot change

secured /sɪˈkjʊəd/ *adjective* used to describe a type of borrowing such as a mortgage where the lender has a legal right to take over an asset or assets of the borrower, if the borrower does not repay the loan

secured creditor /sɪˌkjʊəd ˈkredɪtə/ *noun* a person who is owed money by someone, and can legally claim the same amount of the borrower's property if the borrower fails to pay back the money owed

secured liability /sɪˌkjʊəd ˌlaɪəˈbɪlɪti/ *noun* a loan secured by means of a pledge of assets that can be sold if necessary

secured loan /sɪˌkjʊəd ˈləʊn/ *noun* a loan which is guaranteed by the borrower giving assets as security

securities /sɪˈkjʊərɪtiz/ *plural noun* investments in stocks and shares

securities account /sɪˌkjʊərɪtiz əˈkaʊnt/ *noun* an account that shows the value of financial assets held by a person or organisation

Securities and Exchange Commission /sɪˌkjʊərɪtiz ən ɪksˈtʃeɪndʒ kəˌmɪʃ(ə)n/ *noun* the official body which regulates the securities markets in the US. Abbreviation **SEC**

Securities and Futures Authority /sɪˌkjʊərɪtiz ən ˈfjuːtʃəz ɔːˌθɒrəti/ *noun* in the UK, a self-regulatory organisation which supervises the trading in shares and futures, now part of the FSA. Abbreviation **SFA**

Securities and Investments Board /sɪˌkjʊərɪtiz ənd ɪnˈvestmənts ˌbɔːd/ *noun* the former regulatory body which regulated the securities markets in the UK, now superseded by the FSA. Abbreviation **SIB**

securitisation /sɪˌkjʊərɪtaɪˈzeɪʃ(ə)n/, **securitization** *noun* the process of making a loan or mortgage into a tradeable security by issuing a bill of exchange or other negotiable paper in place of it

security /sɪˈkjʊərɪti/ *noun* **1.** a guarantee that someone will repay money borrowed ○ *to give something as security for a debt* ○ *to use a house as security for a loan* ○ *The bank lent him £20,000 without security.* □ **to stand security for someone** to guarantee that if the person does not repay a loan, you will repay it for him **2.** a stock or share

security deposit /sɪˈkjʊərɪti dɪˌpɒzɪt/ *noun* an amount of money paid before a transaction occurs to compensate the seller in the event that the transaction is not concluded and this is the buyer's fault

seed money /'siːd ˌmʌni/ *noun* venture capital invested when a new project is starting up and therefore more risky than secondary finance

segmental reporting /seg,ment(ə)l rɪ 'pɔːtɪŋ/ *noun* the act of showing in company reports the results of a company or sections of it, separated according to the type of business or geographical area

segment margin /'segmənt ˌmɑːdʒɪn/ *noun* a measure of the profitability of a segment of a business

segregation of duties /ˌsegrɪgeɪʃ(ə)n əv 'djuːtiz/ *noun* the dividing up of responsibilities within a business in order to reduce the potential for fraud or theft, e.g. by ensuring that the person responsible for approving invoices is not also responsible for signing cheques

self-assessment /ˌself ə'sesmənt/ *noun* the process in which an individual taxpayer calculates his or her own tax liability and reports it to the Inland Revenue which then issues a notice to pay ○ *Self-assessment forms should be returned to the tax office by 31st January.*

self-balancing /ˌself 'bælənsɪŋ/ *noun* a situation in which there is equality of debits and credits

self-employed /ˌself ɪm'plɔɪd/ *adjective* working for yourself or not on the payroll of a company ○ *a self-employed engineer* ○ *He worked for a bank for ten years but is now self-employed.*

self-employed contributions /ˌself ɪm ˌplɔɪd ˌkɒntrɪ'bjuːʃ(ə)nz/ *plural noun* National Insurance contributions made by self-employed people

self-financing /ˌself faɪ'nænsɪŋ/ *noun* the process in which a company finances a project or business activity from its own resources, rather than by applying for external finance

self-insurance /ˌself ɪn'ʃʊərəns/ *noun* insuring against a probable future loss by putting money aside regularly, rather than by taking out an insurance policy

self-regulation /ˌself ˌregjʊ'leɪʃ(ə)n/ *noun* the regulation of an industry by its own members, usually by means of a committee that issues guidance and sets standards that it then enforces (NOTE: For example, the Stock Exchange is regulated by the Stock Exchange Council.)

self-regulatory /ˌself ˌregjʊ'leɪt(ə)ri/ *adjective* referring to an organisation which regulates itself

sell *noun* an act of selling ■ *verb* **1.** to exchange something for money ○ *to sell something on credit* ○ *The shop sells washing machines and refrigerators.* ○ *They tried to sell their house for £100,000.* ○ *Their products are easy to sell.* **2.** to be bought ○ *These items sell well in the pre-Christmas period.* ○ *Those packs sell for £25 a dozen.* (NOTE: **selling – sold**)

seller's market /ˌseləz 'mɑːkɪt/ *noun* a market where the seller can ask high prices because there is a large demand for the product. Opposite **buyer's market**

selling costs /'selɪŋ kɒsts/, **selling overhead** /'selɪŋ ˌəʊvəhed/ *plural noun* the amount of money to be paid for the advertising, reps' commissions, and other expenses involved in selling something

selling price /'selɪŋ praɪs/ *noun* the price at which someone is willing to sell something

selling price variance /'selɪŋ praɪs ˌveəriəns/ *noun* the difference between the actual selling price and the budgeted selling price

semi- /semi/ *prefix* half or part

semiannual /ˌsemi'ænjuəl/ *adjective* referring to interest paid every six months

semi-fixed cost /ˌsemi fɪkst 'kɒst/ *noun* same as **semi-variable cost**

semi-variable cost /ˌsemi ˌveəriəb(ə)l 'kɒst/ *noun* the amount of money paid to produce a product, which increases, though less than proportionally, with the quantity of the product made ○ *Stepping up production will mean an increase in semi-variable costs.* Also called **semi-fixed cost**

senior /'siːniə/ *adjective* **1.** referring to an employee who is more important **2.** referring to an employee who is older or who has been employed longer than another **3.** referring to a sum which is repayable before others

senior capital /ˌsiːniə 'kæpɪt(ə)l/ *noun* capital in the form of secured loans to a company. It is repaid before junior capital, such as shareholders' equity, in the event of liquidation.

sensitivity analysis /ˌsensə'tɪvəti əˌnæləsɪs/ *noun* the analysis of the effect of a small change in a calculation on the final result

separable net assets /ˌsep(ə)rəb(ə)l net 'æsets/ *plural noun* assets which can be separated from the rest of the assets of a business and sold off

separate /'sep(ə)rət/ *adjective* not connected with something

sequester /sɪ'kwestə/, **sequestrate** /'siːkwɪstreɪt, sɪ'kwestreɪt/ *verb* to take and keep a bank account or property because a court has ordered it ○ *The union's funds have been sequestrated.*

sequestration /ˌsiːkwe'streɪʃ(ə)n/ *noun* the act of taking and keeping property on the order of a court, especially of seizing property from someone who is in contempt of court

sequestrator /'siːkwɪstreɪtə, sɪ'kwestreɪtə/ *noun* a person who takes and keeps property on the order of a court

series /'sɪəriːz/ *noun* a group of items following one after the other ○ *A series of successful takeovers made the company one of the largest in the trade.* (NOTE: The plural is **series**.)

Serious Fraud Office /ˌsɪəriəs 'frɔːd ˌɒfɪs/ *noun* a British government department in charge of investigating major fraud in companies. Abbreviation **SFO**

SERPS /sɜːps/ *abbreviation* State Earnings-Related Pension Scheme

service /'sɜːvɪs/ *noun* **1.** the fact of working for an employer, or the period of time during which an employee has worked for an employer ○ *retiring after twenty years service to the company* ○ *The amount of your pension depends partly on the number of your years of service.* **2.** the work of dealing with customers ○ *The service in that restaurant is extremely slow* **3.** payment for help given to the customer ○ *to add on 10% for service*

service bureau /'sɜːvɪs ˌbjʊərəʊ/ *noun* an office which specialises in helping other offices

service charge /'sɜːvɪs tʃɑːdʒ/ *noun* **1.** a charge added to the bill in a restaurant to pay for service **2.** an amount paid by tenants in a block of flats or offices for general maintenance, insurance and cleaning **3.** a charge which a bank or business makes for carrying out work for a customer (NOTE: The UK term is **bank charge**.)

service contract /'sɜːvɪs ˌkɒntrækt/ *noun* a contract between a company and a director showing all conditions of work ○ *She worked unofficially with no service contract.*

service industry /'sɜːvɪs ˌɪndəstri/ *noun* an industry which does not produce raw materials or manufacture products but

offers a service such as banking, retailing or accountancy

service life /'sɜːvɪs laɪf/ *noun* the period during which an asset will bring benefit to a company

service potential /'sɜːvɪs pəˌtenʃ(ə)l/ *noun* future benefits that an asset is expected to bring

services /'sɜːvɪsɪz/ *plural noun* **1.** benefits which are sold to customers or clients, e.g. transport or education ○ *We give advice to companies on the marketing of services.* ○ *We must improve the exports of both goods and services.* **2.** business of providing help in some form when it is needed, e.g. insurance, banking, etc., as opposed to making or selling goods

set /set/ *adjective* fixed, or which cannot be changed ○ *There is a set fee for all our consultants.* ■ *verb* to fix or to arrange something ○ *We have to set a price for the new computer.* ○ *The price of the calculator has been set low, so as to achieve maximum unit sales.* (NOTE: **setting – set**)

set against *phrasal verb* to balance one group of figures against another group to try to make them cancel each other out ○ *to set the costs against the sales revenue* ○ *Can you set the expenses against tax?*

set off /ˌset 'ɒf/ *verb* to use a debt owed by one party to reduce a debt owed to them

set-off /'set ɒf/ *noun* an agreement between two parties to balance one debt against another or a loss against a gain

settle /'set(ə)l/ *verb* to place a property in trust

settle on *phrasal verb* to leave property to someone when you die ○ *He settled his property on his children.*

settlement /'set(ə)lmənt/ *noun* **1.** the payment of an account □ **we offer an extra 5% discount for rapid settlement** we take a further 5% off the price if the customer pays quickly **2.** an agreement after an argument or negotiations ○ *a wage settlement*

'…he emphasised that prompt settlement of all forms of industrial disputes would guarantee industrial peace in the country and ensure increased productivity' [*Business Times (Lagos)*]

settlement date /'set(ə)lmənt deɪt/ *noun* a date when a payment has to be made

settlement day /'set(ə)lmənt deɪ/ *noun* **1.** the day on which shares which have been bought must be paid for. On the London Stock Exchange the account period is three business days from the day of trade. (NOTE: The US term is **settlement date**) **2.** in the

US, the day on which securities bought actually become the property of the purchaser

seven-day money /ˌsev(ə)n deɪ 'mʌni/ *noun* an investment in financial instruments which mature in seven days' time

severally /'sev(ə)rəli/ *adverb* separately, not jointly

severance pay /'sev(ə)rəns peɪ/ *noun* money paid as compensation to an employee whose job is no longer needed

SFA *abbreviation* Securities and Futures Authority

SFAS *abbreviation* Statement of Financial Accounting Standards

SFO *abbreviation* Serious Fraud Office

shadow director /'ʃædəʊ daɪˌrektə/ *noun* a person who is not a director of a company, but who tells the directors of the company how to act

shadow economy /ˌʃædəʊ ɪ'kɒnəmi/ *noun* same as **black economy**

shadow price /'ʃædəʊ praɪs/ *noun* the estimated price of goods or a service for which no market price exists

share /ʃeə/ *noun* 1. a part of something that has been divided up among several people or groups 2. one of many equal parts into which a company's capital is divided ○ *He bought a block of shares in Marks and Spencer.* ○ *Shares fell on the London market.* ○ *The company offered 1.8m shares on the market.*

'...falling profitability means falling share prices' [*Investors Chronicle*]

'...the share of blue-collar occupations declined from 48 per cent to 43 per cent' [*Sydney Morning Herald*]

share account /'ʃeər əˌkaʊnt/ *noun* an account at a building society where the account holder is a member of the society. Building societies usually offer another type of account, a deposit account, where the account holder is not a member. A share account is generally paid a better rate of interest, but in the event of the society going into liquidation, deposit account holders are given preference.

share at par /ˌʃeər ət 'pɑː/ *noun* a share whose value on the stock market is the same as its face value

share capital /'ʃeə ˌkæpɪt(ə)l/ *noun* the value of the assets of a company held as shares

share certificate /'ʃeə səˌtɪfɪkət/ *noun* a document proving that you own shares

share disposals /'ʃeə dɪˌspəʊz(ə)lz/ *plural noun* the selling of shares, which is often subject to conditions

shareholder /'ʃeəhəʊldə/ *noun* a person who owns shares in a company ○ *to call a shareholders' meeting* (NOTE: The US term is **stockholder**.)

'...as of last night the bank's shareholders no longer hold any rights to the bank's shares' [*South China Morning Post*]

'...the company said that its recent issue of 10.5% convertible preference shares at A$8.50 has been oversubscribed, boosting shareholders' funds to A$700 million plus' [*Financial Times*]

shareholders' equity /ˌʃeəhəʊldəz 'ekwɪti/ *noun* 1. the value of a company which is the property of its ordinary shareholders (the company's assets less its liabilities) 2. a company's capital which is invested by shareholders, who thus become owners of the company

shareholders' funds /ˌʃeəhəʊldəz 'fʌndz/ *plural noun* the capital and reserves of a company

shareholder value /ˌʃeəhəʊldə 'væljuː/ *noun* the total return to the shareholders in terms of both dividends and share price growth, calculated as the present value of future free cash flows of the business discounted at the weighted average cost of the capital of the business less the market value of its debt

shareholder value analysis /ˌʃeəhəʊldə ˌvæljuː ə'næləsɪs/ *noun* a calculation of the value of a company made by looking at the returns it gives to its shareholders. It assumes that the objective of a company director is to maximise the wealth of the company's shareholders, and is based on the premise that discounted cash flow principles can be applied to the business as a whole. Abbreviation **SVA**

shareholding /'ʃeəhəʊldɪŋ/ *noun* a group of shares in a company owned by one owner

share incentive scheme /ˌʃeər ɪn 'sentɪv skiːm/ *noun* same as **share option scheme**

share option /'ʃeər ˌɒpʃən/ *noun* a right to buy or sell shares at an agreed price at a time in the future

share option scheme /'ʃeər ˌɒpʃən skiːm/ *noun* a scheme that gives company employees the right to buy shares in the company which employs them, often at a special price

share premium /ˈʃeə ˌpriːmiəm/ *noun* an amount to be paid above the nominal value of a share in order to buy it

share purchase scheme /ˈʃeə ˌpɜːtʃəs ˌskiːm/ *noun* a scheme that allows employees to buy shares in a company at a favourable rate

share quoted ex dividend /ˌʃeə ˌkwəʊtɪd eks ˈdɪvɪdend/, **share quoted ex div** /ˌʃeə ˌkwəʊtɪd eks ˈdɪv/ *noun* a share price not including the right to receive the next dividend

share register /ˈʃeə ˌredʒɪstə/ *noun* a list of shareholders in a company with their addresses

share split /ˈʃeə splɪt/ *noun* the act of dividing shares into smaller denominations

share warrant /ˈʃeə ˌwɒrənt/ *noun* a document which says that someone has the right to a number of shares in a company

sharp practice /ˌʃɑːp ˈpræktɪs/ *noun* a way of doing business which is not honest, but is not illegal

shelf registration /ˈʃelf ˌredʒɪstreɪʃ(ə)n/ *noun* a registration of a corporation with the SEC some time (up to two years is allowed) before it is offered for sale to the public

shell company /ˈʃel ˌkʌmp(ə)ni/ *noun* a company that has ceased to trade but is still registered, especially one sold to enable the buyer to begin trading without having to set up a new company (NOTE: The US term is **shell corporation**.)

'…shell companies, which can be used to hide investors' cash, figure largely throughout the twentieth century' [*Times*]

short /ʃɔːt/ *adjective, adverb* **1.** for a small period of time **2.** less than what is expected or desired ○ *The shipment was three items short.* ○ *My change was £2 short.* □ **when we cashed up we were £10 short** we had £10 less than we should have had □ **to sell short, to go short** to agree to sell at a future date something (such as shares) which you do not possess, but which you think you will be able to buy for less before the time comes when you have to sell them

short bill /ˈʃɔːt bɪl/ *noun* a bill of exchange payable at short notice

short-change /ˌʃɔːt ˈtʃeɪndʒ/ *verb* to give a customer less change than is right, either by mistake or in the hope that it will not be noticed

short credit /ˌʃɔːt ˈkredɪt/ *noun* terms which allow the customer only a little time to pay

short-dated bill /ˌʃɔːt ˌdeɪtɪd ˈbɪl/ *noun* a bill which is payable within a few days

short-dated gilts /ˌʃɔːt ˌdeɪtɪd ˈgɪlts/ *plural noun* same as **shorts**

shorten /ˈʃɔːt(ə)n/ *verb* ○ *to shorten credit terms* □ **to shorten a credit period** to make a credit period shorter, so as to improve the company's cash position

shortfall /ˈʃɔːtfɔːl/ *noun* an amount which is missing which would make the total expected sum ○ *We had to borrow money to cover the shortfall between expenditure and revenue.*

short-form report /ˌʃɔːt fɔːm rɪˈpɔːt/ *noun* a standard brief auditor's report summarising the work done and the findings

short lease /ˌʃɔːt ˈliːs/ *noun* a lease which runs for up to two or three years ○ *We have a short lease on our current premises.*

short position /ˌʃɔːt pəˈzɪʃ(ə)n/ *noun* a situation where an investor sells short, i.e. sells forward shares which he or she does not own. Compare **long position**

shorts /ʃɔːts/ *plural noun* government stocks which mature in less than five years' time

short-term /ˌʃɔːt ˈtɜːm/ *adjective* **1.** for a period of weeks or months ○ *to place money on short-term deposit* ○ *She is employed on a short-term contract.* **2.** for a short period in the future ○ *We need to recruit at once to cover our short-term manpower requirements.*

short-term capital /ˌʃɔːt tɜːm ˈkæpɪt(ə)l/ *noun* funds raised for a period of less than 12 months. ◊ **working capital**

short-term debt ratio /ˌʃɔːt tɜːm ˈdet ˌreɪʃiəʊ/ *noun* an indicator of whether or not a company will be able to settle its immediate obligations

short-term forecast /ˌʃɔːt tɜːm ˈfɔːkɑːst/ *noun* a forecast which covers a period of a few months

short-term investment /ˌʃɔːt tɜːm ɪnˈvestmənt/ *noun* a section of a company's account that lists investments that will expire within one year

short-term loan /ˌʃɔːt tɜːm ˈləʊn/ *noun* a loan which has to be repaid within a few weeks or some years

short-term security /ˌʃɔːt tɜːm sɪˈkjʊərɪti/ *noun* a security which matures in less than 5 years

shrinkage /ˈʃrɪŋkɪdʒ/ *noun* **1.** the amount by which something gets smaller ○ *to allow for shrinkage* **2.** losses of stock through theft, especially by the shop's own staff (*informal*)

SIB *abbreviation* Securities and Investments Board

sick pay /'sɪk peɪ/ *noun* pay paid to an employee who is sick, even if he cannot work

sight deposit /'saɪt dɪ,pɒzɪt/ *noun* a bank deposit which can be withdrawn on demand

sight draft /'saɪt drɑːft/ *noun* a bill of exchange which is payable when it is presented

sign /saɪn/ *verb* to write your name in a special way on a document to show that you have written it or approved it ○ *The letter is signed by the managing director.* ○ *Our company cheques are not valid if they have not been signed by the finance director.*

signatory /'sɪɡnət(ə)ri/ *noun* a person who signs a contract, etc. ○ *You have to get the permission of all the signatories to the agreement if you want to change the terms.*

signature /'sɪɡnɪtʃə/ *noun* a person's name written by themselves on a cheque, document or letter ○ *She found a pile of cheques on his desk waiting for signature.* ○ *All our company's cheques need two signatures.*

simple average cost /,sɪmpəl 'æv(ə)rɪdʒ ,kɒst/, **simple average price** /,sɪmpəl 'æv(ə)rɪdʒ ,praɪs/ *noun* the average cost of stock received during a period calculated at the end of the period as the average unit price of each delivery of stock, rather than an average price of each unit delivered as in weighted average price

simple interest /,sɪmpəl 'ɪntrəst/ *noun* interest calculated on the capital invested only, as distinct from compound interest which is calculated on capital and accumulated interest

simple rate of return /,sɪmpəl reɪt əv rɪ 'tɜːn/ *noun* a measure of a company's profitability calculated by dividing the expected future annual net income by the required investment

single-entry bookkeeping /,sɪŋɡ(ə)l ,entri 'bʊkkiːpɪŋ/ *noun* a method of bookkeeping where payments or sales are noted with only one entry per transaction, usually in the cash book

single-figure inflation /,sɪŋɡ(ə)l ,fɪɡə ɪn'fleɪʃ(ə)n/ *noun* inflation rising at less than 10% per annum

single-parent allowance /,sɪŋɡ(ə)l ,peərənt ə'laʊəns/ *noun* a former name for the tax allowance which can be claimed by a single person who has a child of school age living with them, now called the 'additional personal allowance'

single premium policy /,sɪŋɡ(ə)l ,priːmiəm 'pɒlɪsi/ *noun* an insurance policy where only one premium is paid rather than regular annual premiums

sink /sɪŋk/ *verb* **1.** to go down suddenly ○ *Prices sank at the news of the closure of the factory.* **2.** to invest money into something ○ *He sank all his savings into a car-hire business.* (NOTE: **sinking – sank – sunk**)

sinking fund /'sɪŋkɪŋ fʌnd/ *noun* a fund built up out of amounts of money put aside regularly to meet a future need, such as the repayment of a loan

sinking fund method /'sɪŋkɪŋ fʌnd ,meθəd/ *noun* a method of providing for depreciation of an asset which links it to an annuity that, at the end of the asset's life, will have a value equal to the acquisition cost of the asset

sister company /'sɪstə ,kʌmp(ə)ni/ *noun* a company that is part of the same group as another

sitting tenant /,sɪtɪŋ 'tenənt/ *noun* a tenant who is occupying a building when the freehold or lease is sold ○ *The block of flats is for sale with four flats vacant and two with sitting tenants.*

skimming /'skɪmɪŋ/ *noun* the unethical and usually illegal practice of taking small amounts of money from accounts that belong to other individuals or organisations

sleeping partner /,sliːpɪŋ 'pɑːtnə/ *noun* a partner who has a share in the business but does not work in it

slide /slaɪd/ *verb* to move down steadily ○ *Prices slid after the company reported a loss.* (NOTE: **sliding – slid**)

slow payer /,sləʊ 'peɪə/ *noun* a person or company that does not pay debts on time ○ *The company is well known as a slow payer.*

slump /slʌmp/ *noun* **1.** a rapid fall ○ *the slump in the value of the pound* ○ *We experienced a slump in sales* or *a slump in profits.* **2.** a period of economic collapse with high unemployment and loss of trade ○ *We are experiencing slump conditions.* ■ *verb* to fall fast ○ *Profits have slumped.* ○ *The pound slumped on the foreign exchange markets.*

slush fund /'slʌʃ fʌnd/ *noun* money kept to one side to give to people to persuade them to do what you want ○ *The party was accused of keeping a slush fund to pay foreign businessmen.*

small and medium-sized enterprises /ˌsmɔːl ən ˌmiːdiəm ˌsaɪzd ˈentəpraɪzɪz/ *plural noun* organisations that have between 10 and 250 employees and are usually in the start-up or growth stage of development. Abbreviation **SMEs**

small business /ˌsmɔːl ˈbɪznɪs/ *noun* a company which has an annual turnover of less than £5.6 million and does not employ more than 50 staff

Small Business Administration /ˌsmɔːl ˈbɪznɪs ədˌmɪnɪstreɪʃ(ə)n/ *noun* US a federal agency that advises small businesses and helps them obtain loans to finance their businesses. Abbreviation **SBA**

small businessman /ˌsmɔːl ˈbɪznɪsmæn/ *noun* a man who owns a small business

small change /ˌsmɔːl ˈtʃeɪndʒ/ *noun* coins

small claim /ˌsmɔːl ˈkleɪm/ *noun* a claim for less than £5000 in the County Court

small claims court /ˌsmɔːl ˈkleɪmz ˌkɔːt/ *noun* a court which deals with disputes over small amounts of money

small companies rate /ˌsmɔːl ˈkʌmp(ə)niz ˌreɪt/ *noun* a rate of corporation tax charged on profits of small companies

small company /smɔːl ˈkʌmp(ə)ni/ *noun* same as **small business**

SMEs *abbreviation* small and medium-sized enterprises

SMP *abbreviation* statutory maternity pay

social /ˈsəʊʃ(ə)l/ *adjective* referring to society in general

social audit /ˌsəʊʃ(ə)l ˈɔːdɪt/ *noun* a systematic assessment of an organisation's effects on society or on all those who can be seen as its stakeholders. A social audit covers such issues as internal codes of conduct, business ethics, human resource development, environmental impact, and the organisation's sense of social responsibility. ○ *The social audit focused on the effects of pollution in the area.* ○ *The social audit showed that the factory could provide jobs for five per cent of the unemployed in the small town nearby.*

Social Charter /ˌsəʊʃ(ə)l ˈtʃɑːtə/ *noun* same as **European Social Charter**

social impact statement /ˌsəʊʃ(ə)l ˈɪmpækt ˌsteɪtmənt/ *noun* an assessment of the impact of the non-profit activities of an organisation on a specific social area

social security contributions /ˌsəʊʃ(ə)l sɪˈkjʊərɪti kɒntrɪˌbjuːʃ(ə)nz/ *plural noun* regular payments by employees and employers to the National Insurance scheme

society /səˈsaɪəti/ *noun* the way in which the people in a country are organised

soft currency /ˌsɒft ˈkʌrənsi/ *noun* the currency of a country with a weak economy, which is cheap to buy and difficult to exchange for other currencies. Opposite **hard currency**

soft landing /ˌsɒft ˈlændɪŋ/ *noun* a change in economic strategy to counteract inflation, which does not cause unemployment or a fall in the standard of living, and has only minor effects on the bulk of the population

soft loan /ˌsɒft ləʊn/ *noun* a loan from a company to an employee or from one government to another at a very low rate of interest or with no interest payable at all

sole agency /ˌsəʊl ˈeɪdʒənsi/ *noun* an agreement to be the only person to represent a company or to sell a product in a particular area ○ *He has the sole agency for Ford cars.*

sole agent /ˌsəʊl ˈeɪdʒənt/ *noun* a person who has the sole agency for a company in an area ○ *She is the sole agent for Ford cars in the locality.*

sole distributor /ˌsəʊl dɪˈstrɪbjʊtə/ *noun* a retailer who is the only one in an area who is allowed to sell a product

sole owner /ˌsəʊl ˈəʊnə/ *noun* a person who owns a business on their own, with no partners, and has not formed a company

sole proprietor /ˌsəʊl prəˈpraɪətə/, **sole trader** /ˌsəʊl ˈtreɪdə/ *noun* a person who runs a business, usually by him- or herself, but has not registered it as a company

solvency /ˈsɒlv(ə)nsi/ *noun* the state of being able to pay all debts on due date. Opposite **insolvency**

solvency margin /ˈsɒlv(ə)nsi ˌmɑːdʒɪn/ *noun* a business's liquid assets that exceeds the amount required to meet its liabilities

solvency ratio /ˈsɒlv(ə)nsi ˌreɪʃiəʊ/ *noun* the ratio of assets to liabilities, used to measure a company's ability to meet its debts

solvent /ˈsɒlv(ə)nt/ *adjective* having enough money to pay debts ○ *When she bought the company it was barely solvent.*

sort code /ˈsɔːt kəʊd/ *noun* a combination of numbers that identifies a bank branch on official documentation, such as bank statements and cheques (NOTE: The US term is **routing number**.)

source /sɔːs/ *noun* the place where something comes from ○ *What is the source of her income?* ○ *You must declare income from all sources to the tax office.*

source and application of funds statement /ˌsɔːs ənd ˌæplɪkeɪʃ(ə)n əv 'fʌndz ˌsteɪtmənt/, **sources and uses of funds statement** /ˌsɔːsɪz ən ˌjuːzɪz əv 'fʌndz ˌsteɪtmənt/ *noun* a statement in a company's annual accounts, showing where new funds came from during the year, and how they were used

source document /'sɔːs ˌdɒkjʊmənt/ *noun* a document upon which details of transactions or accounting events are recorded and from which information is extracted to be subsequently entered into the internal accounting system of an organisation, e.g., a sales invoice or credit note

spare /speə/ *adjective* extra, not being used ○ *He has invested his spare capital in a computer shop.*

SPE *abbreviation* special purpose entity

special audit /'speʃ(ə)l ˌɔːdɪt/ *noun* an audit with a narrow remit specified by a government agency

Special Commissioner /ˌspeʃ(ə)l kə 'mɪʃ(ə)nə/ *noun* an official appointed by the Treasury to hear cases where a taxpayer is appealing against an income tax assessment

special deposits /ˌspeʃ(ə)l dɪ'pɒzɪts/ *plural noun* large sums of money which commercial banks have to deposit with the Bank of England

special drawing rights /ˌspeʃ(ə)l 'drɔːɪŋ raɪts/ *plural noun* units of account used by the International Monetary Fund, allocated to each member country for use in loans and other international operations. Their value is calculated daily on the weighted values of a group of currencies shown in dollars. Abbreviation **SDRs**

special journal /'speʃ(ə)l ˌdʒɜːn(ə)l/ *noun* a journal in which entries of a specified type are recorded

special purpose entity /ˌspeʃ(ə)l ˌpɜːpəs 'entɪti/, **special purpose vehicle** *noun* a separate business entity created to carry out a specific transaction or business unrelated to a company's main business. Abbreviation **SPE, SPV**

special resolution /ˌspeʃ(ə)l ˌrezə 'luːʃ(ə)n/ *noun* a resolution concerning an important matter, such as a change to the company's articles of association which is only valid if it is approved by 75% of the votes cast at a meeting

specie /'spiːʃiː/ *noun* money in the form of coins

specification /ˌspesɪfɪ'keɪʃ(ə)n/ *noun* detailed information about what or who is needed or about a product to be supplied ○ *to detail the specifications of a computer system* □ **the work is not up to specification** *or* **does not meet our specifications** the product is not made in the way which was detailed

specific order costing /spə,sɪfɪk 'ɔːdə ˌkɒstɪŋ/ *noun* same as **job costing**

specify /'spesɪfaɪ/ *verb* to state clearly what is needed ○ *to specify full details of the goods ordered* ○ *Do not include VAT on the invoice unless specified.* (NOTE: **specifies – specifying – specified**)

spend /spend/ *verb* to pay money ○ *They spent all their savings on buying the shop.* ○ *The company spends thousands of pounds on research.*

spending /'spendɪŋ/ *noun* the act of paying money for goods and services ○ *Both cash spending and credit card spending increase at Christmas.*

spending money /'spendɪŋ ˌmʌni/ *noun* money for ordinary personal expenses

split-capital trust /ˌsplɪt ˌkæpɪt(ə)l 'trʌst/ *noun* same as **split-level investment trust**

split commission /ˌsplɪt kə'mɪʃ(ə)n/ *noun* commission which is divided between brokers or agents

split-level investment trust /ˌsplɪt ˌlev(ə)l ɪn'vestmənt ˌtrʌst/ *noun* an investment trust with two categories of shares: income shares which receive income from the investments, but do not benefit from the rise in their capital value, and capital shares, which increase in value as the value of the investments rises, but do not receive any income. Also called **split trust, split-capital trust**

split payment /ˌsplɪt 'peɪmənt/ *noun* a payment which is divided into small units

split trust /ˌsplɪt 'trʌst/ *noun* same as **split-level investment trust**

spoilage /'spɔɪlɪdʒ/ *noun* **1.** waste arising from decay or damage **2.** the amount of something wasted because of decay or damage

spot cash /ˌspɒt 'kæʃ/ *noun* cash paid for something bought immediately

spot market /'spɒt ˌmɑːkɪt/ *noun* a market that deals in commodities or foreign exchange for immediate rather than future delivery

'…with most of the world's oil now traded on spot markets, Opec's official prices are much less significant than they once were' [*Economist*]

spot price /'spɒt praɪs/, **spot rate** /'spɒt reɪt/ *noun* a current price or rate for something which is delivered immediately. Also called **cash price**

'…the average spot price of Nigerian light crude oil for the month of July was 27.21 dollars per barrel' [*Business Times (Lagos)*]

spread /spred/ *noun* **1.** same as **range 2.** the difference between buying and selling prices, i.e. between the bid and offer prices ■ *verb* to space something out over a period of time ○ *to spread payments over several months*

'…dealers said markets were thin, with gaps between trades and wide spreads between bid and ask prices on the currencies' [*Wall Street Journal*]

'…to ensure an average return you should hold a spread of different shares covering a wide cross-section of the market' [*Investors Chronicle*]

spreading /'spredɪŋ/ *noun* an action of spacing income from artistic work such as royalties over a period of time, and not concentrating it in the year in which the money is received

spreadsheet /'spredʃiːt/ *noun* a computer printout or program that shows a series of columns or rows of figures

SPV *abbreviation* special purpose vehicle

Square Mile /ˌskweə 'maɪl/ *noun* the City of London, the British financial centre

squeeze /skwiːz/ *noun* government control carried out by reducing the availability of something

'…the real estate boom of the past three years has been based on the availability of easy credit. Today, money is tighter, so property should bear the brunt of the credit squeeze' [*Money Observer*]

SSAPs *abbreviation* Statements of Standard Accounting Practice

staff incentives /ˌstɑːf ɪn'sentɪvz/ *plural noun* higher pay and better conditions offered to employees to make them work better

stag /stæg/ *noun* a person who buys new issues of shares and sells them immediately to make a profit

staged payments /ˌsteɪdʒd 'peɪmənts/ *plural noun* payments made in stages

stagger /'stægə/ *verb* to arrange holidays or working hours so that they do not all begin and end at the same time ○ *We asked our supplier to stagger deliveries so that the warehouse can cope.*

stagnant /'stægnənt/ *adjective* not active, not increasing ○ *Turnover was stagnant for the first half of the year.* ○ *A stagnant economy is not a good sign.*

stagnate /stæg'neɪt/ *verb* not to increase, not to make progress ○ *The economy is stagnating.*

stagnation /stæg'neɪʃ(ə)n/ *noun* the state of not making any progress, especially in economic matters ○ *The country entered a period of stagnation.*

stake /steɪk/ *noun* an amount of money invested

'…her stake, which she bought at $1.45 per share, is now worth nearly $10 million' [*Times*]

'…other investments include a large stake in a Chicago-based insurance company, as well as interests in tobacco products and hotels' [*Lloyd's List*]

stakeholder /'steɪkhəʊldə/ *noun* a person or body that is directly or indirectly involved with a company or organisation and has an interest in ensuring that it is successful (NOTE: A stakeholder may be an employee, customer, supplier, partner, or even the local community within which an organisation operates.)

'…the stakeholder concept is meant to be a new kind of low-cost, flexible personal pension aimed at those who are less well-off. Whether it will really encourage them to put aside money for retirement is a moot point. Ministers said companies would be able to charge no more than 1 per cent a year to qualify for the stakeholder label' [*Financial Times*]

stakeholder pension /'steɪkhəʊldə ˌpenʃən/ *noun* a pension, provided through a private company, in which the income a person has after retirement depends on the amount of contributions made during their working life (NOTE: Stakeholder pensions are designed for people without access to an occupational pension scheme.)

stakeholder theory /'steɪkhəʊldə ˌθɪəri/ *noun* the theory that it is possible for an organisation to promote the interests of its shareholders without harming the interests of its other stakeholders such as its employees, suppliers and the wider community

stamp duty /'stæmp ˌdjuːti/ *noun* a tax on legal documents such as those used, e.g., for the sale or purchase of shares or the conveyance of a property to a new owner

stand-alone cost method /ˈstænd ə ˌləʊn kɒst ˌmeθəd/ *noun* a method that divides common costs among all users

standard agreement /ˌstændəd əˈɡriːmənt/, **standard contract** /ˌstændəd ˈkɒntrækt/ *noun* a normal printed contract form

standard cost /ˌstændəd ˈkɒst/ *noun* a future cost which is calculated in advance and against which estimates are measured

standard costing /ˌstændəd ˈkɒstɪŋ/ *noun* the process of planning costs for the period ahead and, at the end of the period, comparing these figures with actual costs in order to make necessary adjustments in planning

standard cost system /ˌstændəd ˈkɒst ˌsɪstəm/ *noun* a system that records costs at standard levels, rather than at actual levels

standard direct labour cost /ˌstændəd daɪˌrekt ˈleɪbə ˌkɒst/ *noun* the cost of labour calculated to produce a product according to specification, used to measure estimates

standard letter /ˌstændəd ˈletə/ *noun* a letter which is sent without change to various correspondents

standard opinion /ˌstændəd əˈpɪnjən/ *noun* an accountant's judgement that a company's financial information has been presented in a way that is both fair and consistent with presentation in previous years

standard rate /ˈstændəd reɪt/ *noun* a basic rate of income tax which is paid by most taxpayers

standby credit /ˈstændbaɪ ˌkredɪt/ *noun* **1.** credit which is available if a company needs it, especially credit guaranteed by a euronote **2.** credit which is available and which can be drawn on if a country needs it, especially credit guaranteed by a lender (a group of banks or the IMF in the case of a member country) and usually in dollars

standing order /ˌstændɪŋ ˈɔːdə/ *noun* an order written by a customer asking a bank to pay money regularly to an account ○ *I pay my subscription by standing order.*

start /stɑːt/ *noun* the beginning ■ *verb* to begin to do something □ **to start a business from cold** *or* **from scratch** to begin a new business, with no previous turnover to base it on

starting rate of tax /ˌstɑːtɪŋ reɪt əv ˈtæks/ *noun* a tax rate (currently 10%) paid on the first segment of taxable income, before the basic rate applies

starting salary /ˈstɑːtɪŋ ˌsæləri/ *noun* a salary for an employee when he or she starts work with a company

start-up /ˈstɑːt ʌp/ *noun* the beginning of a new company or new product ○ *We went into the red for the first time because of the costs for the start-up of our new subsidiary.*

'It's unusual for a venture capitalist to be focused tightly on a set of companies with a common technology base, and even more unusual for the investment fund manager to be picking start-ups that will be built on a business he's currently running.' [*InformationWeek*]

start-up financing /ˈstɑːt ʌp ˌfaɪnænsɪŋ/ *noun* the first stage in financing a new project, which is followed by several rounds of investment capital as the project gets under way

state /steɪt/ *noun* **1.** an independent country **2.** a semi-independent section of a federal country such as the US ■ *verb* to say clearly ○ *The document states that all revenue has to be declared to the tax office.* □ **as per account stated** the same amount as shown on the account or invoice

'...the unions had argued that public sector pay rates had slipped behind rates applying in state and local government areas' [*Australian Financial Review*]

state bank /ˌsteɪt ˈbæŋk/ *noun* in the US, a commercial bank licensed by the authorities of a state, and not necessarily a member of the Federal Reserve system. Compare **national bank**

state benefits /ˌsteɪt ˈbenɪfɪts/ *plural noun* payments which are made to someone under a national or private scheme

stated capital /ˌsteɪtɪd ˈkæpɪt(ə)l/ *noun* the amount of a company's capital contributed by shareholders

State Earnings-Related Pension Scheme /ˌsteɪt ˌɜːnɪŋz rɪˌleɪtɪd ˈpenʃən ˌskiːm/ *noun* ♦ **State Second Pension**

statement /ˈsteɪtmənt/ *noun* something said or written which describes or explains something clearly

statement of account /ˌsteɪtmənt əv əˈkaʊnt/ *noun* a list of sums due, usually relating to unpaid invoices

statement of affairs /ˌsteɪtmənt əv əˈfeəz/ *noun* a financial statement drawn up when a person is insolvent

Statement of Auditing Standards /ˌsteɪtmənt əv ˈɔːdɪtɪŋ ˌstændədz/ *noun* an auditing standard, issued by the Auditing Practices Board, containing prescriptions as to the basic principles and practices which members of the UK accountancy bodies are expected to follow in the course of an audit. Abbreviation **SAS**

statement of cash flows /ˌsteɪtmənt əv ˈkæʃ ˌfləʊz/ *noun* a statement that documents actual receipts and expenditures of cash

statement-of-cash-flows method /ˌsteɪtmənt əv ˈkæʃ fləʊz ˌmeθəd/ *noun* a method of accounting that is based on flows of cash rather than balances on accounts

statement of changes in financial position /ˌsteɪtmənt əv ˌtʃeɪndʒɪz ɪn faɪˌnænʃəl pəˈzɪʃ(ə)n/ *noun* a financial report of a company's incomes and outflows during a period, usually a year or a quarter

Statement of Financial Accounting Standards /ˌsteɪtmənt əv faɪˌnænʃ(ə)l ə ˈkaʊntɪŋ ˌstændədz/ *noun* in the US, a statement detailing the standards to be adopted for the preparation of financial statements. Abbreviation **SFAS**

Statement of Principles /ˌsteɪtmənt əv ˈprɪnsɪp(ə)lz/ *noun* a document in which the Accounting Standards Board sets out the principles governing the carrying out of financial reporting in the UK and the Republic of Ireland

statement of realisation and liquidation /ˌsteɪtmənt əv rɪəlaɪˌzeɪʃ(ə)n ən ˌlɪkwɪˈdeɪʃ(ə)n/ *noun* a statement of the financial position of a company going out of business

statement of retained earnings /ˌsteɪtmənt əv rɪˌteɪnd ˈɜːnɪŋz/ *noun* a statement accompanying a balance sheet and giving details of the movement of retained earnings during an accounting period

Statements of Standard Accounting Practice /ˌsteɪtmənts əv ˌstændəd ə ˈkaʊntɪŋ ˌpræktɪs/ *plural noun* rules laid down by the Accounting Standards Board for the preparation of financial statements. Abbreviation **SSAPs**

state of indebtedness /ˌsteɪt əv ɪn ˈdetɪdnəs/ *noun* the fact of being in debt, owing money

state pension /ˌsteɪt ˈpenʃən/ *noun* a pension that is provided by the state and funded from National Insurance payments

state retirement pension /ˌsteɪt rɪ ˈtaɪəmənt ˌpenʃən/ *noun* a pension paid by the state to people when they reach the statutory retirement age

State Second Pension /ˌsteɪt ˌsekənd ˈpenʃ(ə)n/ *noun* a state pension that is additional to the basic retirement pension and is

based on average earnings over an employee's career, formerly called the State Earnings-related Pension Scheme or SERPS

statistical /stəˈtɪstɪk(ə)l/ *adjective* based on statistics ○ *statistical information* ○ *They took two weeks to provide the statistical analysis of the opinion-poll data.*

statistical discrepancy /stəˌtɪstɪk(ə)l dɪˈskrepənsi/ *noun* the amount by which sets of figures differ

statistical quality control /stə ˌtɪstɪk(ə)l ˈkwɒlɪti kənˌtrəʊl/ *noun* the process of inspecting samples of a product to check that quality standards are being met

statistician /ˌstætɪˈstɪʃ(ə)n/ *noun* a person who analyses statistics

statistics /stəˈtɪstɪks/ *plural noun* **1.** facts or information in the form of figures ○ *to examine the sales statistics for the previous six months* ○ *Government trade statistics show an increase in imports.* ○ *The statistics on unemployment did not take school-leavers into account.* (NOTE: takes a plural verb) **2.** the study of facts in the form of figures (NOTE: takes a singular verb)

status /ˈsteɪtəs/ *noun* the importance of someone or something relative to others, especially someone's position in society

status inquiry /ˈsteɪtəs ɪnˌkwaɪəri/ *noun* the act of checking on a customer's credit rating

status quo /ˌsteɪtəs ˈkwəʊ/ *noun* the state of things as they are now ○ *The contract does not alter the status quo.*

statute /ˈstætʃuːt/ *noun* an established written law, especially an Act of Parliament. Also called **statute law**

statute-barred /ˌstætʃuːt ˈbɑːd/ *adjective* referring to legal action which cannot be pursued because the time limit for it has expired

statute book /ˈstætʃuːt bʊk/ *noun* all laws passed by Parliament which are still in force

statute law /ˈstætʃuːt lɔː/ *noun* same as **statute**

statutory /ˈstætʃʊt(ə)ri/ *adjective* fixed by law ○ *There is a statutory period of probation of thirteen weeks.* ○ *Are all the employees aware of their statutory rights?*

statutory audit /ˈstætʃʊt(ə)ri ˌɔːdɪt/ *noun* an audit carried out on the instructions of, and with a remit set by, a governmental agency

statutory auditor /ˈstætʃʊt(ə)ri ˈɔːdɪtə/ *noun* a professional person qualified to carry out an audit required by the Companies Act

statutory books /ˌstætʃʊt(ə)ri 'bʊks/ plural noun company records required by law, e.g. a register of members

statutory instrument /ˌstætʃʊt(ə)ri 'ɪnstrʊmənt/ noun an order which has the force of law, made under authority granted to a minister by an Act of Parliament

statutory maternity pay /ˌstætʃʊt(ə)ri mə'tɜːnɪti ˌpeɪ/ noun in the UK, payment made by an employer to an employee who is on maternity leave, for a continuous period up to 39 weeks. Abbreviation **SMP**

statutory regulations /ˌstætʃʊt(ə)ri ˌregjʊ'leɪʃ(ə)nz/ plural noun regulations covering financial dealings which are based on Acts of Parliament, such as the Financial Services Act, as opposed to the rules of self-regulatory organisations which are non-statutory

stay of execution /ˌsteɪ əv eksɪ'kjuːʃ(ə)n/ noun the temporary stopping of a legal order ○ *The court granted the company a two-week stay of execution.*

stepped costs /ˌstept 'kɒsts/ plural noun costs which remain fixed up to some level of activity but then rise to a new, higher level once that level of activity is exceeded

sterling /'stɜːlɪŋ/ noun the standard currency used in the United Kingdom ○ *to quote prices in sterling* or *to quote sterling prices*

'...it is doubtful that British goods will price themselves back into world markets as long as sterling labour costs continue to rise faster than in competitor countries' [*Sunday Times*]

sterling area /'stɜːlɪŋ ˌeəriə/ noun formerly, the area of the world where the pound sterling was the main trading currency

sterling balances /ˌstɜːlɪŋ 'bælənsɪz/ plural noun a country's trade balances expressed in pounds sterling

sterling crisis /'stɜːlɪŋ ˌkraɪsɪs/ noun a fall in the exchange rate of the pound sterling

sterling index /'stɜːlɪŋ ˌɪndeks/ noun an index which shows the current value of sterling against a basket of currencies

stock /stɒk/ noun **1.** the available supply of raw materials ○ *large stocks of oil* or *coal* ○ *the country's stocks of butter* or *sugar* **2.** especially *UK* the quantity of goods for sale in a warehouse or retail outlet. Also called **inventory 3.** shares in a company **4.** investments in a company, represented by shares or fixed interest securities ■ *verb* to hold goods for sale in a warehouse or store ○ *The*

average supermarket stocks more than 4500 lines.

'US crude oil stocks fell last week by nearly 2.5m barrels' [*Financial Times*]

'...the stock rose to over $20 a share, higher than the $18 bid' [*Fortune*]

stockbroker /'stɒkbrəʊkə/ noun a person who buys or sells shares for clients

stockbroking /'stɒkbrəʊkɪŋ/ noun the business of dealing in shares for clients ○ *a stockbroking firm*

stock certificate /'stɒk səˌtɪfɪkət/ noun a document proving that someone owns stock in a company

stock code /'stɒk kəʊd/ noun a set of numbers and letters which refer to an item of stock

stock company /'stɒk ˌkʌmpəni/ noun a company that has its capital divided into shares that are freely tradable

stock control /'stɒk kənˌtrəʊl/ noun the process of making sure that the correct level of stock is maintained, to be able to meet demand while keeping the costs of holding stock to a minimum

stock controller /'stɒk kənˌtrəʊlə/ noun a person who notes movements of stock

stock depreciation /'stɒk dɪpriːʃi ˌeɪʃ(ə)n/ noun a reduction in value of stock which is held in a warehouse for some time

Stock Exchange /'stɒk ɪksˌtʃeɪndʒ/ noun a place where stocks and shares are bought and sold ○ *He works on the Stock Exchange.* ○ *Shares in the company are traded on the Stock Exchange.*

'...the news was favourably received on the Sydney Stock Exchange, where the shares gained 40 cents to A$9.80' [*Financial Times*]

Stock Exchange listing /'stɒk ɪks ˌtʃeɪndʒ ˌlɪstɪŋ/ noun the fact of being on the official list of shares which can be bought or sold on the Stock Exchange ○ *The company is planning to obtain a Stock Exchange listing.*

stock figures /'stɒk ˌfɪɡəz/ plural noun details of how many goods are in the warehouse or store

stockholder /'stɒkhəʊldə/ noun US same as **shareholder**

stockholding /'stɒkhəʊldɪŋ/ noun the shares in a company held by someone

stock-in-trade /ˌstɒk ɪn 'treɪd/ noun goods held by a business for sale

stock ledger /'stɒk ˌledʒə/ noun a book which records quantities and values of stock

stock level /'stɒk ˌlev(ə)l/ *noun* the quantity of goods kept in stock ○ *We try to keep stock levels low during the summer.*

stock market /'stɒk ˌmɑːkɪt/ *noun* a place where shares are bought and sold, i.e. a stock exchange ○ *stock market price* or *price on the stock market*

stock market valuation /ˌstɒk ˌmɑːkɪt ˌvæljuˈeɪʃ(ə)n/ *noun* the value of a company based on the current market price of its shares

stock option /'stɒk ˌɒpʃən/ *noun US* same as **share option**

stocks and shares /ˌstɒks ən 'ʃeəz/ *plural noun* shares in ordinary companies

stocktaking /'stɒkteɪkɪŋ/, **stocktake** /'stɒkteɪk/ *noun* the counting of goods in stock at the end of an accounting period ○ *The warehouse is closed for the annual stocktaking.*

stocktaking sale /'stɒkteɪkɪŋ ˌseɪl/ *noun* a sale of goods cheaply to clear a warehouse before stocktaking

stock transfer form /ˌstɒk 'trænsfɜː fɔːm/ *noun* a form to be signed by the person transferring shares

stock turn /'stɒk tɜːn/, **stock turnround** /'stɒk ˌtɜːnraʊnd/, **stock turnover** /'stɒk ˌtɜːnəʊvə/ *noun* the total value of stock sold in a year divided by the average value of goods in stock

stock valuation /ˌstɒk ˌvæljuˈeɪʃ(ə)n/ *noun* an estimation of the value of stock at the end of an accounting period

stop-loss order /ˌstɒp 'lɒs ˌɔːdə/ *noun* an instruction to a stockbroker to sell a share if the price falls to an specified level (NOTE: The US term is **stop order**.)

storage capacity /'stɔːrɪdʒ kəˌpæsɪti/ *noun* the space available for storage

store card /'stɔː kɑːd/ *noun* a credit card issued by a large department store, which can only be used for purchases in that store

straddle /'stræd(ə)l/ *noun* **1.** a spread, the difference between bid and offer price **2.** the act of buying a put option and a call option at the same time

straight line depreciation /ˌstreɪt laɪn dɪˌpriːʃiˈeɪʃ(ə)n/ *noun* a form of depreciation that divides the cost of a fixed asset evenly over each year of its anticipated lifetime

strategic cost management /strə'tiːdʒɪk kɒst ˌmænɪdʒmənt/ *noun* the use of cost information made by management to achieve the aims of a company

strategic management accounting /strəˌtiːdʒɪk ˌmænɪdʒmənt əˈkaʊntɪŋ/ *noun* a form of management accounting in which emphasis is placed on information which relates to factors external to the firm, as well as non-financial information and internally generated information

strategy /'strætədʒi/ *noun* a course of action, including the specification of resources required, to achieve a specific objective ○ *a financial strategy* ○ *a pricing strategy* ○ *Part of the company's strategy to meet its marketing objectives is a major recruitment and retraining programme.* (NOTE: The plural is **strategies**.)

strike /straɪk/ *verb* □ **a deal was struck at £25 a unit** we agreed the price of £25 a unit

strong /strɒŋ/ *adjective* with a lot of force or strength ○ *This Christmas saw a strong demand for mobile phones.* ○ *The company needs a strong chairman.*

'…everybody blames the strong dollar for US trade problems' [*Duns Business Month*]

'…in a world of floating exchange rates the dollar is strong because of capital inflows rather than weak because of the nation's trade deficit' [*Duns Business Month*]

strongbox /'strɒŋbɒks/ *noun* a heavy metal box which cannot be opened easily, in which valuable documents and money can be kept

strong currency /ˌstrɒŋ 'kʌrənsi/ *noun* a currency which has a high value against other currencies

strong pound /ˌstrɒŋ 'paʊnd/ *noun* a pound which is high against other currencies

structure /'strʌktʃə/ *noun* the way in which something is organised ○ *The paper gives a diagram of the company's organisational structure.* ○ *The company is reorganising its discount structure.*

sub /sʌb/ *noun* wages paid in advance

subcontract /ˌsʌbkən'trækt/ *verb* (*of a main contractor*) to agree with a company that they will do part of the work for a project ○ *The electrical work has been subcontracted to Smith Ltd*

subcontractor /'sʌbkənˌtræktə/ *noun* a company which has a contract to do work for a main contractor

subject to /'sʌbdʒɪkt tuː/ *adjective* depending on

sublease /sʌb'liːs/ *verb* to lease a leased property from another tenant ○ *They subleased a small office in the centre of town.*

sublessee /ˌsʌble'siː/ *noun* a person or company that takes a property on a sublease

sublessor /ˌsʌble'sɔː/ *noun* a tenant who leases a leased property to another tenant

sublet /sʌb'let/ *verb* to let a leased property to another tenant ○ *We have sublet part of our office to a financial consultancy.* (NOTE: **subletting – sublet**)

subordinated debt /sʌbˌɔːdɪneɪtɪd 'det/ *noun* a loan that has less of a claim on assets or earnings than another debt

subordinated loan /səˌbɔːdɪnətɪd 'ləʊn/ *noun* a loan which ranks after all other borrowings as regards payment of interest or repayment of capital

subscribe /səb'skraɪb/ *verb* □ **to subscribe for shares**, **to subscribe to a share issue** to apply for shares in a new company

subscription /səb'skrɪpʃən/ *noun* **1.** money paid in advance for a series of issues of a magazine, for membership of a society, or for access to information on a website ○ *Did you remember to pay the subscription to the computer magazine?* ○ *She forgot to renew her club subscription.* **2.** □ **subscription to a new share issue** application to buy shares in a new company □ **the subscription lists close at 10.00 on September 24th** no new applicants will be allowed to subscribe for the share issue after that date

subscription price /səb'skrɪpʃən praɪs/ *noun* the price at which new shares in an existing company are offered for sale

subsequent event /ˌsʌbsɪkwənt ɪ'vent/ *noun* an event with an important financial impact that occurs between the publication of a financial statement and the publication of an audit report, and that should therefore be disclosed in a footnote

subsidiary /səb'sɪdiəri/ *adjective* less important ○ *They agreed to most of the conditions in the contract but queried one or two subsidiary items.* ■ *noun* same as **subsidiary company** ○ *Most of the group profit was contributed by the subsidiaries in the Far East.*

subsidiary account /səbˌsɪdiəri ə'kaʊnt/ *noun* an account for one of the individual people or organisations that jointly hold another account

subsidiary company /səbˌsɪdiəri 'kʌmp(ə)ni/ *noun* a company which is more than 50% owned by a holding company, and where the holding company controls the board of directors

subsidiary company accounting /səb'sɪdiəri ˌkʌmp(ə)ni ə,kaʊntɪŋ/ *noun* the accounting methods that are used at a subsidiary for recording transactions with its parent company

subsidise /'sʌbsɪdaɪz/, **subsidize** *verb* to help by giving money ○ *The government has refused to subsidise the car industry.*

subsidised accommodation /ˌsʌbsɪdaɪzd ə,kɒmə'deɪʃ(ə)n/ *noun* cheap accommodation which is partly paid for by an employer or a local authority

subsidy /'sʌbsɪdi/ *noun* **1.** money given to help something which is not profitable ○ *The industry exists on government subsidies.* ○ *The government has increased its subsidy to the car industry.* **2.** money given by a government to make something cheaper ○ *the subsidy on rail transport* (NOTE: The plural is **subsidies**.)

subtenancy /sʌb'tenənsi/ *noun* an agreement to sublet a property

subtenant /sʌb'tenənt/ *noun* a person or company to which a property has been sublet

subtotal /'sʌbˌtəʊt(ə)l/ *noun* the total of one section of a complete set of figures ○ *She added all the subtotals to make a grand total.*

subtract /səb'trækt/ *verb* to take away something from a total ○ *The credit note should be subtracted from the figure for total sales.* ○ *If the profits from the Far Eastern operations are subtracted, you will see that the group has not been profitable in the European market.*

subtraction /səb'trækʃən/ *noun* an act of taking one number away from another

subvention /səb'venʃ(ə)n/ *noun* same as **subsidy**

succeed /sək'siːd/ *verb* **1.** to do well, to be profitable ○ *The company has succeeded best in the overseas markets.* ○ *Her business has succeeded more than she had expected.* **2.** to do what was planned ○ *She succeeded in passing her computing test.* ○ *They succeeded in putting their rivals out of business.* **3.** to take over from someone in a post ○ *Mr Smith was succeeded as chairman by Mrs Jones.* □ **to succeed to a property** to become the owner of a property by inheriting it from someone who has died

success /sək'ses/ *noun* **1.** an act of doing something well ○ *The launch of the new model was a great success.* ○ *The company has had great success in the Japanese market.* **2.** an act of doing what was intended ○ *We had no success in trying to sell the lease.* ○ *She has been looking for a job for six months, but with no success.*

sum /sʌm/ *noun* **1.** a quantity of money ○ *A sum of money was stolen from the human resources office.* ○ *He lost large sums on the Stock Exchange.* ○ *She received the sum of £5000 in compensation.* **2.** the total of a series of figures added together ○ *The sum of the various subtotals is £18,752.*

sum at risk /ˌsʌm ət ˈrɪsk/ *noun* the amount of any given item, such as money, stocks or securities that an investor may lose

sum of digits method /ˌsʌm əv ˈdɪdʒɪts ˌmeθəd/ *noun* a method of depreciating a fixed asset where the cost of the asset less its residual value is multiplied by a fraction based on the number of years of its expected useful life. The fraction changes each year and charges the highest costs to the earliest years.

sum-of-the-year's-digits depreciation /ˌsʌm əv ðə ˌjɪəz ˌdɪdʒɪts dɪˌpriːʃiˈeɪʃ(ə)n/ *noun* a method of recognising depreciation that assigns more depreciation early in an asset's useful life than in the later years

sums chargeable to the reserve /ˌsʌmz ˌtʃɑːdʒəb(ə)l tə ðə rɪˈzɜːv/ *plural noun* sums which can be debited to a company's reserves

sundry /ˈsʌndri/ *adjective* various

sunk cost /ˈsʌŋk kɒst/ *noun* a cost which has been irreversibly incurred or committed prior to a decision point and which cannot therefore be considered relevant to subsequent decisions. Also called **consumed cost**

superannuation /ˌsuːpərænjuˈeɪʃ(ə)n/ *noun* a pension paid to someone who is too old or ill to work any more

supplementary benefit /ˌsʌplɪment(ə)ri ˈbenɪfɪt/ *noun* formerly, payments from the government to people with very low incomes. It was replaced by income support.

supplementary statement /ˌsʌplɪment(ə)ri ˌsteɪtmənt/ *noun* a statement that elaborates on an earlier financial statement

supplier /səˈplaɪə/ *noun* a person or company that supplies or sells goods or services ○ *We use the same office equipment supplier for all our stationery purchases.* ○ *They are major suppliers of spare parts to the car industry.* Also called **producer**

supply and demand /səˌplaɪ ən dɪ ˈmɑːnd/ *noun* the amount of a product which is available and the amount which is wanted by customers

supply chain /səˈplaɪ tʃeɪn/ *noun* the manufacturers, wholesalers, distributors, and retailers who produce goods and services from raw materials and deliver them to consumers, considered as a group or network

'Only companies that build supply chains that are agile, adaptable, and aligned get ahead of their rivals.' [Harvard Business Review]

supply chain management /səˈplaɪ tʃeɪn ˌmænɪdʒmənt/ *noun* the work of co-ordinating all the activities connected with supplying of finished goods (NOTE: Supply chain management covers the processes of materials management, logistics, physical distribution management, purchasing, and information management.)

supply price /səˈplaɪ praɪs/ *noun* the price at which something is provided

support price /səˈpɔːt praɪs/ *noun* a price in the EU at which a government will buy agricultural produce to stop the price falling

surcharge /ˈsɜːtʃɑːdʒ/ *noun* an extra charge

surety /ˈʃʊərəti/ *noun* **1.** a person who guarantees that someone will do something ○ *to stand surety for someone* **2.** deeds, share certificates, etc., deposited as security for a loan

surplus /ˈsɜːpləs/ *noun* more of something than is needed

'Both imports and exports reached record levels in the latest year. This generated a $371 million trade surplus in June, the seventh consecutive monthly surplus and close to market expectations' [*Dominion (Wellington, New Zealand)*]

surrender /səˈrendə/ *noun* the act of giving up of an insurance policy before the contracted date for maturity

surrender value /səˈrendə ˌvæljuː/ *noun* the money which an insurer will pay if an insurance policy is given up

surtax /ˈsɜːtæks/ *noun* an extra tax on high income

suspend /səˈspend/ *verb* to stop doing something for a time ○ *We have suspended payments while we are waiting for news from our agent.* ○ *Work on the construction project has been suspended.*

suspense account /səˈspens əˌkaʊnt/ *noun* an account into which payments are put temporarily when the accountant cannot be sure where they should be entered

suspension /səˈspenʃən/ *noun* an act of stopping something for a time ○ *There has* *been a temporary suspension of payments.* ○ *We are trying to avoid a suspension of deliveries during the strike.*

SVA *abbreviation* shareholder value analysis

swap /swɒp/ *noun* an exchange of one thing for another

sweetener /'swiːt(ə)nə/ *noun* an incentive offered to help persuade somebody to take a particular course of action (*informal*)

switch /swɪtʃ/ *verb* **1.** to change from one thing to another ○ *to switch funds from one investment to another* ○ *The job was switched from our British factory to the States.* **2.** to change, especially to change investment money from one type of investment to another

SWOT analysis /swɒt ə,næləsɪs/ *noun* a method of assessing a person, company or product by considering their Strengths, Weaknesses, and external factors which may provide Opportunities or Threats to their development. Full form **Strengths, Weaknesses, Opportunities, Threats**

syndicate /'sɪndɪkeɪt/ *verb* to arrange for a large loan to be underwritten by several international banks

'…over the past few weeks, companies raising new loans from international banks have been forced to pay more, and an unusually high number of attempts to syndicate loans among banks has failed' [*Financial Times*]

system /'sɪstəm/ *noun* an arrangement or organisation of things which work together ○ *Our accounting system has worked well in spite of the large increase in orders.*

systematic sampling /,sɪstəmætɪk 'saːmplɪŋ/ *noun* an auditing technique that selects a number of random samples of data in a systematic way, instead of a pure random sample

systems analysis /'sɪstəmz ə,næləsɪs/ *noun* the process of using a computer to suggest how a company can work more efficiently by analysing the way in which it works at present

systems analyst /'sɪstəmz ,ænəlɪst/ *noun* a person who specialises in systems analysis

system weakness /'sɪstəm ,wiːknəs/ *noun* weakness in an accounting system that leads to a risk that financial statements will be flawed or that budgets will be miscalculated

T

T+ *noun* an expression of the number of days allowed for settlement of a transaction

tab /tæb/ *noun* same as **tabulator** (*informal*)

tabulate /ˈtæbjʊleɪt/ *verb* to set something out in a table

tabulation /ˌtæbjʊˈleɪʃ(ə)n/ *noun* the arrangement of figures in a table

tabulator /ˈtæbjʊleɪtə/ *noun* a feature on a computer which sets words or figures automatically in columns

T account /ˈtiː əˌkaʊnt/ *noun* a way of drawing up an account, with a line across the top of the paper and a vertical line down the middle, with the debit and credit entries on either side

take /teɪk/ *noun* **1.** the money received in a shop ○ *Our weekly take is over £5,000.* **2.** a profit from any sale ■ *verb* **1.** to receive or to get □ **the shop takes £2,000 a week** the shop receives £2,000 a week in cash sales □ **she takes home £450 a week** her salary, after deductions for tax, etc. is £450 a week **2.** to perform an action **3.** to need a time or a quantity ○ *It took the factory six weeks* or *The factory took six weeks to clear the backlog of orders.* (NOTE: **taking – took – has taken**)

take away *phrasal verb* to remove one figure from a total ○ *If you take away the home sales, the total turnover is down.*

take off *phrasal verb* to remove or to deduct something ○ *He took £25 off the price.*

take over *phrasal verb* to start to do something in place of someone else ○ *Miss Black took over from Mr Jones on May 1st.*

take-home pay /ˈteɪk həʊm ˌpeɪ/ *noun* same as **disposable personal income** ○ *After all the deductions, her take-home pay is only £600 a week.*

take-out /ˈteɪk aʊt/ *noun* the act of removing capital which you had originally invested in a new company by selling your shares

takeover /ˈteɪkəʊvə/ *noun* an act of buying a controlling interest in a business by buying more than 50% of its shares. Compare **acquisition**

takeover bid /ˈteɪkəʊvə bɪd/ *noun* an offer to buy all or a majority of the shares in a company so as to control it ○ *They made a takeover bid for the company.* ○ *She had to withdraw her takeover bid when she failed to find any backers.* ○ *Share prices rose sharply on the disclosure of the takeover bid.*

Takeover Code /ˈteɪkˌəʊvə kəʊd/ *noun* the code of practice which regulates how takeovers should take place. It is enforced by the Takeover Panel.

Takeover Panel /ˈteɪkəʊvə ˌpæn(ə)l/ *noun* a non-statutory body which examines takeovers and applies the Takeover Code. Also called **City Panel on Takeovers and Mergers**

takeover target /ˈteɪkəʊvə ˌtɑːgɪt/ *noun* a company which is the object of a takeover bid

take up rate /ˈteɪk ʌp ˌreɪt/ *noun* the percentage of acceptances for a rights issue

takings /ˈteɪkɪŋz/ *plural noun* the money received in a shop or a business ○ *The week's takings were stolen from the cash desk.*

tally /ˈtæli/ *noun* a note of things counted or recorded ○ *to keep a tally of stock movements* or *of expenses* ■ *verb* to agree, to be the same ○ *The invoices do not tally.* ○ *The accounts department tried to make the figures tally.*

tally sheet /ˈtæli fiːt/ *noun* a sheet on which quantities are noted

tangible assets /ˌtændʒɪb(ə)l ˈæsets/, **tangible fixed assets** /ˌtændʒɪb(ə)l fɪkst ˈæsets/, **tangible property** /ˌtændʒɪb(ə)l ˈprɒpəti/ *plural noun* assets that are physical, such as buildings, cash and stock. Leases and securities, although not physical in themselves, are classed as tangible assets because the underlying assets are physical.

tangible asset value /ˌtændʒəb(ə)l ˈæset ˌvæljuː/, **tangible net worth** /ˌtændʒəb(ə)l net ˈwɜːθ/ *noun* the value of all the assets of a company less its intangible assets, e.g. goodwill, shown as a value per share

tangible book value /ˌtændʒəb(ə)l 'bʊk ˌvæljuː/ *noun* the book value of a company after intangible assets, patents, trademarks and the value of research and development have been subtracted

taper relief /'teɪpə rɪˌliːf/ *noun* the relief for capital gains on assets sold after being held for some period of time. The longer the assets have been held, the more relief is given against capital gains.

target company /ˌtɑːɡɪt 'kʌmp(ə)ni/ *noun* same as **takeover target**

'...in a normal leveraged buyout the acquirer raises money by borrowing against the assets of the target company' [*Fortune*]

target cost /'tɑːɡɪt kɒst/ *noun* a product cost estimate derived by subtracting a desired profit margin from a competitive market price. This may be less than the planned initial product cost, but will be expected to be achieved by the time the product reaches the mature production stage.

target market /'tɑːɡɪt ˌmɑːkɪt/ *noun* the market in which a company is planning to sell its goods

target pricing /'tɑːɡɪt ˌpraɪsɪŋ/ *noun* the setting of a selling price with the aim of producing a particular rate of return on investment for a specific volume of production

tariff /'tærɪf/ *noun* a tax to be paid on imported goods. Also called **customs tariff**

tax /tæks/ *noun* **1.** money taken by the government or by an official body to pay for government services **2.** an amount of money charged by government as part of a person's income or on goods bought □ **to levy** *or* **impose a tax** to make a tax payable ○ *The government has imposed a 15% tax on petrol.* ■ *verb* to make someone pay a tax, to impose a tax on something ○ *Businesses are taxed at 40%.* ○ *Income is taxed at 35%.* ○ *Luxury items are heavily taxed.*

tax abatement /'tæks əˌbeɪtmənt/ *noun* a reduction of tax

taxable /'tæksəb(ə)l/ *adjective* able to be taxed

taxable base /ˌtæksəb(ə)l 'beɪs/ *noun* the amount subject to taxation

taxable benefit /ˌtæksəb(ə)l 'benɪfɪt/ *noun* a benefit which is included in a person's taxable income and is subject to tax

taxable income /ˌtæksəb(ə)l 'ɪnkʌm/ *noun* income on which a person has to pay tax

taxable items /'tæksəb(ə)l ˌaɪtəmz/ *plural noun* items on which a tax has to be paid

taxable matters /ˌtæksəb(ə)l 'mætəz/ *plural noun* goods or services that can be taxed

taxable person /ˌtæksəb(ə)l 'pɜːs(ə)n/ *noun* a person who is registered for VAT, and who charges VAT on goods or services supplied

taxable supply /ˌtæksəb(ə)l sə'plaɪ/ *noun* a supply of goods which are subject to VAT

tax adjustments /'tæks əˌdʒʌstmənts/ *plural noun* changes made to tax

tax adviser /'tæks ədˌvaɪzə/, **tax consultant** /'tæks kənˌsʌltənt/ *noun* a person who gives advice on tax issues and problems

tax allowance /'tæks əˌlaʊəns/ *noun* part of the income which a person is allowed to earn and not pay tax on

tax assessment /'tæks əˌsesmənt/ *noun* a calculation by a tax inspector of the amount of tax a person owes

taxation /tæk'seɪʃ(ə)n/ *noun* the system of raising revenue for public funding by taxing individuals and organisations, or the amount of revenue raised

tax at source /ˌtæks ət 'sɔːs/ *verb* to deduct tax from earnings before they are paid to the recipient

tax auditor /'tæks ˌɔːdɪtə/ *noun* a government employee who investigates taxpayers' declarations

tax avoidance /'tæks əˌvɔɪd(ə)ns/ *noun* the practice of legally trying to pay as little tax as possible

tax bracket /'tæks ˌbrækɪt/ *noun* the section of people paying a particular level of income tax

tax code /'tæks kəʊd/ *noun* a number given to indicate the amount of tax allowance a person has

tax collector /'tæks kəˌlektə/ *noun* a person who collects taxes which are owed

tax concession /'tæks kənˌseʃ(ə)n/ *noun* an act of allowing less tax to be paid

tax consultant /'tæks kənˌsʌltənt/ *noun* ♦ **tax adviser**

tax credit /'tæks ˌkredɪt/ *noun* **1.** a sum of money which can be offset against tax **2.** the part of a dividend on which the company has already paid tax, so that the shareholder is not taxed on it

tax date /ˈtæks deɪt/ *noun* the date on which a transaction occurs for tax purposes, particularly relevant to invoices on which VAT is charged

tax-deductible /ˌtæks dɪˈdʌktɪb(ə)l/ *adjective* possible to deduct from an income before tax is calculated

tax deposit certificate /ˈtæks dɪˌpɒzɪt səˌtɪfɪkət/ *noun* a certificate showing that a taxpayer has deposited money in advance of a tax payment. The money earns interest while on deposit.

tax dodge /ˈtæks dɒdʒ/ *noun* an illegal method of paying less tax than an individual or company is legally obliged to pay

tax domicile /ˈtæks ˌdɒmɪsaɪl/ *noun* the place that a government levying a tax considers to be a person's home

tax evasion /ˈtæks ɪˌveɪʒ(ə)n/ *noun* the practice of illegally trying to not pay tax

tax-exempt /ˌtæks ɪgˈzempt/ *adjective* **1.** referring to a person or organisation not required to pay tax **2.** not subject to tax

tax exemption /ˈtæks ɪgˌzempʃən/ *noun* **1.** the fact of being free from payment of tax **2.** *US* the part of income which a person is allowed to earn and not pay tax on

tax exemption cut-off /ˌtæks ɪg ˌzempʃ(ə)n ˈkʌt ˌɒf/ *noun* a limit on tax exemption because of high income

tax-exempt special savings account /ˌtæks ɪgˌzempt ˌspeʃ(ə)l ˈseɪvɪŋz əˌkaʊnt/ *noun* a now-discontinued form of interest-free savings account largely superseded by the ISA. Abbreviation **TESSA**

tax form /ˈtæks fɔːm/ *noun* a blank form to be filled in with details of income and allowances and sent to the tax office each year

tax-free /ˌtæks ˈfriː/ *adjective* with no tax having to be paid ○ *tax-free goods*

tax harmonisation /ˈtæks ˌhɑːmənaɪzeɪʃ(ə)n/ *noun* the enactment of taxation laws in different jurisdictions, such as neighbouring countries, provinces, or states of the United States, that are consistent with one another

tax haven /ˈtæks ˌheɪv(ə)n/ *noun* a country or area where taxes are low, encouraging companies to set up their main offices there

tax holiday /ˈtæks ˌhɒlɪdeɪ/ *noun* a period when a new business is exempted from paying tax

tax incentive /ˈtæks ɪnˌsentɪv/ *noun* a tax reduction afforded to people for particular purposes, e.g., sending their children to college

tax inspector /ˈtæks ɪnˌspektə/ *noun* a government employee who investigates taxpayers' declarations

tax law /ˈtæks lɔː/ *noun* the body of laws on taxation, or one such law

tax liability /ˌtæks ˌlaɪəˈbɪlɪti/ *noun* the amount of tax that a person or organisation has to pay

tax loophole /ˈtæks ˌluːphəʊl/ *noun* a legal means of not paying tax

tax loss /ˈtæks lɒs/ *noun* a loss made by a company during an accounting period, for which relief from tax is given

tax loss carry-back /ˌtæks lɒs ˌkæri ˈbæk/ *noun* the reduction of taxes in a previous year by subtraction from income for that year of losses suffered in the current year

tax loss carry-forward /ˌtæks lɒs ˌkæri ˈfɔːwəd/ *noun* the reduction of taxes in a future year by subtraction from income for that year of losses suffered in the current year

tax obligation /ˈtæks ˌɒblɪgeɪʃ(ə)n/ *noun* the amount of tax a person or company owes

tax office /ˈtæks ˌɒfɪs/ *noun* a local office of the Inland Revenue. It does not necessarily deal with the tax affairs of people who live locally.

tax on capital income /ˌtæks ɒn ˌkæpɪt(ə)l ˈɪnkʌm/ *noun* a tax on the income from sales of capital assets

tax payable /ˌtæks ˈpeɪəb(ə)l/ *noun* the amount of tax a person or company has to pay

taxpayer /ˈtækspeɪə/ *noun* a person or company that has to pay tax ○ *basic taxpayer* or *taxpayer at the basic rate* ○ *Corporate taxpayers are being targeted by the government.*

tax planning /ˈtæks ˌplænɪŋ/ *noun* planning how to avoid paying too much tax, by investing in, e.g., tax-exempt savings schemes or offshore trusts

tax point /ˈtæks pɔɪnt/ *noun* the date on which goods or services are supplied, which is the date when VAT becomes is due

tax pressure /ˈtæks ˌpreʃə/ *noun* the financial difficulty that a company may face because of the taxes it must pay

tax rates /ˈtæks reɪts/ *plural noun* percentage rates of tax on different bands of taxable income

tax rebate /ˈtæks ˌriːbeɪt/ *noun* money returned by the Inland Revenue because it was overpaid

tax reform /'tæks rɪˌfɔːm/ *noun* changes to tax provisions made by a revenue authority

tax refund /'tæks ˌriːfʌnd/ *noun US* same as **remission of taxes**

tax relief /'tæks rɪˌliːf/ *noun* reductions in tax liability that are allowed in line with necessary business expenditure

tax return /'tæks rɪˌtɜːn/ *noun* a completed tax form, with details of income and allowances

tax revenue /'tæks ˌrevənjuː/ *noun* money that a government receives in taxes

tax schedules /'tæks ˌʃedjuːlz/ *plural noun* six types of income as classified for tax

tax shelter /'tæks ˌʃeltə/ *noun* a financial arrangement such as a pension scheme where investments can be made without tax

tax system /'tæks ˌsɪstəm/ *noun* the methods used by a government in imposing and collecting taxes

tax threshold /'tæks ˌθreʃhəʊld/ *noun* a point at which another percentage of tax is payable ○ *The government has raised the minimum tax threshold from £4,000 to £4,500.*

tax treaty /'tæks ˌtriːti/ *noun* an international agreement that deals with taxes, especially taxes by several countries on the same individuals

tax voucher /'tæks ˌvaʊtʃə/ *noun* a document detailing various items of financial information, issued to shareholders at the time dividends are paid

tax year /'tæks ˌjɪə/ *noun* a twelve month period on which taxes are calculated. In the UK this is 6th April to 5th April of the following year.

T-bond /'tiː bɒnd/ *noun* same as **Treasury bond**

technical /'teknɪk(ə)l/ *adjective* referring to influences inside a market, e.g. volumes traded and forecasts based on market analysis, as opposed to external factors such as oil-price rises, wars, etc.

'…market analysts described the falls in the second half of last week as a technical correction' [*Australian Financial Review*]

'…at the end of the day, it was clear the Fed had not loosened the monetary reins, and Fed Funds forged ahead on the back of technical demand' [*Financial Times*]

technical analysis /ˌteknɪk(ə)l əˈnæləsɪs/ *noun* a study of the price movements and volumes traded on a stock exchange

technical correction /ˌteknɪk(ə)l kəˈrekʃ(ə)n/ *noun* an adjustment to the price of a share or the value of a currency

technical decline /ˌteknɪk(ə)l dɪˈklaɪn/ *noun* a fall in share prices because of technical analysis

technical reserves /ˌteknɪk(ə)l rɪˈzɜːvz/ *plural noun* the assets that an insurance company maintains to meet future claims

teeming and lading /ˌtiːmɪŋ ən ˈleɪdɪŋ/ *noun* an attempt to hide missing funds by delaying the recording of cash receipts in a business's books

telephone banking /ˌtelɪfəʊn ˈbæŋkɪŋ/ *noun* a service by which a bank customer can carry out transactions over the phone using a password. It may involve direct contact with a bank representative or may be automated using the phone's keypad.

teller /'telə/ *noun* a person who takes cash from or pays cash to customers at a bank

tenancy /'tenənsi/ *noun* an agreement by which a tenant can occupy a property

tenant /'tenənt/ *noun* a person or company which rents a house, flat or office to live or work in ○ *The tenant is liable for repairs.*

tender /'tendə/ *noun* an offer to do something for a specific price ○ *a successful tender* ○ *an unsuccessful tender* □ **to put a project out to tender, to ask for** *or* **invite tenders for a project** to ask contractors to give written estimates for a job □ **to put in** *or* **submit a tender** to make an estimate for a job

tenderer /'tendərə/ *noun* a person or company that puts forward an estimate of cost ○ *The company was the successful tenderer for the project.* (NOTE: The US term is **bidder**.)

tendering /'tendərɪŋ/ *noun* the act of putting forward an estimate of cost ○ *To be successful, you must follow the tendering procedure as laid out in the documents.* (NOTE: The US term is **bidding**.)

tender offer /'tendər ˌɒfə/ *noun* a method of selling new securities or bonds by asking investors to make offers for them, and accepting the highest offers

10-K /ˌten ˈkeɪ/ *noun* the filing of a US company's annual accounts with the New York Stock Exchange

tenor /'tenə/ *noun* the life of a financial instrument, between the time it is taken out and the maturity date

10-Q /ˌten ˈkjuː/ noun the filing of a US company's quarterly accounts with the New York Stock Exchange

term /tɜːm/ noun a period of time when something is legally valid ○ *during his term of office as chairman* ○ *the term of a lease* ○ *We have renewed her contract for a term of six months.* ○ *The term of the loan is fifteen years.*

term deposit /ˈtɜːm dɪˌpɒzɪt/, **term account** /ˈtɜːm əˌkaʊnt/ noun money invested for a fixed period at a higher rate of interest

terminal bonus /ˌtɜːmɪn(ə)l ˈbəʊnəs/ noun a bonus received when an insurance comes to an end

termination clause /ˌtɜːmɪˈneɪʃ(ə)n klɔːz/ noun a clause which explains how and when a contract can be terminated

term loan /ˈtɜːm ləʊn/ noun a loan for a fixed period of time

terms /tɜːmz/ plural noun the conditions or duties which have to be carried out as part of a contract, or the arrangements which have to be agreed before a contract is valid ○ *to negotiate for better terms* ○ *She refused to agree to some of the terms of the contract.* ○ *By* or *Under the terms of the contract, the company is responsible for all damage to the property.*

'...companies have been improving communications, often as part of deals to cut down demarcation and to give everybody the same terms of employment' [*Economist*]

'...the Federal Reserve Board has eased interest rates in the past year, but they are still at historically high levels in real terms' [*Sunday Times*]

term shares /ˈtɜːm ʃeəz/ plural noun a type of building society deposit that offers a comparatively high rate of interest for a fixed period of time

terms of reference /ˌtɜːmz əv ˈref(ə)rəns/ plural noun the specific areas which a committee or an inspector can deal with ○ *Under the terms of reference of the committee, it cannot investigate complaints from the public.* ○ *The committee's terms of reference do not cover exports.*

terms of sale /ˌtɜːmz əv ˈseɪl/ plural noun the conditions attached to a sale

TESSA /ˈtesə/ abbreviation tax-exempt special savings account

testamentary /ˌtestəˈmentəri/ adjective referring to a will

testamentary disposition /testəˌmentəri ˌdɪspəˈzɪʃ(ə)n/ noun the passing of property to people in a will

testate /ˈtesteɪt/ adjective having made a will ○ *Did he die testate?* ◊ **intestate**

testator /teˈsteɪtə/ noun someone who has made a will

testatrix /teˈsteɪtrɪks/ noun a woman who has made a will

theory of constraints /ˌθɪəri əv kənˈstreɪnts/ noun an approach to production management that aims to maximise sales revenue by focusing on constraining factors such as bottlenecks

third party /ˌθɜːd ˈpɑːti/ noun a person other than the two main parties involved in a contract, e.g., in an insurance contract, anyone who is not the insurance company nor the person who is insured

third quarter /ˌθɜːd ˈkwɔːtə/ noun the period of three months from July to September

3i abbreviation Investors in Industry

threshold /ˈθreʃhəʊld/ noun the point at which something changes

threshold agreement /ˈθreʃhəʊld əˌɡriːmənt/ noun a contract which says that if the cost of living goes up by more than an agreed amount, pay will go up to match it

thrift /θrɪft/ noun **1.** a careful attitude towards money, shown by saving or spending it wisely **2.** US a private local bank, savings and loan association or credit union, which accepts and pays interest on deposits from small investors

'...the thrift, which had grown from $4.7 million in assets in 1980 to 1.5 billion this year, has ended in liquidation' [*Barrons*]

'...some thrifts came to grief on speculative property deals, some in the high-risk junk bond market, others simply by lending too much to too many people' [*Times*]

thrifty /ˈθrɪfti/ adjective careful not to spend too much money

throughput /ˈθruːpʊt/ noun the amount of work done or of goods produced in a certain time ○ *We hope to increase our throughput by putting in two new machines.*

throughput accounting /ˈθruːpʊt əˌkaʊntɪŋ/ noun a management accounting system that seeks to maximise the return on bottleneck activity

tied financial adviser /ˌtaɪd faɪˌnænʃəl ədˈvaɪzə/ noun a qualified professional who gives advice on the financial products offered by a single company, as distinct from an independent financial adviser who advises on the products of various companies

tighten /'taɪt(ə)n/ verb to make something tight, to control something ○ *The accounts department is tightening its control over departmental budgets.*

'…the decision by the government to tighten monetary policy will push the annual inflation rate above the previous high' [*Financial Times*]

tighten up on phrasal verb to control something more strictly ○ *The government is tightening up on tax evasion.* ○ *We must tighten up on the reps' expenses.*

tight money /ˌtaɪt 'mʌni/ noun same as **dear money**

tight money policy /ˌtaɪt 'mʌni ˌpɒlɪsi/ noun a government policy to restrict money supply

till /tɪl/ noun a drawer for keeping cash in a shop

time /taɪm/ noun **1.** a period during which something takes place, e.g. one hour, two days, or fifty minutes **2.** the number of hours worked **3.** a period before something happens □ **to keep within the time limits** *or* **within the time schedule** to complete work by the time stated

time and materials pricing /ˌtaɪm ən məˈtɪəriəlz ˌpraɪsɪŋ/ noun a pricing model that takes account of the cost of materials and parts, labour costs, and a percentage markup of each to cover overhead costs, and a margin for profit

time and method study /ˌtaɪm ən 'meθəd ˌstʌdi/ noun a process of examining the way in which something is done to see if a cheaper or quicker way can be found

time and motion expert /ˌtaɪm ən 'məʊʃ(ə)n ˌekspɜːt/ noun a person who analyses time and motion studies and suggests changes in the way work is done

time and motion study /ˌtaɪm ən 'məʊʃ(ə)n ˌstʌdi/ noun a study that seeks to improve efficiency and productivity in an office or factory

time deposit /'taɪm dɪˌpɒzɪt/ noun a deposit of money for a fixed period, during which it cannot be withdrawn

time draft /'taɪm drɑːft/ noun a bill of exchange that is drawn on and accepted by a US bank

time limit /'taɪm ˌlɪmɪt/ noun the maximum time which can be taken to do something ○ *to set a time limit for acceptance of the offer* ○ *The work was finished within the time limit allowed.* ○ *The time limit on applications to the industrial tribunal is three months.*

time limitation /'taɪm lɪmɪˌteɪʃ(ə)n/ noun the restriction of the amount of time available

time rate /'taɪm reɪt/ noun a rate for work which is calculated as money per hour or per week, and not money for work completed

timescale /'taɪmskeɪl/ noun the time which will be taken to complete work ○ *Our timescale is that all work should be completed by the end of August.* ○ *He is working to a strict timescale.*

time sheet /'taɪm ʃiːt/ noun a record of when an employee arrives at and leaves work, or one which shows how much time a person spends on different jobs each day

time work /'taɪm wɜːk/ noun work which is paid for at a rate per hour or per day, not per piece of work completed

title /'taɪt(ə)l/ noun a right to own a property ○ *She has no title to the property.* ○ *He has a good title to the property.*

title deeds /'taɪt(ə)l ˌdiːdz/ plural noun a document showing who is the owner of a property

token charge /ˌtəʊkən 'tʃɑːdʒ/ noun a small charge which does not cover the real costs ○ *A token charge is made for heating.*

token payment /'təʊkən ˌpeɪmənt/ noun a small payment to show that a payment is being made

token rent /ˌtəʊkən 'rent/ noun a very low rent payment to show that some rent is being asked

toll /təʊl/ noun a payment for using a service, usually a bridge or a road ○ *We had to cross a toll bridge to get to the island.* ○ *You have to pay a toll to cross the bridge.*

toll call /'təʊl kɔːl/ noun US a long-distance telephone call

toll free /ˌtəʊl 'friː/ adverb, adjective US without having to pay a charge for a long-distance telephone call ○ *to call someone toll free* ○ *a toll-free number*

top-hat pension /ˌtɒp hæt 'penʃən/ noun a special extra pension for senior managers

total /'təʊt(ə)l/ adjective complete, or with everything added together ○ *The company has total assets of over £1bn* ○ *The total amount owed is now £1000.* ○ *Our total income from exports rose last year.* ■ verb to add up to ○ *costs totalling more than £25,000* (NOTE: **totalling – totalled**. The US spelling is **totaling – totaled**.)

total absorption costing /ˌtəʊt(ə)l əb ˈzɔːpʃən ˌkɒstɪŋ/ *noun* a method used by a cost accountant to price goods and services, allocating both direct and indirect costs. Although this method is designed so that all of an organisation's costs are covered, it may result in opportunities for sales being missed because it results in high prices. ◊ **marginal costing**

total assets /ˌtəʊt(ə)l ˈæsets/ *plural noun* the total net book value of all assets

total asset turnover ratio /ˌtəʊt(ə)l ˌæset ˈtɜːnəʊvə ˌreɪʃiəʊ/ *noun* a measure of the use a business makes of all its assets. It is calculated by dividing sales by total assets.

total invoice value /ˌtəʊt(ə)l ˈɪnvɔɪs ˌvæljuː/ *noun* the total amount on an invoice, including transport, VAT, etc.

total manufacturing costs /ˌtəʊt(ə)l ˌmænjʊˈfæktʃərɪŋ ˌkɒsts/ *plural noun* the total figure for costs of materials, labour and overheads incurred during an accounting period

total overhead cost variance /ˌtəʊt(ə)l ˈəʊvəhed kɒst ˌveəriəns/ *noun* the difference between the overhead cost absorbed and the actual overhead costs, both fixed and variable

total productivity /ˌtəʊt(ə)l ˌprɒdʌk ˈtɪvɪti/ *noun* a figure that represents the value of total output divided by the cost of all input

total quality control /ˌtəʊt(ə)l ˈkwɒləti kənˌtrəʊl/ *noun* a manufacturing approach that aims at turning out products that are consistently defect-free

total return /ˌtəʊt(ə)l rɪˈtɜːn/ *noun* the total percentage change in the value of an investment over a specified time period, including capital gains, dividends and the investment's appreciation or depreciation

traceability /ˌtreɪsəˈbɪlɪti/ *noun* the extent to which a cost can be directly assigned to an activity or object

traceable cost /ˈtreɪsəb(ə)l kɒst/ *noun* a cost that is directly assigned to an activity or object

tracker fund /ˈtrækə fʌnd/ *noun* a fund which tracks one of the stock market indices, such as the FTSE

tracking stock /ˈtrækɪŋ stɒk/ *noun* shares on which the level of dividend payments is linked to the performance of a subsidiary of the company

trade /treɪd/ *noun* **1.** the business of buying and selling **2.** a particular type of business, or people or companies dealing in the same type of product ○ *He's in the secondhand car trade.* ○ *She's very well known in the clothing trade.* ■ *verb* to buy and sell, to carry on a business ○ *We trade with all the countries of the EU.* ○ *The company has stopped trading.*

'…a sharp setback in foreign trade accounted for most of the winter slowdown. The trade balance sank $17 billion' [*Fortune*]

'…at its last traded price, the bank was capitalized around $1.05 billion' [*South China Morning Post*]

'…with most of the world's oil now traded on spot markets, Opec's official prices are much less significant than they once were' [*Economist*]

'…the London Stock Exchange said that the value of domestic UK equities traded during the year was £1.4066 trillion, more than the capitalization of the entire London market and an increase of 36 per cent compared with previous year's total of £1.037 trillion' [*Times*]

'…trade between Britain and other countries which comprise the Economic Community has risen steadily from 33% of exports to 50% last year' [*Sales & Marketing Management*]

trade agreement /ˈtreɪd əˌgriːmənt/ *noun* an international agreement between countries over general terms of trade

trade association /ˈtreɪd əˌsəʊsieɪʃ(ə)n/ *noun* a group which links together companies in the same trade

trade barrier /ˈtreɪd ˌbæriə/ *noun* a limitation imposed by a government on the free exchange of goods between countries (NOTE: NTBs, safety standards, and tariffs are typical trade barriers.)

trade bill /ˈtreɪd bɪl/ *noun* a bill of exchange between two companies who are trading partners. It is issued by one company and endorsed by the other.

trade credit /ˈtreɪd ˌkredɪt/ *noun* the provision of goods or services to another company with an agreement to invoice them later, which is a major source of capital for many businesses

trade creditors /ˈtreɪd ˌkredɪtəz/ *plural noun* companies which are owed money by a company. The amount owed to trade creditors is shown in the annual accounts.

trade cycle /ˈtreɪd ˌsaɪk(ə)l/ *noun* a period during which trade expands, then slows down, then expands again

trade date /ˈtreɪd deɪt/ *noun* the date on which an enterprise becomes committed to buy a financial asset

trade debt /'treɪd det/ *noun* a debt that originates during the normal course of trade

trade deficit /'treɪd ˌdefɪsɪt/ *noun* the difference in value between a country's low exports and higher imports. Also called **balance of payments deficit**, **trade gap**

trade description /ˌtreɪd dɪˈskrɪpʃən/ *noun* a description of a product to attract customers

trade discount /ˌtreɪd ˈdɪskaʊnt/ *noun* a reduction in price given to a customer in the same trade

traded options /ˌtreɪdɪd ˈɒpʃənz/ *plural noun* options to buy or sell shares at a specific price on a specific date in the future, which themselves can be bought or sold

trade fair /'treɪd feə/ *noun* a large exhibition and meeting for advertising and selling a specific type of product ○ *There are two trade fairs running in London at the same time – the carpet manufacturers' and the mobile telephone companies'.*

trade gap /'treɪd gæp/ *noun* same as **trade deficit**

trademark /'treɪdmɑːk/, **trade name** /'treɪd neɪm/ *noun* same as **registered trademark**

trade-off /'treɪd ɒf/ *noun* an act of exchanging one thing for another as part of a business deal (NOTE: The plural is **trade-offs**.)

trade price /'treɪd praɪs/ *noun* a special wholesale price paid by a retailer to the manufacturer or wholesaler

trader /'treɪdə/ *noun* a person who does business

trade surplus /'treɪd ˌsɜːpləs/ *noun* the difference in value between a country's high exports and lower imports

'Brazil's trade surplus is vulnerable both to a slowdown in the American economy and a pick-up in its own' [*Economist*]

trade terms /'treɪd tɜːmz/ *plural noun* a special discount for people in the same trade

trade-weighted index /'treɪd ˌweɪtɪd ˌɪndeks/ *noun* an index of the value of a currency calculated against a basket of currencies

trading /'treɪdɪŋ/ *noun* **1.** the business of buying and selling **2.** an area of a brokerage firm where dealing in securities is carried out by phone, using monitors to display current prices and stock exchange transactions

trading, profit and loss account /ˌtreɪdɪŋ ˌprɒfɪt ən ˈlɒs əˌkaʊnt/ *noun* an account which details the gross profit or loss made by an organisation for a given period

trading account, and after adding other income and deducting various expenses, is able to show the profit or loss of the business

trading account /'treɪdɪŋ əˌkaʊnt/ *noun* a company bank account administered by an investment dealer and used for managing trading activity, rather than for investment purposes

trading area /'treɪdɪŋ ˌeəriə/ *noun* a group of countries which trade with each other

trading company /'treɪdɪŋ ˌkʌmp(ə)ni/ *noun* a company which specialises in buying and selling goods

trading financial assets /ˌtreɪdɪŋ faɪ ˌnænʃəl ˈæsets/ *plural noun* financial assets acquired or held in order to produce profit from short term changes in price

trading limit /'treɪdɪŋ ˌlɪmɪt/ *noun* the maximum amount of something which can be traded by a single trader

trading loss /ˌtreɪdɪŋ ˈlɒs/ *noun* a situation where a company's receipts are less than its expenditure

trading partner /'treɪdɪŋ ˌpɑːtnə/ *noun* a company or country which trades with another

trading profit /'treɪdɪŋ ˌprɒfɪt/ *noun* a result where the company' receipts are higher than its expenditure

trainee /treɪˈniː/ *noun* a person who is learning how to do something ○ *We take five graduates as trainees each year.* ○ *We employ an additional trainee accountant at peak periods.*

training levy /'treɪnɪŋ ˌlevi/ *noun* a tax to be paid by companies to fund the government's training schemes

tranche /trɑːnʃ/ *noun* one of a series of instalments, used when referring to loans to companies, government securities which are issued over a period of time, or money withdrawn by a country from the IMF ○ *The second tranche of interest on the loan is now due for payment.*

transaction /trænˈzækʃən/ *noun* an instance of doing business, e.g. a purchase in a shop or a withdrawal of money from savings ○ **a transaction on the Stock Exchange** a purchase or sale of shares on the Stock Exchange ○ *The paper publishes a daily list of Stock Exchange transactions.*

'…the Japan Financial Intelligence Office will receive reports on suspected criminal transactions from financial institutions, determine where a probe should be launched and provide information to investigators' [*Nikkei Weekly*]

transaction costs /trænˈzækʃən kɒsts/ *plural noun* incremental costs that are directly attributable to the buying or selling of an asset. Transaction costs include commissions, fees and direct taxes.

transaction cycle /trænˈzækʃən ˌsaɪk(ə)l/ *noun* any of three aspects of business activity regarded as occurring in cycles: revenue, buying and production

transaction date /trænˈzækʃən deɪt/ *noun* the date on which control of an asset passes from the seller to the buyer

transaction exposure /trænˈzækʃən ɪkˌspəʊʒə/ *noun* the risk that an organisation may suffer the effects of foreign exchange rate changes during the time it takes to arrange the export or import of goods or services. Transaction exposure is present from the time a price is agreed until the payment has been made or received in the domestic currency.

transfer *noun* /ˈtrænsfɜː/ an act of moving an employee to another job in the same organisation ○ *She applied for a transfer to our branch in Scotland.* ■ *verb* /trænsˈfɜː/ to move someone or something to a different place, or to move someone to another job in the same organisation ○ *The accountant was transferred to our Scottish branch.* ○ *He transferred his shares to a family trust.* ○ *She transferred her money to a deposit account.*

transferable /trænsˈfɜːrəb(ə)l/ *adjective* possible to pass to someone else

transfer of property /ˌtrænsfɜːr əv ˈprɒpəti/**, transfer of shares** /ˌtrænsfɜːr əv ˈʃeəz/ *noun* the act of moving the ownership of property or shares of stock from one person to another

transferor /trænsˈfɜːrə/ *noun* a person who transfers goods or property to another

transfer price /ˈtrænsfɜː praɪs/ *noun* the price at which a transaction is carried out between related companies

transfer pricing /ˈtrænsfɜː ˌpraɪsɪŋ/ *noun* prices used in a large organisation for selling goods or services between departments in the same organisation; also used in multinational corporations to transfer transactions from one country to another to avoid paying tax

transferred charge call /trænsˌfɜːd ˈtʃɑːdʒ kɔːl/ *noun* a phone call where the person receiving the call agrees to pay for it

transferred-in costs /ˌtrænsfɜːd ˈɪn ˌkɒsts/ *plural noun* the cost of switching the processing of a product or delivery of a service from one department of an organisation to another

translate /trænsˈleɪt/ *verb* to put something which is said or written in one language into another language ○ *He asked his secretary to translate the letter from the German agent.* ○ *We have had the contract translated from French into Japanese.*

translation /trænsˈleɪʃ(ə)n/ *noun* something which has been translated ○ *She passed the translation of the letter to the accounts department.*

translation exposure /trænsˈleɪʃ(ə)n ɪkˌspəʊʒə/ *noun* the risk that the balance sheet and income statement may be adversely affected by foreign exchange rate changes

transparent market /trænsˌpærənt ˈmɑːkɪt/ *noun* a market in which financial and operational information is shared openly between shareholders, investors and company officials

traveller's cheques /ˈtræv(ə)ləz tʃeks/ *plural noun* cheques bought by a traveller which can be cashed in a foreign country

travelling expenses /ˈtræv(ə)lɪŋ ek ˌspensɪz/ *plural noun* money spent on travelling and hotels for business purposes

treasurer /ˈtreʒərə/ *noun* **1.** a person who looks after the money or finances of a club or society, etc. **2.** a company official responsible for finding new finance for the company and using its existing financial resources in the best possible way **3.** *US* the main financial officer of a company **4.** (*in Australia*) the finance minister in a government

Treasury /ˈtreʒəri/ *noun* **1.** a government department which deals with the country's finance (NOTE: The term is used in both the UK and the US; in most other countries this department is called the **Ministry of Finance**.) **2.** the department of a company or corporation that deals with all financial matters

Treasury bill /ˈtreʒəri bɪl/ *noun* a short-term financial instrument which does not give any interest and is sold by the government at a discount through the central bank. In the UK, their term varies from three to six months, in the US, they are for 91 or 182 days, or for 52 weeks. (NOTE: In the US they are also called a **T-bill**)

Treasury bond /ˈtreʒəri bɒnd/ *noun* a long-term bond issued by the British or US government. Also called **T-bond**

treasury management /ˈtreʒəri ˌmænɪdʒmənt/ *noun* an entity's method of dealing of its financial matters, including growing funds for business, maintaining cash flows and currencies, and managing currencies and cash flows

treasury products /ˌtreʒəri ˈprɒdʌkts/ *plural noun* any financial items produced by a government for sale, such as bonds

Treasury Secretary /ˈtreʒəri ˌsekrət(ə)ri/ *noun* same as **Secretary of the Treasury**

Treasury stocks /ˈtreʒəri stɒkz/ *plural noun* stocks issued by the British government. Also called **Exchequer stocks**

trend /trend/ *noun* a general way in which things are developing ○ *a downward trend in investment* ○ *The report points to inflationary trends in the economy.* ○ *We have noticed an upward trend in sales.*

'…the quality of building design and ease of accessibility will become increasingly important, adding to the trend towards out-of-town office development' [*Lloyd's List*]

trial balance /ˈtraɪəl ˌbæləns/ *noun* the draft calculation of debits and credits to see if they balance

trillion /ˈtrɪljən/ *noun* one million millions (NOTE: In the UK, trillion now has the same meaning as in the US; formerly in UK English it meant one million million millions, and it is still sometimes used with this meaning; see also the note at **billion**.)

'…if land is assessed at roughly half its current market value, the new tax could yield up to ¥10 trillion annually' [*Far Eastern Economic Review*]

'…behind the decline was a 6.1% fall in exports to ¥47.55 trillion, the second year of falls. Automobiles and steel were among categories showing particularly conspicuous drops' [*Nikkei Weekly*]

'…the London Stock Exchange said that the value of domestic UK equities traded during the year was £1.4066 trillion, more than the capitalization of the entire London market and an increase of 36 per cent compared with previous year's total of £1.037 trillion' [*Times*]

true and fair view /ˌtruː ən feə ˈvjuː/ *noun* a correct statement of a company's financial position as shown in its accounts and confirmed by the auditors

Trueblood Report /ˈtruːblʌd rɪˌpɔːt/ *noun* a report, 'Objectives of Financial Statements', published by the American Institute of Certified Public Accountants in 1971, that recommended a conceptual framework for financial accounting and led to the Statements of Financial Accounting Concepts issued by the Financial Accounting Standards Board in the United States

true copy /ˌtruː ˈkɒpi/ *noun* an exact copy of a legal document, as attested by a notary public ○ *I certify that this is a true copy.* ○ *It is certified as a true copy.*

trust /trʌst/ *noun* **1.** the fact of being confident that something is correct or will work **2.** a legal arrangement to pass goods, money or valuables to someone who will look after them well ○ *She left his property in trust for her grandchildren.* **3.** the management of money or property for someone ○ *They set up a family trust for their grandchildren.* **4.** *US* a small group of companies which control the supply of a product

trust company /ˈtrʌst ˌkʌmp(ə)ni/ *noun US* an organisation which supervises the financial affairs of private trusts, executes wills, and acts as a bank to a limited number of customers

trust deed /ˈtrʌst diːd/ *noun* a document which sets out the details of a private trust

trustee /trʌˈstiː/ *noun* a person who has charge of money in trust ○ *the trustees of the pension fund*

trustee in bankruptcy /trʌˌstiː ɪn ˈbæŋkrʌptsi/ *noun* a person who is appointed by a court to run the affairs of a bankrupt and pay his or her creditors

trust fund /ˈtrʌst fʌnd/ *noun* assets such as money, securities or property held in trust for someone

turn /tɜːn/ *noun* **1.** a movement in a circle, or a change of direction **2.** a profit or commission ○ *She makes a turn on everything he sells.*

turn down *phrasal verb* to refuse something ○ *The bank turned down their request for a loan.* ○ *The application for a licence was turned down.*

turn over *phrasal verb* **1.** to have a specific amount of sales ○ *We turn over £2,000 a week.* **2.** *US* to pass something to someone ○ *She turned over the documents to the lawyer.* (NOTE: In this meaning, the usual UK term is **hand over**.)

turn round *phrasal verb* to make a company change from making a loss to becoming profitable □ **they turned the company round in less than a year** they made the company profitable in less than a year

turnaround /ˈtɜːnəˌraʊnd/ *noun especially US* same as **turnround**

turnover /ˈtɜːnəʊvə/ *noun* **1.** the amount of sales of goods or services by a company ○ *The company's turnover has increased by 235%.* ○ *We based our calculations on the* *forecast turnover.* **2.** the number of times something is used or sold in a period, usually one year, expressed as a percentage of a total

turnover of labour /ˌtɜːnəʊvər əv ˈleɪbə/ *noun* same as **labour turnover**

turnover ratio /ˈtɜːnəʊvə ˌreɪʃiəʊ/ *noun* a measure of the number of times a business's stock is turned over in a given year, calculated as the cost of sales divided by the stock's average book value

turnover tax /ˈtɜːnəʊvə tæks/ *noun* same as **VAT**

turnround /ˈtɜːnraʊnd/ *noun* **1.** the value of goods sold during a year divided by the average value of goods held in stock **2.** the act of making a company profitable again (NOTE: [all senses] The US term is **turnaround**.)

two-way analysis /ˌtuː weɪ əˈnæləsɪs/ *noun* an analysis of business activity that looks at price and quantity in relation to materials and labour, and budget and volume in relation to overheads, but does not consider spending and efficiency

U

UBR *abbreviation* uniform business rate

UITF *abbreviation* Urgent Issues Task Force

ultimate holding company /ˌʌltɪmət ˈhəʊldɪŋ ˌkʌmp(ə)ni/ *noun* the top company in a group consisting of several layers of parent companies and subsidiaries

umbrella organisation /ʌmˈbrelə ˌɔːɡənaɪzeɪʃ(ə)n/ *noun* a large organisation which includes several smaller ones

unaccounted for /ˌʌnəˈkaʊntɪd fɔː/ *adjective* lost without any explanation ○ *Several thousand units are unaccounted for in the stocktaking.*

unadjusted trial balance /ˌʌnədʒʌstɪd ˌtraɪəl ˈbæləns/ *noun* a trial balance that has not yet been adjusted at a period end for items such as closing stock

unappropriated profits /ˌʌnəprəʊprieɪtɪd ˈprɒfɪts/ *plural noun* profits that have neither been distributed to a company's shareholders as dividends nor set aside as specific reserves

unappropriated retained earnings /ˌʌnəprəʊprieɪtɪd rɪˌteɪnd ˈɜːnɪŋz/ *plural noun* retained earnings no portion of which has been assigned to a special purpose

unaudited /ʌnˈɔːdɪtɪd/ *adjective* having not been audited ○ *unaudited accounts*

unaudited statement /ʌnˌɔːdɪtɪd ˈsteɪtmənt/ *noun* a financial statement in which an auditor prepares and presents statistics but does not give an audit opinion on them

unauthorised /ʌnˈɔːθəraɪzd/, **unauthorized** *adjective* not permitted ○ *unauthorised access to the company's records* ○ *unauthorised expenditure*

unavoidable costs /ˌʌnəvɔɪdəb(ə)l ˈkɒsts/ *plural noun* costs that will be incurred regardless of what business decisions are taken and that cannot be recovered

unbalanced /ʌnˈbælənst/ *adjective* referring to a budget which does not balance or which is in deficit

unbanked /ʌnˈbæŋkt/ *adjective* referring to a person who does not have a bank account

uncalled /ʌnˈkɔːld/ *adjective* referring to capital which a company is authorised to raise and has been issued but for which payment has not yet been requested

uncashed /ʌnˈkæʃt/ *adjective* having not been cashed ○ *uncashed cheques*

uncommitted credit lines /ˌʌnkəmɪtɪd ˈkredɪt ˌlaɪnz/ *plural noun* a borrowing arrangement that a bank provides but may choose to withdraw at any time

unconsolidated /ˌʌnkənˈsɒlɪdeɪtɪd/ *adjective* not grouped together, as of shares or holdings

unconsolidated subsidiary /ˌʌnkənsɒlɪdeɪtɪd səbˈsɪdiəri/ *noun* a subsidiary that is not included in the consolidated financial statements of the group to which it belongs. An unconsolidated subsidiary would appear on a consolidated balance sheet as an investment.

uncontrollable /ˌʌnkənˈtrəʊləb(ə)l/ *adjective* not possible to control ○ *uncontrollable inflation*

uncontrollable costs /ˌʌnkən ˈtrəʊləb(ə)l ˈkɒsts/ *plural noun* costs appearing on a management accounting statement that are regarded as not within the control of that particular level of management

uncrossed cheque /ˌʌnkrɒst ˈtʃek/ *noun* a cheque which does not have two lines across it, and can be cashed anywhere (NOTE: They are no longer used in the UK, but are still found in other countries.)

undated /ʌnˈdeɪtɪd/ *adjective* with no date indicated or written ○ *She tried to cash an undated cheque.*

undated bond /ʌnˌdeɪtɪd ˈbɒnd/ *noun* a bond with no maturity date

under- /ʌndə/ *prefix* less important than or lower than

underabsorbed **overhead**
/ˌʌndərəbˈzɔːbd ˈəʊvəhed/ *noun* an absorbed overhead which ends up by being lower than the actual overhead incurred

underabsorption /ˌʌndərəbˈzɔːpʃ(ə)n/ *noun* a situation where the actual overhead incurred is higher than the absorbed overhead. Opposite **overabsorption**

undercapitalised /ˌʌndəˈkæpɪtəlaɪzd/, **undercapitalized** *adjective* without enough capital ○ *The company is severely undercapitalised.*

undercharge /ˌʌndəˈtʃɑːdʒ/ *verb* to ask someone for too little money ○ *She undercharged us by £25.*

underemployed **capital**
/ˌʌndərɪmˈplɔɪd ˈkæpɪt(ə)l/ *noun* capital which is not producing enough interest

underlease /ˈʌndəliːs/ *noun* a lease from a tenant to another tenant

underlying inflation rate /ˌʌndəlaɪɪŋ ɪnˈfleɪʃ(ə)n reɪt/ *noun* the basic inflation rate calculated on a series of prices of consumer items, petrol, gas and electricity, and interest rates. Compare **headline inflation rate**

underspend /ˌʌndəˈspend/ *verb* to spend less than you should have spent or were allowed to spend

understandability /ˌʌndəˌstændə ˈbɪlɪti/ *noun* when referring to financial information, the quality of being sufficiently clearly expressed as to be understood by anybody with a reasonable knowledge of business

understate /ˌʌndəˈsteɪt/ *verb* to enter in an account a figure that is lower than the actual figure ○ *The company accounts understate the real profit.*

undersubscribed /ˌʌndəsʌbˈskraɪbd/ *adjective* referring to a share issue in which applications are not made for all the shares on offer, and part of the issue remains with the underwriters

undertake /ˌʌndəˈteɪk/ *verb* to agree to do something ○ *We asked the research unit to undertake an investigation of the market.* ○ *They have undertaken not to sell into our territory.* (NOTE: **undertaking – undertook – undertaken**)

undertaking /ˈʌndəteɪkɪŋ/ *noun* **1.** a business ○ *He is the MD of a large commercial undertaking.* **2.** a promise, especially a legally binding one ○ *They have given us a written undertaking not to sell their products in competition with ours.*

undervaluation /ˌʌndəvæljʊˈeɪʃ(ə)n/ *noun* the state of being valued, or the act of valuing something, at less than the true worth

undervalued /ˌʌndəˈvæljuːd/ *adjective* not valued highly enough ○ *The dollar is undervalued on the foreign exchanges.* ○ *The properties are undervalued on the company's balance sheet.*

'…in terms of purchasing power, the dollar is considerably undervalued, while the US trade deficit is declining month by month' [*Financial Weekly*]

underwrite /ˌʌndəˈraɪt/ *verb* **1.** to accept responsibility for something **2.** to insure, to cover a risk ○ *to underwrite an insurance policy* **3.** to agree to pay for costs ○ *The government has underwritten the development costs of the project.* (NOTE: **underwriting – underwrote – has underwritten**)

'…under the new program, mortgage brokers are allowed to underwrite mortgages and get a much higher fee' [*Forbes Magazine*]

underwriter /ˈʌndəraɪtə/ *noun* a person or company that underwrites a share issue or an insurance

underwriting /ˈʌndəraɪtɪŋ/ *noun* the action of guaranteeing to purchase shares in a new issue if no one purchases them

underwriting fee /ˈʌndəraɪtɪŋ fiː/ *noun* a fee paid by a company to the underwriters for guaranteeing the purchase of new shares in that company

underwriting syndicate /ˈʌndəraɪtɪŋ ˌsɪndɪkət/ *noun* a group of underwriters who insure a large risk

undischarged **bankrupt**
/ˌʌndɪstʃɑːdʒd ˈbæŋkrʌpt/ *noun* a person who has been declared bankrupt and has not been released from that state

undistributable **profit**
/ˌʌndɪstrɪbjuːtəb(ə)l ˈprɒfɪt/ *noun* profit that is not legally available for distribution to shareholders as dividends

undistributable **reserves**
/ˌʌndɪstrɪbjuːtəb(ə)l rɪˈzɜːvz/ *plural noun* same as **capital reserves**

undistributed profit /ˌʌndɪstrɪbjuːtɪd ˈprɒfɪt/ *noun* profit which has not been distributed as dividends to shareholders

unearned income /ˌʌnɜːnd ˈɪnkʌm/ *noun* same as **investment income**

unemployed /ˌʌnɪmˈplɔɪd/ *adjective* not having any paid work

unemployment /ˌʌnɪmˈplɔɪmənt/ *noun* **1.** the state of not having any work **2.** the number of people in a country or region who are willing to work but cannot find jobs

'…tax advantages directed toward small businesses will help create jobs and reduce the unemployment rate' [*Toronto Star*]

unemployment pay /ˌʌnɪm'plɔɪmənt peɪ/ *noun* money given by the government to someone who is unemployed

unexpired cost /ˌʌnɪkspaɪəd 'kɒst/ *noun* the net book value, or depreciated historical cost of an asset, not yet charged to the profit and loss account

unfair competition /ˌʌnfeə ˌkɒmpə 'tɪʃ(ə)n/ *noun* the practice of trying to do better than another company by using techniques such as importing foreign goods at very low prices or by wrongly criticising a competitor's products

unfavourable variance /ʌn ˌfeɪv(ə)rəb(ə)l 'veəriəns/ *noun* same as **adverse variance**

unfunded debt /ˌʌnfʌndɪd 'det/ *noun* short-term debt requiring repayment within a year from issuance

ungeared /ʌn'ɡɪəd/ *adjective* with no borrowings

unguaranteed residual value /ˌʌnɡærəntiːd rɪˌzɪdjuəl 'væljuː/ *noun* the residual value of a leased asset that a company is not sure it will ever be in a position to sell

uniform accounting policies /ˌjuːnɪfɔːm ə'kaʊntɪŋ ˌpɒlɪsiz/ *plural noun* the use of the same accounting policies for all the companies in a group, for the preparation of consolidated financial statements

uniform business rate /ˌjuːnɪfɔːm 'bɪznɪs ˌreɪt/ *noun* a tax levied on business property which is the same percentage for the whole country. Abbreviation **UBR** (NOTE: The uniform business rate is then multiplied by the **rateable value** of the property to give the total rates to be paid in that year.)

uniformity /ˌjuːnɪ'fɔːmɪti/ *noun* the principle of using common measurements, accounting standards and methods of presentation across different organisations, to ensure comparability

unincorporated /ˌʌnɪn'kɔːpəreɪtɪd/ *adjective* referring to a business which has not been made into a company, i.e. which is operating as a partnership or a sole trader

unissued capital /ˌʌnɪʃuːd 'kæpɪt(ə)l/ *noun* capital which a company is authorised to issue but has not issued as shares

unissued stock /ˌʌnɪʃuːd 'stɒk/ *noun* capital stock which a company is authorised to issue but has not issued

unit /'juːnɪt/ *noun* **1.** a single product for sale **2.** a single share in a unit trust

unitary taxation /ˌjuːnɪt(ə)ri tæk 'seɪʃ(ə)n/ *noun* a method of taxing a corporation based on its worldwide income rather than on its income in the country of the tax authority

unit contribution margin /ˌjuːnɪt ˌkɒntrɪ'bjuːʃ(ə)n ˌmɑːdʒɪn/ *noun* the profit made on each unit sold

unit cost /'juːnɪt kɒst/ *noun* the cost of one item, i.e. the total product costs divided by the number of units produced

unitholder /'juːnɪtˌhəʊldə/ *noun* a person who holds units in a unit trust

uniting of interests /juːˌnaɪtɪŋ əv 'ɪntrəsts/ *noun* the international accounting standards term for merger accounting

unit level activities /'juːnɪt ˌlev(ə)l æk ˌtɪvɪtiz/ *plural noun* business activities undertaken each time a unit is produced

unit-linked insurance /ˌjuːnɪt lɪŋkd ɪn 'ʃʊərəns/ *noun* an insurance policy which is linked to the security of units in a unit trust or fund

unit of account /ˌjuːnɪt əv ə'kaʊnt/ *noun* a standard unit used in financial transactions among members of a group, e.g. SDRs in the IMF

unit price /'juːnɪt praɪs/ *noun* the price of one item

units of production method of depreciation /ˌjuːnɪts əv prəˌdʌkʃən ˌmeθəd əv dɪˌpriːʃi'eɪʃ(ə)n/ *noun* a method of calculating depreciation that determines the cost of an asset over its useful economic life according to the number of units it is expected to produce over that period

unit trust /'juːnɪt trʌst/ *noun* an organisation which takes money from small investors and invests it in stocks and shares for them under a trust deed, the investment being in the form of shares (or units) in the trust (NOTE: The US term is **mutual fund**.)

unlawful /ʌn'lɔːf(ə)l/ *adjective* against the law, not legal

unlimited company /ʌnˌlɪmɪtɪd 'kʌmp(ə)ni/ *noun* a company where the shareholders have no limit as regards liability

unlimited liability /ʌnˌlɪmɪtɪd ˌlaɪə 'bɪlɪti/ *noun* a situation where a sole trader or each partner is responsible for all a firm's debts with no limit on the amount each may have to pay

unliquidated claim /ˌʌnlɪkwɪdeɪtd ˈkleɪm/ *noun* a claim for unliquidated damages

unliquidated damages /ˌʌnlɪkwɪdeɪtɪd ˈdæmɪdʒɪz/ *plural noun* damages which are not for a fixed amount of money but are awarded by a court as a matter of discretion

unlisted company /ʌnˌlɪstɪd ˈkʌmp(ə)ni/ *noun* a company whose shares are not listed on the Stock Exchange

unlisted securities /ʌnˌlɪstɪd sɪˈkjʊərɪtiz/ *plural noun* shares that are not listed on the Stock Exchange

unpaid /ʌnˈpeɪd/ *adjective* not paid

unprofitable /ʌnˈprɒfɪtəb(ə)l/ *adjective* not profitable

unquoted company /ʌnˌkwəʊtɪd ˈkʌmp(ə)ni/ *noun* a company whose shares are not listed on the stock exchange

unquoted investments /ʌnˌkwəʊtɪd ɪnˈvestmənts/ *plural noun* investments which are difficult to value, e.g. shares which have no stock exchange listing or land of which the asset value is difficult to estimate

unquoted shares /ˌʌnkwəʊtɪd ˈʃeəz/ *plural noun* shares that have no Stock Exchange quotation

unrealisable gains /ˌʌnrɪəlaɪzəb(ə)l ˈɡeɪnz/ *plural noun* apparent increases in the value of assets that could not be turned into realised profit

unrealised capital gain /ˌʌnrɪəlaɪzd ˌkæpɪt(ə)l ˈɡeɪn/ *noun* an investment which is showing a profit but has not been sold

unrealised loss /ˌʌnrɪəlaɪzd ˈlɒs/ *noun* same as **paper loss**

unrealised profit /ˌʌnˌrɪəlaɪzd ˈprɒfɪt/ *noun* same as **paper profit**

unredeemed pledge /ˌʌnrɪdiːmd ˈpledʒ/ *noun* a pledge which the borrower has not claimed back because he or she has not paid back the loan

unregistered /ʌnˈredʒɪstəd/ *adjective* used for describing a company that has not been registered on the official list of companies held, in the UK, at Companies House

unrestricted income funds /ˌʌnrɪstrɪktɪd ˌɪnkʌm ˈfʌndz/ *plural noun* a charity's funds that are available to its trustees to use for the purposes set out in the charity's governing document

unsecured creditor /ˌʌnsɪkjʊəd ˈkredɪtə/ *noun* a creditor who is owed money, but has no security from the debtor for the debt

unsecured debt /ˌʌnsɪkjʊəd ˈdet/ *noun* a debt which is not guaranteed by a charge on assets or by any collateral

unsecured loan /ˌʌnsɪkjʊəd ˈləʊn/ *noun* a loan made with no security

unsubsidised /ʌnˈsʌbsɪdaɪzd/, **unsubsidized** *adjective* with no subsidy

unused allowances /ʌnˌjuːzd əˈlaʊənsɪz/ *plural noun* part of the married couple's allowance or the blind person's allowance which is not used because the recipient does not have enough income, and which can then be passed to their spouse

up front /ˌʌp ˈfrʌnt/ *adverb* in advance □ **money up front** payment in advance ○ *They are asking for £100,000 up front before they will consider the deal.* ○ *He had to put money up front before he could clinch the deal.*

upside potential /ˈʌpsaɪd pəˌtenʃəl/ *noun* the possibility for a share to increase in value. Opposite **downside risk**

upturn /ˈʌptɜːn/ *noun* a movement towards higher sales or profits ○ *an upturn in the economy* ○ *an upturn in the market*

Urgent Issues Task Force /ˌɜːdʒənt ˌɪʃuːz ˈtɑːsk ˌfɔːs/ *noun* a committee of the UK Accounting Standards Board that considers major urgent and emerging accounting issues. Its pronouncements are known as UITF Abstracts. Abbreviation **UITF**

usage method /ˈjuːsɪdʒ ˌmeθəd/ *noun* a method of depreciating a machine, by dividing its cost less residual value by the number of units it is expected to produce or the length of time it is expected to be used

useful economic life /ˌjuːsf(ə)l ˌiːkənɒmɪk ˈlaɪf/ *noun* the period during which an entity expects to derive economic benefit from using an asset such as a machine and over which it can be depreciated. Also called **depreciable life**

usury /ˈjuːʒəri/ *noun* the lending of money at high interest

utilisation /ˌjuːtɪlaɪˈzeɪʃ(ə)n/, **utilization** *noun* the act of making use of something

'…control permits the manufacturer to react to changing conditions on the plant floor and to keep people and machines at a high level of utilization' [*Duns Business Month*]

utilise /ˈjuːtɪlaɪz/, **utilize** *verb* to use something

V

vacant possession /ˌveɪkənt pə
'zeʃ(ə)n/ *adjective* being able to occupy a
property immediately after buying it
because it is empty ○ *The property is to be
sold with vacant possession.*

valuation /ˌvæljuˈeɪʃ(ə)n/ *noun* an estimate of how much something is worth ○ *to
ask for a valuation of a property before making an offer for it*

valuation of a business /ˌvæljueɪʃ(ə)n
əv ə 'bɪznɪs/ *noun* the act of estimating the
value of a business. This can be done on various bases, such as an assets basis, its break-
up value, its value as a going concern, etc.

value /'væljuː/ *noun* the amount of money
which something is worth ○ *the fall in the
value of sterling* ○ *She imported goods to
the value of £2500.* ○ *The valuer put the
value of the stock at £25,000.* □ **to rise or
fall in value** to be worth more or less ■ *verb*
to estimate how much money something is
worth ○ *He valued the stock at £25,000.* ○
*We are having the jewellery valued for
insurance.*

value added /ˌvæljuː 'ædɪd/ *noun* **1.** the
difference between the cost of the materials
purchased to produce a product and the final
selling price of the finished product **2.** the
amount added to the value of a product or
service, being the difference between its
cost and the amount received when it is sold.
Also called **net output**

value-added activity /ˌvæljuː 'ædɪd æk
ˌtɪvɪti/ *noun* business activity that improves
a product or service at a cost that the customer is willing to pay

value-added statement /ˌvæljuː 'ædɪd
ˌsteɪtmənt/ *noun* a simplified financial
statement that shows how much wealth has
been created by a company. A value-added
statement calculates total output by adding
sales, changes in stock, and other incomes,
then subtracting depreciation, interest, taxation, dividends, and the amounts paid to suppliers and employees.

Value Added Tax /ˌvæljuː ædɪd 'tæks/
noun full form of **VAT**

value-adding cost /'væljuː ˌædɪŋ
ˌkɒst/ *noun* a business cost that increases
the market value of a product or service

value analysis /'væljuː əˌnæləsɪs/ *noun*
analysis by a producer of all aspects of a finished product to determine how it could be
made at minimum cost ○ *Value analysis
showed an excessive amount of rubber was
used in manufacturing the product.*

value chain /'væljuː tʃeɪn/ *noun* the
sequence of activities a company carries out
as it designs, produces, markets, delivers,
and supports its product or service, each of
which is thought of as adding value

'Competition is no longer limited to the
realm of the enterprise. Entire value chains
are now starting to act as formidable entities, competing against each other for similar markets.' [Harvard Business Review]

value chain costing /'væljuː tʃeɪn
ˌkɒstɪŋ/ *noun* a costing model that takes
into account all aspects of the chain of production, from design to after-sales

value in use /ˌvæljuː ɪn 'juːs/ *noun* the
present value of the estimated future net
cash flows from an object, including the
amount expected from its disposal at the end
of its useful life. Value in use replaces book
value when an asset suffers impairment.

valuer /'væljʊə/ *noun* a person who estimates how much money something is worth

variable annuity /ˌveəriəb(ə)l əˈnjuːəti/
noun an annuity based on funds invested in
common stock, which varies with the value
of the stock, as opposed to a fixed annuity

variable costing /'veəriəb(ə)l ˌkɒstɪŋ/
noun a method of recording inventoried
costs that records only the variable manufacturing costs, not the fixed costs

variable cost percentage /'veəriəb(ə)l
kɒst pəˌsentɪdʒ/ *noun* a ratio arrived at by
dividing total variable costs by total sales

variable costs /ˌveəriəb(ə)l 'kɒsts/ *plural noun* production costs which increase

with the quantity of the product made, e.g. wages or raw materials

variable rate /ˌveəriəb(ə)l 'reɪt/ noun a rate of interest on a loan which is not fixed, but can change with the current bank interest rates. Also called **floating rate**

variable rate loan /ˌveəriəb(ə)l reɪt 'ləʊn/ noun a bank loan carrying an interest rate that varies according to fluctuations in a particular index

variance /'veəriəns/ noun the discrepancy between the actual cost of an asset or business activity and the standard or expected cost

variance accounting /ˌveəriəns ə 'kaʊntɪŋ/ noun a method of accounting by means of which planned activities (quantified through budgets and standard costs and revenues) are compared with actual results

VAT /ˌviː eɪ 'tiː, væt/ noun a tax on goods and services, added as a percentage to the invoiced sales price ○ *The invoice includes VAT at 17.5%.* ○ *The government is proposing to increase VAT to 22%.* ○ *Some items (such as books) are zero-rated for VAT.* ○ *He does not charge VAT because he asks for payment in cash.* Full form **Value Added Tax**

'…the directive means that the services of stockbrokers and managers of authorized unit trusts are now exempt from VAT; previously they were liable to VAT at the standard rate. Zero-rating for stockbrokers' services is still available as before, but only where the recipient of the service belongs outside the EC' [*Accountancy*]

VAT declaration /'væt deklə,reɪʃ(ə)n/ noun a statement declaring VAT income to the VAT office

VAT group /'væt gruːp/ noun in the United Kingdom, a group of related companies that is treated as one taxpayer for VAT purposes

VAT inspection /'væt ɪn,spekʃ(ə)n/ noun a visit by officials of HM Revenue and Customs to see if a company is correctly reporting its VAT

VAT inspector /'væt ɪn,spektə/ noun a government official who examines VAT returns and checks that VAT is being paid

VAT invoice /'væt ,ɪnvɔɪs/ noun an invoice which includes VAT

VAT invoicing /'væt ,ɪnvɔɪsɪŋ/ noun the sending of an invoice including VAT

VATman /'vætmæn/, **vatman** noun a VAT inspector (*informal*)

VAT office /'væt ,ɒfɪs/ noun the government office dealing with the collection of VAT in an area

VAT paid /ˌvæt 'peɪd/ adjective with the VAT already paid

VAT receivable /ˌvæt rɪ'siːvəb(ə)l/ adjective with the VAT for an item not yet collected by a taxing authority

VAT registration /'væt ,redʒɪstreɪʃ(ə)n/ noun the process of listing a company with a European government as eligible for the return of VAT in certain cases

VC abbreviation venture capitalist

VCT abbreviation venture capital trust

vending /'vendɪŋ/ noun selling

vendor /'vendə/ noun **1.** a person who sells something, especially a property ○ *the solicitor acting on behalf of the vendor* **2.** a person who sells goods

venture /'ventʃə/ noun a commercial deal which involves a risk ○ *They lost money on several import ventures.* ○ *She's started a new venture – a computer shop.*

venture capital /ˌventʃə 'kæpɪt(ə)l/ noun capital for investment which may easily be lost in risky projects, but can also provide high returns. Also called **risk capital**

venture capital fund /ˌventʃə 'kæpɪt(ə)l fʌnd/ noun a fund which invests in finance houses providing venture capital

'…the Securities and Exchange Board of India allowed new companies to enter the primary market provided venture capital funds took up 10 per cent of the equity. At present, new companies are allowed to make initial public offerings provided their projects have been appraised by banks or financial institutions which take up 10 per cent of the equity' [*The Hindu*]

venture capitalist /ˌventʃə 'kæpɪt(ə)lɪst/ noun a finance house or private individual specialising in providing venture capital. Abbreviation **VC**

'…along with the stock market boom of the 1980s, the venture capitalists piled more and more funds into the buyout business, backing bigger and bigger deals with ever more extravagant financing structures' [*Guardian*]

venture capital trust /ˌventʃə 'kæpɪt(ə)l trʌst/ noun a trust which invests in smaller firms which need capital to grow. Abbreviation **VCT**

vertical equity /ˌvɜːtɪk(ə)l 'ekwɪti/ noun the principle that people with different incomes should pay different rates of tax

vertical form /'vɜːtɪk(ə)l fɔːm/ noun one of the two styles of presenting a balance sheet allowed by the Companies Act. See Comment at **balance sheet**. Also called **report form**

vertical integration /ˌvɜːtɪk(ə)l ˌɪntɪ ˈɡreɪʃ(ə)n/ *noun* same as **backward integration**

vested interest /ˌvestɪd ˈɪntrəst/ *noun* a special interest in keeping an existing state of affairs

virement /ˈvaɪəmənt/ *noun* a transfer of money from one account to another or from one section of a budget to another

visible /ˈvɪzɪb(ə)l/ *adjective* referring to real products which are imported or exported

visible exports /ˌvɪzɪb(ə)l ˈekspɔːts/ *plural noun* real products which are exported, as opposed to services

visible imports /ˌvɪzɪb(ə)l ˈɪmpɔːts/ *plural noun* real products which are imported, as opposed to services

visible trade /ˌvɪzɪb(ə)l ˈtreɪd/ *noun* trade involving visible imports and exports

void /vɔɪd/ *adjective* not legally valid

volume /ˈvɒljuːm/ *noun* a quantity of items

volume discount /ˈvɒljuːm ˌdɪskaʊnt/ *noun* the discount given to a customer who buys a large quantity of goods

volume of output /ˌvɒljuːm əv ˈaʊtpʊt/ *noun* the number of items produced

volume variances /ˈvɒljuːm ˌveəriənsɪz/ *plural noun* differences in costs

or revenues compared with budgeted amounts, caused by differences between the actual and budgeted levels of activity

voluntary /ˈvɒlənt(ə)ri/ *adjective* **1.** done freely without anyone forcing you to act **2.** done without being paid

voluntary arrangement /ˌvɒlənt(ə)ri ə ˈreɪndʒmənt/ *noun* same as **scheme of arrangement**

voluntary liquidation /ˌvɒlənt(ə)ri ˌlɪkwɪˈdeɪʃ(ə)n/ *noun* a situation where a company itself decides it must close and sell its assets

voluntary redundancy /ˌvɒlənt(ə)ri rɪ ˈdʌndənsi/ *noun* a situation where the employee asks to be made redundant, usually in return for a large payment

voluntary registration /ˌvɒlənt(ə)ri ˌredʒɪˈstreɪʃ(ə)n/ *noun* in the United Kingdom, registration for VAT by a trader whose turnover is below the registration threshold. This is usually done in order to reclaim tax on inputs.

voucher /ˈvaʊtʃə/ *noun* **1.** a piece of paper which is given instead of money **2.** a written document from an auditor to show that the accounts are correct or that money has really been paid

vouching /ˈvaʊtʃɪŋ/ *noun* the process of checking accounting accuracy by matching vouchers and other documents with the details recorded in an account

W

wage /weɪdʒ/ *noun* the money paid to an employee in return for work done, especially when it is paid weekly and in cash ○ *She is earning a good wage* or *good wages for a young person.* (NOTE: The plural **wages** is more usual when referring to the money earned, but **wage** is used before other nouns.)

'European economies are being held back by rigid labor markets and wage structures' [*Duns Business Month*]

'…real wages have been held down dramatically: they have risen at an annual rate of only 1% in the last two years' [*Sunday Times*]

wage adjustments /weɪdʒ əˈdʒʌstmənts/ *plural noun* changes made to wages

wage claim /weɪdʒ kleɪm/ *noun* an act of asking for an increase in wages

wage differentials /weɪdʒ dɪfəˈrenʃəlz/ *plural noun* same as **pay differentials**

wage-earner /weɪdʒ ˌɜːnə/ *noun* a person who earns a wage

wage indexation /weɪdʒ ˌɪndekseɪʃ(ə)n/ *noun* the linking of increases to the percentage rise in the cost of living

wage scale /weɪdʒ skeɪl/ *noun* same as **pay scale**

wages costs /weɪdʒɪz kɒsts/ *plural noun* the costs of paying employees' salaries. Along with other costs such as pension contributions and salaries, these costs typically form the largest single cost item for a business.

wages payable account /ˌweɪdʒɪz ˈpeɪəb(ə)l əˌkaʊnt/ *noun* an account showing gross wages and employer's National Insurance contributions paid during a period

wages policy /weɪdʒɪz ˌpɒlɪsi/ *noun* a government policy on what percentage increases should be paid to workers

wall safe /wɔːl seɪf/ *noun* a safe installed in a wall

warehouse /ˈweəhaʊs/ *noun* a large building where goods are stored

warehouse capacity /ˈweəhaʊs kəˌpæsɪti/ *noun* the space available in a warehouse

warrant /ˈwɒrənt/ *noun* **1.** an official document which allows someone to do something **2.** ♦ **share warrant** ■ *verb* to guarantee ○ *All the spare parts are warranted.*

'…the rights issue will grant shareholders free warrants to subscribe for further new shares' [*Financial Times*]

warrantee /ˌwɒrənˈtiː/ *noun* a person who is given a warranty

warrantor /ˌwɒrənˈtɔː/ *noun* a person who gives a warranty

warranty /ˈwɒrənti/ *noun* **1.** a legal document which promises that a machine will work properly or that an item is of good quality ○ *The car is sold with a twelve-month warranty.* ○ *The warranty covers spare parts but not labour costs.* **2.** a promise in a contract **3.** a statement made by an insured person which declares that the facts stated by him are true

wasting asset /weɪstɪŋ ˌæsɪt/ *noun* an asset which becomes gradually less valuable as time goes by, e.g. a short lease on a property

watchdog /ˈwɒtʃdɒg/ *noun* an independent person or organisation whose task is to police a particular industry, ensuring that member companies do not act illegally

watered stock /ˈwɔːtəd stɒk/ *noun* shares that are worth less than the total capital invested in the company

WDA *abbreviation* **1.** writing-down allowance **2.** written-down allowance

WDV *abbreviation* written-down value

wealth tax /ˈwelθ tæks/ *noun* a tax on money, property or investments owned by a person

wear and tear /ˌweər ən ˈteə/ *noun* the deterioration of a tangible fixed asset as a result of normal use. This is recognised for accounting purposes by depreciation.

web /web/ *noun* same as **World Wide Web**

weight /weɪt/ *noun* a measurement of how heavy something is ■ *verb* to give an extra value to a factor

weighted average /ˌweɪtɪd ˈæv(ə)rɪdʒ/ *noun* an average which is calculated taking several factors into account, giving some more value than others

weighted average cost /ˌweɪtɪd ˈæv(ə)rɪdʒ kɒst/, **weighted average price** /ˌweɪtɪd ˈæv(ə)rɪdʒ praɪs/ *noun* the average price per unit of stock delivered in a period calculated either at the end of the period ('periodic weighted average') or each time a new delivery is received ('cumulative weighted average')

weighted average cost of capital /ˌweɪtɪd ˌæværɪdʒ kɒst əv ˈkæpɪt(ə)l/ *noun* the average cost of a company's borrowing in relation to its total capital

weighted index /ˌweɪtɪd ˈɪndeks/ *noun* an index where some important items are given more value than less important ones

weighting /ˈweɪtɪŋ/ *noun* an additional salary or wages paid to compensate for living in an expensive part of the country ○ *The salary is £15,000 plus London weighting.*

Wheat Report /ˈwiːt rɪˌpɔːt/ *noun* a report produced by a committee in 1972 that set out to examine the principles and methods of accounting in the United States. Its publication led to the establishment of the FASB.

white knight /ˌwaɪt ˈnaɪt/ *noun* a person or company which rescues a firm in financial difficulties, especially one which saves a firm from being taken over by an unacceptable purchaser

White Paper /ˌwaɪt ˈpeɪpə/ *noun* a report issued by the UK government as a statement of government policy on a particular problem. Compare **Green Paper**

whole-life cost /ˌhəʊl ˈlaɪf ˌkɒst/ *noun* a cost calculated as life-cycle costs plus any after-purchase costs

whole-life insurance /ˌhəʊl ˈlaɪf ɪn ˌʃʊərəns/, **whole-life policy** /ˌhəʊl ˈlaɪf ˌpɒlɪsi/ *noun* an insurance policy where the insured person pays a fixed premium each year and the insurance company pays a sum when he or she dies. Also called **whole-of-life assurance**

wholesale /ˈhəʊlseɪl/ *adjective, adverb* referring to the business of buying goods from manufacturers and selling them in large quantities to traders (retailers) who then sell in smaller quantities to the general public ○ *I persuaded him to give us a wholesale discount.* □ **he buys wholesale and sells retail** he buys goods in bulk at a wholesale discount and then sells in small quantities to the public

wholesale banking /ˌhəʊlseɪl ˈbæŋkɪŋ/ *noun* banking services between merchant banks and other financial institutions, as opposed to retail banking

wholesale dealer /ˈhəʊlseɪl ˌdiːlə/ *noun* a person who buys in bulk from manufacturers and sells to retailers

wholesale price /ˈhəʊlseɪl praɪs/ *noun* the price charged to customers who buy goods in large quantities in order to resell them in smaller quantities to others

wholesale price index /ˌhəʊlseɪl ˈpraɪs ˌɪndeks/ *noun* an index showing the rises and falls of prices of manufactured goods as they leave the factory

wholesaler /ˈhəʊlseɪlə/ *noun* a person who buys goods in bulk from manufacturers and sells them to retailers

wholly-owned subsidiary /ˌhəʊlli əʊnd səbˈsɪdjəri/ *noun* a subsidiary which belongs completely to the parent company

will /wɪl/ *noun* a legal document where someone says what should happen to his or her property when he or she dies ○ *He wrote his will in 1984.* ○ *According to her will, all her property is left to her children.*

wind up *phrasal verb* to end a meeting, or to close down a business or organisation and sell its assets ○ *She wound up the meeting with a vote of thanks to the committee.*

windfall profit /ˈwɪndfɔːl ˌprɒfɪt/ *noun* a sudden profit which is not expected

windfall profits tax /ˈwɪndfɔːl ˌprɒfɪts tæks/, **windfall tax** /ˈwɪndfɔːl tæks/ *noun* a tax on companies that have made large profits because of circumstances outside their usual trading activities. A windfall tax was imposed on the privatised utility companies in 1997.

winding up /ˌwaɪndɪŋ ˈʌp/ *noun* liquidation, the act of closing a company and selling its assets

winding up petition /ˌwaɪndɪŋ ˈʌp pə ˌtɪʃ(ə)n/ *noun* an application to a court for an order that a company be put into liquidation

window dressing /ˈwɪndəʊ ˌdresɪŋ/ *noun* **1.** the practice of putting goods on display in a shop window, so that they attract customers **2.** the practice of putting on a display to make a business seem better or more profitable or more efficient than it really is

window of opportunity /ˌwɪndəʊ əv ˌɒpəˈtjuːnɪti/ *noun* a short period which allows an action to take place

WIP *abbreviation* work in progress

withdraw /wɪðˈdrɔː/ *verb* **1.** to take money out of an account ○ *to withdraw money from the bank or from your account* ○ *You can withdraw up to £50 from any cash machine by using your card.* **2.** to take back an offer ○ *When the employees went on strike, the company withdrew its revised pay offer.* (NOTE: **withdrawing – withdrew**)

withdrawal /wɪðˈdrɔːəl/ *noun* the act of removing money from an account ○ *to give seven days' notice of withdrawal* ○ *Withdrawals from bank accounts reached a peak in the week before Christmas.*

withholding tax /wɪðˈhəʊldɪŋ ˌtæks/ *noun US* a tax which removes money from interest or dividends before they are paid to the investor, usually applied to non-resident investors

with profits /ˌwɪθ ˈprɒfɪts/ *adverb* used to describe an insurance policy which guarantees the policyholder a share in the profits of the fund in which the premiums are invested

work cell /ˈwɜːk sel/ *noun* a unit of employees, or a set of machines, assigned to a particular manufacturing task

workforce /ˈwɜːkfɔːs/ *noun* the total number of employees in an organisation, industry or country

working capital /ˈwɜːkɪŋ ˌkæpɪt(ə)l/ *noun* capital in the form of cash, stocks, and debtors but not creditors, used by a company in its day-to-day operations. Also called **circulating capital**, **floating capital**, **net current assets**

working capital turnover /ˌwɜːkɪŋ ˈkæpɪt(ə)l ˌtɜːnəʊvə/ *noun* a figure equal to sales divided by average working capital

working partner /ˈwɜːkɪŋ ˌpɑːtnə/ *noun* a partner who works in a partnership

work-in-process /ˌwɜːk ɪn ˈprəʊses/ *noun* inventory units that are only partially completed at the end of an accounting period

work in progress /ˌwɜːk ɪn ˈprəʊgres/ *noun* the value of goods being manufactured which are not complete at the end of an accounting period ○ *Our current assets are made up of stock, goodwill and work in progress.* Abbreviation **WIP** (NOTE: The US term is **work in process.**)

work permit /ˈwɜːk ˌpɜːmɪt/ *noun* an official document which allows someone who is not a citizen to work in a country

works /wɜːks/ *noun* a factory ○ *There is a small engineering works in the same street as our office.* ○ *The steel works is expanding.* (NOTE: takes a singular or plural verb)

works committee /ˈwɜːks kəˌmɪti/, **works council** /ˈwɜːks ˌkaʊnsəl/ *noun* a committee of employees and management which discusses the organisation of work in a factory

workstation /ˈwɜːkˌsteɪʃ(ə)n/ *noun* a desk, usually with a computer terminal, printer, telephone and other office items at which an employee in an office works

World Bank /ˌwɜːld ˈbæŋk/ *noun* a central bank, controlled by the United Nations, whose funds come from the member states of the UN and which lends money to member states

World Wide Web /ˌwɜːld ˌwaɪd ˈweb/ *noun* an information system on the Internet that allows documents to be linked to one another by hypertext links and accommodates websites and makes them accessible. Also called **web**

worthless /ˈwɜːθləs/ *adjective* having no value ○ *The cheque is worthless if it is not signed.*

write down *phrasal verb* to note an asset at a lower value than previously ○ *written down value* ○ *The car is written down in the company's books.* □ **closing written-down value**, **opening written-down value** the written-down value of an asset at the end or the beginning of an accounting period

write off *phrasal verb* to cancel a debt, or to remove an asset from the accounts as having no value ○ *We had to write off £20,000 in bad debts.*

'\$30 million from usual company borrowings will either be amortized or written off in one sum' [*Australian Financial Review*]

write-down /ˈraɪt daʊn/ *noun* a reduction in the value of an asset as entered in the books of a business

write-off /ˈraɪt ɒf/ *noun* the total loss or cancellation of a bad debt, or the removal of an asset's value from a company's accounts ○ *to allow for write-offs in the yearly accounts*

write-up /ˈraɪt ʌp/ *noun* a deliberate overvaluation of company assets

writing-down allowance /ˌraɪtɪŋ ˈdaʊn əˌlaʊəns/ *noun* a form of capital allowance giving tax relief to companies acquiring fixed assets which are written down on a year-by-year basis

written-down allowance /ˌrɪt(ə)n daʊn əˈlaʊəns/ *noun* an allowance which can be claimed on capital expenditure by a business or self-employed person in the years after the purchase was made. In the first year, the first year allowance (FYA) applies. Abbreviation **WDA**

written-down value /ˌrɪt(ə)n daʊn ˈvæljuː/ *noun* same as **net book value**

written resolution /ˌrɪt(ə)n ˌrezəˈluːʃ(ə)n/ *noun* a decision to be reached by postal vote of the members of a UK private company equivalent to a resolution at a meeting

XYZ

xa *abbreviation* ex-all

XBRL /ˌeks biː ɑːr 'el/ *noun* a computer language used for financial reporting that allows companies to exchange or publish financial information through the Internet. Full form **Extensible Business Reporting Language**

xd *abbreviation* ex dividend

xr *abbreviation* ex-rights

year /jɪə/ *noun* a period of twelve months

year end /ˌjɪər 'end/ *noun* the end of the financial year, when a company's accounts are prepared ○ *The accounts department has started work on the year-end accounts.*

year-end adjustment /ˌjɪər 'end əˌdʒʌstmənt/ *noun* final adjustments to an entry in accounts to ensure complete accuracy in the presentation of a financial statement

year-end closing /ˌjɪər end 'kləʊzɪŋ/ *noun* the financial statements issued at the end of a company's fiscal (tax) year

yearly /'jɪəli/ *adjective* happening once a year ○ *We make a yearly payment of £1000.* ○ *His yearly insurance premium has risen to £550.*

year of assessment /ˌjɪər əv ə 'sesmənt/ *noun* a twelve-month period on which income tax is calculated. In the UK it is April 6th to April 5th of the following year.

year to date /ˌjɪə tə 'deɪt/ *noun* the period between the beginning of a calendar or financial year and the present time. A variety of financial information, such as a company's profits, losses or sales, may be displayed in this way. Abbreviation **YTD**

yen /jen/ *noun* a unit of currency used in Japan (NOTE: It is usually written as ¥ before a figure: ¥2,700 (say two thousand seven hundred yen).)

yield /jiːld/ *noun* the money produced as a return on an investment, shown as a percentage of the money invested

'…if you wish to cut your risks you should go for shares with yields higher than average' [*Investors Chronicle*]

yield to maturity /ˌjiːld tə məˈtʃʊərɪti/ *noun* a calculation of the yield on a fixed-interest investment, assuming it is bought at a certain price and held to maturity

YTD *abbreviation* year to date

zero /'zɪərəʊ/ *noun* nought, the number 0 ○ *The code for international calls is zero zero (00).*

zero-based budgeting /ˌzɪərəʊ beɪst 'bʌdʒɪtɪŋ/ *noun* a method of budgeting which requires each cost element to be specifically justified, as though the activities to which the budget relates were being undertaken for the first time. Without approval, the budget allowance is zero.

zero-coupon bond /ˌzɪərəʊ 'kuːpɒn bɒnd/ *noun* a bond which carries no interest, but which is issued at a discount and so provides a capital gain when it is redeemed at face value

zero inflation /ˌzɪərəʊ ɪnˈfleɪʃ(ə)n/ *noun* inflation at 0%

zero-rated /ˌzɪərəʊ 'reɪtɪd/ *adjective* referring to an item which has a VAT rate of 0%

zero-rating /'zɪərəʊ ˌreɪtɪŋ/ *noun* the rating of a product or service at 0% VAT

Supplement

ACCOUNTING ORGANISATIONS

United Kingdom

Association of Chartered Certified Accountants (ACCA)
64 Finnieston Square
Glasgow
United Kingdom
G3 8DT
T: 00 44 (0)141 582 2000
F: 00 44 (0)141 582 2222

British Accounting Association (BAA)
c/o Sheffield University Management School
9 Mappin Street
Sheffield
S1 4DT
T: 00 44 (0)114 222 3462
F: 00 44 (0)114 222 3348
www.shef.ac.uk/~baa/

Chartered Institute of Management Accountants (CIMA)
26 Chapter Street
London
SW1P 4NP
T: 00 44 (0)20 8849 2251
F: 00 44 (0)20 8849 2450

Institute of Chartered Accountants in England and Wales (ICAEW)
Chartered Accountants' Hall
PO Box 433
London
EC2P 2BJ
T: 00 44 (0)20 7920 8100
F: 00 44 (0)20 7920 0547

Institute of Chartered Accountants in Ireland
CA House
87/89 Pembroke Hall
Dublin 4
T: 00 353 1637 7200
F: 00 353 1668 0842

Institute of Chartered Accountants of Scotland
CA House
21 Haymarket Yards
Edinburgh
EH12 5BH
T: 00 44 (0)131 347 0100
F: 00 44 (0)131 347 0105

Institute of Financial Accountants
Burford house
44 London Road
Sevenoaks
Kent
TN13 1AS
T: 00 44 (0)1732 458080
F: 00 44 (0)1732 455848
www.accountingweb.co.uk/ifa/journal/index.html

International

American Accounting Association (AAA)
5717 Bessie Drive
Sarasota, FL 34233-2399
USA
T: 00 1 (941) 921-7747
F: 00 1 (941) 923-4093
www.aaahq.org/index.cfm

Association of Chartered Accountants in the United States (ACAUS)
341 Lafayette Street
Suite 4246
New York, NY 10012-2417
USA
T: 00 1 (212) 334-2078

Australian Accounting Standards Board (AASB)
PO Box 204
Collins St West
VIC 8007
Australia
T: 00 61 (3) 9617 7600
T: 00 61 (3) 9617 7608
www.aasb.com.au/

Institute of Chartered Accountants of New Zealand (ICANZ)
Level 2, Cigna House
40 Mercer Street
PO Box 11 342
Wellington 6034
New Zealand
T: 00 64 4 474 7840
F: 00 64 4 473 6303

National Society of Accountants (NSA)
1010 North Fairfax Street
Alexandria, VA 22314
USA
T: 00 1 703 549 6400
F: 00 1 703 549 2984

Specimen Co Ltd

Profit and Loss Account for the Year to 31 December 2007

	£000	£000
* Turnover		9,758
* Cost of sales		6,840
* Gross profit		2,918
* Distribution costs	585	
* Administrative expenses	407	
		992
		1,926
* Other operating income		322
		2,248
* Income from shares in group companies	200	
* Income from other fixed asset investments	75	
* Other interest receivable and similar income	36	
		311
		2,559
* Amounts written off investments	27	
* Interest payable and similar charges	26	
		53
Profit on ordinary activities before taxation		2,506
* Tax on profit on ordinary activities		916
* Profit on ordinary activities after taxation		1,590
* Extraordinary income	153	
* Extraordinary charges	44	
* Extraordinary profit	109	
* Tax on extraordinary profit	45	
		64
* Profit for the financial year		1,654
Transfers to Reserves	400	
Dividends Paid and Proposed	750	
		1,150
Retained profit for the financial year		504

About the Profit and Loss Account

While two vertical and horizontal formats are permissible, most UK companies use the vertical format illustrated. The horizontal profit and loss account format may be summarised as follows:

	£		£
Cost of sales	X	Sales	X
Gross profit	X		
	X		X
Expenses	X	Gross profit	X
	X		X

In Germany and Italy only the vertical format is allowed.

According to the UK Companies Act a company must show all the items marked with * on the face of the profit and loss account. It must also disclose the value of certain items in the notes to the profit and loss account, such as:

a) interest owed on bank and other loans
b) rental income
c) costs of hire of plant and machinery
d) amounts paid to auditors
e) turnover for each class of business and country in which sales are made
f) number of employees and costs of employment

Specimen Co Ltd

Balance Sheet for the Year to 31 December 2007

	£000	£000	£000
* FIXED ASSETS			
* Intangible assets			
Development costs	1,255		
Goodwill	850		
		2,105	
* Tangible assets			
Land and buildings	4,758		
Plant and machinery	2,833		
Fixtures and fittings	1,575		9,166
* Investments		730	
			12,001
* CURRENT ASSETS			
* Stocks	975		
* Debtors	2,888		
* Cash at bank	994		
		4,857	
* CREDITORS: AMOUNTS FALLING DUE WITHIN ONE YEAR			
Bank loans	76		
Trade creditors	3,297		
Accruals	20		
		3,393	
* NET CURRENT ASSETS			1,464
* TOTAL ASSETS LESS CURRENT LIABILITIES			13,465
* CREDITORS: AMOUNTS FALLING DUE AFTER MORE THAN ONE YEAR			
Debenture loans		1,875	
Finance leases		866	
Bank and other loans		124	
			2,865
* PROVISIONS FOR LIABILITIES AND CHARGES			
Taxation including deferred taxation	33		
Other provisions	557		
			590
			10,010
* CAPITAL AND RESERVES			
* Called-up share capital		5,000	
" Share premium account		500	
" Revaluation reserve		1,158	
• Other reserves		262	
			6,920
• PROFIT AND LOSS ACCOUNT			3,090
			10.010

About the Balance Sheet

While vertical and horizontal balance sheets are permissible, most UK companies prefer the vertical format as illustrated. The conventional form of horizontal balance sheet can be summarised as follows:

	£		£
Capital brought forward	X	Fixed Assets	X
Profit for the year	X		
Capital at year end	X		
	X		
Long term liabilities	X		
Current liabilities	X	Current Assets	X
	X		X

In Germany and Italy only the horizontal format is allowed.

The UK Companies Act requires companies to show all the items marked with * in the example on the face of the balance sheet; the other items can be shown either on the balance sheet or in the notes to the accounts. In addition, the law requires companies to show the value of certain items in separate notes to the balance sheet, such as details of fixed assets purchased and sold during the year.

The notes to the published accounts almost always begin with a description of the accounting policies used by the company in the accounts, e.g. the depreciation policy. In the UK most accounts are prepared on a historical cost basis but this is not compulsory and other bases, such as current cost or historical cost modified by revaluation of certain assets, are also allowed.

Specimen Co Ltd

Statement of Source and Application of Funds

For the year to 31 December 2007

	£000	£000
Source of Funds		
Profit before tax		2,615
Adjustment for items not involving the movement of funds:		
Depreciation	772	
Profit on the sale of fixed assets	(12)	
Provision for bad debts	3	
Development expenditure	45	
		808
Total generated from operations		3,423
Funds from other sources		
Issue of shares	250	
Sale of fixed assets	75	
Dividends received	240	
		565
		3,988
Application of funds		
Dividends paid	550	
Taxation paid	777	
Purchase of fixed assets	1,437	
		2,764
Increase in working capital		1,224
Increase in stock	82	
Decrease in debtors	82	
Decrease in creditors	545	
		383
Decrease in bank overdraft	297	
Increase in cash balances	544	
		841
		1,224

Specimen Co Ltd

Cash Flow Statement for the year to 31 December 2007

	£000	£000
Operating activities		
Cash received from customers		8,804
Interest and dividends received		276
Cash paid to suppliers		(3,642)
Cash paid to and on behalf of employees		(1,789)
Interest paid		(26)
Net cashflow from operations		3,423
Corporation tax paid		(777)
Investing activities		
Purchase of investments	(866)	
New fixed assets acquired	(1,437)	
Sale of fixed assets	75	
Net cashflow from investing activities		(2,228)
Financing activities		
New share capital	250	
Repayment on finance leases	(65)	
Dividends paid	(550)	
Net cashflow from financing activities		(365)
Net cash inflow		53

Specimen Co Ltd

Statement of Value Added for the Year to 31 December 2007

	£000	£000
Turnover		9,758
Bought-in materials and services		5.233
Value Added		4.525
Applied the following way:		
To pay employees' wages, pensions and other benefits		1,827
To pay providers of capital		
Interest on loans	26	
Dividends to shareholders	750	
		776
To pay government		
Corporation tax payable		961
To provide for maintenance and expansion of assets		
Depreciation	772	
Retained Profits	189	
		961
		4,525

About the Value Added Statement

Value added statements are not required by UK law or the SSAPs and are rarely found in company annual reports. However, many people consider them very useful indicators of a company's operational efficiency and it is possible that they will become more widely reported in future.

'Value added' means the difference between the total value of output and the total cost of materials and services used in production. The value added statement shows how this added value is applied: to pay works and managers, taxes and dividends, to maintain operating capacity (i.e. depreciation) and the amount added to reserves.